HOMEWOOD PUBLIC LIBRARY DISTRICT

3 1311 00461 7753

W9-BUQ-826

Arthur Miller

BIO
MILLER,
ARTHUR

Arthur Miller

1915–1962

CHRISTOPHER BIGSBY

Harvard University Press
Cambridge, Massachusetts
2009

HOMEWOOD PUBLIC LIBRARY
JUN – – 2009

Copyright © Christopher Bigsby 2009
Printed in the United States of America
All rights reserved.

First published in the United Kingdom by Weidenfeld & Nicolson
Library of Congress Cataloging-in-Publication Data

Bigsby, C. W. E.
Arthur Miller, 1915–1962 / Christopher Bigsby.
p.   cm.
Includes bibliographical references and index.
ISBN 978-0-674-03505-8 (alk. paper)
1. Miller, Arthur, 1915-2005.   2. Dramatists, American—20th century—Biography.
I. Title.
PS3525.I5156Z5443   2009
812'.52—dc22
[B]   2009002489

Letters from Tennessee Williams © 1977, 1984, 1990 by the University of the South.
From *A Critical Introduction to the Century American Drama* (CUP, 1984); *Tennessee Williams: Five O'Clock Angel: Letters of Tennessee Williams to Maria St. Just 1948–1982* (Knopf, 1990); and *Tennessee Williams' Letters to Donald Windham 1940–1965* (Holt, 1977). Reprinted by permission of Georges Borchardt Inc., for the Estate of Tennessee Williams.

This book is dedicated to the memory
of Steven R. Centola

CONTENTS

PREFACE

This is the story of a writer, but it is also the story of America. For Arthur Miller, his dramatic model was always the classical Greek theatre, where a society could engage with its myths, its animating principles. The theatre was and is a public art, a present-tense art where the audience shares the same moment as those on stage who act out private passions but do so in a public context. For him that symbiosis was reflected in a favourite metaphor. As he was fond of saying, 'the fish is in the water and the water is in the fish'. It follows that to understand him and his work it is necessary to explore the forces that shaped him, the ideas that he propounded or with which he did battle. For him, son of an immigrant, born into wealth but who watched it disappear in 1929, the key events were the Depression, the Spanish Civil War, the Second World War and the Cold War. They dominated his mind and influenced his writing. So they do in this book whose byways, I hope, lead back to the central subject – a writer who America celebrated but who found himself rejected, threatened with imprisonment, declared Un-American.

At the beginning of his career he thought that art could change the world. Later, he was less sure. He remained certain, however, that it had to acknowledge that the individuals whose lives he staged existed in the world. Their private passions might drive them but they were exemplary in so far as they were in part the product of the values they absorbed, even if they stood ready to challenge or even betray them.

Like many of his generation, he embraced Marxism, believing the capitalist dream to have been exposed by history. He held to that dream longer than many, responding to what seemed, to him, to be the lack of transcendence of a system which valued the material over the spiritual, which turned its back on history as though that were an article of faith for those taught to pursue happiness, if never quite hold it in its grasp. To him, individually and collectively, we are responsible for our lives. He responded to Ibsen because he found in his work a central truth. Past actions have present consequences. The chickens, Miller was apt to say, always come home to roost. If it were not so, the spine of morality would be snapped. It is certainly the strategy of his drama but it is something more than that. It is an assertion of his central faith. How, then, to understand such a writer unless we move back in time, explore passions which now seem inexplicable, convictions seemingly invalidated by time or perhaps simply swept away as so many inconvenient truths? This is, however, a study of a writer and I have endeavoured to offer an analysis of his principal works.

This book primarily concerns itself with the first half of his life for that was when he was being shaped, when he began his conversations with America, when, no matter his later doubts, he did, indeed, change the world and continues to do so. For his plays are performed every day of every year to those remote from America but who discover within them human truths easily translated from language to language, culture to culture. His conversation, it seems, was not so parochial. He spoke and still speaks to the world.

1

FROM HARLEM TO BROOKLYN

We are formed in this world when we are sons and daughters and the first truths we know throw us into conflict with our fathers and mothers. The struggle for mastery – for the freedom of manhood or womanhood – is the struggle not only to overthrow authority but to reconstitute it anew.   *Arthur Miller*[1]

I would venture to say, the garment industry in this century has given birth to more writers, scholars, critics, and professors than any other American profession.   *Mark Schechner*[2]

Arthur Miller's story begins in the *shtetl*: Radomizl. It begins with those who decided to leave the known for the unknown, in search of safety and fortune. In the years between the assassination of Alexander II, in 1881 (which was followed by pogroms and the destruction of synagogues), and the outbreak of war in 1914, one-third of East European Jews left their homes and migrated. As the then head of the Russian Synod, and friend of Dostoevsky, remarked, 'One-third will die, one-third will leave the country, and the last third will be completely assimilated within the Russian people.'[3] For the Jew, the first priority was to survive, but assimilation, even if possible, was not survival. Separation had always been a destiny and a fate.

Two million people moved west, partly from fear of persecution, partly to escape destitution and partly because they saw a better future away from the villages and small towns that had defined their existence. Sometimes they went first into the major cities – Warsaw, Lodz, Minsk – but there was little respite there, little prospect of improvement. So they moved on. An active debate began as to whether this exodus should become official Jewish policy. In his study of the immigrant Jews of New York, Irving Howe recalls the 1882 conference of 'Jewish notables' in St Petersburg that discussed this question. On the one hand were those who declared: 'Pogroms are a result of rightlessness and when they have been obviated the attendant evils will vanish with it.' On the other, the minority, were those who insisted: 'Either we get civil rights or we emigrate.'⁴

In the end, though, public declarations meant very little. People made their own decisions. Architects have a word for pathways worn down by people who ignore those thoughtfully provided by city planners and designers, instead following their own whims and necessities. They are called 'lines of desire'. Those who chose to leave the country of their birth, whatever the pressures to remain, followed lines of desire. There are lines like that in America, still visible a century and a half after wagon wheels wore grooves in rocks as people moved on in search of gold, land, or simply unbounded freedom. Those worn down by immigrants are no less real for being invisible. In 1880 there were 230,000 Jews in America. By 1900 the figure was over a million. In 1917 the figure was 3,389,000.

Individuals would abandon their families and step into the unknown. Sometimes entire villages would band together and set out by cart, train and ship on a journey to a country they knew only by report and whose language was a mystery. A people rooted in the past opted for the future, sure only that it would be better. There was, it seemed, a place of hope. Howe quotes one immigrant to that distant country who arrived in New York in 1891 as declaring: 'America was in everybody's mouth.' In 1880 there were just 14,000 Russian Jews in New York; thirty years later there were nearly half a million.⁵ In the words of a lullaby:

> Your daddy's in America, little son of mine.
> But you are just a child now so hush and go to sleep.
> America is for everyone, they say, it's the greatest piece of luck.
> For Jews, it's a garden of Eden, a rare and precious place.
> People there eat challah in the middle of the week.⁶

They carried their God with them but for some He would be lost along the way or abandoned, on arrival, in the clamour of a society in which ambition and material advance constituted the axial lines. A tension was thereby created between one generation and another. One set about the business of recreating the world they had left behind, with its schuls, ritual observances, Yiddish newspapers; the other threw itself into the new life, anxious to claim the possibilities and identity offered by a strange but seemingly welcoming country. As a result fault lines opened up not only between the past and the present but within families whose alliances began to shift, whose sense of identity derived from different experiences. The role of victim no longer seemed appropriate to a free society. Children married 'out'. Forgetting, it seemed to some, was more important than remembering, when to remember meant to preserve a sense of shame and suffering along with tradition. Miller and his family would enact such a process, while in his work he would inhabit those contradictions – this man who not once but three times married out of the faith.

To join another society is to be invited to embrace its values, to share its myths. For the Jew, however, there was another history, there were other myths, and from the negotiation between the two would be born a life and a literature. At times, as the Jewish writer emerged as a major voice in America, he seemed a paradigm of the modern sensibility, simultaneously within and without, alienated but wishing to be accommodated. Yet in a society for which the past exists merely to be transcended or reinvented as romantic fable, the weight of history, the sheer particularity of experience, could be lost in a celebration of a supposed new self. And that particularity remained, that memory, that awareness that the threat could never be said to have wholly disappeared.

This was a time, in New York, when horse railway carriages moved at five or six miles an hour and horse omnibuses forced their way through streets packed with people and past pedlars selling from handcarts, rented at ten cents a day and with an annual fee of a few dollars. Though such a mass of people would have been a shock after Radomizl, otherwise it was not such an unfamiliar world. There were synagogues. You could buy kosher food and go to the Yiddish theatre. This was an area already known as 'Jewtown', the title of a chapter in Jacob Riis's *How the Other Half Lives*, published in 1890.

Riis, a Danish immigrant, a photographer and journalist, offers an account of the tenements of New York when the Millers and Barnetts (Miller's mother's family) lived there, in the process revealing something of the prejudices that confronted incoming Jews from Eastern Europe: 'No need of asking where we are,' he explains, the 'jargon of the streets, the signs of the sidewalk, the manner and dress of the people, their unmistakable physiognomy, betray their race at every step.' He describes 'men with queer skull caps, venerable beards, and the outlandish long-skirted kaftan of the Russian Jew'. The 'oldest women', he insists, 'are hags; the young houris. Wives and mothers at sixteen, at thirty they are old. So thoroughly has the chosen people crowded out the Gentiles in the 10th Ward that, when the great Jewish holidays come around every year, the public schools in the district have practically to close up.'[7]

Beyond that, though, he characterizes them as a race concerned with only one thing:

> Thrift is the watchword of Jewtown, as of its people the world over. It is at once its strength and its fatal weakness, its cardinal virtue and its foul disgrace. Become an overmastering passion with these people who come here in droves from Eastern Europe to escape persecution, from which freedom can only be bought with gold, it has enslaved them in bondage worse than that from

which they fled. Money is their God. Life itself is of little value compared
with even the leanest bank account. In no other spot does life wear so
intensely bald and materialistic an aspect ... Over and over again I have met
with these Polish or Russian Jews deliberately starving themselves to the
point of physical exhaustion, while working night and day at tremendous
pressure to save a little money ... As scholars, the children of the most
ignorant Polish Jew keep fairly abreast of their more favored playmates, until
it comes to mental arithmetic, when they leave them behind with a bound.
It is surprising to see how strong the instinct of dollars and cents is in them.
They can count, and correctly, almost before they can walk.[8]

With little money, they had no choice but to work as many hours as
possible. Living in squalor, they had to set themselves first to survive and
then, slowly, to prosper. How else to escape the conditions that Riis describes.
Their reputation as money-grubbers, however, stuck and years later Miller's
mother, Augusta, would find any discussion of money by her relatives
repellent.

Miller himself recalled a time when his aunt had asked him to drive her
from her son Morton's place to New York in the pouring rain. She was anxious
to get home because she was afraid that the rent cheques from the property
she owned might get wet if the postman failed to push them sufficiently far
through the letterbox. She was a woman whose fierce concentration on money
simultaneously fascinated and repelled.

Arthur Miller was a child and grandchild of immigrants. Both his paternal
and maternal grandfathers had come from the same Polish town of Radomizl,
near Cracow (though two other Radomizls were suggested to him – the
largest near Lublin – as possible alternatives, making the past more problematic, closer to myth than to history). This was then part of Austria-
Hungary and Miller's father was prone to describe himself as Austrian.
Ross Miller, Arthur Miller's nephew, has explored something of his family's
past:

Radomizl ... became part of Austria after the partition of Poland in the late
eighteenth century ... There were at least 1,000 towns like the one my family
is from. They all have a market square, synagogue square, shops and a
street or two of abattoirs, warehouses and the most rudimentary sort of
manufacturing facilities where artisans worked. Radomizl was an 'urban'
satellite of the local nobleman or magnate. Some Jews lived and worked
directly on the estate. Most were innkeepers and distillers. The richest were
'tax farmers' who collected excise taxes and the like for the state. Radomizl
was a 'private' town to distinguish it from royal towns and cities like Krakow.
In Poland the king was weak, the noblemen strong.[9]

The family name, long assumed to be Miller, now, following research by Mordecai Miller (the son of Arthur's cousin, who met an elderly man who claimed to remember the family), seems likely to have been Mahler (the German form of the same name and also a reference to the trade of milling). Apparently the family made the name change as they set off to America. Miller, though, is a Polish name. Leszek Miller, for example, a communist before Solidarity brought about a revolution, rose to be leader of the Democratic Left Alliance and won a national election in 2001. Nonetheless, as it now seemed in retrospect, the less Germanic 'Miller' was perhaps thought more suitable to ease the transition into America, though in truth this was a country whose own identity was in a continuous state of reinvention.

The Mahlers/Millers had travelled, precariously and apprehensively, from a deeply anti-Semitic Poland. They shared the double impulse of many such in that they were fleeing from and travelling to. The overriding impulse was to become, to forge a new identity. For some, that would mean the pursuit of success. It was so for Miller's father, as it was for the playwright son of another immigrant family, David Mamet, who grew up in a household that seemed designed to obliterate memories of an immigrant past and where he was taught one thing – the need to succeed.

For Miller, looking back over his family history in the 1990s, the journey out of Europe had sorted the adventurous and the ambitious from those who remained. As he explained:

> I had an aunt who told me that she was married in about 1913, and for her honeymoon she and her husband (who was my father's brother) went back to Poland. Can you imagine, a wedding trip to Poland? But they had never been there . . . and my uncle took her to this little village which was a miserable little hamlet. She had been born there, and she said, 'You can't imagine how stupid they were!' I said, 'What do you mean?' She said, 'Well, they were just like dumb animals!' I said, 'Really?' She said, 'They knew nothing about anything. They did not know where Warsaw was!' . . . That made me wonder whether a kind of selectivity had gone on by virtue of the pressure of events in the late nineteenth century.[10]

Those who chose to leave were deeply provincial people for whom going to America was 'like going to the moon', but they were people, it seemed to him, with initiative and drive that in turn, perhaps, explained the success with which many made their way in the new society. This sounds, of course, suspiciously like the familiar justification of the immigrant and descendant of immigrants. There are photographs of those not long off the boats, wearing suits and already exuding the air of prosperity. The suits were mere photographers' props. The purpose of the pictures was to confirm to those who received them that the journey had been justified, the painful breaking of ties vindicated, the feelings of guilt amounting at times to treachery, absolved.

In the case of the Millers the success would prove real enough and the echoes from the past sound ever more faintly. Even so, it does no harm to the psyche to revisit the past and find there still further justification, evidence for the superiority of those who left over those who stayed. America was the green light seen across the bay. It was necessary that it should prove a true beacon.

Isaac Bashevis Singer also left a small Polish town, though he did so in 1935 when the signs of impending apocalypse seemed clear. His mother and younger brother stayed behind. Four years later they were dead, frozen to death in a cattle truck as the Russians deported them. He felt his own journey was necessary to survival, in every way justified. He was escaping a death sentence. Even so, he felt guilty, declaring that 'a man without guilt is not a man at all'.[11] Miller's plays would be laced through with such self-accusing characters, burdened with a barely repressed sense of failure or unjustified success. He knew what their fate would have been had they stayed. The relatives towards whom his aunt had condescended would undoubtedly have been subject to another, more systematic and ruthless form of selectivity. Even survival could carry a sense of blame.

Arthur Miller's father, Isidore, was left behind by his family when, in the late 1880s, his parents took his three brothers and three sisters from their Polish town, as Kermit Miller later recalled, clutching sewing machines. Supposedly, finances would not stretch to a ticket. Isidore was, the story went, left with an uncle who disobligingly died so that he was passed from relative to relative.

The abandonment is so shocking, though, that this account seems highly improbable. Why one child among so many? Why the youngest and hence, by definition, the one least able to fend for himself? How was a child of six – he was born in 1884 – not merely to handle losing everyone closest to him but at some later date make his way across Europe, and then across the Atlantic, on his own? Astonishingly, only in 2000 did Miller and his brother Kermit begin to piece together another version of the story based on half-forgotten conversations that had taken place seventy years earlier.

It now seemed to both of them that their father had been abandoned as mentally defective. In 2001 Miller told me that he remembered him explaining that when he was left behind he had been terrified because he was forced to sleep with 'idiots who pissed all over the beds and howled all night'. He recalled, too, his mother explaining that he had hardly spoken as a child. Kermit remembered his father saying that he had been forced to drink from, and bathe in, a rain barrel. It now seemed to the brothers that their father had been left in an institution from which he was only released when word was sent, in all probability by a rabbi, as the only person of authority, that he was in fact sane, or at least fit to travel.

This was the reason, it seemed to them, that on his arrival he was denied the schooling offered to his brothers, as if he could not be expected to benefit from it. It was the reason, too, for the contempt with which he was treated, from time to time, by his own mother who was seemingly unable to accept the irony that the child she had abandoned should have turned out, at least for a while, to be the most successful. She had, Miller came to believe, left her own son to die. His success was thus a fluke that must have deepened her sense of guilt. By the same token, she seems to have believed that her grandson's later success owed more to his mother than his father. For the rest of his life her son tried to buy her love with expensive gifts. For her part, she seems to have been incapable of offering it.

In retrospect, it appeared to Miller remarkable that his father had survived the experience in Poland, not least because conditions for a young child had been bad enough without, as it now seemed to him, his having been institutionalized in what must surely have been 'some slimy asylum'. Rado-mizl, after all, had been the place where Jerzy Kosinski, admittedly not the most reliable of sources, claimed to have been tortured by peasants and saved by a priest during the Second World War.

The journey from Poland was not an easy one. It involved crossing the German border, legal enough for citizens of the Austro-Hungarian empire but nonetheless frequently involving protracted inspections by German authorities fearful of disease. From there the emigrants would travel to Berlin, where they would join the stream of Russian Jews heading for the ports where they were liable to be held in quarantine for two weeks and were prey to confidence tricksters drawn to those who journeyed with all their possessions.

The numbers involved at each port were considerable. Howe quotes a figure of 2,173,919 emigrants leaving from Bremen alone between 1882 and 1902, though what percentage were Jews is unknown. The sea crossing itself was exhausting. Conditions in steerage were frequently appalling, with dark compartments packed with two-tiered wooden bunks in which those unused to sea travel vomited on one another. With time, the shipping lines effected improvements but it was still physically debilitating and emotionally draining.

At last, a ticket did arrive for the young Isidore and he journeyed first to Hamburg, or perhaps, as Miller later thought, Bremen, and then on to New York, with a label requesting that he should be put aboard a particular ship. The train journey itself was frightening: 'emigrants were herded at stations, packed in cars, and driven from place to place like cattle'.[12] There were frequently no seats so that they had to sit and lie on the floor, resting their heads on their bundles. In Hamburg, he would have been led into a large room with narrow bunks along the wall in each of which two people were expected to sleep. Rose Cohen, en route to New York, recalled that 'the air in the room was so foul and thick that it felt as if it could be touched . . . But worst of all were the insects in the cot.'[13] Isidore would have waited for his name to be called. More than a century later, his son attempted to imagine the scene in what was part memoir and part potential play. A uniformed official reads a note from a rabbi in Radomizl asking anyone who reads it to help the young boy who carries it. In the play fragment it is suggested that he would have been seven weeks on the ocean. The trip probably took closer to three weeks but he did, as the play suggests, travel steerage, next to the ship's steering equipment and below the waterline. He had to sleep on a straw mattress. Shut off from the open air, the passengers lived in a stench from the filthy lavatories, often cleaned only as the ship steamed into port where they might be inspected: 'This pervasive, insidious odor,' recalled one such passenger, 'a distillation of bilge and a number of less identifiable putrescences, settled on one's person, clothes, and luggage and stayed there forever.'[14] Up to 17 per cent of those who left Europe died on the crossing.[15] Miller's father 'arrived in New York with his teeth loose and a scab on his head the size, they used to say, of a silver dollar'.[16]

It is hard to think what must have gone through the mind of such a child, deprived of family and travelling among strangers. If it had been difficult for them, it must have been terrifying for him. It was his first time outside of Radomizl, his first on a train, his first time on a ship, unable to read or write in his own language or that of a city that must have seemed intimidating to a young boy used only to the scale of a small Polish town. He never talked of this. No doubt it quickly sank down into his subconscious, faded into a series of sepia memories. Some residue, however, must have survived, if only a fierce ambition to insulate himself from the anarchy of dispossession and desertion, if only a desire for the love he had been denied, a need for the security of which he had been deprived and would be deprived of again when his new country lost its grasp on destiny in 1929.

When Ellis Island was opened as the reception point for immigrants, things were better organized though still traumatizing, with doctors who had the power to turn back those they suspected of illness, physical or mental. Letters were chalked on them that were designed to define them as ruthlessly as the scarlet A on Nathaniel Hawthorne's Hester Prynne, letters that designated the illnesses from which they were suffering and which would determine whether they were to be Americans or rejected Poles, Russians, Germans.

Until 1892, when Ellis Island opened, immigrants would arrive at Castle

Garden, a red granite fort on the southwest tip of Manhattan in Battery Park, later converted into a saloon where Jenny Lind performed, and later still into an aquarium and then a visitor information centre for New York's National Parks and Monuments. Today you can buy tickets there for ferry trips to Ellis Island and the Statue of Liberty. The building itself looked imposing, with flags flying from its vaulted roof and notices in English and German. The procedures hardly matched the triumphal architecture. Badly organized, their reception was, to many, deeply depressing. In his 1917 novel *The Rise of David Levinsky*, Abraham Cahan describes the arrival of his protagonist in New York:

> We were ferried over to Castle Garden. One of the things that caught my eye as I entered the vast rotunda was an iron staircase rising diagonally against one of the inner walls ... The harsh manner of the immigration officers was a grievous surprise to me. As contrasted with the officials of my despotic country, those of a republic had been portrayed in my mind as paragons of refinement and cordiality. My anticipations were rudely belied ... These unfriendly voices flavored all America with a spirit of icy inhospitality that sent a chill through my very soul.[17]

Confidence tricksters were attracted to those who knew nothing of exchange rates or the proper price of baggage clearance.

Very often the immigrants were bewildered as to the answers they should give to officials. If they declared they had a job, for instance, they were, after 1885, liable to deportation following passage of a law prohibiting importation of contract labour.[18] How, after all, do you read the signs and symbols of an alien country to which you have nonetheless committed your future? And not everybody could take separation from a former life. Alfred Stieglitz's famous photograph 'The Steerage', celebrated as an image of the immigrant, was in fact a portrait of a woman returning to the Eastern Europe from which she had fled, unable, finally, to cut the threads that connected her to her past. As it happens, Jewish re-emigration rates were a fraction of those for other groups. Even as late as the Depression, when a third of immigrants turned back, the figure for Jews was just 5 per cent. They had greater cause to fear the past.

In his novel *Middlesex* (2002), Jeffrey Eugenides imagines the narrative of immigration like a film run backwards, with Europeans and Asians walking back on to a ship that forges stern first across the ocean, nestling back into the European womb, as if this were a secret fear and dream. There were no such doubts in the Miller home. Even the tenement carried a promise that a bleakly rural Poland had not. The polyglot, unformed world that was New York lacked the callous fixities that had embedded anti-Semitism in a merciless history. The whirl of the sewing machines was not a sign of drudgery, though there was to be plenty of that, but evidence of sheer focused energy, and infinitely preferable to the sullen silence of a country whose irrelevance was underscored by borders so easily erased by enfolding empires. In Poland, labour had been to do with survival; here it was to do with advancement. Seeking transformation, they were transformed, though not always in ways they had anticipated.

They were now part of a country supremely confident in its possibilities, assured not only of its own destiny but of its exemplary status. The tall son of a wizened father, Isidore Miller would himself become an emblem of the new generation's status, no matter that his parents would find his triumphs, and subsequently his son's, bewildering. Eventually he became the chief inheritor of a decision made in a country where the Jew's precarious grasp on his own fate was to be taken as a sign of the secure grasp of others.

Not so many years later, as Eugenides makes plain, the golden door edged closed, as 'Henry Cabot Lodge thumped a copy of *The Origin of Species*, warning that the influx of inferior peoples from southern and eastern Europe threatened "the very fabric of our race". The Immigration Act of 1917 barred thirty-three kinds of undesirables from entering the United States."[19] Immigrants from these regions were cut by four-fifths. The gene pool was to be protected. But by then the Millers had already worked their way uptown, away from the promiscuous flow of wide-eyed innocents, standing on the edge of their future, their feet in the mud and manure of a city beyond their imagining. It was a journey, though, whose beginnings were at first bewildering and always difficult.

Isidore was met at Castle Garden by the next-oldest child, Abe, then some ten years of age. He told him that his father owned all the buildings the young boy could see. Many decades later Isidore's son, Arthur, took a trip out towards Ellis Island in the company of the rich and successful, struck suddenly by the fact that though Castle Garden was long since closed, it was over these waters that his father had sailed into a new life, exhausted, frightened and carrying the scars, literal and psychological, of the journey.

Once free of immigration, most Jews made their way to the Lower East Side and it was here, on Broome Street (with its twenty synagogues between Broome and Delancy), that Miller's mother Augusta was born in 1891. Her father was Louis Barnett, a clothing manufacturer. Indeed, by far the greatest proportion of Jewish immigrants gravitated to the clothing industry. Forty per cent, between 1899 and 1914, worked in the trade,[20] Miller's paternal grandfather and father among them. As Irving Howe indicates, of 'the 241 garment factories in New York City in 1885, 234 were owned by Jews, or more than 97 percent'.[21]

The Lower East Side, originally dominated by German and Irish immigrants, largely consisted of tightly packed tenement buildings with one cold water tap to a floor and, in the early 1880s, a death rate nearly double that of the city as a whole. By 1900 the population density, at 700 per acre, was greater than that of Bombay.[22] Some blocks even reached a figure of 1,000 per acre, though most buildings were less than seven storeys high. It was here that pedlars, labourers, tailors, shop workers, struggled to get a hold on their new country. They worked in sweatshops for twelve to fourteen hours a day and more, determined first to survive and then to prosper. Initially, for many, such objectives seemed problematic. It was these conditions that led to the creation, by one Lillian Walk, of the Hester Street Settlement, established to deal with the plight of those debilitated by poverty and ravaged by disease. 'In America,' one immigrant wrote to his family back home, 'one has to sweat more during a day than during a whole week in Poland.'[23]

Isidore was taken to the tenement on Stanton Street (sometimes Miller thought it might have been Christie Street), with eighteen synagogues and, in 1910, more than two thousand Jews on certain blocks, where the family, now nine in number, lived and worked in three cramped rooms. Nancy Foner quotes Samuel Chotzinoff's description of such an arrangement: 'My parents occupied the only bed in the house, in the small windowless and doorless room between the kitchen and the front room. My sisters slept on improvised beds on the floor of the latter, I on four chairs set up each night in the kitchen.' In the morning, the chairs 'would be pulled from under me, one by one, as they were required for breakfast.' In the summer, they slept on the fire escape. It was much the same for the Millers, Isidore sleeping on a bed with three of his siblings.

The toilet, for the Millers as for Chotzinoff, was an outhouse (augmented, in the Millers' case, by a pot on the fire escape): 'This arrangement did not strike us as in any way unusual. The water closets – as they were unflatteringly called (there was no water anywhere around) – were always locked, and each family was given a key ... Sometimes a child could earn a penny by giving his key to a passer-by in distress.'[24] Miller recalled the occasion when one of his aunts, the evening of her first date, had an embarrassing accident as a result of such domestic arrangements. She tripped on the stairs and upset the pot over herself. It was a story recalled in subsequent years when she would excuse herself from a bridge game so as to pee on her hand for luck. For his part, Isidore, known as Izzie, was afraid to go to the outhouse at night for fear of the rats that lived beneath the fire escape and the broken bottles that littered the ground. Stories of inside toilets, meanwhile, seemed little more than fantasies.

The family used either the public baths or a tub placed in the middle of the room. Over half the city's population lived in such tenements (by 1900 the figure for Jews was 90 per cent).[25] That the Miller family had not arrived in America with much money scarcely marked them out from their fellow immigrants. As late as 1910, 87 per cent of Jewish immigrants arrived with less than fifty dollars when the average annual household income for their fellow Jews in New York was ten times that.

Whatever the reason, the young Isidore, fresh off the boat, had only the briefest of schooling, hence the illiteracy that would become his burden and the source of his wife and children's embarrassment (though male illiteracy among Jewish immigrants ran at some 22 per cent).[26] He did, however, of necessity, and in confirmation of Jacob Riis's comments, become competent at maths as, interestingly, his son Arthur did not, failing repeatedly. Speaking in July 2000, Kermit remarked to his brother that those years of labour, the illiteracy, 'made him what he was . . . And to some extent, what I was . . . And you.'

For Miller, if indeed his father had been left behind to die, his pathetic attempts at education as an adult must have been even more painful as he lived with the seemingly insoluble puzzle of why his brothers were literate and he was not, why they were embraced by his parents and he was not. Even at the height of his success, Miller suspected, his father felt a sense of his own undeservedness so that failure, when it came, must have seemed the final justification for the early disregard. No wonder that a sense of abandonment was an essential component of his identity, as, at times, Miller suspected, it was of his own.

It was the theme of abandonment, he thought, that lay at the heart of his play *After the Fall* (1964); it was that which had attracted him to Marilyn Monroe, the figure at the centre of that play, a woman whose early history was one precisely of abandonment. All his life Isidore was to defer to the parents who had once rejected him, at considerable cost to his own family as the Depression bit and their hopes sank back into the broken streets of a distant Brooklyn.

Isidore was quickly set behind a sewing machine and joined the burgeoning clothing industry that would become the basis of the family fortune. Though he did briefly go to school, he was withdrawn in order to help the family finances. He never returned or learned his ABC. But numbers he did understand. He knew prices, wages, profit margins as, later, he knew the box office returns of his son's plays. Arthur, despite conspicuously failing school maths exams, would later note and recall advances on royalties, the cost of rent, the changing prices of meals, quite as if such details gave him a grasp on who he had become and on a world in flux.

Isidore worked seven days a week on the sewing machine from sun-up to sun-down, as did his brothers and sisters when they were not at school, and though this was long before he was born Miller found the image of the sweatshop haunting him in his later years, not least because he had glimpsed this world on visits to his father's company. In the 1980s he travelled to China where, peering into the window of a store in Yenan, he saw a group of women bent over their sewing machines in the gloom, the sight stirring a retrospective anger at the treatment of those, like his own family, forced to spend years struggling to escape a kind of servitude.

By the age of twelve Isidore was employing two other boys who sewed coat parts for him in a basement on Broome Street, but his father had other plans for him. Two years later, already tall for his age and with blue eyes and reddish hair, he was sent on the road with a trunk of coats he was supposed to sell to various stores along the railroad lines. Wearing a blue serge suit (his first time in long trousers) and a tie, he got no further than Penn Station, already missing his mother. By fifteen, though, he was selling, travelling, for Miller & Sons, to Cleveland, Chicago, Minneapolis. Too young to chase women or go drinking, he would sit in hotel lobbies or walk around the town talking to other salesmen.

In an age before houses and offices were heated, coats were sometimes worn indoors. They were a major purchase and women would often keep them all their lives. Coats were full length and made of wool so that salesmen needed to be strong. Isidore would pay others to display them and take down the orders, not least to conceal his own illiteracy. The employment of an assistant, however, also gave added status, though the role of salesman itself carried status in an age and a society in which buying and selling were central to the national ethos. That did not mean, though, that he was independent of his family. He was to be thirty-two when he married and, until then, like his brothers, he handed his pay packet to his mother in return for an allowance.

The garment industry had expanded along with the population growth. The development of a national market led to demand for ready-made women's clothes. The ready-made clothing industry had emerged in the 1830s but by the time the Miller family arrived in the 1880s Jewish entrepreneurs dominated it. Women's wear came late. It was as a manufacturer of women's cloaks, in the 1880s, that the protagonist of Abraham Cahan's *The Rise of David Levinsky* set himself up, Cahan himself (who later helped to found the *Jewish Daily Forward*) arriving from Vilna, Lithuania, in 1882. By 1910 New York City produced 70 per cent of the country's women's clothes and the industry employed some 60 per cent of the New York Jewish labour force.[27] The trade was concentrated below 14th Street. If it gave many immigrants their first chance, however, it was also deeply exploitative, something that would later weigh on Miller's conscience and be addressed in his first student play.

In 1909 there was a strike in the garment industry, the workers' demands explaining something of the conditions under which they worked. What they were calling for was a fifty-two-hour week, no more than three nights' overtime consisting of no more than two hours, and payment for needles, thread and electricity. Nancy Foner quotes labour leader Clara Lemlich, who went to work two weeks after her arrival in 1903: 'Those who worked on machines had to carry the machines on their back both to and from work ... The shop we worked in had no central heating, no electric power ... The hissing of the machines, the yelling of the foreman, made life unbearable.' As Foner points out,[28] when demand was high, women could work for up to seventy hours a week with no overtime pay. When demand was low they were simply dismissed.

Rose Cohen recalled her 'fingers stiffened with pain' as she worked on women's coats. This was the basis of the Miller family fortune, this the world into which Arthur Miller was born, son of a man who was one of the country's leading manufacturers of women's clothes. In his first play, *No Villain*, a line of women silently sew as outside the building dispatch clerks go on strike. At the heart of the play, meanwhile, is a dispute, ideological, moral, between the manufacturer, plainly Isidore Miller, and his idealistic son, Arnold, sometimes inadvertently called Arthur.

Miller's maternal grandfather, Louis Barnett, from the same small town as the Millers, left Poland in the late 1870s, before the main body of emigration. According to Ross Miller, the name had originally been 'Baer – very common in that part of Galicia. The name change was a result of a female relative anglicizing the name to secure domestic work in Britain. She [eventually] returned to Poland but the name change stuck.'[29] Louis travelled first to Vienna, to study tailoring, before moving to New York where Augusta was born in the swarm of life that stretched and shrank and stitched the cloth on Broome Street. For Augusta, as for Isidore, this cannot have seemed such an alien place. This was their country, or almost so, in a way it could never be for their parents, whose fingers were pressed to the Braille of an alien culture and for whom each day must have been heavy with mysteries beyond the confines of the immediate area in which the old language could still be used, familiar rites practised. In a sense they were in neither one country nor another but in the anteroom to a reality which lay somewhere beyond, a place where their children could function more easily than them.

We have a portrait of Broome Street as it was when Augusta was growing up and Isidore employed two boys in a basement sweatshop. Jacob Riis describes a six-storey tenement in which a family live, like the Millers, in two bare rooms, the daughter sleeping in the front room, the older boys and younger children on the floor, while 'under the roof three men are making boys' jackets at twenty cents a piece, of which the sewer takes eight, the ironer, three, the finisher five cents, and the buttonhole maker two and a quarter, leaving a cent and three-quarters to pay for the drumming up, the fetching and bringing back of the goods.'[30] These were the economics of those who slowly lifted themselves out of poverty, saving at first a few cents and then a few dollars and then employing others.

Riis includes a photograph in his book of a black-and-tan dive in Broome Street (there were, by Riis's calculation, 4,065 such saloons below 14th Street). A man sits on a barrel in a run-down room, a woman staring blankly down. Here was the world that greeted the immigrants, the world they would fight hard to escape. This was the street in which Arthur Miller's mother was born and raised.

The older generation drove themselves hard in this new country but emotionally were most fully at home in the past, the world that had shaped them, whose language and rituals had structured their lives. Here, in America, the past was thrown away as suspect, used up, barring the path to the future. The next generation, meanwhile, was already letting go of that language and those rituals. They did not stare in from the outside. They might be coerced or persuaded to continue the old ceremonies but they did so grudgingly and with a sense of their irrelevance. As they grew up and slowly began to establish themselves in the new world, their place at the sewing machines taken by the next wave of immigrants, and the next, so they married outside the faith, forgetting why they were supposedly a chosen people, the status that had made them simultaneously blessed and cursed, and that had set their elders to travelling in despair and in hope. For the most part they had lost that instinct which should have told them it could all disappear.

The final humiliation for the older generation would come when age meant them becoming dependent not only for their daily needs but for that confirmation of their reality which comes from shared memories. Not even the landscape was there to remind them of who they once were and who they might now be. There was a fault line running through their lives, a line between past and present, between the generations, but also between what was fixed and what was changing. Success moved them, physically and emotionally, deeper into the new society, yet if assimilation was what they yearned for it was also, and more importantly, what they feared. It was the negotiation that had always confronted the Jews: to remain separate and yet be a part of the world from which they thus distanced themselves. That balance had defined them. To lose that balance, to embrace too completely the new world in which they had sought safety, was to face a subtler kind of extinction than the one they had fled.

One of New York's gifts, though, lies in the fact that everyone is a stranger and hence everyone is at home. Few have time's sanction; tradition is suspect. All languages and accents seem equally valid, the very babel being definitional. Even today, for some bizarre reason, taxis are driven by Russians with no

English and a mental map of Omsk with which to navigate Manhattan. Elsewhere in the world taxi drivers are expected to be masters of an urban geography. In New York no one expects a cab driver to know where he is going or even to be too sure where he is. Journeys are negotiations, with the passenger throwing out hints, as the man behind the wheel improvises his way through an improvised city, making and unmaking itself daily.

For those who fear change, perversely New York offers a homeopathic remedy. Here, nothing, it seems, is permanent, and in his 1998 play *Mr Peters' Connections* Miller was to acknowledge the vertiginous nature of a disassembling world. So many of Miller's descriptions of the neighbourhoods, the stores, the restaurants he knew when growing up are accounts of buildings long since demolished, replaced and demolished again – as if shadow were cast upon shadow in an urban archaeology which lays down strata of experience, customs, images. What is excitingly dynamic to the new arrival can be disturbingly entropic to those whose lives are winding down and for whom a morphing city can leave memories disturbingly detached.

The fact that in New York cab driving is regarded as an entry profession says something about that city's readiness to grant authority and legitimacy to the foreigner, as if he or she has an equal, and just possibly a superior right to be guide to a city state of nations. In 1900, 37 per cent of people in New York were foreign-born. It was the same percentage in 2000. When Arthur Miller was born, more than 14 per cent of all foreign-born people in America lived in New York. Perhaps the location of the United Nations in Manhattan was a recognition of this fact and a concession to the friendly unfriendliness which is a product of a people whose inflected English is stripped of all grace notes, a place in which many seem to speak English as a second language even if it is their first.

The family company thrived until after the First World War, Isidore working for it until he broke away to form the Miltex Coat and Suit Company, which in turn became extremely successful. Finally, his father dissolved his own company, probably as the result of the death of another of his sons, Morton Miller's father. He died in the great flu epidemic at the end of the First World War and, Miller suspects, was the real brains of the firm. Certainly he recalled his mother saying, 'The rest of them were idiots.' Isidore's other brothers now joined him, much to Augusta's disgust, she regarding them as no more than leeches, especially when what had seemed an endless boom suddenly showed signs of faltering.

Later, Arthur Miller was to recall trips downtown with his mother on which they visited his father in a building with a service elevator, rows of workers at sewing machines, clerks, salesmen and a warehouse area with huge bales of cloth moved around by carts. The women working the machines, he recalled, all on piece work, pushed the needles through the seams at high speed. Lunch, for them, lasted a bare fifteen minutes and consisted of a bowl of sour cream with pieces of onion and a handful of pumpernickel bread. The going rate for those sewing and packing, as for the shipping clerks, was twelve dollars a week.

What struck Miller as a child, though, he told me, was not their attenuated lives but his own position: 'I was rather proud to be the boss's son. I only went there on a weekend, on a Saturday once or twice, because I was at school the rest of the week. I remember pushing all the trucks around with big bolts of cloth. There were big scales to weigh stuff they were going to ship out. He [Isidore] was so excited and proud to have his family in there. It was Sabbath, so not everybody was there.' The Sabbath, however, made no difference either to his father or to his grandfather when it came to work. It was only later that his grandfather became particularly religious. 'He would go around being terrifically godly, but in his working life he hadn't been that way at all.'

When his father had lost his company but, briefly, started another, Miller worked for him for a month, 'until he couldn't stand it any more'.[31] He swept out, arranged cloth, performed minor chores and was thoroughly bored. His father, detecting this, asked, ironically, 'Do you remember where you left off last night?' He was there long enough, though, to absorb the ethos of the Lower East Side: work hard and keep your nose clean. At the same time he recognized the desperation of those who laboured in the ill-lit, oppressive rooms. As he said, 'I usually got involved with failures, of whom I considered myself one, people who didn't fit. And this included a lot of salesmen. Down below was a rough place to be.'[32]

There was, indeed, another side to this part of New York that was initially the site of the Miller family fortune. Eric Lanzetti, son of an Italian socialist immigrant, a man who had served with the anarchists in Spain in 1936 and become a communist, later recalled the nature of the area where Isidore had his first factory:

> The East Side ... was a city within a city, the town of [Michael Gold's novel] *Jews Without Money*: polyglot, teeming, colorful, its heart on its sleeve ... It was a sovereign state, working class and radical to the core, bounded on the south by Chinatown, on the west by Greenwich Village, on the north by the Protestant World, and on the east by the river ... Our republic had its own newspapers (the *Jewish Daily Forward*, the *Day*, the *East Side News*, *Der Freiheit*, the *Daily Worker*) ... The system on the East Side ... was a *gestalt*. It was capitalism in all its complex and tortured detail. The East Side was politically *sui generis* in America: there were practically no conservatives. The right-wingers were the New Dealers, and the political conjugation went on

from there: Social Democrats, Socialists, Communists, Trotskyists, Anarchists. The majority party was the Democratic, the ALP [American Labour
Party], then the Communist Party.[33]

Both Miller's grandfathers were contractors who bought pre-cut material
from the manufacturers (usually German Jews) and made it up into ready-
to-wear clothes for a set price. In order to be competitive, they would
often require their workers to raise their productivity by cutting, sewing
and pressing more garments in the same time. These were the sweatshops
of the Lower East Side. There were occasional, and devastating, fires.
From time to time there were strikes, but with new labour appearing at
Ellis Island with every boat that docked, workers had very little power.
Louis Barnett, Isidore's father-in-law, had been known to throw union
organizers downstairs.

As Irving Howe has pointed out, the majority of East European Jews who
succeeded in business did so in the garment industry[34] and, by degrees, those
who prospered began to move out of the Lower East Side. New communities
were established in Brooklyn and Harlem. By 1910 a third of Jews lived in
Brooklyn and by 1916 only a quarter of New York City's Jews still lived on
the Lower East Side.[35] After the building of the Williamsburg Bridge in 1903,
the anthropologist Nancy Foner points out, so many people moved across the
East River to the Williamsburg section of Brooklyn that the *New York Tribune*
called it the Jews' Highway.

Two of Arthur Miller's uncles, both salesmen, moved to Brooklyn in the
1920s, though not from Manhattan but from small towns in Upper New York
State. There, just across the bridges from Manhattan, of which the Brooklyn
Bridge was the most iconic, they lived in a still largely rural area, in small
wooden houses with flat roofs and three-step stoops and with gentiles for
neighbours. One, Manny, was a partial model for Willy Loman in *Death of a
Salesman*. His sales trips took him up into New England and Miller said of
him: 'It was the unpredictability of his life that wove romance around it. He
was not in some dull salaried job where you could never hope to make a
killing. Hope was his food and drink, and the need to project hopeful
culminations for a selling trip helped, I suppose, to make life unreal.'[36]

When Augusta married Miller's father in 1911, it was potentially the
merging of two commercial empires. It was certainly a decision that the two
patriarchs assumed was theirs to make after an evening in which Augusta's
father had examined the potential suitor's accounts. Physical attraction, Miller
noted, let alone love, was not the issue. What was at stake was the need to
protect an ever-embattled religious identity – that, and the consolidation of
hard-won success.

Augusta's sisters, Annie and Esther, had eloped and were married to what Miller called 'sensuous, impecunious lovers', but she was afraid of her father and unwilling to challenge him. Another young suitor had been chased away. Isidore, from a successful company, was approved. When he came to call, carrying a bunch of flowers, ice cream was served, a luxury. The result was a marriage that was a mixture of love and resentment. In good times it seemed an alliance if not quite of equals then of two people who brought differing talents to a relationship of mutual respect. In the bad times that would come with the Depression, it seemed what it was, an arranged marriage in which Miller's mother Augusta had sacrificed her own talents and potential.

In an early version of *After the Fall* Miller offers a portrait of the two men who had arranged her life, and of his mother's response to the deal done over her head: 'I wasn't allowed to *see* your father till his father and Grandpa had agreed!' She had accepted the arrangement *'because*, I decided for once somebody was not going to break my mother's heart', her sisters having refused to go along with her parents' plans.[37] Back in Eastern Europe, such arranged marriages had been common. In America they would quickly die out, but the two patriarchs who arranged the marriage between Augusta and Isidore had their roots in the old world, even as they determined the best way to succeed in the new.

In the final published version of *After the Fall* Miller includes a lament, by a character called Mother, who was plainly Augusta: 'I'll never forget it, valedictorian of the class with a scholarship to Hunter [College, City University of New York] in my hand . . . *A blackness flows into her soul*. And I came home, and Grandpa says, "You're getting married!" I was like – like with small wings, just getting ready to fly; I slept all year with the catalogue under my pillow.' Miller also offers what is clearly an account of Augusta's shock when she discovered that the man she had married was illiterate (not such an uncommon occurrence – the writer Alfred Kazin's mother, for example, also being illiterate): 'two weeks after we were married; sit down to dinner and Papa hands me a menu and asks me to read it to him. Couldn't *read*! I got so frightened I nearly ran away.'[38] It was, Miller later insisted, an invented detail but it is also to be found in the play fragment from what seems to be the late 1960s in which he recalled these times. The precise circumstance of the revelation was invented, the fact was not. Augusta's sense of dismay was certainly real enough, the feeling on her part that she had surrendered her own future to a man whose charm and business acumen left her entertained and apparently secure but in some fundamental sense frustrated and eventually contemptuous of his incapacities. In fact, Miller insists, she discovered that Isidore was illiterate one Sunday afternoon when, in their living room overlooking Central Park, she watched as her husband asked his lawyer to reread an agreement for the third time. She was nineteen years old and had been married for two months. It was not the only revelation. She had already discovered that he did not know the world was round, asking her, on the boardwalk at Atlantic City where they had gone for their honeymoon, why he could see the smokestack of a ship on the horizon before the rest of it. In his autobiography *Timebends: A Life*, Miller describes his father as still being baffled by this as he sat on the porch of the Long Island nursing home where he died. 'Oh. So it's round!' he reported him as saying,[39] as though it had taken most of his life to penetrate that particular mystery.

He had little in the way of small talk. Conversation was for information. But, his evident admiration for attractive women aside, he was faithful, and this despite his odd habit of pursuing women in the street to check out their clothes, committing details of the design to memory in order to copy their designer coats.

Isidore admired his wife. He acknowledged her talents but thought her naive when it came to the business of living and was afraid that his sons might embrace her values. Like many women, Augusta was the carrier of the culture. Though her sisters had no interest in their European heritage she could name the royal families of a continent her family had long since left behind. She was the only one of them to read for pleasure. Her taste ran to Alfred Lord Tennyson, William Cullen Bryant, Sherwood Anderson and Emily Dickinson. She was also, though, to be the one denied access not to America's wealth, which, for a time, she had, but to the self-realization that was equally its promise. She played music, she drew, but not merely was she married to a man who did neither of these, she was cut off from the education that she later saw as a key to her sons' future.

The wedding, in 1911, was a grand affair, and suggests just how wealthy the family was. Two hundred and fifty guests, the women in evening gowns and the men in tuxedos, attended the reception in a large restaurant-dance pavil-ion. It was the celebration of something more than a marriage. The two families had been in America for not much more than twenty years and here they were, dressed in the costumes of another country, having moved from poverty to wealth, from outside to inside toilets. The two young people being married were the future for which they had themselves left a familiar world that had promised them nothing but poverty and persecution.

Miller was born in Harlem on 17 October 1915, at 127 West 111th Street, the family shortly afterwards moving to a six-storey building at 45 110th Street between Lenox and Fifth Avenues, in his view the handsomest street in New York. Augusta's parents now lived on 118th Street. At that time the only predominantly African-American part of the area was from 130th to 140th Street. Five years earlier, the *Jewish Daily Forward* had called the area 'a Jewish city, inhabited by tens of thousands of Jews ... as busy and congested as our East Side, with the same absence of light and air'.[40] In 1910 there were a hundred thousand Jews living in Harlem, the second-largest concentration of immigrant East European Jews in the country.[41] This Jewish enclave stretched from 97th to 142nd Street. Within this, between Lenox and Seventh Avenue, was a more up-market area of 1890s buildings: 'Private dwellings and apartments, houses of a quality superior to those constructed anywhere in East Harlem, were scattered all along the wide-open thoroughfares of Fifth and Lenox Avenues.'[42] Those who lived there were what Abraham Cahan was to call the 'alrightniks'. And there were fortunes to be made. Samuel Silverman, like Miller's grandfather, and father a coat manufacturer, amassed half a million dollars. Growth in the women's garment business had coincided with Jewish immigration. By 1900 it was worth $159 million, with New York's share $107 million, while by 1914 the clothing industry employed more than half a million people.[43]

In 1915, the year of Miller's birth, William Fox, a former wool 'sponger' in the garment industry, approached Miller's father for a $50,000 loan to help set up a movie studio in California, in return for a percentage of the company. The size of the proposed loan gives some idea of the state of the Miller family finances. But, suspicious of spongers, who were responsible for pre-shrinking wool before it was cut into garments, and who hence were in a position to shrink cloth by other means than steam (simply cutting it for their own use), he rejected the offer and hence lost a fortune. Miller later recalled his father remarking, '"I might have given it to him if they were making films in New York", but to give Bill Fox fifty thousand dollars and have him disappear into California was beyond his credulity, so he didn't do it.'[44]

The decision also ensured that his son would be raised in New York and not California and that he himself would be wiped out by the Depression, when it came, rather than prospering as did the film industry. As Miller caustically observed, 'It would have been inconceivable to him that afternoon, as he told Fox the bad news, that in not so many years he would be finding it hard to scratch up the price of a ticket to a Twentieth Century Fox movie.'[45] It would have been inconceivable, too, to think that many years later his son would meet Marilyn Monroe on the set of a Twentieth Century Fox movie, and later have the head of the company beg him to collaborate with the House Un-American Activities Committee rather than allow the reputation of his star to be damaged by association with communism – a communism, incidentally, that had thrived in the sweatshops of the Lower East Side.

For many years the Millers' experiences in the new country fully validated their family's decision to leave Europe. With an expansive and expensive apartment in a then still fashionable area of Harlem, they had a chauffeur-driven car, a red-headed Polish maid called Sadie (who once pushed a young Arthur Miller's face into his hot breakfast cereal) and a family business employing some four hundred people, with salesmen travelling in more than half of the United States. Arthur's father, a man with curly reddish hair, fair skin and blue eyes, would wear a grey hat and Chesterfield overcoat with a velvet collar, and appeared the epitome of success. They now lived in a society where, for the most part, anti-Semitism took a far subtler form than in the country they had left behind. So long as they moved within their own community they need seldom register its existence.

Isidore and Augusta Miller, like all immigrants or children of immigrants, were precariously balanced between conflicting desires. 'They were certainly Jews,' Miller later observed, 'but they were trying to become, and in some ways did become, indistinguishable from anybody else. You lose roots and you gain something else, perhaps. It's a trade-off. It's a question of what you do lose.'[46] The words 'trying' and 'perhaps' here seem freighted with ambiguity and surely he is implying a sense of loss. At first, though, there appeared to be no conflict.

The community they joined had myths of its own – to do with national destiny, progress, material advancement, personal ambition – that seemed to chime with those of a people who had themselves come west in search of possibility. In truth, though, the most famous historian of the West, Frederick Jackson Turner, had been keen to make a distinction between those immigrants who had opened up the West, in a process that he saw as defining the American identity which lay at the heart of American democracy, and those, largely Jews, who arrived in the late nineteenth century when the frontier was, anyway, closed. In part he was reacting against the new urban life but he reserved a special dislike for the 'swarthy sons and daughters of the tribe of Israel'[47] who raised nothing but a crop of 'pants'.

In America, as elsewhere, the Jew was often seen as, alien, self-contained and hence the subject of suspicion. When another historian of America, Henry Adams, announced 'Westward the course of Jewry takes its way' in 1899, he was doing anything but accommodating Jewish ambitions to those of his country. This, after all, was a man who believed that 'We are in the hands of the Jews' who 'can do what they please with our values', and who confessed to preaching 'the downfall of the Jews'[48] while lamenting his own inability to bring it about. For a young Arthur Miller though, the views of Henry Adams were of little significance. There were more pressing concerns, beginning in the family.

Arthur Miller, then, was not born into the clutter and noise of the Lower East Side. Not for him the social kaleidoscope, the staccato rhythms of streets dense with those whose eyes were dull with work or bright with ambition.

He was born into privilege and a certain elegance, and delivered by the family physician, Dr Plotz (a name which became a family joke), whose son would one day take care of Augusta and Isidore at their deaths and in 1985 shake Miller's hand in an Italian restaurant, a ghost from the past.

Retrospectively, the FBI would interest itself in the birth of this son of an immigrant. In 1951, FBI report NY 100-57673 noted that his 'true name', as reflected in the birth records (Certificate 54449 of the Board of Health, Manhattan), was not Arthur Asher Miller but 'Anton Asher Miller', suitably foreign-sounding and evidence that he had subsequently adopted an alias. This identification was to remain in his file for some time. In November 2002 Miller noted, 'My name was never Anton Asher Miller, who was probably some other nuisance whom the FBI wanted to execute. I have no idea what they're talking about because I have my birth certificate which has my real name.'[49] So he had and so it does, though the first name is written so casually that there is some excuse for the error. It also misspells Isidore's name. The certificate is dated 26 October, nine days after the birth.

His earliest memory, from, he thought, the age of two or three, was of his mother, in a long woollen dress that reached her ankles. She was speaking into a wall telephone. He recalled tugging her dress as a shaft of sunlight crossed her shoe. That was to be the starting point for the autobiography he published seventy years later, long after his mother was dead, a woman he struggled to mourn.

The family's multi-room apartment meant that there was space and privacy. There was a smell of money in the air. There is a picture of the young Arthur Miller in winter, his trousers tucked neatly into long socks. He is wearing a shirt and tie with a fur-collared sheepskin coat and flat cap and gloves. His shoes look suspiciously new. He is about to throw a snowball and looks for all the world like a young Vanderbilt, or F. Scott Fitzgerald before heading east to an Ivy League Princeton. He was, however, allowed to play outside. His cousin Morton, slipping out to play, wearing a jacket and tie even in the hottest weather, was frequently led back indoors by his mother 'to study', the family wanting him to be either a lawyer or a rabbi (at Columbia University he would later have to walk two miles a day for a kosher meal, until, in his third year, he ate a ham sandwich and, in his own mind, became a real American).

Recalling the Harlem of his youth, Miller remembered a sense of space, a cityscape that had briefly emerged from a rural idyll. New York, at least in memory, had boulevards like Paris:

> It is the highest point of the island, so that we got a terrific view of most of the island from our home. It was where people went on vacation back in the nineteenth century. There were German beer-gardens all over the place. In

fact my father remembered that there had been a German beer-garden on the area where our apartment house was standing, and it faced Central Park, which was about the most beautiful part of the island ... There were a lot of trees along the boulevard – big, enormous elms and maples.

Though he would later prefer the woods of Brooklyn, which made Central Park seem 'a tame reproduction', he still regarded Harlem as 'marvellous'.[50] On a good day he could see down to the harbour.

America itself was booming. This was a world in which Lindbergh flew the Atlantic and baseball player Babe Ruth astonished with his home runs. It was a time when, as Lee, Miller's alter ego in his play *The American Clock* (1980), recalls, 'Gertrude Ederle swam the English Channel and Charley Paddock, the World's Fastest Human, won a race against a racehorse – because he believed.' It was a country, indeed, of believers. Its mood was that of Britain at the height of Empire. Every piece of news seemed to confirm that this was an age like no other, and this a country that was specially blessed. As Lee remarks, 'I thought that if a man was ... like my father – hard-working and making the right goods – he got to be well-off ... Life was a question of individuals.'[51] And all this was the gift America offered to the immigrant. Miller was to say:

> the idea then was to disappear into the general American population. The first thing the immigrant groups did, especially the Jews, was to set up schools to teach English, to speak it properly, and to write it properly ... The original impulse of the immigrant was to become an American, not, as is the fashion now, to emphasize the ethnicity of everybody, to show how different people are. There is something to be said for both, because my parents' generation were deformed by having, in effect, to conceal themselves. They tried to eliminate any accent from their speech. There was something called elocution taught in grammar school. You were taught to speak regular English.

Isidore Miller, however, had been denied such schooling as his wife had not, itself a source of friction: 'You couldn't talk to my father about anything that had to do with a book ... My mother read books, played the piano quite well, and sang, so that between them there could be no cultural discussion, excepting about a movie or the theatre.'[52] But these were the 1920s when, as F. Scott Fitzgerald remarked, the snows were not real snows. If you did not want them to be real snows you just paid some money and they went away. To imagine something was to make it so and for the Miller family the sky seemed blue and cloudless.

One generation back, meanwhile, lay another language. Miller's maternal grandfather Louis Barnett 'regarded German, the language and the culture, as the highest reach of human culture ... Consequently he spoke a kind of Yiddish, a medieval German with other languages collected into it', though even he 'was always trying to improve his English ... The idea was to become a citizen of the country in which you lived, not to become some excrescence from it ... that was a very strong thing.'[53] This Yiddish-speaking grandfather was to become a character in his first play.

The Yiddish, the German, however, had to be excised, burned off. It was the unfortunate residue of alien cultures whose sole role now was to be abandoned, acknowledged only as precursor. As five brothers complained to the *Jewish Daily Forward* in 1933: 'Imagine, even when we go with our father to buy something in a store on Fifth Avenue, New York, he insists on speaking Yiddish. We are not ashamed of our parents, God forbid, but they ought to know where it's proper and where it's not. If they talk Yiddish among themselves at home, or to us, it's bad enough, but among strangers and Christians? Is that nice?'[54] The new language was to be a facilitator, a guarantee. And since language is something more than a carrier of values, histories, ways of seeing, the abandonment of prior languages involves renunciation even as it offers induction.

Miller's paternal grandfather was small, and with what his grandson would call a large toppling head. As a child, Miller found it difficult to look at him, afraid that his fascination with his deformity would become apparent. He was nearly a foot shorter than his wife, a single-minded woman who never let anyone or anything interfere with her plans. The two of them lived in a large, elegant house in the Flatbush area of Brooklyn. Years later he recalled visiting them, at the age of nine, with his father, an occasion on which the old man had stared at Isidore as if trying to fathom how someone they had assumed to be an idiot had managed to produce such evidently bright children, a bemusement which only deepened when one of those children grew up to be a successful playwright. Isidore was attractive and that, no doubt, was one reason for his success. His mother was darker-skinned, a fact that worried his mother-in-law who would later anxiously enquire as to the complexion of Miller's children.

Miller recalled his mother as she was in the 1920s, a time of change. He remembered her, in particular, as she was when preparing to go out to a show: 'She wore a cloche hat, beaded dress and looked real slick. She looked like a real swinger ... My mother cut her hair, and that was a great event. She, like most of the women, wore her hair long, and wound it on top of her head. Sometime in the 20s she had it bobbed, which was revolutionary. It was a real shocker! I reflected some of it in *The American Clock*, where the boy bursts into tears. It was like an amputation.' The boy was based on Miller's older brother, Kermit.

The men did not change but the women assuredly did: 'The skirts went up high, and the tops went down. People were bare-armed, where before their clothes were quite Victorian, and it all happened, it seemed to me, in a year.' Even entertainment was changing. Irish tenors were replaced by crooners. When Rudy Vallee sang on the radio, Miller recalled, 'all these married hausfraus ... would ... flock into one house, eight or ten of them, and sit there facing this radio'.[55]

The radio, indeed, was the principal source of entertainment. As he explained to me in 2003, 'we kept track of all the new comedians, the singers – Bing Crosby, Russ Columbo, Rudy Vallee. We sat there judging who was the best.' That was hardly surprising since Russ Columbo's agent deliberately set up a battle of the crooners between his client and Crosby, which came to an end when Columbo fell out with the agent and then, in 1934, was accidentally shot in the head. 'Kate Smith,' Miller recalled, 'was a national heroine. She weighed a good two hundred and eighty pounds in her stockinged feet and she belted out these numbers. I couldn't stand her because she was sort of threatening. Sometimes you would hear Billie Holiday but she never got to be a national figure because she was black and they couldn't stand for that. But one did hear her and it opened up a whole new sound.' Since Rudy Vallee began his radio work in 1928 and Kate Smith in 1931, Miller seems here to be going back in his memory to the age of thirteen to sixteen.

Augusta Miller would play the piano and sing. On occasion, at New Year and on her wedding anniversary, she would even dance on the mahogany table, but long after Arthur had gone to bed. This was the table at which Kermit did his homework and Arthur learned to read, as the radiators hissed gently in the background, the table that would one day appear on stage as a prop in a play that looks back to the 1930s called *The Price*; a token, perhaps, that for Miller his family life, with its ebb and flow of tensions, lay at the heart of his drama.

His mother made pencil sketches of the children, as they tried to do of one another as they sat around the dining-room table. His brother's, he recalled, were clear and precise, his own endlessly erased as he fought for her attention and affection. Augusta was also an avid reader in a house and a community where few people read anything more than the newspaper, if that. The printed word drew her just as it baffled her husband, who was thus cut off from the kind of contact she enjoyed with her sons, a gentle conspiracy that nonetheless seemed bound to breed resentment and, ultimately, even contempt. The idyllic scene recalled by Miller excluded the father, whose own version of the future was to differ radically from his own.

Augusta had graduated from her school head of her class, but her ambitions for further education came to an end with marriage. She was, Miller observed, 'a good example of the way society treated women, especially in that immigrant group'.[56] Suddenly, she had had to give up all thoughts of improvement, the excitement of college. Not for her the New Woman of the 1920s. She had to settle for domesticity. Her identity had to be subsumed in that of a man who was her intellectual inferior. As a substitute for what she could never hope to share with him, she hired students who would arrive clutching books, often those in the news, and the following week they would discuss them. Miller remembered her, sitting against the brightness of the window, with Central Park stretching out into the distance, talking earnestly with these young students, a scene whose pathos would only strike him with the passing years. At the time he did not know what to make of these visits. Later, it became an image of everything she thought she had lost in marrying.

Her family had no interest in anything but business. The public world passed them by. Her husband, who loved her, nonetheless had nothing to offer beyond financial security and material comfort. She was, it seemed to Miller, a kind of prisoner in the life that had been chosen for her. These visits by young men, though, were only one of the many mysteries that confronted a young boy growing up in a family and a community which seemed to hug its secrets to itself.

In 1959 Miller wrote a short story in which, effectively, he tries to re-inhabit his younger self, to convey some sense of his struggle for autonomy and to account for the complex feelings towards his parents that have left him with a residue of guilt. It is a story in which the young boy registers but cannot fully understand the events that take place around him. He feels, above anything else, a sense of exclusion, but he also registers the offer of collusion from a mother desperate to discover a meaning slipping through her fingers. The protagonist of *I Don't Need You Any More*, is five years old. The world remains a confusing place as he tries to relate events to some central meaning. Jewish holidays come and go – Tisha b'Av, Rosh Hashanah and Yom Kippur. They evidently require certain observances but he alone is exempt. It is as though he were being deliberately excluded. He is on the outside of life looking in. He is not taught Hebrew or even piano or violin. When the others fast, he eats. For the moment he feels unneeded and responds in kind by telling his mother that he has no need of her, not realizing the pain he causes. At stake is his relationship with his family, with a religion that mystifies and entices.

This is a story, but Miller acknowledged its personal relevance. The boy, like Miller, is mocked for his protuberant ears. The mother tells him that she had loved a young student – he 'was so in love with me! I was ready to marry him, can you imagine? But Grandpa made him go away. He was only a student then. Oh, the books he brought me all the time!'[57] Instead she had gone ahead with the marriage her father had planned for her, a story Miller had heard from his own mother of course. The result is that the boy feels obliged to share his mother's secret, thereby betraying his father and forging an alliance with his mother which leaves him feeling uncomfortable. Miller confessed to just such a feeling, as he did to the thought expressed by this five-year-old in what is clearly the Millers' seaside cottage at Far Rockaway: 'he knew he would astonish everybody'. Here, then, is a portrait of a young boy trying to understand his place in the world:

> For the first time in his life he had the hard, imperishable awareness of descent, and with it the powers of one who knows he is being watched over and so receives a trust he must never lay down. In his mind's eye there rushed past the image of his angry father, and behind Papa was Grandpa and then other men, all grave and bearded, watching over him and somehow expecting and being gratified at the renewal of their righteousness and bravery in him.[58]

The tradition, it seems, is male. It is his mother with whom he has a problematic relationship, a mother who he senses is trapped, disappointed in her ambitions and desires. One consequence, as it seemed to him, of being raised by a woman who felt trapped and sought to transform her life with literature, with reimagining the world to make it tolerable, was that he felt reality was male, and had to do with business and money, while fiction was female and had to do with retreating into the imagination, surviving, spiritually, by recasting experience into an acceptable and consoling form. The fiction-making impulse was thus ambiguous. It was simultaneously a means of surviving and a desperate evasion. Meanwhile, his father's illiteracy opened a gap between the two of them. Miller would later admit to the conviction that each play he wrote was a reproach to a man for whom words were a mystery, a barrier between feeling and sense, as between himself and those he loved without, seemingly, ever fully understanding.

Isidore Miller was radically different from his wife. For him the business, one of the country's two or three largest women's coat manufacturers, was everything. Such limited reading skill as he had was acquired, with the help of Augusta, because of his need to follow a regular item in the *New York Times* that announced 'The Arrival of Buyers', these being buyers – of shoes, clothing and other goods – who had come to the city from across the country to look at the products they wished to sell in their stores in Minneapolis, Chicago, St Louis and elsewhere. Beyond that, though, he could hardly go.

It is difficult to imagine what his feelings must have been, then, when his wife had to hire students to give her the intellectual stimulation he could not. There must have been a sense of humiliation somewhere, balanced, until his business failed, by his success in offering her access to a cultural world largely closed to him. What drove him, it seemed to Miller and his brother, was a desire to make his mark, to claim his place in a world that once he could have felt he had no right to access, and no skills to master. As a result, even when failure came he refused to accept it, struggling to set up new businesses when this seemed no more than foolishness.

Over the years husband and wife had accommodated themselves to each other. If theirs had never been a love affair, there were points of contact and a mutual respect. Miller's mother was an avid theatre-goer. She would dress up and the chauffeur would drive her and Isidore to watch musicals. Her jewels glittered in the light as she rushed around preparing to leave. If it seemed an empty life compared to the one she had planned for herself, she did not show it, or not until later when things began to unwind. She would come home from the theatre carrying sheet music and the next day would play the songs on the piano, with the young Arthur occasionally joining in, this being the first signs of a career that he nearly followed when he worked briefly, for no pay, as a crooner at the age of fifteen. Even in his eighties he could be persuaded to sing the old songs (as a child he had had piano and violin lessons in turn, but had hated both). Fifty years later, his sister Joan would sort through the sheet music and choose some for the production of *The American Clock*, in which she played the part of her mother.

In 2007, Joan still had the piano at which her mother had played. One day she needed it tuned and the man who arrived at her West Side apartment recognized it immediately as one of a series of seven he had made for various members of the Miller family, starting with Joan's mother who had set the cultural tone for the family. Each ordered a slightly grander grand piano. Nobody bought into the idea of a competitive society more profoundly than the children of immigrants. In 1984 Miller had a piano delivered at his home in Roxbury, Connecticut, despite the fact that none of the family played, as though he were reaching back to his childhood and memories of his mother playing show tunes as they all joined in. Joan, meanwhile, willed her mother's piano to Miller's daughter, Rebecca.

However, if Isidore accompanied his wife to the musical theatre, he offered little in the way of cultured conversation about what they saw, though in later years, when he and his son had largely got over the disputes precipitated by political differences, the playwright would learn to trust his simple but honest and direct responses to his plays and the actors they starred. And Isidore was not without his fastidiousness. He would refuse to eat in any restaurant that had thick water glasses. Decades later, when the marriage between Arthur Miller and Marilyn Monroe ended, one of the few possessions she was anxious to hold on to were just such glasses which, for her, recalled the days of her poverty.

Arthur Miller attended public school (PS 24) on 111th Street between Fifth Avenue and Lenox Avenue, a strict institution where lessons were reinforced

with the edge of a ruler. On the corner was a candy store where he and his
fellow pupils could buy 'two-cent plains'. He was slow to learn. It had even
taken him time to master the art of tying his shoes. He found it difficult to
tell the time, mystified by the cardboard clock face demonstrated by his
teacher, Miss Summers. Seventy years later, he recalled little in the way of
real education but an emphasis on deportment and handwriting. The Palmer
Method, aided or not by a smart blow from the ruler, seems to have left little
trace, since his handwriting then and later remained difficult to decipher. It
was, however, the kind of education his mother, who had attended the same
school, valued.

Miller was three years younger than his blue-eyed, pale-skinned brother
Kermit, who, as an infantry captain, would one day carry a man on his back
in freezing weather until he found medical help, coming close to losing his
feet through frostbite. Six years younger there was Joan, who nearly died
when an infection from a horsefly bite drove her temperature up to a dangerous
level and the family waited for the end.

As a child, Miller played on the oriental carpet in the living room and
dreamed of being a soldier, especially since his mother's Uncle Moe had
brought a German helmet back from the war, a war in which he had driven
an ammunition wagon to the Front behind mules, only to be gassed and
return a broken man, already incubating the tuberculosis that would kill him.
'I used to walk around wearing that [helmet] when I was six years old. Being
a soldier was the greatest thing you could do.' Until he was twelve or thirteen
Miller wanted to go to West Point: 'It was a strong thing, a very strong image,
of being an officer in the army.'[59] He never made it but, fifty years later, did
go to West Point to denounce the Vietnam War in front of a hall full of
uniformed officers.

More practically, he was tempted to be a Boy Scout, not least because,
as Miller recalled, he had seen a photograph in the *New York Times* of
Commander Byrd, famous for his exploits in Antarctica, with a group of
sea scouts. The young Arthur Miller was, he insisted, 'absolutely a regular
citizen'. When he was not fantasizing about his military future, he was
reading *The Book of Knowledge* and marvelling at the world conjured up
by Charles Dickens. Slowly, he was absorbing an aesthetic world by
indirection and partly, he thought, because of the nature of the 1920s with
its popular music and movies. He was surrounded by art, in the form of
magazines, and hence never thought of it as remote, except that he was
aware of another kind that resided in museums and was, ultimately, none
of his business. Art, in all its forms, was to do with fame and excitement
and was part of a society full of a sense of its own energy.

The time came when he was at last granted access to a certain mystery,
when a man arrived to begin his education in Hebrew, 'a language already

associated in my mind with magic'. As he later explained:

> I was six or seven years old and my translator was an ancient man with a long
> yellowed beard who smelled of strong snuff tobacco. I have never been good
> at memorizing and certainly wasn't then, especially Hebrew words. So I had
> to piece together, syllable by syllable, the creation of the world, gradually
> filling out the empty spaces like a jigsaw puzzle, and there was a certain
> suspense and therefore a kind of sensuality in the proceeding. It was heavy
> duty – learning a language and simultaneously how the world was made, and
> the magical was inevitably a relief from having to figure it all out.[60]

It was a world, though, which seemed to have a hard time fitting in the
story of women. As he would observe, 'a certain darkness crept in with the
appearance of the Mother. As a boy I was perfectly happy with Adam and
God; now we had women to deal with, and mothers could see into a boy's
mind and know what he was thinking, which was usually something bad.'[61]
Yet his own mother embraced him and he could feel himself her ally even as
that alliance caused him a sense of unease that would take him years to
understand.

These were the days of icemen with their horse-drawn carts, of butchers'
shops with live chickens waiting for their necks to be cut to order. To buy
fish was to point out a particular flounder as it swam lazily in a tank and
watch it slit open and eviscerated. To go shopping was to choose pickles from
a barrel or horseradish run through a mincing machine. This was a time when
laundry was boiled on the stove and then dragged to the roof for drying,
when carpets were beaten on those same roofs by maids, so that dust would
rise above streets lined with expensive cars, their chauffeurs waiting to ferry
the owners downtown. Each day, Miller recalled, men climbed into those
cars looking grave and businesslike, a ritual that in some way seemed a
guarantee of stability, its rhythm reassuring and confident. Here was wealth,
a wealth that insulated the family from the daily life of those downtown and,
incidentally, from the gentiles, since this was a Jewish enclave.

Admittedly, this was also an era of Klan marches and, eventually, the reality
of prejudice would penetrate the Miller apartment, if only through the radio
and newspapers; but for the moment, and for a child growing up in a
family that seemed to have everything, this was another country. His mother
prepared Jewish food, draping noodles over the back of a chair to dry – as
Marilyn Monroe would do years later, briefly anxious, as she was, to penetrate
the mysteries of a Jewish cuisine that would confirm her in her new, and as it
turned out, temporary role as Jewish wife.

For entertainment, there was Central Park across the road, or fireflies,
released from jars on the top of their apartment building, flashing in the
night sky. In an unpublished short story, 'Ditchy', Miller recalls finding a

fledgling alongside a green stone in Central Park, a stone which as a child he had believed to be part of a star. He carried the bird to the top of his building, tied a May-bug to its leg, and watched as it spiralled down, the light going on and off like a blinking eye. It was on the roof, too, that he recalled seeing his first movie, a ten-minute short projected on to a sheet strung on a line. It was a lesson in illusion. Here, on this tabula rasa, high over New York, pictures flickered and stories unfolded. Life was a kaleidoscope of images.

The young Arthur built himself a racing machine by attaching baby-carriage wheels to a soapbox, speeding down the hill, never quite in control. 'Pretty good for my own making,' he boasted to his brother, who duly repeated the phrase to him in the ensuing years. Later, he would try to build himself a glider in a Brooklyn basement, forgetting, somehow, that he would have to dismantle it to get it out. He would go on bicycle rides deeper into Harlem, once or twice toying with the idea of running away, though from or towards what he was never clear. Time passed slowly, each stifling summer stretching out into an indefinite future.

His was also a protected life, although danger could come from unlikely quarters. As a child, Miller was a sleepwalker, one night waking up to find himself balanced on the edge of the airshaft that angled down to the ground below. He would dislike heights thereafter, watching appalled as his older brother jumped over those same airshafts.

In summer, when the heat became unbearable, people would drag their mattresses out on to the iron balconies and sleep there in their underwear. They slept in Central Park, alarm clocks close to hand to wake them for work. The Millers were too bourgeois to think of doing such a thing, and sweated the night through, secure in their status. Yet extremes of weather could create a camaraderie in New York. For entertainment, he and his brother raced each other around the lake in Central Park, timing themselves with the family clock.

Though Arthur wanted a pet, none was allowed. But there were other pleasures. In winter, children in the nearby apartments would wait for a red ball to be raised in the Park indicating that the ice on the pond was thick enough for skating, at which point they would pour out of the buildings, with mufflers round their necks, and run across the road – though the Park was not always entirely a safe place, as he discovered when some Italian boys stole his skates, an incident he recalls in 'Ditchy' in which the tremor of fear is recaptured in middle age. It was a lesson he also quickly learned in school. To be called up to the blackboard was to risk losing whatever you had on your desk, so that everything had to be automatically cleared away. Even their apartment was robbed, annually, when the family was away at the beach. The culprit, it turned out, was the caretaker. And the neighbourhood was changing. Originally, it had been German and Irish. The Italians and Jews moved in later, to be followed by African-Americans and Hispanics. The Italians lived in an area east of Third Avenue, between 106th Street and 125th Street.

According to his school principal, Miss Fisher, who had also taught his mother and who had kept samples of her handwriting pinned on the bulletin board for years, he was not well behaved, or at least not as well behaved as his older brother, and not very quick, or at least not as quick as his brother. Hardly surprisingly, in the circumstances, he and Kermit developed something of a competitive attitude to one another, though when they ran in the Park Kermit would always contrive to fall just short of the agreed finishing line rather than beat Arthur. Then, and later, he would lack his brother's drive and ambition, even sacrificing himself so that that brother could succeed.

Miller's preference for sport over study would continue throughout his schooldays and, eventually, prejudice his chances of university education and, as a result of a knee injury incurred during a football match, keep him out of the war, despite his efforts to join up.

Once Miss Fisher summoned his mother to discuss her younger son's deficiencies. These included a tendency to giggle (which he would control by recalling the death of his Uncle Hymie). Thereafter, he struggled to behave, as Puerto Rican children sucked penny stalks of sugar cane in class while some of the barefoot black pupils played truant and waved to them from a nearby rooftop as Miss Fisher recited speeches from *Julius Caesar*. Later he would recall learning almost nothing in classes which tended to empty on summer days. When, later, he reached college he had to spend nights teaching himself spelling, fractions and algebra. At this time it was not unusual for classes to be mixed, with Puerto Ricans as well as black and Italian students, not least, Miller would explain, because Harlem was not as yet a predominantly black area but still housed some of the better restaurants, theatres and clubs – some, like the Cotton Club, exclusively white, apart from those who served and entertained.

His mother would visit the Shubert Theatre four blocks away on Lenox. It was there, he recalls, that he saw his first stage play at about the age of eight, as later, like his father, he would go to vaudeville. At the Regent Theatre, on 116th and Seventh, he saw a brief drama set in Chinatown that warned of the dangers of drugs, especially to vulnerable young girls who evidently faced fates that were terrible if barely understandable. What, after all, was white slavery? Interestingly, this was a decade in which articles were published proposing that the influx of Russian Jews had been to blame for white slavery. He was shaken and enthralled. This, then, was theatre, a world that could seem tangibly real and that offered entertainment and moral instruction. Not far from the Miller apartment, meanwhile, was a Yiddish theatre, later to become the Second Canaan Baptist Church. In the 1920s there were twelve Yiddish theatres in New York.

For the moment, along with the rest of America, the Millers seemed to be taking a free ride. The country was booming. And those who were not were out of sight, though not that far, of course, since a few blocks to the north lay a Harlem that consisted of more than the Cotton Club. Seen from the height of an apartment looking out over Central Park, national and private destiny seemed in perfect alignment.

Downtown where the Miller money was made, there were, to be sure, still sweatshops and striving immigrants who stared through the glass, but what they saw was an America apparently exulting in the Jazz Age and reading the ticker-tape reports of stock-market rises as though these were the true word. This was the time when Christ was compared to an advertising executive (by a man who worked for an advertising agency which would one day be involved in NBC's *Cavalcade of America* series, for which Miller would write in the early 1940s and which would be invoked by him in an early draft of his 2002 play, *Resurrection Blues*). Advertisers commandeered the sky itself, projecting slogans from rooftops on to the clouds or writing across the heavens in smoke as aviators twisted and turned their aircraft to spell out the virtues of familiar products.

In their climb up the American ladder, however, the family had not entirely abandoned their religious roots, not least because of the brooding presence of Miller's maternal grandfather whose piety had increased with age and leisure. Once he had left his business behind, the synagogue increasingly offered him a sense of significance. He now lived with his family, spending six months with each daughter, like a downmarket King Lear and almost as resentful. One, Augusta, lived in Manhattan, in an eleven-room apartment, another in what seemed a kind of exile in Brooklyn in a small house with a single bathroom. He did not appreciate this shuttling to and fro. The synagogue offered him the respect he felt lacking in his family life.

Arthur Miller, then, grew up in a world in which Jewishness was part of his identity but in a way, and to an extent, that he could never really understand until he stepped outside the Jewish community that marked the parameters of his experience. In his autobiography he recalls visiting a library on Fifth Avenue and being required to give the name of his parents before borrowing books. He fled. Beyond the normal awkwardness of a child made to offer his parents' first names, was a special anxiety. Looking up at the librarian, 'I could not bring to voice my father's so Jewish name, Isidore'. He pretended to have forgotten it. Asked what his mother called him, he refused to say. This seems only in part to be a reflection of his sensitivity about Jewishness. It was also, surely, the familiar response of a child of immigrants, anxious to be like those around him and hence embarrassed by a family so manifestly unlike them. His parents and grandparents spoke of another time and place. It was not an inheritance he wanted or that seemed particularly relevant. Yet something was being inculcated, beyond the rote learning of the Talmud that was for a while a resented part of his daily life. What was communicated was a sense of vulnerability. Seeing an accident on the street Miller and his brother pressed forward, only to be pulled back by their father with the warning, 'Stay away from crowds', crowds in Eastern Europe often presaging an attack on Jews.

Looking back more than sixty years later, he came to feel that the fear that had stopped him naming his father to the librarian was 'so deeply buried that I can only imagine I had been denying, quietly and persistently, what I surely must have been hearing [as a child] – stories, remarks, fear-laden vocal tones that had been moving me by inches into a beleaguered zone surrounded by strangers with violent hearts'.[62] In a key passage in his novel *Focus*, that fear is rooted more securely in a Polish past, the past from which such stories had sprung. The librarian, he came to feel, had seemed to challenge him to identify himself as a candidate for victimization. If he could not see that at the time, and perhaps if it had not even been true, something of his background, something he had picked up from his family without even realizing it, must have made him respond as if the instinct for survival had been bred into him. Perhaps he registered something of the mood of the country which culminated in the passing of the Johnson anti-immigration bill in 1924, which sought to reduce the flow of immigrants from Eastern Europe, and hence Jews.

In the 1960s, Miller wrote a brief memoir headed 'In an Effort to Penetrate to Feeling'. It was not designed for publication, not corrected for grammar or, indeed, finished, and in it he spoke of himself in the third person as though trying to burrow into his consciousness from the outside. It was an effort, though, to recall what it had felt like growing up in a Jewish household. He remembered, for example, that whenever a pot fell off the stove or she pricked her finger with a darning needle, his mother would cry out: 'A schwartz yu'r on alle goyim!' (A black year on all gentiles). There were other warnings about those not of the faith and of the cabalistic symbols that seemingly had a mysterious power, but even as a young boy he found it hard to take these entirely seriously. He recalled a lighted cross hung on a church front over the sidewalk a few blocks away. His grandfather warned him never to walk beneath it, never to let its shadow fall on him even for an instant. Within a short time he had forgotten the supposed threat. One generation's values meant nothing, it seemed, to another for whom such warnings had no roots in lived experience. Indeed, if anything, they served to open a gulf where his grandfather had thought to close one.

As for his mother, at times she seemed to favour gentiles over Jews, or over

certain Jews with whom she had no desire to be associated. As a result, it
appeared to him that there was a crucial distinction to be made. The good
Jew was a leader, exemplary, pure. The bad Jew was self-interested, deceitful,
sexually aware. Also, there was some implied threat that had to be neutralized
by good behaviour and achievement. There was, in short, a safety to be found
in success, and there is surely a sense in which Miller, like his mother,
internalized this. At the same time it meant that success could never entirely
be separated from a form of self-contempt, a sense that he was being judged
by those whose regard was never quite what it appeared. He was being the
good Jew.

In a way, he argued to himself in his draft memoir, this is no more than
the situation of all children, for whom there are always two worlds, one
within the family and one without, the latter offering possibilities and
threats in equal proportion. But his Jewish memories were not by any
means all associated with threat or fear. There was, he confessed, something
curious but reassuring about the male world of the synagogue, about a
community focused on a single text. The rituals had their own rhythms,
the mysteries a kind of oblique excitement. Even the muttered Hebrew
suggested that language had a power that was not entirely explicable. At
the 114th Street synagogue he used to sit beside his great-grandfather
Barnett as he swayed back and forth in prayer.

The synagogue on Seventh Avenue – the Ansche Chesed synagogue –
which had moved north from Beakman Place near 50th Street in 1893, had a
German Conservative Orthodox congregation. It was one of the grandest in
Harlem. In 1910 the rabbi, Jacob Kahn, had replaced German-born Gustav
Hausman, dismissed for 'not possessing the spiritual uplift which a spiritual
leader and religious teacher must have'. The new rabbi urged the study of
Hebrew and inspired a religious awakening.[63] The building itself, designed
by Edward Shire, was imposing and aimed to reflect the wealth of those who
attended it. It had a neo-classical porch behind six tall columns supporting a
pediment with a decalogue representing the ten commandments. Its corner-
stone was dated 1908 and 5668, the latter according to the Hebrew calendar.
It was designed to impress. When, in the late 1920s, the wealthy moved away,
Ansche Chesed followed them to the west side of the Park.

His maternal great-grandfather, six foot four and with a white beard stained
with chewing tobacco, was a spinner of stories, and though he died before
Miller went to school, sixty-five years later he still recalled not so much the
content of those stories, often recounted in Yiddish, as their intoxicating
power, their ability to place the teller at the centre of the group. This was the
man who, on his deathbed, accused the young rabbi who attended him of
stealing diamonds from under his pillow. Rising from his bed, he walked to
the 114th Street synagogue and confronted him, beating him with a stick until

he confessed. He then returned to his bed, distributed the diamonds to his family, and died. And though this has the feel of a story shaped and polished like the diamonds it features, it seems clear that what a young Arthur Miller later recalled was the fascination of mere experience given form and point by a man whose power came in part from language. This was a man who, in the 1920s, had a special seat in the synagogue and who, in hot weather, when the door was left open, would rock back and forth 'with all the sorrows of Israel', occasionally spitting chewing tobacco out on to the fire escape.

Miller later commented on a moment of revelation when, in researching *The Crucible* in Salem, he suddenly recognized that there was a connection between the severe Puritans, blending a faith in God and justice, a belief in rational process and a dangerous arbitrariness, and the Jewish patriarchs. Those Puritan divines were, he came to feel, 'ur-Hebrews, with the same fierce idealism, devotion to God, tendency to legalistic reductiveness, the same longings for the pure and intellectually elegant argument. And God was driving them as crazy as He did the Jews trying to maintain their uniquely stainless vessel of faith in Him.' A painting of the Puritan judges, seen in the Historical Society at Salem, seemed suddenly to bring to mind the figures he had seen dancing in the 114th Street synagogue: 'I knew instantly what the connection was: the moral intensity of the Jews and the clan's defensiveness against pollution from outside the ranks ... I understood Salem in that flash, it was suddenly my own inheritance.'[64]

Miller was eleven when his great-grandfather died, and he later recalled the scene which took place in a large Flatbush house. Men from the synagogue sat drinking seltzer mixed with red wine while his mother told a familiar story about Madame Lupescu being the brains behind the King of Rumania, an obsession of hers for reasons he could never understand. Outside was a row of cars, a few with chauffeurs. The emotions of the occasion were beyond him, though first his father and then his mother burst into tears. His uncles cried into handkerchiefs, all, except one, tall and balding, whose wife had left him. The young Arthur was then taken upstairs to witness his great-grandfather's death.

The old man seemed small. He had a Vandyke beard and wore a white satin yarmulke on his white hair. They all waited until at last he struggled to rise up in the bed, his blue eyes open wide. The old man looked round at the men gathered around him, spoke his last words – 'So many hats?' – fell back and died. Only then were the women allowed in. His grandmother entered, straightening her wig. Everyone stopped crying, everyone but Arthur, who chose this moment to show the emotion he had seen but not felt. His brother instantly hissed him to stop.

There is perhaps something rather too neat about the surreal last words of this aged patriarch. When Miller's maternal grandfather died he, too,

supposedly obliged with a memorable phrase. By then he had only a single
dollar in the bank and expired with the words, 'So I am even.'

At the age of twelve much was a mystery to Miller, not least sex. He was
bewildered by the thought of men and women in bed together. Girls were,
he confessed, a race apart. He was embarrassed if one even looked in his
direction. In the synagogue women were separated from the men, watching
from the balcony as though the rites performed below were not primarily for
them. Yet he was always drawn to their company.

His Uncle 'Lou', in fact Manny Newman, one of the two uncles who had
moved to Brooklyn in the early 1920s, had no inhibitions with women, his
wife a blowsy figure, sexually provocative, with two sons virile and themselves
successful with the girls. When Miller was a child, he had quietly envied
them. He wore clothes from Fifth Avenue stores; their sweatshirts and
bell-bottom pants came from Sears. He liked theirs better. Lou was an
incorrigible liar. According to Augusta, he was 'so full of shit he's a danger to
the block', though in the end he proved a greater danger to himself, finally
committing suicide. Beyond anything, however, he wanted success for his
boys. If they needed books to study they would be liberated from stores or
libraries.

As young boys, Miller and Kermit would join their uncle and cousins on
camping trips which sometimes had more to offer than an introduction to
the kind of nature they had been expecting. On one such a young woman
appeared in the apple orchard where they had pitched their tents and offered
her services to Buddy Newman. They held a collection and he disappeared
into the tent with her, to be followed by Kermit Miller. Arthur, then twelve,
was not invited, and sat in his tent holding his breath, unsure what exactly it
was that he was missing. And it was this uncle who kept a box of pornographic
cards in the closet. On New Year's Eve, when relatives came round to party,
he would pass these photographs around. Some seventy years later, this scene
would be recalled in his play *Broken Glass* as the sexually impotent Phillip
Gellburg is taunted with memories of just such an occasion. Little in Miller's
life would be lost.

Isidore Miller was heavily committed on a stock market that, it was presumed,
would rise for ever. It was an unreal world, a world of bonds and share
certificates and ticker-tape fantasies. At least on paper, he grew richer every
day. The business of manufacturing women's coats seemed increasingly beside
the point. His attention switched from the Lower East Side to Wall Street.
Money simply materialized. Then it all changed. 1929 marked a sharp divide
not only in the fortunes of the Miller family but in American experience.

One of those interviewed by Studs Terkel for his book on the Depression,

Hard Times, that would later be one of the inspirations behind Miller's *The American Clock*, described it as like a thunderclap. Everybody was stunned. Nobody knew what it was about. 'The Street had general confusion. They didn't understand it any more than anybody else. They thought something would be announced.'[65] As Terkel rhetorically asks, who now could make such an announcement?

The Depression was cataclysmic. This was an economy that had developed a high-wire act without a safety net. There was no social security, no unemployment benefit. There were few unions and those there were seemed powerless before economic forces that swept jobs away overnight. The literal step into the void taken by some financiers, as they plummeted down to the street from their offices above the city, was merely a metaphor for the precipitate downward plunge of those who suddenly discovered all support taken away, who found their social authority and very identity under threat. Isidore Miller's company foundered, leaving him bewildered, no longer in command of his fate, no longer able to invest in the sons who were to have been the mark of his achievement.

An historical process seemed to have run its course. Capitalism had apparently exhausted itself in its own circularities of demand and consumption and collapsed in the face of forces to which it had no response. As Edmund Wilson was to remark, 'The stock-market crash was to count for us almost like a rending of the earth in preparation for the Day of Judgement.' If it came as a shock to those committed to the American system, however, to others it implied the welcome collapse of capitalism. As Wilson observed:

> One couldn't help being exhilarated at the sudden unexpected collapse of that stupid gigantic fraud. It gave us a new sense of freedom ... a new sense of power to find ourselves still carrying on while the bankers, for a change, were taking a beating. With a businessman's president in the White House, who kept telling us ... that the system was perfectly sound, who sent General Douglas MacArthur to burn the camp of the unemployed war veterans who had come to appeal to Washington, we wondered about the survival of representative American institutions; and we became more and more impressed by the achievements of the Soviet Union.[66]

At fourteen, Miller, now six feet tall and very thin, registered the Depression on a more personal level, but within three years he would share Wilson's convictions. Nor was this to be simply a financial disaster. The Crash would redefine the real. There is a metaphysics to sudden loss of any kind. It carries with it a knowledge that nothing, perhaps, is secure, and for Jewish immigrants that knowledge tapped into deeper insecurities. Certainly, in interviews and in many of his plays – most obviously the autobiographical

The American Clock – the Depression would stand out as a national disaster beyond all others, bar the Civil War. For him, it was never simply a matter of money. It was the root of emotional collapse, of social and political upheaval, and of a shift in the moral and ontological ground on which Americans believed themselves to stand.

Why did it sink its roots so deep into his sensibility? It was, he said later, because the Depression was 'my time'. When 'you're fourteen or fifteen you walk into a moment of history. It's your most sensitive moment of consciousness. That's when the world is most inevitable, when you have least perspective on it and consequently it reaches in deeper than anything else.'[67] The Depression taught him that no system was reliable, that everything could disappear. It fostered a feeling of helplessness in the Miller family and a knowledge that, like so many others, they had collaborated in their own fall. They had believed in the something-for-nothing ethos of the 1920s. A solid business had seemingly slipped through their fingers, and that was, in some mysterious way, their fault or, more precisely, Isidore Miller's fault, since his wife had been unaware of the extent of their market exposure. They had embraced the unreality of paper fortunes and were now to be exiled to Brooklyn as a result, a Brooklyn where their poor relations lived. As Miller later explained:

> My father made the great discovery, made by better men than he, that you could make more money on the stock market than you could manufacturing. You could make eighty–ninety per cent in six months. Well, you could not do that in a legitimate business. It was impossible, unless you were mining gold. So more and more of the capital of these businesses went into the stock market, leaving them less and less operating capital. But they were all relying on the ever-rising stock market. So, whenever they needed the cash, they would sell some stock. They would sell it at a much higher price than they had bought it for. So everybody was happy.

When the market turned, however, they 'would have to sell stock at a lower price than they had bought it for. So they took a distinct loss. And then, pretty soon, they needed more cash, because the market was drying up. People were losing their jobs. The amount of purchasing going on was less and less and, within a year or so, a lot of businesses simply folded up.' The Millers' business collapsed. 'It was humiliating.'[68] When, thirty years later, in March 1961, Augusta Miller died of a heart ailment, her husband Isidore was described in the newspaper notices as a salesman, what he had been just a few years after arriving in the country.

As the Depression deepened, so family tensions increased. For Miller himself, loyalties were not so much divided as oscillating and already his own future was seeming less clear. Like his father-in-law before him, Isidore declared bankruptcy but, unlike him, attempted to pay his debts. He acted out of a sense of honour, out of a desire to keep his good name, but the result was potentially ruinous and ultimately futile.

In *After the Fall*, in a play fragment he wrote in the late 1960s and in *The American Clock*, Miller returns to the trauma of this time and to the arguments he overheard as his father's authority was stripped away along with his money. His father had sold his stocks and cashed in his insurance, as well as his wife's bonds. In *After the Fall* the mother cries out, 'You throw good money after bad? Are you some kind of moron?' He replies, 'You don't walk away from a business; I came to this country with a tag around my neck like a package in the bottom of the boat!' Her reply – 'I should have run the day I met you ... I should have done what my sisters did, tell my parents to go to hell and thought of myself for once! I should have run for my life! ... I ought to get a divorce!' – serves in the play, as it did in Miller's life, as a symbol of that abandonment, that cruelty, that broken connection, which destroys the faith of the child who hears it. Beyond that, it becomes an image of a wider collapse of mutuality. All of this came directly from his family life. He heard the arguments, the accusations and the contempt in his mother's voice, the sense of defeat and humiliation in his father's. As Quentin/Miller asks, in a speech from *After the Fall* cut from the final version, 'Aren't there mothers who keep dissatisfaction hidden to the grave, and do not split the faith of sons until they go in guilt of what they did not do?'[69]

Miller's mother was for many years at the centre of his emotional life. He could terrify himself with the thought that he could lose her while finding it unimaginable that such a moment would ever come. Yet at some level he knew he was part of a battle going on above his head. The children were a compensation for something lost along the way. Married to an illiterate man, who at moments could shame her and who came to represent her failed opportunities, Augusta turned to them, encouraging them, as all mothers do, but, in part at least, he came to feel, because they were weapons in some battle never to be fully understood. When she spoke with awe about writers, those who succeeded not by accumulating money but by creating something genuinely new in the world, he knew that it was both a criticism of his father and the expression of a heartfelt hope that he and his brother might achieve something similar, and in escaping carry her with them.

When he began to write it was of his mother he thought. It was to her he would send letters from college; after all, his father could not read them. At the same time, he would begin to resent the fact that somehow he was performing a role in some drama not of his own devising. So it was that in time a gulf would open between them, between two people who loved one another but where love would begin to seem instrumental, as if he were working in some sense on her behalf and as if there was a kind of contract whereby he would redeem her from her inner loneliness and sense of waste. And slowly that burden began to pull them apart even as they were both bewildered that such a bond could be broken.

In a sense the journey from unquestioned love to something approaching an objectivity qualified by that same love, and guilt, is a familiar one. It is complicated here by the sense of her despair over her marriage and the weight she accordingly placed on her children. It is complicated, too, by Miller's awareness of the role into which he had been cast, a role close enough to his own emotional needs to leave him with a residue of guilt. For he, too, felt distant from his father, uncultured, uncultivated, who required of him only success, a success which in truth he craved but which he came to suspect as the source of the false values that had warped his own family and defined the society with which he felt increasingly at odds.

He, too, yearned to become the artistic genius admired by his mother, and hence, when, later, he bought into Freudian theory, that placed him in an ambivalent relationship to the woman who had effectively wooed him away from her husband. There was, perhaps, more than one reason for the references to patricide and incest that scatter his writings.

The family were not impoverished immediately, nor did the money quite disappear overnight, but it was gone within the year. The move from Manhattan came as a shock, though less so for Arthur and Kermit for whom the chauffeur-driven car was scarcely part of their daily experience. Nonetheless, that seven-seat National automobile had set them apart. The Harlem apartment had cost $135 a month, where other middle-class families were paying thirty or forty. There was also the summer cottage on the white sandy beach at Far Rockaway, with a view of the sea, where Miller had once been bitten on the finger by an organ grinder's monkey. That all went: chauffeur, car, cottage. Suddenly, they were living in a world in which, as Miller would remark, there was nobody running the store. To the later bafflement of his wife, Kermit was withdrawn from the Townsend Harris School whose three-year programme was designed for those who scored highly on the Regents examinations (a set of standardised tests used in New York schools) and who had ambitions to go to City College. He could have continued, travelling in by subway, but his mother seems to have decided to make a complete break.

In 2007 Kermit's son Ross, an academic and biographer, observed: 'My father was pulled from Townsend Harris because it became inconvenient for his parents. Once they moved to Brooklyn he transferred to James Madison [High School]. This was a blow to my father. But in his usual stoical manner he accepted the decision. My mother understood it this way: Working class families sacrifice for their children; middle class families expect their children to sacrifice for them.'[70]

Alfred Kazin once remarked that the move from Brooklyn to Manhattan was the longest trip in the world. It was a sign that you had finally made it. The Millers were going the other way, against the logic, so it appeared, that had once taken them from the Lower East Side to the top of Central Park. Now they were moving to the periphery, away from money, away from power. It was a symbol of failure. As it happens, however, this was not the exile it seemed, at least not for a young man with literary ambitions. A number of those who were to shape American literary life also grew up in Brooklyn, so that Hannah Arendt would later speak of 'the boys from over the bridges'.

Besides which, Jewish Harlem had been steadily declining in numbers throughout the 1920s, from 160,000 in 1923 to 88,000 in 1927 and 25,000 in 1930. Later estimates, Jeffrey S. Gurock has suggested, put the figure closer to 5,000.[71] Where did they go? Some went to the Upper West Side, and some to Brooklyn, which had its wealthy sections – Flatbush – as well as its poor. For the Millers, though, theirs did not seem part of a general population shift but exile; however, many decades later Joan would return to live in a luxury apartment on Central Park West, and her brother Arthur to own a pied-à-terre in the East 70s.

When his maternal grandmother, Rose, died, they moved first to their half of a sizeable two-family house on Ocean Parkway and then, in order to be close to other members of Augusta's family, to a small six-room frame house at 1350 East 3rd Street, in the Midwood section of Brooklyn. One of these relatives was her sister who, with her husband Manny, had moved down from the north of New York State and spoke in a rural way, saying 'road' for 'street' and 'fetch' for 'carry'. He had, Miller later discovered from his son, only wanted a business for his boys, one of whom, according to an unpublished and fictionalised memoir, was a fantasist while the other was earning next to nothing down in New Mexico – *Death of a Salesman*'s Happy and Biff Loman in embryo. Miller's parents had slipped Manny money from time to time, as Charley would help Willy in that same play, so that for those who would later wonder if Willy was based on Isidore Miller, Manny was a more plausible model.

East 3rd Street was a cul-de-sac ending at the Friends' School Athletic Field, where a young Arthur Miller would sometimes walk behind the motor-ized mower for twenty-five cents a day. It was there, too, that he would teach his sister to play tennis, she squeezing through the gap left by a padlocked gate or, later, climbing the mesh fence and throwing herself down into his waiting arms. Beyond lay a cemetery. The house, of clapboard and brick, consisted of three bedrooms, a bathroom, kitchen, dining room and living room. Later the gables would be painted white, but at the time few chose to paint them at all. There was a small hedge in front, now gone. The house cost five thousand dollars and was bought with a large mortgage, payments on which became a monthly torment. The three bathrooms of their Manhattan apartment, with its views across the city, had shrunk to one. The city was now a distant prospect.

For the Millers, it represented a fall from grace. For others, though, it was a step up from the slums in which they had been trapped. In some ways, indeed, this kind of neighbourhood lay at the heart of the American experience. It was a modest house. Even a teenage Arthur Miller could reach out his arms and nearly touch the next one. It was the kind of house, though, in which many Americans raised their families. It was, Miller later said, Willy Loman territory. The streets were as muddy as Russian roads. People caught rabbits and snakes in traps and stored sacks of potatoes in their cellars. Children walked to school through tomato fields rented by Italian families. It was a village with village crimes. He and others would steal from the local candy store and play handball against the wall of the druggist's store, breaking his window.

By the end of the 1930s one-third of the borough's population – 850,000 people – would be Jewish, half the city's Jews. It was by no means a poor area. Some neighbourhoods had wide streets and elegant houses; others were more constrained. East 3rd Street was one such and certainly a drastic contrast with what had gone before, an eloquent symbol of the reversal of the family's fortunes.

From here the elevated Culver Line, its wooden carriages heated with coal-fired iron stoves in winter, ran towards Coney Island, two and a half miles distant, the place where a ten-year-old Joseph Heller was growing up. Its racketing rhythm could be heard from East 3rd Street. Indeed it still runs a bare hundred yards away and was clearly visible from the Miller backyard. Long steel stairs led up to the station. In summer it was possible to open the doors and ride in the open air. Alfred Kazin recalled how it felt:

> Groaning its way past a thousand old Brooklyn red fronts and tranquil awnings, that old train could never go slowly enough for me as I stood on the open platform between the cars, holding on to the gate . . . As we came back at night . . . the great reward of the long parched day, far better than any massed and arid beach, was the chance to stand up there between the cars . . . In the summer night the city had an easy unstitched look – people sat on the corner watching the flies buzz around the street lamps, or at bedroom windows openly yawning as they stared past us.[72]

Miller's aunts and uncles had moved to Brooklyn in the immediate aftermath of the First World War when it was virtually countrified. It still had a rural feel to it in the early 1930s. There were few of the conveniences of the city. 'Every twenty blocks or so there would be a grocery store, and people bought food in large quantities, because you didn't just jump into a car and go shopping then. They bought twenty-five-pound bags of potatoes and ten cabbages.' Families, especially the Italian ones, grew their own vegetables and raised their own animals. There was even hunting, of a minor kind (squirrels and small game), in the woods. Manhattan was a nickel's ride away in one direction, while Miller and his cousins would rise at four in the morning and climb around the Culver Line turnstiles, to go fishing for sea bass and flounder off the rocks at Coney Island, the breakwaters that curve out from the white sand. In truth, in 2004 Miller would admit that all too often the hook became stuck in those rocks and he 'never caught anything'.

To a boy in his mid-teens, Brooklyn represented a release. He had cousins there, poorer, but

> terrific athletes ... Their parents bought them these awful cheap shoes which I thought were just terrific. They were punctured with all kinds of designs in the front; they cost two dollars a pair. My shoes were eight dollars, miserable high-class shoes. There was space there. Brooklyn then had empty lots so that you could play football, or baseball. You could get lost. There were areas that still had not been cut up into streets; there were woods, and I loved that.[73]

He played football on a vacant lot on Avenue M and Gravesend Avenue and skated at the rink on Ocean Parkway. At the East 3rd Street house he dug up the small backyard, which consisted of infill, littered with cans and bottles, and planted tulips. In 1931 he added two trees, a pear and an apple, with just enough distance between them so that one day a hammock could be hung there. The apple tree blew down in a storm, as would the apple tree in *All My Sons*, whereas when he returned nearly fifty years later the pear tree had grown as high as the house. In 2004, the modest house was occupied by orthodox Jews, as were those alongside it. An extension had been added, but the pear tree still stood. Indeed, each year the family blessed it. They had themselves lived there for more than twenty years but knew nothing of its past. They did, though, know of Willy Loman, but not of the fact that their house was the one in which Miller saw his ageing salesman as living out his last twenty-four hours on earth.

Like his brother, Miller went to the James Madison High School, between Avenue P and Quentin Road, being enrolled a year before finishing grammar school. He frequently jogged there, anxious to get on the track team rather than shine academically. Later, he transferred to the newly opened Abraham Lincoln High School on Ocean Parkway near Shore Parkway, where, a slight hundred-and-twenty-pound figure, he played end in the second squad of the football team, picking up a torn ligament, the injury that years later kept him out of the army. Today, the school sports field acknowledges the financial support of Donald Trump's parents. Beyond sport, though, Miller always felt something of an outsider, later observing that he had never had much sense of what was going on. If there was a photography club he only heard about it in the middle of the term and never discovered where it met. He was, he confessed, a 'bewildered' student. The Year Book may have listed his ambition to go to Stanford University, but he certainly did nothing to prepare himself for this.

With the Depression, things had begun to change. When the Bank of the United States closed (a Jewish-owned bank, Alfred Kazin lamented), the line of desperate depositors stretched for five blocks along Avenue J, only blocks from the Miller home. It had held deposits of one-fifth of New York Jews and was the largest financial institution ever to suspend payments. It had sixty branches in New York and four hundred thousand depositors, mostly Jewish. Rumour in the Jewish community suggested that anti-Semitic banking officials had allowed it to fail.[74] Miller had himself withdrawn his twelve-dollar deposit only the day before. His sense of triumph was short-lived, however, when the bicycle he had bought from his friend Joey Backus, a Columbia Racer, was stolen the next day.

Years later, after writing about this incident in his autobiography, he was riding a somewhat dilapidated bicycle through New York when a truck drew up beside him and the driver shouted, 'Hey, Miller! At least no one's gonna steal that one.' Now, on the way to and from school, he would pass the unemployed, sitting on the front stoops of houses. Fellow students began to drop out, looking for work. Stores began to close; fewer people came off the Culver Line at Avenue M. Long after, he would write a radio play about the desperation of a subway train driver, driven crazy by the monotony of his journey from Coney Island to Manhattan. But at least subway train drivers had jobs, as did postmen, who now became envied figures. Meanwhile, the mortgage man came to call at the Millers', only to be deflected with coffee and cake. This was not poverty. It was genteel desperation of the kind Tennessee Williams dramatized in *The Glass Menagerie*, and though Augusta Miller was a long way removed from Amanda Wingfield she, too, bore the burden of sustaining the family, concealing her own desperation from those closest to her.

Miller was forced to share a room with his maternal grandfather. The old man would lay his head on four pillows, each smaller than the one beneath, spending five minutes arranging those pillows so that they were exactly in the middle of the bed. He would fold his socks carefully before dropping them in the laundry basket. He paid four dollars a week rent and insisted on sitting at the head of the table. One effect of the Depression was to reassemble families no longer able to sustain themselves in their separate homes. The generations were suddenly forced on one another. Babies and great-grandparents tussled for the same space. A lifetime's possessions had to be pushed into a single set of drawers. And as the space shrank so suppressed tensions bubbled to the surface. Referred to contemptuously by his father as the 'lodger', Miller's grandfather began to be the source of general irritation. He had arrived with his own soup plate, bigger than those used in the Miller household, and insisted on it being filled to the brim. Each week he would remind Augusta of the Sabbath, as though she might otherwise forget it.

To Miller, he had something of the air of a Prussian general, his speech scattered with German and Yiddish expressions. He dressed immaculately and wore a black satin skullcap, with a sharp crease. On hot days he would change his eyeglasses, looking for what he calls a cool pair. For him, there were winter eyeglasses and summer eyeglasses. When the family moved to Brooklyn, he had carried with him more furniture than their new house justified. This he now fussily rearranged. Augusta was afraid of him and rushed to greet him each morning as he descended at seven-thirty.

He was a remnant from another world, the carrier of traditions, prejudices, language, other ways of doing things. He had no desire to be swallowed by the new culture, at least not now he was retired and business no longer required compromises. Like her older brother, Joan Copeland, Arthur's sister, remembered her grandfather as speaking German and Yiddish or a heavily accented English: 'If you wanted to put an advertisement in the newspaper about what you had to sell it would be called an "offertisement".' He was dictatorial: 'Mother was expected to jump whenever he said "jump".' This, she suspected, was the source of her father's resentment. His authority was already undermined by the loss of his business and his reliance on his wife's money. The idea of the old man setting himself up as a patriarch infuriated him. In his first student play Miller would make fun of him but in the East 3rd Street house he was the source of genuine friction.

Grandpa Barnett was also deeply religious. Joan later remarked that he 'spent most of his days, as I recall, in the temple, praying hard to live longer ... because the world would stop if Grandpa didn't go to the temple'.[75] Her brother remembered him in the family home, rocking to and fro. Such behaviour, along with the rituals of the synagogue, dietary rules, shared ceremonies, were, perhaps, offered as a reproach to those who no longer saw their purpose – or saw them, as Miller eventually would, as evidence of precisely those socially and morally reactionary traditions that had to be abandoned in the name of a new religion of man.

For the time being, though, Augusta's father was simply a kind of ancient presence, accepted by the young Arthur, like everything else, as part of a given world. Having once owned his own business, Barnett offered advice to his son-in-law, as his business failed, so that there was a constant tension between the two men. As Miller explained, 'He had that Germanic, dictatorial nature. Everything had to be exactly so. He was very clean. Everything around him was spotless.'[76]

In 1943, and perhaps significantly in a Jewish monthly called *New Currents: A Jewish Monthly*, Miller, described as a 'young short story and radio writer', published an ironic memoir of his grandfather, broad-shouldered and heavy, with 'a belly that forced him to stand stiffly erect, a Prussian head as bald as a stone'.[77] In this, he recalled him announcing: 'Roosevelt ... is a great man. *Grossartik*. Like Abraham Lincoln, like Franz Joseph he is', Franz Joseph, supposedly, having ridden into his village throwing silver kronen to the people *including* the Jews. Though his background should have precluded support for a man whose policies smacked of socialism, he was not out of step. In 1932 almost three-quarters of New York Jews had voted for Roosevelt. By 1940 the figure was nearly 90 per cent. He was, though, a little confused in his political views. Miller recalled him suggesting that his grandson should go to Russia, a land of opportunity, until he learned that private businesses were illegal there. He also remembered how the old man would stride manfully along the sidewalk of Avenue M until he reached the family home, whereupon he began to move with difficulty so that they would be aware of his suffering. He drank 'gallons of mineral water', and ate as many chops as there were. On his deathbed he had announced that he wanted a wider burial plot than had been set aside, asking his relatives to contribute the difference. Then, changing his mind, he dressed and announced that he was going to have a new suit made, 'with two pairs of pants'. He died three weeks later, with eleven suits in his closet. The new one was delivered on the day of his death.

Miller's paternal grandfather, by contrast, had held on to much of his money, and done nothing to help his relatives as they slid into debt, a fact that remained a mystery to Miller as it did to his brother, though it was the cause of considerable and understandable bitterness between Isidore and Augusta, who never got on with her mother-in-law either, not least because Isidore who, as a child, had been effectively abandoned by them, seemed intent on buying the love they failed to offer. When they had still had money, if he had given his wife a jewelled bracelet he also felt obliged to give one to his mother. Even when there were no longer any jewelled bracelets to give, the relationship between Augusta and her mother-in-law remained fraught. '[She] says there's a Depression going on,' remarks the character based on Augusta in *The American Clock*. 'Meantime you can go blind from the diamonds on her fingers. Which he gave her!'[78]

Augusta also blamed her mother-in-law for sending her son out to work after only two weeks of schooling, thus ensuring his illiteracy. And plainly these tensions were registered by Miller, who makes his parents characters in *After the Fall*. In this he has the figure based on Augusta complain of her mother-in-law, 'That's what some women are ... and now he goes and buys her a new Packard every year.'[79] Isidore had put $30,000 into his brother's business. A year later, he had to borrow to buy a coat for his daughter.

There was never really any question of Isidore and Augusta divorcing, though they talked about it, and not only because it was expensive. In fact the divorce rate declined during the Depression as people clung together even in their misery, aware at some level that the fault did not lie with one another but with a machine that had simply ceased to work. Nonetheless, Augusta's conviction that her husband was being used by his parents became ever more acute. His mother seemed, to her, to have no redeeming qualities, being mindlessly materialistic and wholly lacking in maternal feelings. As Joan later remarked to me in 1999, 'I think that she [Augusta] always felt that they were sucking him dry.' Her grandmother 'had absolutely no feeling for what one would refer to as the finer things in life, things that my mother would have loved. She understood money and she understood diamonds.' Even the simplest gesture seemed beyond her. She promised Joan an unset diamond, first for her sixteenth birthday, then for her engagement, then for her marriage, then for her first child. It was never forthcoming. Her son Isidore never having been her favourite, 'she kept taking from him and demanding from him things that really belonged to my mother'.

Miller's parents were caught in a drama for which they did not have primary responsibility, but the fault lines that had always existed now opened and certainties began to fade as the small house, in which there was effectively no privacy, staged the collapse of a marriage and of the security it had once seemed to confirm.

The portrait of Augusta offered in *After the Fall* is of a woman frightened at their new relative poverty, occasionally to the point of hysteria, who suddenly realizes that she has sacrificed her life for nothing. Yet, at the same time, she has no alternative but to battle on, improvising in the face of disaster. As Lee, Miller's alter ego, remarks in *The American Clock*, 'After all these years I still can't settle with myself about my mother. In her own crazy way she was like the country. There was nothing she believed that she didn't also believe the opposite ... money obsessed her but she really longed for some height where she could stand and see out and around and breathe in the air of her own free life.' She would 'lament her fate as a woman: "I was born twenty years too soon," she'd say. "They treated me like a cow, fill her up with a baby and lock her in for the rest of her life."' But then she would warn her son, as Augusta warned hers, 'Watch out for women – when they're not stupid they're full of deceit.'

At the same time, with all her defeats, 'she believed to the end that the world was meant to be better."[80] She would listen to her son's radicalism, when he returned from university in the late 1930s, and seemingly thrill to his vision, only to abandon it for a more patrician view. They came from poor people who became rich and now they had lost nearly everything, including the love which was the name they had given to contentment. The contradictory rhythm of their lives was that of the culture, and it is a rhythm that beats in most of Arthur Miller's plays as hopes are betrayed, ideals compromised, even lives lost while at the same time a current runs the other way, raising death in the direction of tragedy, redeeming the broken, discovering meaning in seemingly lost lives. For hope was never entirely relinquished, and this, too, they shared with the country. Even the jokes, as Miller later recalled, had a certain self-conscious irony: 'A wealthy lady is confronted with a beggar who holds out his hand and says, "Lady, I haven't eaten in three days." To which she replies, "Well, you have to force yourself."'

From time to time Isidore made another attempt to set up a business. For a while he had a small coat company on 39th Street, employing a dozen men who worked the sewing machines, handling thick woollen coats in the heat of summer. Miller later recalled one man who bit off inch-long strands of thread. By the end of the day they sprayed out from his lips like a fringe. One match and his mouth would have flamed. That company, too, went bankrupt. In the end it was Augusta's efforts that would keep them afloat.

Augusta's frustration at what she saw as her wasted life turned into a bitterness at the man who could no longer support them and who she blamed for their predicament. She communicated her frustration to her children. After all, she had sacrificed her own future on the understanding that the trade involved his working for the family, ensuring the success that had cemented the agreement between her parents and his. Instead she was now confronted with a man who seemed powerless to intervene on his own behalf, let alone on behalf of the family he was supposed to head. As Miller remarked:

> Had I been able to side with her wholeheartedly in her disappointment with my father, my course would have been straightforward and probably fairly painless. But I couldn't help blushing for him when she made him her target, since I admired his warm and gentle nature as much as I despaired of his illiterate mind. And her way was never straight and simple; she could veer suddenly and see with a blast of clarity and remorse that what had happened to him had happened to a man of a certain honor and uncomplaining strength. For love of me and all of us she divided us against ourselves, unknowingly, innocently, because she believed – and I was beginning to believe myself – that with sufficient intelligence a person could outwit the situation. Why couldn't he do that?[81]

Isidore had now gone through three bankruptcies in succession and often brought home less than twenty-five dollars a week, when he had a job. Augusta spent her time inventing costless menus while periodically succumbing to anger at herself, her husband, life in general and even God. Every few weeks she would take the Culver Line to Manhattan and have her fortune read in tea leaves. She kept an eye on astrological signs (as Kate Keller would do in an early version of *All My Sons*) as if it might be possible to decode the mystery of her desperation. She was not immune to the craze for mysticism, taking up the then current enthusiasm for ouija boards, which perhaps echoed a half-forgotten sense of Jewish mysticism. She was a believer in invisible forces if not entirely those acknowledged by her Jewish upbringing. She had, for example, she said, sensed the moment of her mother's death (in the years to come Miller himself noted instances of an uncanny prescience in his own life). There was, then, some hidden structure to experience even if her daily life seemed to offer ever less evidence for it. In like mood, she listened to Roosevelt's radio addresses, wanting to believe in the possibilities he summoned out of words. Nonetheless, this woman, battling to hold the family together, bright with intelligence, a woman of taste and ambition, if not now for herself then for her children, would later come to the verge of suicide, despairing of her life, dismayed at what her hopes had come to.

These were the days when elevated trains rattled along Second, Third, Sixth and Ninth Avenues, carrying those lucky enough to have a job, with each passing year fewer in number. In 1930 there were five million unemployed in America, even after apple sellers were redefined as 'employed' on the grounds that those selling apples were earning a good living.

For Miller, to some degree insulated in his own teenage concerns though an unwilling eavesdropper on his parents' arguments, society no longer meant images in the glossy magazines, celebrating the rich and famous. It now meant the daily reality of men asking for work, any work, or sometimes collapsing on the sidewalk from hunger. And that in turn began to change the way he saw the world and literature. He found himself impatient with novels that did not situate their protagonists in a social world that extended beyond the family. He found himself drawn to the suggestion not merely that the world could be changed but that writing might in some way be implicated in that process. A hidden principle seemed to have revealed itself, even if for the moment he was none too clear as to what it might be. But he was seventeen before such thoughts came to him. Earlier, he had been told that the world was structured around religion, even if his parents showed little sign of believing so.

Though he later remembered nothing of the speech he delivered at his bar mitzvah, at the age of thirteen, Miller did recall his father saying, 'Boy, you put it over.' Unlike his brother, he was not required to deliver his speech in three languages – English, Hebrew and German – a flourish that Miller puts down to his mother's desire to establish the family's primacy in the Miller clan. As in much else, it was the oldest child who was required to bear the burden of his parents' ambitions and psychological needs. By the same token, if the younger son was thereby taught a lesson in his own relative insignificance, he was also the beneficiary of a certain freedom which came from diminished expectations.

Though not really religious, Miller later confessed to having a 'mystical feeling about religion' as a child, though 'I never could arrive at where I could stand with other people in a congregation and bow my head to some deity'. He even made a midweek visit to a synagogue in search of enlightenment, to the astonishment of those he encountered there playing pinochle in the entrance corridor. The enlightenment was not forthcoming. He revisited it several times thinking that 'something would speak to me, but nothing did'.[82]

His grandfather, Louis Barnett, 'would have described himself as orthodox' but his parents were not, or hardly so. While a practising Jew, his father was not without his scepticism, though more especially with respect to those who came to the door begging, presuming that a religious connection would inspire charitable feelings:

> My father believed that people should earn a living – that is all he was ever doing in his life – and should not go around begging from other people who did make a living . . . But, at the same time, he was dutiful and orthodox and he regarded the whole thing with respect. He could never keep his place in the prayer book, however. His mind kept wandering, and he would keep asking me where it was, as if I would know.[83]

Arthur Miller was brought up amongst Jews until the age of nineteen, but if he went through the rituals of Jewish life it was in a grudging and uncomprehending way. Though he knew almost no gentiles, his instincts were to follow the codes and values of mainstream America. His father, likewise, refused to see their Jewish identity as lifting them out of the continuum of American experience, a fact that Miller sees as in part explaining his own faith in a human nature transcending the particularities of religion, race, nationality. As he remarked, 'If ever any Jews should have melted into the proverbial pot, it was our family in the twenties.' His own interest was in football or playing second baseman. But, he would point out, 'escape and denial are hardly the monopoly of the Jews', since 'one of the strongest urges in the writer's heart, and perhaps most especially the American's, is to reveal what has been hidden and denied, to rend the veil'.[84]

In 1931, another kind of escape came into his mind. Genuinely oppressed by the world around him, he decided he would go to sea: 'I was crazy about that idea.' He was inspired by the beauty of the American Line ships, berthed

along the piers on the west side of Manhattan, and by his reading of Conrad.
And he was assisted by a man who had taken up residence in his family's
basement and was an ex-purser on the SS *Manhattan*. He offered to get
Miller a job as a cabin boy. Fortunately, or unfortunately, they were fully
crewed; but the idea still appealed, not least because it was a means to get
away from a society that seemed to him increasingly suffocating:

> the idea of simply disappearing from this troubled land we all lived in, which
> was so miserably competitive all the time, dog eat dog, in which you couldn't
> take a deep breath, appealed. There is a mythology about that time which is
> directly opposite to my experience. It's partly a result of literature. The
> mythology is that in those days people helped one another. It may have come
> out of the organization of the first unions, like the auto union and the electrical
> workers' union, and that did take place, but outside of those movements, the
> competition was ruthless, it was murderous. I remember when I did work for
> my father he would ship cartons of clothes to various places in the United
> States and I had to take them to the post office. So I had a little hand truck
> which I pushed along Seventh Avenue to the post office in the 30s, and they
> closed at seven o'clock. So there was a line of guys with their own trucks, and
> they were all climbing over each other to get to that desk before it closed.
> And you had to fight your way through. It was murderous. Later on, I read
> John Steinbeck and he had a scene that utterly astonished me. The Joads
> were on the road and Tom, I think, went into a scraggly little grocery store
> and asked for bread. He only had a nickel and the bread cost eight cents or a
> dime, and the owner said, 'That's all right, you can take it.' I read that and
> thought, 'That's terrific.' I never saw anything like that. They would watch
> you starve to death slowly, in New York at any rate.[85]

Later, a recently married Miller would go to sea in search of stories. He
travelled, though, not as a seaman but as a passenger, paying fifty dollars for
the privilege and travelling not on an American Line ship but a down-at-heel
merchantman working the eastern seaboard.

The story of his family's adoption of the ex-purser turned handyman,
however, would seem to contradict his scepticism about human solidarity.
There was, it seemed, a degree of camaraderie, at least in the Miller family.
One day the man had knocked at the family's door, asking for work. He was
not the first to seek them out. The Miller home seems to have acted as a
magnet to the unemployed. Decades later Miller described what happened:

> You would see these guys come around the corner, walk down the street and
> turn into our house. I often looked around to see if there was a mark
> someplace! My mother was a sucker. She would give them whatever was
> going on the stove, a bowl of soup or a piece of bread with butter, whatever.

They were genuine victims. They came from all over the States ... They couldn't give up the dream. The dream was 'elsewhere'. Elsewhere had to be better.[86]

The man the Miller family effectively adopted was a Lithuanian, who came for a bowl of soup and remained for a number of years. Augusta gave him a dollar to clean the windows and then fell asleep. When she woke the dining-room table had been laid with her best silver, with a folded napkin at each place, and her new, and supposedly temporary, employee was standing at the kitchen door in a starched white jacket with an ironed kitchen towel over his arm. The only false note was the cut-away shoes through which his toes protruded.

By a process Miller himself never quite understood, the Lithuanian managed to charm his way into their basement, together with a bed he had found. He put curtains in the window and, in return for food, cleaned and cooked. Probably homosexual, he was never seen as a threat by the women of the family. He was finally ejected when he drank several gallons of wine produced by Miller's maternal grandfather, only to be passed on by Augusta to one of her sisters (though in an early article this whole story is told as though it had happened not to the Millers themselves but to his uncle and aunt).

Perhaps this generosity to the stranger had less to do with the special circumstances of Depression America than with habits learned in the *shtetl* and handed down to Miller's parents. The Hebrew word for charity – *tzedakah* – means justice. In the Jewish tradition charity was not a gift but an obligation. Some lessons are bred in the bone.

It was at the age of sixteen that Miller experienced his first rite of passage. He was taken by his brother Kermit and a friend called Oscar to a brothel in an apartment building on the Upper West Side. It was, he insists, not a particularly unusual initiation in the 1930s. Nor a decade later, if we are to go by the experience of another Jewish intellectual, George Steiner. He recalls a visit to a brothel in Cicero, Illinois, where he was initiated by a good-natured woman, of a kind much found in fiction but seldom encountered in real life. For Miller, it seems to have been something of a disappointing experience, despite the woman's obligatory flattery of his physiognomy: It was he told me in 2001, very perfunctory. Like going to the dentist. Something was missing! The whole thing was very awkward. It would not be the last occasion on which he would visit a brothel. Next time, though, he was taken as something of a cultural tourist and not, like Chekhov, who confessed that he preferred 'immoral women'.

This was his erotic bar mitzvah in which he learned a new language and underwent a momentary trial, to emerge, supposedly, reborn, a man. If he did not feel particularly guilty he also did not feel transformed. The mystery turned out not to be so mysterious. His memory is that he paid for this initiation with money he had earned working briefly at his father's company. No wonder he was later drawn to Freud.

However, the whole experience had one unlooked-for consequence. Kermit's friend was a student at the University of Michigan and it was he who informed Miller about the literary prizes on offer there. Forty years later, walking down Park Avenue, Miller encountered him again. Oscar now owned an upmarket chain of grocery stores. As Miller observed, 'If you live long enough, everything connects!'

It was in 1931, too, that Miller recognized for the first time that power had shifted from father to son. His father was forced to borrow money from him for a subway ride, an event clearly of such importance that it would recur in an early short story and then again later in his career. Three years earlier, that father had been driven to work with a fur-bordered blanket covering his knees. There had seemed no reason to suppose that his upward rise would ever come to a halt. Now, stripped of his own business, he was seemingly on his way to a new job. Yet his apparent assurance was suddenly exposed for what it was. Walking Arthur part of the way to school, he had stopped and asked, in an embarrassed way, if he could borrow a quarter for the subway fare. This man, still dressed in a topcoat and hat that a year before would have cost five hundred dollars, literally had no money left. Was there a job? Probably not. But as Miller would write in an early unpublished novel, a man has to try to sustain himself in the eyes of his son.

In 1932 the young Arthur Miller was offered a key to the pressures he observed around him: a street encounter now inducted him into the mysteries of Marxism, providing him with another faith, longer-lasting, more closely related to the world he saw around him. These came as a revelation, not least because they caused him to re-evaluate his own father. He might now be stripped of his company, but had he not once employed people and lived on the profits of their labour? Miller long remembered the sense of shock and thrill that this re-ordering of the world gave him, and the transformation it wrought in his family relationships.

His teacher in Brooklyn was a student, like him waiting his turn to play in a street handball game against the wall of Dozick's drugstore. Miller was nearing his seventeenth birthday. That year unemployment reached twelve million, the national income had fallen by a half and eighty-five thousand businesses failed. They continued their conversation on a Coney Island beach where the new poor lived beneath the boardwalk in scrap-metal or wood-slat shacks. He was told that he was part of the narrative of history, that what had seemed so arbitrary to him was in fact the working-out of an economic law, and that, feeling adrift, he actually had his place in the scheme of things. He was, he learned, a member of the declassed bourgeoisie. There were two classes of people: the workers and the employers. All over the world, 'including Brooklyn, of course, a revolution that would transform every country was inexorably building up steam. Things would then be produced for use rather than for someone's personal profit, so there would be much more for everyone to share, and justice would reign everywhere ... This day's overturning of all I knew of the world,' Miller explained, 'revolutionized not only my ideas but also my most important relationship at the time, the one with my father. For deep down in the comradely world of the Marxist promise is parricide.'[87] Despite the family's economic distress, his father was still an occasional employer of labour, upholder of a system suddenly revealed as oppressive. He thus stood as a representative of power without purpose or justification while his failure, stood explained. The system was indeed bankrupt, socially and morally no less than economically.

That conversation in 1932, with a student whose name he could not later recall, seems to have been crucial. Certainly, more than fifty years on he remembered it as marking a change in his attitude to his father and to society alike. At the time, he found himself engaging in fruitless arguments with that father, a seventeen-year-old explaining the injustice and immorality of capitalism to the former owner of a major company. It was, though, the very disjunction between past values and the new truth that was its recommendation.

Nonetheless, when he tried out his new ideas at home he encountered nothing but bafflement and resentment. How, after all, could a company possibly operate without profit? It was as though he had two fathers, the familiar one who now increasingly dozed his way through the afternoon, and this other one who represented hostile forces, who built his success on other people's misery. The fact that he had been stripped of his wealth was beside the point.

For the son, suddenly, there was a spine to history and an explanation for that father's fall from grace, a fall for which he was not really culpable, being a product of a system he did not understand. A salesman, he had, like Willy Loman, been sold a bill of goods. There was, now, an answer to everyone's dilemma which went beyond the bland assurance that prosperity was just around the corner. More than that, Marxism gave Miller a role even as it seemed to give him a purchase on his life. His dissatisfaction with religion now made perfect sense as he was informed of its opiate role.

Marxism, whatever that might turn out to be, made what nothing else at the time did – sense. It was a philosophy rather than a political dogma. It was a myth of new beginnings and hence hardly alien. It charged each moment with significance. Writing in the *New Republic* in 1931 Edmund Wilson had said that America had been betting on capitalism and had lost. By 1932 he was suggesting that 'nine-tenths of our writers would be much better off writing propaganda for Communism than doing what they are at present: that is, writing propaganda for capitalism'.[88]

Marxism was a philosophy that reinvented the future, a future that the Crash had seemed to nullify or foreshorten. And that, too, had an American feel to it, and it is important to realize the extent to which those drawn if not to the Communist Party then to the ideas it propagated could find in Marxism a familiar utopianism. It was an idea that had a special appeal to the young in its idealistic demand for self-sacrifice. It was a philosophy of causes. It stood for that great abstraction, the working man. It was not a substitute for religion; it *was* religion, though drained of the irrational, for at the same time this was science, history restructured as process.

The student on the Coney Island beach explained that the Depression was a consequence of people being underpaid so that it was impossible for them to buy goods. Having been raised to feel that it was better to be a boss than a worker, Miller now met someone who suggested that it was quite the other way round. The progressive force, he learned, was not capital but labour. Since, at the time, he regarded himself as labour, that made him a progressive force. History, at least, it seemed, was on his side. The old men in the synagogue suddenly appeared still more the remnants of another world. For his part, Miller had begun to be sceptical about more than the political and economic system that had led them to abandon the city for a semi-rural suburb. The crack-up had broken something more fundamental. 'The cleavage,' he has said, 'was sudden and terrific between the generations. At one point ... I thought nobody, none of us, would ever go to a synagogue as adults, or Christians would ever go to a church again. I wondered what would happen to these buildings, because Brooklyn was full of churches and synagogues.'[89]

So, at the age of seventeen, Miller came to regard himself as a Marxist. The Depression, he had come to feel, was only incidentally a matter of money. 'Rather, it was a moral catastrophe, a violent revelation of the hypocrisies behind the facade of American society.' This realization prompted moral indignation and nothing, he remarked, looking back from the late 1980s, 'is as visionary and as blinding as moral indignation'. From the perspective of fifty years, he was inclined to see this as in part a product of adolescence which 'is a kind of aching that only time can cure, a molten state without settled form'. The truth seemed to be that at a time when 'the order of society has also melted and the old authority has shown its incompetence and hollowness, the way to maturity is radicalism'. It had the assurance of rationality. It rejected superstition, myth, religion, but nonetheless, as Miller acknowledges, 'engaged some of the very same sinews of faith within me'.[90]

It offered to enrol the individual into a brotherhood as wide as the community of man. It offered the future in place of an exhausted past.

In *The American Clock* he has Lee remark: 'I keep trying to find the holes in Marxism but I can't.'[91] There were, though, implications to Marxism that went beyond an analysis of social class and economic condition. At its heart was a rejection of old authority, an inversion of the natural order. As the young girls of Salem revolted against an older generation, so Marxism seemed to offer power to the young. His father's arguments with his son lacked real force precisely because he was himself trying to account for his own and America's failure. Miller's mother, meanwhile, looked on, increasingly bitter, getting by from day to day and placing her hope in her sons, at least one of whom seemed suddenly to be blaming his parents, at least in an abstract way, not only for their own plight but for that of others.

In reacting against his father, Miller was scarcely breaking new ground. What was different was that he was part of a generation that increasingly believed itself blessed with a special insight, a social, economic and moral grasp of the world that could eventually transform that world and withstand the forces of reaction at home and abroad. The commitments born that day in Brooklyn carried him through college and on through the first years of his career until they eventually landed him before a congressional committee that cited him for contempt and brought him to the verge of a prison sentence.

It was as though he had suddenly been offered a secret formula that made sense of the random tumble of events and relationships that surrounded him. The Depression that had previously seemed like an act of God was now revealed as the logical culmination of a failed system. Elsewhere in the world, meanwhile, other people had solved the problem, bringing human need into neat alignment with social theory. The failure of America was thus revealed as simultaneously a moral flaw and a failure of reason.

Such radical ideas were not entirely discontinuous with the Jewish tradition. The fact is that some immigrant Jews brought with them, on the crowded immigrant ships, not only the Talmud but copies of Marx. Others were introduced to Marxism in the sweatshops. And such ideas did not seem alien, even to those politically at odds with them. As Vivian Gornick has said, 'If a Jew growing up in this world was not a Marxist he may have scorned the socialists or shrugged his shoulders at them or argued bitterly with them, but he did not in the deepest part of himself disown them or find them strange, or alienating creatures. They were there, they were recognizable, they were *us*.'[92] Miller later came to regard himself as a communist, as did his brother and his cousin Morton, raised to be a rabbi but preferring a more secular faith.

Gornick, whose father stood on the floor of a dress factory on West 35th Street, steam-iron in hand, for thirty years, discovered in the Party precisely that sense of belonging and becoming that had driven Miller's father to build a successful factory. He read the Yiddish paper *Der Freiheit* and the *Daily Worker*, his Jewishness and his radicalism seeming naturally allied. And it is necessary to recall just what the Party meant to so many. It was simultaneously a logical response to the industrial world and a moral crusade. It was to do with ideas as much as with passion and it offered a new identity. Gornick again:

> the people at my father's kitchen table could place themselves; and if they could place themselves ... they could *become* themselves. For in order to become one must first have some civilizing referent, some social boundary, some idea of nationhood. These people had no external nationhood; nothing in the cultures they had left, or the one to which they had come, had given them anything but a humiliating sense of outsidedness. The only nationhood to which they had attained was the nationhood inside their minds: the nationhood of the international working class. And indeed, a nation it was – complete with a sense of family, culture, religion, social mores, political institutions.[93]

Miller's father, of course, did not feel alienated, and, until the Depression, had a stake in his new country. If there was a sense of outsiderness, he believed he could insulate himself and his family with money. Under the pressure of their new circumstances, however, family relationships began to change. Miller felt respect for his father turn to pity. He watched, too, as his mother's attitude began to change: 'I could not avoid awareness of my mother's anger at this waning of his powers ... I must have adopted my mother's early attitudes toward his failure, her impatience at the beginning of the calamity and her alarm as it got worse, and finally a certain sneering contempt for him that filtered through her voice.'[94] She was the one who had to institute economies. She was the one who had to confront the mortgage man. It was her jewellery that had to be disposed of, piece by piece.

Speaking in 1999, he observed:

> My mother was smart enough to understand that it was not his doing; but the frustration was so great that she could not help blaming him anyway. She blamed him and pitied him at the same time. It is one thing when everything is going great, and both people are feeling absolutely secure ... but when suddenly they do not know from one week to the next where the money is going to come from, the recrimination begins and the loss of respect, loss of mutual toleration.[95]

Nor were such tensions restricted to his family. Miller recalled three suicides on their block in Brooklyn, 'ordinary people who could not cope'. Years later, researching for *The American Clock*, he was reminded not merely of the extent of unemployment but of the conviction of many that they would never work again. As he said, 'It was not just the money ... It was the illusion. These people were profound believers in the American dream and, when that stopped working, the day the money stopped, their identity was gone. They did not know who the hell they were.'[96]

Miller's contribution to the failing family finances took the form of delivering bread at four o'clock in the morning, having risen at three-thirty and checked the furnace where he had banked up the fire the night before, all this before going to school. He would stare into the flickering blue flames as though they had a life of their own, before venturing out into the bitter early-morning air wearing two sweaters, a mackinaw and a stocking cap, with a pair of heavy wool socks over his hands. These were the days when people expected fresh bread delivered ready for breakfast. In a nostalgic article of the mid-50s, called 'A Boy Grew in Brooklyn' (a reference to the novel *A Tree Grows in Brooklyn* by Betty Smith), he recalled slipping on the unsalted ice on Ocean Parkway and sending his delivery skidding across the street like ice-hockey pucks. His efforts to reassign the various rolls, bagels and loaves to the correct paper bags proved futile, and irate telephone calls from Ocean Parkway reached the bakery before he had finished his rounds.[97] Nonetheless, he took pleasure in being alone on these errands, as he did in watching the few cars venturing out skating in graceful circles on the ice and the cats that would follow him along the early-morning streets.

He worked two and a half to three hours each morning, seven days a week for four months, going to bed at eight in order to be up in time. The pay was four dollars, so that the twelve dollars he spent buying wood to build a porch for their house on East 3rd Street, early evidence of that commitment to carpentry that would last his whole life, represented a major investment. No wonder, perhaps, that Willy Loman, in *Death of a Salesman*, would be most in tune with himself when building a back porch in a play written in a ten-by-twelve cabin built by its author. His father, by contrast, was baffled by such things, being unable to master can-openers or umbrellas as, later, Miller would suggest, the director Harold Clurman was incapable of peeling an orange.

The Depression, meanwhile, bit ever deeper. Brooklyn was changing in ways that inevitably bring *Death of a Salesman* to mind. The woods had gone, and with them the open spaces where Miller had played football. The sense of alarm in *Death of a Salesman*, as refrigerator and car fail and mortgage payments fall due, surely has its roots not in the 1940s, when it is set, but in the 1930s when such things were an immediate and real problem for the Miller family.

Miller's mother felt adrift. With fancy Manhattan apartment and chauffeur-driven car gone, she would shuffle around the small Brooklyn house in carpet slippers 'sighing, cursing with a sneer on her lips, weeping suddenly and then catching herself, in the winters feeding the furnace with as scant a shovelful of coal as will keep it burning, making meal money at high-stakes professional bridge games all over Midwood and Flatbush, which are sometimes raided by police'.[98] In the summer heat, when no air moved, tarred roofs liquefied and the tarmac street became viscous, Augusta and her sisters would take off their dresses and sit in their slips, the uninsulated house offering no protection from the heat and the smell of the attic percolating downstairs. Miller's Downs syndrome cousin, Carl, would bring them glasses of water, carefully wiped down and balanced in his hands as his mother, Betty (married to Harry Barnett), alternated between snapping at him and bursting into tears at the burden laid upon her.

The boy, who had not been supposed to live into his teens, was now nearing thirty. He would dress himself immaculately each morning. He could give change for a dollar and run errands to the store and loved to answer the door, greeting people with elaborate politeness. He loved everyone, from the postman to Mae West, whom he wished to marry. He was teased to the point of tears while his mother struggled to love him, her maternal instincts blocked by the sense of injustice that her life had been so blighted. It was the memory of this boy, and the desperation of the sister who looked after him, that would lead Miller to decide, on the advice of his doctor, that his own Downs syndrome son, Daniel, born in January 1967, could be better served by being placed with others such as himself in a specialist institution rather than raised in the family home.

Augusta was an all but professional bridge player, frequently invited to games in the hope that she would bring her less accomplished neighbours with her. It was a route she dare not take both because it would be an acknowledgement of despair and because she could not afford to lose. Instead she contented herself with afternoon games with friends, relatives and neighbours. 'It was a great escape for her and she had girls over . . . and she probably won more off them than anybody else,' according to her daughter Joan.

From time to time the police would, indeed, raid these games, though without any evident enthusiasm. Everyody knew what people had to do to get by. Augusta's sisters, like Tennessee Williams's mother, and Amanda, the character based on her in *The Glass Menagerie*, would try, without evident conviction and certainly without success, to sell magazine subscriptions. As in *The American Clock*, in which Miller recalls these years, the family had to adopt strategies to avoid the man collecting the mortgage payments, closing the shutters even in the hottest weather and entering through the rear. Nor was this the only man soliciting money. Miller's mentally damaged cousin would be sent to the door to announce to the pale-skinned Orthodox Jew looking for contributions to the synagogue that there was no one at home.

And so the sisters waited out the Depression as if they had never grown up and married, never been disillusioned with life, never had to face the collapse of their dreams. Augusta had done her duty in agreeing to an arranged marriage, her sisters having eloped. Perhaps their disillusionment was the greater as romance gave way to dull routine. Not that they were particularly bright – one, memorably, being baffled by the question, 'Who wrote Gray's *Elegy*?'

The sisters lived within blocks of one another, in virtually identical houses, waiting for the waiting to be over. Irving Howe, albeit from a poorer background, said of his family in the Depression that they were never really hungry but always anxious. For Miller's family, too, it was not a matter of real deprivation but of a continuing and unrelenting anxiety.

What the Depression did was to sandblast away the normal civilities, place under pressure those bonds which, disturbingly, often proved to have been all too fragile. Joan recalled the case of her Aunt Blanche, a college graduate, who, like Augusta, had been forced into an arranged marriage. Joan and she once had a conversation about her brother's relationship with Marilyn Monroe:

> I said, 'But he loved her, really loved her. You know what love is, for God's sake. You love Uncle Sam' – Uncle Sam was in the kitchen and this conversation was taking place in the living room – and she said, 'Oh, no. I don't.' She had been married to this man, and she had two grown children. Her son was a doctor and her daughter was a psychologist. She said, 'No, I never loved Uncle Sam. I loved a young man whom I wanted to marry but my family wouldn't permit it. So I married Uncle Sam because my father wanted that.' She said this in front of her daughter, who had never heard this. It was just astonishing what people's lives turned out to be, how they permitted them to be. But the option of saying 'No' very rarely made itself evident to people of that generation.

Despite the tensions between Isidore and Augusta there were lighter moments. As Joan would recall, Augusta 'was the life of the party. She would entertain, she would sing and play ... She could tell a dirty joke quicker than anybody else and she was a good mimic.' She was uninhibited and generous and Isidore took pleasure in her company. But also, according to Joan, her mother's life had begun to close in.

On the wall behind the family piano in Joan's apartment is one of her mother's paintings: 'I bought her some oil paints and I said, "I don't want to hear any more complaints about how boring your life is." It wasn't until the Depression,' however, Joan said, 'that she felt she had been, so to speak, hagged by life ... she was angry. Hers was not a monumental talent; it was a modest talent that was never permitted to go anywhere. But the life around her became very mean and petty. She wanted different things.' Indeed, she became suicidal: 'She would put her head in the oven, and I think she planned it. I guess she didn't do it because she had a family to take care of. She was very loyal and responsible.'

Augusta thus kept up a front, concealed her disappointments. She encouraged her youngest son to go to college in the face of her husband's opposition and, when he went, Joan recalled, 'painted all these rosy pictures of how dad's business is doing so well, and I am at home seeing this almost suicidal woman behaving quite differently. So what he saw, or thought he saw, what was presented to him by his mother, was not at all what I was experiencing in this house.'

There were other desperations, too. One thing to be avoided above all, in a world of economic hardship and emotional estrangement, was pregnancy. There were no possibilities, then, of discrete abortions, no socially sanctioned solutions to problems of this kind. And Augusta had become pregnant. There is a poignant, even chilling, poem by Miller which recalls this fact and her half-desperate, half-comic attempt to resolve her dilemma – that and her seeming abstraction from her own actions. It tells of the time his mother had jumped off a table in order to kill the child she was carrying. Its poignancy comes from the fact of the young boy – Arthur – who goes to his room unable to reconcile what he has just seen with the protective mother who sits at the same table reading a book. The poem is undated. Was it a product of these stressful years, a pregnancy that ultimately came to nothing? Or does it reach back further and was this child Joan, once to be killed in the womb? Miller confirmed the accuracy of the event but not the moment it occurred. Either way, it must surely have had an impact on the nature of his relationship with a woman willing to dispose of a child with such apparent equanimity or, perhaps, merely resignation.

Joan remembers her mother with affection but has characterized her as a snob. 'She was pretentious, my mother, but she had a right to be a snob. She had exquisite taste in everything . . . She set the standard for what was correct and beautiful in furnishings.' Joan herself was brought up not to the life they were now living but the life they had once had, though she had been only eight when they moved to Brooklyn. Whatever their straitened circumstances, she was not to wash or dry the dishes, clean the sink, do any of the chores. When she offered to do so her mother replied, 'I want you out of the kitchen. You are not to learn how to do this because you are going to marry a rich man and you will have maids.' As Joan remarks, 'Who paid for it all? My poor husband when we got married.'[99]

By 1932, the year Miller graduated from Abraham Lincoln High School, their situation was increasingly grim. After the graduation ceremony, he recalls running the three miles home along the tree-lined Ocean Parkway worried about what lay ahead. There was a distinct possibility that they would lose the house. The $50-a-month mortgage was increasingly difficult to find. They were not, though, alone in their problem. Miller knew a businessman who worked in a laundromat and who dealt with his new circumstances by maintaining an outward show of confidence, betrayed by the fact that he had begun to speak formulaically. His reply to all questions was 'Well, say.' In fact this seems to have been the father of his best friend Sidney Franks, the Franks family having originally lived in the same Manhattan building as the Millers on 110th Street.

The Millers were not poor; they were simply living in a way they had never imagined, unsure whether they could even sustain their new lifestyle. The future was as mortgaged as their house. Perhaps that is why, when Miller graduated, no one from the family attended the ceremony. It was no longer seen as a stepping stone to further education. He had, anyway, seemingly destroyed his hopes through his own dilatoriness. In the play he sketched out in the 1960s but never finished, he confesses that if he had paid attention to his work instead of playing football he might have won a scholarship, though, looking back, he realizes how unrealistic his ambitions had been. He had toyed with the idea of Cornell (which as late as 1950 was still discriminating against Jews in its medical programmes) or Brown University (whose fraternities discriminated on grounds of race and religion until the same date), but this was no longer a credible proposition. Nor was it simply a matter of grades. As he later showed, there were ways of getting round this problem. The issue was primarily one of money and this deepened the sense of betrayal within the family. Not only had they failed to hand the dream on to their son, in the form of the family business, but they had failed to give him the education that might have opened up other possibilities. They had failed, most especially, to realize the immigrant imperative, to see their children, and especially their sons, do better than them.

Many New York Jews who went on to higher education chose the city's public universities. As Beth S. Wenger has pointed out, in the 1930s Jews made up 80–90 per cent of students at City College, Hunter College and Brooklyn College. These, in turn, became the site of ideological debate and cultural ambition. They were the breeding ground of the New York intellectuals. Unlike Michigan, where Miller would go, these were not campus universities in a college town. The harsh realities of Depression New York were a matter of daily experience even if many of the students remained more dedicated to possible careers than to transforming society. Ivy League colleges for the most part remained out of reach. A City College magazine included a cartoon of a young boy about to be circumcised crying out, 'Stop! I want to go to Princeton.'[100] Miller's ambitions, though, reached beyond New York, though his family as yet knew nothing of what he had in mind.

In so far as identity was a product of economic power and social respect the loss of the former seemed to threaten the latter. It was not only the house that became smaller, it was the family. There no longer seemed any basis for hope. As Miller asked, 'What the hell [was] there to hope for?' Yet at the same time hope remained a cultural imperative: 'Americans hope even when it does not work. You keep the hope alive. That is why the movie industry is always so good.' Indeed, to his mind it was not irrelevant that the movie industry was the product of Jewish immigrants: 'These guys really believed that you could magically transform yourself into anything you could imagine.' Isidore Miller had lost his faith in that possibility.

His son, by contrast, was willing to try his hand at anything, including popular music. He had acquired an agent and went for a series of auditions in the cramped back rooms of Tin Pan Alley. Having watched the impact of Rudy Vallee and Bing Crosby on the women of the neighbourhood, he saw himself, briefly, entering show business as a crooner. He later remarked, 'I wanted to be a crooner, sure. I wanted to be anything that was going! I had a radio programme, in fact, that I sang on two or three times. I had a good tenor voice, and I sang all the latest hits. I had a blind pianist who had a lot of dandruff, and he said, "You are the young Al Jolson!" But it got so boring that I stopped doing it after about three times.'[101]

The family were thrilled by his appearance on this Brooklyn radio programme, not least because he was paid. Remarkably, there is a recording of Miller, just turned twenty-six, singing 'Old Man River' in an impressive tenor voice. The song was recorded in October 1941 when he was in Wilmington, North Carolina, on behalf of the Library of Congress. It is still to be found buried in the Library archive. It appears as the equivalent of an out-take on a recording to do with the songs devised by a group of women garment workers striking for higher wages. Listening to it, it is tempting to think that perhaps the theatre's gain was the bobbysoxers' loss.

What he really wanted, though, was to go to college and to pursue his interest in literature. His enthusiasm for writing had been fired in his final year at high school, when he came across Dostoevsky's *Crime and Punishment* (and then *The Idiot*). It must, he later mused, have been raining too hard to play ball. He picked up the book thinking it to be a detective story but quickly found himself absorbed in another world more engrossing than his own. He was inclined to think he might have been responding to what it said about family relationships, but beyond that it engaged with causalities which seemed to him significantly lacking in the world he observed.

Thereafter, despite his various jobs, he spent his time reading, using his subway rides to work his way through Dostoevsky and Tolstoy. It was in 1932 that he produced a short story about a failed salesman that in some ways anticipated his later play. It was that year, too, that he wrote a comedy routine, parodying a radio commentator. It consisted of little more than a series of nonsensical news items. He sent it to the Major Bowes Amateur Hour and was invited to an audition, after which he was approached by a man who claimed to represent the Lord & Thomas Advertising Agency. He handed the man the script and, as he later explained, went home to await fame and fortune. Instead, a few weeks later he tuned into the radio only to hear his sketch delivered by the comedian Phil Baker, and not as well as he thought he had delivered it himself. He was not credited and was never paid. His letters went unanswered. Years later, looking back on this, the first public performance of a piece he had written, he suggested that the reason he had turned to writing tragedies was because he thought no one would steal one of those. As it happens he was wrong – an avant-garde theatre company later used *The Crucible* without permission, leading to a threatened legal suit.

Decades later, when he was introducing Pablo Neruda at the fiftieth annual PEN birthday dinner, he recalled reading Neruda's poems when he was growing up and being struck by the fact that he was a writer who not only seemed to acknowledge that the world was in crisis but evidently thought it the writer's job to address that fact, to engage history and address power, even while remaining true to his own vision.

Initially, though, it was Kermit who seemed likely to become a professional writer. Joan recalled him writing poetry. Arthur, she had supposed, would become an auto-mechanic since this was where his talents seemed to lie. As Miller described it, 'Kermit was always very romantic about writing. He loved Keats. I never heard him refer to an American poet. It was all British romantic poets. He had this flowery writing, nineteenth-century stuff. I could make nothing out of it but in those days I knew nothing about anything and didn't try to make anything of it. But I thought he would be a writer.'[102]

Kermit, having graduated from Madison High School in 1930, briefly went to New York University, only to drop out, assisting his father in one of a number of his attempts to re-establish his coat business. As he himself remarked, 'The money was a problem, just attending school. There were no plans during the Depression ... When I think back, I was not ambition-driven ... I didn't have a goal because things were tough ... Everything was held up ... We were constantly aware of the fact that we had come down.' Besides, as Joan was to say, 'somebody had to stay home and keep the family fed'. As the oldest, Kermit felt a special responsibility: 'I felt as though perhaps I could do something. Coming of age, you know ... So I did what I suppose any of us would do. You want to help your people.'[103]

In his 1960s unfinished play, Miller stages a conversation between himself and Kermit in which his brother decides to abandon college to look after his father and freeing his brother to pursue his own ambitions. His speech ends with a stage direction that calls for Kermit to close the book he has been reading 'forever'. There is a deal of guilt in that last stage direction in that Kermit did, indeed, stay while his brother went off to college and became the writer Kermit himself had wished to be. Kermit did close the book and became a carpet salesman, and though ultimately he would be a successful businessman Miller never ceased to feel guilty about a brother he loved but whom he felt he had in some way betrayed. Once again, Kermit had deliberately fallen before the winning line to give precedence to his younger brother.

The family, meanwhile, seemed to be drifting. His father continued to struggle, but to no purpose. As Kermit remarked, 'it was terribly tough for him ... He was uneducated, so he had run the business by hiring other people to take his role, which normally he had been able to do. But this was the neck of the Depression; they were terrible days. Until about 1935 you couldn't get a job. It was very tough for lots of people.' Finances were getting ever more precarious. Where his mother had once had $100,000 of her own, invested in the stock market, now she was reduced to selling her jewels, sending Arthur on his bicycle to the pawnbrokers at 3rd and 19th Streets, paper bag in hand, a task reminiscent of Charles Dickens, sent on similar errands by his mother. Eventually, there were none left to sell.

Kermit went to work as a salesman, first for his father and, when the business foundered, for others. When his brother did eventually go to university, in 1934, having raised the necessary money himself, he 'kept going' because 'I was the only earner'.[104] Later, when the war broke out, Kermit volunteered for the infantry and, following three months' basic training, became a second lieutenant, arranging for his pay to be sent to his parents.

In *The American Clock* Miller replays the scene between himself and his father when he had gathered together college catalogues and explained the tuition costs, oblivious to the fact that the family had no money for such ventures: 'it was a very strange July. I'd graduated from high school but nobody was mentioning college anymore.' 'I feel so terrible,' says Rose/Augusta in the play, 'all these years we were throwing money around, and now when you need it—' to which Lee/Arthur replies, 'That's okay. I think I'll try looking for a job',[105] which is precisely what, out of necessity, Miller did, though his mother was adamant that he should not; adamant, too, that he should not sacrifice himself for his father. In his unpublished 1960s play he has Augusta say that it is enough that she and her other son have tied their fate to an ignorant man without him doing likewise. It is simultaneously a brutal and a desperate speech as she pins all her hopes on a young son whose own escape will constitute the closest she will ever get to liberating herself.

This may be just a play fragment, written three decades later, but it does reflect his mother's attitude towards him, her sense that he had a special destiny, her almost mystical belief that she could perceive what others could not. The disappointments of her marriage left her believing that he could become what she had been denied the possibility of becoming. She saw in him what she did not see in the ostensibly more literary Kermit – a drive, an ambition, a commitment to becoming.

As Miller had realized, his poor academic record meant that scholarships were out of the question. He had failed algebra repeatedly, been expelled from one class and regarded as unpromising material by several other teachers. Later, he was inclined to think that his poor school performance reflected his desire not to compete with his illiterate father. There was, however, one possibility. He recalled what he had been told of the University of Michigan and its awards for writing, the lowest of which was $250. But before he could get there, apart from persuading university officials that they should accept someone with such an unimpressive school record, he was required to show evidence of $500 savings, so as not to be a burden on the Michigan taxpayer. He would, he knew, have to find a job.

What followed was two years of hard work and a further education in the ways of the world as he struggled to find employment in the depths of the Depression and, in the process, for virtually the first time, became aware of the anti-Semitism that infested New York. He tried for a job at Macy's but many of those ahead of him in the line had degrees. Scanning the small ads in the *New York Times*, he noticed that certain jobs were designated 'Gentile', 'Chr' or 'Protestant'. A firm was 'Cath', or the required workers were 'White'. There was, in other words, an alternative map of New York. This was a world in which tribe separated itself from tribe and though, with help, he did eventually secure work in an auto parts warehouse, with a company that had originally denied it to him, the experience offered an insight into the society he was anxious to join. Nearly sixty years later, when a film version of his novel *Focus* was produced by his son Robert, it was he who suggested that these newspaper ads should be reproduced in an attempt to reconstruct the mood of the period.

For a few months after graduation from high school Miller had driven a delivery truck for Sam Shapse, the father of a schoolfriend: 'I didn't have a driver's licence, but I was driving anyway, because I loved to drive; and I always believed in my luck, that I wouldn't get caught.' He made pickups from auto parts companies, including Chadick-Delamater. But by the summer of 1932, the Shapse firm was in trouble and Miller's work came to an end. By chance, Chadick was advertising for labour. He applied. Nothing happened. When Shapse found out, he was unsurprised, explaining that the company did not employ Jews. Nonetheless, he called them and pointed out that, whatever their employment policy, their customers were frequently Jewish. Miller got the job, 'the only Jew they ever hired and the only one they would'.[106] Chadick-Delamater was scarcely aberrant in this respect. Beth S. Wenger has pointed out that 'the city's telephone and gas companies routinely rejected Jewish applicants. Insurance companies, banks, and law offices also regularly refused to hire Jewish workers.'[107]

Chadick-Delamater, where Miller worked as a stock clerk from 1932 to 1934, was the largest wholesale auto parts warehouse east of the Mississippi. Its five floors of bins and shelving contained parts from vehicles dating back twenty years. The warehouse was on 63rd Street and Tenth Avenue, where the Metropolitan Opera House now stands, in an area then full of bars and boarded-up houses. The job paid fifteen dollars a week and it is a mark of his mother's attitude to his ambitions to go to college that he was allowed to keep the money, sometimes banking all but two dollars of it.

The journey to and from work began each morning at six and involved travelling by trolley bus and subway for an hour and twenty minutes. At first he tried to combine this with study at the nearby City College: 'They wrote and told me I was going to be taking physics, chemistry and mathematics, none of which I had a prayer of ever learning ... by the time I got to my classes, I was sleeping, and I lasted three weeks. I tallied up, no doubt, the worst academic record ever seen on the continent. So I pulled out and decided to save some money.'[108]

The warehouse personnel were almost exclusively Irish and suspicious of Miller. The back of the building faced a whorehouse whose naked inhabitants were at first on display until a newly arrived Irish immigrant insisted on pasting over the windows. For the other workers, it was home and security; for Miller, reading Russian novels and the *New York Times* on the subway ride, it was temporary. Meanwhile, whatever the conditions, no one complained, even when required to work with asbestos or dangerous tools. As he described it to me in 2003:

> We cut brakes. Brake lining came in large rolls. It was an asbestos product that was compressed with some other binder. We had to cut it to specification and if you twisted the material as it was going through the cutter, the cutter would break. The cutter was made of carborundum. Any pressure and it would shatter and spray parts as sharp as broken glass all over the place and you just had to duck. We had no masks. You could replace a worker for ten cents. We were unskilled people, so why bother?

Security of employment was everything, ambition not only a luxury but in some way beside the point.

His response to the generalized anti-Semitism was neither shock nor revulsion. This was evidently the way the world operated. There were rules to the game but the game was not thereby invalidated. He 'denied that Wesley Moulter, my boss, hated my presence',[109] as he denied the initial hostility of his fellow workers, simply keeping himself in the background. His own later explanation for that hostility was that they feared his intelligence, his application, his ambition and his thrift, taking all these as tokens of his Jewish identity.

Miller's desire to save his money and go to college was seen both as confirming his suspect intellectualism and as a judgement on those who squandered their money on more immediate pleasures, though he did squander some of his own, spending three dollars buying a bulldog pup which lasted two weeks before eating one of his mother's chocolate cakes. His time in the auto warehouse plant is recalled in an unpublished memoir called 'Two Years', written, seemingly, in 1945, and in *A Memory of Two Mondays*, but the anti-Semitism does not form a part of that play, which is, instead, a gesture towards those who labour with their hands without opportunity to escape. It was his feeling of solidarity with them that he recalled, not the alienation he had initially experienced. He came to sense that their anti-Semitism was in the end not as important as their contempt for themselves, not least because he saw in this the seeds of that political manipulation that would characterize a deadly century.

In his autobiography *Timebends*, he says of this time: 'I should have exulted in my aloneness and taken heart from Ibsen's signature line in *An Enemy of the People* – "He is strongest who is most alone." But the Jew in me shied from private salvation as something close to sin. One's truth must add its push to the evolution of public justice and mercy, must transform the spirit of the city whose brainless roar went on and on at both ends of the bridge',[110] the bridge in question being the Brooklyn Bridge in whose shadow he was later to set *A View from the Bridge* (though in fact Red Hook, where the play is set, lies two miles further on).

Interestingly, James Parker's 1945 book on anti-Semitism is called *An Enemy of the People*, a chance echo but also a reminder of the tension Miller was beginning to feel between himself and those who casually dismissed what he saw as his kind. In 1936, *Fortune* magazine would announce that the 'apprehensiveness of Jews has become one of the important influences in the social life of our time'.[111] In truth it was not an important influence on Miller who, for the moment, had other and more immediate concerns, but a decade later it would lead him to write his novel *Focus*.

Life at the warehouse was spartan. In the summer the heat was unbearable, while in the winter the radiators were inadequate and there were cracks in the building you could see through so that the twenty young women who worked there would wear several sweaters and bind their legs in newspapers. It was an experience that convinced him of the drudgery of the lives of working people who lived those lives to a deadly rhythm, never glimpsing, never aspiring to and never achieving transcendence. He himself dealt with the monotony and depression by writing letters. They were never addressed to anyone in particular, not even, as he would later say, to the world. They were simply a way of making sense of what he was seeing and feeling, giving order to what seemed the numbing irrelevance of work that meant nothing to him. They were unposted letters to himself.

The day he finished in the warehouse was anticlimactic. Most of the women had already left for the day, as had several of the men with whom he had worked for two years. He walked over to Broadway and then downtown. He had $512 in the bank, just twelve more than he needed to go to Michigan. A week later he was on his way, convinced that he would never go back. Later, though, and on a whim, he did return to the warehouse and found the same man he had worked with decades before. He was performing the same job, in the same oppressive space, and was indifferent to this effort to re-establish a relationship. Miller remarked in 2003, 'I remembered him – vividly – even that on a freezing December night his wife gave birth in their Jersey City tenement under a missing pane in a window which he stuffed with newspaper. His name was Hughie. He had no memory of me.'

In 1934 Alfred Kazin, like Miller, was nineteen and catching the El from Brooklyn to Manhattan, though in his case to college rather than to work. In the heat of that summer, he combined his reading of Russian literature with an enthusiasm for socialism: 'I was a "Socialist," like everyone else I knew.' And why would you not be? 'Trouble was in the air every day now.' He listed the events of what seemed a critical year:

> Hitler and Mussolini had met in Venice in June. And now Mussolini's little man Dollfuss, having fulfilled the bosses' orders to destroy Austrian socialism, was in his turn ambushed by the Austrian Nazis and bled to death on the beautifully polished floors of the Chancellery in Vienna. That summer, Hindenburg died and Hitler took Germany over completely as 'Premier-President.' That summer, Upton Sinclair won the primary nomination for governor in California on the 'EPIC' program – End Poverty In California. That summer, the drought got worse and more and more Okies crawled out of the Dust Bowl in their jalopies.[112]

The writers spawned by those times flourished their social credentials. The American author had always sought to validate his or her work by reference to lived experience, but now it had the virtue of sounding out in harmony with the times. Kazin listed them: Robert Cantwell, who had worked in a plywood factory; James T. Farrell who had been a clerk in an express company and a cigar store; Edward Dahlberg, for a time a hobo before going to college; Daniel Fuchs, who had come from one Brooklyn slum, and Henry Roth from another, Brownsville, also home to Kazin himself. Meanwhile, Richard

Wright had come from a Mississippi tenant farm while John Steinbeck had worked on farms and in a sugar refinery. Nelson Algren found employment in a filling station in Texas.[113] Arthur Miller, delivery boy, truck driver and warehouseman, already seemed qualified for the career he had privately decided on. That he should write his way through college seemed in tune with a period in which others were writing their way out of unemployment.

Kazin quickly found his way into the New York literary world, where Malcolm Cowley was a key figure, wedding radical politics to an enthusiasm for modernism, in a way that would prove so attractive to those drawn to *Partisan Review* and the *New Republic*. It was a world with a proliferation of political groupings. Again, Kazin listed them: 'Norman Thomas Socialists, old-time Social Democrats, Austro-Marxists, Communists who were Stalinist centrists, Trotskyite leftists, Lovestoneite right-wingers, Musteites and Fieldites; Zionists who were Progressive Labor Zionists, left Socialist Zionists and Religious Zionists'. He himself believed in socialism, 'if not in the savage proletarian exclusiveness of the Communists at this time – before the growing power of Hitler and the Spanish Civil War induced a united front'. He thought of socialism 'simply as a moral idea, an invocation of History in its righteous sweep'.[114] Miller never moved in those circles. His subway rides took him from a family home in which radical politics was seen as a threat, to a warehouse in which reading books and the *New York Times* was regarded as eccentric and suspect. His Marxism, though, was like Kazin's socialism, a moral idea.

Irving Howe (from the Bronx rather than Brooklyn, and from a family who laboured in the garment industry rather than employing others who did), like Miller, bought his *New York Times* as an earnest of his seriousness. He, like Miller, was drawn to Marxism because it seemed to render the world into his hands, to provide a language, functioning metaphors, an emotional and seemingly intellectual kinship with others who might otherwise feel deracinated and alone. It was the source of a displaced passion, as religion might have been for an earlier generation. It was a trade of faith for hope. And interestingly, given Miller's subsequent career, Howe chooses to explain his new loyalties in terms of drama:

> Marxism advances a profoundly dramatic view of human experience. Its stress upon inevitable conflicts, apocalyptic climaxes, inevitable doom, and glorious futures gripped our imagination. We were always on the rim of heroism; the mockery we might suffer today would turn to glory tomorrow; our loyalty to principle would be rewarded by the grateful masses. The principle of classical drama – peripeteia, or the reversal of fortune – we stood on its head, quite as Marx was supposed to have done to Hegel. The moment of transfiguration would come, if we only held firm to our sense of destiny.

A movement that raises in the imagination of its followers the vision of historical drama must find ways of realizing the dramatic in the course of its history.[115]

It is tempting to see something of Miller's attraction for the theatre as lying precisely in the inner structure of a form that turned on transformations, a social art in which individual lives were integrated not only in a public forum but in the processes of art itself. A privately consumed poem or novel lacked the significance of a shared event. The temporal limits of drama conveyed the urgency of a process that rushed to conclusion, that relied on revelation, on thought and language transmuted into action.

For the moment, though, not yet in college, he was not part of the 'tireless virtuosi who threw radical arguments at each other morning, noon and night',[116] never fully embraced that alliance with modernism which for many others was the sign that their aesthetic radicalism matched their political convictions. He was fiercely focused on getting to Michigan, sending pleading letters to excuse his poor high school grades as he banked his wages. On the other hand, there was a politics of the street. In Brooklyn, Italian businesses often placed photographs of Mussolini in their front windows. He saw the unemployed sitting on front stoops, listened to the speakers in Union Square (where the Communist Party had its headquarters and the Jewish communist newspaper *Der Freiheit* had its offices) denouncing the failures of capitalism and arguing the virtues of their own ideologies.

By the end of the century, things would have changed in Union Square. Politics had gone, to be replaced by a farmers' market. That sense of a gap between the strenuous commitments of the 1930s – strident, felt rather than thought – and the domesticated and private concerns of a society committed to merely material advancement was to generate the energy behind many of his plays, that sense of a missing transcendence.

His own brief primer in Marxism may have been something of a private epiphany, leading him neither to join with others in political action nor, like Kazin, to find his way into New York's literary circles, but when he set out for Michigan he was already convinced that he held a key to history and an explanation for the failure that had brought his father down. He did have a vision of absolute justice and rhapsodic social living, and if they were not accessible in a country that had once prided itself on its utopian principles, there was another place where a new great experiment was being conducted. It was taking place in the Europe from which his father had once journeyed in hope of a new life.

Money was not the only problem facing Miller in getting to the University of Michigan. His father had other plans, and Miller recalled their conversation in *After the Fall*: 'What the hell are you talking about? We're just getting a business started again. I need him! ... when I was your age I was supporting six people!' In the play, as in life, it is his mother who supports him, thus further opening the breach between his parents and adding to the burden of his guilt. Quentin's remarks in that play are surely not far from Miller's own feelings: 'I felt a power, in the going ... and treason in it. Because there's failure, and you turn your back on failure.' It was a burden lifted from him by his brother, who, having dropped out of college, now planned to stay around because 'I just want to see him [his father] big again.'[117]

This was precisely the situation with respect to Miller's brother Kermit, and the scene is effectively reprised in another of Miller's plays in which two brothers look back to the 1930s, *The Price*. Here, too, one brother stays while the other leaves and prospers, and Miller would return in memory, and in his plays, to this moment when he turned his back on his family, their past, their values, and pursued the education his mother had been denied, a mother who, like Quentin, he could never finally mourn.

In his first play, *No Villain*, written, he claimed (others placed it later), less than a year after leaving home, he offered a portrait of his family life and of the tensions he was escaping in going to university, confessing that his brother's decision had set him free. 'I'm a lucky fellow to be able to go off without having to support you here. There are fellows who even send money home from school let alone make their way. You've got to get out and on top and look down, and see, see what one thing is worth against another.'[118]

Speaking in 2001, Miller acknowledged that he had been able to go to Michigan because, as the second son, he was 'blessed with having no expect-ations. My poor brother was supposed to carry the load. It was he who was the responsible party. I was, early on, regarded as a hopeless case as far as any kind of responsibility was concerned. Consequently, I always felt free to do whatever it was that I wanted to do.' But, in going to Michigan, he left Kermit behind: 'at the time I felt terrible about it, because Kermit had gone to NYU for about a year and he was a pretty good student, while I, of course, was a dreadful student in the early part of my life. It was he who should have been going to university, not me, because I was too stupid. So it was unjust, but I didn't resign my position.' He recalled the moment he parted with his brother:

> I remember when I first went to Michigan I got on a bus somewhere in Manhattan. The fare was eleven dollars and at the last moment Kermit went with me to say goodbye as I went into the Wild West, because people didn't travel around the way they do now. At the last moment he gave me his hat, which was a very good one. He loved hats. I never wore a hat but I took this. I kept it for about three years and I was hitch-hiking back and was somewhere in New York State, having come across Canada to Buffalo, from Detroit,

taking Route 17 toward the city, and I got dropped off next to a beautiful field of grain. A car stopped and I ran down the road and the hat blew off and I didn't go back to get it. It blew into the field.'[19]

The hat and the guilt seemed to come together in his memory.

In many ways, though, it appeared to Miller that his brother's hopes were destroyed by a misplaced loyalty. He was increasingly convinced that his father had wilfully exploited a decent and honest man. As for himself, at the time he felt no sense of obligation. He was following a trajectory of his own and, indeed, had been doing so long before the collapse of the family fortune: 'I always felt to one side of the family. I had my own career from the time I was six years old. I had my own space, psychologically. Kermit was totally occupied by them. He was the man they relied on to carry on.'

In 2007, Kermit's son Ross added another detail: 'My father and uncle agreed that since Arthur had gotten into Michigan (a miracle by all accounts) he should go. The following year Arthur would stay home and work and my father would go back to NYU. When Arthur did so well in his first year at school my father insisted that he continue.'[120]

Had the business survived, Kermit would have run it and did, indeed, help in his father's various abortive efforts to begin again. It never occurred to Miller to make a similar sacrifice. 'I formed my nature to reinforce what I wanted to do, which was to have my own career. I had nothing but the greatest regard for Kermit. He was responsible, and I wasn't.'[121] Kermit had managed to be a businessman while holding to Marxist ideals, a combination that slightly baffled Miller but which he nonetheless respected, as he did the integrity of a man who accepted responsibilities which he, himself, could not. On the other hand he thought that his brother now paid the price of doing so. Kermit was noble but also naive. His father was vulnerable but also manipulative. The future for Miller could only lie elsewhere. Rationally, he knew he had to leave his family behind. Emotionally, it felt like desertion and, in later years, he would recall his parents' lives in the 1930s with a mixture of affection and pity.

On a summer evening, the meal over, his mother would read the newspaper Isidore had brought back from the city, the newspaper he himself could barely decipher. She would sit almost motionless, reading of European royal families or the rise of Hitler and twisting her hair in the through breeze, front and back doors standing open. She had, he remembered, a habit of moving her lower jaw forward as she read.

On the back porch, meanwhile, cooling down from the heat of the city, sat his father, staring blankly ahead into the yard as he had once been able to look out from his Harlem apartment over a city of which he could imagine himself a prominent citizen. The tide of time had retreated and left them, at least in Miller's memory, stranded on the beach. Now, looking back, Miller felt a trace of regret for two people whose hopes had been betrayed and who, while still respecting one another's goodness, never again found in one another the comfort and security they sought.

2

MICHIGAN

We were born at the beginning of the First World War ... As ado-
lescents we had the crisis of 1929; at 20, Hitler. Then came the Ethiopian
War, the Civil War in Spain, and Munich ... Next came the Second
World War ... born and bred in such a world ... what did we believe
in?
Albert Camus[1]

Fascism formed my life.
Arthur Miller

Explaining his choice to go to the University of Michigan, Miller remarked:

I had two reasons for choosing Michigan, apart from its educational repute.
The first was that they did not require mathematics. By the time I graduated
from high school I was possibly the world's greatest expert on algebra, having
failed it twice, and only been passed a third time because they could not bear
to look at me anymore. I came to a certain intimacy with every problem in
the textbook. All I lacked was the remotest idea of how to solve them. The
second was the astounding news of the Hopwood awards. The idea of a
university handing out cold cash to students was, I confess, almost too
glorious to contemplate ... with money so hard to come by in the Depression
thirties, giving it away for nothing more than words on a piece of paper had
miraculous overtones ... But the central attraction was even more mysterious.
The fact that money was given out meant that the judges – unlike your
mother or your friends – could really tell good writing from bad. Thus, the
recognition of an award touched more than the pocket; it might even point
to the future.[2]

Later, he added a third reason. 'Tuition was $65 a year and that, as he
remarked, 'was a great recommendation'.

Miller studied at the University of Michigan from 1934 to 1938. He had
twice been rejected but was eventually accepted following an appeal in which
he declared that he had been working for two years for fifteen dollars a

week and had discovered a new sense of academic commitment. Persistence ultimately paid off, though more than sixty years later he remained amazed that he had talked his way in. His acceptance was conditional on his first semester grades reaching the required level. He had worked hard to get there, 'two years on the subway morning and night, living through the summer heat and the freezing cold in that auto parts warehouse'.[3] He was determined not to throw it all away, though he was terrified of failure even as, at some level, and seemingly paradoxically, he had total confidence in his future, believing there was nothing he could not conquer, nothing that would defeat his boundless self-belief.

Miller, then, left home but that Brooklyn world would stay with him. Without noticing it, he had discovered if not his subject then the site of much of his drama. In play after play he would return to the streets where his parents had lived out their desperation and where he had cycled on cold winter mornings to deliver bread. In a 2002 essay celebrating another writer, John Steinbeck, he remarked that 'it is a very rare thing for an American writer to stay home. We tend to use up the energies of a particular place, then to leave home in the attempt to capture a wider America for our work. But in the end America is perhaps only a lot of little places, the undistinguished streets and neighborhoods and countryside of native ground.'[4] He never really used up the energies of his Brooklyn neighbourhood, to which, anyway, he would return after his time in Michigan. It would appear in his first college play, *No Villain*, as it would in *Boro Hall Nocturne*, *Death of a Salesman*, *The Hook*, *A View from the Bridge*, *The American Clock* and *Broken Glass*, whose Ocean Parkway, with its doctors' surgeries and horse riding he had seen as he ran to school imagining nothing more than success on the football field. The undistinguished neighbourhood of his youth, that he was so anxious to escape, turned out to contain the raw material of his art and the story of America that he would tell over a career lasting through one century and into another.

Miller travelled to Ann Arbor by bus in mid-September 1934, at the end of a brutally hot summer. The journey was by no means direct and it took nearly two days. For his mother it was an emotional moment, though she carried it off with good humour. She had high hopes for her son but was also aware that she was losing an ally, someone who shared her interests, spoke her language. At her insistence, he clutched a bag of home-made cookies to help him survive his trip to Michigan.

Michigan, when eventually he did arrive, was not New York. Political ideas were painted with a broader brush there and, besides, his first objective was to survive, academically and financially. Nonetheless, in a year in which sixteen million Americans were unemployed and a million on strike, it was

impossible to feel insulated from social and political events and such consciousness was liable to be intensified in a university. Michigan might be
remote from the intellectual ferment of New York, but it was close to a
blighted countryside, close, too, to Detroit and Flint where sit-down strikes
in the automobile industry that would change more than American labour
history were just three years away.

He was nearly nineteen, but even so a year older than many of his fellow
freshmen. Also, his experience working as a driver, a waiter, a warehouseman
gave him a sense that he knew more of life than they did. He was at the time
(like Tennessee Williams, then working his way through the University of
Missouri) an intending journalism major, less because he had ambitions in
that direction (though later he flirted with the idea of becoming a journalist
for a radical paper) than because he thought his family might take it as
evidence of practicality.

Michigan was something more than an escape, an adventure taking him
away from obligations he had no desire to discharge. It was the fulfilment of
a dream, a sense that his destiny was not congruent with those who looked
for nothing more than material fortunes, the return of an American normalcy
in which he had no faith.

Ann Arbor, thirty-three miles west of Detroit, struck him immediately.
In his biography of Miller, Martin Gottfried comments on the urban feel
of the Michigan campus but even today, and despite the size of the
university, it has a small-town air to it. To Miller it was the college town
of his dreams, beautiful, far removed from the bleak monotony of subway
rides, dawn to dusk labour, the constraints of a three-bedroom house. In
winter, he would discover, it was possible to skate and ski through the
streets while in summer you could swim, without clothes, in certain nearby
ponds. After the warehouse, it was liberation in every sense. For the first
time he was away from his family, leaving behind him the tensions of the
last years. He was not to know, though, that behind the cheerful letters he
would receive from his mother in the course of the next four years lay a
suicidal woman. He was not to know, either, that his brother, working
hard to keep the family solvent, was quietly joining the Communist Party
of the United States – a step that he himself never took – while paradoxically
trying to sustain a father who looked to restore his capitalist dream.

The Midwest was a foreign country. Its conservatism took a different form
from that of the Jewish community in which Miller had been raised. The
university, meanwhile, was a curious hybrid. While not 'a leftist institution
... In the twenties the faculty had been open to socialists, birth control
advocates and other oddballs'; in the thirties it was 'one of the few universities
where Marxism as such was openly discussed in the classrooms'.[5] Yet it was
also an institution that expelled three student radicals (indeed, in the 1950s,

during the McCarthyite witch-hunts, it would dismiss a number of teachers, finally apologizing forty years later).

Michigan had a curious record, both in the past and in the future. When Cornell dismissed Henry Carter Adams, a German-trained economist, following a speech which seemed to favour the anarchist bombing in Haymarket Square, Chicago, in 1886, Michigan appointed him, though only after he had disavowed the speech. In the 1940s, however, it banned American Youth for Democracy from campus, under pressure from the Callahan Committee, the state Senate's Committee to investigate Communist Activities. In 1948, the Dean of the College of Literature, Science and the Arts proposed that 'the University will not appoint its staff nor continue on its staff any person who is a member of the Communist Party'.[6] In the 1950s the university Dean of Women insisted that radical students were 'seriously maladjusted late-adolescents ... Rather than a group of tightly cohesive, rigidly disciplined Party members I see a pathetic group of emotional misfits, cursed with enough brains to complicate any problem but not enough to go to the heart of it'.

Left-wing speakers were regularly banned from the campus, in 1952 the president dismissing the idea that universities should allow people to say what they liked. The following year a more efficient way was devised to dismiss faculty members charged with disloyalty. The Association of American Universities, composed of the presidents of thirty-seven universities, issued a statement declaring it to be the duty of faculty to cooperate with investigating committees, avoid ill-considered public utterance and reject invoking the Fifth Amendment, the constitutional protection against self-incrimination. Michigan President Harlan Hatcher, who had signed it, was anxious to see it accepted as university policy. He wrote to the House Un-American Activities Committee (HUAC) assuring it of the university's cooperation.

Charles Davis, a professor of mathematics, summoned by HUAC in 1954, would refuse to say whether or not he was a member of the Communist Party and, after a six-year battle, finally served a prison sentence in the Danbury Federal Penitentiary, having been fired by Michigan. Nor was Davis alone. Clement Markert, who had served in the Spanish Civil War, was fired, as was Mark Nickerson. The mathematician M.L. Wilder denounced the administration's cooperation with HUAC as 'beyond all bounds of morality and decency'.[7] Michigan was censured by the Association of University Professors.

Not that political reaction was restricted to Michigan. In 1935, Granville Hicks, the radical academic and literary editor of the communist *New Masses*, was fired from Rensselaer Polytechnic Institute. The following year Morris V. Schappes, who taught English at City College and was a Party member, was dismissed and then reinstated, following well organized protests, while

Jerome Davis was dismissed from the Yale Divinity School. Such actions were limited, apart from anything else, by the fact that it was not always possible to tell that someone was a member of the Party. Daniel Boorstin, later to be Librarian of Congress, kept his membership secret until 1953. As Ellen Schrecker has pointed out, by 1936 twenty-one states and the District of Columbia had imposed loyalty oaths on teachers, some vague, some requiring that a teacher declare he or she would not teach communism.

In the 1930s, however, when Miller arrived, Michigan was relatively liberal, and full of contending ideas. For his part, though, his first priority was to find somewhere to live.

As Enoch Brater points out:

> Miller lived in Elnora Nelson's rooming house on South Division Street. She was the widow of a dentist and made all residents store their luggage in a large wooden barrel in the attic containing old teeth (none with gold crowns, Miller discovered). His housemates included Harmon L. Remmel and Henry Carl Reigler, both from Little Rock, Arkansas; Keith and Bob Duber from just north of Ann Arbor; Paul B. Cares, a doctoral student; Charles S. Cook, who was later killed in World War II; Bob Danse; and William and Mary Tommy Lee from Kentucky, who occupied an apartment on the first floor and were great bridge players.[8]

Miller later took a room in a three-storey nineteenth-century building at 411 North State, a white clapboard house framed by trees. He shared a room with Charlie Bleich, a fellow Jew from New York. Miller dressed soberly. His student ID shows him with dark close-cropped hair, revealing the protuberant ears for which he had been mocked as a child. He is holding a chalked board with his full name in capitals – ARTHUR ASHER MILLER – for all the world like the subject of a police photograph. This was his first time away from home, his first time mixing with people from all over the country. It was an unnerving experience. His next-door room-mate at Elnora Nelson's rooming house, Harmon Remmel, son of an Arkansas banker, filled his room with rifles, packed two .38s in his bag, and made his own bullets. This was decidedly not Brooklyn. Remmel later recalled that Miller was always involved with one cause or another in his Michigan years.

Miller sent a card and a letter home and his mother replied within the hour, cursing herself for not telling him to wire news of his arrival. She wanted to know if his bed was long enough. She was glad, she said, that he had made up his own mind about his future, and that they had made no objections. Meanwhile, his young sister Joan had been promoted to his bed.

Only a few of Augusta's letters survive, but what emerges from them is a deeply affectionate, ironic tone. Like any mother she missed her son (she telephoned him each Sunday evening and sent regular packages of fruit cake and cookies) but, given the increasingly difficult nature of her relationship with her husband, his loss was more significant than it might otherwise have been. Her suggestion that they had not raised any objections is disingenuous. In fact, as noted earlier, Isidore had been affronted. The family company might no longer be in existence but the dream of a father passing the business to his sons still survived. Nonetheless, as Ross Miller has indicated, a compromise seems to have been effected. Augusta was meanwhile sufficiently tolerant of her son's radicalism to make it the subject of mutual jokes (a later letter is addressed to 'Artovsky Millensky'). Four years later, fresh out of college and with his plans not working out as he wished, he would go home to East 3rd Street and live in the basement for a time, a fact not so uncommon in the 1930s and not so uncommon in Jewish households. Emotionally, however, he never went home again. He was not lacking in love for his family, but now felt he shared very little with them. He was in tune with the times – revolutionary, morally committed; they were what they had always been, desperate to embrace an America whose values were not to be questioned, merely accepted as a blessing. And if things were not as they wished, then the thing to do was to await the epiphany of reflation.

In truth, Miller, too, was treading water. All the excitement of starting afresh in a new place with new people could not conceal the fact that, in a sense, university was a relief from the Depression. It was time out. Back home people were fighting for menial jobs. Here, the pressure was off. Now there were four years for the country to sort itself out before he was back on the labour market. One-third of the class of 1933 in America were now unemployed. Others were staying on to do graduate work, hoping things would get better. Twenty-six per cent more PhDs were awarded in 1935 than in 1931, though at the same time academic salaries were being cut.

In *The American Clock*, Lee expresses what was clearly Miller's own view when he says, 'The very best place to be was school. Two pairs of socks, a shirt, a good shirt, and a mackinaw; part time jobs in the library maybe – you could live like a king and practically never see cash.'[9] In fact, Miller did see cash, fifteen dollars a month for feeding experimental mice and whatever he could beg from his parents. He was paying $2.75 a week for his room, bargained down from a higher rate, and smoked two packs of Granger tobacco a week (he would smoke until the mid-1970s). He washed dishes in return for free meals at the Co-op cafeteria. Health care was also free. The dishwashing involved working three times a day. The mice, all three floors of them, were in a laboratory two miles distant, and had to be fed at four o'clock each afternoon, while once a month those that had outlived their scientific use-fulness indoors were taken outside and fed to owls in a further experiment. The project was part of Roosevelt's National Youth Administration.

It took him a little while to get over his loneliness. Home was now over a thousand miles distant. Seven weeks after arriving, he admitted to his mother that he was feeling depressed. Her reply, on 8 November 1934, suggested a hidden fear as well as a reproach, as she asked whether he was suffering discrimination. This was the first time he had ever lived in a non-Jewish environment. First Harlem and then Brooklyn had been Jewish enclaves, and though religion meant nothing to him he had lived in a largely Jewish world that celebrated Jewish festivals and shared a set of values. The small house on East 3rd Street had often been packed with his Jewish relatives. This was now all half a continent away.

Some years later he said something about the prejudice he encountered, though as he describes it, it was some time delayed:

> My first friend there was the boy who sat next to me in the English class. He was tapped by a well-known fraternity. Naturally he wanted me with him but I hadn't the money or inclination for fraternity life so I declined. He was a very rich boy and very affable. Our friendship continued throughout the year. In my sophomore year I wrote a play and it was about Jewish people. It won the literary prize of the year and was produced on the campus. I ran into him again after the play was produced. He pretended not to notice me. I think that was when I knew I was a Jew.[10]

In the same 8 November letter Augusta proposes cancelling Kermit's trip to see him and using the money instead to bring him home for Christmas, promising to send the fare and prepare a turkey for a not particularly Jewish occasion, but with noodles, perhaps to compensate for that. A visit, she suggests, would give him a chance to question his father on his views, views that he had diplomatically decided not to challenge. (Kermit did see him. In 2007, Ross Miller recalled, 'My father visited Arthur in Ann Arbor and remembered that [his] younger brother kept all his dirty socks under his bed, rotating them daily rather than washing them.')[11] Joan (known to the family as Jinks), Augusta then explained in her letter, according to her teacher had a poise so natural that even a professional actress could never hope to rival it, which suggests a certain insight since that was precisely what she was to become, working in the theatre into her eighties. Augusta also asks her son how *Iolanthe* is progressing, which suggests that he had at least flirted with the idea of signing up to perform (hardly surprising, given his earlier ambition to be a singer), though nothing seems to have come of this.

Plainly, behind this letter was a certain sense of alarm. Less than two months after his arrival he was admitting to unhappiness. The casual change of plans smacks of a hasty strategy to bring him home into a protective environment. At the same time, money was an issue. Even that student fare was clearly a problem.

It is tempting to think that, finding himself on a campus with something
of a radical reputation, he would quickly throw himself into the various clubs
and political organizations that thrived there. But he had other priorities. His
twin objectives were to make enough money to survive and, after past academic dilatoriness, to pass his exams. Indeed, as far as the university was
concerned he was effectively on probation. In letters home, he confessed to
the burden of his work. He would fall into bed each night exhausted. In
November, he admitted to being worried about his grades. His mother assured
him that she herself was not at all disappointed in them. What she was
disappointed with was the fact that he had expressed no enthusiasm for
returning to Brooklyn.

His academic work posed a real problem. At school, Kermit had excelled
at Latin, French, science and mathematics. Arthur had excelled at nothing.
It was not so much that he had fallen out of the habit of study as that he had
never fallen into it in the first place. Despite his subway reading of Dostoevsky,
two years in the warehouse had hardly sharpened his analytic skills or prepared
him for the examinations that lay ahead. As he later explained:

> during the first two years, I was under the impression that I had better keep
> my nose to the books or they would throw me out of there. I had practically
> to memorize the entire textbook. I had an examination in European history
> in my freshman year and I sat there and my brain froze. The teacher came
> over to me and I said, 'I know all the answers to these questions, in fact I can
> tell you the pictures on the page of the textbook where all these questions
> appear, but for some reason I'm unable to write them.' He said, 'Why don't
> you go home and have a nap and just promise me not to confer with the
> other students', which wasn't difficult because they didn't know any more
> than I did. He said, 'Come back tomorrow and I'll give you the exam', which
> I did. The next day I was perfectly fine. I guess it was a form of hysteria.[12]

The exam that paralyzed him took place at the end of his second semester.
He scored a C grade for the course, his second-semester grades being worse
than his first, in part because of the hours spent earning money. The ABCC
of his first semester gave way to the ACCD of his second, but at least he was
free of algebra. 'C' was defined as 'fair' and 'D' as 'deficient'.

Nonetheless, he found himself eager to learn, and after two years in which
he had had no one to talk to about his literary and political enthusiasms – his
mother aside – suddenly he was in an environment in which everyone had an
opinion, naive or not. The university, he quickly discovered, was 'full of
speeches, meetings and leaflets. It was jumping with issues.'[13] Everybody he
knew, he said later, was a radical and in his eyes those who were not did not
count. The University of Michigan registered the largest number of student
signatories of the Oxford Pledge, a peace movement founded at Oxford

University in England. Those adding their signatures undertook not to fight in any future war: 'We pledge not to support the United States government in any war it may conduct.' In a 1933 poll at Columbia University, 31 per cent of undergraduates had declared themselves pacifists while another 52 per cent said they would not fight unless the country were invaded.[14] In the first play he wrote while at Michigan, a family, based on his own, expresses alarm that their son, based directly on Miller himself, has fallen in with just such an anti-war group, and Miller did indeed sign the Pledge. 'They were all left-wing people,' he observed, 'because the world war was to be a war of capitalists using innocent boys for their own ends.'[15]

The head of the movement on campus was C. Mennen Williams, known as 'Soapy' because he was heir to a shaving-cream fortune. Miller listened to speeches he made from the library steps. Twenty years later, as Miller recalled, he was Governor of the state and as such in charge of the state police who, in the 1950s, would file reports on student activists at Ann Arbor – one of many examples listed in *Timebends* of those who traded their radical convictions for power and success as the decades passed.

For the moment, the peace movement was the only one in which Miller showed any interest. Even then, he attended no meetings. At the University of Chicago, by contrast, and in that same year, a young Saul Bellow was part of a Trotskyite-run socialist club whose magazine carried a quotation from William Randolph Hearst: 'Red radicalism has planted a soapbox on every campus of America.'[16] He was in 'Cell Number Five'.

Miller steered clear of such groups. He was still by no means sure that he would survive his first year, either academically or financially. Indeed, he had to renegotiate the price of his room down from $2.75 to $2.50. He had looked at two-dollar rooms but they were 'uninhabitable'. He recalled two medical students in his house on State Street who lived on bananas, buying them by the whole stalk convinced that they could survive on fruit alone. Meanwhile, he explained to his mother in January 1935, he had made a deal with that landlady to have a free room for a month if he could find her two roomers for her empty rooms. His grades, he told her, were good enough to be able to take psychology the following semester, along with sculpture, an idea he subsequently abandoned. He was enthused enough by some of his work to encourage his brother to read *The Education of Henry Adams*, the last four pages if he could not manage the whole book. More mundanely, he remarked that his laundry had yet to arrive but that this was not a problem since he was still wearing the same shirt he had come with. If he had been lonely before, he was so no longer. There was, he wrote, no time.

That same month, he received a letter from his brother which must have served as a reminder of the price Kermit had paid for his own escape:

Dear Arty,

Sorry for delay in writing you but have swell excuse. Arty I've been initiated into that most honored fraternity: the travelling salesman! Left Friday afternoon with old Sy Rothschild ... and only got back this morn at 9 o'clock. Trip takes 5 and a half hours one way and made it to see Fowler Dick Walker when we sold some forty spring coats and suits. One inspired remark of Sigs has me in stitches whenever I think of it. It was 3 o'clock in the morning Saturday ... I slept none too soundly. And the sound of ever present fire sirens seemed to emanate from just below my window. However after a few minutes, being assured after proper investigation that the hotel was not on fire went back to bed and sleep. The next morning the conversation, in effect ran:

KERM: Sig did you hear the racket of the fire engines last night?
SIG: No, Kermit but dats awright they've got a office around the corner.

Good 'nuf. What a man. 79 yrs old and young as 20.

Got some inside information that might interest you. This from one of the hotel lounge-lizards identity unknown. This gent is convinced A. Hitler will meet his end at the hands of Goering on April 7th. Inquiry further failed to divulge any additional infom. So pass it on as it was given me.

Arty the women in this burg seem to have no scruples or the men either. Went out Saturday night with several of the women from the store. And you can imagine the change in my facial expression when I discovered the gal I was with was not only espoused but had a 21 year old at home. Well I understand that the male of the species goes on a tear at one end of the town, while his 'beloved' goes about a similar course at the other end.

Another, a widow of 26, with a kid of 2 or 3 made it known rather discretely she would like to marry again. And maybe I'm the guy, eh? Very pretty, she, but me no unerstan'. After imbibing about 25 beers, no exaggeration, found it 1.30 Sunday morn, and with the aid of several cranes made way to the depot, and the 2.00 for New York made in nick of time after checking out of hotel. Have been invited back to that coal town. But I don't know. Let it be known that tho' nothing serious transpired there might well have, and maybe – ah, well.

Aside from the pose of the older brother, it is tempting to hear in this letter the origins of the figure of Dave Singleman in *Death of a Salesman* and of Happy Loman, romancing other people's fiancées. The reference to Hitler is a reminder, at the very beginning of 1935, of what would become a central concern of the two brothers, both of whom were drawn to communism as the only effective response to fascism.

By January 1935 Miller had already begun to think about the Hopwood Awards, which seemed to offer the only hope of raising money, a hope he shared with his mother in a letter, as he did the fact that his landlady had raised the rent. His mother sent an understanding response, following a large parcel of food. She was, she wrote, praying for success in the Hopwoods. In that same letter, though, is a suggestion of the problems still facing the family back home and a hint, too, that he continued to be reluctant to go home, something that would become a regular complaint in the coming years. His father's latest attempt to relaunch his company, under the name 'Miller Made', still limped on but he was moving it to cheaper accommodation.

Whatever his preoccupation with exams and part-time work, however, Miller did slowly find himself pulled into the political ferment of Ann Arbor, in the second semester of his freshman year beginning to write for the student newspaper the *Michigan Daily*, located on Maynard Street, which had its own building, printing presses and staff and subscribed to the Associated Press, Reuters and other agencies. It had a circulation beyond the campus, being daily reading for many in the surrounding area. When he arrived it was 'in the hands of the fraternity guys ... the Jazz Age bums as we called them',[17] those who had gone to Michigan when the Depression was barely under way. By contrast, he and the others who now began writing for it 'were already Depression kids'. It became a liberal paper, a forum for political debate as well as the usual parochial concerns of undergraduates.

Now he was balancing academic work with reporting and beginning to get more involved in politics and, rather more surprisingly, through his course on psychology, hypnosis. On Sunday, 1 March 1935, he wrote to his mother. He had, he told her, been listening to a symphony concert in his room. He itemized the reading he had done for his courses in history and psychology, together with details of his attempt to hypnoptize a friend. Along with the letter went a clipping from the *Michigan Daily*, a front-page piece he had written about a possible investigation of campus communists. Beyond his college work, he had been nominated for the steering committee of the Michigan branch of the Farmer-Labor Party (founded in 1920 and with a socialist programme) in Washtenaw County, southeast Michigan.

The major issue he tackled first as a young reporter was the New Deal and, as a succession of New Deal measures were challenged in the Supreme Court, he found himself sent to interview academic historians, economists and sociologists. In his 3 March letter he wrote about a 20–25 per cent cut in local relief payments and sent the article, together with others, to his mother, posting it immediately after receiving a phone call from home. He had, he confessed, forgotten to tell her to listen to *Carmen* on the radio, an indication of how much he and his mother shared in terms of cultural interests. He would be an enthusiast for classical music throughout his life, a regular attender at concerts.

Work on the *Daily* was giving him valuable experience, not only because of the subject matter he found himself dealing with but because of the technical skills he was picking up. But his mind was full of something more than the paper. In a handwritten note (his letters, in contrast to his mother's, are typewritten) he urged his mother to see *Chapayev*, a Russian film that he thought the best he had seen and which seemed to him to catch what he assumed to be the spirit of the new society. He had seen it in one of the university theatres and despite the paucity of communists in the audience it had been enthusiastically received. It was, he told his mother, showing in New York, suggesting that she should see it – not on the whole, surely, a likely prospect.

In New York that summer Alfred Kazin would see the film, replete with the voices of stern and virtuous Soviet military commanders, in the Acme Theater on Union Square. This was where radicals could take their fix of Soviet cinema before walking into the heat and the dense crowds, some arguing the need for an American soviet, some looking up, as girls, incredibly, modelled fur coats behind lighted store windows. Union Square was head-quarters for a number of Party front organizations and publications.

On 12 March Miller was reporting, in the *Daily*, on a speech by Professor John F. Shepard in which he described the psychology of the fascist: 'the psychology of the cheater'. The 'whole basic psychology of Fascism', Miller reported Professor Shepard as saying, 'is that of deceit'. The speech was delivered at a symposium on war and fascism sponsored by the Michigan Student Alliance, which attracted an audience of five hundred. This would become a subject of more than journalistic interest to Miller when, the following year, the Spanish Civil War broke out. Nor, according to Miller's report on the remarks of Professor Slosson, a Michigan history professor, was fascism external to the United States: 'The true seeds of Fascism are in this country . . . but you can't establish such a regime unless the internal conditions are ripe for it.' In Slosson's opinion, William Randolph Hearst was 'the example of the nearest approach to a Fascist who could appeal to the American mind. His clever, jingoistic, chauvinist appeal to nationalism is at the bottom of his whole career.' Fascism 'is preparation against a threat . . . a struggle against Socialism and Karl Marx's teaching'.

Slowly, Miller's reading, and still more the events he attended, were confirming his Marxist views; and his letters, alongside their domestic information, were beginning to include more elaborate accounts of his own position. On 15 March he reported that he had the chance to buy a $16 tennis racket for $12.95. Acknowledging that finances were difficult at home, he nonetheless suggested that the offer was a bargain since he could play free at the university. This, however, was not the main thrust of the letter, which instead, inspired by a visit by the British Marxist John Strachey, who had been arrested in Chicago before coming to Michigan, was dedicated to an explanation of his new enthusiasm for communism, which seemed to him the only solution to America's problems. He now for the first time declared himself to be a communist. If this letter had been placed in front of the House Un-American Activities Committee twenty years later it would have confirmed their suspicions, even though the letter ends with a renewed request for twenty-five dollars to cover rent and the tennis racket; the time for play, he observed, being necessarily short given the new political realities.

Speaking in 2003, Miller was inclined to distance himself from such beliefs:

> The word 'communist' was a generic name for people who were militant, and cared about all this, because the majority of students didn't. They didn't know what was happening. They were studying dentistry. It was the difference between those who were conscious of what was happening, particularly in Europe, and those who were not. Fascism then was the coming movement. Lindbergh's wife said that it was the wave of the future. But there didn't seem to be any resistance to it in America. So I would have used that word 'communist' more vaguely. I did know many who were Marxists but not communists as such. I'll never forget, there was a professor of economics who at one point asked 'Who has read volume two of *Das Kapital*?' Somebody stuck his hand up and he said, 'There isn't one.' I'm sure nobody read it. It was just taken as an article of faith that we understood what this was all about. I would certainly have described myself as a Marxist, or at least a would-be Marxist.

On the whole, this seems a distinction without a difference. It is no doubt true that his friends were not members of the Party, though the Party was active in universities, but they did identify with the views of those who were, and his letter to his mother seems to leave no room for doubt.

He was nineteen and a half and wholly confident that he held the key to the future. What had started as a gossipy letter, in which he justified spending thirteen dollars on a tennis racket (nearly five weeks' rent), becomes a cross between a lecture and a manifesto, until, with a final flourish, he remembers who he is writing to. At the beginning of the letter communists are described as 'them'. By the end he identifies himself as among their number. Communism was, he insisted, the only solution. The twenty-five dollars were eventually delivered by a friend.

There is a sense of earnestness in the letters he sent home, perhaps even of self-righteousness, but it was surely a product of the times as well as of his youth. He genuinely felt he had stumbled on the truth, and was scarcely alone in doing so. Ironically, an ideology which required an abnegation of the self was proving a route to the self.

A month later, he sent the long-suffering Augusta Miller his front-page interview with the Washtenaw Federal Relief Administrator, explaining that the night editor, ideologically at odds with him, had cut out his reference to the inadequacy of relief payments. Another article had suffered a similar cut, with references to the low pay of building workers being excised. As he informed Augusta, by now he was becoming an expert on the radical politics of Michigan; he told her that the National Student League was under threat, with the *Michigan Daily* refused permission to print announcements of their meetings. The legislature, he noted, had passed a bill requiring oaths of allegiance to the Constitution for teachers and students. He was, he confessed, feeling increasingly guilty about his own failure to lend his weight to the battle. Quite what he thought his mother would make of this evidence of his radicalism is not clear, though in the play he was shortly to write (*No Villain*) he acknowledges that it must be the source of alarm. For the most part, though, he was too full of his new enthusiasms not to share them.

Many years later, he jotted down ideas and dialogue for a play that never came to anything. These included a speech that seems to have the force of autobiography in so far as it presents his youthful radicalism as less an attempt to break out than to break in, to be accepted by the brightest who, almost by definition at that time, were Marxists. It is a speech, too, which suggests that his commitment was part of his battle with his father – and beyond him, with an adult world for which he felt contempt, not least because its authority was seemingly undermined by the manifest failure of its values and beliefs.

The speech is that of a character, not yet fully developed, but it seems to bear more than a little relevance to Miller himself. It is written from the perspective of the postwar world and of his own early success, and it is clear that Marxism did offer Miller not only a way of understanding the world but also a kind of club in which shared certainties created a comfortable social environment. As a student at Michigan he felt part of the movement for justice that gave him a role and a place and which distinguished him from his father's generation. As Irving Howe remarked of his own discovery of Marxism, 'One revelled in the innocence and arrogance of knowledge, for even in our inexpert hands Marxism could be a powerful analytic tool and we could nurture the feeling that, whether other people realized it or not, we enjoyed a privileged relationship to history. The totalism of the Marxist system seemed attractive because we wanted a key to all doors of knowledge.'[18]

The very fact that Miller spent so much time on the paper (he ended up as night editor) played a crucial role in politicizing him, as did the various assignments on which he was sent and which he proudly reported to his mother, sending her regular clippings. He recalls that the *Michigan Daily* building 'was home to every disputatious radical splinter group, along with the liberals and conservatives shouting back at them, since all political groups inevitably wanted to dominate *Daily* editorial policy on the issues of the day'.[19]

By the end of his first year, Miller had all but exhausted his hard-won $500 savings, and the university required evidence of further funds before allowing him to proceed, hence his part-time work. His academic record, meanwhile, continued to be somewhat patchy, though sufficient to continue. In his first semester his only A grade was in English Composition, as it was again in his second. He was no more than 'fair' in history and political science. In his second year, once again the only As would be in Composition and the English Essay, with a B in one Shakespeare class and a C in another. There were Cs, too, in journalism, psychology, history and anthropology. In his final two years, however, he would switch his major to English and his grades would edge up as he began to see a connection between academic study and his new enthusiasm for the theatre. He scored straight As in Drama to 1600, Playwrighting, Play Production and Ibsen and his Contemporaries, along with Acting and Aesthetics. In the first semester of his final year he scored A in four of his courses.

One incident that occurred in Miller's first year provides evidence of a commitment that would intensify once he had left Michigan, as he found himself embroiled in something that exposed the extent of American racism. Enoch Brater offers details:

The Wolverine football team, which included an undergraduate from Grand Rapids who later went on to become President Gerald R. Ford, was scheduled to play against Georgia Tech. The team from Atlanta refused to play on the same field with Ford's African-American teammate, Willis Ward. The official story was that Ward chose not to play after Georgia Tech protested his presence. Michigan administrators backed down; Ward was sent off to scout another game in Wisconsin. Miller's friends from Arkansas, Remmel and Reigler, knew one of the Tech players named Pee Wee Williams from high school, and took Miller to meet with members of the Southern team, to protest and appeal to their sense of fair play. Not only did the visiting team rebuff 'the Yankee' Miller 'in salty language,' but told him they would actually kill Ward if he set foot on the Michigan gridiron. Miller was furious. He 'went immediately to the office of the *Michigan Daily* and wrote an article,' Remmel said, 'but it was not published.' Years later President Ford, who graduated from the University of Michigan in 1935 and considered Miller 'a lifelong friend,' referred to the same incident when he spoke in support of affirmative action at the School of Public Policy named in his honor.[20]

One possible source for the money Miller needed to continue his university career was the Hopwood Awards. They were named after Avery Hopwood, successful author of such comedies as *Getting Gertie's Garter* and *Up in Mabel's Room*. He had drowned in 1928, the University of Michigan being a major beneficiary in his will, netting $300,000. This was invested and prizes were established in drama, fiction, poetry and the essay (a generation later, Miller's nephew Ross would win a Hopwood essay award). Miller later explained that, attracted by the prize money, in March of his first year he decided to write a play, knowing nothing at all about drama, his first classes in which came in his second year: 'Why it had to be a play rather than a story or novel I have never been sure, but it was like the difference, for an artist, between a sculpture and a drawing – it seemed more tangible ... But it may mainly have been my love of mimicry, of imitating voices and sounds: like most playwrights, I am part actor.'[21]

Thus, he later claimed, in the spring break of 1935, rather than go home he sat in his room and wrote a play, though despite his protestations at the suggestion it seems more likely that he wrote it a year later. He certainly referred to working on it in his sophomore year in his 1948 article in *Jewish Life*, while mentioning the earlier date in interviews several decades later. The first person he showed it to was Jim Doll, son of his landlord, who lived across the landing where he designed and made costumes for the theatre. It was to Jim Doll, too, that he had to turn for advice as to the correct length for an act. To his surprise, his acts exactly matched Doll's answer.

Miller wrote what he called *No Villain* having seen only two other plays, both before his fifteenth birthday. His reading had extended only to a few Shakespeare tragedies, while his acting career was somewhat abbreviated. He performed the nonspeaking role of a bishop in a college production of *Henry VIII*: 'On cue I had to nod.' Beyond that, he had played a somewhat inglorious part in a play called *Excursion*, by Victor Wolfson. In this he was a coastguard officer who boards a New York ferry-boat that the captain has taken out to sea, with the consent of the passengers, because he is bored going from Staten Island to Manhattan and because they are all trying to escape the Depression. Speaking in 2002 he recalled this, his last venture as a stage actor (though many decades later he would appear in the film of his own novella, *Homely Girl*):

My part consists of my banging on the door of the lounge and yelling out, 'United States coastguard!' and 'Open up!' Throughout rehearsals I was banging this .38 calibre gun on the floor, because you couldn't hit the set, which would shake. It made a loud noise. On opening night I banged on the floor and it didn't make any noise. I looked down and the whole revolver had simply fallen apart. I was in the dark, off-stage. So here I was, on my hands and knees, yelling 'Open up! United States coastguard!' The Captain was played by an Irish actor who came every year to direct a play at Ann Arbor. He was a great grave-digger in many productions. He, of course, was a professional. And he opened up the door and I stood up and I had the barrel of the gun in my hand to conceal the fact that it had no handle. By this time I was in total confusion. He put up his hands. My next line was 'I want everybody up against that wall', but I couldn't think of it. So he said, 'You want everybody up against that wall?' I said, 'Uh huh.' So they all moved up against the wall and I entered the set. I was standing there, completely out of it. So he said, 'You going to tow us back to New York?' because my next line was 'I'm going to tow you back to New York.' I said, 'Uh huh.' And I had one other statement, which he supplied, and he then led me off the stage. That was my last acting.[22]

Miller wrote the first act of *No Villain* in a day and a half and the rest in the following three and a half, before showing it to Jim Doll who thus became the first person ever to read a Miller play: 'I was close to despair that he might make nothing of it, but I had never known such exhilaration – it was as though I had levitated and left the world below ... Finally his door opened, and he came across the corridor into my room and handed me the manuscript ... "It's a play, all right. It really is! ... I think it's the best student play I've ever read."' Thrilled, Miller went out into the night-time Ann Arbor streets and ran 'uphill to the deserted center of town, across the Law Quadrangle and down North University'. For the first time he felt 'the magical force of making marks on a piece of paper and reaching into another human being, making him see what I had seen and feel my feelings'.[23] And what the gangling six foot eight inch Jim Doll had seen and felt others did, too.

Miller later submitted it as part of his requirement for an English class. The professor, Erich Walter, 'loved it and read it to the class. He was so enamoured of it. I had to cringe because his pronunciation of the lines was so stiff that instead of "Oh, yeah" he said "Oh, yay".' Nonetheless, the class responded with enthusiasm, laughing and even crying. He had, it seemed, the power to move strangers. 'Walter suggested that I should join Professor Rowe's class. He taught playwrighting. I had never heard of him. But that's how I ended up in Rowe's class.'[24]

Kenneth Rowe was an inspirational teacher with connections into the New York theatre (he spent much of 1936 on leave at the Theatre Guild) and his influence would ultimately prove crucial to Miller's development as a writer.

It was the reaction of his fellow students but, still more, Rowe's support, that not only convinced him that he might have a future in the theatre but also gave him a sense of his own purpose and direction. From the beginning, he says in his autobiography,

> the idea of writing a play was entwined with my very conception of myself. Playwriting was an act of self-discovery from the start and would always be; it was a kind of license to say the unspeakable, and I would never write anything good that did not somehow make me blush. From the beginning, writing meant freedom, a spreading of wings, and once I got the first inkling that others were reached by what I wrote, an assumption arose that some kind of public business was happening inside me, that what perplexed or moved me must move others. It was a sort of blessing I invented for myself.[25]

The surprising thing is that this appeared true even of this first effort, written in his bedroom.

No Villain begins with an epigraph from Friedrich Engels: 'Now for the first time a class arose which, without in any way participating in production, won for itself the directing role over production as a whole and threw the producers into economic subjection; a class which made itself the indispensable mediator between every two producers and exploited them both.'

To be a playwright in the mid-1930s was to be, or seem, radical. In Missouri at the same time, Tennessee Williams was writing ostensibly radical plays for a radical theatre group, though the nature of his radicalism was a touch uncertain. In June 1936 he would be baffled by what he called the hullabaloo about fascist repression and capitalism and complained about what he called 'professional againsters'. A month later, however, the Spanish Civil War broke out and in 1937 he claimed, none too convincingly, that he would gladly enlist in the Loyalist army. Looking back in the 1950s, Williams would insist that he was living in a world threatened by totalitarianism, in which reactionary opinion threatened the writer who chose to challenge orthodoxies. He even suggested, with characteristic brio, that artists were trembling before the spectre of investigating committees and even mindful of Buchenwald if they so much as considered supporting Henry Wallace, the third-party left-wing candidate for whom Miller would himself vote. But, in truth, in the 1930s Williams wrote student plays about strikes and conditions in prison because he thought there was a market for them, also turning out a gangster play and a drama about ghosts for much the same reason. Indeed, when Erwin Piscator rewrote his *Battle of Angels* as an anti-fascist work, Williams withdrew it.

In 2004, Miller said of his contemporary that 'he had begun as a writer in the midst of the Depression and his work echoed an awareness of the social as well as the personal elements affecting his themes and stories – his people were both alive and shadows on the larger world'.[26] His radicalism, though, did not go deep. Miller's did. It was passionately felt. In contrast to what he called Williams's radicalism of the soul, Miller's had an intellectual basis.

No Villain is set squarely in a world Miller knew – the garment industry of New York. For his characters, as so often, he drew on his own family. Indeed, the central character was plainly himself, described as over six feet tall and angular. From time to time, he forgets the characters' names and substitutes those of the people on whom they are based. The play opens in what is plainly a version of the Miller home on East 3rd Street in Brooklyn as the family await the arrival of their son Arnold, hitch-hiking home (as Miller did) from the University of Michigan. The father, Abe Simon, is the illiterate head of a coat-manufacturing company that has fallen on hard times. His wife's father, who in one version of the play retains Miller's father-in-law's name, is a figure of fun, slipping into German and Yiddish from time to time. The other members of the family, Abe's wife Esther, Arnold's brother Ben and sister Maxine, are versions of Augusta, Kermit and Joan.

When Arnold arrives, the tension in the family becomes clear. His mother is concerned at Arnold's 'communistic ideas'. He does, after all, write for a 'communistic paper', plainly the *Michigan Daily*. Both sons are at odds with their parents. Abe Simon is a businessman, suspicious of unions: Arnold and Ben are radicals who believe that the world has to be reinvented and that it is, in fact, being reinvented in the Soviet Union.

The immediate crisis is precipitated by a strike in the Simon Coat and Suit Company and it is to the office of the factory, and the shop-floor, that the action now moves. The question is whether Arnold, out of family loyalty, will help to break the strike ('A boss's son is a boss's son') and thus enable the company to survive, or whether he will be obliged by his politics to join with the workers. It is a question of loyalty. Is he to be concerned with the family or the family of man – exactly the dilemma, of course, that would fuel Miller's first Broadway success *All My Sons*? Joe Keller would ask his son to 'see it human.' The question is whether Arnold will, and what precisely that might mean, since we never see the strikers but do see Abe Simon's anguish. A loan is due. If it is not paid it means ruin and the end to his hopes for himself and his sons.

Even this early in his career Miller has discovered the dramatic tension contained within the family and the essential connection between the private and the public worlds. In *No Villain* Arnold rejects his father's values. He accuses his parents of a blind materialism serving nothing but itself. In return they blame the 'communist books' he has been reading. Beyond the boundaries of the play, that was precisely the tension that existed between Miller and his parents and in fact Miller did once join the picket line outside his father's company, with what effect on family relations can only be imagined.

The play ends as the grandfather dies and Ben rejects the idea of an arranged marriage with the daughter of another manufacturer who is willing to rescue the family firm. The bank forecloses and Ben dedicates himself and his brother to fighting for change. There is, as the play's title indicates, no villain in this play, beyond a system whose injustice seemed so self-evident to a young Arthur Miller and, indeed, to a generation of those who had seen that system fail on every level.

What he would later say of *All My Sons* is equally true of this, his first play. It was concerned with 'the destruction of the hermetic seal around the family – the conflict between being a father and being a citizen. I've always been interested in writing about the family but also the family of mankind.' He wrote the play in hope of securing his future at Michigan, but the issues it dealt with were real enough. As he would say, 'the theatre is a bit like a newspaper. Suddenly there is an issue that is imperious.'[27]

The strength of *No Villain* lies in the fact that alongside the sometimes truculent assurance of the two brothers, so certain of their presumptive rights to possession of the future, is a doubt about the human cost of such certainties. Miller may have felt free to use his family for his own dramatic ends but his own loyalties sharpen the dilemma on which the play appears to comment. He was himself restrained by love of his family from deploying them as mere ideological markers. Their very human reality exerted a pull against the political logic being adumbrated. The parents stare with bewilderment at the future so casually invoked by their sons, and Miller feels the human force of that bewilderment. Here, at the beginning of his career, is a sense of that ambivalence which would give such force to his work.

In his biography of Miller, Martin Gottfried dates the writing of *No Villain* to the spring of 1936, the year in which it won the prize. Miller was adamant that it was 1935. His memory was that he missed the closing date for submission in 1935 – then in April, now at the beginning of the year. Certainly his mother's references to the Hopwood in January 1935 seem to substantiate this and he had, after all, chosen Michigan precisely because he had hopes that he might win a prize that would enable him to stay. That being so, however, it seems unlikely that he would have missed the entry deadline, so that the date of composition remains unclear, though 1936 would appear more plausible.

Meanwhile, in May 1935, and with examinations approaching, he received apparently reassuring news from home. His mother wrote assuring him that business was good but that, ominously in view of *No Villain*, there was a possibility of a strike (perhaps itself further evidence that Miller wrote the play the following year). His father, meanwhile, was showing signs of tiredness, withdrawing from a family gathering and sleeping the afternoon through. His grandfather, she explained, was reading the Torah aloud as she wrote. Here was a reminder of something else he had left behind.

Apart from worries about whether he had received money to redeem his laundry and hence whether he was wearing his underwear, his mother was concerned that his efforts to earn money might mean that he was spreading himself too thin. She also chided him for his brief and infrequent visits home, though he was now only three weeks away from his first summer break. The next day Miller wrote to his brother (whom he congratulated on his sale of coats, suggesting that they might both end up in the family business) confessing that he was, indeed, feeling overcommitted, working from nine to midnight at what he called a ritzy local bar where he was learning to distinguish between the various beers on offer but saving money on meals. The ritzy bar was called the Pretzel Bell, where a glass of beer cost the owner two cents and was sold for five. There was, of course, no question of Miller joining Kermit in the business, though, like Biff and Happy Loman in *Death of a Salesman*, they did sometimes fantasize about it. It was, after all, precisely to escape that fate that he had come to Michigan.

In the letter to Kermit he enclosed a copy of the *Daily* and explained that he was writing a piece on what struck him as the confused political views of the professors. Meanwhile, he told him, he was at work on a one-act play for his English course (possibly a reference to *No Villain*) and rapidly learning respect for professional dramatists who had to produce works in which dialogue and action had to seem realistic even as they contributed to a contrived climax. It was 8 May 1935.

So ended his first year at university. Academically, he was still bumping along the bottom. The *Daily*, however, had given him an outlet for his political views and the Hopwood, perhaps, a spur to his invention. Financially, he was barely surviving, but he was increasingly confident of his own abilities and of political opinions that were now more completely formulated. Whereas earlier in the year he had spoken of communists as though they were a breed apart, now he counted himself among their number even if not enrolling in the Party. The university, meanwhile, had agreed to offer him a loan so he could continue with his course, and at home Kermit reconciled himself once more to surrendering his own chance of university education in favour of his younger brother.

For all that Michigan had furthered his political education, there is no doubt that from the end of his first year what mattered most to Miller was his writing. As he said in interview in 2003, 'I was involved in the idea of how to become a writer, how to succeed, how to get published. I remember reading that Sidney Kingsley, I think, had gone nine or ten years writing without any recognition. When I read that, I thought it was incredible.' He himself was in a hurry for recognition.

When he returned to Michigan in September 1935 after a summer at home, working, briefly, for his father who was once again trying to re-establish himself, he had a double commitment. He still needed to keep at his work, his grades being too borderline for comfort, but he also determined to commit himself to writing. On 13 November he wrote home announcing an A grade in an economics paper, admitting that the *Daily* continued to occupy his time. Having stayed at Michigan, as he later claimed, to write a play in his Easter break, he now confessed that he would not be going home for Christmas either, planning instead to work on a bigger project, a novel. The novel came to nothing but it was already clear that the links to his family were becoming attenuated. In a 1986 interview, somewhat chillingly, he says of this time: 'I left home when I was eighteen or nineteen. I lived in the middle west. My home ceased to interest me.'[28]

Along with his wages from the Pretzel Bell and the mouse laboratory he had also been receiving cheques from home, where money was more of a problem than his mother ever allowed herself to admit. On 29 November, writing on the headed paper of the Art Cinema League, he replied to Kermit, defending himself against accusations of extravagance and speculating on his future. He wanted, he explained, to be a journalist and had been told that there might be work on radical papers. He seems to have been preparing himself for such a job in writing an editorial in the *Daily* complaining at the scarcity of proletarian literature on campus. The English Department, he told his brother, had itself called for contributions so that it could buy left-wing books, not least because it was requiring book reviews of such literature from its students. The letter is a curious mixture of defensiveness and self-assurance but it also betrays a continuing sense of guilt. Having justified his spending habits and expressed gratitude for the money sent from home, he ends his letter by confessing that he thought his brother, rather than he, should be at university.

The following spring he was still working on the *Daily*, even as his exams approached, when he sent a letter to his mother apologizing for not writing and explaining that once again he would not be home for the holidays. He had, he told her in a letter dated 26 March 1936, some literary work to finish and a thesis on Freud for his course on abnormal psychology. There is no copy of her reply, but by now she must have been inured to holidays without him.

He itemized his work: an essay for his English course and a thesis on Walter Lippmann – who, incidentally, had remarked that 'the rich and vulgar and pretentious Jews of our big American cities are perhaps the greatest misfortune that has befallen the Jewish people. They are the real fountain of anti-Semitism.'[29] Miller had also, and intriguingly given the subject of *No Villain*, written an essay dealing with what he called the 'scabbing' of his two cousins who had crossed picket lines (as he himself was to do). Despite impending exams (he was taking one in economics an hour after writing his letter), he had, he went on, been to a speech given by Toyahiko Kagawa [a Japanese pacifist] the previous night and was to hear Smedley Butler speak on 'War is a Racket' that night and interview him for the newspaper.

Butler was a retired marine major-general who lectured on his role in various marine expeditions in Central America and the Caribbean and on his conviction that he had, in effect, been serving the interest of American monopoly capitalism. He had proposed a constitutional limitation prohibiting American involvement beyond the twelve-mile limit, and it is clear that Miller found this persuasive if not politically plausible. It certainly seems to have fed his own isolationist instincts that would lead him to oppose American involvement in the Second World War until Pearl Harbor. Fifty years later he was still struck by 'the poverty and misrule in Central America, the rebellion against it, and an American resolve that nothing fundamental ever change except to our liking'.[30]

His piece on Lippmann had duly appeared (his name misspelled) in an issue of the *Daily* for which he was acting night editor, standing in for Bob Cummins who a year later would go to fight in Spain. The big news story of the day, however, lay beyond the campus. He and others on the paper had waited by the teletype machine for news of the Hauptmann trial to come through (he had allegedly kidnapped the Lindbergh baby). He ends his letter by wishing his mother a happy Passover.

When he had sat down to write *No Villain*, Miller later wrote, he 'felt alone, of course, and I was scared of making myself ridiculous, and I felt light-years away from any suggestion of professionalism, for I was painfully aware that I knew very little about plays and nothing at all about the theatre. My only hope was that the other plays being written for the Hopwood contest would be worse. This thought was the only one I had at the time that approached reason. The awards provided a world small enough to grapple with.'[31]

It had been a long wait, but his problems finally came to an end in May 1936, when *No Villain* received the Avery Hopwood Award, which he has described as the student equivalent of the Nobel Prize. The news, he said, was 'like an artillery shell fired right through the ranks of my opposing army – down went all my old algebra teachers'. The judges included Edith Isaacs (editor of *Theatre Arts Monthly*, a charter member of the Provincetown Players and director of the Manhattan–Bronx Federal Theatre Project) and Alfred Kreymborg (poet and editor of the annual *The American Caravan*). They were not unanimous but finally settled on this play as the winner. Kreymborg submitted his suggested list of winners on 13 May. He placed *No Villain*, entered under the pseudonym 'Beyounm', first among the contestants for minor awards, with 'Jay Sebastian' second. It was, he said, 'an excellent modern theme, handled with a tender insight into character'. Alexander Dean placed Miller second to 'Sebastian', as did Edith Isaacs, with the dismissive comment that 'I may add regretfully that all the Minor submissions seem to be quite without indications of talent.'[32] In fact Miller shared the year's prize with the man who had first read *No Villain*, Jim Doll, though he makes no reference to this in *Timebends*. Each received $250, Miller blowing $22 on a Model T Ford.

It is not surprising that he subsequently decided to expand the play. There was enough here to convince him that it could find a place in the professional theatre and for the next five years he revised it with that in mind. As a result, it survives in various forms and, under the title *They Too Arise*, was finally produced on 12 and 13 March 1937 by the Hillel Players in the Lydia Mendelssohn Theatre at Ann Arbor, and seven months later, on 23 October, in a single performance by the Federal Theatre in Detroit (at the Jewish Community Center). The contract, signed six weeks earlier, specified that he was to be paid $10 per performance. This was the first money he ever earned for the professional performance of one of his plays.

A subsequent version submitted to the New Plays Bureau in 1937 received an award of $1,250 (his friend Norman Rosten and Tennessee Williams received similar awards), while in 1939, after graduating, he produced yet another version, now called *The Grass Still Grows*, double in length and very different in tone, in hope that it might be accepted by the Federal Theatre (to be abruptly closed down by Congress that same year), or by Broadway, where it was rejected as 'too Jewish'.

On 29 May 1936 he sent a telegram, significantly addressed to his mother rather than his father, announcing not so much the award as its cash value: 'JUST WON TWO HUNDRED FIFTY DOLLARS FOR MY PLAY LOVE ARTHUR.' To make doubly sure, he called home long distance, anxious to announce his new status, now no longer feeling it necessary to present himself as a journalism major. His mother screamed and left him on the telephone as she rushed around the neighbours announcing his success, even as the cost of the call mounted ever higher. On East 3rd Street he was now famous; in Michigan, he was confident he had found his vocation. What he seems not to have revealed to his family is that he had drawn directly on their lives in writing his play. Many years later, he would own up to a passing doubt about the legitimacy of appropriating other people's experiences for his art, building fame and success on the lives he had stolen. At the time he felt no such scruple – nor, in truth, would he, in a career in which he mined his own life and those of his family and others, in which he inspected each experience for its utility. In *After the Fall* his parents would be required to restage their arguments from these Depression years, as they would again in *The American Clock*, in which his sister Joan, by then an actress of considerable reputation, would play the part of her own mother while herself contesting the accuracy of the portrait she was required to enact.

Later, he would explain something of his approach to his source materials: 'I don't think a dramatist creates anybody simply out of a real person. The real person only supplies the surface. The character comes from inside yourself and all of it is a distillation of everything you know up to that moment about a certain kind of situation.'[33]

In fact, there would be few Miller plays that did not reach down into real experience, his own or that of others, from *All My Sons* through to *Broken Glass*. Some are based on stories he was told (*All My Sons*, *A View from the Bridge*), some on people he knew ('Some Kind of Love Story', 'I Can't Remember Anything', *The Last Yankee*). His unpublished plays, stories and novels would often press even closer to private truths, that being one reason no doubt for their remaining unpublished. To him, this was not evidence of a failure of imagination, but a guarantee of authenticity. His plays, he often said, were not so much imagined as recalled. Indeed for some years he feared exhausting his supply of memories, experiences, half-forgotten stories.

That he should start his career by turning to his own family was understandable. From the beginning, however, he acknowledged the necessity to reach beyond his immediate models for a social truth and saw in private tensions the roots of social revolt. As he remarked twenty years after writing his first play, whether it was Tolstoy, Dostoevsky or Hemingway, or indeed a woman writer, all were formed first as sons and daughters; and built into that relationship for the writer, as for everyone, is a battle for mastery of identity and for independence. That struggle with authority, it seemed to him, lay at the heart of aesthetic and political revolt alike.

Without the Hopwood money he would almost certainly have had to leave. It is unlikely that the university would have offered him a further loan. He would have had few options, the most obvious being the least acceptable. He could have returned home and joined his brother in helping a father whose values were not his own. He might well have tried to find some employment of a practical kind, having always been adept at working with his hands. But this would have been a crushing defeat.

The Hopwood Award revealed to him that he had the talent to succeed. He had come to Michigan believing himself intellectually the inferior of many of those he encountered. For the first time he now excelled, and in writing discovered the kind of satisfaction he had never felt before. Now, and for the next two decades, he was confident of the theatre's power to describe, dramatize and transform the social world. The announcement of the award was a ratification of what he believed he already knew. He ceased to fear academic failure. He was not yet content, though, with what he had written. Even as his name was read out he had 'felt pleasure, of course, but also something close to embarrassment, praying that everybody would soon forget my poor play in favor of my next one, which would surely be better'.[34]

Miller had now moved to 122 North Thayer Street and it was while he was here that he set himself to revise *No Villain*. The play now carried a new title, *They Too Arise*, the 'they' not meaning simply those on the picket line fighting for their rights but a bourgeois family suddenly alerted to the necessity for social change.

A strike is still at the centre of the play, but the issue now is less the conflict between Abe Simon and his workers than between Simon and the larger companies, though it is this external battle that eventually heals the wounds in the family. An arranged marriage is still offered as a way out, but this time the proffered bride is revealed as the daughter of a fellow manufacturer who has stolen their business. The tension between the generations builds. The grandfather berates his son, goading him to the point at which he physically pushes the old man aside, thus exacerbating a heart condition. Abe, meanwhile, feels alienated from his son Arnold, bewildered that he should side with the strikers who are threatening his livelihood. When the grandfather subsequently dies it is as though the family were turning against itself. Eventually, though, it becomes clear who the real enemy is. Miller now effectively sidesteps the divisions within the family by uniting them against those who are as interested in crushing the small manufacturers as in defeating the workers.

When the Manufacturers' Association proposes to hire strike-breakers Abe Simon refuses to go along, insisting that he wants to leave his sons a clean name, a statement which prefigures a number of similar statements in subsequent plays. His problem is that, like Willy Loman, he believes that his name is implicated in his success. By the same token, however, he insists that he will not agree to violence because it is no way for Jewish men to act, not least when, as Arnold observes, anti-Semitism is on the rise.

Now it is the father who acknowledges the need for change. He expresses an ambivalence missing in the earlier version and the family end up united against the forces of reaction. He acknowledges that he has wasted his life trying to get rich.

They Too Arise is not a significant improvement on *No Villain*. Helen, the girl offered to the other son Ben, is less a character than a proposition. The play has altogether too much in the way of unexamined rhetoric, unexamined by the playwright as well as by the characters. Yet there are also signs that

Miller is tightening the dramatic structure, and developing that blend of humour and social drama that would characterize much of his later work. Here, too, is that concern with power and the language it accretes to itself, with the need to develop a social ethic, that would prove fundamental concerns of his subsequent plays. The Simon family come to understand the extent to which their fate is in their own hands. In the end they are victims of nothing but their own failure to confront the nature of their situation and to understand that the drive for success, or even unprincipled survival, is of no purpose if human values are not sustained.

Miller was now a prize-winner, but he faced a problem: 'I had spilled out into that first play everything I knew or could imagine about life. For I had hardly lived at all. I must invent something, I thought with sinking heart, and for this I supposed one had to have some kind of objectified technique. So, I promptly groped my way into Professor Kenneth T. Rowe's play-writing class.'[35]

It was, indeed, Kenneth Rowe who took this enthusiastic young writer, suddenly full of his own potential, and helped to educate and shape him, as a similar professor had helped Eugene O'Neill and another was helping Tennessee Williams. It was Rowe who exposed him to Greek drama, to Ibsen and to the new radical playwrights, but who also inducted him into the practicalities of playwrighting. Long after leaving Michigan, Miller maintained a correspondence with his mentor which reveals him as anxious to justify himself in the eyes of a man who had been one of the first to acknowledge his talent and offer him advice. When an edition of his essays was published in 1978, Miller included a dedication, 'To Kenneth Thorpe Rowe – teacher, friend, scholar – whose lifelong devotion to drama and the theater has made a difference'.

'It is hard to define what I took from Professor Rowe's classes,' he later reflected – perhaps

> it was, above all, his enthusiasm for the catholicity of dramatic literature, the sheer variety of forms that time had developed. And, indeed, there was no single overriding style of writing in his class as there would be in the coming decades when fashion, for some reason, had so dominated and, I think, in many cases crushed invention ... It did not yet seem that there had to be obeisance to a prevailing mode. Perhaps fewer people were reading the arts section of the *New York Times* then.[36]

Rowe was not only a teacher. He later became a consultant to the Theatre Guild and had good connections in the professional theatre. 'He was the closest I had gotten yet to any professional, serious theatre group, because we had no theatre in Ann Arbor, except the Hillel Players that mostly did comedies.'

The year after Miller's departure from Michigan, Rowe published *Write That Play* (1939), which summarized some of the ideas he had passed on to his students, ideas that Miller clearly seems to have taken to heart. There was, Rowe insisted, 'a great deal to be said for a realistic play in traditional form at the start. Fantasy, symbolism, expressionism all have their traditional place', particularly in an era of experiment, but it 'is a good idea for the beginner feeling an impulse toward radical experiment to make an earnest effort to cast his material into established form, and only then, if it won't work, go ahead with the experiment'.[37] Beyond this pragmatic approach, realism, he believed, encouraged observation and practice in creating credible dialogue. Miller's first play, though written before his exposure to Rowe's ideas, was realistic, its dialogue closely modelled on his family's conversations. His desire to experiment was, indeed, deferred.

There is also a perhaps unremarkable coincidence between Miller's decision to write about his own family and Rowe's observation that 'It is a curious fact that a young person with a high degree of dramatic talent is likely in his first play to base the characters on members of his own family, following the right instinct for what he knows and understands most intimately.' He seems not, though, to have heeded Rowe's warning that 'if he includes himself, that character is especially liable to be colorless', since 'the more truly dramatic the talent the more unsuccessful the attempt at self-portraiture tends to be, while the young person with the inherent talent often shows startling penetration into mature experience in others'. Certainly, the character he did model on himself in *No Villain* is the most lifeless.

It was Rowe who directed him to the work of Clifford Odets, to whom he attributed 'a flair for putting a finger accurately on a certain kind of reality' and whom he praised for 'a picturesque virility of theatre speech which is quite his own', an aspect of Odets's work that Miller would himself later praise. It was Rowe, too, who advised that 'an incident in a newspaper ... or a story one has heard may be the starting point as well as events directly observed. The dramatist,' he suggested, 'must develop a keen nose for plot suggestions whenever they pass his way. A notebook is almost certain to be helpful.' Miller kept such notebooks and once he had exhausted his family and his own immediate experiences, did indeed rely on newspaper articles and stories told to him by others.

He perhaps also took his cue from Rowe's assertion that they were living at a time when the 'public forum as part of theatre is strong. People are thinking about social problems, the problem of labor versus capital, of economic oppression, the problem of ... what drives people to crime, of the effects of prisons upon their inmates'. Miller, after all, concentrated in his first two Michigan plays, *No Villain* and *Honors at Dawn*, on the conflict between labour and capital; and in his third, *The Great Disobedience* (originally entitled *A Three-Act Prison Tragedy*, begun in October 1937 and submitted the following March), on the effects of prison on prisoners, while his first Broadway success, *All My Sons*, had at its heart a crime and a consideration of the pressures that led to it.

Perhaps, too, he derived from Rowe his tendency to write in verse. For Rowe, the reason for verse in drama was 'to give fuller expression to the significance of profound moments in human experience than the convention of realism allows'. He adds – significantly, given Miller's subsequent fascination with the tragic – that the 'convention of poetry is especially needed for tragedy'.

To a certain extent Rowe was doing no more than identify essential elements of theatre; hence, for example, his insistence on conflict; yet the way in which he does so seems to have a special relevance to Miller's work. Thus, he insists, a play opens with the presentation

> of a situation that in some way is poised, in a state of unstable equilibrium. The audience recognizes a potentiality of conflict which creates a minor state of question, of suspense, but the question is not formulated; conflict is not yet assured, nor do we know the form and direction the conflict will take. We only recognize, more or less definitely, that the status quo of someone on the stage is vulnerable. Then some new element enters which precipitates the conflict.

Basic though they are, Rowe's comments seem to bear directly on a play such as *All My Sons*, in which Miller works hard to create that sense of an unstable equilibrium, that intuited sense of vulnerability that waits only on a catalyst to precipitate conflict and disaster.

Miller also responded to Rowe's enthusiasm for Ibsen, then undergoing a revival in America. He saw Jed Harris's 1937 production of *A Doll's House*, the text of which was adapted by Thornton Wilder (Harris was later to direct the premiere of *The Crucible*). He also saw *Ghosts* at the Brighton Theatre in Brooklyn. Rowe's reasons for referring his students to Ibsen are themselves of critical interest in relation to Miller's career. He suggested that they should study his plays in part for their dramatic construction but more especially because he 'made character the heart of his drama. In writing a problem play he subordinated thesis to a consistency of character', while 'the general social problem is always the problem of a living individual, and developed accordingly'. This, of course, was to be precisely the strength of Miller's own work and a key to his success as a playwright, though he was subsequently determined to underline the experimental nature of a number of his early works.

Ibsen had played a crucial role in the development of American drama. O'Neill had been inspired by watching Nazimova in *Hedda Gabler* while, in 1936, Tennessee Williams went to see the same actress in *Ghosts* and was required to study Ibsen's work for his drama course at Washington University. Ibsen, in the radical 1930s, was himself seen as a radical. It might be Clifford Odets and Sean O'Casey, lyrical prophets of Marxism, who primarily appealed, but Ibsen wrote, as Miller and his fellow students thought, social plays that confronted society with its hypocrisies. He was a believer in change, and what better qualification could a man have? His characters acknowledged the power of the past but did so in order to purge it of that power and refuse its orthodoxies.

In 'the Leftist tide of the Thirties', Miller asserted, Ibsen's stance 'was translated into an anti-capitalist militancy',[38] a curious piece of sleight of hand but convincing to those concerned to accommodate art to their own needs. To be sure, there were debates about what some saw as his potential fascist impulses. Certainly, his apparent endorsement of an intellectual elite in *An Enemy of the People* would still give Miller pause for thought when he adapted it in 1950. But, for his part, Miller found in Ibsen's work a sense of indignation about the given, a rejection of social hypocrisies, in tune with his own rigorous rebelliousness. Ibsen was for dragging the hidden into the full light if not of day then of a Norwegian drawing room which otherwise acted as an image of constraint, order and a pallid hypocrisy.

Beyond that, though, Miller saw in him a kindred spirit to the Greeks. 'To me,' he said later, 'he was a reincarnation of the Greek dramatic spirit, especially its obsessive fascination with past transgressions as the seeds to current catastrophe.' Ibsen and the Greeks seemed to him related through 'their powerful integrative impulse which, at least in theory, could make possible a total picture of a human being ... Present dilemma was simply the face that the past had left visible.'[39] Unsurprisingly, he related this to his own approach in *Death of a Salesman*. In the 1930s, though, Ibsen seemed a powerful voice for change – if, Miller confessed, something of a difficult read and short, as it seemed to him, on entertainment: not many laughs, simply ironies in which to revel.

Ibsen, only thirty years dead when Miller wrote his first play (as Chekhov was only thirty-five), carried a tragic sense into the modern age. It was Ibsen who had declared his wish to write a tragedy of the contemporary age, and his colleague, the Danish critic Georg Brandes, who called for a literature subjecting social problems to debate. Ibsen had also been drawn to dramatic poetry, and declared drama to be a public art addressing public issues while seeing the past as organically implicated in present concerns, all of which would become markers of Miller's work. Beyond this, though, what drew Miller to Ibsen was his revolutionary spirit. Ibsen and Brandes preached Truth and Freedom. They had called for a change in social values. They were in revolt against a conservative, Victorian, society. They recognized the dilemma of the individual trapped within national and social myths. So, too, did Miller. Ibsen speaks of the reforming nature of theatre, or at least its power to 'shed light' on aspects of society, a phrase also used by Miller.

Ibsen staged the drama of a society in which money sustained a culture that subsisted on denial, that treated with suspicion and more the free spirit, the critical voice. In a world in which private behaviour and public forms diverged, Ibsen was concerned to underscore that divergence and insist on the tragic implications consequent upon that gulf. For him, the family was deformed by its social role, becoming an agent not simply of repression but of false values. So it was for Miller and, of course, for Marx.

For Miller, the leap from Marx to Ibsen was not so great and, indeed, in an 1886 amateur production of *A Doll's House* the part of Nora, who slams the door on family and convention alike, was played by Eleanor Marx, daughter of Karl. The same production saw William Morris's daughter as Mrs Linde and Bernard Shaw as Krogstad. Eleanor Marx even learned Norwegian so as to translate Ibsen.

In later years Miller was uncertain as to the extent of Kenneth Rowe's influence, feeling that he had been following a trajectory of his own. However, given how little he knew of the history of drama, Rowe was a crucial figure. As Miller explained in 2003, 'In those days there weren't any writing courses that I knew about. I don't think they existed. Rowe was probably the only one in the United States who taught playwriting [in fact, both O'Neill and Williams benefited from such courses]. He was a great audience. He loved whatever was good and what was bad he minimized.'

But that raised its own difficulties. Would-be playwrights of varying abilities gathered to study drama and read their work. Writing in 1951, Miller admitted his frustration at having 'to sit around a table and listen to the reading of utterly talentless plays written by people who were merely indulging themselves, who had paid tuition, in effect, in order to guarantee themselves a forced audience for works that ought not to have been written'.[40] His chief criticism of his mentor was that he was altogether too tolerant of such bores. He was 'capable of running into the ground the slightest ray of hope in the most hopeless of plays'. Looking back, Miller said, 'I don't know of anybody else, besides myself and Norman [Rosten, his friend and rival], who came out of that whole thing. But he was invaluable as a warm, encouraging presence and he knew a lot about the history of the theatre which was a deep, dark secret in the English Department. Nobody knew anything. You could talk about styles to him. One on one he was wonderful. He was a great man to be with. But when he got into the class he was hopeless.'

These were harsh words considering that he was talking about under-graduate students, but Rowe's seemingly uncritical response to his fellow students led Miller gradually to lose the feeling that he was a proper judge of anything. Some sixty-five years after taking his class, though, he 'still prized his affection and love for the theatre', together with the fact that 'he saw the theatre as having a voice which was its own. You were in a unique area. He made playwrighting seem terribly important as a social and moral force. That was important.'[41] It was Rowe who alerted him to the possibilities of drama in a time of change and political commitment. In New York, Clifford Odets's *Waiting for Lefty* seemed to be making a claim for the centrality of theatre in presenting America with an analysis of its domestic failings and the need for radical change. Miller did not see the production but he did read the theatre magazines in the university library and found there accounts of the politically committed plays that were helping to define what seemed a new theatre.

He did see the Chicago production of Odets's *Awake and Sing*, a play that had a major impact on many on the left. Alfred Kazin saw the New York production and enthused over its 'lyric uplifting of blunt Jewish speech ... I wanted to write with that cunning anger and flowing truth; the writer would forget his specialness, his long loneliness, and as he spoke to that mass of faces turning in the dark, the crowd would embrace him, thank him over and over for bringing their lives out into the light. How interesting we all were, how vivid and strong on the beat of that style! Words could do it.'[42] Miller felt no less. It was a world and a language he recognized.

For Miller, at that time, Odets 'seemed pure, revolutionary, and the bearer of the light'.[43] His commitment to socialism and the Soviet ideal allied him with the new forces that appeared, if not to galvanize American society at large, then at least to impact on the intellectuals, the artists and the young. Miller went to see Group Theatre plays in New York because these were by writers who brought him news of the world as it was. It was, he recalled, like rushing for a newspaper.

Writing later, he confesses to forgetting which Odets play he saw at the Group:

> all I remember was seeing actors who for the first time in my experience were physically vivid ... I found myself believing that offstage – and I had never set foot on a stage but could imagine what it must be like back there – offstage

was not offstage at all but the city itself, the New York I knew. So that the play was not like a little isolated cell where things went on disconnected from the city around us, but was one cell among the myriad, part of the sound and the anxiety and the almost universal frustration of life at that time. Had I been capable, as I was not, of rationalizing the experience, I should have called it an experience of theatre as life, as much a part of life as going into the subway or bringing home a bottle of milk or sitting in the back yard and wondering anxiously what was ever going to become of me failing algebra three times.[44]

One of those Group Theatre actors was Elia Kazan, later to become a crucial figure in his life. Miller did not feel the same about the work of Eugene O'Neill, who won the Nobel Prize in the same year that Miller picked up his first Hopwood Award. He came, it seemed to Miller, from an altogether different world. He was a product of the Theatre Guild which, until Miller won one of its awards, he regarded as smelling of Art and serving the interests of the elite. This was not the man who wrote *The Hairy Ape*, *All God's Chillun Got Wings* or *Desire under the Elms*, which lay a decade in the past, but the author of *Strange Interlude*, *Lazarus Laughed*, *Mourning Becomes Electra*, *Ali Wilderness* and *Days without End*. O'Neill's effective withdrawal from the theatre after 1936 merely seemed evidence that he had exhausted his talent, as the Theatre Guild had handed the baton to its spin-off, the Group Theatre.

Later Miller would revise his opinion of both Odets and O'Neill, coming to recognize his own tendency, and that of his contemporaries, to judge writers by their commitment to a cause, their ability to protest at a seemingly stifling social system, rather than by their qualities as dramatists or their ability to address more fundamental concerns. What he saw in O'Neill at the time, was 'his fossilized individualism, his dirgelike longing for private salvation redolent of the alcoholic twenties'.[45] What he admired were those writers who took up the conflict between fascism and democracy. Other writers seemed to speak from a past now invalidated by events.

Ironically, Miller's first stage success, *All My Sons*, would coincide with the premiere of *The Iceman Cometh* which, despite a poor first production, he eventually came to see as more profoundly revolutionary than anything Odets had written. Now the O'Neill he recognized was the man who had written about those peripheral to the thrust of American society, those spun off from the centre of a culture content to define itself by myths rooted in material ambition.

There was, Miller eventually came to feel, a tragic grandeur to him, as, in his later work, there was an absurdist poetry. There was also, in *Long Day's Journey into Night*, a recognition that the family could be the site for a drama that explored fundamental tensions within the psyche. In other words, Miller came to feel that O'Neill rather than Odets breathed the same air as him. Odets, who had once proclaimed himself a stormbird of the working class, now seemed an American romantic, a reformer rather than a radical, never willing to chase down his own increasingly evident ambiguities.

For the moment, though, Odets was his primary model. O'Neill smacked of Broadway and commerce, and that allied him with the forces of reaction. The Theatre Guild, which presented his work, also produced *Porgy and Bess* (1935), *Idiot's Delight* (1936) and *The Philadelphia Story* (1939) – a sign, to Miller, of its lack of seriousness. Odets, by contrast, was a product of the Group Theatre, which he found inspirational. Miller has spoken of seeing their productions in New York while on vacation from university:

> I had my brain branded by the beauty of the Group Theatre's productions. With my untamed tendency to idealize whatever challenged the system – including the conventions of the Broadway theater – I was inspired by the sheer physical spectacle of those shows, their sets and lighting by Boris Aronson and Mordecai Gorelik . . . To this day I can replay in memory certain big scenes acted by Luther and Stella Adler . . . Elia Kazan, Bobby Lewis, Sanford Meisner, and the others, and I can place each actor exactly where he was on the stage.[46]

For fifty-five cents, sitting in his balcony seat, he was entranced by the interpretative use of colour by Gorelik and Aronson, the fierce concentration of the actors, and the apparent integrity of their aims. Later, in *The Golden Years*, he would make use of that colour and light, as he would of the lyricism he detected in their productions. For the moment, though, such productions, and particularly those of Odets, convinced him that the theatre was in tune with the times and had something to say to those looking for new ideas, new loyalties, new forms.

Of the Group Theatre's internal tensions he knew nothing. Kazan would later admit before the House Un-American Activities Committee that it was thoroughly infiltrated by the Communist Party, while Stephen Spender spoke of the difficulties he had when they produced his verse play, *Trail of a Judge*. He was denounced for creating a play which seemed to sympathize with a liberal point of view when what was required was militant communism.

The doctrinaire nature of some of those who ran the theatre was invisible to Miller, as to other theatre-goers, though he would hardly have been dismayed had he been aware of it. What was important was that it stood in contrast to Broadway and that it staged socially committed drama. Theatre seemed to him the cockpit of all literary activity:

There was the audience, here were the actors, and you could talk directly to the audience, and radicalize everybody ... Whereas a book, prose, you dropped it into the well and you heard the thing go 'plunk' in the water, and that was the end of it. You had immediacy in the theatre, and you were working against time. Everybody thought that either the Second World War was going to happen, or we were going to have fascism, so whatever you were going to do, you had better do it quick.[47]

To look back on that period, and to look back on Miller in his early twenties, is to feel that sense of urgency, of large issues waiting to be engaged. History, it seemed, was in the making; the future was in the balance. It is to be aware, also, of a confidence amounting to hubris that his was a generation charged with a special responsibility and possessing a unique insight. The impatience of youth now had a historic legitimacy. The crudeness of much of the drama of the period, and of Miller's early plays, is in part a product of this urgency, a need to rush out the news, seize audiences by the collar. They themselves might feel alert to the major forces at large in the world, but America seemed, to the politically committed, to be in denial, at home and abroad.

He, and those to whom he now gravitated, saw themselves as embracing a new idealism born out of the exhaustion and evident failure of capitalism and the aggressive individualism it seemed to validate. And their heroes were people of their own generation, or almost so. Odets was twenty-nine in 1935, George Sklar (who co-wrote *Stevedore* with Paul Peters) twenty-seven. And when, in August 1935, the Seventh Comintern Congress in Moscow formally adopted the Popular Front, all progressive forces suddenly seemed to be working in harmony for the common good. The old schisms were healed overnight. From now on the essential battle was less for socialism than against fascism. It was through this shift that, according to Ellen Schrecker in her book *Many Are the Crimes*, 'the party made a strong appeal to what was to become its most important constituency: urban, upwardly mobile, second-generation American Jews',[48] like Arthur Miller.

At the time, however, he was confused as to the role of the writer once socialism had been ushered in. It was clear that in 1930s America there was no point in planning for success, no expectation of wealth, and that socialism was the rational solution. But, once that was achieved, where would the conflict be that seemed to him the necessary precondition to drama and the essential business for the writer to provoke? For the moment, until the arrival of socialism, the stage and the political platform seemed essentially alike, hence the hortatory tone of many of the plays produced in this period. Theatre existed to change the world. Miller's was to be a theatre of praxis. The proletarian novel, by contrast, seemed almost a contradiction in terms. Certainly it was privately produced and privately consumed, if consumed at all (most sold in the hundreds). Theatre spoke the language of the people. It was dialogic. Prose fiction seemed to him too oblique, less responsive to the moment, less open to the spoken word. As he has remarked of that period, 'I heard language, and I could reproduce what I had heard ... So it was a thrill for me to write down what I was hearing, whereas to reduce it to prose was to formalize it, and the blood left it, the pulse left it ... with drama you pick up the real language. It was thrilling to write that.'⁴⁹

It was, he later said, not precisely the presumed Marxism of Odets and his contemporaries that appealed. It was

> a convenience to call their message Marxist or revolutionary; but for me it was more like being provided with an emotion, an emotion appropriate to the frustrations of living in the early thirties, specifically, the verb, if you will, for protesting the cursed irrationality of our lives. For people were starving then in America, while food was being burned up on the farms for want of a price. Odets seemed to provide a license for outrage, which has to be the first step toward a moral view.⁵⁰

Beyond the Group Theatre, meanwhile, was the Federal Theatre Project, established by Act of Congress under Roosevelt's Works Progress Administration. Its Living Newspaper productions, a documentary theatre that set itself to expose the evils and problems of the age, placed daily reality on stage. Here was an organization that took as its premise the centrality of drama. Spread across the country, it was capable of opening the same play in twenty-six cities simultaneously. It engaged formerly marginalized groups, including black Americans, and addressed social problems in a direct, way. Perhaps unsurprisingly, therefore, at the end of 1936 Miller submitted *They Too Arise* to the New Plays Bureau of the Federal Theatre at its West 42nd Street headquarters.

The play had changed once again. Arnold is now a would-be writer and an acknowledged communist, declaring that he wishes to take power away from the capitalists and hand it to the working class who will bring socialism to America. A strike, such as that in the garment industry, is a means to that end. Arnold, his brother Ben explains, feels this. He resolves his conflict with the family by insisting that they belong with the working class.

As noted earlier, Abe Simon has something of Willy Loman about him. He has Willy's desperate desire to leave his mark, if necessary through his sons. Here, too, is to be found a speech that will echo in Miller's later work – in *The Golden Years*, *The Man Who Had All the Luck*, *Focus*, *The Crucible*, *Broken Glass* – a speech which insists on a link between the private and the public world, which underscores his resistance to what he sees as moral and political disengagement. Thus Arnold asserts that it is impossible to close the door on the world, that the world will only be changed by those determined to act. Ben, indeed, waves a gun around, effectively promising the fire next time. It is a gesture that sits uneasily in a play as much about personal as political transformation. Miller's, though, was to be a drama of cause and effect, in which individuals were brought to confront the nature and consequences of their own actions. Certainly, at this stage, he believed that the theatre could change the world. Decades later he was to be less sure, aware that change is incremental, ambiguous. But for the moment the call for a transformed world carried the full force of his political and moral convictions. The result was less than convincing. The rhetoric was overblown, the characters too often simple mouthpieces.

The reports from various readers took almost a year to come in, the first dated 4 January 1937 and the last in December. The responses were varied.[51] For John Rimassa, the play deployed authentic Jewish dialogue but lacked 'humor or melodrama', an odd complaint in a play that struggled against its melodramatic tendencies, the gun aside, and was, in fact, at times comic. For Rimassa, though, it was 'an unbearably dull play'. Leo Schmeltsman dismissed it in two sentences. It was 'plotless, incoherent, undramatic and uninteresting' with 'a few lines of good humor' but 'pointless dialogue'. Fanny Malkin agreed. For her, the author 'has no knowledge, training or dramatic sense'. She rejected the script 'without reservation'. Three other reports, however, took a wholly different line.

A reader identified as Lipschutz found it 'an exceedingly promising play, just fitted for the Anglo-Jewish theater' [a Federal Theatre unit directed by Boris Thomashefsky] with 'the most convincing [characters] I have found in any script coming into the Bureau for some time'. It was recommended for acceptance, subject to revisions. Another reader insisted that the play 'should be given an immediate tryout' because of its 'original approach to the contemporary picture', while another found it 'an honest, human reflection of life and the contemporary scene . . . almost certainly heart-warming, moving and entertaining', and suggested that the play 'should be done' by 'one of the Experimental Groups'. Yet another recommended it for 'Jewish labor audiences' and all 'adult socially alert groups'.[52]

The result was the single performance of the play, in October of that year, in front of just such an audience. After graduating, Miller found himself on the payroll of the Federal Theatre for six months and, indeed, wrote a play he hoped would be performed by what was the boldest theatrical experiment ever conducted in America. By then, however, Congress had voted to close it down because of its supposed and, in some cases, actual subversion by communists.

His enthusiasm for the Federal Theatre was scarcely diminished when, home from college for the summer in June 1937, he heard about the cast of Marc Blitzstein's *The Cradle Will Rock*, a Federal Theatre production, parading through the streets looking for a theatre in which they could perform, having been banned from doing so by the Theatre's hierarchy under pressure from Washington. A musical about labour unions in 'Steeltown USA', it was finally performed in a bare-stage production at the Venice Theatre, under the direction of Orson Welles. A few years later Welles would appear in one of Miller's radio plays. Two decades later, Blitzstein stopped Miller on Fifth Avenue to congratulate him on *The Crucible*.

At Michigan, Miller took his Marxism seriously enough to do some extra-curricular reading. He read pamphlets by Lenin, including *What Is To Be Done?* which he regarded as

> a marvellous title. You've got to do something. I read some of the polemics that were going on between Trotsky and the Leninists. I thought he was a nuisance. He was getting in the way of this great experiment. I read some histories of the Russian Revolution, both by the Americans and the Russians. I read John Reed – and I would have been with him – who saw the romance of this whole thing. I read a lot about the period between 1900 and the 1920s. As for the Stalin time, there wasn't much to read. It was boilerplate.[53]

What Is To Be Done? may have been a marvellous title but it was somewhat heavy reading, so that his willingness to tackle it suggests a genuine commitment.

Miller may not have joined any of the political groupings on campus, but the social and moral convictions he shared with those who did offered a sense of belonging which was far from uncommon to those drawn to the radical cause. In the Soviet Union, Konstantin Simonov would later confess: 'I, personally, cannot bear loneliness ... If you ask me what the Soviet system has done for the writer I should answer that, first of all, it has erased from his inner self all trace of loneliness, and given him the feeling of complete and absolute "belonging to society and the people".[54] Stephen Spender, likewise, remarked: 'My sense of the equality of men was based not so much on an awareness of the masses as on loneliness.'[55]

For Anthony Ehrenpreis, child of a well-to-do family and a distinguished book editor interviewed by Vivian Gornick, loneliness had also been a fact of life. His sometimes troubled twenty-five years in the Party gave him a shared language as well as shared objectives. To him, Thomas Mann had possessed an insight into the triumphs and weaknesses of the bourgeois world. As he remarked, 'Mann saw as clearly as we did the meaning of human loneliness at the center of the bourgeois world. But what he observed with philosophical distance we experienced with a sense of imperative. That, as far as I can see, is the difference between Mann and Marx, the difference between the nineteenth century and the twentieth. That imperative became the characteristic emotion of our century, and for better or worse the Communist Party embodied it.'[56]

It is a crucial insight. The Party acknowledged historical inevitability. It dealt in revolution. It understood, as liberal democracy seemed not to, the urgency of the moment. Ehrenpreis's statement about his own dilemma can stand equally with Miller's, anxious as he was for a world at moral attention: 'So, here I stood in my youth, poised between these two worlds, each with its mixture of barbarism and beauty, falling finally to the left because to the left lay the future while to the right lay the past.' And to the right, of course, in Miller's case, lay Jewish tradition and a father still desperately trying to reinvent the capitalist enterprise that had failed but that might yet be massaged back to life.

Alfred Kazin wrote of that supportive network of institutions and assumptions that had characterized the Jewish community and which went beyond the particularities of religion: 'We had always to be together: believers and non-believers, we were a people; I was of that people. Unthinkable to go one's own way, to doubt or to escape the fact that I was a Jew ... The most terrible word was *aleyn*, alone.'[57] Miller was not denying his Jewish identity, but in stepping out of one community he was in search of another that would address his sense of momentary deracination and which anyway seemed to have organic links to Judaism, albeit radically redefined in terms of secular transcendence. The Communist Party of the United States was not a product of Jewish immigrants, or its instrument. Later attempts to make it such themselves smacked of anti-Semitism. But it did have its attractions to people whose loyalties had always transcended those of their immediate circumstances.

Diana Michaels, a Philadelphia lawyer interviewed by Gornick, who had been a member of the Party for eighteen years until Khrushchev's speech to the 20th Party Congress (which exposed a number of Stalin's crimes) ended her allegiance, recalled going to the University of Wisconsin in 1938, the year Miller graduated from the neighbouring state: 'I think practically the first thing I did in Madison after I checked into the dorm was to join the Communist Party. In 1938, on every college campus in America, it was easier to join the Party than it was to join a posh sorority, and at Wisconsin, well, the best and the brightest were in the C.P.'[58] For Miller himself the Party had few attractions. The ideas for which it stood, however, and about which he read, did. Speaking in 2001, though, he remarked that,

I was totally misled by the whole business. I don't think there's been such a snow job done in history as was done then but it was self-intoxicated people who were writing these things. It was not done, for the most part, cynically. High up it was done cynically, I am sure of that, but down below it was people passion. There was an excitement about it all. You felt that this had got to change, what we were in. One knew one was in a disintegrating situation. The whole thing was coming apart. How and when was a different question but it was certainly not going to be there very long.

The disillusionment would come later, but for the moment there was total assurance. Indeed, it was that very assurance that seemed to give authority to Marxism and those who embraced it. In terms of his flirtation with Marxism, Miller's case was no different from thousands of others. Indeed, looking back it is remarkable how similar they were. It scarcely mattered whether you joined the Party or not. Some did, some did not, the former suffering rather more crises of the soul than the latter. What mattered was that you believed in a fundamental shift in human relationships.

You can take almost any life as paradigmatic of those drawn to the Party in the 1920s and 30s. Arthur Koestler, for example, ten years older than Miller and born on another continent, was otherwise a spiritual twin. Like Miller, he was born of a wealthy family that lost its money. His father, too, had worked in textiles and, when he was ruined, in his case in 1914 rather than 1929, tried to recover with a series of business ventures that came to nothing, as did Isidore Miller. Miller would have recognized him immediately, as he would Koestler's sense of guilt. Koestler was nine when he became aware of the economic disaster affecting his family; Miller was fourteen. Both generalized a personal anxiety into a social ethic.

Koestler, in Germany, watched as produce was destroyed to keep prices high. Miller watched the same process in America. Koestler joined the Party in 1931, at the age of twenty-six; Miller began his flirtation with Marxism in 1932, at the age of seventeen. Where Koestler set himself to read the classic works of the Marxist canon, Miller gave up when *Das Kapital* proved too daunting, though he did, as we have seen, read other Marxist texts.

Across the world, Brecht, Auden, Isherwood, Spender, Dos Passos, Sinclair, Steinbeck, Wright, all signed up to the new gospel if not to the Party. The world, it seemed, was full of writers' congresses, radical theatre groups, committees for peace and solidarity. This was where the energy was. Who would not have wished to see themselves as the agents of progress and the principals of a new Jerusalem? Artists, writers, sculptors willingly offered their labour for something more than self-aggrandizement and formalist satisfactions. As Koestler observed, 'The new star of Bethlehem has risen in the East, and, for a modest sum, Intourist are prepared to allow you a short and well-funded glimpse of the Promised Land.'[59] He went to that Promised Land. Miller did not, until three decades later. But, as Thoreau remarked of the American West, knowing it existed was enough.

Marxist rhetoric had a powerful appeal, not least because it tapped into a certain guilt about Miller's own upbringing. As Arthur Schlesinger Jr observed of the Party in his anti-communist book *The Vital Center*, 'Its appeal lies partly in the progressive intellectual's sense of guilt over living pleasantly by his skills instead of unpleasantly by his hands, partly in the intellectual's somewhat feminine fascination with the rude and muscular power of the proletariat, partly in the intellectual's desire to compensate for his own sense of alienation by immersing himself in the broad maternal expanse of the masses.'[60]

The sense of solidarity, of the need to find common ground in the face of economic and social adversity, which is a mark of both *They Too Arise* and his second play *Honors at Dawn*, as later of *All My Sons*, was, though, a product of something more than a then fashionable ideology. As Miller was to say in *Timebends*:

> It often seems that the impoverished thirties were the subliminal fixed point from which all that came afterward is measured, even by the young who only know those years from parents and reading. It was not that people were more altruistic but that a point arrived – perhaps around 1936 – when for the first time unpolitical people began thinking of common action as a way out of their impossible conditions.[61]

On New Year's Day 1937, Arthur Miller, now twenty-one, was sent by the student paper to report on the sit-down strikes in the General Motors Fisher body plant in Flint. The *Daily* was fast off the mark. It was on that day that all Chevrolet and Buick plants were closed down. It seemed to him that fascism abroad had its counterpart here in Michigan, the heartland of the new trades union movement: 'Spain was in Detroit. We knew what that was about. Spain was a battle of very rich people against very poor people. That is the way we saw it, and we could see it on the streets of Detroit.'

Ann Arbor was some fifty-two miles from Flint, 'where the big war was going on. It was literally a war, with guns going off. Mr Ford had gas piped into his sprinkler system, so that if ever there was a sit-down strike he would turn on the gas. It was murder. He had real fascist-type storm troops running that factory.'

By 1937, he confessed, he had been

> well radicalized about the United States, about Europe, about everything in the sense that the prevailing view among students and faculty was that we were approaching some kind of apocalypse because the Depression hadn't

ended. It was supposed to end but instead it got worse. What's forgotten
now, too, is that there was a fantastic amount of racism in this country, not
just against blacks but against Jews, especially in Detroit where there were a
lot of Southern workers. Ford had recruited whole towns in Alabama and
Mississippi. I had a temporary job doing a census of the auto workers for the
sociology department and we went to addresses and asked them a series of
questions. I was really shocked at the way these people were. I remember, I
went to one family and heard this rustling under the porch and it turned out
they were raising pigs under there and it smelled a little funny. The sanitation
they had in the middle of Detroit! There was running water and there were
sewers but they were living like animals. And they were working in the auto
plants because they were preferred by Ford who liked them good and dumb.
But finally these guys got organized too.[62]

Nor was it only the workers who were prejudiced. Henry Ford was himself
deeply anti-Semitic. In the 1920s his newspaper, the *Dearborn Independent*,
had run a scurrilous campaign, even reprinting *The Protocols of the Elders of
Zion*, a turn-of-the-century invention of the Russian secret police. As
Leonard Dinnerstein points out, 'During Ford's lifetime, no Jewish physicians
served on the staff of the Henry Ford hospital in Detroit and few Jews were
on hospital staffs anyplace else in the country.'[63]

The Flint strike, which involved General Motors rather than Ford, was
in part an attempt by the union to organize the unskilled workers, many
of them, indeed, from the South, and to secure union recognition. Police
were called and National Guardsmen manned machine-guns. Six weeks
later, the company recognized the United Automobile Workers' Union and
the strike was ended. By this stage, Miller had already returned to Ann
Arbor but he did so with a new respect for unions and a new faith in the
possibility of communal action: 'It was fiery stuff. It was very moving, very
touching.'[64]

Miller hitched a ride from Ann Arbor with a young man who was test-
driving a Ford car. He recalls police cars overturned by hoses manned by the
strikers. He remembers, too, National Guardsmen who had, he was told, shot
at strikers. The covered overpass joining the two Fisher plants had
been blocked by several Chevrolet bodies welded together and standing
vertical.

In fact he seems to be eliding memories from later in the sit-in. Until 11
January no attempt had been made to move the strikers. It was on that day,
with the temperature standing at 16 degrees Fahrenheit, that the heating was
turned off and a group of plant policemen forced their way past the main
gates. Later in the day police attacked with tear gas and the workers responded
with hoses. The police then fired into the group of strikers as they found

themselves pursued. Fourteen strikers and their allies were wounded, thirteen of them by gunfire, while nine policemen, a sheriff and deputy sheriff were injured, all but one by missiles or gas. This was what came to be known as the Battle of Bulls Run, 'bull' being slang for police officer.

It was at this moment, and not before, that Victor Reuther, of the Auto Workers Union, ordered the barricade of Chevrolets across both ends of Chevrolet Avenue in front of Fisher body plant no. 2. This was designed to prevent police driving along the road shooting into the building. In other words, in Miller's account, eleven days seem to have been telescoped into one. The National Guardsmen, moreover, were responsible to the state's Governor, who was largely sympathetic to the strikers and at various stages in the strike acted implicitly in their support.

There is no doubting the centrality of this event or the impact it must have had on the young Miller. This was a battle for union rights that involved people risking their lives. In the early days of the New Deal, Section 7(a) of the National Industrial Recovery Act – the NIRA – which became law in June 1933, stipulated the right of workers to organize and bargain collectively through representatives of their own choosing. From that moment onwards large corporations had done their best to evade this requirement. The action by the Automotive Workers' Union was thus part of a wider battle to do with the New Deal. The NIRA had been declared unconstitutional by the Supreme Court, but was replaced by the National Labor Relations Bill in June 1935.

In an attempt to undermine the unions, General Motors hired a large number of company spies. As Sidney Fine has shown, at least fourteen detective agencies were employed for espionage services between 1933 and 1936. These included the famous Pinkerton agency. The job of these spies was to join the union and attempt to get into positions of power while betraying their new colleagues. At the end of December 1936, Roy Reuther had exposed a company spy who was serving as chairman of the union's welfare committee.[65] Miller would feature company spies in his second Hopwood play, while the issue of informing and betrayal was to remain central to his work. This was where he experienced it for the first time.

Miller recalls a meeting with Walter Reuther, the third brother involved in the strike, and it is tempting to think that it might have been the memory of two of them, Walter and Victor (who decades later was to receive CIA money channelled through the Agency's International Organizations Division), that supplied the names for the two central characters in *The Price* (a play with echoes of the 1930s). Interestingly, the Reuthers had picked up their socialism while in college in the early 1930s, in what is now Wayne State University, then gone on a bicycling holiday through Europe, working for sixteen months in Gorki at an automobile plant built by Ford, despite Walter having been fired by Ford back in the United States as an agitator. Later, Walter would turn against the Party when it double-crossed his brother in a Congress of Industrial Organizations (CIO) election.[66]

According to Miller's account, Victor insisted that the union had three hundred members. In fact, membership had been claimed, somewhat incredibly, to be 26,000 in 1934, shrinking to 120 in the summer of 1936, in part because of company espionage, three of the thirteen members of the executive board of the union's local branch being company spies and at least two others Pinkerton agents. However, by the end of 1936 UAW membership in Michigan as a whole was in the region of 10,000, while by the end of October the two Fisher body shops accounted for some 1,500. The 300 figure quoted by Miller thus sounds somewhat wide of the mark. Indeed, 500 had joined on a single day, 14 November, in plant no. 1 and fifty in no. 2.[67] Michigan was the centre of General Motors power and General Motors was one of the country's largest and most dynamic companies. The battle thus had far more than local significance. Fisher body plant no. 1 employed 7,300 workers and produced 1,400 Buick bodies; no. 2 employed 1,000 and produced 450.

The sense of transforming not only one plant or one industry but a society was strong. The strikers' favourite song was 'Solidarity Forever'.[68] When an injunction was granted against the strikers, the judge – Edward D. Black – was shown to be a stockholder, so that it looked as though business and justice were working hand in hand, that there was a conspiracy against the working man. Meanwhile, newspapers were welcomed in, and that evidently included the *Michigan Daily* and its young reporter, Arthur Miller.

Indeed, University of Michigan students played a significant if minor role in the conflict. In the third week of January a mimeographed strike bulletin called the *Punch Press* appeared, edited by Michigan students known as the union's 'Baby Braintrust'. As Sidney Fine has pointed out, 'The editor of the *Punch Press*, Ralph Segalman, and his student associates ... were concerned about Fascism abroad and injustice at home and, like many college students of the yeasty New Deal years, felt an obligation to become personally involved in the effort to fashion a better social order.'[69] Back in Ann Arbor they had supported a strike for higher wages by pin-boys. In Flint, they went first to observe and then to participate. They also worked in the welfare office and helped in the union's educational work in the striker-occupied plants, while graduate students taught classes in journalism and creative writing.

One edition of the *Punch Press*, published on behalf of the United Automobile Workers of America local No. 156, and calling itself the 'Official Strike Bulletin', reprinted an advertisement from the *Detroit News* that was plainly an attempt to recruit what the newssheet called 'stools and strike breakers'. The advertisement called for 'industrial secret service operatives and investigators with and without experience as operatives, and with and without

trades'. They were to be employed 'by an old established company in anticipation of increased business, and for purposes of interviewing and teaching
our methods of operation to a selected number of interested men'.[70]

The strike consolidated Miller's Marxist views about labour and capital.
As he has said, the victory of the strikers on 11 February 1937 'made me feel
safer on the earth, and as it did to others trying to write or make art in that
time, it seemed to me a new beauty was being born',[71] albeit one that would,
as he equally admits, one day be threatened by the gangsterism that began to
dominate unions. Indeed, he himself saw one of his own projects, a film
script, destroyed by the threat of unions in alliance with a new reactionary
spirit. However, those days in Flint never left him, even if at the time he had
become aware that there was another side to these supposedly progressive
forces. Over forty years later, in *The American Clock*, he has Lee, a figure
modelled closely on himself, recall:

> I was in Flint, Michigan, when the sit-down strikes started ... It was a
> confusing experience. The solidarity was enough to bring tears to your eyes.
> But I interviewed about thirty of them afterwards ... They're not backward,
> they're normal. Normally anti-Semitic, anti-Negro, and anti-Soviet. They're
> building unions and that's good, but inside their heads it's full of fascism ...
> I found one man who knew what socialism was. There's an openly fascist
> organisation in Detroit – the Knights of the White Camellia ... It's full of
> auto workers.[72]

Set in the 1930s, the play bears evidence of Miller's later disillusionment
but also of the source of the passion that carried him through that decade
and on into the 1940s. He was aware of the contradictions at the time, but
they seemed far less significant then, when the battle lines appeared clear.
Lee has a perspective that the youthful Arthur Miller could not permit
himself, caught up as he was in his enthusiasm for working-class solidarity.

It is true that the workers in the Flint strike were not revolutionaries, but
behind them stood organizers who were, supported by socialists – particularly
those in the CIO and UAW – and by the Central Committee of the
Communist Party, which called on its members to support the strike as well
as operating through its more clandestine representatives. Miller remarks that
while he understood that communists had been responsible for some of the
organizing, nobody knew where he could find them. In fact communist
involvement was considerable, but this was a period in which individuals
worked under cover or through various front organizations so that there were
doubtless occasions on which undercover company spies and undercover
communists sat side by side on committees, oblivious of one anothers' true
identities. Indeed, the Flint strike was cited as an example of communist

infiltration by Martin Dies on the House Un-American Activities Committee in 1938.

For Miller the success of the strikers, who had secured the recognition they sought, was evidence of the power of men working in concert for a common goal. He returned to Ann Arbor before the signing but full of the excitement of the occasion. America was changing, and he had been there to see it.

The Flint strike has been called 'the most critical labor conflict' of the 1930s and 'perhaps in all of American history', part of what *Fortune* magazine described as 'one of the greatest mass movements in our history'.[73] Three decades later the sit-down strikes of the 1930s were echoed in the sit-ins of the civil rights movement. 'We Shall Not Be Moved' was sung both by Flint strikers and, slightly modified, by civil rights workers while, as Fine points out, university students would borrow the tactic that had worked so well in Flint when they occupied university buildings to secure their demands. And one of those who would take part in the teach-ins at the University of Michigan in the 1960s was Miller, back at his alma mater where the tactics and songs of the Flint strike were being reprised.

How did Miller reconcile his admiration for the strikers with their manifest racism? 'It took a lot of doing. You had to cancel out a lot of what you knew, as you did with a lot of other things, too. My favourite president is Roosevelt but the fact is that he helped to destroy the Spanish Republic ... He was betraying people, or so it seemed. What we all forgot was that he had to get elected.' The Flint strike, though, remained 'the class struggle, *par excellence*. It couldn't', he explained, 'be more classic.' The physical layout of the plant, with the executive offices on one side of the road and the plant itself on the other, with the connecting overpass blocked by welded Chevrolet bodies, 'was sure pure as a symbol, it was melodramatic: the workers on one side and the bosses on the other. And the fact that I came from the bosses helped to alienate me.'[74]

For Miller, as for so many others, the principal political and moral cause of the 1930s, though, was Spain. It was a commitment born out of reports of bombs spilled out of aircraft and swaying down towards what only a day before had been the quiet irrelevance of Guernica. Spain might be geographically distant from Michigan, but it seemed the central issue of the age. Even sixty-five years later, in a new century, he felt obliged to recall this time to a Spanish audience for many of whom it was no more than a distant history, now best forgotten. He was in Spain to receive the Prince of Asturias Award. His mind, though, was not on the present but on those days of his youth when the cause of Spain was worn like a badge of honour and the names of the smallest towns in that divided country were known to young Americans who had never left their own country or even their own state.

He recalled: 'I had just entered my twenties when the Civil War broke out ... There was no single event as powerful in the formation of my generation's awareness of the world. To many it was our initiation into the twentieth century, probably the worst century in history ... For nearly four years the first news we looked for in the morning newspapers was the news from the Spanish front.' The very word 'Spain' 'was explosive, the very emblem of resistance not only to the forced return of clerical feudalism in the world but to the rule of unreason and the death of the mind'.[75]

Several of his contemporaries joined the Spanish Civil War, one dying there. As he remarked, 'In '36 and '37 we had been certain that if Franco could only be defeated a new world war might be averted.'[76] Harvard students and teachers were not the only ones to buy an ambulance for the Loyalist forces.

In accounting for his own enthusiasm for a Party that he formally joined only for a few weeks, during the winter of 1936–7, Stephen Spender offered an explanation that centred on the Spanish Civil War and did so in a language that would have appealed to Miller. Spain, Spender said, 'became a theatre where the drama of the struggle of Fascism and anti-Fascism was enacted', and was 'dramatised in Spain as a theatre'.[77] It was, he suggested, 'a poets' war'. Not only did a number of writers perish there but their death drew intellectuals to the cause. André Malraux went there, as did Arthur Koestler and Hemingway, who, before *For Whom the Bell Tolls* appeared in 1940, made a propaganda film, *This Spanish Earth*, to raise money for ambulances (Dorothy Parker, now radicalized, bought one for $1,000). Darwin's great grandson John Cornford, a student at Cambridge, died there. It was as significant a symbol as the revolutions of 1848 had been.

Spender later abandoned his temporary loyalty, as would Koestler, while Hemingway's unflattering portrait of communists would lead to his vilification. But for the moment, for a newly converted Marxist and a writer-in-the-making, the cause of Spain, no less than the domestic failure of capitalism, seemed the justification for Miller's politics. As the radical Howard Fast remarked, 'Spain was the passion of our generation ... This was a great conflict, where fascism could be stopped. I guess every writer of the time was deeply moved by Spain.'[78] Alfred Kazin later recalled his own feelings in 1936:

History was going our way, and in our need was the very life-blood of history. Everything in the outside world seemed to be moving toward some final decision, for by now the Spanish Civil War had begun, and every day felt choked with struggle. It was as if the planet had locked in combat. In the same way that unrest and unemployment, the political struggles inside the New Deal, suddenly became part of the single pattern of struggle in Europe against Franco and his allies Hitler and Mussolini.

The daily rush of events, he suggested, 'fitted so easily into a general pattern of meaning, seemingly supplied by the age itself, that every day was like a smoothly rushing movie of the time'.[79] Support for Spain was also the quickest way to earn an FBI file, and that would prove true of writers as diverse as Pearl Buck, Edna Ferber, Maxwell Anderson, William Faulkner, Moss Hart and, indeed, Arthur Miller.

The civil war in Spain broke out in July 1936, when Miller had just finished his sophomore year, and more than sixty years later he still remembered the shock with which he received news of the bombing of the Basque town of Guernica, on 26 April the following year: 'I'll never forget that, because the idea that in broad daylight, with the sun shining, an airplane would fly over an occupied town, where people were going about their business, and drop bombs on it, was something indigestible, incredible. How to deal with this? It is easy enough to say that it was barbarism, but it unhinged the mind that this could happen. So you reached for anything that would combat these fascists.' His was a revulsion, though, not shared by everyone. As he admitted, 'Ninety-nine per cent of the American people, including the students, didn't know where Spain was and certainly didn't know what the issues were. But enough of the vocal, conscious people were aware that a contest was going on for the future.'[80]

Despite the Neutrality Act, promulgated by the Roosevelt administration, in August 1936 various left-wing publications published advertisements asking for funds to support volunteers. *The Nation* was one such, but it eventually backed off in the face of legal advice, though not without what turned out to be a vain appeal: '*The Nation* hopes that United States law will not be applied against American volunteers to Spain as it has been so loosely interpreted in the past. We have ourselves used foreign volunteers. If we stop our volunteers for Spain it will only help fascism.'[81] A young Doris Lessing, growing up in Rhodesia, felt the urgency of Spain and shame at the failure of European governments to intervene: 'Everyone I knew was ashamed, bitter, about the way our Government and the French Government pursued "non-intervention" so the democratic forces had no arms, except minimal ones from the S[oviet] U[nion], and Franco was handsomely supplied by Hitler and Mussolini.'[82]

'As I got the news,' Miller recalled, 'if Spain fell then the next world war was imminent because Hitler would now have a fascist state on his flank. This [the Republican administration] was an elected government, which everybody forgets, and the Russians seemed to be the only ones who were helping. We knew nothing of the internecine fighting that was going on in the Loyalist camp. It was all gloriously unified.'

As Enoch Brater has pointed out, in a signed editorial in the *Michigan Daily* on 11 October 1936 Miller responded to remarks made at the Michigan Union by the vice-chairman of the Chrysler Corporation, James C. Zeder, in which he had declared that 'Hitler is doing a great job ... getting his house in order', by offering his own gloss: 'In other words you mean labor in concentration camps working for whatever you choose to pay them. You mean that labor strikes and efforts of labor to make a living wage under decent conditions are "crimes against the state".' Fascism, Miller added, 'has not one iota of "responsibility for the welfare of others". So thanks again, Herr Zeder. But we advise, if we may, that you change your opinion of the college man. HE is not a sap!'

In 1937, Miller drove from Michigan to New York in a 1927 Model T coupé he had bought from a graduate student for twenty-two dollars, taking with him a fellow student, Ralph Neaphus, the only man, he later remarked, he had ever met who parted his hair down the middle and wore octagonal glasses. The soft-spoken Neaphus had worked side by side with Miller in the student cafeteria. He had been raised on a New Mexico ranch and had never been east of the Mississippi before going to Michigan. He was now en route to Spain, with an address in New York where he was to report. Miller himself toyed with the idea of going, asking Neaphus how to go about applying. He was given the address and told that the Communist Party would make the necessary arrangements, the Abraham Lincoln Brigade being, Miller later recalled, an illegal recruiting organization. Neaphus was a graduate of twenty-three, Miller still a twenty-one-year-old undergraduate.

In *Timebends*, he speaks of carrying his indecision within him 'like a kind of sinfulness. One moment I was ready to break loose and go off and join the Abraham Lincoln Brigade in Spain, the next I was too appalled at the idea of not living to write a great play. Worst of all was the blinding prospect of informing my mother that I was off to war.'[83] Though he wrote of beginning to hate his mother for her selfishness in restraining him, speaking in 2001 he acknowledged: 'I never thought I would go.'

As they drove through the rain east of Buffalo, with a single manually operated windscreen wiper, the rain began to obscure their vision. Miller pulled off the road and questioned his friend about the procedures. He said nothing of his motivations. As Miller said later, 'I did not think it unusual for someone of the left to suppress personal feelings, which after all were of no real significance – only duty was. There was something of the psychology of priests in this.'

The car began to disintegrate and they completed the journey only by virtue of tackling hills in reverse. The battery failed, as did the brakes: 'We had to get to New York and the Spanish war so that Ralph could die there.' As they crossed the George Washington Bridge in New York, the front wheels began to collapse, but they were waved on by a tolerant policeman. They arrived home in one piece and Augusta Miller made up a bed for Neaphus on the couch, stiffening with alarm when they told her why he was there. Miller was tempted to go too, but contented himself by recalling that his friend was a graduate and that he himself still had a year left. Time enough, perhaps, when he had a degree. It was not so much fear that stopped him as a sense of what he would be giving up. He was already anxious to be on his way, to return to New York and conquer Broadway. Politics and ambition were at odds with one another and there was, in truth, little doubt which would win out. The next day he walked Neaphus to the Culver Line. They said goodbye at the turnstile. He never saw him again.

The death of Neaphus – killed in Spain – left him with the sense of an undischarged responsibility, a conviction that he had, perhaps, failed in a duty that others had acknowledged, a feeling later intensified when he failed to enter the military during the Second World War. No wonder he would cling to his radical beliefs long after logic and historical process suggested they were misguided. In a sense, he would never accept that the feelings that inspired his radical commitments were ever invalidated. After all, what had he believed beyond the idea of human unity? What was his faith if not a conviction that we are responsible for our own actions and the state of our society?

In the 1990s, Miller returned to this period in a play he worked on for several years. Provisionally called 'Imitations', it is set partly in 1936, partly in the 1960s and partly in what appears to be the late 1980s. It begins with a conversation between two young men, one, Aaron Steiner, about to leave for Spain, the other staying at home. It is, as Miller tells himself, a play about talent and its arbitrary nature, but it is Spain that first sets the two apart. Aaron, who has won literary prizes but wishes to experience war, leaves for Spain, riven with doubts about his courage, never having been tested. Jacob, meanwhile, envies him, especially his ability to override his mother's objections, and considers the possibility of joining the Communist Party, feeling that if he does not fight now he will have to later.

The play, involving two actors for each of the principal characters, one young, one old, seems to run together aspects of its author and of Ralph Neaphus in a work that is not, finally, about the Spanish war but in which the war is the starting point for an exploration of changing personal and public values. In a way, it is as if Miller were imagining himself as the one who went rather than the one who stayed. Certainly it is Aaron who is Miller's age and Jacob, Neaphus's. The former's relationship with his girlfriend, with whom he has been living for three years, seems remarkably close to that which Miller would have with his wife-to-be, since we are told that it was she rather than Aaron who is anxious to be married, and who is subsequently betrayed. The two are long divorced when, as an older man, he looks back on these events.

The conversation recalls what are surely details that will have passed between Miller and Neaphus as Aaron explains the procedures for his trip to Spain, which involve telephone calls to secret numbers, a last-minute arrival on the pier for fear of FBI intervention and, in Europe, a trip through the mountains before training. His motivation is a hatred of fascism and a conviction that a victory for Franco will signal a fascist Europe and the end of the Jews. That last observation seems informed by later knowledge, as is their acknowledgement of the in-fighting between Republicans, but what Miller is anxious to do is to recapture the passion that would send one young man to his death and instil a sense of guilt in another. That he should choose to return to this moment is evidence, too, of his conviction, expressed by the older Aaron, that this was a critical time whose signifance would scarcely fade.

Neaphus went on board the ship that was to take him to France with another Michigan student, Bob Cummins. When the latter returned, he brought news of his friend's capture by Moorish troops. Asked why he himself had not been captured he explained that he was 'too fast'. His job had been to carry messages rather than serve in the front line. He had, he said, 'spent the whole war in sneakers'.[84]

Miller responded by scrawling three pencil verses in his notebook, verses devoid of literary worth but expressive of his romantic celebration of a man who had seemingly died for a cause. It is entitled 'Song for a friend Who Died by Moors', and ends with a memory of their parting, Neaphus walking away to his death. He later recalled the moment news of Neaphus's capture reached the campus. Three weeks later came news of his death. This, he explained, 'was one of the debts I would carry in my heart', one that would keep him loyal not just to a lost cause but to a sense of himself threatened by his own equivocation placed beside the total commitment of a young man in octagonal glasses who parted his hair down the middle.

Neaphus was one of 2,800 Americans to fight in the Abraham Lincoln Brigade. Curiously, years later, in the 1990s, Miller met a veteran of the Brigade who denied all knowledge of Neaphus. His name, it turned out, appeared on no records. It was as though he had disappeared into the air. One day Miller received a telephone call from a man who claimed to have served in the Lincoln Brigade with Neaphus, but when he came round he was merely intent on selling stocks in oil wells. In 2001, after further inquiries, Miller had still drawn a blank: no survivor, he noted, seemed to have known him.

In fact, Ralph Lawrence Neaphus, of Clovis, New Mexico, did leave traces. He shipped to Spain where he became a member of the Third Company of the McKenzie-Papineau Battalion (the Mac-Paps) of the 15th International Brigade, the last English-speaking battalion established. This was supposed to be a Canadian battalion, and was known as such, but most of its men were

Americans. Arthur Landis, in his study of the Abraham Lincoln Brigade, describes it leaving its training base at Tarazona, northwest of Zaragoza, where it had been for four months, on 9 September 1937, to join the 15th International Brigade which had fought at Belchite.

The battalion reorganized at Azaila, to the east of Belchite and southeast of Zaragoza, names which now have little or no resonance but which at the time, and for those who saw Spain as the crucial battleground between two ideologies, were as familiar as the battles of the Second World War. It was at Azaila that they were visited by Ernest Hemingway and Martha Gellhorn. According to Landis, the Battalion stayed here from 20 September to 10 October before marching fourteen miles to Albalate and on through the wooded countryside of the Teruel region singing, 'We are the fighting anti-Fascists ... We'll set those Fascist bastards on the run ... And when we get home once more, we'll do the same thing there.'[85] They then manoeuvred back and forth until they came first to Quinto and then to Fuentes del Ebro, where they became involved in a disastrous encounter with rebel forces. The Brigade arrived after travelling ten miles from Quinto and immediately came under fire as they took up their positions in daylight.

Neaphus's company took several casualties immediately, before the attack had begun. His was a machine-gun company. Ahead of him, as he set up his gun, lay 'an open field, almost flat, leading to the crest of a ravine ... some six or seven hundred metres distant'. The fascist fortifications lay another two or three hundred yards further.[86]

When the attack came it was ill-coordinated. Tanks did penetrate the town but were easily picked off in the narrow streets. Neaphus's company took heavy casualties, its commander killed. Their bodies were strewn across the field to the ridge. Neaphus (wrongly identified in a first-hand report as coming from Seattle) set up his machine-gun with Robert Collentine from Milwaukee. Their gun was a Russian-made Takarev. They opened fire from the near-suicidal distance of a hundred and fifty yards: 'We had no for-tifications, foxholes, or anything else.' By nightfall on 24 October, the 'Can-adian' Battalion had sixty dead and over a hundred wounded. They stayed on the line for another ten days, but the battle was lost. Nonetheless, the lines were 'then stabilized until the great Rebel offensive of March, 1938',[87] the offensive in which Neaphus was to lose his life.

At the turn of the year his brigade was two miles from Teruel, in Teruel Province, a Nationalist salient seventy miles from the sea and 'a place resem-bling a blackened Goya etching. A city frozen and stark, surrounded by burnt, bomb-blasted hills. Its reputation – of being the coldest spot in Spain – held true.'[88] Temperatures dropped to 18 degrees below freezing. They were in a poor condition. Alvah Bessie described his first encounter with the Lincoln Brigade: they had week-old beards, 'were filthy and lousy; they stank; their clothes were in rags; they had no rifles, no blankets, no ammunition, no mess kits, no pack-sacks. They had nothing but the rags in which they were dressed and the filth with which they were covered.'⁸⁹ Up against them were 60,000 men, the fascist forces having regrouped. Some of these were Moorish cavalry, many of whom were killed by machine-guns, including those of Neaphus's company who themselves once again took heavy casualties. They were withdrawn from the line on 3 February 1938, only to be thrust back into the fight again a few days later as things became ever more desperate.

On 9 March, three Nationalist armies attacked along the front. The 15th Brigade was in their path. The Brigade now moved on to Belchite and Azuara and it seems likely that this was where Neaphus was captured.

By 15 March, six days after the attack started, the Lincolns and the Mac-Paps had each lost four-fifths of their complements. Despite orders to fall back on Alcañiz, they marched on to Hijar, which they found in fascist hands, and fought back encircled by some of the 30,000 Moors in the rebel army. The road was cut in several places. As Arthur Landis remarks, 'Many men had been lost, killed, or wounded; many had been captured. Most of these, it was found out later, were summarily executed on the spot where they were taken. John Blair, of the McKenzie-Papineau Battalion, himself a prisoner for many months, recalled that a number of captured Americans were shot and their bodies thrown into the irrigation ditches outside Belchite.'⁹⁰ It was certainly common practice for members of the International Brigade to be shot rather than held as prisoners.

This could have been Ralph Neaphus's fate but in fact he was taken prisoner and executed at Calanda, in March 1938. This village of three thousand, birthplace of Luis Buñuel, earlier in the war in the hands of Anarchists, lies close to Hijar and Alcañiz. Given that in his last battle Neaphus was indeed faced by Moroccans, the story brought back to Miller seems to have been true. He was, it seems, probably, killed by Moors.

Given this account in 2001, Miller was struck again by how much Spain had seemed the spine of his politics and how much of him had been invested in the fate of a friend whose journey to war had been one he had himself once contemplated.

Neaphus was killed as Hitler entered Vienna and the Americans and British did nothing – indeed, as Britain negotiated to legalize the Italian intervention in Spain. This was why people like Neaphus chose to give their lives, not just for Spain but for what Spain represented. Arthur Landis quotes a speech by David Lloyd-George earlier in the campaign:

Bilbao, Santander, the Asturias, were all defended by as brave men as ever went into battle – traditionally so, historically so, and racially so. But they had no munitions; they had no guns. Who is responsible for that?

Nonintervention. Who is responsible for keeping nonintervention alive? His Majesty's Government. If democracy is defeated in this battle . . . if Fascism is triumphant, His Majesty's Government can claim the victory for themselves.[91]

And not His Majesty's Government alone. Roosevelt's America stood by as the Republic succumbed to the fascists. In 1948, long after Franco's victory, Camus defended his own decision to set his play *State of Siege* in Spain rather than, as Gabriel Marcel had suggested, in Eastern Europe:

Why Spain? May I confess that I am somewhat ashamed to ask the question for you. Why Guernica, Gabriel Marcel? Why that event which for the first time, in the face of a world sunk in its comfort and its wretched morality, gave Hitler, Mussolini, and Franco a chance to show even children the meaning of totalitarian technique? . . . For the first time men of my age came face to face with injustice triumphing in history . . . some of us will never wash our hands of that blood.

He had spoken out against Russian concentration camps, he stressed in that same 1948 essay, having been accused of doing otherwise, but 'they will not make me forget Dachau, Buchenwald and the nameless agony of millions, nor the dreadful repression that decimated the Spanish Republic . . . I cannot forgive that hideous plague in the West of Europe because it is also ravaging the East on a vaster scale.'[92] Miller was perhaps slower to lift his eyes to the evils of Eastern Europe, and, in fact in later life accused himself of such, but he felt much as Camus did with respect to Spain.

Reviewing a book in 1972, which recounted the life of Manuel Cortés, a former mayor of a Spanish village called Mijas, who had concealed himself in a small space within the walls of his own house in 1939 and not emerged until thirty years later, Miller described the Spanish war as 'the watershed of our age'. In that struggle, 'the terms of social and political evolution in this century were set'.[93] Beyond that, the story itself offered a powerful metaphor in that this literally immured man had finally emerged into the light of a different world.

Though old resentments might still smoulder in some of the other villagers, what struck Miller was, first, that Cortés's wife and daughter perforce were turned into actors, playing the roles of widow and orphan, while he alone retained his integrity locked within a prison of his own choosing, a prison ironically constructed out of his own humanistic ideals. Second, he emerged into a world so much more trivial, a world without transcendence, materialistic, historically ignorant. The Spanish war may have led to the Second World War and the Holocaust, and on to Vietnam and a hundred other conflicts, as though nothing had been learned, but as spiritually debilitating was the fact that there no longer seemed to be any awareness, even in his native country, of the moral issues that had sent Manuel into hiding in the first place, and millions to their deaths.

He emerges into a post-political world, a world in which power is exercised in the name of nothing but itself. The man who finally appears in the Spanish sun, Rip Van Winkle-like, carries with him the air of another time, only to discover that passions have long since been traded for comfort. The contrast is instructive. He encounters, as Miller sees it 'lobotomized products of 30 years of depoliticalization'.[94] In Manuel Cortés's own words, 'They stand there with eyes wide open looking at me . . . they don't even know if one thing or the other is better or worse.' This was, and is, precisely Miller's own analysis.

It is reflected in *The Price*, in *Mr Peters' Connections* and in *Resurrection Blues*. What is missing from the world, as he implies, particularly in the last two of those plays, written at the end of a century of violence and at the turn of the millennium, is a sense that anything in particular matters. In Spain, as in the world war that followed, there was a principle at stake; nor was it, finally, an ideological one. It went deeper than that. When he speaks of politics he is not invoking particular ways of organizing society. Indeed he praises Manuel Cortés precisely for judgements 'unclouded by the ideological fantasies common to the left', fantasies, of course, that Miller had himself once embraced. He is referring to a politics of the soul that places the fate of individual human beings at the centre of concern.

The war in Spain was not a battle about the future of capitalism. The politics of fascism took second place to the fact of its systematic disregard for human life. The Spanish Republic, after all, was not communist, merely defended by communists when they were not involved in frighteningly violent internecine theological disputes. What appalled was mankind's conspiracy against itself. It was what would make Miller come to regard the Soviet Union as equally repellent, though he did so in the same spirit as that of the incarcerated Spanish mayor who, in Miller's words, 'mourns the withering of humanist illusions about the Soviet Union as a human defeat'. Those illusions, Miller reminds us, were 'the realism of another age which illuminates the road to where we are now'.

Mayor Manuel was elected by the Popular Front alliance of left-wing parties and was alarmed by the violence that erupted from within as well as without. He was thus not a man blinded by party allegiance. He was a humanist who looked beyond the warring factions of his own country for a model in which he could believe – learning, like so many others, and only with the passing years, that he had embraced if not a false religion then a false church.

It is no wonder that Ronald Fraser's *In Hiding: The Life of Manuel Cortés* appealed so directly to Miller. It was not only a reminder of old passions and a highlighting of present indifference. The book echoes the structure of his plays which in turn reflect a fundamental belief in causality and hence moral order, in that past and present are here brought into immediate confrontation; for, to Miller, Manuel Cortés 'carries the past alive into our world', as memories perform the same function in *Salesman* and *After the Fall*.

Miller's opposition to fascism was a revolt against the notion that power has its own sanction, that the individual must submit to historic process, that the weak deserve their fate. If he was blind to the systematic cruelties of communism, he was scarcely alone in that. If, later, he resisted the idea of involvement in a European war he did so in part because he saw the First World War as a bloody collision of competing empires and believed the next might be the same. The real place to stop fascism was Spain, and only the Communist Party had shown any awareness of this. There was no doubt in his mind that fascism was the real and principal enemy, a fascism also evident in a racist, anti-union America. It seemed to him, looking back, that it was this threatening atmosphere, at home and abroad, that lay behind all his plays and that had set him apart from the mainstream of American theatre, which appeared to him not to acknowledge the depths of racial and class hatreds of the kind he himself had seen at first hand.

Albert Camus remarked: 'Every artist ... preserves deep within him, a single source from which, throughout his lifetime, he draws what he is and what he says. When the source dries up the work withers and crumbles.'[95] For Camus, the source was the world of poverty in which he was raised, as it was also the war that distilled so many of his views. Not a single source, then. If, for Miller, it was the Depression, Spain and the Holocaust, it was, above all, fascism, whose effects scarcely stopped with the end of the Second World War.

In 2001, he read an interview with an author he and his wife had come to admire and whom he had met for the first time the year before. The German-born novelist W.G. Sebald, whose life would be cut short a few months later in a car crash, was born in 1944, a year before the end of the war and hence, one would have imagined, free of any sense of guilt or responsibility. Yet the shadow of that war fell over Sebald. His father had been among those who crossed the Polish border on the first day. He would never speak to his son of his experiences, never offer to explain his attitude to the cruelties unleashed by a system whose orders he obeyed. For him, it seemed, history had simply been restarted after the war, purged of its horrors and hence void of moral meaning.

Arriving in England in his early twenties, Sebald met Jews for the first time, only then becoming aware of their absence in his homeland. It was the return of the repressed – repressed not by him but by his culture. He had been raised on denial. When he began to write he chose to use the initial letters of his first names – Winfried Georg – rather than spell them out in full because his had necessarily been names on the approved list published by the Third Reich, and he needed to create a distance between himself and such tainted authentication. But he was not denying the past. Far from it. In his books, past and present would bleed into one another. His books tell Jewish stories, among others, precisely because he feels a guilt that should not be his own, and they do so because what happened before his birth is all but insupportable.

For Miller, reading the interview, Sebald's story was yet another reminder of how long-lasting and profound were the scars left by the fascism that had first galvanized him to political activity nearly seventy years before. As he wrote to me in a letter, of 18 April 2001, 'The interview was yet another reminder of the *permanent* damage that Fascism did to Germany and Europe from which I don't think there will ever be a recovery. Anyway, what is to recover *to* once you realize that Fascism was merely the blossoming of the deadly tendencies of the past?' He continued, 'I guess I'm reflecting in this, a book I've been reading, "Constantine's Sword" by a former Catholic priest, James Carroll ... The present book is scholarship, over 600pp., a study of the Christian war on the Jews from the beginnings, an incredible piece of work. I've decided to give up being Jewish so I can sleep better at night.'

It was increasingly fascist anti-Semitism that drew Jews into the Party. Ellen W. Schrecker has estimated that at least half if not more Party members in the academic community were Jewish.[96] It was not what had first attracted Miller to Marxism. He responded to the social chaos, to a theory which offered both to explain and to solve economic collapse and social injustice. But as the decade proceeded so it became increasingly important, until fascism became the heart of a darkness he was determined to light through political action and through writing.

There was a moment during the American rehearsals of *Broken Glass* in 1994 when, for the benefit of a Jewish cast born after the war and themselves not fully aware of the details of Nazi cruelties, he suddenly became visibly angry, pounding the table in front of him, when he recalled fascist atrocities of the 1930s. As with Manuel Cortés's experiences, it was as if a door had suddenly opened on the past and the foul air of another time drifted through. For Miller, the smell of that corruption had never been fully purged. It would take a lifetime for the bruise to fade. Fascism as fact, fascism as metaphor, structured his sense of the dynamics of betrayal and denial, those twin themes of his work. It was the fact of fascism, as it would be the wartime sacrifices of Russia, that kept him loyal to Marxism not merely when others had abandoned it, but when it had become dangerous to declare loyalties now at odds with a new and vindictive orthodoxy.

At the time, though, it was compelling precisely because history seemed to be creating its own logic. The forces of reaction were at large everywhere, and who else was opposing them but the Party? In America, between 1933 and 1939, there were one hundred and fourteen anti-Semitic, pro-fascist organizations. Father Charles E. Coughlin was echoing Hitler, the British elite were flirting with the Nazis, and the Soviet Union alone seemingly set its face against anti-Semitism. By 1937, the war in Spain was reaching a climax.

Miller's reading at college was not restricted to drama, nor, despite *No Villain* and the play he would next submit for a Hopwood, did he have any particular attachment to realism. Decades later, he would write of his discovery of Karel Čapek. There was, he insisted, 'no writer like him – no one who so blithely assumed that the common realities were not as fixed and irrevocable as one imagined. Without adopting any extraordinary tone of voice he projected whole new creatures and environments onto an oddly familiar non-existent landscape. He made it possible to actually invent worlds, and with laughter in the bargain.' In Čapek he found a social satirist but also a writer who was suspicious of the very commitments that attracted Miller himself. 'We were,' he recalled, 'great believers in Science in the Thirties, the Depression time. Our problem seemed to be that scientific objectivity was not being applied to social problems, like that of scarcity in the midst of plenty, for instance, or unemployment. But here were stories warning against the tyranny and unreasonableness of the rational. They were fancifully put, to be sure, but surprisingly easy to imagine as the oncoming reality.'[97]

Čapek was a man of contradictions, and that seems in part what attracted Miller, whose own works have a dialectic, whose characters, indeed, are often divided as to the right. The certainties on offer in a society that seemed to polarize along the line of conflicting ideologies disturbed him, not least, as his first play made clear, because his own family seemed neatly situated along the dividing line between capital and labour. If he was an enthusiast for Marxism, then, there was at another level a distrust of his own convictions.

He returned to Čapek in 1990 not least because it seemed that his prophecies had proved accurate enough. A man whose heart is said to have been broken by Neville Chamberlain's betrayal at Munich (he died on Christmas Day, 1938), he satirized the European dictatorships (*War with the Newts*). 'We have', wrote Miller in 1990, 'evolved into his nightmare. In our time his Faustian conviction that nothing is impossible makes him very nearly a realist.' The pollution of cities 'sickens and kills' while science is 'shorn of moral purpose'. Perhaps what really attracted him, though, beyond the sheer exuberance of Čapek's imagination, his ability to function with seemingly contradictory ideas, was the belief, expressed by the narrator of *An Ordinary Life*, that 'Each of us is we.' In the 1930s that, perhaps, meant to Miller that the individual contained the social world. In the 1990s (with 'Some Kind of Love Story', *The Ride down Mount Morgan*, *Broken Glass*, *Mr Peters' Connections*), it would be a clue to his conviction that the self is a composite, a series of roles not always in alignment.

In 1937, Miller won his second Hopwood Award, this time for a play called *Honors at Dawn*. Like *No Villain*, it has a strike at its centre and, like *The Man Who Had All the Luck*, *All My Sons*, *Death of a Salesman* and *The Price*, focuses on two brothers who represent contrasting attitudes to life. For the Marxist, the family was suspect, its loyalties taking precedence over wider commitments, but more important than that to Miller was the fact that he understood the psychology of the relationship between brothers and between fathers and sons.

In truth, the brothers of *Honors at Dawn* are remote from Arthur and Kermit Miller, but they do represent contrasting attitudes to life. They are, like the Miller brothers, sons of a Polish immigrant. One, Harry, is a believer in the American dream, prepared to compromise his values in order to succeed. The other, Max, works as a mechanic at the Castle Parts Factory. The two brothers clash over the strike.

Max is invited to turn informer and refuses, joining his brother at university, but the company's influence extends even here. As a major donor, it insists that radicals should be dismissed from the university as the price of the company's support – not, in fact, a Miller invention since precisely this did occur in the 1930s. As part of this process informers are recruited, Harry among them. Max refuses again and returns to the factory, where he joins the workers and is killed, a secular martyr to the cause of social justice.

In many ways the play is as crude as it sounds, but again this is apprentice work and not without interest. While dying for the cause, Max is aware that those he dies for lack ambition and vision, precisely what Miller had found when he worked for the auto parts warehouse back in New York, a scene to which he would return in *A Memory of Two Mondays* (1955). There is a gap, in other words, between Max's experience and his politics, his observation and his rhetoric, which suggests Miller's awareness of an as yet unresolved tension between his political convictions and what he knew of working-class America.

He also introduces another key character, a Polish immigrant called Smygli, an intellectual whose linguistic incapacity makes it impossible for him to secure a job commensurate with his education (he is a graduate in philosophy). Ironically, his vision of America has a purity that contrasts with the reality of a society in which money transmutes into power and the individual is invited to betray personal and social values.

Honors at Dawn is a play, in other words, in which language is suspect even as we are asked to accept the rhetoric of radicalism as offering an adequate account of the world. There is a counter-current flowing. American values, it seems, have been sold to the highest bidder. Reactionary politics prevail. Neighbour is turned against neighbour. Only those without access to power retain their grasp on national verities. But language, even that of those fuelled by revolutionary zeal, seems to have less force and even less legitimacy than action or the felt idealism of a man unable to rise to the level of rhetoric deployed by the representatives of capital and labour. How far Miller was conscious of these tensions or contradictions is less clear. That he was not satisfied with the apparent polarities he identifies, however, seems apparent.

Miller submitted the play under the pseudonym 'Corona' (he was typing on a Corona and, in fact, his noms de plume all derived from the names of typewriters). Susan Glaspell, Director of the Midwest Play Bureau of the Federal Theatre, placed it first for the minor award. It was, she said, a 'faulty play as it stands, but says something in feeling'. She found 'real possibilities' for the author and a 'sense of theatre',[98] though it was three submissions for the major award that she thought should be submitted to the Federal Theatre. Had he known this at the time, Miller would doubtless have found it particularly frustrating, since Glaspell insisted that she was 'out here to try to find new playwrights of promise'. He, plainly, did not yet fit into that category.

Allardyce Nicoll, at that time chairman of the drama department at Yale, appears to place Miller third in his minor award list, while another judge (name illegible) places him first and suggests that if he had been a candidate for the major award (given to seniors) he would have placed him second in that category, since he had a 'genuine dramatic instinct'. With a little more study of technique, he felt, 'he should win the major contest next year or the year after, and that will determine whether or not he should take up authorship'. Miller had

> the ability to work out an idea, interestingly, logically, and dramatically. His writing is honest, fresh and stimulating, and particularly commendable as that of a lower classman. He has either an instinctive feeling for technique, or has studied it seriously. He has not mastered it, but there are many examples of his capacity: the adroit use of preparation . . . the ease with which the dialogue handles its content, and the artistically unaccented curtains.

Paul Mueschke, an English treacher at Michigan acting as an internal judge, placed Miller's play first and noted: 'Corona's manuscript is superior to the other entries and compares quite favorably with other full-length proletarian plays of recognized merit. *Honors at Dawn* should be carefully revised and given a campus performance if possible.' It was also placed first by another judge, H.J. Price.

As before, Miller sent a telegram to his mother at 1350 East 3rd Street: 'JUST WON HOPWOOD PRIZE FOR PLAY HONORS AT DAWN. ARTHUR.' This time it was the award and the play's title, rather than its cash value that featured. This time the word 'LOVE' was missing from the telegram.

Though not as convincing as his first effort, the play confirmed him in his conviction that his future lay in the theatre. It also gave him added status on campus. When, later that year, he wrote a comic piece for the student magazine *The Gargoyle* (on the predatory nature of landladies and the suspect nature of the accommodation they offered),[99] he was billed as 'Arthur A. Miller: Twice Hopwood Winner, Author of *They Too Arise*'. A year later his prison play, *The Great Disobedience*, researched at the nearby Jackson State Penitentiary, would just miss the prize. He was runner-up. This was the first of Miller's plays to owe less to experience than to research. One of his student friends, Sid Moscowitz, was the psychiatrist at the nearby penitentiary. His qualification for the job was the fact that he had taken a single course in abnormal psychology at the University of Michigan, the same course that Miller had taken. He was responsible for the mental health of eight thousand prisoners.

Miller found his visits to the prison bizarre. On one occasion he met a man who assured him that he was receiving radio programmes by way of the metal fillings in his teeth. Understandably, he was regarded as insane. Several decades later Miller discovered that this was entirely possible. The man had perhaps, after all, been receiving Detroit radio programmes through his molars.

Curiously, Tennessee Williams also wrote a prison play at this time. It was inspired by a case of ill-treatment that he had read about in a newspaper account. Unlike Miller, he had no direct experience of prison, just as he had no experience of mining, of strikes, of doss-houses, all of which he wrote about. Neither *Not About Nightingales* nor Miller's play *The Great Disobedience* was produced at the time; both later finding their way to the Harry Ransom Center at the University of Texas at Austin. It was there, decades later, that Vanessa Redgrave read Williams's play, subsequently persuading Britain's National Theatre to stage a production featuring her brother Corin as the vicious warden. Like Miller's play it is a melodrama. So impressive was the production, however, that it was later taken to New York.

The Great Disobedience has never been produced. As with *Honors at Dawn* it turns on the power of capitalism. In the earlier play that power extended to the universities. Here it extends into the prison system, in which many are already incarcerated for offences provoked by economic need. Others are in jail because they are seen as a threat to a system sustained by and operating in favour of those who exploit others for their own advantage.

The inexperienced prison psychiatrist, Karl, is an idealist, but he slowly comes to realize that his function is simply to control the prisoners, not least because a cure would involve changing the social system that has provoked their illnesses. Seeing himself as a progressive, he gathers information and files it as if this were in itself a form of action. The drama is precipitated by the arrival of a former student friend of his. Caroline is in love with one of the prisoners, a former company doctor whose job had been to undermine compensation claims. When he rebelled he had been imprisoned at the instigation of the company, charged with carrying out an abortion on a young woman who was herself a victim of the system.

By degrees, the imprisoned doctor drifts into insanity and the psychiatrist is prompted into action. He succeeds in having the corrupt warden dismissed on the grounds of drug-trafficking – itself a perfect image of the capitalist system which simultaneously creates and satisfies demand, while pacifying the citizenry. The warden, however, is simply replaced by another company man, as the psychiatrist himself is replaced by another liberal idealist who seems likely to fall foul of the same system that has come close to destroying Karl.

Karl, meanwhile, calls for a revolution to smash the system. With the Marxists, he comes to believe that psychiatry is concerned primarily with adjusting people to the given rather than changing the world. His own liberation, he now recognizes, has been ineffectual. Whereas the head of the corrupt company insists that a man's duty is to seize what he wants, which he characterizes as an idea that made America, Karl proposes action to redeem America from this distortion of the national utopianism.

This, Miller's third assault on the Hopwood Awards, was submitted for the major award under the name 'L.C. Smith' (another typewriter manufacturer). He did not top the critic John Mason Brown's list in a year in which Mason found the submissions for the minor prize so bad that he thought there should be no award. Burns Mantle placed him third, commenting of *The Great Disobedience* that it was 'the most thoughtful of the list, indicating the most careful research, but a little rambling in construction, and somewhat muddled as a crusading drama; story uneven; dialogue spotty; philosophies varied in statement and quality; characters incompletely developed; indicates more promise as a novelist than as a playwright, but a strong possibility in either field. Could reasonably split second award with Richard Lawrence.' Richard Lockridge, of the New York newspaper, the *Sun*, thought *The Great Disobedience* 'much more interesting and promising' than his first choices, but found the play 'hopelessly turgid'. He put it third.

This relative failure, though, did not dent Miller's confidence. He would go on working on *The Great Disobedience* when he left Michigan, sure that it would soon find a theatre and an audience. He still believed both in his own talent and in the power of theatre to transform society. Had Stalin, after all, not called it a weapon of revolution, and writers engineers of the soul?

*

If Michigan was important for turning Miller into a playwright and consolidating his Marxist faith, it also had other crucial significances. It was where he forged a friendship with another would-be writer, Norman Rosten, whom he met in the February of his sophomore year and with whom he would write a play, cited twenty years later when he was summoned before the House Un-American Activities Committee.

Rosten was born on New Year's Day in 1914. He came from a farming family in upstate New York, and had once assumed that he would himself become a farmer, even attending the agricultural college of Cornell University. He and the family, however, had then moved to Coney Island, where he graduated from Brooklyn College in 1935, intending to be a teacher. Teaching jobs, though, were no easier to find than any other, so after working in a garage and after a brief period with the Federal Theatre he went to Michigan where, like Miller, he had heard of the Hopwood Awards.

As Miller explained in a comic piece in the 2 January 1938 edition of *The Gargoyle*:

> From the grease pit, comes Norman to New York where Federal Theatre pays him money for reading lousy plays. Then he hears of the Bureau of New Plays National Playwriting Competition, and being on strike in one of the Federal Theatre offices with some forty others at the time, he writes himself a three-act play (first act in the office because they wouldn't leave until their demands were granted). The play wins a prize and Norm collects a scholarship to Michigan for $1,250.[100]

It was the reverse of Miller's story, as prize money from Michigan set him writing and, on leaving, briefly, to membership of the Federal Theatre. To Miller, Rosten must have seemed something of a phenomenon, and there was a sense of competition as well as friendship between the two of them, a competition doubtless heightened by the fact that, during his time at Michigan, Rosten published poems in *Poetry Magazine, Partisan Review* and *New Masses* while writing one play for the university radio station and another, *This Proud Pilgrimage*, staged by Professor Valentine Windt at the university theatre.

Miller later wrote an unpublished novella in which he revisited this time and in which he speaks of two ambitious young writers who were as desperate for fame as they were baffled as to how to achieve it. For one of them, Marxism appealed because of its commitment to justice. It was an abstraction to be embraced for its human poetry. The other still recalled an affluent past now lost to him and hence wanted to see the abolition of private property. Miller was presumably the latter, though in truth the distinction was not a sharp one since he, too, responded to the poetry of Marxism. Like Rosten, he embraced an idea whose appeal lay precisely in the seeming simplicity of its fundamental principles. But that was the essence of Marxism. It could bring together the working-class radical and a member of the middle class and for the moment, at least, leave them unaware of the underlying tensions that would later define their relationship.

More important than this friendship, however, was his meeting with Mary Grace Slattery whom he would marry four years later, though he had, for a while, pursued someone else, the girl who later married Rosten. She was a young shapely blonde called Hedda (born Hedwig Rowinski) who had what he called a big-eyed gaze. At twenty, she seemed unreachable and had 'a terrific body' but was naive, a fact which scarcely decreased her attraction. It was not the last he saw of her. In subsequent years, Norman and Hedda, now married, remained his friends (and, in Norman's case, increasingly, his rival), even providing a meeting place for Miller when he was conducting his affair with Marilyn Monroe. Norman won Hedda, but Miller won the success, and this later seems to have rankled with Rosten, despite the fact that he would eventually rejoice in the title Poet Laureate of Brooklyn. Over the years their relationship slowly devolved into a petty rivalry without purpose.

The novella (reworked as a play), which features his version of Norman and Hedda, also deals with his relationship with Mary. It runs to some forty pages and looks back through what seems to be the later unequal competition between the two men, Rosten never quite, in Miller's eyes, fulfilling his ambitions, his youthful optimism slowly eclipsed. It is in part an account of the collapse of a relationship, as it is about a time when they were, as Miller observes, wrong about practically everything. He abandoned it because he could find no way to express the mixture of love and contempt he felt for the characters. The play itself, he realized, was merely the latest round in a competition that had begun so many years before at Ann Arbor. The novella, however, is also an attempt to recapture something of the mood and spirit of the Michigan years when the competition between them had less to do with their careers than with Hedda. For him she would always be the young woman in a white blouse hurrying across the campus. At some level she was never quite purged from his mind. As late as 1989, when she was long dead, he was still thinking of her.

She eventually died of the cancer caused by the cigarettes she had begun smoking back in Ann Arbor. Miller recalled her smoking Chesterfields, unfiltered in the 1930s, and, in subsequent decades, Regents, then Camels, then Chesterfields again, in the 70s defiantly breaking off the filters. Her smoker's cough began in the 1950s.

In the mid-1930s, though, she was young and exciting and prone to hysteria when tickled. But Hedda was quickly replaced by Mary, in some ways equally naive and also a smoker who, like Miller, was working her way through college and like him glad to be away from home. Her father, in particular, she regarded as deeply reactionary. She was majoring in Psychology with a minor in English and, unlike Miller, was a voracious reader. In the abandoned novella he offers a portrait of her as a black-haired Irish-German Catholic with clear green eyes, paper-white skin and a bright smile. Like Miller, she embraced Marxism and like him despaired of her parents' religion. She was stubborn, principled, an admirer of the Russians but, according to Miller, self-pitying, the last a persistent and ultimately, it seems, debilitating fault.

Miller had first met her at a basement party. She struck him as pretty and funny. Two weeks later they met again and he asked her to the movies. She paid. The affair quickly developed, with Miller even writing one of her term papers (on Roosevelt). 'I was always able to write about anything if I knew three things about it. I could write entertaining things and get away with it.' Besides, he insisted, 'she knew all that stuff. I was only writing what she knew.'[101]

Mary Slattery, who loved every moment of her time at Michigan, was if anything more radical than him. In 1944, when she was giving birth to their daughter Jane during the German invasion of Yugoslavia, she cried out, 'Oh, those poor Yugoslavs!' During the 1940s, when Miller attended the Communist Party meetings that would give him trouble before HUAC, Mary was attending similar meetings, a fact that seems to have slipped HUAC's attention, but by then they were too interested in his second wife to care overmuch.

They met in their junior year, 1937. Mary, the first girl, Hedda aside, in whom he had shown any real interest, already a radical, had revolted against her Catholic upbringing in Lakewood, a suburb of Cleveland, and stopped going to church in her early teens, as had her older brother. It was less simple scepticism, though, than a function of her politics. The Church, after all, was conservative and, as the decade progressed, often in contention with Roosevelt – more especially as fascist but Catholic Franco became a key issue. In 1933, Pope Pius XI had signed the Reichskonkordat 'in the recognition that the new Germany had fought a decisive battle against Bolshevism and the atheist movement'.[102] She found her family's Catholicism oppressive, matched, as it was, by deeply conservative social and political views.

That neither of them, despite their views, was particularly active in campus politics was a function of their need to work. 'The rich kids,' Miller explained, 'did all the organizing.' The less affluent were often on scholarships and had to maintain their grades, or leave. He himself worked sometimes for five hours a day. She had no more money than he. Michigan was, she later said, the only place she could go.

She, too, had saved for two years and relied on financial support from her parents. She also had to earn money at Michigan, working at stenographic jobs in the university, but was a good student and intellectually sharp. 'By the time I met her, she was a rebel already.' She was also forthright or, as he would later come to feel, obdurate. 'People were either right or wrong to her. She saw things pretty black and white. She had a stubborn streak. You couldn't budge her. She was awesome. She was granite, and that was her undoing with me, finally. But at the time I admired it, because I was not that way. It was rock and water. I was the water; she was the rock.'[103] The very elements of her character that attracted him at Michigan, and in the early years of their marriage, would later be the focus of an irritation deepening into bitterness. For the moment, though, bright, vivacious, opinionated, witty and attractive, she made a natural companion while she, in turn, responded to Miller's humour, his evident pleasure in storytelling.

Part of their attraction for one another, then, lay in the fact that they shared the same political passions. At the time, though, neither thought of marriage – or, rather, she may have done but he certainly did not. 'I would never have thought of getting married,' he said later. He had no job in prospect and no wish to tie himself down. He wanted to be a professional playwright and marriage did not fit in with his plans. It is not so clear that they did not fit in with hers. 'We never discussed it,' he explained, 'because she knew that it was impossible, but women are always thinking of getting married.' As far as he was concerned, they would, seemingly, go their separate ways, he to Brooklyn and she to Ohio, except that when the time came she could no longer face the idea of returning to the narrow world of her parents. She, too, opted for New York and as a result their paths quickly crossed again.

At Michigan, she was sexually naive, resistant to Miller's physical approaches. Night-time visits to the Arboretum, a familiar setting for student affairs, proved frustrating, not least because she had only the vaguest idea of the physiology of sex and was overcome with embarrassment at revealing as much. Desperate, she and Hedda, equally uninformed, together sought out a young man and confessed their ignorance. The incident comes from his novella but it is clear that this bizarre consultation did take place, though it was only later that Miller discovered as much.

For the politically committed these could anyway be confusing times with respect to sexuality. At first, reaction against the family as a bourgeois institution had led to promiscuity, until Lenin denounced the so-called glass-of-water theory whereby the sexual act was dismissed as of no more significance than the quenching of one's thirst with a glass of water. Thereafter, Proletarian Morality was invoked and the family rescued from the bourgeoisie. This, of course, was different from bourgeois morality in that it favoured a nourishment of the revolutionary class and not of the self-evidently corrupt. There is a scene in *The American Clock* in which a young communist woman refuses sex precisely on the grounds of proletarian morality, and it is tempting to feel that Miller, on whom the male character is based, himself discovered that the limits of proletarian solidarity were drawn just short of where he wished to go.

By the end of his final year at Michigan, Miller already thought it time to move on:

> I felt that I'd had it there, that whatever I needed to know I could find out, just get the books. Because that was what the education consisted of. Lectures, such as they were, taught me very little. I only hung out there because I had nowhere to go. What was I going to do? I lived on very little. You could always find a job at the university and it was a very pleasant environment, but as for pursuing some intellectual aim, I didn't think that was happening. It's when I got out that I began to percolate.[104]

What did Michigan, then, mean to Miller? It was 'the testing ground for all my prejudices, my beliefs and my ignorance, and it helped to lay out the boundaries of my life. For me it had, above everything else, variety and freedom.'[105] Beyond that, it was the atmosphere created by the presence of fellow students such as Norman Rosten, of Professor Rowe, together with the existence of the Hopwood Awards, the *Michigan Daily* and *The Gargoyle*, that set Miller on the way to his career as a playwright. It was the social and political ferment of the times that helped shape the values that he carried through the rest of that career. Nor had his confidence been dented by his failure to win a third Hopwood. As he later wrote:

> I failed to win the big one as a senior. Nevertheless, it seemed possible to hope that I might become a professional playwright. The theater I was trying to enter seemed as always to be dominated by its critics, just as our immortal souls are dominated by our decaying flesh. But there was a certain illusion, shared, I think, by everyone involved, that I think helped to form a certain kind of play, and that kind, if I am not mistaken, was in the high tradition of the art. The illusion I speak of was that there was one single audience containing within itself in some mystical fashion the whole variety of America and Americans.

It was that audience he wished to address, the audience that paid fifty-five cents for a balcony seat. For him the theatre's 'desire to make contact with the mass was not really different from that of the New and Old Testaments, the classical Greek theatre, and the best of the Elizabethans. It was a brutal challenge and could be a brutal confrontation, even unfair; but to accept it was to know the difference between grace under pressure and grace before dinner.' This was the Miller of 1982, looking back on his younger self, when he was less inclined to intellectualize his ambition. He was a student ready to make his mark on Broadway and confident of his ability to do so. Later he might remark that a playwright was a man with his own church, the 'vessel of a community's need to talk to itself and the world'.[106] For the moment he would have settled for a chance to talk to anybody who was prepared to listen to what he wished to say.

Above all, Michigan had taught him that he could write. The young man whose ambition had once lain in football and track, and who had failed to make any kind of a scholarly mark in high school, emerged as a confident author with, it seemed to him, a subject and the talent to do it justice. Nonetheless, the Marxism to which he was wedded left him ambiguously placed, since it encouraged a sacrifice of the needs of the individual to the group even as the writer in him was ambitious to make his mark. The self was simultaneously to be denied and proclaimed. It was a conflict that he felt marked not only the writers of his generation but their wives too as they were forced to deal with people who were deeply conflicted, guilty at the notion of a success which potentially separated them from those whose fate they believed themselves to be embracing.

For young writers in search of fame, self-abnegation scarcely came easily, and social commitments would quickly be accommodated to the necessities of the market – a fact which he insisted left scars on their own souls, as well as on those of their wives. In these remarks he hints at some of the pressures that would undo his relationship with Mary and do so more quickly and profoundly than he could ever have imagined, had he then been able to imagine marriage at all.

Miller graduated from Michigan in the summer of 1938, hitching a ride back to New York with a salesman of saddles and riding equipment. He later recalled waving goodbye to Mary as she stood in front of the Women's League.

Unbeknown to him, he also left Michigan with a first entry in an FBI file that would eventually grow to 654 pages. He owed his first appearance in J. Edgar Hoover's extensive filing cabinets to membership of the American Youth Congress and sponsorship of the American Relief Ship for Spain. The Bureau, at least, was already interested in a virtually unknown young man now heading off to New York determined not to get married but prepared to conquer the American theatre and confident that art could play its role in transforming America and the world.

3

BEGINNINGS

Miller left Michigan, he explained, with 'little money and many debts', but, carrying a letter of recommendation from Professor Rowe to the Federal Theatre. He was no longer the person who had climbed on to a bus four years earlier, uncertain whether he could survive the first year. His degree mattered very little. What did was that he had discovered his vocation, and, somewhat incredibly, just months after graduating, was offered $250 a week by the delightfully named Colonel Joy of Twentieth Century Fox, then desperate for new writers. As he explained to me:

> They were turning out a picture a week and they needed stuff to put into those movies. So somebody got the bright idea that maybe they ought to get some young guys in who had never done this. So they sent Colonel Joy to New York to ride herd on a group of writers who they would corral on to a train and take to Los Angeles. And I knew a couple of those guys. They offered me a job and I just couldn't think of doing that because the movies then, despite the legends that have grown up since, were junk. They were known as junk. They were made to be junk. They've now become classics. They're classic junk. Anyway, I didn't want to do that. I had higher ambitions.

It was an offer suffused with irony, given William Fox's earlier request for investment funds from the Miller family, but it seems difficult to believe that a young graduate would turn down the chance to make a fortune in Hollywood. After all, even his dramatic model, Clifford Odets (whom he deeply envied), had taken the train west, as had many of the other smart young talents of the period, some, at least, convinced that the movies offered them a chance to spread their left-wing views directly to the people. But turn it down he did. As far as he was concerned, the theatre seemed the place for someone dedicated to changing rather than merely entertaining America, and he felt sure in his ability to make a mark.

He craved success no less than others, but the thought of Odets's expensive New York apartment, high above Washington Square, offered a lesson not entirely to do with a just reward for talent. Besides, his success at Michigan had gifted him the conviction that breaking into the New York theatre would present no particular problems. He was also full of a sense of his own talent, and was far from wrong if we judge not by a play but a short story he wrote, in 1938, in the basement of the family's house on East 3rd Street where he was obliged to live until he could start selling his work and become independent.

The move back to his family home was not a welcome one. He was stepping back into the tensions between his parents that had so distressed him as a teenager, and was reminded of the brother whose sacrifice had made his own liberation possible. He had no other option though, and believed that it would only be a temporary stay as he revised his Michigan plays and wrote a series of short stories aimed at the thriving magazine market.

For all his later achievements, one of these, called 'Schleifer, Albert: 49', must count as among the most fascinating pieces of fiction he ever wrote. He submitted it to a number of magazines. None responded. It lay forgotten for over sixty years and is still unpublished. In one sense it is not to be compared to the plays, with their complex interactions of language and action, the social density of the worlds he summons into being, the characters who speak themselves, but there is something in this short story that is original and compelling. It also shows the influence of a modernism he was later accused of shunning.

It is a story that foreshadows the lyricism of *Salesman*. But there is a glimpse here of something else. For a man whose progressive views had led him to write radical works that moved towards a moment of epiphany, as social process was revealed as susceptible of transformation, here, suddenly, was a writer conscious of the absurd. He creates a figure overwhelmed by a sense that meaning is neither imminent nor deferred but simply dissolving, little by little, in his hands. His protagonist is a man who has gone on a journey and discovered that it leads nowhere but back to himself and to a central unanswered question that he has come to believe is, ultimately, unanswerable being itself without meaning. This is a figure who feels a sense of vertigo as he stares back through his life, and Miller forges a language that reflects the dislocations, the momentary and deceptive consonances, the slowly evacuating coherence for which the ageing salesman at the story's centre had looked and which he now despairs of finding. In a cascade of images and a smother of words, he looks for a clear sense of himself and the world, and finds nothing. He is a failure in his job, but this is a story about a far more profound failure as things fall apart and finally language itself fails to break open the mystery of a life.

'Schleifer, Albert: 49' is a clear precursor of *Death of a Salesman* but it is remarkable less for that or, indeed, its apparent subject, than for its style, a stream-of-consciousness threnody. It tells the story of a man, like Miller's own father then on the verge of his fiftieth birthday. He is a salesman. Clothed in black and with a high, stiff collar, he sets off on a hot September afternoon to make a sale, accompanied by what is described as a young Negro boy who helps carry his samples of women's coats (the Millers, of course, had made women's coats). He is in a strange state of mind and hardly speaks. His conversation is, for the most part, with himself. He seems on the edge of breakdown. He toys, indeed, with the idea of suicide, though even this is referred to obliquely, hinted at in seemingly random images, momentary visions. It is as if death would be a welcome break from the monotony of a job in which he is plainly not successful, as if a submission to fate might offer the only kind of available coherence. His employer is thinking of firing him. But his sense of anomie goes deeper than that. There no longer seems to be anything to hold the pieces of his life, of life itself, together.

He takes the El train, mind in a fever, one thought crashing into the next. As in the story Miller had written at the age of seventeen, this salesman, too, has to borrow money, this time from the young Negro boy. It is a mark of his failure, of a humiliation he can no longer conceal, even from himself. The narrative passes in and out of the minds of the salesman and the boy, each one free-associating. The boy recognizes something wrong in a man who jumps from thought to thought as though to avoid a truth pressing too directly on him.

In a style he would never attempt again, he simultaneously creates a pointillist picture of New York as seen from the El, and a portrait of a man on the edge of breakdown. This is a prose poem in which regrets, anxieties, stultified hopes swirl around. The language spills out in a mesmerizing way, an internal monologue in which image presses on image, memory segues into fractured present. Along with this is a yearning, on the part of its protagonist, for it all to stop, this coinciding with a fear that it will.

The real anxiety of this failed salesman is that there is no meaning to serve, no centre to hold. Preparing to make his pitch, he is simultaneously readying himself for a disappointment that echoes back through his life, a life of regrets compacted within a few sentences on a flying train, images and sights snatched away by an onward rush that reminds him of foreshortened time. Like Saul Bellow's dangling man, he is tempted by the idea of regimentation, submission, the end finally of this restless search for meaning and direction, the end, indeed, of everything.

The relative absence of punctuation in the story echoes the lack of connection that obsesses him, as run-together words reflect the collision of thoughts that crowd in on him so fast they can barely be disentangled. The loss of a sale triggers the idea of loss itself. Success would seemingly have reordered the randomness around him, pinned down the meaning that slides away from him even as he contemplates it. Knowing, however, that selling coats will say nothing about the absurdity that overwhelms him, he feels that absurdity whelm up again. The exchange with the buyer lasts no more than three sentences as he is told that his price is too high.

He is left alone in the booth, the rejected coats set out on hangers. A moment later he is seemingly back on the train, watching others perhaps as lost as himself, as bereft of answers because as unsure of the question. Finally, he disembarks and stands on the platform as another train approaches, ready now to step in front of it and end the striving and the unanswered questions.

This portrait of a life unspooling, achieved not through narrative but through language, is an accomplished one. What we are left with is the husk of a man, a newspaper fact, a name in a register, his name and age being all that is publicly known of him (hence the title, 'Schleifer, Albert: 49'), information that conveys nothing, certainly not the deeper nothing that he feared and to which he finally submits.

The story now stands as no more than a curiosity, a suggestion of a path Miller might have taken, and, perhaps, to advantage. He was experimenting, trying out his skills, but the result still impresses more than sixty years later. Asked by me in May 2003 where that might have come from, he recalled reading Gertrude Stein, as early as 1930–1: 'I didn't understand any single page of it but I just loved the way it was written, incomprehensible as it was. I didn't know what she was talking about but I liked listening to the music. That is the only clue I have as to where I might have connected to that kind of writing.'

Though he would devote much of his energy to revising an existing play and writing a new one after leaving Michigan, he had plainly not given up on the short story. Within a year, in fact, he began another, in which the narrative line is clearer and the plot more central, but in which there is still that same fascination with letting language do the work, a story that also ends with an ironic dying fall, not so impressive this time but still a more than workmanlike piece and accomplished enough to suggest that at this moment the short story or the novel might have won him the success he later found in the theatre.

'See the World First' is narrated by a man hitch-hiking to Albany, as Miller had done from Michigan to Brooklyn. He is picked up by an inexperienced driver at the wheel of a car transporter. It is not the ride he had wanted, trucks being so much slower and this one too old to keep up much of a speed, but in the rain he can hardly choose.

The character of the narrator slowly emerges from his own narrative. He seems confident, experienced, yet, hitch-hiking in the middle of nowhere, for no reason he ever divulges, also vulnerable. The driver, meanwhile, is barely in control of a vehicle itself in a state of disrepair. The hitch-hiker fears that the truck will jack-knife on the wet road, and that once it begins there will be no stopping it. So, too, with the story, which has a momentum of its own. Its essence, however, again lies not in the narrative itself – the truck does, eventually, jack-knife – but in his skill in creating character through dialogue, precisely, of course, what would distinguish his plays.

The young man at the wheel is on only his second trip, lonely, uncertain about his future. His sense of the world comes from *True Story Magazine*, whose title he believes validates the stories it contains. He is tempted by the idea of marriage, but uncertain about going ahead, having read a story in which a marriage fails when the man has a series of affairs, a story which has clearly planted an idea in his head.

Shortly afterwards, they stop at a roadhouse where they pick up a 'road whore', selling sex to the long-haul drivers. For this driver, though, it is as if his 'true story' were, indeed, true. As they drive off through the night so she begins to seduce him and he to lose control of the vehicle, as though the two had become synonymous. He insists of the truck as it begins to go into a skid that he can handle her, but he can handle neither the truck nor the woman. Her head disappears into his lap and the truck begins to swing wildly across the road. What follows is a page-long paragraph in which their plunge down the hillside is matched by the cumulative momentum of the sentences.

The truck smashes into a railroad bridge, the cars it is carrying crushed flat. The woman is killed. The driver's nose is broken. The sentences shorten as he heads towards an ironic final line in which he can do nothing more than express surprise as the dead woman lies on the magazine with its true stories, a magazine now smeared with blood.

This is a writer full of writing, trying out different styles, exploring different genres, and the result was impressive, though evidently not to the major magazines to which he submitted these stories. It is not hard to see why. The first was too radical in style, the second too frank in subject matter. Back in Ann Arbor, he had focused on drama, and that remained his central interest, but for the next several years he was as liable to turn to the short story and the novel and it was as a novelist that he would first make his mark, though to his dismay not until seven years after leaving Michigan.

From November 1938, and with some regularity thereafter, Miller reported on his progress to his old Michigan teacher, Professor Rowe. This correspondence, for a while, at least, seems to have been important to him. As he wrote in a letter of May 1940, he had to have somebody to listen, and Rowe fulfilled that function, though to read these letters is to hear somebody primarily talking to himself, expressing his enthusiasms, confessing his disillusionments, his growing sense that his career was foundering before it had started. At first, however, the letters are full of confidence.

Writing from the family home on 10 November 1938, he outlined what he had been doing for the six months since leaving university but, probably because he was writing to Rowe, made no mention of his attempts at fiction. He had, he explained, been revising *They Too Arise* and *The Great Disobedience* and believed, certainly with respect to the former, that he had suceeded. And he seemed to have reason for his hubris. After all, Lee Strasberg, director of the Group Theatre – and a man with whom he would later find himself at odds when Marilyn Monroe joined the Actors Studio – had cited his play in a lecture and written a letter of recommendation to the Federal Theatre.

He had finished *They Too Arise* in August, three months after leaving Michigan, and sent it to an agent, Paul Streger, who a few days later called to enthuse about it. Miller signed a contract with the company and waited. Every few days he would find himself in conversation with potential producers, but no production emerged. To his surprise and chagrin, the Group Theatre he had admired during his student days turned it down on the grounds that they 'didn't want to do another Jewish play', an interesting observation in view of those subsequent critics who would accuse him of failing to acknowledge his ethnicity and the fact that Jewish playwrights had won Pulitzer Prizes for drama in 1929, 1932, 1934 and 1937 (none were awarded during the war). Nor was the Group Theatre alone in this. For his part, Miller was baffled. As he explained to Rowe, it seemed confusing to him that a Broadway producer would refuse to stage a play that would make money simply because he believed that it was better not to show Jews on stage. To him, only members of the German-American Bund (whose head, Fritz Kuhn, had been appointed by Hitler) would be offended. But the Jewish producers he spoke to, he explained to Rowe, were Zionists and believed it better to keep a low profile. Nonetheless, he insisted that writing the play had been reward enough, though he was in debt.

In 2003, he remarked to me that, 'I quickly found that my confidence was misplaced and that this was going to take longer than I had thought. The first thing I needed to do was find some means of survival and I managed to get on the roster of the Federal Theatre which was then on its last gasp as an institution', though getting on that roster proved more difficult than he had anticipated.

The Federal Theatre was set up for unemployed writers, directors, actors and technicians as part of Roosevelt's Works Progress Administration (the WPA). To qualify, it was necessary to be on the welfare rolls and that, in turn, required that he should be homeless and without support. Yet, of course, he was living in the family home in Brooklyn. As a result he had to resort to subterfuge, supposedly sharing an apartment with a friend (arranging for a bed, in which he never slept, to be available for inspection) and even bringing his father to the Welfare Department, located in a warehouse near the Hudson

River, to explain why it was impossible for him to stay at home. Together, they staged a private drama of disaffection for the benefit of the official whose signature they required. This was the humiliating scene that he replayed in *The American Clock* in which his father appeared as Moe and he as Lee:

RYAN: You gonna sit there and tell me you won't let him in the house?

MOE: [*with great difficulty*]: I won't let him, no.

RYAN: You mean you're the kind of man, if he rang the bell and you opened the door and saw him, you wouldn't let him inside?

MOE: Well, naturally, if he just wants to come in the house—

LEE: I don't want to live there—

RYAN: I don't care what *you* want, fella. [*To MOE*] You will let him into the house, right?

MOE [*stiffening*]: ... I can't stand the sight of him.

The welfare official remains sceptical until the father cries out, 'He don't believe in anything!" precisely Isidore Miller's complaint about his own son, who seemed to have abandoned faith in anything that made any kind of sense to him.

The apartment in which he was supposedly living was on 47th Street and Sixth Avenue above a tobacconist's shop. It was the home of Mr Franks, whose son Sidney was an old schoolfriend. It was he who had joined the young Miller to release fireflies from the roof of the Miller apartment in Harlem. Franks himself was evidence of the deprivations of the Depression. A former banker, like Isidore Miller with a chauffeur and expensive car (a beige-coloured Locomobile tourer with wire wheels), he had lost his job only to see his wife die and his daughter commit suicide. The contents of his eleven-room apartment were now piled high in a room in the four-storey walk-up, and had been since he had moved there in 1932.

His son, with a Bachelor of Science degree from Columbia, had worked as a salesman but despised his success in a world he held in contempt. He was now a policeman. Here, perhaps, is one source for the figure of Victor in *The Price*, written thirty-five years later, though there are several unfinished scripts that show Miller trying out plays in which a policeman, plainly based on Sidney, performs a significant role. For Sidney, it was a temporary job that became permanent; and this was one of those relationships, once so close, that would later slowly dissolve over the years as Miller became increasingly successful. In *The Price*, Victor the policeman settles for a job he mostly despises because he wants to protect his father. That element comes from Kermit Miller, but the sense of drifting into a job he once meant to leave but now holds on to for the pension comes directly from Sidney Franks. He, like his father, was a victim of the Depression, so fearful of another collapse that he opted for a secure but unfulfilling job.

The inspector did come to check out Miller's story of sharing an apartment, and by luck Miller was there when he arrived. A cursory inspection proved sufficient and the necessary fraud was complete. As a result, Miller joined the Federal Theatre in its dying days, finding himself among forty or fifty playwrights drawing $22.77 a week ('real heavy pay') who wrote plays that he characterized as, for the most part, 'execrable, totally incompetent',[2] and who were never subsequently heard about.

Perhaps it is hardly surprising that fifty years later he still recalled that weekly rate. Years of saving for college, awareness of family arguments over money, worries about mortgage payments, had sensitized him to the facts of economic life. His plays, indeed, are full of financial details, from the cost of coats in *They Too Arise*, through the dollar-a-day man Biff in *Death of a Salesman*, to haggling over the precise cost of furniture in *The Price* and the hourly rates of plumbers and carpenters in *The Last Yankee*. If there is one lesson the Depression offered, it was not only the value of a dollar but the fact that money seemingly constituted the measure of value and time. In the late 1980s Miller expressed surprise that a main course of pasta in a restaurant cost $9, quite as if this were in some way evidence that the fixities of life had been abandoned.

Arthur Miller never forgot the not so genteel poverty he witnessed in his teenage years. He inherited his father's work ethic and, though he rebelled against many of his values, inherited too a fear of failure, of the precipitate fall. A failed play was like his father's failed businesses, a blow to who he was, but like his father he felt the need to get up and try again because failure invited vulnerability. It was the family's wealth that, as a child, had protected him from knowledge of anti-Semitism. It was his later relative poverty that exposed him to it. Success was a mark of individual achievement but it was also what insulated him from contingency.

He was not the only one in the Miller family reliant on the federal government. His sister-in-law to be, Frances, worked for the National Youth Administration. As she explained, 'Nobody we knew had a job. I didn't know anybody who had a car, but I went to college ... to a free school ... There was a competitive race to get grades to get free education in the city colleges.' Through the National Youth Administration she was paid fifty cents an hour: 'and that was enough for you. A subway ride was only a nickel, and I lived at home so that I was able to go to school.'[3] In 2007, her son Ross added a footnote: 'My mother was awarded a scholarship to Cornell but couldn't afford the room, board and travel. She was accepted into the engineering program at Cooper Union but didn't attend because engineers couldn't find work during the Depression. That's why she wound up studying biology at Brooklyn College.'[4]

In his letter of 10 November Miller told Professor Rowe that he was only a day away from being on the Federal Theatre payroll, along with Norman Rosten, later author of the Broadway hit *Mister Johnson*. With Rosten, he wrote a revue sketch for the Workers' Alliance, which would be invoked by the House Un-American Activities Committee in 1956 as evidence of Miller's radicalism. The first work he intended to offer to the Federal Theatre was his prison play. This, he indicated to Rowe, was now to feature two choruses and verse. His interest in verse, he pointed out, initially lay in its practicality. And as he wrote so he came to feel that his prison play in particular required a rhythmical speech, and that led him in the direction of writing metrically. Only two weeks earlier he had written his first poem, and he had been so struck by it that he had immediately begun work on a verse play for radio.

Though he would persevere with *The Great Disobedience*, nothing would come of it, but his experiments with verse would prove significant, and not simply in respect to a radio play called *Thunder from the Hills*, broadcast by NBC, and verse plays such as *The Golden Years* and *A View from the Bridge*. Writing in verse frequently gave him precisely that control over rhythm that he was reaching for, as is evident from the *Death of a Salesman* and *The Crucible* notebooks in particular. There are speeches with the stresses marked in, as if this were a poet determined to adhere to strict form.

This letter is also the first sign that he had identified another market for his work – the radio, for which Norman Rosten was already working and for which Alfred Kazin also wrote, dramatizing *The Pickwick Papers* and Edgar Allan Poe stories for a Brooklyn station. Miller's idea for a play, though, as outlined to Rowe, was rather less than convincing. It was a pacifist play featuring a blind man who returns from war and names his newborn son Pax.

This is the Miller of the Oxford Movement, writing at a time when the pacifist play had its place on Broadway, but the confidence his letter exudes speaks directly to his state of mind. He was now plainly no longer shy of taking himself seriously and, for all the abstract didacticism of his proposed play, his optimism was not entirely misplaced. Two weeks later, he wrote to confirm that he had been accepted into the Federal Theatre and that as a consequence he now felt he had a new status in the community. He also had a cheap apartment in an old brownstone at 24 East 74th Street, a large white room with two windows and little heat, a few yards east of Central Park, right off Fifth Avenue and, as he explained, 'on' the Works Progress Administration. What he did not add was that this was one of the places where he would conduct his affair with Mary Slattery, who by now was working as a sten-ographer at a medical publishing house (an offshoot of Harpers) and earning $25 a week, but living, for the moment, in Brooklyn Heights with three other women.

It was here that he wrote a curious short story with the still more curious title, 'Barcelona, Aristotle, and the Death of Tragedy'. This reflected his continuing concern with Spain but did so in an innovative way.

A man is told that he is going to die of cancer. In explaining the disease, the doctor suggests that it is the result of a kind of internal anarchy. The man wanders out on to the streets of New York, in his head a line from a news dispatch about the bombing of Barcelona and the apparent calmness of its citizens ... The man, we are told, thought of himself as being like Barcelona yet aware of the fact that, even as death might be coming to the city, Spain itself still represented order. Can the word 'tragedy', then, he asks himself, be applied either to himself or the city? Are either of sufficient magnitude to warrant use of the word? Confused, he wanders into a burlesque show.

In a state of high anxiety, he registers the show as little more than a series of surreal images, the suppressed sexual energy seemingly allied to an anarchic spirit. The floating fragments of his concern come together in a one-and-a-half-page paragraph that outdoes the ending of Nathanael West's *The Day of the Locust*, a painful aria in which desire and death are drawn together, the private and public fused.

An almost nude dancer now appears on stage in a purple light, though her breasts are two circles of red. The men begin to scream out as the woman begins an ever more provocative and frenzied dance. Then they all rise to their feet as she simulates intercourse. One man throws lighted matches towards the stage, another, in the balcony, screams until a spotlight swings on him and his scream turns into a plea for Barcelona, an hysterical denunciation of fascism as a form of cancer now metastasizing. The dancer stops as the man in the balcony falls into the orchestra and lies face up, bleeding. The dancer then resumes her dance, her eyes on the apparently dead man, whose face now appears blue in the spotlight.

It is an oddly impressive piece of writing, though it is difficult to believe he thought he could find a market for it, and, unsurprisingly, he did not. Nonetheless, it serves to underline his radical aesthetic instincts, the degree to which those who would later choose to characterize him as by nature a realist were wide of the mark.

For the moment, the story was just one more item for the drawer. He was by now, anyway, as he indicated to Professor Rowe, writing his verse radio play, finding the writing of verse easier than prose. As he would later explain:

> I made the discovery that in verse you are forced to be brief and to the point. Verse squeezes out fat and you're left with the real meaning of the language. I could say more, more quickly, than stringing out fully articulated grammatical sentences. I wanted to use the language so that people thought I was using regular language. What I was slipping over was a hidden pattern, which permitted me to say much more in fewer words than I could otherwise.[5]

The play was called *Of Time and the Sword* and was completed in December 1938 at his East 74th Street address. It ends with the blind man unfurling a banner on the battlefield inviting the combatants to beat their swords into ploughshares and put down their arms. They duly oblige.

Happily, he decided to lay his pacifist play aside and to contemplate the situation in Europe and the paralysis that seemed to affect the Western powers when confronted with fascism and its charismatic leaders. He was now beginning what he called his 'Montezuma play', which he hoped to research, at Federal Theatre expense, in the mornings while continuing to work on his prison play in the afternoons and evenings. He intended to place the latter with the Mercury Theatre, under the direction of Orson Welles, whom he would soon encounter in a radio studio. The Montezuma play, meanwhile, he was confident, would 'stand Broadway on its ear'.

As he understood it, the deal with the Federal Theatre would vest ownership of the plays in their author. His only duty was to get on with his own work. If that interpretation proved incorrect, he decided, he would simply resign and return his pay. His Federal Theatre supervisor estimated that research for the Montezuma play, then called 'Conquistador', would take two months. Miller thought it would take rather less but prepared to stretch it to three to cover his work on the prison play. He was beginning to be aware, though, that the Federal Theatre itself, indeed the whole WPA, was under threat.

Ben Russak, first director of the Playwrighting Department, remembered things slightly differently. Miller, he recalled, was reluctant to work for the Department because ownership in the plays would be vested in the government and hence be in the public domain; 'So, he decided to read plays and bring in a report every day ... He very quickly realized he could ... use it to earn enough to live on.'[6]

Norman Rosten, then developing a play called *Iron Land*, described his time in the Playwrighting Department with Miller: 'We all would wait around outside the building to wait for Arthur Miller to roll in from Patchogue where he was living on Long Island – he was out there somewhere writing. He'd be rolling in in an old beat-up car just to make it on time to sign in. And I remember we all used to wait and cheer, "Here comes Miller and on time" ... Of course nobody was known then at all.'[7] In 2002 Miller, too, remembered driving into the city in a Ford Roadster that had cost him $35, from a Long Island home without water or electricity, which cost him $75 for the season. Once again, some sixty-four years on, he still remembered precise financial details. Money mattered. It also seemed significant to him later that he had been writing in the countryside: 'I have always connected writing with the country and not the city. Most of what I have written, I have written in the country.'[8] In fact he spent ten weeks in the summer of 1939 sharing a four-room cottage on Long Island's south shore with his cousin, Morton. He had restored the car by searching out parts in Brooklyn's automobile graveyards.

As for *The Grass Still Grows* (his latest version of *No Villain/They Too Arise*), the Jewish situation that had seemed to threaten production now appeared more conducive to it. After Kristallnacht, it seemed, Jews were the object of pity, though he was depressed at the thought that the very people who had rejected it for one specious reason would now embrace it for another, hoping to gain credit for their supposed courage. And, indeed, the day after his letter to Professor Rowe, *Life* magazine carried a seven-page spread on Kristallnacht. This was the moment to which Miller would return in 1994 with *Broken Glass*, when copies of that issue of *Life* were pinned on the rehearsal room walls in New Haven.

He worked for a bare six months before the Federal Theatre was brought down by those who saw it as a threat to the American way. During that time he and Rosten wrote a comedy called *Listen My Children*, though this, too, came to nothing. Meanwhile, he continued work on his Montezuma play, sending Rowe an interim report on 7 January 1939, having just, as it seemed to him, finished it. He mailed one copy to the Theatre Guild and another to the Group Theatre. He had, he told Rowe, received an enthusiastic response from Morris Carnovsky, an actor whose work at the Group he had much admired, while he himself had come to think that it was 'a major opus'. But his career had not so much stalled as failed to begin, though he did now manage to place a brief radio play.

His first script for radio, *Joe, the Motorman*, was about a rebellious subway driver on the line on which Miller himself had travelled every day on his way to work from Brooklyn in the early 1930s. After eleven years of driving back and forth between Times Square and Coney Island, the motorman has lost the point. He seems to have no identity outside of his role. Tonight, he decides, he will fight back and drive his train without stopping at the 34th Street station.

As rebellions go, it seems modest, and the play, indeed, is a gentle comedy. But as he hurtles along at sixty miles an hour he regains a sense that he is in control of his life. The automatic brakes slam on at the 14th Street stop and he opens the door and walks away, free to be his own person. It is a slight enough work but humorous and a well crafted radio play. More importantly, for the moment, it earned him $100 and suggested a way he might get by until the theatre proved more receptive to his work. *Joe, the Motorman* was transmitted on *The Rudy Vallee Hour* on NBC on 14 July 1939. Nonetheless, with no other income, he was back working at home, not something he could be happy about. He was thinking about looking for a job, if only so that he could afford a room of his own.

*

Meanwhile, the issue that had so commanded his attention back in Michigan was resolved, though not in the way he had wished. On 29 March 1939, the Spanish Civil War ended. Hitler and Pope Pius XII offered Franco their congratulations. Those on the Left who had seen Spain as a dry-run for a world war were about to be justified. It was here that Germany perfected the Messerschmitt 109. Among those Germans who had served in Spain and who now paraded through Berlin was Wolfram von Richthofen, who had masterminded the attack, by Junkers-52s and Heinkels, on Guernica. Von Richthofen would subsequently command Air Fleet VIII, which led the assault on Poland.[9] Karl von Knauer, who led the Guernica raid, subsequently wrote a manual for Luftwaffe bomber pilots and served in the German military until 1975.

Spain, Hitler told his returning warriors, had been a lesson for Germany's enemies. It had also, as many on the left had suspected throughout the second half of the 1930s, been a lesson to Germany, a lesson it put into practice a few months later – though, oddly, Miller himself, having denounced non-intervention in Spain, would resist the idea of American intervention in the Second World War until Pearl Harbor and Hitler's suicidal declaration of war against the United States. He had written a letter of protest to President Roosevelt, denouncing America's attitude towards Spain. In reply came a brief note informing him that his letter had been turned over to the FBI. As he would later observe, not merely did the President turn him over to the secret service, he told him he had done so. About Germany's actions in Europe, Spain aside, Miller had nothing to say beyond a slavish endorsement of the Party line.

In terms of his writing he had nothing to show for his efforts. He and Mary had little money, though they had treated themselves to a 1928 Ford Convertible. They also allowed themselves a visit to the New York World's Fair, opened by President Roosevelt in April 1939. Spain and Germany were absent, but the Soviet Union was there. The Ford Motor Company offered a feature called 'Futurama', in which visitors could make their way through tunnels and get a glimpse of what cars and roads would be like in 1960. They could also see 3-D films, while the Kodak exhibition introduced Kodachrome and NBC showed experimental television. Miller, though, dutifully made his way to the Soviet pavilion. It, after all, represented the true future. It was disappointing, with heavy, dull sculpture. As for Ford, Kodak and NBC, they might be offering a vision of the future, but it was a vision lacking in that utopian social commitment that kept him loyal not just to the rhetoric of Marxism but to its rigorous principles. Dull sculpture spoke of a stripped-down aesthetic, a utilitarianism that placed the self at the service of an idea. Ford and Kodak were mere commerce, NBC vacuous entertainment (though he would be happy writing for it).

The press agent for the Soviet exhibition was Jim Proctor (whose father was what Miller called 'a professional revolutionary'), a committed Marxist and later to become the press agent for all Miller's early plays. Proctor never regretted his service to the Soviets, acting, as he believed, out of the highest motives and responding to the idea of a rational structure to history and hence to human actions. He died of cancer in 1983.

In August 1939 Miller made one last effort to rewrite his first Michigan success. *The Grass Still Grows*[10] is, as its subtitle declares, 'A Comedy'. The most significant aspect of this final version is that it is drained of ideology. The strike has gone. The working class is no longer celebrated. Arnold is neither a student nor a writer but a doctor. It is now Ben who is the writer, though he has just destroyed his novel because the world no longer needs writers but doctors. The social drama is now pushed into a subplot while the Simon company is saved when Abe agrees to borrow money from his workers and create a cooperative.

The main emphasis is on comedy, which focuses on romances between Arnold and Helen Roth, daughter of a rival manufacturer, and between Ben and the company bookkeeper. The grandfather is reprieved as a comic character. What Miller seems to be doing is shaping his much revised play to a new political environment and to a Broadway with little interest in earnest social dramas. His new model appears to be Philip Barry rather than Clifford Odets. It made little difference. He could still find no market for the play that in its original form had first convinced him that he had a future as a playwright.

Then came an event that was a body blow to those, like Miller, on the left, when on 23 August 1939 Stalin signed a non-aggression pact with Hitler. In Article I the two countries declared that they would not attack each other and in Article II that neither would lend its support to belligerent action by a third power. It was to last for a period of ten years. This much was openly declared. But there was also a secret protocol carving Poland up along the line of the Rivers Narev, Vistula and San. Three weeks later, with the destruction of the Polish Army imminent and Warsaw about to be occupied, a joint communiqué was proposed declaring that the two powers would act in order to 'restore peace'.

The full details of this arrangement were not made public, but the declaration alone put the American Left into anaphylactic shock. Ostensibly, it represented a betrayal of everything Miller believed. The Soviet Union was the paradigm of a socialist state, a workers' paradise in which social justice at home was wedded to anti-fascism abroad. It was the one state in the world that seemed to appreciate the nature of the threat posed by the fascist idea. Eric Lanzetti later recalled the personal effect of the Pact. 'After *Der Pakt*, overnight we became "Communazis". People practically spit in my face when I walked down the street.' He recalled being harangued by an old Jewish woman who cursed him in Yiddish. It was not until Hitler tore the Pact up that the Party regained respectability: 'When the Germans invaded Russia, everyone went wild. Pure relief ran, like a fever, through the neighborhood.'

The Pact threw everything into disarray. Lanzetti recalled attending a Party meeting in which it was presented as evidence of the Soviet Union's commitment to peace. When he stood up to complain he was accused of disrupting and undermining the Party: 'I was a Trotskyite, a bourgeois lickspittle, possibly an FBI agent.'[11]

Alfred Kazin remembers hearing the news and shouting, 'No ! . . . It's not true!' at the radio. At the signing of the Pact Stalin had toasted Hitler's health: 'I know how much the German nation owes to its Führer.' For his part, Elia Kazan rationalized the betrayal:

> This alliance, I told myself, is what a war of survival makes necessary. Despite resigning in disgust from the Party four years earlier, I still had protective feelings about Russia . . . What finally did turn me off was the flip-flop of the leading comrades two years later when Hitler turned his Panzers east, invading Poland, then Russia itself. Many left-wing intellectuals vaulted shamelessly – in twenty-four hours – from considering the war imperialist to proclaiming it a war to save civilization.[12]

Looking back on this period, Kazin wrote:

> I now saw that the ideologues . . . had no moral imagination whatever, and no interest in politics. They were merely the slaves of an idea, fetishists of an ideology; the real world did not exist for them, and they would never understand it. . . . Day after day I followed the *Daily Worker* with savage joy at its confusion as those who had been eloquent about the Okies, the unemployed, the victims of Fascism, now tried to explain the secret contribution that the noble Stalin, the great Stalin, the all-wise and far-seeing Stalin, had made to the cause of world peace.[13]

Molotov spoke of 'short-sighted anti-Fascists' as in later years, in America, the Left would be hunted down, accused of premature anti-fascism. The impact on Miller, and those who shared his convictions, was, he admitted:

> devastating . . . the first of the great moral dilemmas . . . Political orientation was impossible . . . German fascism was an expression of the capitalist class in its last throes, as it tried to survive. Socialism was the systematic expression of the working class. How could both of them come together in the same bed? So it was catastrophic, the whole thing, and I do not think that ideology, as such, ever recovered . . . but it took a generation to confront the signs.[14]

In an unpublished piece called 'Scenario: Ohio Marriage' (dated April 1972), he commented that if Napoleon had been exposed as a secret agent of the British king or St Paul had been revealed to be Lucifer in disguise, it could not have had a more traumatizing effect or done more damage to the notion of opposing forces. Yet at the same time he suggests that he and Mary had tried to put the implications of the Pact out of mind and certainly not to raise the issue with one another but, like many others, wait for this tear in the universe to repair itself.

Looking back from the 1980s, he saw the Pact as marking the end of his generation's innocence, the moment when equivocation and doubt for the first time clouded the certainties that had carried him through his Michigan years. He did not, though, regret these youthful passions or see them as entirely misdirected. During a celebration of his eighty-fifth birthday, in October 2000, he remarked: 'I don't think of myself as having been fooled. Either you stand on the shore and watch the river go by or you jump in and swim. And if you jump in you are going to get wet ... you are probably going to make mistakes but they are mistakes, at best, of credulity, of believing things you need not have believed.'

Those on the left, desperate to rationalize this astonishing volte-face, blamed the Western powers, who had refused overtures from the Soviet Union. The historian Henry F. May later recalled:

> In long arguments with my friends and still longer ones with myself, I persuaded myself of the truth of the following propositions: That the Soviet–Nazi Pact was a brilliant coup for peace, once one really understood it. That the war was phoney and that ... Goering was in contact with British imperial and conservative elements. That in the long run British imperialism and American capitalism were an even more serious menace to the world than Hitler ... I was more active in support of these positions than I ever had been in support of the earlier easier ones. Part of the reason was that I needed to be, in order to persuade myself against my better judgment.[15]

Ellen Schrecker has argued that in fact surprisingly few intellectuals left the Party. Miller, not in the Party, nonetheless remained loyal to the Party line, offering the same rationalizations. To his surprise, the following year he was to hear Mary's grandmother, wearing a gingham bonnet familiar from covered-wagon days, adopt this same view. She regarded the Hitler–Stalin Pact as a consequence of French intransigence, she being from German-speaking Alsace. To hear such an opinion in the middle of Ohio seemed to confirm his own equivocation.

The effect of the Pact, however, was that some abandoned if not their radicalism then at least their faith in the Soviet Union as the embodiment of that faith. For others, a faith tested was a faith strengthened. Miller, though

confused by this development, like many others rationalized it either as a
shrewd delaying strategy or as a gesture born out of frustration with the
Western powers. The cynical division of Poland between Germany and the
Soviet Union was explained as no more than a wise and necessary defensive
tactic. It was, perhaps, an extension rather than a denial of the Soviet Union's
idealism. Seen thus, it underscored not Soviet treachery but Western equivocation and myopia, and the not yet abandoned imperial ambitions of another
age. It would be a decade and more before Miller finally abandoned his faith
in the socialist dream, a dream he had sustained in the face of the show trials,
the Pact and news of Soviet repressions.

In truth, he never fully bought into the Marxist model, merely responding
to its universalism. He certainly resisted its discipline, which others submitted
to as to a dominatrix and with much the same baffling sense of fulfilment.
The problem was that in order to transcend boundaries – economic, class,
social – that model insisted on their historic inevitability. Accordingly, even
the withering away of those boundaries would follow a scientific logic. Miller's
instincts lay elsewhere, in humanism, in a native transcendentalism, a Judaistic
faith in the imminence of past in present, a past that is something more than
a mechanistic history. He believed in Rousseau's social contract.

Nonetheless, there is no doubt that he regarded himself as a Marxist at
least from 1932 to 1950, member of the Party or no. He was drawn to Marxism
by its confident propositions, its seeming sensitivity to the plight of those
discarded by capitalism, a system that had foundered and lost its capacity to
beguile. He was drawn to it, too, as noted earlier, by the fact that it seemed
so resolutely to set its face against anti-Semitism, and not least because this
opened clear water between the Soviet Union and Nazi Germany.

This was the period of the Popular Front (which dissolved on news of the
Hitler–Stalin pact) when, as Solomon M. Schwartz would point out in an
article in *Commentary* magazine, Maxim Litvinov made eloquent pleas for
humanitarianism and peace at the League of Nations and when Molotov,
speaking on the draft of the new Constitution at the Eighth Soviet Congress
in November 1936, contrasted Stalin's attack on anti-Semitism with the
'cannibalism' of the Nazis: 'Whatever may be said by present-day cannibals
from the ranks of fascist anti-Semites, our fraternal feeling towards the Jewish
people is determined by the fact that it gave birth to the genius who created
the ideas of the Communist liberation of mankind, Karl Marx.' The Jewish
people, he asserted, had produced outstanding men of science, technology
and art as well as contributing 'many heroes to the revolutionary struggle
against the oppressors of the working people ... All this determines our
attitude to anti-Semitism and anti-Semitic bestiality wherever they may
arise.'[16]

The idea that the Soviet Union was dedicated to a war on anti-Semitism was widely shared by those in and outside the Party, but American Jews proved particularly impressed, not least because the Party worked so hard to convince them. In September 1936 the National Conference of Jewish Communists demanded respect for Jewish culture, and when Trotsky (whose real name was Lev Davidovich Bronstein) spoke of Soviet anti-Semitism Rabbi Stephen S. Wise used his remarks as a reason for rejecting an invitation to join his Defence Committee (a committee, chaired by John Dewey, set up to clear Trotsky of charges levelled against him in the Moscow trials which began that same year). Writing to Sidney Hook, a philosophy professor at New York University who had described Trotsky as the most brilliant Marxist in the world, he claimed that 'to invite me to join your committee on that ground savors of Trotsky's own disingenuousness in introducing the Jewish issue in the present situation. If his other charges against the Soviet government are as unsubstantiated as his complaint on the score of anti-Semitism he has no case at all.'[17]

In 1938 the National Conference of Jewish Communists staged a meeting at Carnegie Hall. It was an impressive affair, drawing delegates from thirty-two cities. That same year, *Jewish Life*, a communist publication for which Miller wrote, declared, 'In the Soviet system . . . the burning Jewish question has been solved. Anti-Semitism is a crime, punishable by fine and imprisonment. The USSR has given the Jews opportunity, security, and a respectable life.'[18]

It was such propaganda that helped to determine Miller's attitude to the Soviet Union and perhaps kept him loyal to it when others defected. He had tasted anti-Semitism in America. In 1940, a Brooklyn court released a group of Christian Fronters (an anti-Communist organization of followers of the Rev. Charles Edward Coughlin) who stood accused of anti-Jewish acts, an incident seized upon by the Yiddish-language communist *Der Freiheit* newspaper as evidence of an American anti-Semitism to which the Party at least – and perhaps, it implied, alone – was sensitive. He therefore responded to a doctrine and a state that seemingly outlawed it. The Moscow trials may have involved a number of prominent Jews – Zinoviev, Trotsky and Kamenev among them – but to Miller this seemed less evidence of anti-Semitism than of an internal battle for power that left him uneasy, but little more, since a threat to Stalin then seemed a threat to the state that had come to represent hope.

Looking back, it appeared to him that one curious result of growing up during the Depression was that it led not to a new realism but to a revived romanticism. This was the story of Wordsworth and the French Revolution all over again. Everything seemed possible and bliss was it to be alive at such a time. Personal qualities mattered far less than whether or not one signed up for the new Jerusalem. And the writer had a special function. He could change the world, and that was the only objective worth embracing. Moreover, to abandon Marxism and a faith in the Soviet Union in 1939 would be to acknowledge that his father had been right, that his own interpretation of the world was awry; that his generation, far from possessing a special insight, was uniquely deceived. It would be to lose his sense of the social function of the art to which he had committed himself.

The Moscow trials had been easily assimilated, blotted out, as they were, for Miller, by the Soviet Union's heroic role in Spain. The Pact was a more fundamental challenge requiring a proportionately greater degree of denial, especially when it was followed, in September 1939, by the German Treaty on Borders and Friendship, a splendid piece of newspeak (though the term was not yet available), which led to the invasion and partition of Poland. In November came the annexation of western Ukraine and parts of Belorussia and the attack on Finland. In December, the USSR was expelled from the League of Nations. More annexations followed six months later. All of this Miller swallowed. It is true that details of such appropriations were quickly subsumed in the assault on Western Europe, the collapse of the democracies, but it would be twenty-two months after the Pact before Hitler's assault on Russia removed the problem and it was possible to resume an untroubled commitment. By the end of that September, however, the Pact was not what was on Miller's mind, though the threat of Nazi expansion was.

He had now completed further revisions to his Montezuma play. It was called *Children of the Sun* and it seemed to him to be 'a beautiful play'. In a letter to Professor Rowe dated 6 October 1939, he wrote that the previous night he had read it to a group of people who included three playwrights, two actors and Norman Rosten. They listened for three hours, on a hot night. At the end, he told Rowe, they had sat in silence for two minutes, one of the playwrights in tears. The play, he now felt sure, was bound to be produced.

It was not. In fact, it would be more than half a century before *Children of the Sun*, renamed *The Golden Years*, found an audience. As he admitted, he had no illusions about the difficulty of finding a producer, not least because history plays seldom seemed to appeal to those whose eyes were on the bottom line. And in truth the fact that it was not produced does say more about the state of the theatre than about the play. The Federal Theatre would have been a natural venue, but it was now dead. The Group Theatre showed no interest and even lost its file copy. (The typescript later ended up in the air-conditioned vault of a university research collection, before I retrieved it for a radio production by the BBC in 1987.) For the moment, the fact of writing it had to be its own satisfaction. The play was, though, a considerable achievement, poetic, subtle and with an immediate relevance to the situation in Europe.

The Golden Years was written between 1939 and 1941. It took as its subject the encounter of Montezuma and Cortés, agent of the Spanish empire and rapacious materialist. Miller's Montezuma is caught at a moment of self-doubt. His is an empire built on blood whose meaning he is beginning to think suspect. Cortés's appearance potentially changes everything since it seems he may be the fulfilment of a prophecy which speaks of the return of the gods. If Cortés is, indeed, a deity then Montezuma becomes the acme of historic process. Uncertain of the meaning of events, he is paralysed and so becomes the victim of something more than a band of brigands.

Cortés is untroubled by doubt, uncharacterized by ambiguity. His power is a product of his single-mindedness. He has no more than a few hundred soldiers to deploy, adventurers like himself, but those who confront him, though their own hands are stained with blood, are undone by uncertainty.

The play is epic in pretension, with twenty-two speaking parts, but the essence of it lies in the confrontation between two men whose conception of the world is wholly different. Cortés is blunt, prosaic, and speaks a language that reflects that fact. Montezuma is touched with poetry, a man of war who longs now for a future time of peace, the golden years of which he dreams. Cortés is a betrayer; Montezuma is a denier. They contest something more than the fate of an empire. They contest meaning itself.

For Montezuma, any event, every action is a sign to be understood in terms of an imminent truth. There is a spine to existence. Sacrifices are brutal (a young boy's throat is slit so he can be sent as a messenger to the gods), but serve a higher purpose. He glimpses a utopia that justifies the stern rituals practised because necessary. Cortés is practical. The world is no more or less to him than a backdrop to his own necessities. The beauty of Aztec art means nothing to him, serves no purpose other than to be rendered down, its gold melted in a crucible and shaped into ingots to be carried away. He seeks a life of ease, power and self-satisfaction.

A young Aztec princess offers love, but the beauty of her feelings is similarly rendered down as she becomes no more than an agent of his conquest, a facilitator of cruelty. Too late, Montezuma realizes the extent of his self-deceit, his historic treachery. He is struck down by his own people, but they are already doomed.

Miller subtitled the play 'A New World Tragedy', but it was offered as a comment on an Old World tragedy then unfolding three thousand miles away, as the price of appeasement was paid in blood. Hitler had offered a spurious friendship while planning conquest. He, too, was prepared to reduce civilization and its evidences to chaos and desolation to serve his own rapacity. Eventually, the European powers, no less than Montezuma, were struck by the sheer fact of 'unreasonable, relentless force'. The fear was that in both cases the result could only be that the desire for compromise would precipitate defeat and destruction. As he confronts his death, at last clear as to his acquiescence in his own annihilation, Montezuma observes:

> Let the history tell how an emperor died in search of the golden years. And
> by no hand but his own. For while his eyes were searching heaven for
> meanings and signs, a sword was pointing at his breast, and as it caught the
> light with such brilliant glare, it seemed to hold the sanction of the sun, and
> he dared not turn the killing blade away. And when the sun was set, and the
> light was gone, the emperor felt for the face of the god but the steel stood
> turning in his heart.[19]

Years later, when at last the play made its way into print, Miller saw its
energy as having been a product of his own fear of the systematized power of
fascism and his awareness that there is a seductive quality to submission. In
his own country the Depression, it seemed to him, had sapped the will. It
had bred a generation of victims who saw themselves as helpless in the face
of events. Hitler had prompted a similar sense of of acquiescence, a feeling
that history was in some ways a natural force, the new dark age inviting
nothing but a masochistic surrender as if that in itself were a form of meaning.

The play took him far beyond the realism of his early college plays (though
he had tried to rewrite *The Great Disobedience* in verse), far beyond the analysis
of social and political process he had offered there. When eventually it was
released from the university archive in which it had lain for nearly fifty years,
to be broadcast on the radio, it received a series of positive reviews. It was
'mesmeric', 'exciting', 'elegant'. Peter Davelle of the London *Times* said, 'This
early Miller has flashes of insight (and certainly of poetry) that are worthy to
stand alongside anything in later Miller. His chronicle about the confrontation
between . . . Montezuma and . . . Cortez inevitably calls to mind Peter Shaffer's
The Royal Hunt of the Sun . . . Put the two plays side by side, try to forget
the breath-taking staging of Shaffer's play, and Miller has the edge in the
competition.'[20]

Following the radio broadcast it was presented, less successfully, on television and then in the theatre. The first time he heard it sound forth from a
stage, was when Ronald Pickup and John Shrapnel presented a brief scene at
the Theatre Royal in Norwich, in 1989, in a gala evening marking the opening
of the Arthur Miller Centre. He was transfixed, and not without reason.
Poetry that had lain on the page in the climate-controlled environment of
the Harry Ransom Center in Texas now lived on the pulse as actors breathed
life into words written at a time when his career, radio drama aside, had
seemed to be floundering. The typescript of *The Golden Years* bears the
Brooklyn address of his family home: 1350 East 3rd Street.

Part of the interest of the play lies in the fact that it was his attempt to
reinvigorate poetic drama. He started writing it just two years after Archibald
McLeish's radio play, *The Fall of the City*, starring Orson Welles and broadcast

on CBS's experimental drama series the Columbia Workshop, the first verse play on radio and itself inspired by the Spanish conquest of Tenochtitlan. It was repeated in 1939. Miller himself has said that it was this play that convinced him that 'radio was made for poetry' and that McLeish had 'lifted it to a gorgeous level'.[21] In 1939 Norman Rosten also wrote a verse play for radio, *Prometheus in Grenada*, about the execution of Federico García Lorca, as he would later write another, *The Unholy Three*, about Goering, Goebbels and Himmler. Miller himself as noted earlier, would write *Thunder from the Hills*, a verse play for radio.

In 1973, distant now from the events in Europe that had, in part, originally inspired it, he toyed with the idea of reshaping *The Golden Years* for the screen, with Marlon Brando as Cortés, and wrote notes for him should he decide to appear in it.

The failure to place *The Golden Years* was a disappointment, perhaps the more so when, in July 1943, Morton Wishengrad, former director of the AF of L (American Federation of Labor) Shortwave Bureau, wrote a play for NBC's *Lands of the Free* series, *The Lost Inca* (later, ironically, published in the same volume as Miller's own *The Story of Gus*). This, too, offered an analogy between the Spanish encounter with the natives in South America and the situation in Europe, a fact underlined by the book's editor, Joseph Liss of the Radio Bureau, a friend and collaborator of Miller's:

> Here is a play of purpose out of yesterday's history that tells us that yesterday's tyrants are the blood-and-money brothers of today's tyrants. If this drama were a mirror in Hell, Hitler and his cronies would see that their murderous deeds were not original. They would see themselves and other cruelties reflected in the image of the Corregidors and the Viceroys of sixteenth-century Spain who came to exploit the Incas.[22]

Miller was not, though, to be so easily discouraged. He had other plans. Together with Norman Rosten and two other playwrights, Oscar Saul and Lou Lantz (authors of *The Beavers*, produced two seasons earlier but whose new play, *Poets Die Young*, had been rejected by the Group Theatre), he attempted to create a production company, even raising $11,000 towards a venture that would open with *They Too Arise/The Grass Still Grows*. They were to be sponsored by the Playwrights' Company, with the support of Elmer Rice and Robert Sherwood.

Saul had written much of the Federal Theatre's Living Newspaper production, *Power*, and now was to offer *Milk*, also a Living Newspaper originally scheduled for the Federal Theatre but never produced because of its collapse. Rosten's play *Iron Land* was as yet incomplete but Miller was more than ready to fill the void with *Children of the Sun*. Lee Strasberg, Miller reported to Rowe, was willing to drop everything and join them as director. The new company, he was sure, would show a jaded city what a vital theatre could be. The jaded city was to prove remarkably resistant.

In the meantime, on 8 February 1940 Miller was reporting the sale of a brief sketch to the *Rudy Vallee Hour* and transmission of his half-hour radio play *William Ireland's Confession*, about a nineteenth-century forger of Shakespeare manuscripts, on Columbia Workshop. It had been broadcast on 19 October 1939 (sixty years on, he was still playing with the idea of expanding this into a stage play). He also mentioned a planned production of a further revision of *The Grass Still Grows* by a new group (an offshoot of the Group Theatre), directed by Lee Strasberg, while a revue piece written with Rosten was announced for production by the Five Arts Committee. Miller was also busy rewriting his Montezuma play.

By mid-May 1940, however, he confessed to having reached a standstill. It seemed impossible, he now conceded in another letter to Professor Rowe, that he had spent so long on a single play. Though he had received some praise from Morris Carnovsky and John Gassner, no one could see any Broadway potential in it. He was, he said, not surprised by the reactions, knowing that it would be a difficult sell, but had felt unable to let it go. Hence, a year's worth of wasted effort.

He had also been at work on a Jewish comedy, with no better results. As for radio, a few months earlier, he went on, he had written two scripts which were refused and as a result he felt disinclined to try again. Hopes for the production company had also subsided. He had, however, to his surprise, been engaged to write the narration for a Sergei Eisenstein documentary on Mexico, but contract difficulties between producer and distributor had halted the project. His total pay for this was $75. His irons he remarked, had thus all frozen in the fire.

His short stories, meanwhile, had also come to nothing. The first (presumably 'See the World First'), his agent explained, she was sure no one would print because the magazines would regard it as obscene. The second (probably 'Schleifer, Albert: 49') had been rejected by *Esquire*, *Story* and *Atlantic*. His total output since leaving Ann Arbor, he thus calculated, was two plays (not produced), a revue (not produced), a four-minute radio sketch and a half-hour radio play, together with those three unpublished stories 'and three post cards'. His net receipts he put at $200, less 10 per cent commission, plus $75 for the film script, a total of $255. This was all he had to show for the career on which he had so confidently launched himself two years earlier. As he was to say in 2002:

> Oh, it was tough, very hopeless. There was no Off-Broadway theatre. There were some Broadway producers, like Herman Shumlin, who were open to social plays, plays that were not pure entertainment, but the dominant

playwrights were entertainers. I felt completely out of it. Totally. I didn't know where you could go with anything I was interested in. They were interested in my talent but not in what I was writing. The only one who would really be interested was Joe Fields, who directed *The Man Who Had All the Luck*. Now Joe Fields, and this is symbolic, wrote plays like *Dough Girls*, really blatant farces, but in his pocket he always had Baudelaire and Verlaine. He read and spoke French. He loved *The Man Who Had All the Luck*. He had an illegitimate brother who was a manufacturer of men's perfume, and he put up the money and when it closed in a week he said, 'You go right on doing it because you've got it.' But outside of him it was a hopeless theatre.[23]

The Man Who Had All the Luck, though, still lay four years ahead.

In his letter to Rowe he explained that, aside from his six months with the WPA, for two years he had been supported by his father and brother, neither of whom could afford it. Now he was twenty-four, the same age as the protagonist of 'Schleifer, Albert: 49' who had 'stopped moving'. He now felt forced to ask himself whether he had justified his self-identification as a writer. There was just so long that he could convince himself of this without a story published or a play produced. He had begun to think that his kind of writing was too alienating, too politically committed, too demanding.

As though to provide further evidence of this, he then mapped out a possible play – more truthfully, an impossible one – set in the near future, in an air-raid shelter at the corner of Wall Street and Broad. Beginning as a comedy, it darkened into something else, and is worth recalling for what it says of his state of mind as for the first time he confronted the possibility that his ambitions for a career in the theatre might be grinding to a halt.

The play opens to the wail of sirens. It is a practice drill, America not yet having been drawn into the war. Those thus gathered together form a kind of ship of fools, all working their way towards some understanding of themselves and their existence. They include a cynical Czech doctor who sells toys on a street corner, an Irishman who runs an elevator, a woman with what he describes as 'an idiot son', a figure that was to recur in his work and which, when his wife Inge Morath gave birth to a Downs syndrome child, would seem to him a strange prefiguring of a traumatic moment, though in truth more clearly an echo of his learning-disabled cousin.

The play as outlined is a strange, visionary work which, he realized, would almost certainly never find its way on to the stage, not least because he was unwilling to make the compromises he was told were necessary for success. He wanted to expose the inner workings of a capitalist society in a play that would be part comedy, part tragedy. It was, though, he knew, likely to be one more for the bottom drawer. Once again, he noted, he would spend months on a futile project, supported by a brother whose own sacrifices stood as an accusation.

As he describes it, it is a breathtakingly bad drama, and the letter in which he outlines it reveals an odd blend of personal depression alongside a continued commitment, which says a great deal about the sense of personal crisis Miller was experiencing. If anything, he had gone backwards. What had seemed his imminent success had receded. Broadway was a dream, while the companies he had relied on to produce his work had either closed down or showed little interest. He was, he mused, thinking of taking a job. What he wanted was to find a place for himself in the world, to become independent. To accept such a job was to accept failure, but to pretend he was a writer when everything he wrote was rejected was scarcely better.

He had always, he told Rowe, despised the kind of writer who settled for the odd radio piece, rewrote earlier stories, but otherwise spent his time with other failed writers complaining about their plight. The problem was that this was a good description of what his life showed signs of becoming. Now, approaching twenty-five, he contemplated the fate of the writer of twenty-seven to thirty who was forced to defer his hopes of fame to an indefinite future. How, he asked, could such people admit defeat, with a decade lost and nothing to show but a pile of unproduced manuscripts? Was this something he could contemplate? Unsurprisingly, his answer was No. It was, he went on, necessary for him to break out of his hermetic life rather than simply recycle his own limited experience in plays that nobody wanted. Even as he was admitting to his depression, however, he still took pride in what he had written, still planned future work which, he had decided, would now focus on the contemporary world, not least because it would make the writing of dialogue easier.

The job he did envisage taking would be one that might tire him but would not so exhaust him as to make writing impossible. Besides, to throw himself back into the life of working people again, it seemed to him, would generate more material as well as putting him in touch with those he most wished to address. He even approached Professor Rowe's wife, an executive in a New York advertising agency. She was horrified that he should seemingly be thinking of abandoning his ambitions to be a writer, or at least compromising what she had assumed to be his full-hearted commitment.

The problem was that in retreating into his basement study in the Miller family home he had cut himself off from precisely those who he felt might energize his work – the figure in *The Man Who Had All the Luck* who perfects skills in his basement that paradoxically disqualify him from his chosen career perhaps had a personal relevance. He needed, he said, to move out into life again. Clement Greenberg once made the same point about the Jewish writer who 'suffers from the un-availability of a sufficient variety of observed experience. He is forced to write,' he suggested, 'the way the pelican feeds its young, striking his own breast to draw the blood of his theme.'[24]

On the other hand, Miller continued in his letter to Professor Rowe, he was not a man of action, admitting that even as a child he had never been tempted to fight. There were, anyway, few objectives that required force to attain. The writer's function, or at least his own inclination, was to become coldly objective. But here, too, he suspected was a weakness. The problem with intellectuals, it seemed to him, lay precisely in their unwillingness to throw themselves into life, a process that he felt vital to his own work.

His immediate temptation was to travel, to see things he had not seen before. He had just received a last instalment of $150 on his Hopwood prize and a trip to Mexico seemed a possibility. After all, he had been working on the story of Montezuma and on the Eisenstein film and there were elections pending in Mexico in which revolutionary and counter-revolutionary forces (the latter led by Standard Oil) were likely to come into collision. He was looking for a subject, for something that would satisfy equally his political and aesthetic commitments.

As he acknowledged, a simple letter to his former professor had again turned out to be a letter to himself, but he needed, he said in justification, someone to listen to him. You might have thought that that person would be Mary. After all, they had just decided to marry. Following graduation, Miller and Mary had lived together, either in the run-down rooming house on 74th Street and Madison Avenue or at her apartment in a converted brownstone at 102 Pierpoint Street in a Brooklyn Heights that Auden would declare was as quiet as the country. 'At Michigan I never heard of anybody doing that,' Miller later commented, but in Brooklyn 'it was very common,' – though not so common, Mary later remarked, for them to inform their parents. Eventually, though, he 'wanted to have a regular relationship. She certainly did. She was tired of all this commuting.' Nor did radicalism and marriage seem antithetical, not least because, as he put it, 'the most conformist people, in that sense, were radicals'.[25] Two years earlier, Alfred Kazin, living in Brooklyn Heights, had married a woman he had known for only two weeks, explaining that 'we were both in a terrible rush to get away from everything we had grown up with'.[26]

There was an element of that in the marriage of Arthur Miller and Mary Slattery, which took place in August 1940. They would certainly not have been the first couple to build affection around an assumed mutuality of beliefs only to discover that shared convictions are not sufficient justification for a shared life. And to a degree they do seem to have married because they shared the same politics – then, as he has pointed out, much more of an organic part of daily life, in the way that religion had once been. Lionel Abel has remarked of the 1930s: 'In the city of New York – the choice of a party became one of the important spiritual decisions one could make. In choosing a party one often chose whom one would marry.'[27] Mary's determined and inflexible views attracted Miller and chimed with his own. He admired her strength.

In a brief unpublished sketch, written in 1985, he described a marriage, clearly his own, and a woman, equally clearly a version of his wife, a severe woman, whose honesty first attracted and then repelled, a person whose idealism and commitment were the other side of the coin to an accusatory self-abnegation. He was now Mary's cause, having also liberated her, evidence that in leaving the Church and her reactionary parents she had found other causes to serve. Speaking to me in 2001, Miller acknowledged: 'Left to myself I would not have gotten married. But I really admired Mary a lot. I loved her. I had a great feeling of companionship with her. And we got along great and she was really anxious to get settled down so I thought, well, it's probably a good idea. I didn't want to lose her but I didn't terribly want to get married. Marriage, to me, didn't mean all that much, anyway. But I didn't want to lose her.'

Somehow these phrases – 'admired her', had a 'feeling of companionship with her', 'got along great' – have something of a dying fall and, together with his suggestion that the marriage was partly inspired by Mary's irritation at commuting, seem to modify his declaration of love for her. Though the comments were made nearly half a century after the marriage had ended, they nonetheless hint at a reluctance that goes some way towards explaining the tension that would soon invade their relationship. He had seized on Marxism as a response to the general social and political drift of the time. Yet, sitting on a porch in Ohio on the evening of his marriage he would suspect that he had himself merely drifted there rather than making a willed decision or submitting to a genuine passion.

That August, he and Mary set out for Ohio, and marriage. It had been a scorching summer, and this was the hottest week. The couple travelled to Cleveland in a train full of soldiers. The journey was constantly disrupted. They spent the night stopping and starting, for no apparent reason. The carriage was full of cigarette smoke. He wore uncomfortable new shoes. She slept through the night, her blue cotton dress hardly disturbed. He was wearing his only suit. The day before he had deposited a hundred dollars in the bank but the tickets had already eaten into that. In an unpublished story, 'Ohio Marriage' (written in 1972), he has the tall and angular twenty-four-year-old Jew, who is a patent portrait of himself, admit that he is not entirely convinced that the marriage is a good thing. The protagonist, far from wanting to be married to Catherine May Muldoon (read Mary Grace Slattery), is in fact sure that he does not, but she, for her part, sees it as a logical consequence of the fact that they have lived together since leaving college. What marriage offered Miller was a secure base from which to operate as a writer, though with only a hundred dollars in the bank it was not without its problems. For the moment, though, the pros and cons of marriage seem evenly balanced, a somewhat stunning revelation of his state of mind on the eve of his wedding. Interestingly, another reason he offers for the marriage is that it will keep him out of uniform a little longer, should America enter the war. Nonetheless, the protagonist of the story resented having to travel, expensively, to Ohio to undergo a ceremony in which neither of them believed.

An earlier version of the same story, 'The Dispensation', also unpublished, evidences the same equivocation with regard to marriage when the protagonist confesses to his guilt at feeling nothing when he kisses the woman he is about to marry – aware, indeed, of his lack of feelings beyond a sense that she is necessary for his work.

The young couple were met at the station by Mary's parents, her mother, heavy-hipped, in a green summer dress and 'hospital-like' white shoes. She wore silver-rimmed glasses and was crying, though quite why we are not told. Her father, bald and sweating, wore a short-sleeved striped shirt. They walked back to the three-year-old green Studebaker sedan, parked two blocks away, Mr Slattery insisting on carrying the heavy cases. The family home was at 17320 Fries Avenue, in Lakewood, six miles south of Cleveland.

Miller wrote to Rowe from Ohio, but listing his New York address – 62 Montague Street, a Queen Anne building divided into what were known as 'French flats'. In the first sentence he noted that he was enclosing the script of, presumably, *The Golden Years* which he had been promising for some time. In the next, he explained that he was about to marry. In fact, following delays that had nearly prevented the ceremony taking place at all, he wrote the letter in a stationery store just before the service. Despite the imminent marriage, however, he devotes most of the note to an account of the fate of his plays. The Playwright' Company, he reports, is to stage his play in the fall. He had also just received an advance for an as yet unwritten play and was off to South America the following week.

Years later he wrote an untitled, undated short story, never published, about a character called Rufus Solomon, in which he plainly revisited his marriage in an attempt to understand what had drawn him and Mary together and what eventually pushed them apart. It is a story in which the marriage is seen as less a product of love than of a momentarily shared sensibility, a natural reticence. Her reticence was a product of a natural timidity and social awk-wardness, his of his fierce commitment to his work which necessitated with-drawal from everything but a young woman with whom, at first, he felt he could share his dreams. In the story the protagonist had spent most of his wedding morning and what he describes as a good part of the night working. It seems that the same was true of Miller.

Cleveland, in 1940, was one of the most anti-Semitic cities in America.[28]

Mary's maternal grandparents, originally from Alsace, had travelled there by wagon from New York State. Rejecting a prime position by the river (situated in what would later be the centre of Cleveland), they settled on land that recalled the fields of Alsace but that turned out to be a great deal harder to work. By 1940 all six daughters had left, and the family now rented the land they had once owned.

The marriage was not welcomed by either family. When Miller's mother told her father of it he threw an alarm clock at her. His grandson, after all, was betraying the faith, marrying out. A decade later, still only 6 per cent of Jews married non-Jews. The two families shared almost nothing except their profound doubts about the marriage and a hostility towards trade unions. Mr Slattery, a retired boilermaker, had, in Miller's words, 'fiddled around at the edges of a German-American anti-Semitic organization in Cleveland whose meetings he liked to attend'.[29] In 'Ohio Marriage' he points out that, being Irish, he would have had to go out of his way to join it. The only other point of contact between the families was that both were against the war. Mary's parents had evidently assumed, that 'as a Jew he would be interventionist'. Their points of agreement, however, left him disturbed, given what seemed to be their instinctive anti-Semitism.

Miller regarded Mr Slattery as bigoted and stupid and Mrs Slattery as compliant, though humane, a portrait Mary would later reject as unjust. It was, though, he later suggested, their initial resistance, and the fight he had to put up to ensure that the marriage went ahead, that brought Mary and himself more completely together. Indeed, in his autobiography he hints at doubts about the marriage which were overcome precisely because of their sense that they were mutually embattled.

Miller's Jewish education had been largely at the prompting of his grandfather, his own parents not being particularly religious, so that he was hardly turning his back on a living faith. Joan, six years younger than Arthur and nine years younger than Kermit, did not go to a Hebrew school, and when she encountered anti-Semitism found her mother entirely pragmatic on religious matters:

When I wanted a part-time job to pay for piano lessons, they used to ask what your religion was. You had to put it on the application. And I said to my mother, 'When I put that down they just seem not to be interested.' She said, 'Well, you don't put it down.' I said, 'Well, what am I?' She said, 'You are a universalist', something dumb like that. I put it down and immediately got a job. She said, 'See, you have got to pay attention to what I tell you.' She was wily ... But in that way we had to protect ourselves. It would have been terrible if she [had been] religious, really religious, or if I [had been] brought up to be that way, but I was not. I would go to the temple on the high holidays, because that is where everybody went. It was just not part of my upbringing. I think my brothers were a little bit more aware because they had to go to evening school to learn to prepare for their bar mitzvahs.[30]

But, religious or not, for Miller to visit the Slattery home was like entering alien territory. This was heartland conservative America and while his own Jewish faith had been laid aside, the statue of Christ crucified (by the Jews, of course) in the Slattery living room was a reminder of something more than separate traditions. Ironically, though, it was precisely such evidences of tribalism which suggested that beneath the surface the two families perhaps shared more than they appeared to. This was, after all, neither a Jewish nor a Catholic country. Until John F. Kennedy was elected, the idea of a Catholic president seemed as unlikely as a Jewish one. Both groups were outside the White Anglo-Saxon Protestant imperium even while laying claim to national myths of inclusion and endeavour. Both were accused of loyalties that lay outside the country and both, perhaps, therefore declared their loyalty with greater vehemence.

Thus, even while Miller felt increasingly irritated at the processes he was required to go through to appease people whose views he rejected and even despised, he nonetheless recognized a level on which there was an affinity that neither side would willingly concede. Even so, Mary was acutely aware that in marrying a Jew she was asking a lot of her parents. As a result she held out for a Catholic marriage, though one which, in a spirit of compromise, was not actually to take place inside a Catholic church. As it happened, it was nearly not to take place at all. Not only were they forced to collude in the usual lies then required by the Church, as couples swore to raise their children as Catholics and abstain from birth control, having no intention of doing so, they were also told by the youthful priest that such marriages usually failed. It was a gratuitous remark and served to reinforce them in their sense of detachment from the process they were having to go through.

Miller, then, was less than impressed with the new family into which he was being inducted, with Mr Slattery whose yellowed dentures forced his lower cheeks out,[31] and Mrs Slattery, who explained to him that it was necessary to secure special permission for her daughter to marry a Jew. A dispensation would be required from the papal delegate, and he was unreachable – occupied that day, as he was, on a golf course.

For her part, Mary was in a seemingly permanent state of apology – for her family, with their right-wing views, and for the charade they were about to go through. The news that the Catholic Church had now thought of a new way of obstructing them was a final irritant. The required dispensation, Miller learned, delayed because the priest had filled it in incorrectly, was not likely to come through in time for the ceremony, scheduled for Friday. The Slattery family seemed to take this as an unchallengeable decision. This meant that he would have to prolong his stay, which was costing him six dollars a day since he was spending each sweltering night in a nearby boarding house rather than in the Slattery home. As Miller comments indignantly in 'The Dispensation', apparently he had no right to sleep under the same roof as his bride-to-be despite the fact that he had been living with her for two years. His hundred dollars, in fact now eighty-two, would be leeching away to no purpose.

The irony was that the Slatterys seemed unaware that he was unemployed. In 'The Dispensation' he says that they would have found this inconceivable, given the fact that he was Jewish and hence would have been presumed, by them, to be adept at money matters. There is obviously a deal of bitterness in the remark and it serves to underscore the gulf between him and the family into which he was marrying.

Mary sat, drinking coffee and smoking Chesterfields, waiting for him to make a decision. Then, as he has explained, 'something snapped'. Miller announced that he could not possibly wait until Monday, to his surprise finding himself supported by a father-in-law himself about to lose his \$200 deposit for the reception. The next day he and Mary visited the Monsignor. They were turned away. In 'Ohio Marriage' he remarks that it was the Jew in him that responded not only to what seemed to be a slight but to the sense of an authority somewhere exerting its rights over his life. Suddenly, the compromise to which he had agreed seemed a bargain struck with the very people at whose hands the Jews had historically suffered. Personal irritation gave way to indignation and alarm.

Attempts to hurry things along seemed to be failing when, to everyone's astonishment, including his own, Miller, in a state of anger, telephoned the Monsignor:

> I felt an uproar rising in me, an anger fed in part by the long hot train ride from New York, the tasteless unseasoned food in this house, the idiocy of sleeping in a hot furnished room, the appalling mood of unrelieved blame that emanated from my crucified kinsman hanging on the wall, the repression of every human instinct in these people, my insecurity about my unknown future as a writer, the fall of France to the Nazis just weeks before, and guilt about marrying without my family present – for they had made no mention of wanting to come, and the expense of it all was beyond my means anyway. Anger created a new reality here, the reality of Mary, whom I felt myself falling in love with in a way I had not when she had seemed so strong and resolute a girl rather than the foundering and vulnerable young woman she was now.[32]

He would, he informed the Monsignor's office by telephone, be marrying the next day whether the dispensation arrived or not. In 'The Dispensation' he offers an account of the conversation in which he countered the peremptory decision of the Church with the announcement that if the dispensation was not forthcoming they would simply secure a licence and marry at City Hall. When he tried to replace the receiver, the protagonist (plainly Miller) missed the hook, his hands shaking, but, to general surprise, the dispensation was immediately forthcoming and the marriage took place.

What is interesting about his account is not only the complex of insecurities that he recalls but most strikingly, surely, the idea that only under this pressure had he really fallen in love with, or, more precisely, 'felt' himself falling in love with, the woman he was about to marry. Even then, this fact comes at the end of a list in which the fall of France takes priority. Recalling these events nearly fifty years after they took place, he seems to slide over the most significant truth. In 'The Dispensation' he observes that after his battle with the Church he was marrying not merely out of passion but out of a desire to rescue his wife-to-be from her passivity. Significantly, the word 'merely', written in ink, was added later.

It is true that the world was changing, and that in the depths of Ohio everyone seemed in thrall to outmoded dogmas in which neither he nor Mary believed. Nonetheless, the marriage was surely the central focus of the moment, even if his own family was to be absent. He suggests that they showed no desire to attend, but according to Joan, she, at least, knew nothing of the wedding until it was over. In 'Ohio Wedding' he admits that he had done nothing to facilitate his parents witnessing the wedding, but Joan, who never met any of Mary's family, later explained that 'in those days you just didn't pick up and travel to see people, anyway'. Mary, meanwhile, she regarded as 'very smart and cool', though, coming from a family that, Arthur aside, were effusive, she found her 'removed'.

Many years later Mary took exception to the portrait her former husband drew of her parents and the wedding in his autobiography. They were, she recalled, kind to him while he had not even got the details of the event right. The wedding reception did not take place at the family farm in the country, as he suggests in *Timebends*, while he never had the conversation with her grandmother that he describes there with such touching detail. This, she insisted, was invented, though she herself was also speaking some fifty years after the event. She was right about the reception. Miller is confusing it with the grandmother's eighty-sixth birthday party, celebrated shortly after he and Mary arrived. The conversation, though, does seem to have taken place. Certainly it enters his unpublished fiction as well as his autobiography, and Mary had not been present.

The details of the Ohio marriage of 5 August 1940 were later retrieved and duly noted in 1951, when the FBI was gathering data. It recorded Mary's age – twenty-five – and her Ohio address. She was listed as a stenographer and the daughter of Matthew and Julia Slattery. The file even includes the name of the presiding priest – Clarence Padva.

After the near-debacle in Cleveland, the young couple returned to New York, broke. But Miller had glimpsed another America, one that shared his own isolationism though for very different reasons. He continued to see the war in Europe as merely a continuation of an imperialist battle for territory and power; they, he suspected, saw it as a conflict in which the forces of international Jewry were trying to enmesh the country. The result was a deal of confusion in Miller's own mind, though it served to reinforce his desire to write for something more than New York intellectuals.

'The end of all this inner turmoil,' he later wrote, 'was that it reinforced the weld between my personal ambition as a playwright and my hopes for the salvation of the Republic. More, it deepened the presumption that should I ever win an audience it would have to be made up of all the people, not merely the educated or sophisticated, since it was this mass that contained the oceanic power to smash everything, including myself, or to create much good.'[33] In 1940, newly married, he still believed this was possible and that the theatre would be a mechanism for such a transformation.

He was not the only one in the family drawn to Marxism. Years later, in 1999, and much to his surprise, his brother Kermit admitted to having been a card-carrying communist in the 1930s, a fact equally unknown to HUAC for which this detail might have been of considerable interest. As Kermit remarked, 'Today, you talk about the Communist Party, it sounds like some-body with a flag; it was a point of view and lots of people were involved in that kind of thing.' Bizarrely, he was converted to communism by a group of rich but radical dentists, who later persuaded him of the necessity for winning the war against fascism by signing up for military service. He signed up. They stayed at home. Fifty years later it still rankled with his wife Frances.

Kermit and Frances (maiden name Resnick) met at Lake George in the Adirondacks in 1943 and married two years later. She was as radical as her new husband. She was from a working class background. Her mother came from Odessa while her father, educated in Russian schools, had been a Bolshevik. They were intellectuals who settled in Newark and Port Elizabeth, New Jersey, living in a tenement rather than a family home. The Millers came from another world. As Frances explained, she 'had never met a family like this. The families that I knew, my relatives, I guess, were all working-class except one aunt. This was a new experience for me . . . my father was a radical and I was a radical . . . everybody in Brooklyn was a radical.'[34] Her father, indeed, was a member of a group that met on 14th Street and had been asked by federal authorities to spy on the anarchists next door, as they, doubtless had been asked to spy on them. Later, a young Arthur Miller would be drawn to Frances's parents, providing, as they did, a model of Marxist commitment.

Frances, too, had signed the Oxford Pledge. She regarded the Millers as inherently middle class and well-to-do, despite their straitened circumstances. They, after all, ate store-bought cake while her own family ate no cake at all. Kermit, by that stage, also had a car, and a new one at that. It was a $600 Plymouth. To her, her putative mother-in-law was typically bourgeois and not at all keen on her son marrying a poor girl: 'She was always interested in money, looks, and conventional things.' A Catholic had been bad enough, and she was not keen on Mary, though always too polite to show it – but now a working-class girl!

Augusta Miller, though, had another reason for not favouring the marriage. Frances was already married. At the age of seventeen she had secretly married an Italian-American called Sal, son of a Mafia don. His family owned a bakery, lived in a cold-water flat but drove a Cadillac. In 1939 he went to Italy to study medicine, and perhaps something more: 'They used to carry money to the priests. They used to change money. A lot of things went on during the Depression.'

Kermit and Frances married on his return from the war, following a Mexican divorce. But New York did not recognize such divorces. According to Frances, Augusta was 'very polite about it ... I don't think she ever confronted Mary, either, but she didn't approve of Mary. She never confronted me, but she didn't approve of me ... Nobody was good enough for her boys.'

Mary got on reasonably well with her new in-laws, though Miller acknowledged that it must have been somewhat difficult since his mother 'didn't get on too well with most women ... There was a certain competitive streak in her.' She did, grudgingly, respect Mary as a graduate, and later as a good mother, but never quite reconciled herself to her. Fifty years on, in a conversation which included Miller, Frances recalled, too, her conviction, on joining the family, that her brother-in-law would be a success: 'Coming in from the outside you could see one thing about Arthur. We never thought he would be unsuccessful, never.' She also recalled the pleasure that Augusta had taken in his achievements, confessing to her own embarrassment when she stopped at a bookstore 'and loudly said, "Do you have my son's book?"' Of Isidore she said, 'Your father was very proud of you when you started to make money. They would count the box office.' The implied rebuke is hard to miss. This was a family in which success was a primary value.

In 1940, though, Miller was a long way from being successful. He had a wife but virtually no income. They were, his wife later recalled, married without a dime. His confidence had been dented in the two years since leaving Michigan. He needed, he felt, to find a new subject, to look beyond his family and beyond his own experiences, not least because he felt the need to write a play that engaged the new realities of America in time of war.

This was the conviction behind the decision to abandon Mary and ship on board a freighter, researching a new project that would address the present war in a more direct way than *The Golden Years*. It was impossible to sign on as a sailor because of union restrictions, so he travelled, for fifty dollars, as a passenger. Mary came to see him off at the Hoboken Pier on the SS *Copa Copa*, a Waterman Line freighter scheduled to dock at various ports on the Gulf of Mexico. In one sense perhaps this curious action (even he confessed that it was 'somewhat odd') was less significant than it appears, in that the couple had already been living together. Also, the trip had been arranged some time earlier and Mary later admitted that she had been too busy to go along. He, however, was clear. He needed to go alone. It was as if he were making a statement of intent at the beginning of the marriage and, oddly perhaps, he later remarked that 'I loved her more in the leaving than if I had hung around merely dreaming of the sea.'[35] He was going off to research a possible play or novel, and that simply took primacy. After all, having just sold a radio play, a political satire called *The Pussycat and the Expert Plumber Who Was a Man*, to the Columbia Workshop, he had hopes that his luck was about to change.

In his autobiography he explains his choice to take a trip immediately after his marriage as an expression of his sense of the seemingly infinite possibilities available to his generation, for which the stability of marriage was balanced by a determination to hold on to a sense of freedom. As he later observed, 'This early parting, like our marriage – and perhaps most marriages in our time – was a refusal to surrender the infinitude of options that we at least imagined we had. I would not yet have believed that our characters leave us far fewer choices than we like to concede.'[36] The fact was that if he was attracted to an ordered life, as represented by marriage, he also experienced what he called 'a lust for experience'. He felt that artistically he had been living at second hand, that too much of his knowledge came from books. Hence this trip down the coast to New Orleans and beyond.

In the unpublished and undated story in which he later tried to recapture this moment, and the failed marriage that followed, the central character Rufus Solomon, within a week of marriage embarks on a five-week voyage to Mexico in order to undertake research, feeling that he had given his wife what she wanted in marrying her and that now he had to resume his planned career as a writer. On board ship he writes every day, giving no thought to the oddity of a honeymoon that separated husband and wife in this way. It is a story in which he accuses himself, in retrospect, of a disabling self-concern, but it is also a story in which Solomon (clearly an alter ego of Miller) confesses that he loves his wife more when separated from her, that in some way she represents little more than a necessary adjunct to his career, the stability that seems a precondition for his work.

The ship, a run-down merchantman, travelled south towards the Gulf in a heat that made the deck almost unbearable. It was under the command of a captain hated by everyone on board, but Miller made friends with a man on whom he was to base both the play that came out of this trip – *The Half-Bridge* – and an unpublished novel – *The Bangkok Star*. He was a handsome Irishman, Mark Donegal, with an infectious sense of humour, who had served in the Air Force in the 1930s, only to be discharged because of his drinking. He had once flown an Airforce plane under the Brooklyn Bridge, which can only have hastened his departure. He served as a steward until he upset a bowl of soup over the Captain (who himself ate nothing but breakfast cereals three times a day) and ended up in the engineering room.

In New Orleans, Miller joined Mark on a tour of the city that took in the jazz joints of Bourbon Street. They ended up in a brothel a block long, which, bizarrely, required its customers to sign their name in a ledger on arrival. The first thing that Miller's new companion did was to check the names to see if any of his friends were there and then disappear to find them. Left alone, Miller wandered around until he came upon the surreal sight of a wrecked room, its wall half collapsed, in whose ruins sat a comatose man with a bottle of whisky and a woman wiping his face with a wash cloth. He later recorded the scene in an unpublished note.

Neither the play nor the novel that emerged from this trip came to anything. The play remained unproduced and the novel unfinished, but *The Bangkok Star* is a remarkable book and not only because of its subject. In 1945 Miller would publish *Focus*, one of the first novels about anti-Semitism in America. *The Bangkok Star* is also about racism and is as direct a denunciation of it as is to be found in the work of any white American author outside of Faulkner or James T. Farrell (in his *Studs Lonigan* trilogy). Had it been published, it would have caused a sensation, not least in the middle of a war in which segregation was still a fact of life in the military as it was in society at large.

Miller had been sensitized to the issue in Flint, when he discovered the racism of the auto workers battling for their union rights, as he also would be on his visits to North and South Carolina for the Library of Congress in 1941, and again when he researched material for *The Story of GI Joe*, research that took him into army camps across America. In these instances, though, racism was seen as a minor irony; in *The Bangkok Star* it is at the centre of his concern. As he explained to me in an interview in 2002:

> I was brought up in Harlem for the first twelve or thirteen years of my life and my school had a lot of black kids in it, although most of them didn't stay.

They just disappeared. I can't say I was ever a friend of theirs because they hung together, but they were always to me figures of great anguish. I always felt badly about them. I had a very instantaneous feeling of identification with them. I felt close to them. We lived on 110th Street. By the time you got to 116th Street there were a certain number of black families and I used to ride my bike through there a lot and they were always very nice to me. The ones who were not were the Italian kids, who were always looking for a fight. The blacks were absolutely the opposite. I was writing out of my own experience. I had no idea what was going on in the literary world. I didn't know there was such a thing.

The first section of the book is narrated by a writer and begins as a portrait of the ship's captain, plainly modelled directly on the man he came to know on the *Copa Copa*. Miller then seems to have changed his mind and the narrator becomes Mark Donegal, an experienced sailor like his real counterpart, who witnesses events on the ship as it sails out of New York and travels south first to Florida and then South America. At the last minute two Negroes (then the preferred term), sent by the National Maritime Union, join what is largely a Southern crew, drawn from Alabama rednecks. They are, in seamen's jargon, 'sailing southern', sailing with 'boll weevil émigrés'. Throughout the voyage there is a tension between the Captain and the crew over conditions on board. More central, though, is the question of the fate of the Negroes.

The men refuse to allow them in their quarters and resent their presence. It is partly instinctive racism, and partly the product of a dispute between the bosun and an ignorant chief mate, hostile to the union (which, as Miller knew, was racially integrated and had a black General Secretary, a Jamaican immigrant called Ferdinand Smith who was a member of the Communist Party and would later be deported). Even the bosun, however, believes that the union is wrong in this instance, that justice for the working man is one thing but working with 'niggers' is another. His decision to protect them has less to do with radical principles, which, his faith in the union aside, he seems to lack, than with his battle with the mate, who rejects the idea of sleeping in the same bunk as 'fuckin' niggas'.

For Miller, there is plainly a connection between these domestic bigots and a distant war, but this is a minor theme, as is the invocation of the 'clean' union that has won the seamen rights even while saddling them with black shipmates. There is no doubt what the novel is about.

In struggling to account for his own feelings, but also to explain his understanding of the irrational hatred of the men, the bosun recalls an incident from his youth which underlines the self-destructiveness of the prejudice he confesses to sharing. His father had owned a grocery store in Chicago and one day his daughter, the bosun's sister, disappeared. The store was in the black area and he became convinced that she had been taken by 'some nigger'. Thereafter, he would allow no Negro in his store, though they represented his principal customers. Eventually she returned, married to an Italian bookie, but the bosun-to-be could not get the idea out of his mind and now whenever he sees a black face recalls the trauma.

Nonetheless, he insists of the men, and beyond them of the whole of American society, that with thirteen million Negroes in America it is necessary to accept them, and that acceptance has to begin with the working man. In part the novel seems a lament that the working class, who Miller had been taught were the agents of revolution, were in fact not only reactionaries but adrift, easily distracted by women, drink, trivial entertainments. In part it is an acknowledgement that these deracinated men are no more than the raw material for demagogues.

The Negroes who come aboard are a father and son, the former trying his best to protect his son from knowledge of American racism and his own resulting humiliation. It is a hopeless task, as they have to hide out each night in the bilges to avoid being beaten. Nor is it the fact that this is a Southern-crewed ship that explains their plight. As the fifty-seven-year-old Negro, William, explains, if you are black all ships are Southern. Now, in the face of the crew's apparent hatred, he has to confront the fact that for the first time his son will be a witness to his humiliation.

For the bosun, the battle is to stop his black crewmen being put off in Florida, to bring them back to New York. Partly, this is because he is answerable to the union but, beyond that, his own manhood has become entwined with the fate of those he struggles to protect.

Then they are beaten. William is blamed for an accident, but they stay on board, still sleeping below while working alongside the whites during the day, though those around them keep up a litany of racial abuse. When a strange bird lands on the top of the mast, the mate uses this as an excuse to work the superstitious men up into a lynch mob, suggesting that the bird is responding to the smell of the Negroes, the only solution being either to incarcerate them in the hold or kill them. In order to drive the crew to murder he tells a story of a kind for which there was then no parallel in the contemporary novel, no model that Miller could have been using. In an aria of racial abuse, the mate celebrates the cruelty of the slave owners and traders. The murder is momentarily deflected, however, by the realization that whatever story they concoct in their own defence, the union might ban them from putting to sea again. The book breaks off as they try to kill the bird instead.

The *Bangkok Star* of the title is not the name of the vessel on which they sail. (That is the *Calhoun* (John C. Calhoun having been an advocate of slavery).) It is the ironic name of the ideal ship on which William has told his son he once served, a ship on which there was no prejudice and black and white worked happily together. It is the lie that he tells, like the lie America tells itself, a utopia with no roots in the real.

The Bangkok Star, unfinished though it is, is an impressive piece of work. At times lyrical in its evocation of the sea, it is also a powerful indictment of American racism whose authenticity derives in large part from the demotic language he gives his characters. It is a novel about the struggle to live with dignity, about the power of the irrational in human relationships. It is, like Richard Wright's stories, and like his *Native Son*, inherently melodramatic, but that melodrama is a product of the subject he addresses. Nor, though he fills his ship with Southerners, is it offered as an indictment of the South alone. Miller had read and been disturbed by *Native Son*, despite the attacks launched on it by the Communist Party. He felt a profound emotional identification with Bigger Thomas and a sense of shock at what it evidently meant to be a black man in America. The contempt for Wright's book expressed by those on the left seemed to him a reflection of their desire for a committed art devoid of ambiguity and a sense of the tragic.

Miller's novel was begun shortly after his brief trip on the SS *Copa Copa* and continued into 1942 – a year, incidentally, in which his FBI file registered his membership, along with his wife's, of the American Labor Party, later declared a front for the Communist Party. The typescript runs to 151 pages. He never approached a publisher with it. Indeed, astonishingly, speaking in 2003 he had forgotten even writing it: 'I probably didn't have the confidence ... I would have deferred to Richard Wright and Countee Cullen [the black American poet] who certainly knew [the racial situation] a lot better than I did. But it always made me uncomfortable, the thought of those people.'

This was not his only comment on American racism. In an undated and unpublished short story called 'Dedication', based on an incident referred to in *Situation Normal*, his first published book, he describes an attempt to dedicate the parade ground of a military base in the South to the first man from that base to be killed in war. The idea is that the parents are to be located and made the guests of honour at the dedication ceremony. By chance the man's last name is that of the commanding officer and of a nearby plantation. The problem is that the man turns out to have been black and hence, by implication, a relative, by way of slavery. The ceremony has to go ahead but the officer wants nothing to do with the parents of the dead man. Race was plainly on Miller's mind.

For the moment, with both his plays and stories rejected and his novel incomplete, his best hope seemed to lie with radio plays; and though he came to despise them, thinking of them as journeymen pieces that he could run off in a few days, some had a touch of originality. In one he even played the part of a drunk. On 24 September 1940, meanwhile, he wrote to Kenneth Rowe, having just delivered a new play to his agent. The play (probably the first act of *The Half-Bridge)* was never produced.

That month, CBS transmitted one of his plays as part of the Columbia Workshop and he sent them the first part of *The Half-Bridge* – featuring Mark Donegal, the Gestapo, a homosexual ship's captain once a U-boat commander, émigrés, a wronged woman, a kidnapped Jew, a plot to discover hidden treasure in South America and another to sink Allied shipping. It was, in other words, a brantub of plots and bizarre characters, and it is hardly surprising that neither then nor later did he find any takers for what he had somehow convinced himself was a marketable product.

Mark Donegal also features in a fragment of what was to be another novel, *Tenth Man*, begun in 1943, which never got beyond the first few pages of the first chapter, called 'A Word on the Man'. The story is set ten days after the burning of the *Normandie*, the luxury liner of the 1930s that waited out the first two years of the war at a pier in the North River, and which caught fire in February 1942 as it was being converted into a warship. The narrator is shocked by the scene and finds himself talking to a drunken seaman, a handsome young Irishman with red hair and a scar, Donegal.

They both assume the ship to be the victim of arson and retreat to a bar where Donegal begins to spin the stories that will be the basis of the novel. Miller had himself witnessed the burning of the *Normandie* and at the time he wrote this piece it was widely believed to be a victim of sabotage. In fact it burned as the result of an accidental fire caused by those carrying out the conversion. The novel fragment breaks off before the first of the stories has begun. The *Normandie*, incidentally, had another claim to fame. It took the first Abraham Lincoln Brigade volunteers to the Spanish Civil War.

Brooklyn, then as now, was a racially mixed world. Through his back window Miller could watch Moslems holding services in a backyard which they had turned into a Moorish garden, planted with curving lines of white stones. Twenty or thirty of them would eat at a long table, served by women in purple and rose robes. While living on Schermerhorn Street he wrote another story, never published, which once again picked up the question of race, though this time more indirectly. [Miller lived at a number of Brooklyn addresses, all within a few blocks of one another].

'The Test For It' tells the somewhat implausible story of a young black man, who works in the Brooklyn Navy Yard and who persuades a friend to attempt to seduce his girlfriend, as a test of her loyalty. In fact he is afraid of the logic of his relationship – afraid, in particular, of marriage and children because he fears that the end of the war will see a return of unemployment. He keeps an atlas to hand as a reminder that in South America the colour of his skin would be no barrier. Happily for him his girl sees through the ploy and understands his fears. The story lacks conviction but underscores the degree to which the racial problem remained at the centre of Miller's concern. He was still having no more luck with fiction, though, than with plays.

In April 1940, Miller spent some time at the Playwrights' Dramatic Workshop at the New School, open to students with previous training and presided over by John Gassner and Theresa Helburn, who with Lawrence Langner was head of the Theatre Guild. It was here that he sat across from Tennessee Williams, who had a scholarship and was staying at the YMCA on 63rd Street. Williams was trying to interest Gassner in his *Battle of Angels* as Miller was trying to place his own work. There is a photograph of the two men at the seminar, both wearing a suit and tie, with Williams assiduously taking notes and Miller smoking a pipe. Again, nothing came of this.

Miller and his wife were living frugally at Schermerhorn Street, occupying a whole floor in a newly remodelled building and paying $35 a month (out of Mary's income of $100 a month), as he struggled to complete the novels and plays he hoped would win him recognition. It would be some time before his income would support them both. In his first year writing radio scripts, he earned $300. In his second, he pushed that up to $1,200, at last matching his wife's income. In the meantime, they had relied on her secretarial job.

Despite the collapse of the Federal Theatre, however, he did still qualify for employment under the WPA and was contacted via Kenneth Rowe in Michigan who had received a telegram from Jerry Wiesner: HAVE ART MILLER CONTACT CHARLES HARREL LIBRARY OF CONGRESS WASH-INGTON DC IF HE IS INTERESTED IN WRITERS JOB WITH RADIO PROJECT SALARY 3200 DOLLARS PER ANNUM IN LIBRARY OF CONGRESS.

Writing to Kenneth Rowe in November 1940, Miller admitted that the telegram had caught him off guard because it came at a moment when he thought his career might be about to take off. He was, he explained, waiting by the telephone for his agent to call with a reaction to the third act of *The Half-Bridge*, which he considered the best in the play. He thought it a good sign that they had sent him an unsolicited $4 shirt from Saks Fifth Avenue. He had, meanwhile, despaired of the Theatre Guild, which had recently dropped their option on Norman Rosten's next play and whose contracts demanded 15 per cent of the take of any productions of plays they had previously produced. He was in high hopes, though, for *The Half-Bridge*.

Paul Muni was being contacted with a view to playing the principal role, with Morris Carnovsky playing the second male lead. Harold Clurman, it was hoped, would direct. All this shortly after sending his agent the third act and before any revisions. No call came from his agent. In the end, the play was never produced.

In the circumstances, he decided to accept work offered by the Library of Congress, though not that offered to him by Wiesner. Instead, he secured a commission with the Library of Congress Folklore Division which wanted someone to travel in the South collecting recordings, interviews with ordinary people. The commission, supposedly for four months, in the end lasted only some three weeks, and would be delayed until the autumn of 1941.

Then in November 1940, Miller received his draft number, 5163 – his friend Norman Rosten drew 5683 – but there was no immediate likelihood of military service. Pearl Harbor still lay just over a year away. As to his domestic life, he was, he assured Rowe, happy. Mary was now secretary to the head of the medical books department at Harper Brothers, having left Harcourt Brace. She was currently, he explained, typing a book on brucellosis and was the keel to an otherwise wayward ship. Within seven years, however, she would come to resent performing the role of keel and accuse him of giving her nothing, obsessed as he was with his career. If she was happy at first, in time she came to feel that she was invisible, keeping the family home going for a man who worked night and day. A fellow graduate, she found herself doing work that could never satisfy her.

He worked in a makeshift workroom where, behind a closed door, he dedicated himself to his various projects while Mary did little other than wait for him to emerge. After a time, she began to resent his withdrawal, and when success arrived she came to fear it as it bred a different kind of discontent and opened up possibilities for him but not for her. Meanwhile, she was increasingly intolerant of his sometimes disreputable friends. A relationship that began with some passion, if an uncertain love, would end up with scarcely any contact. 'We were not on the same track. We were on parallel tracks, waving at each other.'[37]

In 1941, the Millers moved to an old apartment at 62 Montague Street on Brooklyn Heights. From here he could walk down a long, steep, cobbled slope until, to the right, Brooklyn Bridge soared upwards across the East River, its cables singing in the wind, as it seemed to the poet Hart Crane, like a harp. It was, in part at least, unchanged since the nineteenth century. He walked and cycled across it as he had once travelled on a trolley that would take you in both directions for the same nickel, being swung round by the driver at either end. As a young man his father had hired a horse and gig to drive from the Lower East Side across the bridge to Coney Island and back to the stable on Rivington Street.

It was a bridge on which, in 1950, he would come close to death when, driving across it from the Manhattan side at one in the morning, amidst a river fog, he suddenly found himself sliding towards a parked car. The bridge was only one and a half car widths wide and paved with wooden blocks, slick with oil and water. Seeing the rear lights of another car, he applied the brakes, only to continue at the same speed down the Brooklyn side of the bridge. He was driving the green Studebaker convertible to which he had treated himself after the success of *Death of a Salesman*. Ahead of him was not only the parked car but people standing on the roadway behind it.

He tried to press his wheels against a containing girder, hoping it would slow him down as, years later, in rural Connecticut, he would drive down roads covered with sheet ice, slowing himself by nudging into the snow banks pushed to the side by snowploughs. This time, though, he snagged a break in the guard rail and was spun around, finding himself facing back to Manhattan, but stationary. He had killed neither himself nor those standing in the road. At that moment the people climbed back into their car and left him to watch as the headlights of another car came into view, a car which in turn was about to start a slow slide towards him.

Miller ducked down on to the floor on the passenger side and prepared for the impact, rather than climb out and risk being pitched into the East River like an ice-hockey puck. The collision duly occurred. His car had been hit by a Ford. The impact was such that both its front wheels turned from the vertical to the horizontal. Neither he nor the driver of the Ford had been injured, but the other driver insisted that Miller had been crossing the bridge in the wrong direction, and continued to so insist when, after half an hour driving round the neighbourhood in the still-functioning Studebaker, they finally located a policeman to whom, by law, they had to report the accident. It is scarcely surprising that Miller would regard the Brooklyn Bridge as having played a significant role in his life.

It was also on this bridge, after all, just along from where Hart Crane used to cruise for sexual partners, that in the early 1950s he would see messages scrawled in chalk asking, 'Dove Pete Panto?' ('Where is Pete Panto?') which would set him inquiring along the Brooklyn waterfront, researching the life of a longshoreman killed by the corrupt unions whose power he was challenging. The messages must have been there for some time, since Panto had been murdered in 1939. Miller later met Albert Anastasia who had ordered the hit. Later still, the story would prompt a film script that would take him to Hollywood and his encounter with Marilyn Monroe. From this, too, would come a play about an Italian-American called Eddie Carbone, who would betray two men out of an illicit love for his niece: *A View from the Bridge*.

If things did not seem to be going as well as he had hoped there was always enough encouragement to maintain his momentum. One project came to nothing but another was always in development. Indeed he was writing and rewriting plays and short stories, talking to his agent, receiving sufficient feedback from admired directors to feel that he must surely see some return for hours spent at his desk. In January 1941 he applied for but did not receive a Rockefeller Fellowship, but on 4 May he received an encouraging letter from Paul Muni, who in 1949 would play the role of Willy Loman in the

London production of *Death of a Salesman*. Muni wrote from the Château Elysée in Hollywood:

> Please believe that I did not neglect reading your play also that I enjoyed reading it. My reasons for not writing are numerous. I had too much to say about it and could not quite get myself to explaining all in a letter ... I would appreciate the opportunity to read your other play as I sincerely feel anything written by you is worth reading. As also good plays are so scarce. As also I am incidentally looking for a play, so you see I have a perfectly selfish reason for being interested.

On 8 October Muni wrote again: 'I am terribly sorry we could not get together on the script. I had every intention to do so upon my arrival from California ... The play left me feeling that great merit lay inherent in it yet I could not see it for myself. Perhaps at some future time we will run into one another and I may still get the opportunity of discussing the play with you.' It was a disappointment, but in meetings with other writers, Norman Rosten principal among them, he still found reason to hope.

So dedicated to his work was Miller that it comes as a surprise to discover a commitment to the international plight of the Jews of quite the range and depth of that apparent in an article entitled 'Hitler's Quarry' which appeared under the name Arthur Miller in May 1941 in a magazine called *Jewish Survey*. It detailed the suffering of Jews around the globe and advanced a Marxist solution: an uprising of the working class against occupying Nazi troops. Viewed retrospectively it would seem to throw an interesting light on a playwright otherwise so preoccupied with trying to secure a production for his plays, were it not for the fact that this was another Jewish, Marxist Arthur Miller, a New York attorney whose mail Miller continued to receive for several years. As he later told me, material in this essay was beyond anything he had been concerned with at that time. He was not unaware of the current plight of the Jews, of course, but this was a far-reaching description of presecution not only in occupied Europe but in England, America and South America.

In truth, his concerns were more immediate. He needed money. So it was that on 15 October 1941 he headed south, accompanied only by a sound engineer, on the project to be paid for by the Library of Congress. He had never been to the South before. He was hired by Joseph Liss, editor for the Library's Radio Research Project, who had previously worked for the Columbia Workshop series. The project, as Matthew Barton has pointed out, was the idea of the playwright Archibald McLeish and was funded by the Rockefeller Foundation. One of those involved, Alan Lomax, twenty-six-year-old director of the Archive of American Folksongs, was interested in using the venture for his own purposes and proposed a documentary series to be based on field recordings that would demonstrate 'a new function for radio, that of letting the people explain themselves and their lives for the entire nation.'

That summer Liss and others had travelled, with a sound truck, to talk to people around the country. It was this venture that Miller joined, though Lomax had his doubts. As he observed, Arthur Miller 'making the trip means for the project to make other sacrifices. Mr Miller is an awfully nice lad, but if his ability to handle regional materials is evidenced in the New Orleans script [he had written a script about that city] and in the Buffalo Bill script [a brief piece called *Buffalo Bill Disremembered*], I say he needs some more work before we spend $400 on him.'[38]

His job was in part to record the variety of regional accents, but what emerged was something more. He created a portrait of a Southern town on the verge of war and an oral history which threw light both on labour relations and on the racial situation in a town which half a century earlier had been the site of an explosion of racial violence. He travelled to Wilmington, North Carolina, which had once been a receiving port for the slave trade. It struck him as 'very primitive'. They were, he explained in an interview in October 2003, 'still reacting fairly violently to labour organizations and hunting down labour organizers'.

On his return in December 1941 he wrote a radio script which begins with him receiving his instructions for the trip: 'Get on the Library Sound Recording Truck and go down to North Carolina. There's a boom town called Wilmington ... Ask the folks there what's going on, what they think is wrong and what's right. Talk to the people. Get records of their answers, their questions ... Get Wilmington, North Carolina, into that sound truck.'[39]

The recorder itself was a large affair designed to cut acetate records. It was housed in a green Chevy van with federal insignia on the side and the words 'United States Government'. Then, as now, these were not words to guarantee a ready welcome, certainly not in rural North Carolina. Miller recalled:

[Johnny] Langenegger [his driver and sound engineer] and I were looking for a quarry where we were told we would hear all kinds of strange accents. We went to a heavily wooded area where there was just a track and came to this enormous pit. It was probably a quarter of a mile in diameter. And down the bottom, maybe six storeys down, were these workers, mining stone. And I was wondering how we could get down to them when I turned my head and there was a truck right next to us. And from the truck was protruding a large shotgun. It was octagon-shaped. I'll never forget it. It was about two feet away from my face. And at the end of it was this infuriated man. He began railing against the Jews. I'd never laid eyes on this idiot. Johnny, who was driving the van, put it in reverse and we went backwards at about thirty miles an hour along the track. And this idiot – who was obviously boozed up – had his wife pulling on his arm so that the gun was waving all over the place. So we got out of there. But I wondered how he knew I was Jewish. Johnny, who wasn't Jewish, had the answer. We had this Library of Congress Washington DC insignia in gold on the door. They thought that everybody in Washington was Jewish. They used to call Roosevelt, Rosenveld. There was fierce anti-Semitism down there.[40]

But, as he would discover, it was not only Jews who found themselves the victims of prejudice.

Wilmington had suddenly been expanded by the arrival of workers to clear land for the new shipyard owned by the Carolina Ship Building Company. Miller interviewed everyone from policemen, cab and bus drivers to those responsible for public health and the water supply. He talked to housewives in the local wash houses and to those who were beginning the process of building the ships that were to sail to England. Were they aware of the importance of their work, he asked? What was the difference between the American way and fascism? He was in pursuit of the same idealism he had carried with him to Michigan and back, and he listened for an echo of it here as he would later when he travelled around military bases to research a film script. In both cases what he heard was simple pragmatism. People were glad of a job, any job, their women making do as prices rose and they were forced to live in trailer parks, in 95-degree heat. Fascism, in these weeks before Pearl Harbor and the German declaration of war, was no more than a foreign term for a vague sense of menace.

What emerges from his recordings is a Studs Terkel-like portrait of a town in transition. What emerges, too, is a snapshot of race relations as he talks to unemployed black workers and the descendants of plantation owners and reveals a sudden enthusiasm for those, black and white, who are staging a strike, the first since 1934.

One evening soon after he arrived in October 1941, he came on a thousand black workers filling the town square. He recorded their comments. They had, it transpired, been building the new shipyard at Cape Fear, in the swamps and white sand around Wilmington, and, now their job was finished, had been fired so that white workers could take over the new shipbuilding work. It was not a strike. They had no jobs from which to withdraw their labour. They were not even meeting in the hope of changing their situation. They were simply gathered there in a state of shock, unsure where to go. Perhaps because he was white and seemed to have some connection to the federal government, they appeared to imagine Miller might have some power to help. Calling him 'Cap'n', one asked:

Do you have any idea why they won't let a coloured man have a go at the
welding? We build it up and then they put you out. If you'd just get us a first-
class job we wouldn't be standing around . . . just as it's a good ordinary job
. . . just a common labourer. I could easily work myself up but they wouldn't
allow me the chance. Hard as we worked down there, a little while they just
turned us off. Now they are running the shipyard. I feel that we haven't been
treated right, especially the men that built it. Now we out and they won't
allow us inside the gate. The men come in and they get the jobs.[41]

By the next morning they had all disappeared. There had never, it appeared,
been an issue to be addressed. This was simply the way things were. This was
Miller's introduction to Southern racism.

After meeting the men on the square, Miller had gone to interview the
head of the shipyard:

He said, 'Well, their work is done.' And I said, 'Couldn't they have been
hired as labour in the building of the ships?' because the available white
labour wouldn't have had any experience either. They were probably illiterate.
'Oh, no the whites wouldn't work with them.' And that was the end of that.
I was astonished. I don't know why because it wasn't a hell of a lot better in
New York. The admixture of black and white. But this was such an overt act
of discrimination that it was breathtaking. It was fierce. It was total.[42]

He travelled briefly with Dr Vestal, head of North Carolina's health service.
With him he visited a talc mine, where he saw the poor conditions of those
who laboured there. Talc is manufactured from crushed stone and talc miners
suffer, effectively, from the same disease as coal miners. He jotted down the
beginnings of a poem about a woman sitting by the mineshaft with her
children at sundown. He was plainly moved.

He also visited a forging shop where they manufactured iron stoves. Here,
Miller encountered a friend, Oscar Saul, who was making a film about health
issues for the federal government. In the shop, they were shooting a row of
machines and Miller was asked by the cameraman to move a man out of
frame. He walked over to a sixty-year-old black man and said, 'Excuse me,
mister, could you just step back a little.' He observed later:

I came back to Vestal who was white with anger. He had been a very friendly
guy, but he asked me to step outside. And when we were outside he said,
'You must never address a Negro as mister.' So I said, 'What am I supposed
to call him?' and he said, 'Boy.' I was twenty-five years old and this man was
sixty! Later, I was driving with him when a report came on the radio that
Hitler had replaced the cross in some church in Germany with the swastika.
He was out of his mind! He was ready to go to war that morning. This led
me into the complications of real life! He was a sweet guy. For breakfast he

had four small bags of peanuts and two Coca-Colas. In the corner of his office were cases of Coca-Cola. He was the head of the health service of the state of North Carolina![43]

In contrast, he recalled a farmworker's wife who had brought her children to see her husband work. She had had a breakdown after three years working in a silk mill. He was struck by her beauty.

The trip south was proving an education, and certainly an affront to his sense of human decency. As he later noted in the draft of an unpublished article, before Pearl Harbor there were those in America who welcomed fascism and racism alike. One Southern woman explained something of the racial situation as she saw it:

In 1898 men had come to Wilmington who were political, exploiting the Negroes. The men of Wilmington rose up. Racial riots were quietly nipped in the bud by the men of Wilmington. Each block had a captain and the people were protected. We were told where to go, which church to go to if trouble came. My father was captain of my block. The men went to the printing press where the paper was printed that was stirring up the strife and trouble and burned it to the ground. The leading men of our town, the gentlemen with generations of aristocratic blood behind them, took the white leaders to the railroad station and bought them tickets and told them to leave and not to come back.

In fact the 1898 incident had seen the murder of nine African-Americans, the burning of virtually the only national black newspaper and the intensification of segregation. The gently spoken 'aristocratic' woman who told the story was seemingly oblivious of the truth behind her reminiscences, as, at the time, was Miller himself.

If race was one theme he pursued in his portrait of Wilmington, another was labour unrest. The Amalgamated Clothing Workers of America had called a strike against a shirt-manufacturing company. A previous strike, in 1934, had failed. Now, one hundred and fifty women, black and poor white, had been on strike for four months. The minimum wage was also the maximum wage: 30 cents an hour, $12 a week for a forty-hour week (a bus driver earned $25–30, shipyard workers $45–50). Prices had risen by 40 per cent since the strike began, a strike not only about money. As one woman put it, 'The boss man would cuss us out ... Sometime we wouldn't be on time and they would send us straight home, in the cold, rain and snow. We make a mistake and he wouldn't let us check in.'

What most struck Miller, though, was the fact that the women had composed a series of songs, some derived from spirituals, others specially created to reflect their feelings of solidarity and determination as well as to intimidate their employer. One was called 'We'll Pull Through' ('We'll pull through, yes we'll pull through/ We'll pay the price, whatever others do/ We started the union and we'll pull through'). As one of them explained, 'We were out on strike for twelve weeks and the boss seemed to fight us so hard until we got together and pulled that song [together], "We'll Pull Through", and sang it in front of the plant to show him that we were determined to stay out until we win.'

Miller recorded half a dozen of their songs. He described the circumstances:

> Upstairs is a dance hall; downstairs a beer hall with a regular modern jukebox in it. In this corner of the hallway that enters on to the wooden stairway I've listened to the songs of a few people in this neighbourhood. Upstairs the meeting goes on of the strikers in the Block Factory. Below are soldiers from the nearby encampment. And the inhabitants of this neighbourhood come and drink their beer and talk about the news of the day on the corner of 6th Street and Brunswick.[44]

Later, inspired by those North Carolina women, he recorded himself singing 'Old Man River', unaccompanied and in a clear tenor voice, as downstairs a jukebox played Glen Miller and upstairs the strikers met.

Miller returned to Washington on 5 November 1941 and wrote a memo to Lomax:

> Just to remind you, Alan … in the Negro jobless scene my aim was to keep their talk going in as spontaneous a fashion as was possible. So the dubs should be as close together as possible. In between cut pieces, of course, we don't want dead silence. Now I remember several pieces of the Negro records which were barren of voices and only the general street and outdoor noise was recorded. If those could be slipped in between the dubs, the realism of the scene could be maintained. Of course the sound of a car passing would do if the above is too difficult.[45]

The script based on his trip was completed on 11 December, but key sequences were deleted, the very sequences that had meant so much to him. America was now at war and priorities had changed. On 21 December Lomax wrote to Miller to explain that Philip Cohen (in charge of the Radio Research Project of the Library of Congress), 'for reasons which he will explain to you (considerations of National Defense Policy), decided that the strike sequence, Negro unemployment sequence and material about the gay times of defence workers would have to come out of the show. That meant cutting the show down to twenty-four minutes and I saw nothing else to do but cut it further and make a fifteen-minute programme out of it.' The programme ends with Miller remarking, 'And this is Wilmington, North Carolina. A hundred voices talking free and one voice over all the rest, the voice that will keep men free.'[46] This was not a time to acknowledge striking workers, unemployment or racism.

The programme was transmitted on 28 May 1942. Alan Lomax later wrote a report for Archibald McLeish:

> Mr Miller shows the town of Wilmington which, since the beginning of the defense program, has more than doubled its size. It is a shipbuilding town and full of contrasts between the old leisurely way of life and the new trip-hammer tension that the defense program has brought on. Mr Miller was more direct than we had been in other field efforts and simply walked up to people that he met in trailer camps, factories, and on the streets and interviewed them about what was going on in the city. From this material, we developed an interesting script about this Southern boomtown. This script was written and narrated by Mr Miller and it is up to now the most stirring program which we have completed.[47]

Though his theatre career seemed to be stillborn, a new avenue had evidently opened up, and since this little-known area of Miller's work would turn out to be so important to him in the early 1940s, it is worth considering it in some detail. Radio drama had first come to America in 1935–6. The Columbia Workshop was based on British and German models. By 1940 nearly a third of available air time went to drama (10,000 hours). The normal procedure was for networks to sell time to advertising agencies who produced shows for the sponsors. Miller's first play, *Joe, the Motorman*, earned him $100. Following this, he wrote a fifteen-minute sketch for NBC and his then current employer, the Library of Congress, the Buffalo Bill script referred to by Alan Lomax. *Buffalo Bill Disremembered* was originally a pure improvisation, transcribed for the actors who were to perform it. It was broadcast on 12 October 1941, on the eve of Miller's departure for North Carolina. Hardly an impressive piece, it is effectively a monologue in which Buffalo Bill reminisces, and among his memories are those of his father who had died fighting against slavery, a fact not much known but in line with Miller's own anti-racist sentiments. Even at the beginning of his radio career, it seems, he was happy to infiltrate his political views, sometimes into the most unpromising material.

Buffalo Bill (William Cody) lived well into the twentieth century (he died two years after Miller's birth), and at the end of the play the announcer invites anyone who has known him to write to the Library of Congress with their reminiscences. Many responded with family stories.

By degrees, Miller now found himself in demand as a radio writer, and for all his inclination to dismiss much of this work, buried among the many scripts he turned out are some with more than a touch of originality, scripts which, in comic or serious form, manage to convey the values he had carried forward from Ann Arbor and which would find expression in his later plays. One work, a light comic satire called *The Pussycat and the Expert Plumber Who Was a Man*, proposes the existence of a talking cat who secures his election as mayor by blackmailing anyone who might oppose him with information derived from a network of domestic cats who have easy access to such material. He is on the verge of election as Governor (a stepping stone to the presidency) when his cover is blown by a plumber who stumbles on his secret and is appalled by the deception and corruption. Unbribable and secure in his skills, he brings about the downfall of this feline Tammany. The moral is: 'A cat will do anything, the worst things, to fill his stomach, but a man ... will actually prefer to stay poor because of an ideal ... Because some men, some useful men, like expert plumbers, are so proud of their usefulness that they don't need the respect of their neighbors and so they aren't afraid to speak the truth.'

The cat's analysis of human nature, meanwhile, would find an echo in several subsequent plays. The one thing a man fears, the cat observes, next to death, 'is the loss of his good name. Man is evil in his own eyes ... worthless, and the only way he can find respect for himself is by getting other people to say he's a nice fellow.'[48] Like Willy Loman, in other words, he wants to be well liked.

No more than a comic time-filler, the play nonetheless contains a few seeds of what was to follow and, indeed, was presented as part of the 1997–8 Signature Theatre season dedicated to Miller's work. Speaking in 2003, Miller recalled his thrill at hearing the play live on air. 'It was,' he observed,

> a political fantasy but everything was politics in those days. But that set me off thinking that I might be able to make a living. I had no agent. Nobody knew me. I can't remember how I got it to them. I may have dropped it off at CBS for all I remember. But hearing it on the radio was thrilling. As a matter of fact I heard it at sea. I was on a freighter to the Gulf [of Mexico] and I could only get snatches of it from the ship's radio. The crew couldn't care less. Then again I had friends who were already writing for radio. Of course you have to remember that in those days hack work was regarded as essential if you were going to be a writer. Faulkner used to write mystery stories and haunted tales. Fitzgerald worked in the movies. Of course if anybody had offered me work in Hollywood then I probably would have taken it.

Miller wrote for a number of radio series but the most significant was NBC's *Cavalcade of America*. Norman Rosten also began writing for the series that same year, on a recommendation of another *Cavalcade* author, Stephen Vincent Benét, whom he had met as a result of winning a Yale Younger Poets Award. Rosten, like Miller, had been a committed leftist, in his case contributing to *Mainstream* and *Soviet Russia Today.* In 1937 he had written a poem on the Haymarket riot in Chicago, and a pageant on the lives of Lenin and other radicals for the Young Communist League. Now he wrote for a series which celebrated American heroes and which, when the war broke out, saw itself as part of the national war effort.

Miller's and Rosten's careers seemed to parallel one another, a reason both to consolidate their friendship and to foment their rivalry, a rivalry that was to continue until Rosten's death. Like Miller, Rosten had won a Hopwood Award at Michigan. Now, not only were they working for the same employer but, like Miller, Rosten declared that he would undertake war work, in his case in an aircraft factory. His plan came to nothing, while Miller worked for more than a year at the Brooklyn Navy Yard. In 1942 Rosten received a $1,000 Guggenheim Award, while the Rosten home became something of a salon. Those who attended were known as the 'Broken Wing Society'. The Millers' house never quite became the same kind of focus. Mary lacked Hedda's enthusiasm for writers.

Rosten was an engaging man. Norman Mailer observed that he was 'the most easy decent man, totally relaxed and affable. Norman's manner was one of the models of behavior for me ... He was a guy who'd treat the postman with the same dignity as a world famous author.'[49] Perhaps it was something of that charm, along with talent, that consolidated his position as one of the eleven-writer team that created *Cavalcade of America*. It was a charm, though, that Miller would come to suspect.

Radio was then what television is today – indeed, in some senses it was more important. Today, there are hundreds of channels to choose from. The audience is fragmented. Broad-casting has given way to narrow-casting. In 1941 certain radio programmes were listened to by a significant proportion of the population. It was possible to walk down a street, Miller commented, and hear the same programme coming from every house. Few were more popular than NBC's *Cavalcade*, which began broadcasting in 1935.

Cavalcade of America was a weekly series of plays, with patriotic themes, starring major figures from the New York theatre and Hollywood. Its writers included Stephen Vincent Benét, Robert Sherwood, Maxwell Anderson and Carl Sandburg. The plays were staged in front of a live audience and featured a full orchestra. Miller describes it:

> They had a forty-piece orchestra; imagine, to play those little ditties that they did between scenes they had a real symphony orchestra! Some of those guys were out of the New York Philharmonic ... and there would be, maybe, ten or fifteen seconds of music [specially composed by Ardon Cornwell] between scenes. They cooked up enough music to fake it and these guys were playing all kinds of tunes. It was wonderful. It was a hell of a show.[50]

The programmes were transmitted twice, once at eight o'clock for East Coast listeners and then again at 11.30 p.m. for the West Coast. For actors appearing on Broadway, cabs would rush them from the Rockefeller Center to the theatres. Orson Welles used an ambulance.

As Miller recalled in 2003, 'It was some production. They had big movie stars who they flew in from the West Coast. It was probably the best of the kind they had at the time. You rehearsed two days, all day in the big studio at NBC, and then they broadcast, live of course, on the evening of the third day.' In fact rehearsals began on the Tuesday, with microphone rehearsals on the Thursday. The Hollywood actors were paid up to $3,500.

The series was sponsored by DuPont ('Makers of better things for better living, through chemistry'), which maintained a Radio Division. The transmissions featured a sponsored message, lasting some three to four minutes, designed to link the company's products to war work and, if possible, to the play, though Miller's first play for the series, a potted biography of Joel Chandler Harris, made this difficult. Instead, the announcer extolled the virtues of DuPont's nylon ('fifty million brushes a year are used for washing bottles').

In his book on Second World War drama, *Words at War*, Howard Blue explains the origin of DuPont's interest in radio. After the First World War a committee had investigated DuPont, which had made $238 million profit producing gunpowder and propellent powders. It was not an image the company favoured. In response, DuPont hired the advertising agency Batten, Barton, Durstine & Osborn, who suggested that it should sponsor a radio series on American history, one that should avoid war themes and the use of black actors.

In 1940 the America First Committee, a group of isolationists, hired BBD&O to produce a series of recorded programmes opposing aid to Britain, a view shared by the writer Theodore Dreiser, who remarked: 'The English have done nothing in this war thus far except borrow money, planes, and men from the United States.'[51] With the outbreak of war, the series began to focus on contemporary events. What seems not to have changed was the company's anti-Semitism. The programme's director, Homer Fickett, confided to Miller that he had been told that they would 'rather you and Rosten not be around here'. Erik Barnouw, NBC's director of scripts, recalled that when the name of another writer, the Jewish Morton Wishengrad, came up he was told that he would not be considered 'because he's a Jew. His career would be hampered because he wouldn't be able to work on the DuPont account.'[52]

Joel Chandler Harris, Miller's first script for the series broadcast on 23 June 1941, was an account of a visit by the author of the *Uncle Remus* stories to the White House and an encounter with President Roosevelt. Later that same year, on 27 October, Claude Rains starred as John Paul Jones in *Captain Paul*, a play to celebrate Navy Day. Miller, speaking in 2003, recalled the process

behind this and other *Cavalcade* plays: 'They would call me in the morning
and say they were going to send over a book about John Paul Jones, the guy
who started the American Navy. And you had never heard of John Paul Jones
and you read the book fast on Monday morning. On Tuesday morning you
started writing. I wrote the whole damn thing in a day. I made $250, which
was a lot of money.'

Set at the time of one war, the Revolutionary War, it is offered as a comment
on another: 'America is going to be free ... There's going to be a war.'[53] The
series was already registering a threatening international situation. Once the
war was under way, its function as cheerleader became even more evident. In
The Battle of the Ovens, transmitted a year later, in June 1942, and again set at
the time of the Revolutionary War, Miller has a character insist that he wishes
'to do instead of to watch', because 'I feel like a stone in a river that's rushing
over me.' 'I can,' he maintains, 'fight with my own weapons ... We will fight
with our trade.' Miller was doing no less. At the end of the show the star,
Jean Hersholt, made an appearance, to celebrate those in his native Denmark
who were 'valiantly struggling to crush the evils of Nazis that hold them I
pray only temporarily in their grasp'.

DuPont were, in Miller's words, adept 'in helping to refashion the necessary
profit motive into themes of high-minded service'.[54] The company, indeed,
was the sponsor of the Liberty League, a right-wing pressure group, but its
politics sometimes proved difficult for Miller to fathom. It was as bitterly
opposed to the New Deal as Miller was in favour of it, but the fact of the war
created an ambiguity within which the radio series operated, bringing together
a conservative company and a radical playwright, albeit a radical playwright
who was careful not to advertise himself too obviously as such. Miller recalled
having to conceal his copies of the *Nation*, *New Masses* and *Partisan Review*
when he entered the corporate headquarters.

For all his own doubts, his radio work arguably contributed as much to the
war effort as his job as a ship-fitter, grade three, in the Brooklyn Navy Yard –
a job which he deliberately took at this time to serve the cause – in that the
programmes he worked on were often designed to raise morale by celebrating
American personalities and values. Increasingly the war would become a
central subject. According to the contracts, Miller netted between $150 per
script in 1941 and $375 in 1945, which only goes to show how maverick was
his decision to work in the Navy Yard. His house at 31 Grace Court would
later cost him $28,000 and his Nash-Lafayette car $250.

Much of the time the plays were inconsequential, often marking otherwise
forgettable anniversaries. As he explained,

The man in the advertising office has a calendar with all the national holidays
and celebrations and so on marked on it. I come in and we talk until I get

depressed, and then go home and do the script and then try not to think of Washington's birthday coming up. I will not deny though that I had a desire to make people realize that the Statue of Liberty [at the centre of his play *Grandpa and the Statue*] was erected to signify America's former open-door policy. If people get the idea from the show that, Jew, Irish, Italian or whatnot, we were all welcome here once, that will be a great satisfaction to me.[55]

Occasionally, however, Miller was offered the chance of writing plays on more significant topics. One took as its central figure Sacajawea, the Native American who acted as guide to Lewis and Clark and hence spelled doom for her own people. This was transmitted on 25 August 1941. The *Cavalcade* radio log lists Robert L. Richards as the author, but the Miller script has survived. It bears his Montague Street address.

It was a play in which he revealed his interest in mixing poetry and prose and took a somewhat sceptical view of a move west accomplished at a high cost to Native Americans. It begins and ends with an aged Sacajawea looking back on events that have shaped her and her people's destiny. The opening speech recalls the first encounter:

> They came from the Eastward, their wet canoes balanced easily on
>   their shoulders . . .
> I was young then; I saw them between the trees;
> I saw them with the West at my back. Over my shoulder
> Lay the West, and their blue eyes gazed at the hills
> When they questioned me. I am very old but the memory
> Is like a pickerel shining in a pool, and I reach under,
> Holding it bright and living across my palm.

Her closing speech balances hope and regret:

> . . . no man remembers the year of the long march,
> Nor woman the name of the Indian, Sacajawea,
> And the sun still rises on the bleeding flesh of man,
> The hour we prayed for when the air will sing at morning
> With the clasping of hands over boundaries
> And the mingling of different colored eyes
> And the slash of the dagger in the water of the sea.
> We wait for it in prisons. How we watch for the dawn! [56]

Poetry would also be evident in what was probably his best radio play. He was sent a book on the life of the Mexican peasant leader Benito Juárez, an unlikely choice for a show sponsored by DuPont, except that the company had factories in Mexico and needed a script to celebrate Pan-American Day – not an occasion that had exactly burned its way into the American consciousness. By chance, it was produced on air by Orson Welles, whose Mercury Theatre Company was famously responsible for the broadcast in October 1938 of H.G. Wells's *The War of the Worlds*, which caused panic among listeners but left Miller unmoved. Out of the six million listeners 1.7 million thought it authentic.

Welles was a committed leftist and a member of a number of front organizations. Fiercely anti-fascist and anti-racist, in 1935 he had appeared in Archibald McLeish's play, *Panic*, and in 1936 headed the Negro unit of the Federal Theatre. He was also a key figure in Marc Blitzstein's *Cradle Will Rock*. In March 1944 an agent in the New York office of the FBI wrote to J. Edgar Hoover saying that the office would be sending reports on Welles to the Dies Committee (the House Un-American Activities Committee headed by Senator Martin Dies). His dispute with Hearst newspapers as a consequence of *Citizen Kane* had led to Hearst sympathizers contacting the FBI. Of one radio series in which he was involved, *The Free Company*, an FBI report insisted that it threatened the national defence system, while Hoover sent a memo identifying the communist character of the organizations to which Welles belonged. In 1941 Welles also directed a production of Richard Wright's *Native Son*, the book admired by Miller.

Welles had been directing another play for *Cavalcade of America* when he objected to historical inaccuracies in it that had turned an American defeat into a victory. As Miller later recalled:

> I brought it [the script of *Thunder from the Hills*] in to the producer who was in Radio City and I went into that studio, which was the big studio – 8A. It was a gigantic studio, and I walked in and there was Orson Welles screaming his head off, and calling someone behind the glass window a goddamned liar and a cheat and a fake and a phoney ... He was flying ... I just stood there transfixed, and all the actors (he had all his famous Mercury Theatre actors, some of the best actors in America at the time) were just standing there waiting for him to cool down.
>
> The director, a man called Homer [Fickett], who weighed about three hundred and ten pounds ... came out to quiet him down. Next to Homer was sitting a Yale historian, who was the official historian for *Cavalcade of America* [Professor Frank Monaghan]. He vetted all scripts to make sure they were not inaccurate. Welles's point was that they were dealing with something in Latin America and Welles's grandfather had been Secretary of State, so he knew all about this situation. He said, 'You have just whitewashed America here! We murdered a lot of people down there. It was the usual American imperialism, and I'm not going to do this!' ... The historian was slightly pickled so Homer turned to me and said, 'Can you write something for tomorrow night?' I said, 'Well, I've got this thing about Juárez ...' So Welles,

who I had never met before, picked it up and started to read it. He said, 'Hey, this sounds pretty good! Let's do this!'

The typescript still had pencil corrections, but 'he passed out pages to the rest of the actors. They rehearsed it for ten minutes or so and he glanced through the rest of it and decided to go ahead.'[57] He embraced Miller. It was broadcast forty-eight hours later, on 28 September 1942, with Welles as Juárez (the play replaced *The Man Who Wouldn't Be President*, by Hector Chevigny, a drama about Daniel Webster which was eventually transmitted three months later).

For Miller, Welles was a key figure:

They might not have done it except for Orson. Orson understood the microphone like nobody before or since. He would wrap himself around that microphone and come out through the wires. So if it was in verse or not you never knew. He managed to make it sound marvellous, as did the others. They were trained in Shakespeare. They understood language. Otherwise I doubt they would have done it. It's the only time that I felt it was right to use it [i.e. verse – he had plainly forgotten *Sacajawea*]. Most of these stories wouldn't have supported verse.

There was, though, one scene that DuPont was not ready to accept:

It was a hell of a show. But I have to tell you that there was a scene in there, and the DuPont people intervened immediately ... one of the big shots came in, Russ Applegate, and said, 'You can't do this!' 'Why?' He said, 'Well, you've got a scene here where Abraham Lincoln is leaving a pile of arms on the north side of the Rio Grande for the Mexican revolutionaries to steal at night, with the permission of the United States.' In effect they were supplying the revolution to drive the French out of Mexico. They were not interested in having the French in Mexico, naturally. I said, 'You gave me a book to dramatize, and that was in the book.' He said, 'Yes, but we can't have that.' I said, 'Why can't you have it? It's a great scene. It shows you are trying to demonstrate how America is friendly with Latin America.' He said, 'Because DuPont owns Remington Arms, and we're always being accused of gun-running in Latin America.' But they left it in, anyway.[58]

In *Timebends* he had found it 'impossible to remember whether I pulled the scene or not'.[59] In fact, as he suggests above, they did indeed leave it in.

The play (based on Nina Brown Baker's *Juárez, Hero of Mexico*, published earlier that year) was transmitted under the title *Thunder from the Hills*. It reveals not only Miller's interest in verse drama but his considerable facility with it. He was finding virtues in a form that gave discipline and shape to his language. The story of Juárez also chimed with his own revolutionary instincts. *Thunder from the Hills* celebrates the life of a man 'with labor toughened hand', who rose to be first a lawyer and subsequently President of Mexico when he overthrew Ferdinand Maximilian, the last emperor. To Miller, he was Mexico's Abraham Lincoln, and, indeed, the play makes much of the parallel. Lincoln, he reminds us, was a farmer's son, another man of the people:

> Listener, there were two men who lived a century ago,
> And it is a strange and marvelous thing,
> But if they were to stand side by side before the sun
> They would have cast two identical shadows!

Lincoln, the narrator tells us (a narrator, like the protagonist, played by Welles), lives in Salem, Illinois:

> Now travel your eye down the spine of our continent
> Two thousand miles south of Salem, across the Rio Grande,
> Across the high spikes of the Sierra Madre.
> This other lawyer lived a century ago,
> This other Lincoln, this Indian man
> With the narrow Indian eyes ...

Juárez, in Miller's play, fights against those for whom 'a peasant is made for working and dying'. He supports the poor against the rich, and eventually gathers his troops in 'a greener Valley Forge'. For DuPont, he was a suitable symbol of the fight for freedom; for Miller, he was also a man of the people, a believer in social justice and revolutionary change.

Thunder from the Hills is a play that reflects something of the language of *The Golden Years*, and it is not difficult to see what appealed to Welles in the poetic arias that he delivered in an only faintly suspect Mexican accent:

> The land is on fire! The sky burns!
> The people lift up like lions,
> Roaring their anger from the coast, from Mazatlán
> And Atoyac, from the towns of the Spaniard
> And the Indian towns! They came from Tehuantepec,
> Durango and the river there, from the bay of Banderas,
> The fishermen with salt on their lips
> As once the fishermen of Marblehead came
> In their boats to crash the Heights of Washington!
> The sowers of corn and the makers of bread,
> The black-eyed and the fair, the forest men
> Whose backs were bent like the trees they cut –

They came, they came, sweetening with blood
The deserts of long-dead centuries,
And they scrawled new names on Mexico's face!
Dios y Libertad! For God and Liberty!
And the stones rang like bells from Guadalajara
To the Gulf.

After the play Welles was brought back to offer a personal coda, remarks which bore directly on the play and perhaps explain something of his enthusiasm for a script by an unknown writer. 'A few weeks ago in Mexico,' he explained, 'I attended a great celebration in his [Juárez's] honour with many speakers. The last of these was a humble citizen of the Mexican Republic. He was also a very old man. I'll never forget what he said. "I am eighty-seven years old and I have the honor to be one of those who shot and killed the Emperor Ferdinand Maximilian."'

The DuPont representative who closed the programme, no doubt finding it difficult to spot a link between their products and a Mexican revolutionary, contented himself with quoting from the company president: 'The momentum of America will not be stopped, says the President of the DuPont company in the current issue of the *DuPont Magazine* ... there is nothing awaiting us of America, either in business or the nation's battle lines, that we cannot overcome with fundamental study, effort, initiative, vision and daring.'[60] Listeners were then invited to write for a free copy of the magazine, which came complete with colour photographs of a chemical works. The mixed messages of *Cavalcade of America* could sometimes defy decoding.

That same month a new series was proposed that would have paired Miller and Welles. *Ceiling Unlimited* was to be a celebration of the aircraft industry, sponsored by the Lockheed Vega Company and with Miller as principal author. In the end, Miller conceded, Welles hardly needed such support.

In his autobiography Miller describes another play he wrote, which to him seemed to expose the rapacity of John D. Rockefeller. Rockefeller had acquired the rights to the world's largest opencast iron deposit, diverting the profits from the poor and the Native Americans, who the original owners had wished to see benefit, into his own pockets. To Miller, it was a story of corporate greed, of a robber baron at his worst, and as such not likely to be approved. To DuPont, it was a play that celebrated corporate enterprise and as such was well received. There was, it seemed, no way of second-guessing the company's reactions.

Miller followed *Thunder from the Hills* with *Toward a Further Star* (now held in the Harry Ransom Center), the story of the aviator Amelia Earhart, starring Madeleine Carroll. It was this play that Miller admitted having written to a sceptical fellow ship-fitter in the Navy Yard. When he tuned in, the man was unimpressed because it was 'all true'. Though she had died in 1937, Earhart's exploits were dramatized as a means of celebrating the achievement of the twenty-two thousand women then piloting civilian air-patrol planes as well as those ferrying bombers or working in factories, shipyards and aeroplane plants. In Miller's hands, it became a play about the liberation of women: 'Isn't it time,' he has a character ask, 'to unlock the kitchen and let women out?'

> Try and imagine how much richer it [America] would be if half its population, if all its women, were free to do their part of the world's work. Right now . . . it must be true that a woman can live out her personal dream and still be a wife. Women must have the right to lead the way once in a while, to search for new things instead of sitting home waiting for men to do the work of the world.

In 1940 thirteen million women had been in the industrial workforce. By 1944 the figure was nineteen million. In 1943, CBS launched a drama series called *American Women*.

Toward a Further Star, which was transmitted on 2 November 1942, was followed by *The Eagle's Nest* (28 December), with Paul Muni, the actor he had earlier tried to persuade to appear in his stage plays. Later radio plays for *Cavalcade* include *Bernadine I Love You*, starring William Bendix, and *The Philippines Never Surrendered* with Edward G. Robinson, who would later appear in the film version of *All My Sons*.

By now Miller was a mainstay of those putting together the weekly schedule of plays. As he explained in an interview in October 2003:

> Very often they would be in rehearsal for some play. I think they began on Tuesday. By Wednesday afternoon they realized it was a dead horse. There was no way they could broadcast this script. So they would call me up and say, 'We've got a subject and we've got to go on tomorrow night.' And they'd send a messenger over with a book. It would arrive at two o'clock in the afternoon and they had to be rehearsing the thing the next day at three. And I would sit down – and these were not electric typewriters – and I'd write the whole damn thing and get it off. I took great pleasure in being a good mechanic.

Cavalcade of America was not the only series in which Miller was involved. He also placed a number of scripts with the Theatre Guild, whose radio shows were sponsored by US Steel: 'I only worked for the best!' These included his adaptations of the Hungarian Ferenç Molnár's *The Guardsman*, John Cecil Holm and George Abbott's *Three Men on a Horse*, both extremely funny, and *Pride and Prejudice*, the latter adapted, none too faithfully, for an American audience – an adaptation that lays rather greater stress on comedy than even Jane Austen, though it was based on a then current stage production rather than the book.

Miller had to be present for the transmission of the plays in order to make last-minute changes in scripts that had already had to be condensed: 'I remember having to wrestle that terrific plot of *The Guardsman*, which took about two hours and fifteen minutes on stage, into less than an hour. Mind you, they spoke at a rate which for Americans anyway was extremely fast, but you heard every syllable. So I had to be there.' In the case of *The Guardsman*, which starred Alfred Lunt and Lynn Fontanne, that meant travelling to Chicago.

Another series for which Miller was recruited prompted several excellent scripts. CBS decided to launch *The Doctor Fights*, a series that would celebrate the achievement of the sixty thousand doctors serving in the military. The programme was sponsored by Schenley Laboratories, responsible for, among other things (including the production of liquor), the manufacture of penicillin. He wrote plays for this series from June 1944 to July 1945. They were mostly based on actual cases and frequently concluded with the doctor concerned appearing for a brief, often embarrassingly stilted, interview. The series featured Raymond Massey and (Captain) Robert Montgomery, among others.

Miller's scripts for *The Doctor Fights* also included two set in England, and though he was dealing with sometimes brutal situations what is striking is his evident desire to reach out for a poetic prose. In *Glider Doctor*, for example, he sets the scene for a night attack:

> The moon was round as a barrel head that night; poured her icy light on the English coasts. On the choppy sea England floats like a great moored ship. Along the dark and hidden piersides from Plymouth to the Scottish coast, men stop in the dark to study the moon. In the flared bows of waiting cruisers, doctors lift up equipment for the hundredth inspection, like old women fussing in their shopping bags. Further inland where the concrete carpets of the airports have thrust through woodland, where King Arthur rode, doctors stow plasma in grossly shadowed bombers whose silent motors even now nose toward the wind.[61]

The play concludes with the text of an address by Major General Norman T. Kirk, stressing the reduction in infection rates in the armed forces and including a commercial for Schenley Laboratories 'maintaining the health of all of us at home'.

The following week he wrote of a plane 'roaring out of the mouth' of a 'pastel English dawn', on its way to Germany, while far below the English Channel seems 'too silver to drown you'. The bomb-aimer is crouching over his bomb-sight 'like a kid over a gopher hole. And time is a knife turning in your flesh.' When the bombs are released, the 'plane banks stiffly like an iron gull'. It is a play that celebrates the brotherhood of those in the plane and that laments the likelihood that such feelings may not survive the mission and, more seriously, the war. This would be precisely the lament of his nonfiction book *Situation Normal*, and of his first successful play, *All My Sons*.

A week later, Miller was the author of another play in the same series, *The Magic Drug*, starring Ronald Colman and telling the story of penicillin (interestingly, Morton Wishengrad wrote a similar play for *Cavalcade of America* with George Coulouris as Fleming). It concluded with an interview with the real Sir Alexander Fleming, then in the United States to work on a further development of the drug (at the time available only by injection).

The Magic Drug[62] is more prosaic than his previous week's offering, but here too he was determined to punch home his central message. Penicillin had been discovered in England, but its industrial-scale production was a function of a massive and urgent investment in plant in America that required the kind of cooperation that plainly, to him, was symbolic of that sense of brotherhood that was something more than a wartime expedient: 'It should have taken ten years to do what was done in ten weeks. This is what happens when the life of man becomes the most important thing instead of the least. This is what happens when we live like brothers.'

Similar sentiments expressed in wartime films would lead screenwriters to be hauled before HUAC barely three years after this play was broadcast. Nor, they discovered, were wartime exigencies to be seen as a defence. Appeals for brotherhood were decoded as Marxist slogans. No one, however, either then or later, seems to have registered the Marxist tinge to Miller's radio work, not least because it was to remain largely forgotten.

These plays, perhaps because they often involved the stories of those doctors who struggled to deal with the effects of war, seem to have engaged Miller more profoundly than much of his other radio work. In 1945, preparatory to writing two plays for the series which tackled the question of plastic and reconstructive surgery, he wrote a note to the producers:

Before outlining this story of plastic surgery a few observations are perhaps in order. Having written several of the programs last year and two this year I feel now – after having spent three days at Valley Forge General Hospital – that the attitude of the program has not been a sufficiently responsible one. We have written and produced too much from the point of view of the audience and not enough from that of the doctor and the patient. As a result we have tended toward the jolly without preserving the undertone of tragedy which is always there, we have made our doctors more unfeeling than they are and our patients – they have acted as though they knew their troubles would clear up at the end of the broadcast. The heroism of doctor and patient

as I saw it at Valley Forge does not lie in their ability to remain cold to
suffering. When they are heroic it is because they do feel and yet drive
themselves on to do the best they can in a horrible situation. To shut our eyes
to this situation is to commit a travesty, and in my opinion, will lower both
the sponsor and radio in general in the estimation of those who know the
facts of life.[63]

He was determined that the true story of wartime injuries and their
treatment should be told. The producers were at first resistant. As he noted
in 2003:

They didn't want it that way. It was dangerous. It would put people off the
military. But I felt it was better to tell people the truth. I remember one guy
who was hit by shrapnel and he ended with his face on the floor of the
bomber. And the floor froze and his face froze to that floor. I'll never forget
that. And they had to cut him away from the floor. And this doctor restored
that guy's face. And I saw the photographs of the procedure, which went on
for a long time, for months and months. He never went to sleep, that surgeon.
This man must have worked eighteen hours a day, seven days a week. They
were heroic. It was very moving for me. They were all very young, younger
than I was, and marred for life. You couldn't turn your back on them and I
just felt I owed it to them. I was moved terribly by the whole experience, as
remote as I was from it. I wasn't flying over Europe being shot at.

A script from June 1945, *Mare Island and Back,* shows what he had in mind.
A doctor insists that 'This is no tale designed to inspire for twenty minutes
and leave you staring through your tears at the trouser leg hanging empty
from your hip. I have laced too many steel and leather forearms to your elbows
to promise you'll play Chopin in ten easy lessons.'[64] Nonetheless, the play
does tell the story of an injured pilot who takes to the air again, despite the
loss of his leg, and a subsequent play recounts the plastic surgery that enables
a trumpeter to resume playing. The former play featured Robert Montgomery,
now in real life a lieutenant commander (he would later appear as a friendly
witness before HUAC), as Captain Henry H. Kessler, director of the
Rehabilitation Division of the Naval Hospital at Mare Island, himself interviewed at the end of the programme. Broadcast on 19 June 1945, it looked,
the announcer said, to the end of the war in the Pacific, and meanwhile
assured listeners that Schenley Laboratories were working on new products
which would become available with the peace.

In 1946, Miller published a short story based on his experience at the Valley
Forge Hospital. Called 'The Plaster Masks', it concerns a writer's visit to a
hospital in which servicemen's faces are reconstructed. It is forthright in its
description of the various injuries suffered by the men and ends with his visit

to the part of the institution where the plaster masks are made, showing how the patients looked before and after their treatment. 'There they hung now on the wall, ten square yards of wall covered with their broken faces. The boy with the triangular hole in his face that obliterated everything from his nose to the angles of his jaw. The man whose left cheek was bundled up like the mouth of a tobacco sack. The boneless foreheads, the tongues hanging down to the Adam's apples, the eyeless, the lipless.'[65] The writer discovers that, disturbingly, one of the masks seems to fit him, and has a sudden vision of what it must be like to suffer such traumas.

The last play in the series, *Dr Rehm's Story*, written by Miller, was transmitted a bare three weeks before the end of the war and featured a doctor who had deliberately flown fifty missions in order to understand the process involved in operational fatigue.

In one of these last scripts Miller seems to have registered a change in mood and to have seized the opportunity to register his resistance to it. In *Lips for a Trumpet* the narrator remarks, 'I tell this story in the hope that a certain group of four people will be listening . . . I was in New York at the time on business . . . In the afternoon I was having my lunch in a restaurant. There were four people at the next table, talking over their food.' What he had heard, he recounts, was a man remark, 'I say before we demobilize the Army we ought to finish the job. Russia's big but without our lend lease . . . I hate war, but everybody *knows* we're in for another one; I say have it out now and get it over with!'[66] In the context of the play, about the damage done to the human body by war, the comment is unexceptionable, but the reference to Russia is a pointed one and in line with his earlier attempt to introduce his social and political views into patriotic radio drama.

He did, of course, have the cover of major American companies. He was effectively writing for the large chemical and pharmaceutical firms of America and producing plays that celebrated doctors, nurses, the average man and woman. Somewhat surprisingly, though, there were also plays sponsored by the trades union movement, and these might have been expected to attract rather more attention than they did, either then or later.

CBS collaborated with the Congress of Industrial Organizations (the CIO), whose leadership included communists. In a series called *Jobs for Tomorrow*, writers were invited to celebrate today's workers in the context of tomorrow's possibilities. Miller's contribution, in which he drew directly on his experience in the Brooklyn Navy Yard, was transmitted on 3 February 1945. It told the story of the massive increase in shipbuilding during the war, a feat achieved by the cooperation of everyone concerned through a labour-management committee. As one of the characters remarks, 'One thing that's come out of this war is this – a lot of bosses are learning that the man on the job has got eyes and ears to see and hear what's wrong. And if he's got an organization – a union – to come to he can improve things. A man all alone don't like to open his mouth sometimes.' This echo of Hemingway's *To Have and Have Not* was a 1930s truism, to be carried forward here into the soon to be postwar world.

The union, we are told, is now negotiating with government for a new housing project: 'They ain't going to listen to me, no, or to you, but they sure listen to half a million and that's how many members we got.' Another character observes: 'I realized then that something had got into this country during the war that I thought had died when I was young.' A toast is offered to the Industrial Union of Marine and Shipbuilding Workers of America and the CIO. The following week's programme was to be about the clothing industry, the industry that had once made the Miller family fortune via a company that was fiercely anti-union.

Aside from a lyrical passage which celebrates the building of ships, Miller's play is a shameless plug not only for the union but for the President's sixty-million-job programme which the CIO supported. In part, of course, he was writing to order, but the play surely also reflected his loyalties. Perhaps surprisingly, however, it failed to attract the attention of HUAC, as did another script, about a convoy of military hardware on its way from New York to Murmansk.[67]

Here, once again, is an invocation to brotherhood: 'You stick your fingers in the ocean and you're shaking hands with all men everywhere.' But here, too, is evidence of his own politics, as a sailor observes: 'There wasn't a sailor didn't know that the German and Italian ships were pouring munitions into Franco's ports from the very beginning.' There are calls, too, for a second front to relieve the beleaguered Russians. The sailor, after all, is aware that 'a corps of Russian tank crews [is] waiting for these machines'. The play ends with a kiss between the sailor and a Russian woman.

HUAC later invoked what it regarded as suspect radio plays as a reason for investigating writers and actors, including Fredric March and his wife Florence Eldridge, along with writer Norman Corwin. In 1950 *Red Channels*, published by American Business Consultants, an organization that worked closely with HUAC, listed those with supposedly subversive views. Norman Rosten's name appeared there as did that of Norman Corwin, Langston Hughes, Arthur Laurents and Edward G. Robinson. *Red Channels*, Miller commented in 2003, 'was a racket. The man who published it had a long list of people who should be barred from writing radio for the innocent American public. It involved every good American radio writer there was. That began a real massacre. Producers would avoid using those people. The way to get off that list was to go and pay him. The producers cleaned out Leftism from radio quite early and without much ado.' In 1955, HUAC would open hearings on the broadcasting industry, at which point the American Federation of

Television and Radio Artists abandoned its own members. Miller was never questioned, nor did he appear in *Red Channels*, though he was listed in *Aware*, a similar publication, allegedly paying $300 to get himself cleared by its publisher, Vincent Hartnell.[68]

The script about the Russian convoy was not Miller's most direct statement of his political priorities. There is a synopsis for another play, *In the Beginning Was the Word*, that is even clearer in that regard, even more of a challenge to America's priorities.

In the Beginning Was the Word is the story of what might happen to an ordinary American should he wake up one morning to discover that the Bill of Rights has been abolished. An agent of the Internal Security Department tells the protagonist that citizens who mind their own business have nothing to fear. Those who argue are in trouble. Only one newspaper is allowed. Teachers are not to mention the existence of the Bill of Rights, whose first article is a guarantee of free speech. The protagonist is assaulted for failing to salute the flag. He ends by rearranging lightbulbs in an electric sign that previously read 'Mind Your Own Business' so that it now reads 'Freedom'.

Scarcely a profound piece of work, it nonetheless speaks to Miller's frame of mind. There is no date on the surviving typescript but since he hardly wrote any more radio plays after the success of *All My Sons*, it would seem to suggest that he was responding early to tendencies in American society that would eventually reach out to him. It is tempting to surmise that the play may have coincided with the founding of the Committee for the First Amendment, which sponsored an ABC broadcast called *Hollywood Fights Back*, attacking HUAC's 1947 hearings on Hollywood. By 1950, CBS had initiated a loyalty oath indicating that employees were not and never had been members of the Communist Party. Batten, Barton, Durstine & Osborn, meanwhile, seem to have adopted an aggressively anti-communist policy.

Miller was involved in yet another series. This was a product of the Office of War Information Domestic Radio Bureau and was designed to celebrate the men of the Merchant Marine – the series title. It was to be a recruiting programme that would secure free air time on a commercial network. Miller was one of the team assembled. Though he wrote several plays, he found himself at odds with some of those responsible for the series. One vice-president protested that there was 'too much character' in stories that struck him as radical. For his part, Miller interviewed men in East Coast and Gulf ports. One of the plays, *The Story of Gus*, was rejected. He was not pleased. 'No medium of expression can fulfil itself,' he objected,

> if its form and its content are proscribed beforehand. There is so much you can't say on the radio that for a serious writer it represents a blank wall. The

answer is freedom, which is tightly circumscribed in the present setup. I mean not only freedom of speech, but freedom to write a radio play without a format. I have tried to do this in *The Story of Gus* and as a result it was one of the few things I have ever done that was never produced. Radio today is in the hands of people most of whom have no taste, no will, nothing but the primitive ability to spot a script that does not conform to the format. Give the medium to the artists and something might happen. As it is – death in the afternoon and into the night.[69]

In later years, Miller tended to dismiss his radio plays. Some of them were, indeed, hack work, produced to order. Some, though, remain impressive. Wartime required and validated that call for brotherhood that recurs in his plays, but this clearly still had a political dimension for Miller, who could see his radio work as continuous with his personal commitments. The constraints and necessities of radio drama, meanwhile, were teaching him something about plot, language and character. As he later remarked, learning how to condense is invaluable: 'If you can condense a four-hundred-page book into twenty-eight minutes then you might be able to condense your own elaborate fantasies into a time that people would be willing to sit there and listen to. I learned how to condense and to do it gracefully. Radio drama could be a terrific but minor form.'[70]

In 2003, he remarked:

The model is the Book of Genesis. You read about the Creation and in about a page and a half you've got the human race. And that's pretty hot stuff. That is the way to tell a story, and a story that never dies. It is the imprint of a hot iron on the soul. [Writing radio plays] taught me a lot about how to tell a story. Less is better. Why? It's very simple. It's like dreams. Dreams are very brief and some of them you never forget because they are very discrete. Nothing is wasted. No dream has got excessive material. It all counts.[71]

By June 1941, however, he had barely dipped a toe into radio, and Broadway was proving more resistant than he had imagined when he left Michigan. But when he wrote to Kenneth Rowe from a friend's farm in Bethel, Connecticut, it was to announce that he had received an advance of $500 on the first 10,000 words of a novel – the novel version of *The Man Who Had All the Luck*. The money came from Atlantic Monthly Press, an editor from which wrote to Miller's old university professor back in Michigan, R.W. Cowden. He replied that Miller was a 'wide awake' Jewish boy whose commitment to writing had sometimes been at the expense of his academic success. In fact Miller's grades had consistently improved after he started writing, so it seems that he had either forgotten this or was shaping his reply to underscore his ex-student's writing as opposed to academic achievements.

Miller expected to finish quickly but was already formulating an idea for a play he expected to work on in the autumn. His deadline for the novel was September, with publication expected in January. In the end, work on the novel stretched into the spring of 1942 and, as with so many other projects, nothing came of it, though one further radio play was scheduled for McLeish's Library of Congress regional series and another for *Cavalcade of America*. Meanwhile, in a letter to Professor Rowe he noted that his draft status was deferred, just six months before America entered the war. He was beginning to rethink his isolationist stance before Pearl Harbor invalidated it.

Three years after leaving Ann Arbor he still regarded himself as a radical. Indeed, on the evening of 8 October 1941 he stated in his notebook that he was still a revolutionary, that after four years of indecision and torment, four years of taking part in the usual bourgeois struggle to succeed, he had now left all this behind him. From now on, he told himself, he would cease to draw on his personal experiences and set himself to fight for a revolutionary future, creating portraits not of the damned but of those who battle for the future.

On 7 December 1941 came Pearl Harbor, and immediately thereafter Hitler's declaration of war on the United States. Suddenly, he had rejoined his country – or his country, perhaps, had rejoined him. Now anti-fascism, he presumed, would be the common bond, though he knew that he still treasured a loyalty to an idea that might, and did, attract the attention of the FBI. Cheering Russians was permitted and his exclusion from the national project was at an end. His political beliefs were now respectable. His pacifism was laid aside. For Elia Kazan, likewise, it 'was not until ... Pearl Harbor ... that I began to feel allegiance to our side in the war'.[72]

Miller's brother Kermit enlisted in the infantry, later emerging with a purple heart. As his wife Frances explained in a 1999 interview, 'He was in the volunteer corp. In other words, if he volunteered to go into the Infantry and passed officers' training he would immediately become an officer after three months' basic training and his family would get the money, which was a second lieutenant's pay, and that money was sent to [his] parents', which, as Kermit added, 'wasn't a lot of money' but 'at least they weren't dying of thirst'.

Both Miller and Kazan had tried unsuccessfully to enlist (600,000 Jews served in the war, winning two Congressional Medals of Honor, 74 Distinguished Crosses, 37 Navy Crosses and 2,391 Distinguished Flying Crosses),[73] their failure to do so leaving, in both cases, a residue of guilt. Miller once described to me the low farce that accompanied his attempt to discover how to join the Navy. He presented himself to a recruiting centre, in search of information, but instead of being handed a leaflet, found himself swiftly passed from office to office, in each one of which he was asked questions before being passed on again. Finally he was asked, by a man in a white coat, to undress. Thoroughly confused by this time, he complied and, some minutes later, found himself outside, his non-existent application rejected by the Navy because of his college football injury.

He never did find the leaflets he had been seeking. Subsequent attempts to enlist proved equally futile. He was classified 4F, according to his Selective Service Board because of his 'weakened and impaired use of wrist due to accident. Swelling and stiffening of right knee joint as of 3/17/41'. The detail, interestingly, comes from his FBI file.[74] His Selective Service Board record was requested by the Bureau and duly recorded in September 1944. It included far more than details of his medical condition. The Bureau noted in particular that in 1941 his wife had earned $850 a year and he just $30, a wholly inaccurate figure. More ominous, though, was the information, noted earlier, that he and his wife had registered with the American Labor Party in 1942. His file also contained the information that he had worked at the Brooklyn Navy Yard from November 1942, which fact had been notified to his selection board on 28 February 1943.

The agent compiling the report had checked that the names of both husband and wife appeared on the apartment register at 18 Schermerhorn Street and added, 'General inquiry was made at this address, but it was ascertained that no superintendent [caretaker] resides at that address, and the neighbors contacted under pretext did not know the subject.'[75] It was noted that 'none of the informants in Brooklyn or Manhattan had reported any Communist activity on the part of the subject. In view of this fact, further investigation does not appear warranted at this time. This case is being closed, therefore, on the authority of the Special Agent in Charge subject to being opened on the receipt of pertinent information.'

The file helpfully listed his Social Security number and offered a description. He was six foot two and a half inches, weighed one hundred and sixty pounds, with brown eyes and hair. He was of a dark complexion. In a 1950 report he had shrunk by half an inch and gained weight, with further weight gains in subsequent years. The file, as is evident, would not remain closed for long.

Martin Gottfried has suggested in his biography of Miller that he may have dodged the draft. There is absolutely nothing to substantiate this. He was rejected for his leg injury, as Tennessee Williams was for his poor eyesight. Instead of going to war he had to watch as his brother left for overseas. In 1948 he tried to recall his feelings in the form of a poem, but drew a line through it and wrote no more than a couple of strained paragraphs about the pain he felt as his brother left for the war, unable to explain where he was going. The two shook hands and Kermit walked away into a crowded street.

To an extent Miller could feel he was doing his bit for the war effort by writing plays like *The Half-Bridge* and another wartime play, *Boro Hall Nocturne*, as well as the patriotic radio scripts for *Cavalcade of America* but he was also acutely conscious that he remained in New York while others risked their lives in battle. Besides, those two plays found no producer.

He wrote *Boro Hall Nocturne* in 1942. (Boro Hall was the sector headquarters of the Air Raid Protection Service.) It is a play which highlights the fact of anti-Semitism even in wartime America. It envisages the infiltration of American East Coast cities by Nazi saboteurs. It is set 'tomorrow morning, at three o'clock', as an indication of the sense of urgency that provoked the play, and that drives it. In fact, eight Nazi agents did land on Long Island and in Florida, in 1942, with the intent of blowing up installations, though one of their number immediately informed the police, a fact that did not stop the Director of the FBI from claiming credit for their arrest. They were tried before a military tribunal, a procedure not subsequently invoked until President George W. Bush reinstituted it following the terrorist attacks on 11 September 2001. In a broadcast in September 1943, Walter Winchell predicted that the Gestapo would blow up American railroads, prompting J. Edgar Hoover to write a note denouncing Winchell's hysterics – which 'do more to sabotage the war effort than saboteurs have ever done'.[76]

Beyond this, on 19 February 1942 Roosevelt signed Executive Order 9066, authorizing the War Department to intern 110,000 Japanese as potential saboteurs, while in July twenty-eight writers and publishers were arrested on charges of sedition. Lights were even dimmed on Broadway for fear of air raids. There would in fact be no cases of Nazi sabotage during the Second World War, but in 1942, with reports of the arrest of Nazi saboteurs, things seemed rather different.

Boro Hall Nocturne is a war drama about Nazi saboteurs but also about those within the country who sympathize with them. It is set in Boro Hall itself. The building is dilapidated and largely unoccupied. The only object of significance is a piano. Plainly, air raids do not seem an immediate possibility. Even the man in charge, Mr Goldberg, a piano tuner, is asleep, it being three in the morning. Transports are leaving the nearby dockyard, where Miller himself worked, to join the Atlantic convoys. The Japanese have reached out across the Pacific. Ironically, though, this store-front office is about to become the centre of a drama, or more precisely a melodrama.

Goldberg is relieved by Alexander Kelley, a disaffected musician with little belief in the war. Drafted into the Army, he is supposed to report for duty but has decided not to go. He tears up his draft card, refusing any responsibility to others, any duty beyond himself. All that matters to him is his music. The two men are friends, not least because in the depths of the Depression Goldberg rescued Kelley from destitution. This, indeed, is one of the reasons

Stanton Street, where the Millers lived on arriving in the United States.

East 3rd Street, the Miller family home in Brooklyn.

The Student Publications Building at 420 Maynard Street, Ann Arbor, as it looked in the 1930s when Miller was on the staff of the *Michigan Daily*.

Arthur Miller (front row, seated right) as the Bishop of Lincoln in a student production of Shakespeare's *Henry VIII*, Ann Arbor, 1934-5.

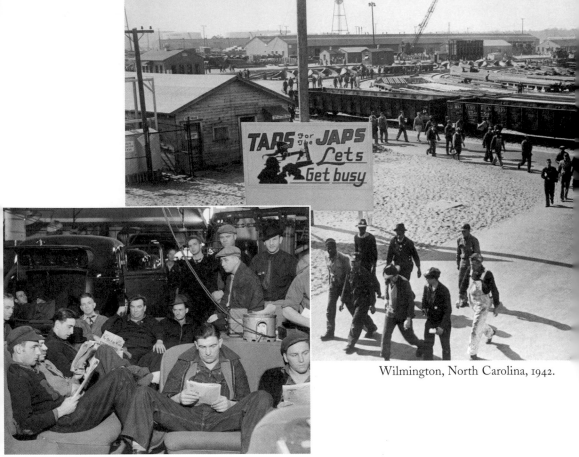

Wilmington, North Carolina, 1942.

Sit-down strike at General Motors
plant, Flint, Michigan, 1935.

RIGHT: *The Man Who Had All the Luck*
(Broadway, 1944) directed by Joseph
Fields. (from left) Karl Swenson as
David Beeves, Eugenia Rawls as Hester
Falk, Dudley Sadler as Amos Beeves.

Norman Rosten, poet,
novelist, playwright (1914-1995).

Actress Marsha Hunt and
Arthur Miller present the
first flag of the new Jewish
state to Yakov Riftin,
member of the Palestine
Military Defence Council,
May 1948.

Arthur Miller and his
wife Mary, March 1952.

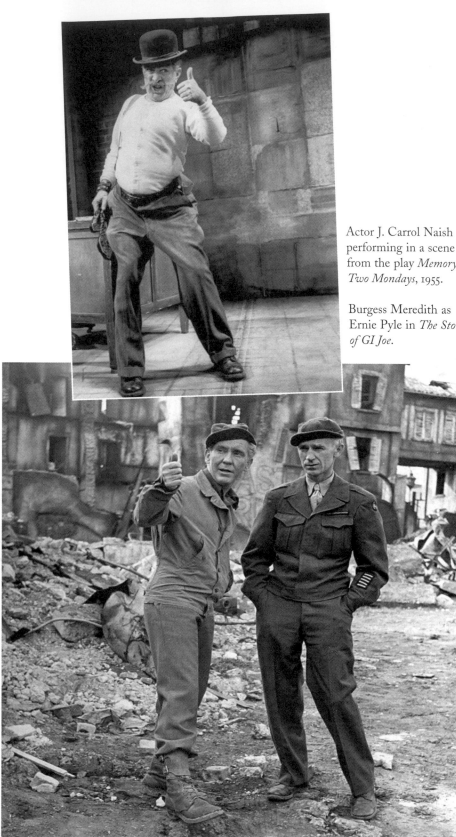

Actor J. Carrol Naish performing in a scene from the play *Memory of Two Mondays*, 1955.

Burgess Meredith as Ernie Pyle in *The Story of GI Joe*.

Brooklyn navy yard, where Miller did war work as a fitter.

Recording a play in the *Cavalcade of America* series.

Edward G.
Robinson in
Miller's radio play
*The Philippines
Never Surrendered.*

*An Enemy of the
People* (Broadway,
1950-1) written by
Henrik Ibsen; the
book was adapted
by Arthur Miller.
(from left) Anna
Minot, Ralph
Robertson,
Fredric March,
Florence Eldridge
and Richard
Trask.

that Kelley has refused to join the anti-Semitic group that courts him.

At first the mood is humorous, but they are then interrupted by an anti-Semitic drunk and a supposedly drunken bar owner, who in fact has been a minor player in the imminent Nazi invasion. He is a member of an organisation, presumably the German-American Bund or its equivalent, though it is never specified. The Jews, he maintains, are monsters. He tries to persuade Kelley to join, but he resists because he has seen a Jew beaten by them on Atlantic Avenue. Kelley, though, is clearly on the verge of collapse. He lives for his music, playing the piano not simply to pass the time but to hold his world together, unsure how people identify and fulfil their destiny.

The play turns on the arrival of one of the saboteurs, a man calling himself Claire who claims to be and, it transpires, is, a professor of music, though he conceals the fact that he is based at Berlin University. He is part of the invading force, waiting out the night to play his role. Bizarrely, though, he is peculiarly inept in that not only is he happy to insist on the primacy of all things German, including its music, but he also betrays a highly implausible ignorance of the music of all other countries. In short, he is both an unconvincing agent and an unconvincing professor. Now enter a group of Italian workers, one of whose homes is destroyed by the attack which is now unleashed the length of the eastern seaboard. Miller relies on the device of a radio to move the action on and to explain the wider context of the action in the office. This conveniently keeps us informed of the actions of the saboteurs and of their ultimate failure.

Claire is finally unmasked, kills in an attempt to escape, and is arrested. The play ends as Kelley tries to piece together his torn-up draft card, having learned that the war is not some distant venture but is being fought out on the streets of Brooklyn.

Boro Hall Nocturne is a contrived piece, a melodramatic gesture, but, as Lillian Hellman's *Watch on the Rhine*, Robert Sherwood's *There Shall Be No Night* and Alfred Hitchcock's *Saboteur* attested, these were melodramatic times. *Saboteur* (1942), indeed, was inspired by the same sense of paranoia as had prompted Miller's play. As far as Miller's craft was concerned, *Boro Hall Nocturne* hardly edged it forward. But for those who thought that his assault on anti-Semitism in *Focus*, in 1945, came out of nowhere, that Miller was hesitant to deploy Jewish characters, this play, together with *The Half-Bridge*, provides evidence to the contrary. In both, the Jew lies at the heart of works whose principal concern was to stage the drama of those who regarded the conflict then going on as in some ways remote from themselves.

It is not that he was proposing that this was a war about anti-Semitism. In neither play was the Jew a main character. It is that the attitude of the characters to the Jew is an indicator of the extent of their commitment to values at real risk of collapse. The result of cynicism, self-regard, isolationism, the plays suggest, is that the Jew is once again dispossessed (the drunk in *Boro Hall Nocturne* awaits a Nazi victory so that he can lay claim to Jewish property), but more fundamentally that there is no longer any resistance to a power that will, ultimately not, distinguish Jew from non-Jew because the fate of the Jew will become the fate of all.

Boro Hall Nocturne, like *The Half-Bridge*, was to some extent Miller's effort not only to rally people to the flag but to recognize that the world was their backyard. Martin Gottfried suggests that *The Half-Bridge* was the last of his plays to go unproduced. It was not. Beyond lay several more written in the ensuing decades.

If *Boro Hall Nocturne* sparked no interest, however, another of his plays did. *That They May Win* was first performed for the Victory Committee of the Welfare Center at Albemarle Road, Brooklyn, a road which intersects with East 3rd Street, site of the Miller family home.

The play, which exists in more than one version, was written for Stage for Action (called in one draft Stage Door to Action), a radical dramatic group whose declared aim was to 'wake people up', to 'help them realize that the war, the peace, and their entire futures depend on what they themselves do – now'.[77] The productions were confessedly propaganda 'for sound social thinking'.

That They May Win concerns Danny, an injured soldier back from the war, who discovers that his wife, Delia, now finds it impossible to make ends meet. Prices are rising, despite government controls. He urges action; she shrugs at what seems an inevitability. To survive, people are leaving their children to roam the streets as they themselves seek work. As the two argue, they are interrupted by a member of the audience, identified as Distressed Man, who objects to Danny's treatment of his wife. Soon they are joined by a 'Man Who Knows', another member of the audience, who calls on them to take control of their own fate. 'You gotta watch your storekeeper like a hawk. Don't let him get away with any price violations. Report him every time he tries to.' Told by the Distressed Man that women are too dumb, he replies:

> They ain't dumb, my friend; look what they learned to do in this war. They learned how to weld, how to run a drill press, how to build a P-47, how to hold a home together while their husbands are away fighting to win the war … Their army is the Consumers' Council and their machine guns are market baskets, and someday, when Johnny comes marching home, they'll be able to say to him, 'Okay, soldier, I was a soldier, too!'[78]

The play concludes as Danny confesses that this was how, indeed, it was to have ended. Lou Gilbert, who played the part of the Distressed Man, found himself ejected from the theatre on several occasions by those who failed to understand that he was part of the play. An earlier version was subtitled, 'A Short Play on the Need for Child Care Centers'.

Surprisingly, *That They May Win*, with its invitation to inform on shop-keepers (this from a playwright who would later denounce the informer), was one of the most popular productions of Stage for Action, attracting an audience of 100,000. When it was published, in a collection of one-act plays in 1945, one of its companion pieces was by his old college friend and Federal Theatre colleague, Norman Rosten. *Concerning the Red Army* (written to mark the twenty-sixth anniversary of the Red Army, and sponsored by Russian Relief and the Writers' War Board), as its title suggests, is a celebration of the achievements of the Red Army and was originally broadcast by CBS in cooperation with Russian War Relief Inc. The accompanying music was drawn from the work of Soviet composers. No wonder, perhaps, that Rosten would later find himself blacklisted.

In August 1942, the novel version of *The Man Who Had All the Luck* was finally turned down, this time by Doubleday, Doran & Co. The letter to Miller's agent commented on what struck them as its strangeness. It required, it seemed to them, a complete rewrite. It did have some virtues. In particular, his characters seemed strong. They were, they assured the agent, very interested in the author but felt that the book as it then stood was confused and uncon-vincing. If he were willing to undertake a thorough rewrite, they suggested, they would be willing to reconsider. A rewrite, though, was not what the author had in mind.

Miller was still desperate to do something concrete for the war effort, applying to the Office of War Information, an agency concerned with propa-ganda and intelligence. Once again, though, he was rejected. As he has said, 'I seemed to be part of nothing, no class, no influential group; it was like high school perpetually, with everybody else rushing to one or another club or conference with a teacher, and me still trying to figure out what was hap-pening.' He felt 'the inevitable unease of the survivor'.[79]

Aware of the need, his own and others, to make some sense out of the sacrifices reported in the newspapers, and the contrast between such sacrifices and the business of daily life, he became ever more determined to find some war work in which he could serve the cause, at the same time aware that many others who found themselves exempt from war service were lining their pockets. He would later see in this the origins of *All My Sons*: 'psychologically situated as I was – a young, fit man barred from a war others were dying in, equipped with a lifelong anguish of self-blame that sometimes verged on a pathological sense of responsibility – it was probably inevitable that the selfishness, cheating, and economic rapacity on the home front should have cut into me with its contrast to the soldiers' sacrifices and the holiness of the Allied cause. I was,' he said, 'a stretched string waiting to be plucked.'[80]

He was doubly blessed and therefore doubly responsible. His parents had left Poland and thus survived destruction. He was a bystander in the war and hence protected from its consequences, while his own brother was exposed to danger just as his friend had died in the Spanish war while he stayed at home. Perhaps this was one reason why he wrote the novel-turned-play *The Man Who Had All the Luck*, but it was also this sense of non-involvement, this feeling of not contributing, that led him to the Brooklyn Navy Yard. Here he laboured for thirteen out of fourteen nights, from four in the afternoon to four in the morning, sometimes in sub-zero temperatures. Occasionally he would work on Navy ships in the Hudson River. It was a voluntary move, a seemingly quixotic gesture, since he was now, at last, earning good money, but it answered his need to feel involved.

At the end of his time there, on 12 April 1943, he received a form letter from the Commandant of the Yard addressed to 'Arthur Miller, Helper Trainee Ship-fitter, Check No. 87172 (New 123127)' which noted: 'As you have been inducted in the United States Armed Forces, you are hereby placed on furlough during the period of your active service in the US Armed Forces, effective April 16, 1943, at which time all accrued leave, with pay, due you will have been taken.' It also promised that on receipt of 'a certificate of satisfactory service from the military authorities', he could apply for 'restoration to a civilian position within forty days' of his discharge, and that 'you will be restored to your former position, or to a position of like seniority, status, pay, providing you are still qualified to perform the duties of your former position'.[81]

Patriotic radio plays were one thing; working on navy ships showed a more direct commitment to the war effort. But because of his draft status he did not, of course, serve in the military; nor was he ever likely to reclaim his job as fitter, third-class.

His experience of the Yard was not without its low comedy. It began with his having his photograph taken for a security pass but ending up with someone else's face on his identity card. In peacetime, it took between two and seven years to qualify as a ship-fitter. Once the war started that time was cut to six months, as grocery clerks, haberdashers, truck drivers, bookies and would-be playwrights were supposedly given the skills that would enable them to build warships like the *Missouri* and *Iowa* from the ground up. His own estimate was that no more than one man in twenty really knew what he was doing.

Ship-fitting involved the erection of bulkheads, decks, doors and hulls. Conventionally, a ship-fitter was a jack-of-all-trades, a welder, a pipe-fitter, an electrician. This was explained to him on his first day in what was now to be a four-week course in which he joined another thirty men, a mixture of ages and ethnic backgrounds, many of whom never mastered the difference between perpendicular and horizontal, despite the teacher turning his desk on edge and back again as a visual aid. The group included a young Jewish boy, outside his community for the first time and baffled by the fact that the Yard did not respect the Sabbath or Yom Kippur. As Miller recalled in an unpublished memoir, it took him more than two weeks to explain that the Jewish religion was not the dominant one and that for most people the Sabbath took place on Sunday rather than Saturday.

When the fourth week had passed, with many in the class no wiser than when they had entered, another week was added for no apparent reason; and while they tried to make sense of blueprints, outside the Navy tested warning whistles. Desperate to justify what, increasingly, seemed a waste of time, their teacher, with an air of desperation, staged a poetry competition.

Next, they were told that there was an over-supply of ship-fitters and that they would have to retrain as welders. Ten days later, having been inducted into the mysteries of welding, they were told there was an over-supply of welders but that ship-fitters were now in short supply. As a result, Miller finally found himself on board a ship, working with a man whose complex love life required him to make a series of telephone calls, setting up and cancelling dates, a procedure in which he enrolled Miller, who was now required to take time off from winning the war to assist his new boss in his complex two-timing. That boss, known as Ipana Mike, specialized in stealing brass clocks from the walls of captains' cabins and then smuggling them past security. He became the basis for a story about a man trapped in a marriage to a woman he hates because of fear of his Italian grandfather, who alternately beats him when he strays from his wife's side, and offers him a fortune if he has a child. When he does, the fortune in Italian lire turns out to be practically worthless in dollars. The incident finally emerged not only as a short story, 'Fitter's Night', but also as an anecdote in *Timebends* and a full-length, though untitled, unpublished and unproduced play running to two hundred pages. The first two are no more than light-hearted tales. The play is rather different, a naturalistic work with Mike trapped in his loveless marriage but lacking the will to move in with his mistress.

The Yard, no more than fifteen minutes' walk from Miller's home, was a curious place, rather like a medieval town, with narrow, twisting streets and brick workshops covered with soot. The streets, behind the huge dry-docks facing the bay, carried naval names: Perry Street, after the admiral; Paul Jones Street. There was a blacksmith's shop and, at the entrance, a display of early attempts at submarines (one called *The Whale*), with plaques noting the dates on which they had sunk, somewhat bizarre icons for a navy yard.

Fresh-faced Marines searched lunchboxes and Thermos flasks as the workmen passed through the turnstiles. Facing the gate was the Eagle Nest, a café where the dockworkers could eat and where sailors would collect huge bags of fried-egg sandwiches for those about to set sail. Miller later recalled standing in a dry-dock under the stern of a cruiser, a hundred steps up the ladder below the deck. Underneath, river water leaked in from the caisson, ice-cold. In the ships themselves men would stand around waiting for the pressure to mount inside the oil tanks, or hammer steel amidst a curtain of falling sparks. In winter it could be bitterly cold, and they would search out snug places they could sleep rather than wait around as one job was completed before another craft could begin work.

It was here that Miller, a graduate, son of a once wealthy man and himself now financially secure, laboured through a New York winter alongside men who knew nothing of his background. This was not Teddy Roosevelt, swinging an axe to demonstrate his prowess and his common touch, nor yet the Marxist convinced of the dignity of labour and kinship with the working class. He was paying his dues, purging a sense of guilt, contributing to a common cause.

Patriotism, however, frequently made way for more immediate concerns. When the yardmaster announced a shortage of cadmium, the metal immediately disappeared as workers began to fashion it into rings and bracelets. I personally saw one on the wrist of a Brooklyn woman sixty years later. The Yard was largely manned by Italian Americans who had a penchant for beating up British sailors who were fighting their compatriots and whose ships were being refitted. It was also tainted with anti-Semitism. Indeed, it seemed to Miller that in this immigrant country there was more than one war going on. The South, scarred with racial prejudice, supported England against Germany because England had supported the Confederacy in the Civil War. The Irish, meanwhile, sided with the Germans against the English, even as their American loyalties led them to enrol in the Allied cause.

The Yard's chief machinist was a German who could hardly speak any English. He was responsible for installing sixteen-inch cannon on a battleship in for refitting. Miller later recalled the occasion:

There were higher officers, admirals, everybody standing around this one lone machinist with a black worker's cap on. He looked like he was right out of Bremen. He marched up the gangplank with five 'ducklings' behind him, his assistants. He never touched a tool. It took about a day to do this. He was the king of the ship, and I heard him speak with a distinct Deutsche accent. The whole thing was crazy. We had wonderful British officers in there one night. We were in a lunatic asylum! Here was the Captain of this marvellous cruiser, and I had to go down and do some welding on a bulkhead. You were not allowed to weld unless you could see round the back of the bulkhead, because there might be electrical connections back there and you would destroy them by heating the metal. The ship's officer said, 'You can't go in there.' I said, 'I've got to go in there.' 'No, you can't go in there. That is the Captain's locker.' I said, 'I'm sorry, but if you want a welder here that is what has got to happen.'

So I went up to the Captain, who never left the ship (it was in dry-dock). He looked like John Bull, a short man with a crushed cap, smoking his cigar, walking up and down with a riding crop, which he would slap against his thigh as he walked. He was guarding this ship against God knows what in dry-dock, within sight of the skyscrapers of Manhattan ... he called a sailor over and the sailor got the key out of somewhere. It was a gigantic medieval-type key. You would never see that on an American ship ...

We opened the door and walked in and there was this store room of lockers filled with canned goods, nuts, candy, polo equipment, tennis equipment, golf equipment. But the main thing was all these nuts. He had this marvellous cache of nuts from all over the world, and sardines, and things you could not buy for love nor money. And this kid said, 'Son of a bitch! We are starving on this fucking ship!' No wonder he looked so good.[82]

Nonetheless, for all the conflicts going on a millimetre below the surface, Miller did discover a sense of comradeship in the Navy Yard. Here was the embodiment of that sense of solidarity he had celebrated at college, the practical reality behind the rhetoric of 1930s idealism. If there were those who saw such work as a safe alternative to military service, banking their overtime pay and avoiding the supervisors who roamed the ships, there were also those who rose to the challenge of repairing the ships that limped into port, heavily damaged by enemy action, and readying them for convoy work. His story, 'Fitter's Night', published in 1962, was in part his acknowledgement of the skill and commitment of those he served beside. It was here, too, that he heard the story of an Italian longshoreman sexually attracted to his young cousin and unable to see his feelings for what they are, a story that would resurface as *A View from the Bridge*.

In the meantime, he had not given up on the theatre. Along with his radio plays, he had now written three in which he addressed his sense of the paralysis that had seemingly been induced by the implacable power of fascism. *The Half-Bridge*, *Boro Hall Nocturne* and *The Golden Years* formed a trilogy of unproduced, unpublished plays that, for much of his career, would remain unknown. These plays were something more than efforts to come up with a commercial success. They were, at least in part, the acknowledgement of a responsibility to engage with issues raised by the war.

In 1957 Susan Frank (maiden name Heiligman), also known as Sue Warren, of Christopher Street, New York City, would be called before the House Un-

American Activities Committee. A graduate in dramatic arts from Rutgers University (she left in 1938), she had appeared, she admitted, in a summer theatre production of Odets's *Awake and Sing*. Beyond that, the Committee could not get. She declined to answer all further questions on the grounds of the First and Fifth Amendments. The Committee showed her a *Daily Worker* review of a production of Odets's *Waiting for Lefty* by the New Labor Theatre on East 78th Street. Sue Warren was listed among the cast. The Committee, though, had little interest in her thespian skills. They wished to confront her with a Communist Party application form which carried the slogan 'Victory in 1943'. The name on the application form was A. Miller. The address was 18 Schermerhorn Street. The occupation of the applicant was given as 'Writer'. The candidate for membership was sponsored by a Sue Warren. She was asked a series of questions. She refused even to confirm where she had lived in 1943. The fact is that Miller did attend Party meetings but he never signed the application form that had been typed out for him. Had he done so, the House Un-American Activities Committee might well have summoned him before it did.

In other words, Miller had simultaneously been working in a supposedly secure defence establishment and attending meetings of the American Communist Party. Quite why this dimension of his life was not pursued by those who eventually summoned him before HUAC is not clear. His questioners seemed unaware of his work in the shipyard or, if aware, not interested in pursuing the potential damage he might have done given that by 1956 he was apparently being seen as a threat to the republic. Still more surprising was their failure to probe the possible danger represented by what they believed to be a card-carrying communist being given virtual free run of US army bases when he was commissioned to write the screenplay for a film.

While he could persuade himself that his radio work was serving the war effort, albeit indirectly, and that his employment in the Brooklyn Navy Yard did likewise, in 1943 he was given a chance to apply his skills more directly to the cause. Herman Shumlin, who had produced and directed Lillian Hellman's plays and was later to turn down *All My Sons*, recommended him to Lester Cowan, a Hollywood producer, as a possible screenwriter. He was to work with him on a film based on the columns of war correspondent Ernie Pyle (who, incidentally, had his own FBI file, for a derogatory comment about Hoover made by his paper's owners). Shumlin had heard some of Miller's radio scripts and read several of his unproduced plays. The provisional title of the film, like that of Pyle's collected columns, was *Here is Your War*, later changed to *The Story of GI Joe*. It was a considerable piece of luck since, for all his radio work, Miller was effectively an unknown. The pay was $750 a week, a welcome boost to family finances.

His parents, meanwhile, still living on East 3rd Street, seemed to be getting back on their feet. Isidore Miller had created the Bestex Coat Company, manufacturing coats and suits and working out of 1261 Broadway, though he relied on other family members to do much of the work. Miller's mother found herself finishing coats in 90-degree temperatures, rewarding herself with her son's favourite meal, chopped steak at the Roxy. Kermit, she reported in a letter dated 11 August 1944, was at Fort Jackson and had just sent his watch home, having been issued with an army model. Writing to Joan, she explained that the now pregnant Mary was fine. She and Arthur, Augusta reported in her letter, were wonderfully happy and it was only a matter of time before she became an aunt.

During 1944, the film project took Miller on a tour of placement centres, military bases and officer training schools in North and South Carolina, Florida, Kentucky, Texas, Oklahoma, Colorado and California. Mary stayed behind. It also took him to Washington where he had a disturbing experience, encountering a young woman whose Navy husband had been reported missing on the Murmansk run. Her desperation had provoked a curious response. 'She told me she was sleeping with young sailors now.' He found her confession simultaneously shocking and moving. Unsurprisingly, perhaps, he felt drawn to her, 'stimulated almost as much by the poetry of the idea as by her body . . . My own vulnerability, which normally I kept carefully shielded, responded to hers, and I knew that I was no longer as safely high-minded as I had tried to imagine.'[83] Nothing, he insisted, happened, but on his return he confided his feelings to his wife, seemingly believing that she would be impressed by his restraint. The result was predictable if not predicted. She was shocked and repelled. It was an incident that scarred their relationship for some years. Quite why he decided to tell her that he had resisted the temptation to sleep with another woman is hard to say. It was a mistake he would repeat a decade later with respect to his relationship with Marilyn Monroe.

If he was trying simultaneously to assert his virtue and his attractiveness to other women, the gesture backfired. What Mary derived from what was a half-confession, half-boast, was that he was not to be trusted. What seemed to him a trivial episode, to her was evidence of contempt for herself and a self-absorption already evidenced in his subordination of private life to career. Just four years after their marriage, there were already signs of estrangement. So significant was this event that he would refer to it several times in his published and unpublished work, and yet Miller's sexual indiscretion amounted to confessing not to an act of adultery but to the imagined possibility of an act of adultery.

Compare that with Mary McCarthy, who loved attacking Miller for his plays. She catalogued the number of men she slept with, three in twenty-four hours on one occasion. She did not so much devour men as try them out and file them away under penis size (small men, like *Commentary* magazine's

Norman Podhoretz, failing to measure up). Nor was marriage any bar to this adventuring. The fact is that Miller and Mary, by contrast with many of their contemporaries, were puritans.

Love, which in this relationship seems never quite to have overwhelmed him, even at the moment of their marriage, appears to have been replaced by desire wedded to a sense of duty. For Mary's part, passion did not lie at the centre of their relationship. Perhaps the Catholicism she had abandoned so many years before had not quite lost its grasp on her. Certainly, from this moment onwards, the relationship between them was never quite the same. There were clearly many times when they were happy, when something approaching love did seem to hold them together, but what was lacking was a relaxed assurance, an instinctive trust, an unquestioned commitment. For all their early radicalism, theirs was a relationship increasingly characterized by repressions, and later, as he became successful, so her fears that he would be exposed to new temptations grew, and alongside this his own sense of desiring liberation from a puritan ethic that had seen him work for a success that he knew Mary felt increasingly threatened by.

The trip to Washington also resulted in three attempts at short stories, all centring on the same idea and all focusing on an illicit sexuality: 'The Girls From New York', 'The Independents' and 'A Matter of Suspicion'.

A writer is in Washington to outline the details of a scenario for a film to a group of military officers, pitching an idea he has yet to work out in any detail. He is accompanied by a producer. The two men stay at the Statler Hotel where they are to be joined by a cameraman, himself seconded from the forces. The producer explains that the latter is about to be married and that his girl will herself be coming to the hotel. He asks whether the writer will mind surrendering his room, rooms being difficult to get in wartime Washington. Accordingly, the writer moves in with the producer. To his surprise, the cameraman also joins them, seemingly respecting the proprieties. In fact, though the cameraman is indeed getting married, the young woman has nothing to do with him. She turns out to be a prostitute brought down from New York by the producer.

Nothing came of the stories, which were based on fact. Lester Cowan had, indeed, secured the services of a New York hooker.

Though it was published in April 1946, following research for his radio play about plastic surgeons, his story 'The Plaster Masks' explains something of his approach to writing the scenario for what was to become *The Story of GI Joe*. As the writer in the story explains to a surgeon, 'What I'd like to do . . . is to find out the actual attitude of these men toward the country and toward themselves and their injuries. I have never been in the Army or in combat . . . I would like the program to avoid clichés; I would like to feel that when you hear it you'll feel it true, and the men the same.' – 'But you want the program to have a lift. You want to send the audience away with hope,' observes the surgeon. – 'But the right hope,' the writer replies. 'I would like the hope to be based on reality.'[84] That is essentially the problem that confronted him in writing the film script. It quickly became apparent not merely that his object-ive was not quite in line with his employer's, but that a gulf was opening up between the kind of hope he carried into the project and what he found.

For two months he joined troops on exercises, talked to men who had been hospitalized, interviewed generals, in an attempt to understand something of military life and the attitude of those involved in the war, a war which, at least in terms of the European theatre, was still in its early stages as far as American troops were concerned. He was looking for people fired by idealism, those whose 1930s vision of human solidarity had transferred effortlessly into the context of war. He felt, or wished to feel, as did Mary McCarthy, that in war 'Class barriers disappear or tend to become porous; the factory worker is an aristocrat in comparison to the middle-class clerk ... The America ... of vast inequalities and dramatic contrasts is rapidly ceasing to exist.'[85] That was not what he discovered. What he found were raw recruits being honed into fighting men, soldiers for whom this was no more than a task to be accomplished – indeed, in some cases a relief from unemployment. They did feel that they were fighting a worthwhile cause, not least because Pearl Harbor had revealed a disturbing vulnerability, while German U-boats, for a while, seemed to operate with impunity off the eastern seaboard. But they did not see it as an ideological conflict.

What he also found was a casual and sometimes virulent racism in an army that was segregated. He recalled a white captain, John Wrabel, who had volunteered to command a black infantry company in an Alabama training camp and who was nearly killed when he rescued two of his men from a lynch mob. They had laughed at a display in a women's hat shop and two white women had taken exception. A mob had quickly gathered. In an unpublished memoir, he noted what had happened. Wrabel, he recorded, had driven into town in a jeep, with only one man in support. He drove his jeep into the crowd, where the two black soldiers, hands tied behind their backs, were being prepared for hanging. He stood on the seat, drew his pistol, and ordered the crowd to surrender their prisoners. Astonished, they complied.

The research conducted on his various visits led to his first book, *Situation Normal*, an ironic title derived from the familiar Army expression, SNAFU, situation normal: all fucked up. The screenplay proved more obdurate. Miller's idea was to place the ordinary soldier at its centre, but he was dealing not only with Hollywood but the military top brass whose support and approval were necessary. So it was that in his late twenties, and still with no major work to his name, he found himself meeting with generals before taking a train out to the West Coast to continue work on the script in Hollywood. This work consisted partly of further interviews with soldiers rounded up by the studio. But it also involved a meeting with Laurence Stallings, author, with Maxwell Anderson, of the anti-war play *What Price Glory*, and of the film *The Big Parade*.

Years later, Miller recalled the meeting and his own insistence that Russian resistance was based on ideological commitment, only to have Stallings correct him by pointing out: 'This is one thing you've got to watch in your script – don't try to make it mean too much. Battle is never about beliefs or ideas, it's about your buddy and you and not coming off a shitass or a coward.'[86] The studio, Stallings warned him, was not going to use his script unless it conformed to the familiar structure and content of the genre – unless, that is, it looked remarkably like *The Big Parade*. But to Miller this was not what Ernie Pyle was about. His reporting, like the script he was anxious to write, focused on the individual, and it was to Ernie Pyle that he was now sent by the studio, not least because they were still awaiting his signature on the contract, Miller arrived having been on what turned out to be a terrifying flight on a C-47. Pyle agreed to go ahead with the project, provided that the film featured not him but the serving soldiers he wrote about in his columns.

Miller found the encounter strangely disappointing. To Pyle, Miller's idealism seemed beside the point. He, after all, was a reporter. Like Frederic Henry in Hemingway's *A Farewell to Arms*, he distrusted abstract nouns. He was concerned with places, names and actions. He had no desire to project emotions, ideas, thoughts on to men who were simply surviving from moment to moment, doing what they did either well or badly. Miller realized that 'Ernie knew most soldiers were not being visibly changed by ideas. He understood completely that they could be, but it was not his business to write about what could be. He had enough to write about what is. Now.'

But Miller knew, too, that, to him, the war was of a piece with the values he had embraced up in Michigan. To him, 'the truth is a larger thing than what a man feels or knows at any particular time in his life'.[87] Pyle, he was sure, knew this too. The difference between them lay in what they saw as their immediate job. It was Miller's double commitment to describe accurately what he saw and to propose a broader sense of society, and the individual's place in it, that disturbed many reviewers, who saw in *Situation Normal* precisely that sentimentality which Miller had found in many war films and that he had told himself he would ruthlessly excise. Nonetheless, as he was to explain in his autobiography, he had 'determined to conquer whatever problems there were in the screenplay and to make sure it strengthened support for our men fighting the enemy'.[88]

The critic and biographer Jackson Benson recalls another meeting with Pyle when he and Miller were taken to dinner at the 21 restaurant by United

Press. They were joined by John Steinbeck, whose drunken wife had recently fallen off the balcony of their apartment. The boy from Brooklyn was suddenly introduced to the writer as celebrity, an author who, in *The Grapes of Wrath*, had precisely succeeded in relating individual lives to a broader sense of social values: 'The wire service [UP] men were hard drinkers, and by the time they had dinner and wine, the bill came to several hundred dollars – but Steinbeck insisted on paying it.' Afterwards, Steinbeck and Miller walked the streets of the city together and talked.[89]

Years later, Miller recalled the embarrassment caused by Steinbeck's grand gesture. Here was a West Coast writer who knew nothing of the ethos of those he found himself among. The journalists insisted on tossing a coin to see who paid, but Steinbeck won. It was one sign, among many, in the years that followed, that in unplugging himself from California Steinbeck had lost touch not only with the country but with himself. It was something that Miller, briefly travelling in the opposite direction, was determined not to do.

Back in Hollywood, he was overwhelmed by the surreal nature of his position, writing the screenplay that was to celebrate the lives of real people risking their lives for democracy, while outside his window the kaleidoscope of inanities that constituted the movie business was played out in front of his eyes. He was, for example, taken for a drive by a man who had to have his attention drawn to the existence of windscreen wipers when it suddenly began to rain. Here, money was spent carelessly. Writing was a product. Relationships were temporary alliances. This was Nathanael West territory.

He resigned when another writer, Alan LeMay, was hired as his collaborator in an effort to produce a film more amenable to Hollywood needs. He did, though, produce an outline for the film. Elements of his original script survived the various writers who replaced him, and the film does draw on the work he had done in the field. He confessed to an odd satisfaction with the final film, which received four Academy Award nominations. Nonetheless, it was no longer an account of a series of individuals but of a lieutenant, played by Robert Mitchum, who loses his life for the cause, and of a reporter, played by Burgess Meredith. Miller's name does not appear on the credits.

By then, however, he was involved in his first Broadway production, a play whose plot he had outlined to Ernie Pyle, who had recognized something of himself in the portrait of a man whose life seemed specially blessed. The play was called *The Man Who Had All the Luck* (originally 'Something Like a Fable').

Ernie Pyle, though, did not prove especially blessed. He died in 1945, shot in the head in the American advance across the Pacific towards Japan. Miller wrote an appreciation of him in *New Masses*, dead on a Pacific island 'with a tiny name, a name that is like the initials of distance – ie.' [Ie Shima] Pyle, he explained, understood 'that the life of a man is made up of details, and he could build a column on a thumbtack'.[90] It was a quality he had admired and reflected in his own work.

On 12 March 1953, one of those who replaced Miller in writing the script of *The Story of GI Joe*, the screenwriter Leopold Atlas, found himself summoned before HUAC in executive session, where he named thirty-seven names, a fact his daughter did not discover until sixteen years after his death.

Miller's account of his time researching the film *Situation Normal*,[91] was published in 1944. It was recommended for publication by Frank E. Taylor, editor-in-chief of Harper's Reynal & Hitchcock division. This was where Mary now worked. The book is dedicated to his brother, Lieutenant Kermit Miller. It was a long way from the kind of story Hollywood had been looking for. Surprisingly, for a publication of that time, it emerges as something of an indictment of America. What was to have been a celebration of the fighting man turns out to be in part an attack on American racism and a lament over the lack of values in a country going to war with no clear idea as to what it is fighting for.

Laced into Miller's account is an awareness of the casual racism that infects the Army. The world of his aborted novel *The Bangkok Star* is not far away. Recalling a soldier accused of 'raping a colored girl', a group of white officers dismiss this as 'an impossibility on the face of it', so that the accused man is 'freed by both present and past juries'.[92] Meanwhile, a 'buck nigger' is accused of grabbing the wife of a white officer. Miller is plainly shocked. Indeed, he has to 'keep remembering that some of the most aggressive-minded officers I have met, men who want to come to grips with the enemy at the earliest possible moment, are men who betray strong traces of home-grown Fascist complexes'.

On his travels he discovered white men who objected to 'being instructed by negroes', and Negroes forced to sit on their own, shunned by their supposed comrades. He admitted: 'From the time I left the reception center, the problem of bringing the Negro into this picture has been bothering me.' For the most part he had seen him in menial roles. 'I just couldn't see anything hopeful in the situation and I couldn't get myself to lie about it.' The stories he heard seemed to come straight out of burlesque, with the Negro supposedly shaking, wide-eyed, in the face of danger. As to the reality, he found this difficult to ascertain, being steered away from black soldiers. He did meet one African-American – a lawyer from Nebraska – who shared a barracks with whites. He had volunteered 'Because if this country loses, my people are going to fall back five decades'. At the same time, he acknowledged the outrages that regularly occurred: 'the uniform highlights all the irony of our position; we are asked to die for a country that doesn't always let us live'. 'I want,' Miller says, 'in the picture, a man like this in the officers' school. I will show how ridiculous is the claim that the races absolutely cannot tolerate each other after prejudice has been instilled.' The only false moment comes when he praises a black soldier who puts a platoon through its paces for 'the sense of rhythm that a Negro has'.

It is hard to believe that he thought either the Army or Hollywood would have the slightest interest in turning their movie into a plea for racial tolerance; but that he should choose to make this a central theme of his first published book, as he would of *The Bangkok Star* and *Focus* (originally titled 'Four Eyes'), reveals both the nature and the intensity of his commitment, a commitment to racial justice that has largely passed unremarked because unknown. There is a greater irony, however, and that is that Miller would later play virtually no role in the civil rights movement. Asked why he had not, he replied that he had left it to a younger generation, and this from a man who made his opposition to the Vietnam War a central part of his life. But the civil rights movement still lay a decade and more ahead when he published *Situation Normal*.

Situation Normal received mixed notices, praised for its journalistic observation and criticized for its digression into moral speculation. For Russell Maloney, in the *New York Times*, he was convincing in his descriptive writing but not in his philosophizing. The same was true for Herbert Kupferberg in the *New York Herald Tribune*. To Miller, though, the fascination of the exercise lay precisely in trying to understand not only the daily experiences of those preparing for, or involved in, war but also their motivation and the implications of moving suddenly from civilian life to a world in which they were expected to kill and, potentially, lay down their lives.

Louis Falstein, who served in the Air Force, wrote, in *Face of a Hero*, of the Jewish narrator fighting fascism because he 'hated Hitler, hated fascism, and feared they would come to America', while his crewmates 'fought on nothing. They fought without anger', having no idea what the war was about, 'for the army had kept our cause a deep, dark secret'.[93] Miller did not accuse the military of such an act of suppression, aware as he was of the familiar charge that this was a Jewish war, but he did encounter the same sense of detachment, the same lack of passion.

What he found was men, and one man in particular, a veteran called Watson (he never recorded his first name), who had already experienced brutal fighting in the Pacific, and for whom loyalty to those in his unit meant far more than any military engagement, far more than the abstractions in whose name Miller in particular wished them to be fighting, and far more than the materialism driving American society: 'Friendship,' Watson says, 'is the greatest thing out there. I mean real friendship, not because a guy can give you something you want.' He would, he asserts, 'die for any one of thirty or forty men out there just as easy as I'd flick out this match. I swear that's the truth. I don't expect you to understand it, but I swear it. It never seemed a terrible thing or a sacrifice after a while. I would die for them. I love them with everything in my heart.'[94]

This is surely the origin of Chris Keller in *All My Sons*, a man who returns from war with an idealism forged out of shared danger and rooted in mutual responsibility. Watson had found, as Chris was to find, that returning home was like entering a dream. Nothing had substance. And it is worth remembering that *All My Sons* was written during the war, to be produced, as he assumed, during the war.

Watson, who feels guilty at having left his comrades behind, is sexually impotent because he feels he has no right to live fully when they cannot. Chris Keller carries a similar burden of guilt, heightened by the fact that men under his command have died, and while not impotent has denied himself the relationship he craves not only because of his mother's brooding presence but because he, too, is conscious in particular of his brother's death. He, like Watson, feels he has no right to a full life, though it is doubtful if the Hollywood that commissioned Miller, or the US Army, which presumed the project was designed to bolster morale, would have appreciated Watson's comment that 'the real heroes never come back. They're the real ones. They're the only ones. Nobody's a hero if he can still breathe.'

When an officer tells Miller that Watson 'will do things for his unit that a larger organization could never get him to do, things he would never dream of doing as an individual – you might say, as an individualist', it chimed with Miller's own faith in communal action. Indeed the logic he was developing was leading in a dangerous direction, as far as the book was concerned, as the war began to seem an irrelevance and he edged towards a denunciation of American values:

> I wondered for the first time whether I ought not to be wandering through St Paul and Kansas City, New York and Los Angeles instead of through the camps. For as far as Watson was concerned it was in America as much as in the [Pacific] island where he fought that his wholeness had been wrecked and his mind distracted. It was not only the Japanese who had shaken his wits. We here did our part in that, and with terrible effect.

What Miller really seems to have feared was the possibility of fascism in America – or if not that, then a soulless and ultimately divisive capitalism.

His comment, of Watson, that in returning to civilian life, as he would eventually do, he would be abandoning this sense of human solidarity for something altogether less worthy, is essentially what Chris Keller would try to articulate. For, as Miller suggests in *Situation Normal*, he will, thereafter, have to 'live unto himself, for his own selfish welfare. Half of him, in a sense, must die.' What awaits him is family and business, and Miller knew what to think of them. In the book he speculates about returning to a society riven by class and race differences, with 'rich and poor again, white and black again ... Jew and Gentile again' pursuing their separate destinies, an odd observation in a book supposedly extolling the American war effort, but early evidence of Miller's compulsion to swim against the tide. Here, still, is the familiar language of political radicalism as he writes of the need to serve the 'mass of men'.

There is, Miller remarks 'a great and deep sense of loss in that ... Civilian life in America is private, it is always striving for exclusiveness. Our lifelong boast is that we got ahead of the next guy, excluded him. We have always believed in the fiction – and often damned our own belief – that if every man privately takes care of his own interests, the community, the nation will prosper and be safe.'

What is needed, he maintains, is a social goal worth his sacrifice. He suggests that 'the immediate danger of being inundated by a flood', which would necessitate everyone working together for the common good, might do the trick – as it had briefly done in *The Grapes of Wrath*. But, he acknowledges, such a common peril is too rare to guarantee the kind of solidarity he is looking for. In reality, Watson and his kind will return to a world in which 'every group in town' excludes 'the proximate group ... a morass of little groups each of whose apparent goals in life conflicts with the goals of the next group'. What lies ahead is an aimless and alienated life, a deracinated existence. The irony is that in seeking to create a portrait of the fighting man, in fact Miller creates a portrait of American society as he saw it then and, in a sense, as he was to continue to see it, a society of alienated individuals wedded to myths of self-aggrandizement, isolated from one another not so much by prejudice itself as by a failure of moral imagination.

The British and Russians, he suggests, knew why they were fighting. Their bomb-ravaged cities had forged a unity out of necessity. He finds no such unity in America, and its lack clearly goes beyond a concern with wartime morale. The war was most certainly not fought for free enterprise or the status quo. What it was fought for is by no means clear. The attack on Pearl Harbor had seen people rally to the flag but what that flag stood for was less evident. What it should stand for, he suggests, is the idea of equality, an American virtue become no more than an American piety.

In a revealing aside he accepts that the idea may seem simplistic, lacking as it is in 'economic factor', a reference beyond American millennialism to a more clearly Marxist model, a fact equally underlined by his stress on the need for what he calls a 'great social goal'. It is the lack of that social vision which makes his everyman figure, Watson, feel so isolated and guilty. Returned to civilian life, he will 'wall himself in from his fellow man', live his own 'little life' and revert to what Miller calls 'the stale and deadly competition with his fellow men for rewards' unconnected to his human needs, cut off from the 'great movement of mankind'. Watson is a 'man alone', isolated in his guilt.

Nobody, Miller maintains, 'ever fought a war in order to keep everything the same, and certainly never for free enterprise or jobs'. What they are fighting for, did they but know it, is equality, but in a society which invests its money and energy selling mouthwash rather than democracy, this is lost in 'the chaos of mind that is America today'. In this America, Watson, he suggests, is a 'misfit', a word that would later resonate in his mind as he drew a portrait of a group of men and women lost, like him, in their own compromised dream of perfection.

Miller's desire to idealize the serviceman, his sense of the potential corruption involved in the fact of building a career while others risked their lives, may have something to do with the fact that he felt his own contribution to the cause was insufficient. His patriotic radio plays, his painful work in the Brooklyn Navy Yard and now his work on the movie were his attempt to balance the scales. The irony is that the real truth of *Situation Normal* lay less in a damaged idealist than in those soldiers who resented the draft, understood little of the forces against which they were fighting, and longed for precisely that civilian life, replete with materialism, ambition and self-concern, that Miller himself was inclined to castigate.

There is, in short, a sentimentality to this book that is a product of his desire to find what he seeks. It is the homage he pays to those who face risks he does not. Thus the soldiers, understanding or not, must be presented as the agents of moral principle and not tainted with a love of violence, a sullen acceptance of the given, a contempt for other races, creeds, ideas, despite the fact that he provides ample evidence for these.

The damaged soldier, Watson, meanwhile, emerges as a version of Melville's Bartleby, preferring not to accommodate himself to a life of striving and ambition (he persistently fails his officer-training programme), in the process seemingly devoting himself to a slow but inevitable drift towards self-destruction. It is for him, as it was for Saul Bellow's 'dangling man', civilian life that carries the real threat. In 2003, however, Miller added an ironic note: 'Watson actually existed. The officers attending him thought him riddled with grief for having survived terrible conditions, etc. But he was actually in dread of having to return to battle and was acting crazy.'

It is hardly surprising that aspects of *Situation Normal* disturbed reviewers and that it did not lend itself with ease to translation into film. The rhetoric of wartime does clearly account for much of its tone, but there is a level on which this book is the clearest statement of Miller's political convictions to date, albeit dressed up in a generalized transcendentalist language. What was lacking in America, it seemed to him, was precisely a sense of serving any cause beyond the self. That cause, he implied, should be a commitment to equality and that kind of connectiveness that Watson had discovered in war while hating the circumstances that provoked it.

His outline of the screenplay for *The Story of GI Joe*, unsurprisingly, is also peppered with idealistic statements, albeit in the context of a film that follows the exploits of a group of soldiers whose personal failings stretch from cynicism to desertion. The tension between the two is established in an opening scene in which eight men are inducted into the Army, one expressing 'postwar hopes' and another 'wry pessimism'. Beginning with basic training and manoeuvres, the film, as Miller planned it, moves from the North African campaign to Italy and on to the invasion of France. Along the way the men become battle-hardened. There is, though, no equivalent to the figure of Watson.

To the natural melodrama of war Miller adds his own touches. In a 'Kasserine sequence' American and British soldiers in a bar discover a hidden microphone, whose wires they trace to an upstairs room where two 'Fascists' are listening to their loose talk. The British stab them out of pure hatred. The Americans kill fascists out of a desire to purge the world of evil. Given that in *Situation Normal* he acknowledges that few American troops had any sense that they were fighting fascism, the dialogue of the screenplay owes more to Miller's own politics than to those of the men on whom his characters were supposedly based.

In an Italian sequence, a fascist mayor is deposed by his own people and another man summarily appointed at the behest of an American captain. When a soldier deserts he is upbraided by one of his companions, who insists that the racketeers of the world must understand that the world belongs to the people. It is scarcely surprising that such a scene did not find its way into the final script. Then, as the invasion fleet sets sail for France, Ernie Pyle is made to observe that at last the world is waking up and that the people are through with being pushed around. A new day, he suggests, is about to dawn.

It is hard to believe that such rhetoric would so quickly make way for the controlled prose of *All My Sons*, which he began to write just a year later. For the moment, Miller's attitudes and language were still shaped by the previous decade. A year earlier he had attended a Marxist study course, and that seems to have coloured his language no less than his approach. His preference for the term 'fascists' over 'Nazis' or even 'Germans' is a reminder that for him, still, the war was an extension of a more fundamental conflict.

4

ALL MY SONS

Despite its somewhat ambivalent reception, *Situation Normal* marked a significant moment in Miller's career. He was in print. He also had a moral part-ownership of a film, even if little of his material would survive. He had been to Hollywood and learned enough of its attitude to writers to enable him to resist its blandishments a few years later when, after the success of *All My Sons*, he was offered a contract. Six years on from Michigan, he at last had a career and, suddenly, the prospect of a Broadway opening for *The Man Who Had All the Luck*, a work he had been struggling with for several years, but which was finally lined up for production towards the end of 1944.

He was also to be the father of a child. On 15 May, Kermit wrote to 'Art and Mary' from South Carolina where he had been in training, marching twenty-five miles in eight hours:

> Mary, you must be gaining weight and from here even I can see you're looking fine, as Dad would say. Remember, I buy his first choo-choo trains. Yes, I've decided it will be a boy. Hope he resembles its Mom, and thinks like his Dad and Mom ...
>
> Arty, read something about 'G.I. Joe' in a local paper i.e. that Pyle was to appear in the movie. How's about your work?

On 25 August he wrote again, after a brief reunion:

> Voicing my gratitude in this manner is a very meager way of showing you how deeply moved I was at our last meeting. Your understanding and solicitude softened the blow of frustration, Fran's and mine. If the little one takes after you both, you may well be proud, you must know how proud of <u>you</u> I am.
>
> Told Mom to-night, in a letter, that I am looking forward to spoiling the baby, and there is little either of you can do to stop it. I am with you always.

The baby was not a boy. The Millers' daughter, Jane, was born on 7 September 1944. On the 14th Kermit wrote again, this time in a letter headed 'Somewhere in France', unaware, as yet, of the birth of his niece. This and the other letters he sent do a great deal to explain the respect in which Miller held his brother, risking his life in Europe and expressing that sense of idealism which he himself had hoped to find in researching *Situation Normal*. For the moment, though, Kermit was waiting for a battle to begin:

> Am writing in our company orderly tent this mild autumn evening (19.30) with the sun still very much in the sky sending a shaft of light across the typewriter. Outside the fruit laden apple trees in perfect pattern cry out to be relieved of their fruition but the law of the area states they will not be touched by G.I. hands ergo no picking . . . Tasted a few fallen ones and they are very bitter which I suspect is the reason for the strict obedience to the spirit of the law.
>
> Haven't heard, as yet, from either you or Mom, and am therefore completely in the dark as to events at home . . .
>
> Hereabouts the war has left its tell-tale marks in many ways. Craters, fox holes, gaping roofs all testify to the barbarity of our civilization. I remember when reading of Caesar in Gaul my reaction to his exploits and those of his legions and never one moment suspecting I would some day stand on the same ground under circumstances not entirely dissimilar.

Finally, word got through, both of the birth and of the impending publication of *Situation Normal* and the opening of *The Story of GI Joe*. Kermit wrote on 30 September:

> Heard from Fran that Jane Ellen has arrived. That makes me an Uncle and am proud as hell; pretty nearly as thrilling as being a father. How about that Art? Mary, my sincerest congratulations and if Jane is as great a gal as her mother she will be a mighty lucky little girl. You have made an elderly uncle (32 before you get this) very happy. Can just picture Izzy and Gus [Augusta], and remember what I said a while ago about not letting them spoil Jane Ellen. They will if you're not careful.
>
> Hey Art, that book should be in the mail in short order, and it goes without saying that it will be my Best Book of the Year . . . Have told our Supply Sergeant, a fatty by the name of O'Hare, about the opening in Boston. His home is in Holyoke, and he has written his wife to try to see it . . . Wouldn't be surprising if other members of the outfit do the same. You'll have to see Ernie Pyle personally what with the little man having returned to the States for a rest. He's done more for the doughfoot than anyone past or present and the boys think the world of him. Tell me more about the picture. As you can readily understand we're always hungry for news, and especially news of the picture inasmuch as it will mean so much to the infantry. Hope they didn't mangle it beyond recognition.

In fact, Miller had heard from his agent, Paul Streger, in April that the film-makers were 'more or less shooting from the cuff' and that 'there is

nothing of your material in the script, as a matter of fact, they have had seven
different writers on the story since you worked on it, so there.'[1]

Kermit was still 'parked in an apple orchard in the most beautiful scenic
country I've seen since the Adirondacks and Berkshires'. As to the shooting
war, 'Jerry is tricky as hell, but don't get the impression that we've seen
him yet on a battle set. He left these parts hell bent for election as is
obviously evidenced.' A week later the tone had changed, and from now
on Miller's sense of the immediate meaning of the war came less from the
New York Times than from his brother. Kermit had, he wrote on 9 October,
seen

> a mass of rubble unimagined in your wildest departures from the everyday
> norm of civilized life. In the dark, I see it in the early morning hours, it
> presented a visual and ... graphic representation of war's controlled fury,
> controlled because of the almost hellish accuracy of aimed artillery fire ...
> our men are magnificent.

At the beginning of November he wrote to Miller:

> Have been out of the line several days but will be back shortly. There is much
> ahead of us and you can do your bit by throttling talk of the kind that says
> the war is over. It definitely is <u>not</u>. The bastards still have plenty of fight left
> and we are not taking them for granted.
>
> It will be a rough winter and even now the weather is crisp ... In the line
> we eat only C and K rations, and after a few days these can be mighty
> repetitious.
>
> We continue to receive weekly rations of cigarettes candy etc. The officers
> get a monthly liquor ration at 100 francs [*sic*] per (200) at present exchange.
> It's damned good stuff.

As Kermit prepared to go back into the line, his brother was readying
himself for the opening of his new play, *The Man Who Had All the Luck*.
Looking back later, he was inclined to see its roots in the Depression, at least
in terms of the terror of failure and guilt at success experienced by its central
character. Beyond that, though, its theme, of a man who is unaccountably
lucky when others are suffering misfortune, must have seemed close to his
own experience – exempt from military service, building a career and now
with a child of his own.

Despite its harking back to Depression America, this was not to be, like
his early plays, a celebration of those excluded from the dream. On the
contrary, and perhaps paradoxically, it was to explore the sensibility of a
man who had it all but for whom success would be a burden too great to
bear. Nor was it, like *The Golden Years*, to offer an epic account of
conflicting values, expressed in poetic terms. He had set out to write a

fable, though uncertain, for a while, as to where its heart might lie. He was unsure as to whether its central character was to be seen as a tragic hero, destroyed by some self-created inevitability, or whether he was to find redemption by walking the edge of authenticity, reprieved by love and an understanding born out of suffering. Either way, this was to be a modern-day Job.

The Man Who Had All the Luck was prompted by a story told to Miller by his mother-in-law. A relative had hanged himself in a barn. Successful, even in the middle of the Depression, he had become paranoid, obsessively checking the books of a filling station he had acquired. Miller's interest was aroused not because he wanted to dramatize a psychotic individual but because it recalled the incident in which his cousin's husband Moe, also successful, had one day dropped dead on Brighton Beach. In later years Miller made several attempts to shape the latter into a story, not least because of what had followed. A passing doctor had rushed to help the fallen man only to discover that he was already dead. That same doctor, whose hunchback gave him a sinister appearance, had unaccountably chosen to drive the body to his home on East 3rd Street, a delivery service not appreciated by the hysterical relatives, who screamed whenever he came near them.

These stories came to nothing but the two incidents, taken together, prompted him to write a novel designed to explore the arbitrariness of fate. Where, he asked, did meaning reside if we are subject to such capricious pressures? Why were those two individuals so successful when others were not, and why did one choose to end his life and one die unaccountably? These were questions raised, it seemed to him, both by the Depression and by the war, in both of which sheer contingency seemed to prevail, the absurd to have its triumph. Was there no greater order and purpose to existence than birth followed by death, with no structure of meaning, no moral spine to existence?

With reports of the Holocaust already in the public domain (details of the camps had been known since the end of 1942, when the Allies made coordinated announcements), he chose to create a portrait of a man, unaccountably favoured by the gods, who seeks some reason for his success, for his survival, while others suffer. Aware of his own unworthiness, he sees his life as evidence of simple chance, a suspicion that drives him to the edge of madness and beyond. There being, seemingly, no moral structure to experience, identity itself is put under strain and finally snaps.

In the novel version, the protagonist commits suicide, acting out that absurd logic as if also trying to propitiate the gods in whom he does not believe. *The Man Who Had All the Luck*, Miller explained, tried to engage 'the question of the justice of fate, how it was that one man failed and another, no more or less capable, achieved some glory in life'.[2] He saw a connection between the novel, later turned play, and *The Golden Years* in that both works seemed to him to centre on someone destroyed by an illusion of powerlessness. The implications of that for the Holocaust would take several decades to work out, but he would never let go of his conviction that the individual retains control over his or her fate, hence his curious remark many years later to the House Un-American Activities Committee about not being the kind of Jew who would go easily to his death.

He wrote several versions of the novel but none seemed to work. They told the story of a young mechanic whose career is based on a deception as he claims to have repaired a car in fact repaired by someone else. From this stems a seemingly unending series of successes while those around him fail, unwilling to accept responsibility for failure. By degrees, however, the mechanic is disturbed by the arbitrariness of his good luck, and waits for some compensating disaster which he finally rushes to meet by taking his own life.

It is a curious work, the prose style reflecting the mental state of his protagonist. Staying close to his source, Miller creates a portrait of a man spiralling down towards death, offering to sacrifice himself while, Lear-like, challenging the cosmos. He finally set it aside and tried again, this time as a play. The protagonist is still disturbed by his own success, by what seems to him the manifest injustices of life, but now he is more inclined to accept his own agency, something he learns partly from an Austrian refugee out of a Europe in which millions have come to feel they are no more than the playthings of fate, victims of a power over which they have no control.

The novel survives in manuscript. It is not hard to see why it was never published. It is over-written, its scenes overextended, its themes needlessly underscored, its metaphors suspect, its dramatic events signalled. The various elements of the story seem to coexist rather than be integrated. There is, also, a rather too calculated and precise contrast between the success of the central character and the failure of those around him, as if this were a quasi-scientific demonstration. Perhaps it is simply that, despite the success of his later novel, *Focus*, there are aspects of the form to which he did not respond.

Miller has, indeed, confessed to impatience with descriptive writing, recalling his experience of reading Dostoevsky as a teenager: 'I found the parts I enjoyed most were where they were talking. I would skim down pages and see the dialogue, and that was what I loved to read ... it seems as though the speech is the evidence of the person's being. The rest of it is commentary.' For him, texts of any kind only come alive when the voice of an individual sounds from them, whether it is a piece of journalism or 'a study of housing'. As he remarked, 'They have some guy who lives in one of these houses who says, "I think this house is beautiful, excepting that the toilets don't work." That tells you in one sentence what it would probably take a lot more to do.

I love the concision of it, the compression ... you come to climaxes more cleanly. The dialectic is shorter.'[3] Fiction seemed to him 'boundless' and un-economical. In drama, he explained, he could 'feel the walls'.

The novel version of *The Man Who Had All the Luck* seems to bear this out. In the dialogue he is careful to reproduce the rhythms of speech, the syntax of spoken language. In the narrative sections he is inclined to a self-conscious prose. The precision and directness of the one tends to underscore the vagueness and occasional callowness of the other.

The play was altogether more convincing, a fable in part addressing America's belief in its exceptionalism. However, where in the novel the central character is drawn towards suicide, overwhelmed by evidence of a life without transcendence, lacking in moral logic, the play was to head in the direction of redemption. 1944, after all, was not a good year to confront American audiences with the idea that they were victims with no command of their fate. As it turned out, 1944 was not a good year to confront American audiences with *The Man Who Had All the Luck*, either.

The play opened for its try-out run in Wilmington, Delaware, home of the DuPont Corporation, sponsors of *Cavalcade of America* which had established his reputation as a writer. On 8 March Miller had received a letter from William A. Hart of DuPont in which he remarked: 'I am interested to hear about your new stage show and hope that you will keep me informed, particularly if you are going to rehearse and open in Wilmington. Why don't you autograph and present me a copy of "Situation Normal" if it is really something I should see?'[4] The omens, therefore, might have seemed good.

He had high hopes for the production which opened on 23 November 1944 in a not very distinguished Broadway season (whose hits were Mary Chase's *Harvey*, Philip Yordan's *Anna Lucasta* and Norman Krasna's *Dear Ruth*, an adaptation of John Hersey's *A Bell for Adano*). He had arrived at the destination he had plotted back in Ann Arbor when he had been so confident that the New York theatre would respond to plays through which he meant to transform America. His fall from grace was thus the greater when the play was withdrawn after three days, losing investors $55,000.

Reviews of the play, whose first British production took place sixteen years later, were negative or, in Miller's words, baffled, and he himself came to feel that both he and the director had failed to understand its anti-realist thrust: 'I thought it was realistic but I was such a numbhead that my idea of what was real was completely absurd. So I wrote this play thinking I was writing about reality but in fact it was a deep metaphor which has no clues as to how it is going to proceed. The events are simply stated one after another. It is working on a metaphorical level where no psychological basis is necessary.'[5] It needed a style of presentation they never found. But though mainly discouraging, some of the reviews were not without a kindly if slightly condescending prophecy of better things to come. George Freedley regarded it as an honest failure, while Lewis Nichols in the *New York Times* on 24 November regretted the confusion of the script and 'somewhat jumbled philosophies', which he attributed in part to Miller having read too much Saroyan. Nonetheless, he conceded that it had 'a certain amount of merit' and 'some good dialogue in spots'.

For Howard Barnes, by contrast, writing in the *New York Herald Tribune*, the play was 'an unpleasant, unexciting and downright mystifying maze ... incredibly turgid in its writing and stuttering in its execution'. The reviewer of the *New York Post* found 'a lot of ideas knocking around the stage' but had little to say for 'three addled acts', while John Chapman in the *New York Daily News* discovered elements of interest but regretted their failure to 'stick together'. 'I hope,' he added, that 'Mr Miller will go right back to work writing another piece, for he has a sense of theater and a real if undeveloped way of making stage characters talk and act human'.[6]

Ward Morehouse, reviewer for the *New York Sun*, found it 'an ambling piece, strangely confused at times and rather tiresome', though with 'some engaging moments and several likable characters'. He wished him 'better luck with his next one'. The *Boston Science Monitor*, as befitted a Boston newspaper, took a rather more highhanded approach. 'This melodramatic comedy,' observed a staff correspondent, 'has a wholesome theme, which is given an unwholesome presentation. Vulgarity is used without point ... The exercise of a vigorous blue pencil is indicated.' The *Brooklyn Citizen* was more friendly. Edgar Price, though feeling it did not quite come off, nonetheless praised the 'excellent dialogue' and suggested that it 'just misses being good theatre'. Once again, good wishes for the future: 'Better luck next time, Mr Miller.'

Understandably, Mr Miller was far from convinced that there would be a next time. A note at the bottom of the *Variety Review* for 29 November, which itself attacked the play for 'toting in information about which the average person doesn't know and cares less', announced: '*Withdrawn Saturday after four performances*'. It would be over half a century before a full production was staged again in the United States, and even then only after a British publisher had put it back into print and a major British theatre had staged it. In 1988 there was a staged reading in the United States, as there was in Los Angeles in 2000. Finally, in 2001, it was briefly presented at the Williamstown Festival in Berkshire County, Massachusetts, with Chris O'Donnell as David Beeves, a production that reached Broadway in 2002, fifty-eight years after its precipitate failure, the set dominated by a 1929 Marmon car (discovered five miles from the theatre in Williamstown, one of only five hundred remaining). Play and car alike were getting a second chance.

Now, the reviews were rather different from those that had so dismayed the twenty-nine-year-old playwright in 1944. The local *Berkshire Eagle* welcomed it as 'a fable about the American dream; a fable that wrestles with issues of responsibility for what happens to us in life; how responsible we are for our fate and the consequences of life acts'.[7] The *Morning Call* headed its review 'A Fortunate Revival', though its reviewer Michael Kuchwara noted, in what had long become a familiar refrain, that it had previously been successful in Britain 'where audiences are more receptive to Miller's work'.[8] The *New York Times*, which half a century before had regretted its lack of 'care', now hailed a 'compelling' production and asked 'how it could have been so easily dismissed 57 years ago' – dismissed, that is, by the same newspaper. Bruce Webber saw in it 'an admonitory work, one that pleads seriously for a national admonishment that we are not a chosen people but a fortunate one and that declares that our fortune must be wielded with responsibility'.[9]

One answer, of course, is that the original production had been of a play by an unknown author. In 2001–2 it was received as the work of America's foremost playwright. In other words, what had changed was the attitude of critics. Greater attention was now paid to a work that could be seen in the context of his later plays. The question of the individual's and, by extension, America's responsibility for its actions also had a greater relevance. Seen from the view point of the rest of the world it was indeed a country that had had all the luck. Seen from its own perspective, it had created itself. Somewhere in between was a country that managed to be both confident and yet endlessly seeking assurance as to its identity and values.

The critics of the 1944 production, then, were on the whole bemused. Trying to analyse its failure, Miller later wrote, 'I had struck upon what seemed a bottomless pit of mutually cancelling meanings and implications.' In the past, he explained, 'I had had less difficulty with forming a "story" and more with the exploration of its meanings. Now, in contrast, I was working with an overwhelming sense of meaning, but however hard I tried I could not make the drama continuous and of a piece; it persisted with the beginning of each scene, in starting afresh as though each scene were the beginning of a new play.'[10]

These remarks date from 1957. The problem, it seemed, had had less to do with the play than with the production, less to do with his failure to make the drama continuous than with the fact that he was choosing to explore the problems of success at a time of price control, wartime austerity and anxieties generated not by irrational fears but by wholly rational and immediate concerns.

Perhaps audiences might have chosen to see its concern with contingency as echoing their own new awareness of the arbitrariness of fate, but that required a leap from the domestic setting of the play to the real site of their alarm. And in so far as it suggested that we are ultimately responsible for creating our own fates, this was not entirely plausible when the draft snatched sons from mothers and telegrams announced the end of hope. Add to that the fact that the voice of reason is that of an Austrian, and there were clearly equivocal aspects to his text. However, the truth is that not many people got to see the play and work out how they felt about it.

Nonetheless, one critic, John Anderson of the *New York Journal-American*, invited him for a drink and advised him to write a tragedy, detecting something in the play that had been dissipated in the production. Earlier drafts suggest that this was, indeed, what he had been reaching for. He also had another enthusiastic supporter, though his comments came too late to make a difference. In *The Best Plays of 1944–5* Burns Mantle, who had been one of the judges of the Hopwood Awards back in Michigan, remarked: 'An unusually interesting and well-played comedy called "The Man Who Had All the Luck", written by Arthur Miller, was mistakenly withdrawn, it seemed to this writer, after only 4 performances. It was at least worth a three-week chance to find itself and its public.'[11] It is doubtful whether Miller himself saw it as a comedy, and by the time the *Best Plays* volume had appeared it was no more than another of the season's failures.

Miller sat in on only one of the four performances, an experience that rivalled that of his friend-to-be Harold Pinter who was one of only six people to attend a matinée of *The Birthday Party* in 1958. The production seemed to Miller a 'well-meant botch'. Later, he would recall Chekhov's sense of devastation after the catastrophic first night of *The Seagull*. Chekhov had fled to bed with a blanket over his head. Miller felt hardly less destroyed.

However, the director Harold Clurman read the published text of the play in an anthology called *Cross Section* and, on 2 July 1946, immediately sat down at the table in his office and wrote to Miller: 'I am interested in your work. If you have a new play I would be very happy to read it quickly. Let me know.' It sounded like an offer to produce his next play. He did. That play was *All My Sons*.

Two days after the play closed, on 27 November, Kermit wrote from France, four thousand miles away from Broadway and in a way that must have given pause to his brother, who had written of war without seeing it and for whom failure was merely a matter of bad reviews and wasted effort. Kermit was fighting under Patton and, while anxious for news from home – news, in particular, of what he hoped would be Miller's success and his father's thriving business – was thinking beyond the danger of his present circumstances, the terrors of the front and the bravery of his fellow soldiers. Again, it is not hard to see why Miller always respected his brother. From Kermit he heard what he had listened for in researching what became *Situation Normal:*

Am feeling fine and resting for a little while behind the lines after quite some time on the front lines with the finest troops fighting in this war. You must not worry as everything is going OK. Met General Patton, under whose command our outfit is now operating, and he is as colorful as you must imagine from all the news reports. With others had my picture taken while he addressed us. You may see the photograph some day.

Am awaiting excitedly for reports of Art's play and book. Mail has been held up lately and consequently have not heard from home folks ... Have asked a WAC [member of the Women's Army Corps] to get any information she might be able regarding the play's reception, but have not seen her since the request some five days ago. Perhaps she has forgotten. Haven't seen a newspaper from the States in months.

By the time you receive this the coat industry will probably be undergoing its habitual holiday slow season and hope Dad has been able to clear his racks of sports garments before the new year. Give the good guy a kiss and tell him I am always thinking of him. You may not believe it but when things were tough, in a completely non-understandable way my mouth began to mutter: Dad, Mum, Art, Joan, Fran, Mary and Jane Ellen. Even at that dangerous moment I could not bring myself to pray to God although all about me men prayed who am certain never prayed before. In all my living days I shall never forget what my eyes have seen, nor shall my memory forget the courage of those still alive, or that of my buddies no longer among the quick.

The 3rd, along with the British 2nd, French 1st, American 1st, 7th and 9th continue to advance. You cannot, in your wildest wanderings of imagination, picture the fortitude of our boys against the most adverse weather and other conditions. It is beyond my powers of description. And this I know incontrovertibly, that no one who has not seen can possibly tell of it. Remember that every little mile on your map has cost tremendously in all ways and that we must not pay so dearly for nothing. This peace that follows we must never yield. Statesmanship of the leaders alongside an educated citizenship prevailing is the only bulwark worthy of construction.

Tears and heart thumping will not bring the dead back to life nor assure the good life. Only a clear eye and cold understanding will assure your grandchildren and great-grandchildren their places in the sun with all the people of the universe.

Perhaps I shouldn't have sounded off as I have but couldn't deny the urge.
I love you all.

A week later he was in hospital in Britain, not wounded but with trouble to his feet. He was already preparing to return to his unit but still concerned for his men, still trying to fathom the meaning of the experiences he had had. In the process he arrives at a vision of man as his own god which is remarkably close to that which his brother had proposed in *The Man Who Had All the Luck* and would develop in his subsequent works. His thoughts are worth quoting at length not merely for the insight they give into Kermit Miller, but for what they tell us about the brother to whom this letter and others were addressed. Chris Keller, in *All My Sons*, was going to echo many of Kermit's sentiments. In Kermit, Miller found that idealism, that sense of the need for a changed world, which would be echoed in that play and which, arguably, was the basis for his own continuing commitment to a model of social action that would begin to seem outmoded as the Cold War began and yesterday's sacrifices were forgotten in the name of a new potential conflict. When Miller appeared at a peace conference in 1949, perhaps something of Kermit's experiences informed his decision, along with the political commitment they had shared.

On 5 December Kermit wrote:

Much can be written about the boys up on the lines but I must wait to catch my breath. Unheralded bravery, and courage which must remain unrewarded are commonplace. My subconscious has tucked away, ineradicably, detached shots that must wait for interpretations, and then again perhaps never.

By now everyone back home must be bustling about anticipating the holidays. Can picture very vividly 34th St. and Macys with the days to Christmas growing so short. Happy holidays to you 3!

He did not return to his unit, writing again on the 29th:

Am still here in England living a life of comparative luxury and boredom. For the first time in $2\frac{1}{2}$ years I am completely divested of responsibility and am a ward of Uncle Sam. Having been as close to knowing myself as man is ever likely to be I am [hard?], peculiarly so. The luxury of clean sheets, a roof above and absence of shell and small arms fire, with all its sordid implications, is not hard to take however.

Am proud to say, and I hope without boasting, that under fire I acquitted myself as every thinking man hopes he will. There is no preparation for this test except a mental flexibility combined with a figurative 'great hope and prayer'. The hellish cacophony, human screaming, rattle of gunfire and deathly artillery bracketing is far beyond my power to describe.

I'll go even further and say that no man, whether having experienced it or not and regardless of his perspicacity, can aptly describe it in all its nuances of human anguish. For this reason I do not reproach myself too seriously.

Can say now that even when death was closest I did not pray to a God whose existence I've grown to deny. At that moment my mind would not yield to hypocrisy and the reasons, as I remember them, were these. They might not make sense to you, and you may doubt that rationalization at such a time, so short a time, is possible but believe me it is. First, I could not admit what in easier moments I had denied, the existence of a deity. Secondly, if there was a God why should he hear me and not the bleeding and dead all around me? Thirdly, how could a beneficent deity allow such barbarous carnage to visit the good and innocent without regard. And lastly, though to my mind most important, the thought once vague now took full possession and asserted that my belief was not in one god but in many. Every man about me was a God. He was something intrinsic not ethereal. His valor and basic goodness now relieved of all subterfuge became for me an altar and something man did not have to accept blindly because he could recognize it within himself. I recognized and was all peace awaiting what seemed the inevitable, uncomplainingly. No prayer, no incantations, no regret.

Strangely I am completely whole and my excuse for residence here is a common, occupational disease of the infantryman, trench feet. There is no need for alarm . . .

Art, to date I have had no news of your several ventures as you must have gathered by my lack of comment. It is several months since mail from home last reached me.

In fact, Kermit was minimizing his suffering. According to his son,

his 'trenchfoot' nearly lost him his legs. In the weeks preceding the Battle of the Bulge my father gave his men his dry socks. The first time he was evacuated from the front he went back to the lines. His combat experience was so harrowing that he returned to the States 'shell-shocked'. He kept this secret from the Army so that he could be discharged on time. In civilian life he underwent ECT treatments and was clinically depressed for most of his life. All my relatives spoke of the change in his personality after the war.[12]

Miller did not entirely give up on his play. At the end of the year he entered into discussion with the Laboratory Stage in Los Angeles, a group which included Morris Carnovsky and Phoebe Brand of the Group Theatre, along with Lee J. Cobb who would later play the part of Willy Loman in *Death of a Salesman*. They had just established themselves and were planning a season which included *Volpone*, Pirandello's *Henry IV*, Shaw's *St Joan* and *King Lear*, with Cobb playing the king. They were interested in *The Man Who Had All the Luck*. Despite its planned repertoire, the political commitments of the group seemed clear – hardly surprising, since both Brand and Cobb were members of the Party. Miller received a letter from Bud Bohman that must have left him feeling ambivalent:

I see it as a morality play, dealing with the twin sins of our time – Laissez-faire (Dave's theme) and the Corporate State, or Fascist culture (Amos's theme).

> I want to have Hanns Eisler to share the overall concept and to have him
> write a rather unearthly score, perhaps only for one instrument, like the
> electrical guitar, and to use this music in the play the way a geography teacher
> uses a pointer on a map.

In explaining his conception of the play, his correspondent offered a somewhat
fanciful account:

> The best way for me to describe to you the quality I would like to give the
> production is as follows: I have a beautiful tiny daughter, who hates the japs
> and loves the russians, and brings jew stories from the street . . . lets imagine
> her in high school, and lets imagine the time moved ahead about 30 years.
> Its 1975. She's in her room with lots of books, trying to figure the weirdness
> of the world before the 'people's war'. And she asks me to explain to her what
> was that old laissez-faire idea, and what was the lack of freedom under fascism
> . . . So I start to spin a yarn for her . . . I say 'well all those books tell you the
> score about national policies during that period, but in order to understand
> it properly you must see that these policies were a reflection of the approach
> to living that individuals had in their personal lives at that time. It will seem
> incredible to you my dear, in this newer and better world, but let me tell you
> about a fellow named David, and another fellow named Amos and all the
> life around them at the time. It may help you understand all these books.'

It was an odd mixture of perception and reductiveness, which must have
given Miller pause for thought, no matter how desperate he was to redeem a
failure. This will have intensified as what had seemed a crucial aspect of the
play was vigorously rejected:

> In the Broadway version, the play went out the window, structurally, the
> moment Amos and David were made brothers. Jesus Christ! The father of
> Amos cannot produce a David! This killed the larger meaning of all three
> characters, for my money.
>   I am really unhappy about the overwrought handling of the psychiatric
> business in the last act, child versus mink etc [In the play the protagonist
> raises mink. His neighbour's die but his survive. Paradoxically he had been
> hoping for a disaster as if this might balance the scales and thus protect his
> new child who might otherwise be the one to pay the price]. etc. . . . There
> is no solution through acting, directing, or Hanns Eisler, or two dozen
> electrical guitars for this flaw in the play. Its something only the writer can
> fix . . . will you entertain some proposals in this respect?[13]

The answer was No. The Broadway failure was bad enough. The idea of
dismantling key aspects of the play for a speculative production was not one
he could face. This company, however, renamed the Actors' Lab, would later,

briefly, be home to Marilyn Monroe in search of actor training, and then effectively be destroyed when Elia Kazan named Carnovsky and his wife Phoebe Brand as communists.

So depressing was Miller's experience with *The Man Who Had All the Luck* that he later confessed: 'I didn't think I would write another play.' He had been responsible for half a dozen and, aside from the curious popularity of his wartime propaganda piece in support of price controls, they had got nowhere. The very public disaster that was his Broadway debut seemed a last signal that he was wasting his time: 'Standing at the back of the house ... I could blame nobody.' It was 'like music played on the wrong instruments in a false scale ... After the final performance and the goodbyes to the actors, it almost seemed a relief to get on the subway to Brooklyn Heights and read about the tremendous pounding of Nazi-held Europe by Allied air power. Something somewhere was real.'[14]

He now decided to abandon the theatre for prose fiction, despite the fact that behind him lay two failed novels, for one of which he had had to return the advance. In fact, he had been working on one during 1943–4. As he would later observe, 'With the abject failure of my first Broadway play ... I resolved never to write another play but to give novelistic form this time to the assault, figurative and sometimes literal, that was coming at me from the streets.'[15] Publishing suddenly seemed a more fertile soil than Broadway and in 1945 came *Focus*, a study of American anti-Semitism – the first such, he thought, with the exception of Laura Hobson's *Gentleman's Agreement*, also published in 1945 and later filmed by Elia Kazan.

As late as 1962, when an NBC dramatization of *Focus* was transmitted, a note in his FBI file described it as 'strictly Communist propaganda' which aimed to 'foster race hatred between Jews and Gentiles'.[16] In fact an investigation by the Los Angeles FBI office, inquiring into communist infiltration of radio and television, was triggered by nothing more substantial than a telephone complaint by a single person who took exception to the play's theme of 'alleged anti-Semitism in New York' and to the fact that it 'placed non-Jews in an extremely bad light'. The programme, the complainant insisted, was by 'a known communist'.[17] The logging of this telephone call and its incorporation into Miller's FBI file says a great deal about the nature of the records kept on America's supposed subversives.

The book had its roots, in part, in his experience of the Brooklyn Navy Yard, with its tumble of different racial groups. He recalled working with a Czech welder who one day over lunch, not realizing that Miller was Jewish, unleashed a tirade of anti-Semitism that left him aghast. There were those who suggested that Jews controlled the federal government and that this was essentially Roosevelt's war. Such people referred to the 'Jew Deal'. As Miller remarked in the 1990s, 'As the war approached, and during the war, we had a very dense anti-Semitic movement, certainly in New York, which I knew about personally. I ran into it all the time. It was strong in Chicago. The Middle West was very much that way. So this whole theme became dominant in my mind.'[18]

He recalled listening to Father Charles E. Coughlin, who considered Roosevelt a stooge of Jewish bankers and who broadcast his views to ten million listeners, views he had culled from Joseph Goebbels' propaganda broadcasts. In 1934, he had founded the ironically named National Union for Social Justice, which gained five million members in two months. He thrived in Depression America, attacking what he called godless capitalists, the Jews, the communists, international bankers and plutocrats.

Coughlin's political platform was originally a curious amalgam of prejudice and New Deal policies. He favoured the nationalization of public services, the creation of a government-owned central bank and unionization of all workers. He even supported Franklin Roosevelt in 1932, though in 1936 he switched to William 'Liberty Bill' Lemke on the Union Party ticket, now calling Roosevelt 'Anti-God' and a communist. He himself ran for a seat in the House of Representatives and promised he would secure nine million votes for Lemke. He was roundly beaten, as was Lemke in a Roosevelt landslide.

Coughlin's main power, though, lay in his radio broadcasts. Forty-five radio stations carried them. He had a listenership of three and a half million. When an American cardinal tried to control him he was overruled by the Vatican. He had been haranguing listeners since 1926. His Shrine of the Little Flower published an anti-Semitic weekly called *Social Justice*. In 1938, like Henry Ford's magazine, it published the fraudulent *Protocols of the Elders of Zion*, and declared in an editorial that almost without exception the leaders of 'Marxist atheism' in Germany were Jews.

Father Coughlin organized the Christian Front, which included a number of Catholic priests in Detroit. Bizarrely, this was an armed group. Miller recalled members with machine-guns being arrested. Among its strongholds was Brooklyn. The Brooklyn *Tablet* was an enthusiastic supporter as were a number of Irish Catholic policemen. In 1939, the *Nation* reported that 'anti-Semitism in New York has ceased to be whispered and has become an open instrument of demagoguery, a vast outlet for idle energies'.[19] Coughlin was finally, and belatedly, restrained by the Church hierarchy. *Social Justice* was banned in 1942 under the 1917 Espionage Act. It was this organization that Miller featured in *Focus* as James T. Farrell did in *Studs Lonigan*, where Coughlin appears as Father Moylan, and Norman Mailer did in *The Naked and the Dead*, where the Christian Front becomes Christians United and Coughlin, Father Killian.

In the face of pressure to accept European refugees, meanwhile, Americans preferred to keep the doors closed. In a 1938 survey in *Fortune* magazine, only 4 per cent favoured raising quotas, while over 67 per cent voted to exclude refugees entirely. In 1939 8 per cent said they would favour easing quotas, while 83 per cent said they would not[20] – hence the subversive overtones of Miller's otherwise anodyne radio play, *Grandpa and the Statue of Liberty*. In August 1941, four months before Pearl Harbor, the *Catholic Telegraph-Register* published an editorial declaring that 'Jewry seems committed to a war program for our country ... Yet if this country goes to war, we predict that opposition to Jews will gain uncontrollable momentum.'[21]

Nor had Miller forgotten his experience in North Carolina, when he had found himself at the wrong end of a shotgun, or the hiring policy that nearly blocked his path to a job and, through the *numerus clausus* (Latin: 'closed number') stood ready to block his entry into Ivy League universities should he have been qualified to go. He recalled, too, a trip through New Jersey in which he saw signs outside hotels announcing a 'restricted, Christian' clientele; he said later that this was the experience that set him to writing the novel. New Jersey, anti-Semitic as well as anti-black, was Ku-Klux Klan territory. In Congress, Southern politicians denounced 'niggers' and Jews with equal vehemence. It was not until photographs of the concentration camps in Europe began to appear that any kind of awareness of what Nazism might mean came home to those for whom Hitler's persecution of the Jews had seemed no more than a footnote to an unfolding history.

Focus, Miller noted, was written when 'a sensible person could wonder if such a right [of Jews to exist] had reality at all'.[22] There was a curious silence on the subject, a silence embraced by Jew and non-Jew alike, embraced, indeed, by Miller himself as war had approached. 'It was like a dropped vase,' he explained,

> cracked in all directions; touch it and it might shatter. And the silence covered the Jews and their fate. More Jews than not were on the left side of the political spectrum, but here was the Soviet Union lying down with the Jew-hunting Nazis. And Roosevelt, friend of Jews, had denied landing privileges to the *St. Louis*, the ship carrying a couple of hundred Jews allowed to leave by the Germans ... Along with a lot of others, what I made of the silence was that everybody, not excluding myself, was afraid of an outbreak of anti-Semitism in America should that shipload of refugees be allowed to disembark. The writing of *Focus* was an attempt to break through that silence ... It was like some shameful illness that was not to be mentioned in polite society, not by gentiles and not by Jews.[23]

There was considerable pressure for Jews to adopt non-Jewish names. The actor Kirk Douglas changed his and, thus disguised, heard conversations that horrified him; but it was not merely a matter of filmstars. Journalists and

broadcasters were invited at the very least to disguise their racial identity, as
did some in the armed services. In *New York Jew* Alfred Kazin said, of 1943,
when Miller was already writing his novel:

> Now, began the nightmare that would bring everything else into question,
> that will haunt me to my last breath. The Nazis had organized the killing of
> every Jew in their grasp. Three months before Pearl Harbor, Charles Lind-
> bergh at an America First rally had threatened the 'Jewish *race*', [insisting
> that] 'instead of agitating for war, the Jewish groups in this country should
> be opposing it in every possible way, for they will be among the first to feel
> its consequences' ... The systematic murder of Europe's Jews had not yet
> begun by the time we entered the war. But by the end of 1942 and especially
> the spring of 1943, when the Warsaw ghetto was destroyed ... it was clear to
> me what was not clear to 'progressives' with their whimpers for a 'global New
> Deal'. The Nazis planned what even Edmund Wilson called the 'exter-
> mination' of every Jew on earth. But to everyone but us – and by no means
> all of us – this was unreal.

By the time he wrote *Focus*, Miller was fully aware of what had happened
in Europe, but the sheer implacability of the camps precluded a direct portrait.
What interested him were the processes whereby anti-Semitism functioned
and, beyond that, the mechanism whereby, as Kazin put it, 'the Jews were
just a people *accused*, as of old; a people whose only mission was to feel
guilty'.[24]

It was at this time, too, in 1945, that Miller wrote an article in *New Masses*
(three of whose founding editors had been Jewish) denouncing Ezra Pound,
one of whose wartime broadcasts he had heard on the radio. As he later
described it, 'I turned on the short-wave, and there was a voice which I
had never heard but which spoke perfectly good American advocating the
destruction of the Jewish people and justifying the cremation of Jews, and I
was quite astonished because it was such a common American accent, and I
waited to the end, and it was being broadcast from Italy, and it was Ezra
Pound.'[25]

Miller had listened to the broadcast on a new radio and heard Pound claim
that the war was the result of a Jewish conspiracy and that Hitler was right
in seeking their destruction. Eleven years after Pound's trial for treason, Miller
apologized for his 'excitement' at that time, but added: 'In a world where
humanism must conquer lest humanity be destroyed, literature must nurture
the conscience of man.'[26]

Pound broadcast twice weekly on the Italian fascist radio. He attacked
Eleanor Roosevelt for associating with 'niggers', while his attitude to Jews
was unequivocal. On 7 December 1941, he had observed that 'things often do
look simple to me. Roosevelt is more in the hands of the Jews than Wilson

was in 1919.' Just over a year later, he had railed against the idea that 'any Jew in the White House should send American kids to die for the private interests of the scum of the English earth ... and the dregs of the Levantine'. In March 1942, he advised:

> Don't start a pogrom – an old-style killing of small Jews. That system is no good whatever. Of course, if some man had a stroke of genius, and could start a pogrom up at the top, there might be something to say for it. But on the whole, legal measures are preferable. The 60 kikes who started this war might be sent to St. Helena as a measure of world prophylaxis and some hyper-kikes or non-Jewish kikes along with them.[27]

On 23 April, he commented: 'Had you the sense to eliminate Roosevelt and the Jews ... at the last election, you would not now be at war.'[28] In May he added: 'England will certainly have nothing whatever to say about the terms [of the next peace]. Neither, I think, will simple-hearted Joe Stalin, not wholly trusted by the kikery which is his master.'[29] Hitler, he declared, was a saint and a martyr.

Pound had been taken into custody on 3 May 1945. On 25 November, just five months after the end of the war in Europe, he was tried for treason. On 25 December, *New Masses* published an article somewhat lacking in the Christmas spirit entitled 'Should Ezra Pound Be Shot?', a response to a 25 November issue of *PM* magazine in which four poets and a critic had supported him, the four poets being E.E. Cummings, William Carlos Williams, Conrad Aiken and Karl Shapiro. The critic was F.O. Matthiessen.

Among the *New Masses* contributors was Norman Rosten, who asserted that Pound, 'the poets' representative', had 'cheapened us, degraded us. Because he was a poet his crime is millionfold. Because he was a traitor, he should be shot.'[30] Miller, while stopping short of calling for a firing squad, was no less forthright, suggesting: 'In his wildest moments of human vilification Hitler never approached our Ezra ... he knew all America's weaknesses and he played them as expertly as Goebbels ever did.' He had undermined the fight against fascism while his supportive fellow poets were presenting themselves as 'poseurs and harmless clowns, facile entertainers', disavowing their responsibility to themselves and society. While not challenging Pound's significance as a writer, he attacked the idea that he should be released:

> If I may be pardoned some nonpolitical language, the boys are cutting the baloney pretty thick. Shapiro ought to know that Pound is not accused of not 'reversing his beliefs' but of aiding and abetting the enemy by broadcasting propaganda calculated to undermine the American will to

fight fascism. And Mr Aiken ought to know by now that Pound did not betray himself to 'man in the abstract' but to Mussolini, whose victims are, to be sure, now buried and abstract, but who was a most real, most unpoetical type of fellow.

He concluded:

Without much effort one could find a thousand poets and writers who understand not only why Pound was dangerous and treasonous, but why he will be even more so if released ... A greater calamity cannot befall the art than that Ezra Pound, the Mussolini mouthpiece, should be welcomed back as an arbiter of American letters, an eventuality not to be dismissed if the court adopts the sentiments of these four poets.

Years later, before the House Un-American Activities Committee, while no longer feeling the issue quite so intensely, Miller explained the reason for the vehemence of his feelings in 1945: 'I am a Jew. He was for burning Jews.'[31]

This is perhaps one source for *Focus*, one explanation for what might otherwise have seemed a strange topic to be addressing as America moved towards the end of the war. But the fact is that beyond the special case of Ezra Pound, Jews were still seen in deeply ambivalent ways. They were intellectuals in a country which, at the level of myth, celebrated equality and the man of action. They were businessmen contaminated by money and alternately admired and despised for what were assumed to be their sharp business practices. They were bankers, living lives that others could only aspire to. On the other hand, and in contradiction, they were radicals threatening the state with alien theories and practices. They were criminals, if not running then acting as bookkeepers to the underworld: 'Einstein and Freud and/or Meyer Lansky or another gangster; Karl Marx and/or Rothschild; the Prague Communist chief Slansky running Czechoslovakia for Stalin and/or the Jew Slansky hanging by the neck as tribute to Stalin's paranoid anti-Semitism.'[32] And, disturbingly, as he later came to realize, that ambivalence went to the very heart of communism.

Karl Marx, descendant of three generations of rabbis, was baptized a Protestant and was anti-Semitic. 'Isn't that wonderful?' Miller observed to me in 2001. 'The Jews were looking to Marxism as a release', but 'he [Marx] saw the Jew as capitalism. Right through my whole left-wing years there were echoes of this bifurcation. Wherever you looked there was a Jew. He was on the right; he was on the left. It's a real shocker. Some of the things he said were violently anti-Jewish.'

In America, prejudice was intensifying. In answer to a *Fortune* poll asking respondents if they had heard any criticism of the Jews in the previous month, 46 per cent responded positively in 1940. By 1944 the figure was 60 per cent and by 1946, 64 per cent. In 1944, the army magazine *Yank* decided not to run a story about Nazi atrocities against the Jews, the reporter being told to find something less Jewish to write about. In 1945 *PM* magazine reported on the contents of a US armed forces correspondence course which observed that 'the Jew is an offensive fellow unwelcome in this country ... The Gentile fears, and with reason, the competition of the Jew in business and despises him as a matter of course.'[33]

Focus was a provocation. Designed to expose to public view what was known but not openly discussed, it was a challenge to a country that was just concluding a war supposedly fought in the name of liberty and justice for all. Writing on the occasion of a reissue of the book, Miller observed:

> I cannot glance through this novel without once again feeling the sense of emergency that surrounded the writing of it. As far as I knew at the time, anti-Semitism in America was a closed if not forbidden topic for fiction – certainly no novel had taken it as a main theme, let alone the existence within the Catholic priesthood of certain militants whose duty and pleasure was to stoke up Jew-hate.[34]

Its protagonist, Lawrence Newman, is a gentile who, forced to wear spectacles, suddenly appears Jewish, at least to the anti-Semitic company he works for. Having himself acquiesced in such prejudice, not least because it seems to give him a feeling of solidarity with those he lives and works with, he now finds himself excluded. He marries a woman who herself appears Jewish but has, like him, flirted with anti-Semitism. She urges him to throw in his lot with his would-be persecutors, but this does little to save him. Eventually, he declares his solidarity with a local Jewish shopkeeper called Finklestein and resists. They stand back to back with baseball bats in their hands, challenging their attackers. The book ends as Newman refuses to contradict a policeman who assumes that he is Jewish. He accepts an identity that is not his own but which he claims rather than accommodate himself to the prejudice of those who have abused him.

Finklestein is a key figure. He recalls a story told to him by his father. The serfs on a great estate were kept in ignorance of their emancipation for several years. They killed a brutal overseer, then those who had been sent to punish them for the offence. Breaking into the baron's mansion, they stole what they could carry away, including what they took to be portraits of the king – in fact paper money, of which they knew nothing. The baron had then forced a Jewish pedlar called Itzick to enter the estate and offer his pots and pans for sale in exchange for the money. Itzick recognizes the trap but sees no way to avoid it. He will recover the baron's money only to become a victim of a pogrom in which he will lose the money and quite possibly his life. Nonetheless, he goes ahead and his wife and children are murdered.

To Finklestein's father, who first told the story, it was a fable about fate. We do what we must do and suffer accordingly, seemingly the fate of Jews through the centuries. Finklestein offers a wholly different interpretation. Itzick, he maintains, should have refused to do what the baron wished. The pogrom might have been inevitable, but Itzick's acquiescence should not have been. Finklestein stresses the necessity of fighting back, of being responsible for one's own fate and hence one's own identity. That is the truth he passes on to a man who believed he could buy immunity by validating prejudice. Newman is, indeed, a new man and as such he decides to embrace the identity that had placed his life at risk. By accepting identification as a Jew, he refuses the supposedly secure anonymity he had once courted.

Newman's earlier, largely borrowed, anti-Semitism was one source of meaning for a man who had hesitated to advance a personality of his own. Jean-Paul Sartre, in *Anti-Semite and Jew*, said of the anti-Semite that 'he sees in the eyes of others a disquieting image – his own – and he makes his words and gestures conform to it. Having his external model, he is under no necessity to look for his personality within himself ... What he flees even more than Reason is his intimate awareness of himself.'[35] For Newman, though, anti-Semitism is symptom rather than cause. By degrees, and at first by sheer chance, he begins to understand something of the qualities of those with whom he had imagined he could ingratiate himself. For Sartre, the anti-Semite was 'the man of the crowd', innately mediocre: 'The phrase, "I hate the Jews", is one uttered in chorus.' He is a man in retreat from freedom and responsibility: 'Without respite from the beginning of our lives to the end, we are responsible for what merit we enjoy. Now the anti-Semite flees responsibility as he flees his own consciousness ... He chooses the irremediable out of fear of being free.'

Miller never met Sartre but found in his existential rigour precisely an echo of his own beliefs, the basis of a theme that would resound through his work. Miller, like Sartre, saw in anti-Semitism a coercive inhumanity easily extended beyond the Jews. *Focus* begins with an assault on a Puerto Rican woman. Sartre observes: 'The Jew only serves him [the anti-Semite] as a pretext; elsewhere his counterpart will make use of the Negro or the man of yellow skin.'

Perhaps the most striking echo of Sartre in *Focus* lies in his observation that 'the Jew is in the situation of a Jew because he lives in the midst of a society that takes him for a Jew'. This is the premise on which Miller based his novel. The 'Jew' is a construction in so far as his identity is offered to him by those who despise him. The struggle is to resist such a factitious identity, to act and create oneself through action. And is there, at the heart of the book, displaced on to the person of a gentile who comes to accept himself as a Jew, a comment on Jewish self-hatred rooted, George Steiner would say, in theology? The shadow of Job falls not only over *The Man Who Had All the Luck*. Job was required to prove his faith by submitting to suffering. The Old Testament, Steiner observes, could be implacable. The lesson Newman learns is the need to break the connection between suffering and being.

Lawrence Newman, though, was an emblem of something more than a man suddenly unsure of who he might be. He was the American, no longer secure, no longer confident as to his identity or role in a national destiny. It was, Miller would write in 2001, 'the way we were, difficult to understand as some of our behavior may now appear'.[36] Perhaps not so difficult, though. In 2002, some of the tape recordings made by Richard Nixon in the early 1970s in the Oval Room of the White House came into the public domain. They revealed Billy Graham, unofficial pastor to a succession of American presidents, as remarking that 'the Bible says there are satanic Jews and that's where our problem arises', while Nixon claimed that 'the Jews are an irreligious, atheistic, immoral bunch of bastards'.[37]

At one level *Focus* is about identity, about the demonization of the Other, but it is also about the need to relinquish suffering as the evidence of obedience to an authority yet to reveal itself. George Steiner has described Marxism as Judaism grown impatient. Ultimate justice being endlessly deferred, it proved necessary to enact it in a present drained of theological content. The war, though, had mocked that presumption. The victory concealed a more profound defeat. Jews died in their millions still awaiting the arrival of redemptive meaning. Even in America Miller noted a pragmatic silence, a tactical acquiescence in prejudice designed to secure if not immunity then at least provisional safety. *Focus* was a denial of this logic.

Yet there is, perhaps, too casual an assumption that the baseball bat swung in the face of killers will prove an adequate defence. Miller would speak of Jews who went unresisting into the gas chambers, as if desperate retrospectively to invent the possibility of resistance. But the physical battle against anti-Semitism in *Focus* is a symbol of the deeper resistance for which Miller called, the need to throw one's whole self into the business of living in the world. If it were anything else it would risk becoming a simple plea for reactive violence of the kind he would criticize decades later when discussing Israel's response to the Palestinians.

Nor was *Focus* merely a comment on a prejudice that would dissolve with the collapse of fascism. More than fifty years on he would read the diaries of the Rumanian author Mihail Sebastian, who died the year *Focus* was published. There he found not merely an account of the bone-deep and vicious anti-Semitism of pre-war and wartime Rumania, admittedly distant from his own experience, but a reminder of the continuing plight of the Jew and of the respectability to which the anti-Semite could aspire in postwar America.

Asked to write a preface for one of Sebastian's books, Nae Ionescu wrote an anti-Semitic diatribe in which he warned that the Jew could never be part of a national community: 'It is an assimilationist illusion, it is the illusion of so many Jews who sincerely believe that they are Rumanian ... Remember that you are Jewish! ... Are you Iosif Hechter, a human being from Braila on the Danube? No, you are a Jew from Braila on the Danube.' One of Sebastian's close friends, Mircea Eliade, prophesied that Rumania would be 'invaded by Jews' and 'eaten by syphilis'. He proposed that enemies of the fascist Iron Guard, such as the foreign minister Nicolae Titulescu, should be 'riddled with bullets. Strung up by the tongue'.[38] After the war, Eliade moved to the United States where he taught the history of religion at the University of Chicago, in which position he was both influential and honoured.

Lawrence Newman, travelling through the underground tunnels of New York on his way to work for an anti-Semitic company, was in touch with a secret America whose power derived as much from the unspoken as from the spoken, which relied on the silent acquiescence of victim and oppressor alike. Occasionally the assault was open and direct. More often, it was heavily coded. Either way, it represented a challenge to the integrity of the self, as in other places and other times it represented a challenge to the very existence of the individual.

The critic Leslie Fiedler hinted that the tactic of making Newman a gentile derived from Miller's conviction that while Jew-baiting was real, Jews were imaginary, just as he would suggest of *The Crucible* that witch-hunting was real but witches not. This seems an odd comment. Miller was certainly suggesting that the public notion of the Jew is a construction, a projection – and not only of gentiles. He was not suggesting that Jews are unreal, merely that they transcend a reductive taxonomy.

Finklestein himself feels the pressure to conform to traditional roles but what Miller primarily insists on, through Finklestein, is that faith, ideology, racial group are secondary to individual existence and identity. To allow oneself to be determined either by membership of a group or by resistance to it is to be diminished, literally or figuratively to render one's self into the hands of others. And this was an observation by no means limited to the Jew, as he detected what seemed to him to be a conformist impulse in America of a kind that de Tocqueville had noted over a century earlier.

What the book also registers is a feeling of unease and insecurity, a sense of being a victim of forces that seem beyond control. America had entered the war from a state of Depression and Miller was not the only one convinced that it might return to it with the war's end. Just as Bellow's 1944 novel *Dangling Man* had featured a man not so much living as existing in an anteroom to life, so Miller pictures a man who has no purchase on anything, no sense of transcendence, a self so plastic that it moulds itself to the world as it is presented to him. At the same time, whatever is the desired model of behaviour or being seems beyond him until in defending what he is not he discovers who he is, coming into being, a new man. It is an act of paradoxical liberation that leaves him ambiguously poised in that he ends by building his new self on a lie. It simply happens that within that lie he discovers a meaning and a humanity that he had been content, if not happy, to sacrifice to nothing more elevated than routine and shared prejudices which he mistook for camaraderie and acceptance. Smeared with blood, he is reborn, having claimed a freedom he never realized he had lost.

In *Focus*, Miller wrote about a culturally displaced, marginalized figure. Unlike Bellow's intellectuals, who worry at their situation, step from experience into thought, for much of the time Lawrence Newman refuses to process experience at all. Things are as they are. It is only when his world jumps the rails, when he is forced to see things differently, that he begins to think at all.

He had once served in a war that had momentarily given him a role. This time the war is for others and hence his life is evacuated of a meaning it might have had. Speaking in the context of *All My Sons*, but with relevance, too, if not to Newman's plight then to the sensibility that created him, Miller remarked: 'The city I knew was incoherent, yet its throttled speech seemed to implore some significance for the sacrifices that drenched the papers every day.'[39]

In *Focus*, the contrast is between idealism abroad and bigotry at home but there is the same sense of incoherence that would lead to *All My Sons*, the same refusal of experience to render any meaning that can be grasped. The paranoia that Newman detects and experiences seems little more than an attempt to imprint some pattern, no matter how bizarre and self-contradictory, on a disturbing social flux, on a mix of languages and broken histories. The summer heat triggers anger that needs a subject, a desperation that searches out a cause. As the war comes to an end, so the enemy, which had given a shape and direction to effort, is relocated within. There must be a reason for dislocated lives, for thwarted ambitions, for the sense of inconsequence and marginality gifted by the city. It is the Jew, or the Puerto Rican or the Black American. They represent a repressed sexuality, an exploitative personality, a hidden principle of opposition and subversion. Root them out, move them on, force them to accept the exclusion that all feel but they deserve, and all will be well.

For his part, Newman becomes the man no longer confined or defined by creeds, no longer blown by the wind of received opinion, no longer playing out a role in which he is cast by others. A spirit of resistance is born and from that resistance is created an existential self, generated from willed action. His, it turns out, had been a quest essentially like that of Bellow's Joseph in

Dangling Man: 'to know what we are and what we are for, to know our purpose, to seek grace'.[40] The separateness in which he had once taken pride, the primness, cleanliness, precision which were his attempt to delineate his distance from the messy business of human relationships, are now, it seems, laid aside.

This is not the solidarity of political theory, a romantic merging with the common people. It is a spontaneous recognition of need and from that need is born a new necessity. He is not exceptional, either in the sense in which he had once believed or in that asserted by others. His blood has mixed with others. He has stood back to back with the Other and discovered that the Other is himself.

Focus is scarcely an attempt to understand the mind of the anti-Semite. We never penetrate into its fastnesses, though Miller does suggest the extent to which anti-Semitism is a displacement of other anxieties. In some sense he is content to leave it opaque. It exists in the distorted faces of a hostile crowd, a rasping voice, a street violence which echoes that on another continent. For Lawrence Newman it is simply part of the air he breathes. It is literally inscribed on the society he inhabits. It has become a part of him by stealth. What interests Miller far more directly is the Jew's, or the proto-Jew's, response to it.

Newman is forced to act out the role of the Jew. He resists, but his resistance at first is not to anti-Semitism but its application to himself. By making him a gentile Miller forces his protagonist to have a double consciousness, to turn against himself. He is Cain and Abel and, indeed, that is the novel's subtext. It is not a question of guilt and innocence but of the capacity to project the one in order to claim the other.

In *Focus*, the difference between a Jew and a gentile is a pair of spectacles, a truth that Newman at last begins to see, pressing those very spectacles to his face as he is attacked, as though they had now become a part of his body as well as an agent of understanding.

Miller has commented on Kafka's terrifying proposition that 'there was no bottom', that 'everything was permitted', and this is the deeper concern in *Focus*, as it had been in *The Man Who Had All the Luck*. The concentration camp had been the technological evidence of this contingency, but it was merely a logical extension of anti-Semitism itself which condemned its victims for the sin of life. Miller's first play and his first novel, whatever else they were doing, were staking out his refusal to accede to a view of life which declared human agency void and the Jew as a victim sanctioned as such by history.

It proved difficult to place *Focus*, though, ironically, less because of its subject than because of its language. As Miller recalled in 1990, there 'had never been a novel which had anti-Semites actually talking about Jews the way they talked about them in life. It was feared that this would only make it worse for Jews since they were very convincing anti-Semites. But of course there would hardly be a danger in anti-Semitism if they weren't convincing. We were fighting Hitler at the time but everybody knew there was a subculture of pro-Hitler anti-Semitism in New York, you just couldn't talk about it.'[41]

Reynal & Hitchcock, a gentile publisher, had recently opened and was looking for new work. As it happened, Frank Taylor, friend and ex-colleague of Mary Miller, who was now working for a medical publisher, had been hired to find new authors. He responded immediately to *Focus*, whose controversial subject matter appealed to him. It was subsequently adopted by the left-wing Book Find Club, but even here there were some who objected to it because of the anti-Semitic language of some of the characters.

On the day he was supposed to turn up at the publisher's to have his photograph taken for the dust jacket, Miller forgot. He was still at his Brooklyn home when Mary walked in. In the rush to put on a suit, he walked into the open closet door and hence arrived with a black eye, which is why he appeared in profile on the jacket. 'That long-ago photo, of a young man with hair,' he later recalled, 'looking confidently into the distance, brings back some of the excitement of the imminent publication date and, for all anyone knew, outraged public condemnation.' It seemed to him, writing at a time when the book had finally made its way into film at the turn of the millennium, that its relevance had not diminished. 'The current attacks on people for their appearance – Middle Easterners this time – runs right down the middle of the book's theme. This time around, however, silence is out of fashion, and a lot of us find ourselves struggling very consciously with our fears.'[42]

Focus was extremely successful, despite a *New York Times* review that praised it for its observation but saw it as a novel in which character was subordinated to subject matter. It rapidly appeared in France, Germany, England and Italy. In America it sold a reported 90,000 copies. It would be reissued in 1964 and then again in 1984 and once more in 2001. In February 1946, Harold Hecht, of the Harold Hecht Company in Beverly Hills wrote to him suggesting that he might act as his agent and that *Focus*, which had 'created so much interest here', might make a good film and was a subject that many would like to see on the screen. Nothing came of it, but in 2001 the film version, starring William Macy and produced by Miller's son Robert, did have its first showing. It ran in New York for several months.

It is a remarkably faithful and powerful film that changes very little of the original, beyond the elimination of Itzick's story of the peasant revolt. Miller was anxious that the film-makers should recreate the conditions and mood of the 1930s and suggested, among other things, that they should reproduce those advertisements that had once confronted him when he was looking for work, advertisements that specified Christians or Catholics, as a means of excluding Jews. He worried for a time that William Macy did not look at all Jewish, even when wearing spectacles. In the end, though, that was, as he realized, partly the point. It was not what he actually looked like that mattered but what he looked like to those who believed themselves experts in Jewish physiognomy, as others had been in a distant Europe.

Two small changes in the film version do slightly vitiate Newman's final decision to self-identify as a Jew. A woman who had been raped at the beginning of the story dies and thereby he suddenly gains power over his neighbours, who know that he can appear as a witness against them. The point of the original ending is not that he has power over others but that he has it over himself. He is no longer afraid, no longer trades conformity for acceptance. His resistance does not take the form of a legal prosecution of those who seek to intimidate him. It is a matter of will.

Then, in the film, he is joined by his wife when he goes to the police station to report the assault on himself and Finklestein, and the final image is of the two of them reunited. In the novel, Newman has to confront his wife's fear and contempt and walk alone to the police station, thereby giving greater weight to that final gesture. By standing on his own in the glare of the overhead light he joins himself not to the unthinking crowd but to those he had once believed justifiably excluded from society and humankind. Despite these changes, though, the film remains a work of integrity – like the novel, the more effective for its understatement.

Writing in 1984, Miller offered his own sense of the novel, as

> a view of anti-Semitism that is deeply social in this particular sense: the Jew is seen by the anti-Semitic mind as the carrier of the same alienation the indigenous people resent and fear, the same conniving exploitation. I would only add that they fear it because it is an alienation they feel in themselves, a not-belonging, a helplessly antisocial individualism that belies fervent desires to be a serving part of the mythic whole, the sublime national essence. They fear the Jew as they fear the real, it often seems. And perhaps that is why it is too much to expect a true end to anti-Semitic feelings. In the mirror of reality, of the unbeautiful world, it is hardly reassuring and requires much strength of character to look and see oneself.[43]

But despite the book's success, it was not what Miller wanted to be doing. He had long since committed himself to the theatre. He was, he confessed, part actor, needing to see his audience: 'You wrote the book and it disappeared. That was not much fun.'[44] Besides, he had already begun a new play and decided this time to get it right.

As to American anti-Semitism, it began a steady decline. Now when

Americans were asked whether they had heard any criticism of Jews in the previous six months the figure dropped from 64 per cent in 1946 to 24 per cent in 1950 and 16 per cent in 1951.[45] Those returning from the war were less willing to sustain old patterns of prejudice. The film version of Laura Hobson's *Gentleman's Agreement*, whose subject was also anti-Semitism, won an Oscar in 1947, while the federal government under President Truman began the business of unpicking legal restrictions affecting Jews. When Miller wrote *Focus*, however, he did so at a moment when anti-Semitism was at its height. He went into the eye of the storm.

The war ended with twin suns over Japan. Dwight Macdonald, one-time Trotskyist and later member of the anti-Stalinist Americans for Intellectual Freedom, declared that this 'atrocious action' put '"us", the defenders of civilization, on a moral level with "them", the beasts of Maidanek'.[46] Like most other Americans, however, Miller rejoiced. He had friends serving in the Pacific and experience suggested that an assault on the mainland would lead to half a million American dead. Kermit's letters had told him of the price being paid by those required to fight overseas. Now it was over. There would be no more deaths in the newspapers. But it was something more than relief he felt. He took pride in the bomb as an expression of human intellect.

Later he would be bewildered at what seemed to him to be a hole in his heart, a dark area of his consciousness. Beyond that, he would accuse himself of a failure of imagination. In time, he would try to write a play about it, even interviewing nuclear physicists. In 1969 he jotted down the first pages, in which President Truman discusses with a scientist how best to deploy the bomb. The scientist proposes a demonstration of its power by exploding it at sea; Truman favours its immediate use against a city. The play fragment is set out in verse. Truman acknowledges the opprobrium that will follow the first use of the new weapon but insists that since the Japanese had been the first to strike, America itself stood justified in being the first to use a nuclear bomb. He asks the scientist to select a city. He lowers his finger on to a map of Japan and points to Nagasaki. These speeches, though, were written in 1969, at a time when Miller was speaking out publicly in favour of a nuclear freeze. In 1945, he was unequivocal in his support of the bomb.

In 1945, Miller was thirty years old and five years into a marriage with a woman who had lost none of her radical instincts. He himself remained attracted to the Party which in 1943 had dissolved the Comintern and which, the following year, dissolved the American Communist Party itself, replacing it with the Communist Political Association, a name less likely to scare the horses. A year later, the Party was resurrected. It made little difference. The point was that its anti-fascism had set the tone for the 1930s, and the gallant behaviour of the Soviets during the war (the little local difficulty of the Hitler-Stalin Pact notwithstanding) had consolidated the view of those who had yet to jump ship that Marxism remained the best hope for the future. In 1946 the Party had fifty thousand members; the following year, seventy-five thousand. Miller was not one of them but he was attracted to the idea of joining, attending meetings again in 1947.

In terms of his own career, meanwhile, at last the breakthrough he had been waiting for had arrived. The money from his work on *The Story of GI Joe* and *Situation Normal*, from his radio work and now from *Focus*, made it possible for Mary to give up her job to look after one-year-old Jane. Even so, there was nothing financially secure about their situation and Miller remained frustrated at his failure to write a play that would appeal to Broadway. The disaster of *The Man Who Had All the Luck* was not purged by the success of his novel.

It was now seven years since Michigan, and the theatre had changed along with society. In 1938 he had returned to New York at a time when he could still convince himself that drama could be culturally and politically central. This was the year of the Federal Theatre's Living Newspaper production *One Third of a Nation* and Theodore Ward's *Big White Fog*. Even his own historical play, *The Golden Years*, had not been out of line with a theatre that in 1939 produced *Abe Lincoln in Illinois* by Robert Sherwood, the first production of the Playwrights' Company, to which Miller had hoped to link himself. Lillian Hellman's *The Little Foxes*, meanwhile, staged an attack on capitalism of a kind that seemed wholly in tune with his own work. T.S. Eliot's *The Family Reunion* (1939) even suggested the continuing popularity of verse drama, to which, as mentioned earlier, he was himself drawn.

With the war had come Sherwood's *There Shall Be No Night* (1941) and Hellman's *Watch on the Rhine* (1941), which would have given him hope for his own wartime melodrama *The Half-Bridge*. But things were changing. Thornton Wilder's *The Skin of Our Teeth* may have scored a success, but otherwise those who had dominated the pre-war scene had begun to fade away. The musical now seemed central – *Pal Joey* (1940), *Oklahoma* (1943) and *Carousel* (1945). Also in 1945 came someone of Miller's own generation, a one-time author of radical plays, staging a work of lyric intensity in which the question of financial hardship had become subplot, indeed in some ways a metaphor for other kinds of needs. Tennessee Williams's *The Glass Menagerie* won the New York Drama Critics Award. Miller had been beaten to the post.

America, meanwhile, was booming. The gross national product was double what it had been in 1929, just before the Crash. There were twenty-two million cars on the roads. Hitler had committed suicide on 30 April 1945, and the war in Japan had ended in August. The troops were coming home.

As for Miller, *Focus* had brought some attention, though Saul Bellow saw its protagonist's heroism as clipped to his lapel like a delegate's badge at a liberal convention. He longed to get back to the theatre, but for the moment the closest he got was writing theatre reviews for the communist *New Masses*, not under his own name but that of the decidedly non-Jewish Matt Wayne.[47]

It is possible that this is the root of suggestions that he abandoned his Jewish identity. In fact, according to Miller, the name was chosen by the magazine's editor while several other, non-Jewish, contributors also assumed pseudonyms. Speaking in 2002, he explained that he had taken the job 'simply in order to get free tickets' and 'had no desire to be known as a critic', hence his request for anonymity. Though Matt Wayne continued to write, only one or two of the reviews, as Miller remembered it, were by his hand. Otherwise, the pseudonym provided cover for anyone who was available. Thus it was, he maintained, not he who reviewed Tennessee Williams's Broadway debut with *The Glass Menagerie*, though Matt Wayne was on hand to praise its 'faithfulness to life' if also to deplore its 'evaporative ending'.

In 2007 Alan M. Wald, a professor at Miller's alma mater, published *Trinity of Passion: The Literary Left and the Antifascist Crusade*, an excellent study of the literary Left in America. He had stumbled on the figure of Matt Wayne as a result of interviews with two former communists, A.B. Magil and Lloyd Brown, editors of *New Masses*. These confirmed that Miller had published under this name, the latter even suggesting that he might have belonged to a writers' group of the Communist Party under the same pseudonym. Wald's claim that circumstantial evidence is overwhelming that Matt Wayne was, indeed, Arthur Miller is thus simultaneously right and wrong. He was. But so, at least according to Miller, were others, and he denied writing the specific pieces invoked by Wald as evidence of his views, though the fact of his writing for *New Masses* would suggest that the opinions expressed in those pieces would hardly be out of line. Wald could certainly not have known that in 2002 Miller had privately confirmed writing under that name, but since he was perfectly happy to write contentious pieces under his own name in the same magazine Miller's description of the pseudonym as a generic convenience would seem to be true.

By the same token, Wald's suggestion that Wayne played a specific, if short-lived, role in the Party and the magazine would seem to be a speculative bridge too far, based on the presumption that Wayne was cover for a single individual. Equally understandable is his conviction that Arthur Miller had written the article 'Hitler's Quarry' in the first issue of the magazine *Jewish Survey*, unaware, as he was, that another Arthur Miller had been responsible. (Moveover, the later author of *All My Sons* was not even the only Arthur Miller at the University of Michigan between 1934 and 1938.)

Thus, when Miller went walking down Broadway in the autumn of 1945, it was not as a playwright – the memory of *The Man Who Had All the Luck* being too fresh in his mind – still less as a drama reviewer, but as a man in search of the past or, more precisely, his father's past. In a handwritten note in 1992, Miller returned to this moment just as he was writing another play in which he addressed the Jewish experience, *Broken Glass*. He suddenly recalled a moment in which he and his father, alienated from one another politically, briefly came together.

His father, then in his mid-sixties, had taken him to the Lower East Side where he was raised, and the two of them walked along streets that were still part of a Jewish area, which in turn had once been German. Here, his father had been at home, seemingly in control of his life, respected. It is not clear why Isidore chose to take his son to the place where he was raised and in turn raised himself to prominence, albeit a prominence now stripped away. Or perhaps it is. He wanted to show him how far they had travelled, even if their expensive Central Park apartment had long since gone. He wanted to remind him of another world, now slipping away, in which he had once been acknowledged for what he still believed himself to be. As he stood in a doorway and tried to summon up the past, that past was one of chauffeur-driven cars, fur coats for Augusta, and hopes for a dynasty that was no longer to be.

In the end, though, it was a private reverie. His son no longer felt his connection to that place or that time, nor even to the man who had taken so much pleasure in the thought that that son might one day join him in the family firm, the literal or figurative '& Sons' he had so wished to see above the door. Indeed, at that very moment Miller was planning a play in which the conflict between father and son – one a pragmatic businessman, the other an idealist, albeit cruel in his idealism – would be central. They retraced their steps following the route that Isidore had once taken as he returned to what was then home, carrying with him a dream of America that he had thought would never end.

Meanwhile, Miller remained in demand as a radio dramatist. In February 1946, he was approached by the Radio Writers' Guild with a proposal that he should take part in a new project to be called 'This Is My Best' or 'This Time I Write as I Please', a title that suggested the frustration of many writers at the constraints placed on them. The fee was to be $750. And although he was now committed to another project, *All My Sons*, this did not inhibit his political commitments, which remained undiminished despite the first evidences of modest success.

In May that year his anti-HUAC play *You're Next* was performed by the Philadelphia Stage for Action at the Communist Party's May Day rally in Philadelphia. In July he attended a meeting to protest against anti-Semitism. In December, his FBI report noted that the 'author of "Focus"' was scheduled to speak at a meeting entitled 'The Theatre and Propaganda' under the sponsorship of the Jefferson Book Fair, itself an activity of the Jefferson School of Social Science which, despite its name, would find its way on to the Attorney General's List and be classified as a communist front organization. He was also noted as a contributor to the Book Find Club, an organization cited as a communist front by the California Senate Fact-Finding Committee on Un-American Activities in 1948.[48] Nor, despite his pseudonym, had his work for the Communist *New Masses* gone unremarked.

Miller first heard the story on which he would base *All My Sons* from his mother-in-law in Ohio. She had read of a young girl who informed on her father, who had been defrauding the military. Miller has said, 'It stuck in my head that that child would be able to do so, that she would have the moral courage to do that.' In the context of his later career – of his resistance to informing before the House Un-American Activities Committee, and his dramatizing of the life of an informer in *A View from the Bridge* – it is fascinating to think what he might have made of a play based on an act of informing, but this element swiftly disappeared. The young woman became a man, 'because I didn't know much about girls then',[49] and a new family context was created.

Joe Keller is an industrialist who has allowed faulty cylinder heads to be forwarded to the Army Air Force and who thus becomes responsible for the deaths of a number of young airmen. Rather than accept the blame, he allows another man, his business partner, to go to prison. Eventually, his surviving son Chris – the other son, Larry, having (as we later learn) committed suicide out of shame at the news – confronts him and Joe Keller, too, commits suicide as he realizes belatedly that moral responsibility extends beyond the family. That latter death provided something of the impetus for the play. 'I began the play,' Miller remarked, 'with that idea and everything in the play moves like the bow of a ship toward that point. So it was there from the very beginning. I don't see how he could have survived this psychologically. He would have had to destroy himself.'[50]

Miller had been working on the play sporadically since the early 1940s. It took two and a half years to write, far longer than anything he had done before, an investment of time that, given his track record in the theatre, was a high-risk strategy.

After the failure of *The Man Who Had All the Luck*, he set himself to write a realistic play confessedly modelled on Ibsen. Just how closely is evident from the fact that in early drafts of the play a character is given an Ibsenesque name – Ekhart (in *The Wild Duck* a character is called Ekdal; in *John Gabriel Borkman*, Erhart), while *The Wild Duck* is the source both of characters and thematic concerns.

To read the early drafts of *All My Sons* is to see his radical revisioning of the play over the years. Indeed in some respects he turned it on its head. At an early stage, it is Kate, Joe Keller's wife, who insists on the need for the family to accept the death of her son, and the rest of them who are in denial. Ann and Chris are neither planning marriage nor romantically drawn to one another. Though Joe Keller is guilty of the same crime as in the final version, the focus is more clearly on his son, Chris. His experiences in the war were originally more significant. At the front he had presented himself as poor, already distancing himself from the family. His sense of guilt, in other words, pre-dated a suspected crime.

This early Chris Keller is so absolute in his attitudes that in his unit he was known as 'killer Keller', ruthlessly pursuing the enemy even when others were prepared to relent. Miller reminds himself to establish Chris's anger against the Nazis, an anger which frightens his mother Kate. Here, clearly, are the seeds of the Chris Keller who hounds his own father to death. The central contrast in the early drafts is between the brotherhood of wartime service and the soulless materialism and ruthless individualism of the commercial world. To make the contrast more apparent, a member of Chris Keller's military unit is introduced into the action. Chris has returned home wishing to be 'a new man' only to find a manufacturing plant three blocks square where once there had been a tin-roofed machine shop, and a huge house where once had been a six-room building not unlike the Miller family home on East 3rd Street in Brooklyn. The central moral crime, then, focused on the dilemma of Chris Keller rather than on Joe, as he returns to a civilian life that evidences none of the idealism that had taken him to war and that had been consolidated by the comradeship of battle. There is much of Watson from *Situation Normal* in this Chris Keller, as, perhaps, of Kermit Miller whose letters from the front spoke of precisely this sense of brotherhood.

In an early draft, Ann Deever, daughter of Joe's business partner, realizes that Chris suspects his father. Indeed, for a while, it seems, Miller toyed with the idea of Joe Keller having served time. After release, he had been keen to give employment to veterans, as though to compensate for his actions, or perhaps as evidence of the depth of his denial. In this version, the family have left Toledo, where the crime occurred, in the hope of starting again. Miller seems quickly to have abandoned the idea.

Ann Deever levels what was initially the central accusation when she says, not simply of Joe but more tellingly of Chris, that it was not the pursuit of money that appalled her but the failure to mourn for their dead son, Larry, his death being morally connected to the betrayals on which their money had been based. When Kate calls Chris 'as neat as a priest' this is not a positive description. There is a self-righteousness to him that survives into the final text, in which a neighbour complains about the difficulty of living next door to the Holy Family. His standards are too absolute. Not only does he inspire discontent in his neighbours, he drives his own father to the grave.

In the course of two and a half years *All My Sons* (originally called 'The Sign of the Archer', a reflection of Kate's desperate interest in astrology) changed substantially. It is a play concerned with the return of the repressed, with George Deever, Ann's brother, in some way its symbol as he brings into the Keller household the conviction that his own father had been framed for Joe's crime. As Miller has said, 'The function of George is that he is the return of the truth, the notion of the repressed. He is what you wish you could forget, what you wish would disappear from the earth. He is the evidence of the facts – a frightening figure always. He also reveals to us some of the original pre-crime atmosphere of that house.'[51]

All My Sons established what were to be continuing themes in his work. Joe Keller had seen his action as essentially private, concerned primarily with sustaining what he saw as the family business. Miller observed: 'One of his psychological supports is that he is a provider. He is the father of the house. He is the man from whom all power and energy grow. The thought that he would not be able to provide something to his sons is more than he can bear. It is one of his great prides in life that he can leave everything to his boys.'[52] For Miller, though, the private and the public were inextricable: beyond the family was the family of man, and Joe has left that family nothing but shame.

Miller is, in essence, an existentialist who not only sees his characters as the sum of their actions but insists that private acts have public consequences. From this follows his sense of the importance of the past, something he had learned from Ibsen but which was central to his sense of a morally responsive society. What he had admired in Ibsen was the fact that in his work past and present were drawn into a single continuity and that a secret order was 'limned'. Cause led to effect and if this in turn generated guilt, a self-reflexive emotion, self-referring and self-condemning, what really mattered was responsibility. 'Dramatic characters, and the drama itself,' he remarked, 'can never hope to attain a maximum degree of consciousness unless they contain a viable unveiling of the contrast between past and present, and an awareness of the process by which the present has become what it is.'[53]

In *All My Sons* the past shapes the present. With the death of Larry and the conviction of Joe Keller's partner, the clock stopped. When Chris Keller decided to marry his brother's fiancée it started again. Now his mother will have to accept that her eldest son is in fact dead, and to accept that fact is to accept that in some way she cannot yet understand her husband bears responsibility for it.

As in Ibsen's work, the apparently mundane nature of daily routine, its seemingly untroubled surface, not only conceals the tensions that will tear it apart but is the source of the ironies that slowly unfold. The Holy Family –

the Kellers – are, we discover, anything but that. The play takes place in a matter of hours. The opening conversation is inconsequential, light-hearted. We are in the garden of the family's suburban house. The natural world is on the turn. An apple tree, still bearing fruit, has been felled by a storm. This month marks Larry's birthday an irony waiting to be explored. There is a sense of secrets about to be exposed.

There are hints, too, that those who live next door to the Kellers have secrets of their own, that the battle between idealism and pragmatism is also being waged beyond the Keller household. Those neighbours are, we are told, 'uncertain' and characterized by 'sadness'. They are not, we slowly learn, what they once believed they might be. They are something more than a chorus. They extend the action out into the community that Joe Keller is presumed to have threatened. If Chris Keller has something in common with F. Scott Fitzgerald's 'spoiled priest' Dick Diver in *Tender Is the Night* so, too, do those who look on and who have compromised their own principles in the name of materialism – the money that seems a recurring word in the play.

Almost everyone is in denial. Joe Keller denies his crime; Kate, the death of her son. Chris denies his complicity through membership in the family firm, while Ann and her brother deny their abandonment of their imprisoned father. They all act in their own interests, serve their own psychic needs. For all Chris's doubts about the family business and his distaste for money-making, he is not anxious to leave it, merely to negotiate the basis on which he can stay. He will stay, he implies, if his marriage to Ann can proceed without objection.

Chris and Joe Keller are survivors. Chris has survived the war and feels guilty for having done so. His father has survived by offering another man up for punishment in his place. Kate, too, Miller has said, is a survivor herself, reinventing the world and insisting that others inhabit it, give it true sub-stance. Survival, in other words, is an instinct but not a value. There is, indeed, a price to be paid.

It is Kate who holds the key to the play. Besides her husband, she is the only one who knows the truth of the incident of the faulty cylinder heads. It is that knowledge that gives her power. Somewhere love becomes invested with other qualities, contaminated, compromised. She loves her husband but forces him to accede to her demands. She loves her son Chris, but requires him to sacrifice his future so as to sustain her love for her first son whom she will not surrender. In the end it is she who is bereft, her husband and son dead. Earlier, she had said of Larry, 'If he's not coming back, then I'll kill myself.'[54] One pistol shot has rung out. Will another sound when the curtain has finally descended?

There is another level to the play which Miller himself has identified. Why else does Chris hound his father but for a sense of vengeance, killing in his father qualities for which he condemns himself? Why else does Joe Keller kill himself, beyond an acknowledgement of responsibility and a fear of punishment? He does so, Miller has suggested, as a counter-blow to his wife and son. Kate is now abandoned and Chris saddled with an inescapable guilt: 'Chris would feel the burden of guilt until the end of his life because it would have taught him that he really knew better way back when he was denying all this – that he should not have participated in the business without clearing this up earlier on. I think the recrimination against himself would have continued.'[55]

In some ways *All My Sons* invites analysis as a bridge back to the 1930s. The Joads, in *The Grapes of Wrath*, have to learn that the family can be an obstruction to a social ethic. The very title is an echo of that call for social solidarity that had been a principal clarion call of a committed decade. Joe Keller has committed a crime against his fellow man, hence the original title: 'But Cain Went Forth'. *All My Sons*, though, goes far beyond that precisely because it is threaded through with irony and ambiguity. The idealist is tainted. Love is compromised by power. Justice and the law are at odds. Joe Keller's call to his son to 'see it human' is self-serving, but not thereby an inauthentic demand. Joe is guilty of a crime, an offence against the community. The accusations levelled at him, though, are directed by those themselves guilty of offences, if not against the criminal code.

In an early draft, the imprisoned man was to have returned to confront his betrayer. As in many other respects the final text avoids such a polarization. It is, indeed, the layered nature of the characters that is their strength. This is no 1930s morality tale about the corrupting power of capitalism or the warm brotherhood of those only awaiting the circumstances for a revival of a communal spirit. Instead it stages the drama of a group of people, none of whom is what they would be, deeply ambivalent in their motives and increasingly aware of the gap between their language and their convictions. This is not a play that ends with a pistol shot, though Joe's death had been Miller's starting point. The action continues, and in that continuance comes something more than sentimental regret. It is the jagged and complex motives and emotions which have shattered the apparent equanimity of this suburban community in middle America.

He had begun work on the play in 1943, though it would be 1947 before it was produced. In other words, in origin at least it pre-dated both the production of *The Man Who Had All the Luck* and the novel with which he had sought to purge the failure of that play. He wrote it when there was a sense of solidarity against a foreign dictator. There were no longer ideological splits of the kind that had characterized the 1930s. They were at war with the Devil. On the other hand, barred from the war by his suspect knee, Miller had a degree of objectivity and saw, with dismay, the profiteering that was making so many rich while others, like his brother, risked their lives. Nor was he blind to the fact that he, for all his early struggles, had thrived. There was, it seemed to him, something tragic in this dislocation, this moral discrepancy, which made idealism co-exist with self-interest. The writer's task was, at least in part, to identify the process whereby betrayals were justified even as denials were exposed. There were, he insisted, connections between private needs and public actions – acts seemingly detached from human content, and individuals, conflicted, desperate to retain a sense of their own integrity, who performed such acts not because they were cynical but because they were motivated by what seemed to them, at the time, wholly justifiable values. War simply served to raise the stakes, and the play carries that wartime mood. Miller thought that had it been produced at that time he might have faced attacks over his apparent lack of patriotism. As it was, it was produced after the war and he was instead attacked as a communist, a maligner of capitalist morality.

Miller worked on the play in a rented cottage in Port Jefferson, Long Island, writing on the porcelain-topped kitchen table. When he finished he gave a copy to his actor friend from Michigan, Ralph Bell, and his wife, the singer and actress Pert Kelton (later fired from a television show because her husband had once attended a May Day rally). Both responded positively, in contrast to Herman Shumlin, the Broadway producer of Lillian Hellman's plays and therefore, Miller thought, likely to be responsive to work with a social dimension. He rejected it.

Another copy went to Miller's then agent, Leland Hayward, who failed to read it. In mounting despair he sent it to another agent, Kay Brown, who immediately telephoned, enthusing and offering to represent him. She suggested that they meet. The Millers, Mary now pregnant again, were, anyway, scheduled to return to New York that day, which they did in an old Nash-Lafayette car which blew a tyre, costing them twelve dollars.

At Brown's suggestion, the play was sent to Elia Kazan and Harold Clurman, and also to the Theatre Guild, the same organization that had given him a New Plays Award for *They Too Arise* nearly ten years earlier. But there was still a possible problem. The text arrived on the desk of Flora Roberts, the producer Kermit Bloomgarden's reader. She was enthusiastic, as was Bloomgarden, but Lillian Hellman, whose *Another Part of the Forest* he was about to produce, threatened to take that play away from him if he undertook *All My Sons*.

Harold Clurman was the first to read the play. For Miller, he represented the very epitome of the kind of theatre he admired. Ever since seeing the Group Theatre at work, he had ranked Clurman as the best of America's directors. Clurman, impressed, passed it to Kazan, who responded enthusiastically: 'It had a strength not found in the work of any dramatist of this time except Lillian Hellman, but Art's play was warmhearted instead of hateful, as hers were.'[56] To his surprise, Miller now found himself asked whether he would prefer the play to be directed by Kazan or Clurman. Suddenly, the Theatre Guild no longer seemed the best option and his career appeared back on the rails.

The first notice of the play came in an announcement in the *New York Times* declaring that 'Harold Clurman, Elia Kazan and Walter Fried announce the formation of a new production company ... Scheduled for the first presentation by this new partnership is an untitled play by Arthur Miller, formerly known as 'The Sign of the Archer'. It is reported that [the actor] Franchot Tone will have an important interest in the new production.'[57] In fact, nothing had been discussed with Tone. The announcement was a piece of skilful publicity by Clurman. The production company staged only two plays, Miller's and Maxwell Anderson's *Truckline Café*, before dissolving. *Truckline Café* featured a new young acting talent, Marlon Brando.

Kazan's family were Greek and had come to America from Constantinople and to Constantinople from the back country of Turkey. He himself was brought to America at the age of four by his uncle who, in common with other Greeks raised in Turkey, concealed his first names on arrival in New York, being known not as Avraam Elia Kazanjoglous but as A.E. Kazan. As part of a Greek minority in Turkey, the family had learned how to survive. In some senses, like Jews, they had been both inside and outside the culture they inhabited. Kazan's parents, like Miller's, were brought together in an arranged marriage. The family business was a carpet company.

Kazan, five feet six inches tall and boundlessly energetic, was known as 'Gadget' or 'Gadg', a nickname he hated but which reflected his ability to handle minor crises and, Miller claimed, his sexual prowess. He and Miller became close friends, not least because their lives seemed to run in parallel: 'By all distinctive features of behaviour, we were the same fellow, or so it seemed ... We were strictly lower-middle-class neighbourhood kids with a college education who'd swung to the left and were new to money and to pleasure.'[58] Kazan had been expected to join his father's company (located in the Textile Building at 295 Fifth Avenue) which, like Isidore Miller's, had run into financial difficulties, though in 1926 rather than, as with Isidore's, in 1929. Both fathers had chosen to invest in the stock exchange, in the Kazan case stock issued by the National City Bank, bought at $300 and sold at $23, and both felt responsible for the ruin they had brought on their family, while their sons blamed the capitalist system that had given them their own start in life but which had now left them with a patina of guilt.

Both Miller and Kazan had set their minds on going to university against the wishes of their fathers, and it was at university that Kazan, like Miller, encountered an inspiring teacher who introduced him to the theatre. Both were drawn to Marxism, Kazan briefly joining the Party.

Rather than follow in his father's footsteps, he went to Williams College in Massachusetts, a move that so infuriated his father that when he heard about Elia's plans he struck his own wife in the face, knocking her down. At university he was something of a loner, not joining the Zeta Psi fraternity but serving drinks there as a waiter. After graduating, he moved on to the Yale drama school and from there, in 1932, joined the new Group Theatre (run by the triumvirate of Cheryl Crawford, Lee Strasberg and Harold Clurman), whose productions Miller would watch, as a student, in New York. There, Kazan worked first as an actor, appearing in Clifford Odets's *Waiting for Lefty*, at the time a defining production of left-oriented theatre. He also featured as a gangster in a film called *City for Conquest* (1940) opposite James Cagney. His real ambition, though, was to become a director, and in 1945 he directed *A Tree Grows in Brooklyn*, based on the novel by Betty Smith.

While at the Group Theatre he had joined a communist cell (affecting a workers' cap as a badge of his new loyalty). Unbeknown to Cheryl Crawford, this met in Joe Bromberg's dressing room every Tuesday night after the performance. Its members included Bromberg and Paula Strasberg, whom he would later name before the House Un-American Activities Committee. At the age of twenty-five Kazan was teaching directing at the New Theatre League, a communist front organization, and directing at the Theatre of Action, a collective who lived together in a Lower East Side walk-up and which zealously followed the Party line.

Clurman was born in New York and began his career at the Greenwich Village Playhouse before working for the Theatre Guild that had in turn spawned the Group Theatre. His directing credits included Odets's *Awake and Sing* (which opened in February 1935, Miller's freshman year at Michigan) and *Golden Boy*, both greatly admired by Miller.

Thus, nine years after leaving Michigan, nine years in which, as far as the theatre was concerned, he had failed to make his mark, Miller was suddenly confronted with a choice between two men whose work he had admired throughout that time. Kazan was the ultimate theatrical pragmatist, less intellectually engaged with the texts he directed than instinctively able to draw out of actors the performances of which he believed them capable. Clurman was the intellectual, incisive at analysing a text, inspiring, but not always as adept at the dynamics of production.

Miller settled on Kazan with whom he had other things in common. His new director quickly detected that he was having marital difficulties of the kind that he himself was experiencing. A few years later, Mary Miller was surely not wrong to see in him a bad influence, the director having the morals of an alley cat and seeing the power that accreted to him as theatre and film director as giving him a sexual allure he was entirely happy to embrace. There was a feral, predatory aspect to Kazan, a lack of inhibition that surfaced, in his work, in a ruthless drive to achieve his objectives and, in his private life, in a series of sexual betrayals.

Both Kazan and Miller would, under pressure from their wives, enter psychoanalysis in an effort to save their faltering relationships, in the latter case to no avail, though Kazan, after a painful separation, would return to Molly, albeit without significantly abandoning the affairs that seemed to combine pleasure with vindictiveness. Miller grew to admire Kazan's directorial skills and more than fifty years after their first encounter still regarded him as one of the best directors he had ever worked with. But in time, and after Kazan's decision to betray former colleagues to HUAC, he could no longer regard him as a friend. They would work together again, with *After the Fall* in 1964, but the trust had gone.

Replying to a letter, some years later, from Joseph W. Reed Jr of the Wesleyan Film Program asking for a description of Kazan's strengths as a director, Miller stressed the extent to which, for Kazan, all aspects of a production, including casting and tempo, served a play's central theme. He admired his ability to meld together actors with different styles and different training. What mattered to him was to serve the author and the play and he called for the minimum of changes in the text, and even then only after he had explored all possibilities of the play as originally written. For all his egotism, when it came to the theatre that took second place to the work he sought to interpret for the audience. It is for this reason that, even after their estrangement, Miller continued to regard him as an outstanding director. Nor was he the only one to do so. Alfred Saxe, co-director of the radical Shock Troupe, had predicted that he would become 'the greatest actor's director in the American theatre'.[59]

At first, Miller admired Molly Kazan's feistiness, but he eventually came to see in her the same stubbornness he felt he was experiencing at home – what Kazan called her Yankee intransigence. In the accounts of both men the words 'rigid' and 'intransigent' recur, though to 1930s radicals such traits would once have seemed entirely admirable. Kazan's comment that his wife had no 'give' in her would have been echoed by Miller in relation to Mary. By the same token, at first Miller listened to Molly's opinions of his work, not least because of the confidence with which she delivered them. Eventually, though, he came to distrust her as she advised him to remove the Requiem scene which concludes *Death of a Salesman* and urged him not to write *The Crucible*, a play that could only reflect badly on her and her husband when once they had effectively decided to embrace the witch-hunters.

Molly came from an aristocratic background but shared her husband's radicalism, being an instructor at the Theatre Union where she had witnessed

at first hand the coerciveness of the Party, working out of its 12th Street
headquarters through dictats issued by V.J. Jerome, the Party functionary in
charge of the arts. She thus shared both her husband's commitments and his
subsequent disillusionment. Following a cell meeting at the Strasbergs', Kazan
was denounced for failing to embrace the Party line and resigned, while still
joining his former comrades on a May Day demonstration.

Miller, if not a Party member, was still loyal to his Marxist principles. No
wonder, then, that he warmed to his chosen director. He had written a play
in part about the necessity for, but equally the coercive nature of, idealism,
about betrayal yet also about the need still to acknowledge a responsibility
beyond the self, and here was a man who, like him, had done more than
observe the pressures that had deformed the hopes of another age.

At the time Miller first met Kazan, he was making a film called *Boomerang*,
an overly schematic thriller with a background of business corruption. Miller
watched him – for all his earlier suspicion of Hollywood, expressing an
interest in working in film himself, even floating the idea of a movie set on
the Brooklyn waterfront (this was to become *The Hook*). So impressed was
Miller that several of the actors in *Boomerang* – Ed Begley, Arthur Kennedy
and Karl Malden – would be cast in *All My Sons*. Miller himself is to be seen
in the film, albeit momentarily, taking part in a line-up with the chief suspect
in the murder. It is a non-speaking part lasting no more than a couple of
seconds.

Overwhelmed by Kazan's and Clurman's enthusiasm, he watched in awe
as, over a six-week period, actors were summoned to their office on 57th Street
to be auditioned by Kazan. At the end of this process Arthur Kennedy and
Karl Malden were chosen to play George Deever and Chris Keller respectively.
The play was to be designed by Mordecai Gorelik, also a former member of
the Group Theatre and subsequently, reflecting his radicalism, of the Theatre
Collective.

Miller has described both Gorelik's perceptiveness and his ferocity in
defence of a design concept. When actors complained about an unexplained
mound in the middle of the set of *All My Sons*, supposedly the backyard of
the Keller family home, they were told that it was the grave of the dead son –
a son without a grave since he flew into the earth on a distant battlefield.
When Miller himself was enrolled to complain about an obstruction over
which the actors were repeatedly stumbling, he was told, 'You have written a
graveyard play ... The play is taking place in a cemetery where their son
[Larry] is buried, and he is also their buried conscience reaching up to them
out of the earth. Even if it inconveniences them it will keep reminding them
what the hell all this acting is really *about*. The bump stays!'[60]

Kazan has spoken of Clurman's disappointment at being rejected as director. During rehearsals, he recalls, 'he acted abominably',[61] sitting at the rear

of the auditorium, with his secretary, dictating notes. One suggestion he made was that the part of Kate Keller should be rewritten so that she would be seen as sharing her husband's guilt more directly, and Miller attempted this, only to return to the original text. The leading lady nearly left the production, shocked that Kazan and the cast turned up for rehearsals in jeans and sweatshirts.

The part of Joe Keller was given to Ed Begley, a reformed alcoholic. To Miller, it seemed a fascinating piece of casting in that, like Keller himself, he carried a secret sense of guilt that perhaps might be reflected in his performance. Kate Keller was played by Beth Merrill, who had worked for David Belasco, master of stage realism, in the 1920s.

The play opened in New Haven. To many of the cast its social drive, and even its title, recalled not only wartime solidarity but that mutuality celebrated a decade earlier. For Ward Morehouse, drama critic of the *New York Sun*, it was also baffling. Miller recalls him coming to New Haven and, over a drink, asking director and author for an explanation. It did not seem a good sign.

From there it went to the Colonial Theatre in Boston, where Miller had his first experience of the censorship that was to dog this and his next play. The Catholic Church, all-powerful in Irish Boston, exercised considerable influence over the theatre, if not over the burlesque shows that dotted the city. Unsurprisingly, it was especially vigilant for signs of blasphemy. Thus Joe Keller's remark that 'A man can't be a Jesus in this world!' had to go, or the Church would condemn the play. Years later, the same objection would be raised with respect to Edward Albee's *Who's Afraid of Virginia Woolf?* Miller refused, less on principle than because he could think of no alternative. The line survived, and so did the Catholic Church. The shockable Irish Catholics were not, it seems, unduly shocked.

Reviews were reasonable but the theatre seldom full. Miller, after all, had only a three-day flop to his name and was scarcely a draw. Audiences were, he remarked, silent throughout, in a condition of what might be called 'stubborn spiritual stateliness'.[62] None of those involved was yet convinced that they had a hit. Indeed, when the reviews came out they seemed justified in their caution. Following its Broadway opening on 19 January 1947, however, and despite further mixed reviews, it proved quickly popular with New York audiences even as it attracted the ire of those on the Right.

Miller was denounced for supposedly attacking capitalism – and not unreasonably, he confessed, since he certainly did blame capitalism for the profiteering that went on. At the time, he was still under the illusion that such crimes could not happen under socialism, an error that would take him several more years to concede. As it was, even 1947 was not the best of times to be suggesting that America had been subverted by profiteering capitalists. To add to his offence, just a week after the play's opening he published a short story in *Collier's* magazine[63] subtitled 'An Ironic Story of Human Greed', in which a rich businessman allows a thief to escape with $91,000 rather than admit that he has evaded paying tax on it.

America was shifting to the right and *All My Sons* and, subsequently, *Death of a Salesman*, were seen by some less as forceful dramas than political gestures. For the fact is that not merely was the Roosevelt consensus at an end but the Cold War was heralding a Manichean politics of which he would become a victim.

Two months after the play opened, President Truman signed Executive Order 9835. This authorized a loyalty investigation into every person entering civilian employment in any department or agency of the Executive Branch of the federal government, and further authorized suppression of the names of informants. This was a first brick in what Gore Vidal was to call 'the National Security State'. Nor was culture to be exempt from this new call for conformity. In May, the House of Representatives denounced paintings that the State Department had sent abroad as part of its programme presenting American culture. Representative Rankin insisted that 'No American drew those crazy pictures', while HUAC files 'revealed' that of the forty-five artists 'no less than twenty were definitely New Deal in various shades of Communism'.[64] The last phrase was a telling one, not only in its revealing confusion but in its explicit admission of the real target behind many of the assaults by HUAC. One of the artists was denounced as 'one of the signers of a letter sent to President Roosevelt by the United American Artists which urged help to the USSR and Britain after Hitler attacked Russia'.[65]

Already, in other words, a revisionist view of the war was on offer, one that saw American war efforts subverted not by wayward capitalists but by liberals and leftists in league with foreign powers. So quickly had the wartime ally become the enemy. Thus, the idealism in Miller's play, the implicit call for human solidarity, could sound subversive even though the war was only some eighteen months in the past.

In truth, Miller had not yet entirely broken with his earlier loyalties, any more than had many others. In the May Day march in 1946 a thousand communist veterans marched in their uniforms with their officers leading them. Lou Goodstein, an immigrant from Russia, radicalized in 1935 when he watched Eisenstein's *Strike*, an experience that led him to join the Young Communist League, chose this moment to rejoin the party after his wartime service. Miller's continued flirtation with the Party was not, then, so aberrant. Indeed, it was an act of deliberate resistance to the new political logic that now began to emerge. Even as the Cold War began to dominate political thought he, personally, had failed to abandon old loyalties, having not as yet, he explained, climbed on board the bus speeding towards the Third World War.

Nor was he simply sitting in his study, signing whatever was put in front of him. He was also attending regular meetings. With whom? In 1956 he would refuse to tell the Committee when they demanded names. The fact is that Miller was part of a more general debate going on in liberal circles, symbolized by the establishment in December 1946 of the Progressive Citizens of America, a merger of the National Political Action Committee and the Independent Citizens' Committee of the Arts, Sciences and Professions. This was a pro-Soviet group, presided over by Henry Wallace, editor of the *New Republic* and future presidential candidate, whose establishment prompted the founding in January 1947 of Americans for Democratic Action (whose members included Joseph Rauh Jr who in 1956 would represent Miller before the House Un-American Activities Committee).

Both groups saw themselves as liberal. Where they diverged was in their attitude to the Soviet Union and the emerging Cold War. Both supported the New Deal and were concerned to protect its residue from attacks by the Right. However, where the PCA wished to keep the old wartime alliance with the Soviet Union alive and saw itself as dedicated to peace, the ADA, some of whose members were former Trotskyites, was fiercely anti-Stalinist and anti-communist and hence increasingly supportive of a foreign policy that saw Russia as the potential enemy. The ADA also had connections with the anti-communist labour movement.

In truth, the ADA had the more impressive line-up, including Eleanor Roosevelt, Walter Reuther (President of the United Automobile Workers and a member of the Congress of Industrial Organizations (CIO), whom Miller had met in Flint, Michigan, in 1937), David Dubinsky (President of the International Garment Workers), Chester Bowles of the American Federation of Labor (AF of L), Hubert Humphrey, Walter White of the National Association for the Advancement of Colored People (NAACP) and Reinhold Niebuhr (a professor at the Union Theological Seminary). It was not, however, without its confusions. It would be in favour of Eisenhower before anyone knew what his politics were, and hence was embarrassed when he declared himself a Republican. It would be in favour of Adlai Stevenson, who, though admired by liberals, supported the Smith Act (which made it a criminal offence to advocate the violent overthrow of the government) and the imprisonment of communists and showed a cultured disdain for the messy business of being elected (later, at the UN, he would front for people whom liberals would naturally despise).

The ADA excluded communists from its membership whereas the PCA did not. The ADA endorsed the Attorney General's list of subversive organizations, though with reservations; the PCA opposed it. The ADA was for the Marshall Plan; the PCA denounced it, not least because the Soviet Union refused to join. They even disagreed on metaphysics. For the PCA, man was rational, optimistic, utopian; for the ADA, he was flawed and favoured a utopianism linked to tyranny and totalitarianism.

In one sense, Miller should have been drawn to the ADA, but he associated it with Trotskyism and in particular was not ready to endorse its anti-Soviet stance, which could make it seem the ally of a resurgent Right. Instead, he auctioned the manuscript of *All My Sons* on behalf of the PCA. Forty years later he praised Joe Rauh, a leader of the ADA and by now a long-term friend, but sought to distinguish his motives from those of some who had shared his views half a lifetime before. He noted that Rauh, still alive in the late 1980s, 'is anti-Communist for no other reason than his passionate love of democracy; he is uninterested in ideology or even philosophy except as they lead people to a respect or disdain for individual human rights. He is interested in American power abroad, but without the double standard of those who shut their eyes to the crimes of "our" dictators while hurling their thunderbolts at the ones who follow the Soviets' lead.'[66] That last was what had made him keep his distance from an organization whose anti-Stalinism had, it seemed to him, blinded some of its members to the threat to freedom at home. He himself was listed as a sponsor of the PCA in his FBI file.

Interestingly, the British Embassy regarded the development of a split in the liberal left as of sufficient importance to merit a secret memorandum sent from Lord Inverchapel to Ernest Bevin at the Foreign Office on 16 January 1947: 'Left-wing elements in the United States,' Bevin was informed, 'shaken by their reverses in the November elections, have now given birth to two organizations, each bent on recapturing the initiative for progressive policies.' There follows a detailed and accurate summary and analysis which lays emphasis on the fact that the ADA stressed its support for 'freedom-loving peoples the world over', an aim to be pursued 'within the framework of present American foreign policy', a policy, of course, that was now aggressively anti-communist. As Lord Inverchapel observed, 'Considering the anti-Soviet feelings of most American newspapers and, to a lesser extent, wireless commentators, the Americans for Democratic Action had naturally received a much better reception than the Progressive Citizens of America.'[67] It was the former, he suggested, that was closer to the main current of American progressive thought.

Lord Inverchapel's observation about American newspapers and radio commentators could have been extended to the world of literary and cultural magazines, which also divided along the same fault line – a fact which would, in Miller's view, impinge on the reception of his work in America. One such was *Partisan Review*, all twelve of whose original editors had been Jewish, and which had been founded as a house organ of the communist John Reed

Clubs, enlisting in 'the struggle of the workers and sincere intellectuals against imperialist war, fascism, national and racial oppression' and the 'defense of the Soviet Union'.[68] Its principal editors, William Phillips and Philip Rahv, broke with the Party in 1936 and relaunched the magazine the following year. In 1937 Edmund Wilson, who wrote for them, was on the Trotsky Defence Committee, while between 1937 and 1940 *Partisan Review* conducted a correspondence with Trotsky with a view to soliciting his involvement. It was, Philip Rahv explained to him, to be the first anti-Stalinist left literary journal in the world. Trotsky, who thought Stalin the equivalent of cholera, flirted with them but found them insufficiently rigorous. After the Hitler–Stalin Pact, the magazine became chiefly an anti-Stalinist organ whose left-wing views later became accommodated to those of the liberal centre.

It was, indeed, the figure of Trotsky that proved pivotal. His analysis of the betrayal of the Revolution by Stalin, his literate and sophisticated sense of cultural dynamics, proved attractive to those newly dismayed by the evils of the Soviet Union and their own naivety, men like Lionel Trilling, Edmund Wilson, James Burnham, Sidney Hook and Philip Rahv. Stalin had charged Trotsky with treason in 1937 but John Dewey, Chair of his Defence Committee, exonerated him. His followers quickly fell away but neither the schism between them and those who had clung to Stalin, nor the version of the Soviet Union he represented, faded so quickly. The meeting point of the two groups may have been liberalism, but it was a contested liberalism in which no one seemed too ready to forget former loyalties.

To be a Trotskyite was neatly to sidestep those disturbing volte-faces of Stalinist communism. It was – no matter how ironically, given Trotsky's involvement in the brutalities of the Bolshevik Revolution – to embrace the ideal supposedly stripped of its criminalities. The Revolution had been betrayed, but socialism/communism still retained its inner logic. The subsequent step from there to outright rejectionism was altogether less painful than for those who had to jump from what they had believed to be the moving escalator of history on to the seemingly solid soil of American capitalism, especially if the resultant fall could be cushioned, for a while, by the language of liberalism.

Within a very few years, many of these former Trotskyites, like the country, drifted to the right (Burnham ended up on William Buckley's right-wing *National Review*), and never forgot the bitterness of the disputes they had had with their fellow Marxists when the world had seemed young and its making in their hands. When, in 1940, Elizabeth Gurley Flynn was thrown off the board of the American Civil Liberties Union it marked the beginning of a fight within the liberal community that was both vicious and long-lasting. In 1946, William Barrett published an unsigned article in *Partisan Review* which described a liberal fifth column and denounced as Russian patriots or 'pink friends of Russia' Henry Wallace, Eleanor Roosevelt and those associated with the *New Republic*, the *Nation* (for which Miller had written) and *PM*, though that same year the *New Republic*, sounding increasingly like *Partisan Review* itself, changed its attitude following the overthrow of the Czechoslovak government.

Miller would accordingly find himself attacked by *Partisan Review, New Leader* and *Commentary*, both for his politics and for plays which their reviewers insisted on seeing as Party-line works in thrall to realism. In truth, *Partisan Review* studiously failed to review *All My Sons, The Crucible* and *A View from the Bridge* at all, though it did publish a virulent attack on *Salesman* as a Party-line product. *New Leader* and *Commentary* were altogether more forthcoming in their hostility.

When, in March 1947, President Truman had instituted his loyalty oath and directed the Attorney General to compile a list of subversive groups and organizations, it was the kind of tactic that liberals, and, of course, the Party members and fellow travellers they had virtually all once been, would have been likely to oppose. But this was a mark of how things had changed. Arthur Schlesinger Jr (who in 1949 would attack the 'doughface progressive', the fellow traveller whose sentimentality made him a natural target for the communists) agreed with the loyalty programme and the ADA sanctioned it, though both he and it had reservations about its procedures. When the Progressive Party candidate, Henry Wallace, lost out to Truman in the 1948 elections, this was welcomed by both the ADA and the CIO.

Miller, on the other hand, supported Wallace, even though he was a man clearly out of his depth and surrounded by fellow travellers and, indeed, Party members. He supported him, he later explained, 'because he was resisting the Cold War enthusiasm and trying to retain the wartime relationship with the Soviets as far as that was possible'.[69] Miller was one of seventy signatories of a message to French political leaders insisting that Henry Wallace's visit to France 'set a pattern in this One World for the free interchange of opinions between the leaders and the people of all nations of good will'. The fact of the message and its wording were duly recorded in his FBI file.

As the Cold War intensified so the rift in liberal ranks widened. The Alger Hiss case (Hiss being suspected of espionage but ultimately convicted of perjury), which limped on from 1948 to 1950, found Schlesinger, rightly as it later turned out, convinced of his guilt where other liberals saw him as no more than a victim of right-wing anti-New Deal sentiment. When, in 1949, eleven members of the Communist Party were charged with violating the Smith Act (passed in 1940), the American Civil Liberties Union supported the prosecution. Increasingly, those on the left found themselves divided and those divisions proved increasingly useful to one institution in particular – the House Un-American Activities Committee.

Where did Miller locate himself in all this, at a time when Max Eastman, biographer of Trotsky, was becoming an enthusiast for investigating committees, Lionel Trilling was suggesting that liberalism had failed because of its too complete embrace of utopian radicalism (the view, also, of Reinhold Niebuhr, once a member of the Socialist Party), and when liberals were embracing the virtues of the American and political institutions they had once criticized? He clung to the vision that had drawn him to Marxism. He resisted the embrace of Cold War values. Schlesinger might argue, in his book *The Vital Center* (1949), that fascism and communism were simply two versions of totalitarianism, but Miller still carried in his mind what in truth were beginning to sound like sentimentalities.

He was not yet ready to abandon beliefs he had held from the early 1930s. And he paid the price for refusing to do so, not only in attracting the attention of the American Legion (at the heart of the 1919 red scare and fiercely anti-communist), the Catholic League of Decency as well as the House Un-American Activities Committee, but in provoking those ex-communists (some in league with the CIA), predominantly Trotskyites, who now became militantly anti-Stalinist and frequently denounced his work no less than his political views. Indeed, looking back more than fifty years later, he was inclined to believe that the battles between those who described themselves as Trotskyites and the Stalinists had had a distorting effect on his reputation in America and that he had been provoked into defensiveness by these Cold War intellectuals.

His own commitments were clear enough, and were duly chronicled by the FBI. In February 1947 the communist newspaper the *Daily Worker* had noted the success of his play attacking HUAC. It was sponsored by the communist group Stage for Action. *You're Next* was performed four hundred times in twelve months. In September, he attended an open rally sponsored by the Jewish chapter of the Congress of American Women, at which he made a presentation of money to Mrs Eugenia Brunawa, Head of the League of Women in Poland. The Congress was to be placed on the Attorney General's list and classified as a communist organization. In November, he gave a speech 'Concerning Jews Who Write' to the American Committee of Jewish Writers, Artists and Scientists, a speech published the following March in *Jewish Life* which the California Senate Fact-Finding Committee on Un-American Activities designated as a communist publication. He also attended a dinner of the American Russian Institute, an organization which, his FBI file noted, fell within the purview of Executive Order 9835 and which had been classified as communist. He did all these things in the year that he finally, after nearly a decade, successfully broke through into the Broadway theatre.

*

On 30 January 1947, the *New York Herald Tribune* reviewer Howard Barnes in a review headed 'Two More Duds', while conceding that the author of *All My Sons* had a 'feeling for the theatre' and a 'certain sense of form', suggested that he had tried to superimpose a 'classical tragic outline on subject matter which is, at best, confused'. The play, Barnes accepted, 'pulls few punches', but they seemed to him 'scattered badly around the stage at the Coronet'.[70] The *Daily Mirror* reviewer, Robert Coleman, asserted that Miller 'has underwritten. He seldom succeeds in bringing his characters to life and their speech is stilted and choppy, failing to illuminate satisfactorily their actions.' The subeditor's headline was '"All My Sons" Not Very Convincing'[71] The *Daily News* offered a variation: 'A Lot Goes On But Little Happens in Backyard Drama "All My Sons".' The review, by John Chapman, was brutally direct: 'I experienced a disturbing lack of interest in the many affairs which were going on in one small back yard ... long before they got through talking and Mr Begley had shot himself I was ready to go home.'[72]

Reading the reviews must have seemed like a repeat of the morning he opened the papers after the debacle of *The Man Who Had All the Luck*. Then he read the most important review of all and everything changed. Brooks Atkinson, writing in the *New York Times*, welcomed a new talent and praised *All My Sons* as an honest and forceful drama, identifying Miller's talent for unselfconscious dialogue, for creating characters as individuals with hearts and minds of their own. At last the playwright had found a champion – he went on to become Miller's chief defender – and an audience.

In April the play won the New York Drama Critics' Circle Award as best play, in doing so beating Eugene O'Neill's *The Iceman Cometh*. The award was given, according to the citation, 'because of the frank and uncompromising presentation of a timely and important theme'.[73] It did not win a Pulitzer. (In fact, none was awarded that year.) A year later, he sold the film rights only to discover that the company thereby acquired the rights in perpetuity. As a result he would derive nothing from the future television version. Watching the film nearly forty years later, he found the result, starring Edward G. Robinson, a laughable melodrama that ought to be burned. His speeches had been rewritten and all subtleties sand-blasted away.

On the other hand, a review of the play in the *Nation* by Joseph Wood Krutch hinted at problems ahead, suggesting that he 'seems rather unnecessarily careful to express explicitly his warm respect for all the leftist pieties'.[74] What Miller cannot have anticipated at the time was that the play, successful at home, would run into problems abroad, precisely because of its 'frank and uncompromising presentation of a timely and important theme'.

In fact, as the run continued so a controversy began over whether the play could be performed by the US Army in Europe. A work written in wartime, when the United States and the Soviet Union were allies, was suddenly presented as a potential weapon in the Cold War. A play about war profiteering became a foolish confession of the venality of capitalism that played into the hands of a militant communism now anxious to expand its influence throughout postwar Europe. What might be acceptable in the United States became an unnecessary and foolish concession of vulnerability staged in a Europe still bearing the marks of the sacrifices of war.

The *New York Journal-American*, in an article entitled 'Plays Purchase of "Pro-Red" Play', revealed that Miller, 'member of several Red Fascist organizations and a contributor to the New Masses, official Communist magazine', had sold the play to the Army.[75] *Counter-Attack*, an anti-communist newsletter, insisted that 'it would help Stalin in his efforts to convince the Germans that the US is controlled by heartless plutocrats'. Miller, it explained, was a 'COMMUNIST PLAYWRIGHT'. Who, it demanded, 'is responsible for choosing Communist Miller's play? Some innocent in the Army? Or some Communist?'[76] In August, Max Sorenson, National Commander of the Catholic War Veterans, sent a telegram to Kenneth C. Royal, Secretary of War, requesting him to investigate Army plans to produce communist propaganda in the form of *All My Sons*. He demanded to know who was responsible. The New York office of the Catholic War Veterans explained that Sorenson, being busy, had not had time to see the play but had read a résumé. A memo in Miller's FBI file notes: 'Apparently the . . . case has already been taken up with the Army.'[77] Sorenson claimed to have a file on Miller. Two years later, the FBI was asked if such a file had been handed to the Army. If it had, the Army was clearly not sharing it with the Bureau.

The Civil Affairs Division of the American Military Government accordingly refused to license the play for what were then known as the occupied areas in Europe. The *New Leader* supported the ban, objecting to Brooks Atkinson's defence in the *New York Times*. Its executive editor, S.M. Levitas:

> The objection is not so much to such a play's representation here, but to its being sent abroad by an official government unit. The play was to be sent to Germany, Austria and other lands where we are now meeting a rising tide of misunderstanding, resentment and indeed deliberate misrepresentation and hatred. Such a play as 'All My Sons' is fuel for those in Europe that would inflame feeling against the United States; they would say that this prize play is typical of capitalist attitudes in decaying bourgeois America. It is one matter to accept, even to welcome, self-criticism at home; it is quite another matter to parade such problems where millions are being taught to hate us. To send such dramas abroad would be literally playing into our enemies' hands.
>
> Your critic says that 'to quote against Mr. Miller the dialogue of his villain is irresponsible demagoguery'. True! What we warned against is that the

irresponsibles who in Europe are sowing hatred of this land would quote Mr. Miller's dialogue against the United States. The 'calumniators' of this country have enough ammunition ... without our wrapping it in 'prize' packages for foreign convenience in propaganda and gloating.

For Atkinson, in his *New York Times* article, European attitudes to America were more likely to be formed by food shortages and economic paralysis than by a play. He noted, too, that the ban did not extend to England, where 'thousands of people do not like us'. The ban, he maintained, was simple censorship, and censorship would prove effective only if extended beyond the matter of an individual play and enforced by a repressive police force such as existed within the Russian zone. Such censorship, anyway, could only corrode the very American freedoms the US Army was designed to protect:

> This is not the time to be cautious about our most durable asset. As the group loyalty of Americans proved in the war, Americans would rather go down with the principles in which they believe than survive in a world that is afraid. The answer to the 'calumniators' is a more passionate belief in basic American principles and the courage to act on them in every situation. Let's control our own civilization; let's not fritter it away under fire.[78]

For those who challenged the plausibility of the crime that Joe Keller had committed, meanwhile, a Senate committee had obligingly drawn attention to a company guilty of precisely the same crime and cover-up. The Wright Aeronautical Corporation of Ohio, the same state in which the play is implicitly set, was revealed to have forwarded defective engines by the hundred. But it made no difference to those who saw *All My Sons* as a dangerous slur on American business. Forty-three years after the play had been banned from production by the US Army theatre, Miller met a former officer who told him that he had been instructed never to produce *any* Miller plays in future.

The Left, meanwhile, found itself facing in several directions at once. For the *Daily Worker*, the play was by turns a truthful work that could never hope to succeed in a capitalist society and then, when it did succeed, a regrettable celebration of capitalism. Success, anyway, as had been well established in the left-wing theatre groups of the 1930s, was thought to be inimical to radicalism.

This kind of reversal was standard procedure for the *Daily Worker*. Indeed, in the HUAC hearings, Committee members, always avid readers of communist newspapers, would be prone to point out such volte faces, though with quite what in mind is hard to say. Thus, it was Committee members who noted that Budd Schulberg's *What Makes Sammy Run?* was reviewed in the *Daily Worker* of 8 April 1941 as 'the best work done on Hollywood', but by 23 April it was pointing in the opposite direction, the reviewer abjectly apologizing: 'On the basis of quite lengthy discussion on the book,' he explained, 'I've done a little re-evaluating.' Weaknesses in the book had been called to his attention. He duly reversed his position. The same Pauline conversion was observable in *People's World*. On 12 April the book was 'the Hollywood novel'. On the 24th 'The first error I made was in calling the book *the* Hollywood novel.' He, too, it turned out, following 'quite lengthy discussion' had 'done a little re-evaluating'.[79] Different reviews, the same wording.

What happened with Schulberg's work happened as well with Clifford Odets's *Waiting for Lefty*. In a January 1935 review in the *Daily Worker*, this showed 'burning revolutionary fervor', a 'clear guiding idea' and 'sincerity of dramatic utterance'. The following month it revealed 'a woeful looseness of ... structure' and 'strident overtones' that 'all but vitiate his message ... exhortations which now and then deteriorate into mere sloganism or rhetoric'. *New Masses* also required two bites of the ideological cherry, but in the opposite order. A first glimpse had not convinced, but a second viewing provided 'sufficient for discerning in the juxtaposition of sense a clear logic, binding into a solid dramatic role'.[80] For the communist press, it was never worth holding the front page; you could always revise it a few weeks later.

In the Soviet Union, meanwhile, home of ideological gymnastics, the play ran successfully for three weeks and was then precipitately withdrawn as a 'cosmopolitan' work to be deplored because it regarded criminality by a capitalist as a deviation from the norm. For the extreme left, drama was wholly utilitarian. As Odets ironically said of his own *Waiting for Lefty*, it was 'at one time a kind of light machine gun that you wheeled into use whenever there was any kind of strike'.[81]

Miller's early student plays might have lent themselves to this kind of small-arms use; *All My Sons* could patently not, and perhaps the Communist Party was shrewd enough to recognize it. He might have come close to suggesting that capitalism and criminality were closely allied, and, indeed, his suggestion that the family and business were antithetical to idealism is far sharper here than in *Death of a Salesman*. At the same time Joe Keller's actions are seen as aberrant, as the source of a guilt turned finally into remorse and responsibility. Chris Keller's values, meanwhile, are too unfocused to serve the purposes of the Party, but this did not stop an FBI report, compiled between 12 September and 12 October 1947, denouncing the screen version as communist propaganda.

Report number 100-15732, filed on 20 October 1947, was compiled by an FBI special agent and an anonymous writer, part of an ongoing investigation of the communist infiltration of Hollywood. *All My Sons* was being shot at Universal International Studios, and a copy of the script was obtained by an agent designated as T-1, then reviewed by T-2 (the T designation, supposedly, indicating a usually reliable source, though in this case clearly not noticeably so). The twelve-page document offers fascinating reading, less because it makes much sense than because it offers a glimpse of the nature of the material going into Miller's file:

> This story [the report indicates] is the product of a thorough-going Collectivist philosophy. It presents two basic tenets of the real Collectivist philosophy: that man has no right to exist for his own sake, and that all industrialists are criminal monsters. This is pernicious political propaganda, the more pernicious because it deals with fundamentals and never refers to politics as such nor to any political issue of the moment. There is no mention of Communism by name nor of Soviet Russia. But what the play accomplishes is to tell the audience that capitalism is a horrible evil and that a man's concern for himself or his family is a form of depravity.
>
> ... The technique employed here is one used very frequently in stories written by Reds; the plot, ostensibly, deals with the evil of making money through fraud; but the whole piece is slanted and twisted into an indictment of money-making as such; under guise of denouncing 'dishonest greed', the story denounces honest profit and all profit.

It was important to note, the report went on, that 'in all the actual cases of war frauds involving defective munitions (such as the cases that made newspaper headlines recently), the men involved were not professional, established industrialists, but fly-by-nighters and shiftless speculators'. The play, it concluded, was written by a sophomore with no experience of business. Such fraud was, anyway, impossible thanks to government inspectors.

The play was also, clearly, 'a plain, open attack on the family as an institution. It uses the terms of a man's proper, decent concern for the support of his family ("You needed money ... to buy clothes and food and send them to school") and presents this concern as a murderous evil. It stresses that there is "something bigger than the family". What? Why, the collective, of course.'

The document identifies one of the cast, Lloyd Gough, as a member of the Los Angeles County Communist Party. However, of Miller it remarks, 'T-1 was unable to identify ARTHUR MILLER except to say that in his opinion the latter is a New York playwright.' To this insight he offered another: 'in his opinion it will not make money, and ... pictures of this type are not in the same class with pure amusement stories when it comes to profits'.

Miller's response on first seeing this document in December 2001, was to say:

I guess this must be as close as this country ever got to the Stasi in East Germany. What's striking is the sheer ignorance of whoever wrote this report ... the biggest scandal during the war involved the Wright Whirlwind Engine Company which actually changed the tags which had been attached to defective engines and substituted 'Passed' tags on them. A number of high executives went to jail and of course the instigator of the investigation was a senator named Harry Truman. There were numerous other cases but this one would be sufficient to indicate the hysteria implicit in this idiot's report. I had not seen this particular document but I think it will give you a pretty good sense of where things were leading up to with *The Crucible*. How but in fiction could anyone respond to this madness?[82]

Nor was right-wing alarm at the film limited to FBI agents and informers. In his appearance before HUAC, Jack Warner, head of Warner Brothers, in a supposedly closed session, explained his reaction on seeing it:

Of course, if you drop them out of pictures then the Communists have other ways of doing it. In New York I saw All of my Sons [*sic*] written by Arthur Miller. Here are some of the lines: 'Rich men are made ambassadors. Poor men are strung up by the thumbs.' Another line: 'You can't walk along the street and spit unless you hit a college man.'

They write about 21 cylinder heads that were broken. They can't write about the 1,500,000 good airplane motors produced. These are the kind of things they write about. That play disgusted me. I almost got into a fist fight in the lobby. I said, 'How dare they?' They wrote about 21 cylinder heads that were cracked. And the play is a good play but it has all of this stuff in it. In fact, it won the critics' award in New York and was directed by a chap named Elia Kazan who is now at Twentieth Century Fox as a director ... Can I say something off the record? ... This fellow is also one of the mob. I know of him. I pass him by but won't talk to him.[83]

The July–August issue of *Youth* magazine, a product of American Youth for Democracy, offered a free copy of *All My Sons* to the most provocative letter published in each issue – as if Miller had become a by-word for controversy, a fact noted in his FBI file.[84]

All My Sons, however, proved important in another way. Tennessee Williams went to see it. In a letter to the director he wrote, 'This tops any direction I have seen on Broadway. Incidentally, the play is dynamite.' It had, Williams wrote, 'the sort of eloquence this country needs very badly now. I will write Miller my congratulations (though tinged with envy).'[85] He was responding to precisely those qualities that Miller would credit Williams with introducing into the modem American theatre – a blend of the realistic and the non-realistic, the lyrical and the prosaic. And when Miller reciprocated by going to see the New Haven try-out of *A Streetcar Named Desire* he felt liberated by its language, which he saw as giving him permission, as he later said, to speak out with full voice in the play that he was already calling *Death of a Salesman*.

5

DEATH OF A SALESMAN

Ironically, the attention Miller now attracted, and had in part craved, he also fled. A few weeks after the opening of *All My Sons* he applied to the New York State Employment Service, asking for any job they might have. It duly obliged, sending him to Long Island City to assemble beer-box dividers for the minimum wage, forty cents an hour. It was, he said, an attempt to ensure continuity with his past. He lasted only a few days: 'I couldn't stand the idea that I was making money without working. It was morally disgusting . . . But I couldn't get past a week. It was not the work; it was the boredom . . . I wanted to be with the salt of the earth, and the salt was in that factory. But these people were totally depressed. It was just awful being there and I would have gone crazy finally.'¹ It was a gesture, though, that revealed his sense of guilt – ironic, given Chris Keller's equally ambivalent feelings.

Still committed to the values he had embraced in the 1930s, he was uneasy about the gap that had suddenly opened up between himself and those whose fate he had convinced himself was important to him. He felt that his future as a playwright depended on maintaining a connection with those whose lives he instinctively believed would provide his themes and characters. He was also potentially isolated both by his wealth and by his success from his brother and from his father, whose early success he had once taken as a given, and then found the source of a certain political dismay.

In an unpublished sketch/story, written in 1979, the narrator concludes that his sense of guilt had come from his parents and upbringing. The family's wealth meant that when their fortune was lost he had felt ashamed of his clothes, and still more of his failure to succeed. Yet when he became rich he became guilty that he now had more than he could justify. The Marxist playwright was now earning $100,000 a year for as long as the play ran.

Certainly, he had assumed that he and his family would maintain their current lifestyle and not rise up the real-estate ladder. Jews become puritans by way of Marxism, and Miller was an ideological puritan, suspicious of evidence that he might be distancing himself from others. For the moment, then, he and his wife were still living in an apartment in a converted brown-stone at 102 Pierpoint Street in Brooklyn Heights. It was here that he would later recall meeting a young man in Army uniform engaged in an argument with his upstairs neighbour. He was equally pugnacious with repect to Miller, claiming that he could himself have written a play like *All My Sons*. He did, indeed, go on to be a writer, many decades later writing a study of Marilyn Monroe that Miller especially despised. His name was Norman Mailer. Speaking in February 2002, Mailer denied the incident but recalled his time living in the same brownstone ('in fact grey') as Miller. 'He was writing *Death of a Salesman* and I was writing *The Naked and the Dead*. We would talk and then we'd go away, and I know he was thinking what I was, which was, "That other guy is never going to amount to anything".'[2]

The thought that royalties might be accruing, whatever he might choose to do, was both a pleasure and an accusation. As Miller explained, 'The word *royalty* took on a more exact meaning. I had been scratching on the glass from the outside for thirty-one years, until now I was scratching on it from the inside, trying to keep contact with the ordinary life from which my work had grown. For the slow dread was descending on me that I might have nothing more to say as a writer.'[3] Hence his visit to the New York State Employment Service. He was growing rich, but trying to think poor. Success evidently brought its own temptations.

Perhaps to balance his sense of guilt, his became a familiar name on petitions and statements, not least, of course, because his success gave him a new utility to those soliciting support for various left-wing causes. In October 1947 he added his name to an advertisement in *Variety* protesting against HUAC's inquiries into alleged communist subversion of Hollywood. He joined one hundred and fifteen other people in announcing: 'We hold that these hearings are morally wrong because: Any investigation into the political beliefs of the individual is contrary to the basic principles of our democracy.' The advertisement would be duly noted in a 1956 HUAC report on 'so-called "Blacklisting" in the Entertainment Industry', which identified its signatories as either 'out-and-out pro-Communist' or 'aiding and abetting the Com-munist conspiracy'. The same report identified Hollywood films that included 'recently exposed Communists and collaborators'. The list included *Death of a Salesman*, produced by Laslo Benedek, who 'taught at the Los Angeles Communist training school in 1947', and Arthur Miller, who 'has a long record of supporting Communist fronts'.[4] Among these was the Waldorf-Astoria Conference he would attend in 1949 and whose sponsors, the report notes, were forty-three 'Hollywoodites', twenty-three of whom had been identified as members of the Communist Party, the remaining twenty having records as 'collaborators'.

But Miller went further than signing protests and petitions. It was in 1947, a year after Winston Churchill's speech in Fulton, Missouri, in which he had spoken of an iron curtain descending across the continent of Europe from Stettin in the Baltic to Trieste in the Adriatic, and the year in which President Truman ordered loyalty checks on federal employees, that he and his wife, separately, attended a series of Party meetings. According to a Party member who was also an FBI informant, designated T-9, 'ARTHUR MILLER was a playwright in New York City and a member of his Communist Party cell in New York City, during the period September or October, 1946, to early 1947.'[5] The same informant indicated that Jerome Robbins attended meetings during the same time, and we have Robbins's confirmation of this. Miller had no recollection of Robbins being present, but this is easily explained in that the latter was a member of what was known as the 'theatrical transient group', so named because its membership shifted along with its venue. Robbins left the Party when he was asked to explain the influence of dialectical materialism on his ballet *Fancy Free*, which subsequently became the film *On the Town*, starring Frank Sinatra and Gene Kelly.

Pressed, in 1956, during his appearance before the House Un-American Activities Committee, for details of who attended these meetings, Miller recalled 'five or six' people, but refused to identify them. He had gone, he explained, 'in order to locate my ideas in relation to Marxism because I had been assailed for years by all kinds of interpretations of what Communism was, what Marxism was, and I went there to discover where I stood finally and completely'.[6] Where he stood, he decided, was not only outside the Party but outside Party notions of the function of the writer and the nature of literature.

Having presented a paper at one of these meetings, which set out his views on art and its relation to politics, and in particular his conviction that the writer's obligation was to truth rather than to a programmatic version of the real, he found himself regarded with deep suspicion. In the silence that followed, he understood that what he had taken to be his commitment to Marxism was regarded as no more than a naive desire to dissociate ideal from practice, a failure to distinguish the real from the pragmatic necessities of revolution.

He had simply failed to understand the source of authority, which lay not in the self but in those who served a faith whose objective truths were determined as much by an approved text and a cabal of priests as had been those of seventeenth-century New England. The man who had once turned his back on the synagogue, and on those who seemingly nodded agreement in their prayers to precepts that defined the parameters of thought and action, was unlikely to rest content with a secular version of the same. The surprise lies in how long it took him to come to this conclusion, for even now he did not entirely let go of a dream that had driven him since that day in 1932 when a student had first offered him a glimpse of the promised land, or that other day when he wrote to his mother identifying himself as a communist.

A later FBI report, evidently prepared with his HUAC hearing in mind, helpfully lists the 'communist-type organizations' of which he was a member or with which he was connected, a formulation which is itself not without interest. The restricted main file identifies him as having been 'under communist discipline [in the] 1930s and a member of the Communist Party 1943, 1946, 1947'. The list, which stretches beyond 1947, runs as follows:

> American Committee of Jewish Writers, Artists and Scientists; American Jewish Congress; American Labor Party; American Relief Ship for Spain; American Russian Institute; American Youth Congress; American Youth for Democracy; Bill of Rights Conference; Book Find Club; Civil Rights Congress; China Welfare Appeal; Committee for Equal Justice for Mrs. Racy Taylor; Congress of American Women; Cultural and Scientific Conference for World Peace; Frontier Films; Hollywood League for Democratic Action; Hollywood Ten; International Workers Order; Jefferson School of Social Science; Jewish Life; League of American Writers; Mainstream; National Committee to Defeat Mundt Bill [Mundt-Ferguson Bill of 1949 that required the identification and labeling of all material thought to be communist as 'communist propaganda']; National Council of American Soviet Friendship; National Council of Arts, Sciences and Professions; Progressive Citizens of America; Russian War Relief, Inc.; Stage for Action; Veterans Against Discrimination; Voice of Freedom Committee; World Congress for Peace, Paris, May 1949; World Youth Festival in Prague, 1949.

The author of the memorandum notes that Miller was the subject of Bureau file 100-333798 but that there were two hundred references to him in other files. The above list was drawn only from the main file. A more complete summary, it was suggested, could be made available later.

Before HUAC and, again, in conversation in 2001, he could not recall the details of the many manifestos and petitions he signed. They were, indeed, numerous but each, as it seemed to him then, valid. Perhaps his signature, though, was less a sign of his adherence to particular causes than an attempt to assure himself that in rejecting the Party's notion of the role of the writer he was not turning away from Marxism or from the need he had once taken it to address. It was an attempt to convince himself, rather than others, that there was a continuity to his life, that youthful ideals were not invalidated by disillusionment with Party dictats about literature. And it is worth noting, too, that his disaffection was presented as a writer's argument over the nature of art rather than as a political rejection of Soviet policies.

Among the documents he signed was a statement released by the Civil Rights Congress which read, 'The Communist Party is a legal political party.

We see nothing in their program, record, or activities, either in war or peace, to justify the enactment of the repressive legislation now being urged upon the Congress in an atmosphere of an organized hysteria.'[7] There were, indeed, many who were alarmed by attempts to outlaw what was then still a legitimate political party; but the Civil Rights Congress was itself a patent front organization, the result of a merger, in 1946, of the International Labor Defense and the National Federation for Constitutional Liberties. Its sponsors included the confessed communist Paul Robeson and Harry Ward, described by Walter Goodman in his book *The Committee* as 'the model of a model fellow traveler' and by Ward himself as 'a critical student'[8] of communism. The statement was also released through the *Daily Worker*, in April 1947.

There is no reason, of course, why someone of Miller's background, who had regarded himself as a Marxist for twelve to fifteen years and who was himself attending communist meetings, should take any other line, but it would come back to haunt him less than a decade later. He did not, however, restrict himself to signing documents and issuing public statements. He was quite prepared to make his views known in the national media.

On 8 May 1947 he took part in an ABC programme called *Story from the Stars*, which led to his receiving a note of thanks from William Green, President of the American Federation of Labor: 'You and those associated with you rendered most valuable service to the American Federation of Labor and to the millions of members associated with it in the fight we are making against anti-labor legislation. I commend you and all associated with you in the preparation and presentation of the highly impressive educational program which you presented.'[9] The programme, produced with the cooperation of the AF of L, was an attack on the Taft-Hartley Act of 1947, under which employers were no longer required to recognize unions and the President could seek an injunction to end strikes that 'imperil the national health'. The effect was to undermine the power of the unions. *Story from the Stars* was written by Miller, Joe Stein, Aaron Rubin and Peter Lyon and featured, among others, the comedian Milton Berle. It consisted of a series of sketches, musical and comic, beginning with a statement from Berle:

> Good evening – and welcome to 'STORY FROM THE STARS', the A.F. of L. Show. A.F. of L. You know what that is. If some of those anti-labor bills go through A.F. of L. will mean American Federation of Layoffs ... In just a moment you'll hear the DeMarco Sisters sing 'There's No Business Like Show Business'. And I've got a little news for you. The folks in show business have pretty much the same interests as the folks in other businesses – electrical workers, garment workers, teamsters, waitresses. And we've found out that what's bad for them is bad for us. Today we've all got a mighty important thing in common – and that's hanging onto our rights as working

people. Because if we <u>don't</u> watch out for our interests all I can say is – the progress and security we've gained up until now will be completely destroyed and abolished ... And now – may I present five lovely young ladies – holding five union cards in their hot little hands.

There was no pretence that the programme was anything but propaganda. Following the lovely ladies and their union cards the announcer, Clayton Collyer, explained:

Today in this beloved country of ours a crime is being contemplated. It is a crime to enslave 15,000,000 unionmen and women who represent organized labor – to strip them of their dignity and the rights for which they have fought for generations. There is a plot afoot to smash the free unions of American working men and women ... [In] the <u>debate</u> on the Hartley Bill, Representative Hartley said: 'The purpose of this legislation is to break the unions down to the local level.' Those are the words used by the sponsor of the bill, '<u>Break the unions</u>'. And Senator Taft, chairman of the Senate Labor Committee, said: 'The purpose of this bill is to weaken the power of the unions.' ... Wages will be slashed; purchasing power will be diminished sharply ... millions will lose their jobs ... What can you do to stop it? That's up to you. We're not trying to sell you anything ... But make your voice heard – because your voice, the voice of the American people, is the only thing that can kill these slave-labor bills.[10]

This was followed by the comedian Henry Morgan – another union member, the listeners were reassured, as were all those working on the programme, from the writers to the sound effects man.

Miller felt sufficiently engaged to write another piece attacking the legislation. Speaking in 2003, he recalled: 'The AF of L people called me and asked if I would write something for the campaign. I assume what happened was that they bought time on the network, but I wanted to protect the unions. The attack was on, that's for sure.' *The Hiccuping Mr Higgins* concerns a worker whose hiccups are a consequence of his employer making him work ever harder at a machine as a result of the Taft-Hartley Act. Unions could be sued if their members went on strike and effectively bankrupted, leaving, a character called 'Boss' explains, nothing but some old Roosevelt buttons.

On 20 May 1947, the *Washington Post* carried an advertisement protesting against punitive measures taken against the Communist Party. Miller again appeared as a signatory. Five days later, the *New York Times* carried an article about efforts to see that American dance was represented at the World Youth Festival to be held in Prague under the auspices of the World Federation of Democratic Youth. Miller's name appeared as one of its sponsors, thus later leading one of his interrogators on the House Un-American Activities

Committee to believe that he had himself visited Czechoslovakia. A month later the *New York Times* reported efforts to raise funds to send an *All My Sons* production to the same festival. At a meeting of those involved in the company, Miller proposed that a telegram be sent to the State Department, the text of which was to read 'Urge you seriously to reconsider refusal to sponsor availability of transportation for students and participants attending World Youth Festival in Prague this summer. To my knowledge the participants have no special political affiliations.'[11]

Before the Committee, in 1956, he would say that he was doing no more than promote his play and that he would have done so wherever the festival was held. His awareness of the political sensitivities, though, is apparent from the final sentence of the cable, a sentence that was at best disingenuous, though it would be another year before the Communist take-over in Czechoslovakia, a fact that his questioners on HUAC evidently failed to register.

It was, though, Miller's support for Gerhart Eisler that, nine years later, would capture the attention of the Committee. In February 1947, HUAC summoned Eisler before it. He was an Austrian-born communist who had arrived in the country in 1941 and was now denounced by Louis F. Budenz, a former editor of the *Daily Worker* who had turned fervent Catholic and anti-communist and who was also to denounce Miller. In the autumn of 1946, in a radio programme, Budenz had referred to a mysterious agent who took his orders from the Kremlin. A few days later, a newspaper revealed the agent as Eisler. He and his wife had been scheduled to leave the country on a ship for Leipzig but their exit permit was immediately cancelled. When Budenz appeared before the Committee his evidence against Eisler appeared something less than wholly convincing, but by the time Eisler himself was summoned the case had strengthened.

On 6 February 1947, he appeared before the Committee and immediately refused cooperation, declaring himself a political prisoner of the United States. He was duly cited for contempt and escorted back to his cell on Ellis Island where he had been held, but there was now a great deal more evidence against him. His own sister Ruth, summoned before the Committee, which included Richard Nixon, denounced him not only as a communist but as responsible for the deaths of former comrades. She had herself broken with the Party because of her opposition to Stalin and had come to regard Gerhart as a 'dangerous terrorist'. She declared that he had used the sympathy of the American people towards the victims of Nazism to mask his real activities. In Moscow he had denounced anti-fascist Germans to the GPU, forerunner to the KGB, while in China he had brought about the deaths of large numbers. While presenting himself as a German anti-Nazi refugee, he had in fact not lived in Germany since 1929, she insisted, and had been in the service of the Comintern since 1928.

It was a petition concerning this man, organized by the Civil Rights Congress, protesting against 'the shameful persecution of the German anti-Fascist refugee, Gerhart Eisler', that Miller signed. The statement, which would be solemnly read out to Miller by the Staff Director of HUAC Richard Arens in 1956, continued: 'The hysterical atmosphere contrived around the case indicates that this incident involving a German communist kept here against his will is intended as the initial phase of a sweeping attack upon the entire labor and progressive movement in the United States.'[12] It called for Eisler's release and urged that he should be allowed to return to his homeland. On 30 October, Eisler was scheduled to speak at a Communist Party meeting in Newark to protest against the action of HUAC. Stage for Action was scheduled to perform Miller's anti-HUAC play, *You're Next*, at the same event.

The resolution to cite Eisler for contempt was proposed to the House by Richard Nixon, in his maiden speech in February 1947. Whatever Miller's views, as Walter Goodman makes clear, there was no doubt that Eisler 'had been a hard-working Comintern emissary for years under various names, had lied his way into this country, and had traveled, on behalf of the Party, on a forged passport'.[13] Leon Josephson of the International Labor Defense (the Communist organization that had supported the Scottsboro Boys, nine black teenagers charged with rape) was accused of helping Eisler to fake a passport application, perhaps not implausibly, given some of its tactics in the Scottsboro case.

How, then, to account for Miller's support of Eisler, when the facts of his activities were known through his sister's deposition and statements in the House? The case made headline news. Eisler would later be the subject of the Cold War film *I Was a Communist for the FBI*, nominated for the 1951 Academy Award. His was one of the best known cases in the period from 1946 to 1949, when he fled to Eastern Europe. Newspapers were full of details of the hearings and subsequent events, though much of the material supposedly unearthed was in fact manufactured by the FBI.

In his appearance before HUAC, Miller offered no explanation beyond acknowledging that he had been something of a serial signer, merely accepting the suggestion that he would have had no knowledge of the fact that Eisler had been a top-ranking agent of the Kremlin. He would not, he insisted, 'have had the mood of investigating these things'.[14] He was, in other words, claiming naivety, a familiar enough disease at the time. The Eisler case, though, and his response to it, along with the numerous petitions he signed in 1947, suggest a man more seriously embroiled with the Party than at any other time in his life, and this precisely at the moment when he had finally achieved the success he had been seeking since leaving Michigan. Miller's forgetfulness over the case is therefore difficult to account for, even given his obsessive working habits.

His attacks on HUAC itself, however, albeit through communist front organizations, would have resonated with many to whom this was, indeed, a sinister development in American public life. He was, thus, a signatory to a letter released under the letterhead of the writer Millard Lampell on behalf of the Veterans Against Discrimination (on the Attorney General's list) demanding that HUAC be abolished, and was listed as a speaker at a rally organized by the Civil Rights Congress, held at the Manhattan Centre in New York, to denounce HUAC. His name also appears in connection with a protest in Washington against the Committee's hearings with respect to figures from Hollywood, and with a protest meeting on 16 October 1947 on behalf of Howard Fast, a communist writer and member of the board of directors of the Joint Anti-Fascist League. Sent to jail for contempt, Fast had announced 'the beginning of fascism in America'.[15] He would later interpret *The Crucible* as a direct comment on the Rosenberg espionage trial of 1951.

These last activities Miller was happy to claim. He had, he would explain to the Committee in 1956, been responding to an atmosphere of fear and apprehension, especially among artists. In a sense, that explanation might be expanded to include all his public actions in 1947, as, in 1949, his decision to attend the Waldorf Conference – a gesture that he knew would attract considerable opprobrium.

The success of *All My Sons*, meanwhile, affected all aspects of Miller's life. His newfound wealth enabled him to look for a summer home. Accordingly, he and Mary bought a house in Roxbury, Connecticut, some two hours' drive from Brooklyn. His first introduction to this eighteenth-century settlement (with fewer than seven hundred and fifty voters) was sliding into the back of another car, sending the man who had just got out of it carrying a box of groceries sprawling – a man who, it turned out, was already suffering from a slipped disc. He was the owner of the house he had come to see and which he now bought, he observed, partly out of embarrassment. His name was Philip Jaffe, a greeting-card manufacturer, editor of a magazine about China called *Amerasia* and the person for whom Mary had been working as secretary.

The land around the house stretched for some forty-four acres and the whole plot cost $21,000. He and Mary were to live there for nearly ten years. In his autobiography Miller later recalled that Jaffe had subsequently been put on trial for the unauthorized publication of State Department reports on China (leaked by a State Department official, John Stewart Service) in his magazine, evidence against him including what could only have been transcripts of conversations recorded using long-range microphones on the roads near his Connecticut home. Jaffe was fined but not sentenced to prison.

The old farmhouse, would be where he would write *Death of a Salesman*, but before doing so he built himself a ten-by-twelve office–studio, working from his own plans. In buying the house he was following Kazan's example. He and his wife had bought a Connecticut farmhouse, together with 113 acres, a pond and a barn for $17,500. It was there that Miller and Kazan would meet on the eve of the latter's second appearance before HUAC and where Kazan would explain his intention of naming those who had been part of his Party cell in the Group Theatre some fifteen years earlier.

In July, 1947, Miller was once again courted by Hollywood, being offered a one-picture deal to be directed by Alfred Hitchcock. At the time, he was working on a love story of working people in an industrial city – a project that came to nothing – so that he felt little temptation. Besides, having failed to go there when he was fresh from college, and, more recently, having seen just how low the writer's status was in movies (through his work on *The Story of GI Joe*), he found it easy to decline.

He emerged from his success free and clear, as Linda would say in *Death of a Salesman*, but he trailed behind him an ideological baggage that made it difficult for him to rest content. He thought of himself as a shy man, but now found himself in the public world. His retreat, not only into manual labour but into lonely walks around the neighbourhood, was evidence of a confusion that simultaneously disturbed and thrilled him. He had, he realized, become desirable, and in more ways than one. He was a property. The very words warned against the pleasures they implied. In a frank, if still somewhat oblique, passage in his autobiography he remarks:

> Naive as I was, I knew that there was almost no space for me between sexuality and art. I even sensed, without being able to explain the reasons, that while fiercely protective of what I wrote, I was also vaguely ashamed of it, as though it were a sexual secret. On these walks flashes of accusatory truth would sometimes fly at me, showing up my fraudulent pretensions to monogamous contentment when my lust was truer and bewilderingly taunting. At moments it seemed that my relation with Mary and all women was thin and cautious out of some fear that surpassed sex itself. With no more Freud than rumor brought me, I could afford to admit into consciousness what a bit more sophistication might have caused me to suppress: I knew that somewhere behind my sexual anxieties lay incestuous stains that spread toward sister and mother.[16]

That last is a curious remark, but references to incest recur in his papers and in *Timebends* as if he were trying to account for the failure of relationships that collapsed, in part, at least, because of a confusion of realms. It was not literally his mother and sister who disturbed his emotional and sexual equanimity, though he was conscious of the ambivalent role in which his frustrated and disillusioned mother had cast him – as an ally against his less cultivated father. At the same time, in both *All My Sons* and *Death of a Salesman*, the father is killed off, leaving the son alone with the mother. What seems to have been in question was how to relate to his wife when his energies and desires were sublimated in work which for nearly a decade had dominated his life.

Ironically, then, 1947, which saw his first public success, also marked a crisis in a marriage which in truth had already been in trouble for some time. He would later seek to explore the nature of the breakdown in this relationship both in fiction and in prose. In 1956 he wrote a novel, never published, called *The Best Comedians*, which in fictional terms offers a remarkable insight into his marriage. He also explored it in the unfinished short story about a character called Rufus Solomon, the latter in many ways a version of himself, while Mary becomes a character in both *After the Fall* and *The American Clock*. In the Rufus Solomon story, the protagonist realizes that he has hitherto been happy to remain in his room, writing, but that now he must try to communicate with his wife and make some attempt to be happy with her. For both fictional character and author, drift was no longer possible.

After the Fall was written when he had just emerged from a second failed marriage, to Marilyn Monroe, and was about to enter a third, that to photographer Ingeborg Morath. Like his central character, he seems to have been ravaged by self-doubt, afraid to commit himself before understanding the reason for his earlier failed relationships. The play thus seems a conscious and deliberate attempt to analyse himself. It is also a good deal more than this, but it offers as unfettered an assessment of his personal life as he has ever presented, in a work which in many ways is his equivalent of O'Neill's *A Long Day's Journey into Night*.

Quentin, the character modelled on Miller, recalls a confrontation with his wife Maggie, seven years into their marriage (in what would have been 1947 in terms of the Miller marriage), in which their mutual alienation becomes clear. She accuses him of growing away from her, becoming wrapped up in his work, typing behind a closed door, failing to offer the small courtesies which seem to her a mark of the respect she needs. He seems to believe, she suggests, that reading his work to her is sufficient sign of commitment: 'Do you ever *ask* me anything? Anything personal? . . . You don't know me. I don't intend to be ashamed of myself any more. I used to think it was normal, or even that you don't see me because I'm not worth seeing. But I think now that you don't really see any women. Except in some ways your mother.'[17] She accuses him of retreating into silence.

Unwisely, Quentin justifies himself by reference to his confession, six years earlier, that on a trip to Washington (the one Miller undertook in researching *The Story of GI Joe*) he had met a woman he was tempted to sleep with, a confession that had led to a long distancing between them (a similar incident occurs in *The Best Comedians*). In the play he is inclined to grant the justice of her complaints.

Speaking to me in 2001, Miller remarked of his marriage at this time and the strains it had suffered:

> there were two forces. One was that I was totally immersed in my work. When I look back at it I don't know how anybody could have lived with me at all. It was day and night, all day, all night. That's all I ever did, so I probably paid little or no attention to her. And at the same time she was feeling, no doubt, that she could be doing other things. She was very bright, and she could have, instead of waiting around for me to pay attention to her. So I think that both things were working against the marriage. And also, at that time, to my basic surprise, I was becoming well known as a writer, something I really hadn't believed in. And so my horizon simply opened up into other ways of expressing my dominance. I thought I could do anything. And we kind of broke apart there. I was very naive about fame. I was not at all sophisticated. I remember being shocked, or taken aback, when I heard that Marlon Brando had a business manager. An actor, an artist having a business manager! That's the kind of mind I had. An artist was somehow treading on different soil. I wasn't fooling around, but I wanted to. And she was outraged when I mentioned this. So in a way she didn't exist [for me] as another ego.

His relationship with his father also changed after his early success. One day in 1948, in a meeting with a producer, Miller received a call from Isidore asking to see him straight away. He was calling from his office in the garment district, where he was running the latest of half a dozen companies he had tried to set up since he had lost the original twenty years earlier. Imagining news of illness, Miller left the meeting and went downtown. The news that his father offered was that he intended to wind up the company, as he had wound up all the others, despite the fact that, in the postwar boom, this one seemed to be prospering. It had, he explained, been a bad season and anyway he lacked the capital to survive for more than a few months – a year at the most. He was also getting older.

It was still unclear to Miller why he had been summoned. The matter hardly seemed urgent. Was his father after some commiseration, or was he about to reveal a fatal illness, either his own or his wife's? To Miller's surprise and discomfort he began to cry for the first time in his son's presence, asking him for money, not out of desperation but as a debt owed. Oddly, Miller's response was less sympathy than anger. With no catastrophe imminent, he seemed simply to be giving way, surrendering. Indeed, worse than that, he was putting on a display of helplessness, a vulnerability that was performed, calculated.

Then, in an anticipation of *Death of a Salesman*, his father insisted that he could live on two hundred dollars a week, before reducing the amount as Willy Loman was to do. Convinced that his son was now making a fortune on Broadway, he evidently thought the time had come to receive his due, as his own mother had once required him to deliver his pay cheque to her every Saturday until he married in his thirties. At the time, his business was flourishing and he was well but, assuming that five thousand dollars a week was coming through the box office, he presented himself as in need, as he had a decade earlier to his other son Kermit, who had accordingly sacrificed his education to support him.

A stunned Miller found himself explaining that the box office was worth less than three thousand dollars, and was anyway subject to 60 per cent tax, and that he had a family to keep. There was also, he explained, no guarantee that he would write another play. Nonetheless, he would help. He would, he assured him, never starve. But as he travelled back up town he now thought his father contemptible for having set up the occasion, for having staged this drama.

In later years he was inclined to see the episode as expressing his father's fear of ageing. He was simply a man who had supported his son and now expected, if not restitution, then at least a reward. Beyond that, though, was the fear that if his father had proved so vulnerable, might he himself not prove equally fragile? His father's impotence, he felt, carried a threat. Isidore left project after project unfinished. Miller's own notebooks were no less full of uncompleted plays, as if his energy might be leaching away. The occasion festered and left him with a feeling of rage.

In retrospect, he felt that he had perhaps never fully trusted his father. Over the next twenty years father and son became more relaxed in one another's company, but Miller was convinced that on that day the last of his filial feelings dried up, to be replaced with a kind of friendship. Isidore was no longer the fount of wisdom, source of strength. His subsequent contributions to his father had the feeling of charity, the fulfilment of an obligation. Of love there was no trace. This incident, which he later came to view as touched with comic irony, reminded him of the gulf that had long existed between the two of them, since in a sense Isidore had long represented everything against which he had rebelled. Yet, despite the death of love he still found himself looking to his father for approval, as if he could not easily let go of a love that had simply transmuted into an unfocused need.

In later years both Miller and his brother contributed to their father's upkeep, only for Kermit to discover that he had had resources of his own all along. He called his brother about it, and later this fact made its way into *The*

Price, a play which Frances Miller recognized as in part a portrait of the two Miller boys and their relationship with their father.

Mary was nearly four months pregnant when *All My Sons* opened. She gave birth on 31 May 1947. On the 19th, Professor Rowe had written noting that while Miller had supplied the precise date of his play's production, he had not offered a date for the baby's appearance:

> Here it is May and Helen and I have been wondering if the second first night of your and Mary's year has just been or is about to be. If we had had the date for Mary's baby as precisely as for your play we would have sent or be sending a telegram for that occasion too. We are looking forward to news of the event.
>
> No need to say how pleased we were with your letter with all its good news of 'All My Sons', and with all the news of the play since. Especial congratulations for the Critics' Award. I was all prepared to say if the Pulitzer Award went to someone else that I thought that was just as well – it would look better for the country to have two playwrights. To the Pulitzer announcement as it was, I don't know what to say.
>
> I was especially pleased with what you wrote about the smoothness of the process of production and publication of your play – remembering what you said last year about really writing the play, getting it as exactly right as you could, before releasing it.

Miller had in fact given them the month if not the exact date in a letter in which he had announced the possibility of writing a novel rather than a play as his next venture. On 16 June he wrote to Rowe announcing the birth of their son Robert Arthur, who had weighed nine pounds. Meanwhile, he was in rehearsal for *All My Sons*, replacing three actors. Since Kazan was on the West Coast, Miller had had to step in. He had, he explained, just sold the film rights to Universal International which meant he could work without worrying about money, something that perversely he saw as purifying his motives for future works. He now felt the need for solitude, which could hardly have come as good news to Mary barely two weeks after Robert's birth. Already, he had three stories in his mind. More significantly, however, earlier in the year he had begun to explore the background for what would turn into a movie script, a script that never made its way on to film but that was to take him to the West Coast.

Despite his social convictions, Miller, with Mary and their two children Robert and Jane, now moved to a two-family house, at 31 Grace Court purchased with royalties from *All My Sons*. At the end of the street was the East River and across that the tip of Manhattan. You could hear ships' fog horns, as O'Neill had from his new London home. It cost, he later recalled,

$28,000 and contained two duplex apartments. He remembered taking a photograph of the children from a window, in the bitter winter of 1947. The Millers lived on the upper two floors while the ground floor was rented out to the head of a Brooklyn savings bank. If you are going to be a Marxist, as Odets had discovered, there are advantages to being a rich one.

Miller had taken to walking around the neighbourhood, in particular strolling across the Brooklyn Bridge. Down below were the docks, and it was on one of his restless walks through Brooklyn that he had come across the graffiti saying 'Dove Pete Panto?' A few blocks below Brooklyn Heights was the waterfront, controlled by gangsters and corrupt unions. Pete Panto was the young longshoreman who had led a revolt against Joseph Ryan, then in charge of the International Longshoremen's Association, before being murdered.

The idea of a screenplay based on this material appealed to Miller. Once again he was in contact with working men as he wandered the waterfront bars in the small hours, and here was a story that seemed to speak to a moral issue. Beyond the question of the fate of Panto, he was appalled by the treatment of the longshoremen as they gathered to be selected and occasionally scrambled for the brass checks, tokens that they had been hired, tossed on to the ground by the hiring boss.

Research for the script, to be entitled *The Hook*, brought him into contact with members of the American Labor Party (the ALP) in the area who had worked with Panto and were themselves trying to bring about union reform. He learned from them the nature and extent of corruption on the docks. As Miller later recalled, this was for him a momentous experience, not for any immediate impact it had on his career – *The Hook* was never produced – but because it led eventually to *A View from the Bridge*, while his trip to Hollywood in an attempt to sell *The Hook* led to his encounter with Marilyn Monroe. It was from one of his waterfront contacts, a man called Vincent Longhi, six feet tall and a member of the Bar, with political ambitions, that he learned the story of a longshoreman who had betrayed two illegal immigrants living in his own home in order to prevent a marriage between one of them and his niece.

Slightly bizarrely, Vincent Longhi, though a member of the ALP (in fact, as noted earlier a communist front), ran for Congress on the Republican ticket in a piece of remarkable opportunism on the part of all involved, and when he came close to winning ran again in 1948, this time for the ALP. It was Longhi who introduced Miller to the mobster Albert Anastasia and who, as an attorney, defended Communist Party leaders accused of violating the Smith Act. Miller raised funds for Longhi's campaign from Tennessee Williams, whose lover Frank Merlo knew the waterfront situation as well as anyone, being himself the son of a Mafia chief. Williams, certainly at that time, regarded himself as a radical and offered to contribute $500.

It was in connection with his candidacy that Longhi decided to visit Italy in order to meet the relatives of some of his voters, a somewhat curious campaign strategy but one from which Miller benefited, going with him to Calabria and Sicily. He later described his own reasons for going: 'America was where you got rich, but Europe was where the thinking was going on, or so you tended to imagine. America was becoming suspiciously unreal.'[18]

Interestingly, the language he uses to describe his visit to Italy is once again stained with sexuality. Leaving his family behind, he suggested, was 'implicitly erotic and renewing',[19] an opening of the self to the unknown. It was also a visit made in search of inspiration in that he was by no means confident that he would be able to repeat his success with *All My Sons*. He was now a professional writer all too aware that one play was not a career.

Nor was it an exotic trip, beginning, as it did, with a far from comfortable transatlantic voyage in February 1947 on the SS *America*. The slate-coloured sea set the ship wallowing. He was not a bad sailor but even he spent part of the time feeling sick. He arrived in a France still marked by the scars of battle, oddly shocked to see and experience the aftermath of war. What he found was an exhausted people. Whatever the privations of family life in Depression Brooklyn, they were as nothing to what he found in France, as people improvised their lives. The dollar was strong against the franc and lira. It was possible to stay in the Grand Hotel in Rome for a dollar, not that Miller did so. The dollar was worth 650 lire one week and 900 the next. Nobody accepted the official rate. Money was changed on the street or on hotel stairs. He was the American abroad, able to command the limited resources for his own comfort while those who served him watched, he presumed, with a mixture of envy and curious satisfaction. After all, he brought money and, less than two years on from the war, was a representative of the liberating forces. In Paris, a prostitute sat in the lobby of his hotel, available to transatlantic visitors who seemingly alone had the necessary purchasing power. The dollar was king. It could buy anything.

To Miller, Europe had the air of a 'failed continent',[20] though he was aware that already a debate over the function and direction of literature was being waged, a debate of a kind that was, as yet, unthinkable in America, not least because in Europe there was, through the person of Sartre in particular, an entirely respectable and intellectually coherent version of Marxism on offer and, through his arguments with Camus, an active discussion of the future both of society and of writing.

He did not meet Sartre, though he was aware that he held court at the Montana Bar; but he did, at the instigation of the French publisher of *Focus*, Vercors (original name Jean Bruller), attend a reunion of writers who read from their work and made speeches. He saw Sartre across the room. It was the closest he would get. Vercors had worked with the Resistance. Writing later, Miller would characteristically look back to the time of the Resistance as a moment when the moral, the literary and the political were synonymous, not least because this was his own conviction, irrespective of the stimulus of wartime urgencies.

From France he went to Italy, a surreal trip on which, in Rome, for the third time in his life, he was taken to a brothel, a grand palace now somewhat the worse for wear, a kind of municipal facility with no trace of shame. A line of men sat there, as if in the waiting room of a somewhat wayward doctor's surgery.

Travelling south, he crossed the Straits of Messina to Sicily where he met a fellow Brooklynite and one of America's more notorious gangsters, Lucky Luciano, deported from America and living like some Napoleon on St Helena. Italy seemed drained of energy, human and otherwise. The people were thin, struggling to reconstruct their lives. In Foggia, a single twenty-watt bulb illuminated the living room of an otherwise attractive apartment. It was a country that seemed ripe for communism and, indeed, travelling through the country south of Rome he saw the red flag flying from one town hall after another. Meanwhile, the people stayed alive on the wheat delivered from the United States every Monday and which, the American ambassador announced, would end if they failed to vote for the Christian Democratic Party which his country was busy funding. Miller later recalled sitting with a crowd of Calabrian peasants, who watched as a communist organizer indicated on a map the free land they would gain after the 'Revolution'. The Russians, however, were in no position to help, so that while people voted in communist mayors, nationally they voted for the Christian Democrats and the wheat kept flowing. On his return, Miller was one of those who signed a protest against American interference in Italian elections.

It was while he was in Italy, too, that he encountered concentration camp survivors waiting to move on to Palestine, staying in the shadows because the British were committed to their interdiction. For them, he was an irrelevance; for him, they were curiosities, at a tangent to his present concerns which were to do with 'the Italian play' that was beginning to form in his mind. 'Their mistrust,' he said, 'was like acid in my face; I was talking to burnt wood, charred iron, bone with eyes.'[21] Later he would castigate himself for not recognizing his kinship to them, for failing to understand where they had come from and whither they were bound. For the moment, though, they were simply one more European mystery, like the wrecked buildings, the flickering candles at roadside shrines, the gaunt-faced people, the collaborators fast fading into the background. What had happened in the camps would take another fifteen years fully to enter his consciousness. For now, he registered their reproach, but little more. Their stories were not for others, or even for themselves. They were not living. They were waiting out time, so many survivors unsure what survival might mean. For his own part, in later years he accused himself of a failure of imagination, meaning by this a moral failure, so close did it come to invalidating not only his craft but his social and ethical vision alike.

He also saw other men, gathered silently together awaiting work, as he had seen those black men in Wilmington, North Carolina, whom nobody hired, and longshoremen in Red Hook standing in groups, hoping against hope to be chosen. There is a background noise to the stories Miller tells and it has to do with those invisible people who exist on the margin, unacknowledged, judged in some way as irrelevant to the logic of social action. It was these who particularly fascinated him and exerted a moral leverage on his imagination. These were the people who in some part he would celebrate in *A View from the Bridge* and *A Memory of Two Mondays*. These were the people who had animated the dry theories of the Left and whose existence had set him to manual labour after the success of *All My Sons*.

His European visit was a shock. He was, he confessed, aghast at what he saw; and bewildered in particular by those figures, survivors of the camps, who had emerged from an experience beyond his understanding – though *The Crucible*, he later thought, carried its imprint, just as McCarthyism, in his view, replicated some of the procedures of the early Hitler years.

They did, however, cast a longer shadow than he later remembered. There is an unpublished short story from this time that registers something of his awareness both of the casual arrogance of the Americans, who suddenly discovered that they could buy whatever they liked, and of the sufferings of those who emerged from the war morally and spiritually stunned. The story is called 'Winter Crossing', and is set on a ship steaming to Cherbourg in the aftermath of the war. It is February, and those on board are evidently travelling out of necessity rather than for pleasure. It is not clear what necessity drives the American at the centre of the story (at thirty-two precisely Miller's age when he, too, took a ship to Cherbourg in February 1947 – in fact, 'thirty-four' has been crossed through by Miller and 'thirty-two' substituted), but we do learn about the desperation of the seventeen-year-old Jewish girl he encounters. She has been to America in search of a husband. Even now she is flirting with a young Yale graduate, who has come across from First Class.

The other man, the protagonist, is Jewish but, like Miller, has married outside the faith. He is upbraided by the girl. In France, she explains, there are no Jews. What, then, she asks, will become of the Jews? It is a telling question, and one which suggests that Miller was now more acutely aware of an embattled Jewish identity threatened in one direction by the Holocaust and in another by assimilation.

The details of the girl's survival are unclear but the implication is that she has made what seemed the necessary compromises. Americans had thought they were badly off because there were restrictions on the sale of gasoline. Her parents had been trapped in their apartment for over three years, afraid to go on the street, her father eventually being killed, under what circumstances she never explains. With no money, what were they to do, what, in particular, was she to do? Now her mother is anxious only that she should marry somebody, anybody, provided he can support them in their desperation.

As she crosses the deck to greet the young man she has met on board, a group of Jews playing cards gesture to the protagonist. They recognize his kinship to them. When the ship docks the young woman has, it seems, been abandoned by the smart young man from Yale, though she has given him her address so that the unequal trade with American men may be about to continue. For the moment, though, she sets off to Paris on her own, from a destroyed railway station, abandoned by the protagonist no less than by the young man, one of many on whom she has pinned her hopes.

It is a story that surely does register Miller's shocked awareness of what had happened in Europe. Crossed through in the typescript is a description of American men in their thick coats pacing the platform amidst the wreckage of war, anxious only to be on their way, a fictional version of his own experience in Cherbourg's desolated station. The pain is equally crossed through by the young girl whose brittle smile is her desperate attempt to summon a rescuer to her side. It is a story, too, that acknowledges Miller's own Jewish identity, his sense of a responsibility not discharged and perhaps even a residual guilt about his marriage, legitimate enough in an American context but touched with a sense of betrayal in the context of the destruction of European Jewry.

There is another story, though, not published until 1951, which suggests that he had indeed made a connection with those ghosts he had seen in Italy, whose experiences may have been beyond his understanding but whose identity forged a connection with this Jewish-American writer who had abandoned his religion but not, it seems, a sense of shared identity: the story is 'Monte Sant'Angelo' (which he described as the only one for which he had any liking). It clearly emerged from his visit to Italy. It was not *about* those concentration camp survivors, though their shadow perhaps falls on it. It is, rather, a story about origins and therefore also a story about survival, connection, identity. It is also, one suspects, a story about Miller himself and his need to acknowledge the world from which he sprang and from which he could never finally separate himself.

A Hemingwayesque tale, its seemingly neutral descriptions and simple declarative sentences slowly reveal something of the inner lives of the two central characters. These are Americans, and, at first, unproblematically identified as such. They are being driven across the plain of Foggia to Monte Sant'Angelo, the family home of one of them. He is identified only as Appello; his companion, as Bernstein. The town is set, 'comically', on top of a butte rising squarely out of the plain. As Bernstein remarks, again with a Hemingwayesque touch in the ironic pseudo-Britishness, 'Whoever built that was awfully frightened of something.'[22] Just what they were frightened of is in some senses what the story is about, as the journey by one man to discover his roots turns into a journey by the other to do the same.

Bernstein, who has mocked his friend for his quest, nonetheless recognizes what drives him on, grudgingly acknowledging an historical continuity that offers both identity and consolation. If he could do the same, he feels, he would be 'somehow less dead when the time would come for him to die'. 'Wouldn't you like to go back to Austria or wherever you came from and see where the old folks lived? Maybe find a family that belongs to your line, or something like that?' Appello asks. It is a disingenuous question because, as Bernstein points out, 'I have no relatives that I know of in Europe ... And if I had they'd have all been wiped out by now.' It is the only direct reference to the war and the Holocaust, to the absence whose pressure Bernstein feels but has difficulty communicating. He is described as turning away from people, aware of a potential danger that he never articulates or even acknowledges, though we are told that he often 'had the pleasure and pain of resolving to deny himself no more'. Deny what? This becomes clear only by degrees, and indirectly.

Appello discovers the links he seeks, except that his living relative appears barely sane, herself linked to nothing but God. She is aware of a vague feeling of obligation to the visitor but is unable to discharge it because unable to conceive of the world from which he has so suddenly appeared. Appello is the subject of the encounter but the subject of the story, at this point and later, is Bernstein, who watches and recalls a similar encounter with a relative in the Bronx, equally out of touch with his family.

The fact is, though, that while his friend welcomes even this doubtful evidence of connection, Bernstein resists such a link, both in retrospect and prospect, 'even though he had always gotten along with his people'. The more content Appello becomes, as he searches for the graves of his family dead and imagines the past to which he so confidently relates, the more abandoned Bernstein feels, the more stranded in a doubtful present. His parents had recalled a European past, but not with pride, just as Miller's own father had been bemused that his son should have chosen to take a trip to Italy and the continent the family had so enthusiastically abandoned. 'Then I am an American,' Bernstein says to himself, the mere formulation suggesting the extent of his self-doubt, the unease that determines so much of his character.

His links with the past seem broken but his hold on the present appears no more secure. His sense of himself is problematic and that, perversely, is the source of his Americanness.

The two now retreat to a café, only to be joined by a man with whom Bernstein feels a sudden affinity. Mauro di Benedetto has come for his meal and to collect a loaf of bread. Slowly, from small details of dress and behaviour, Bernstein becomes convinced that he is Jewish. He wears a black hat, sells cloth and, as it seems to Bernstein, ties a knot on the bundle which contains that cloth in a way that is familiar: 'It's exactly the way my father used to tie a bundle – and my grandfather ... That's a Jewish man tying a bundle.' For no reason that the man can explain to them or himself, he has a habit of carrying bread home, always making sure to be back before sundown, an action he has simply copied from his father and grandfather before him. 'Shabbas begins at sundown on Friday night,' insists Bernstein. 'He's even taking home the fresh bread for the Sabbath. The man is a Jew I tell you.' Even his first name, Mauro, seems to him to be Jewish.

The suggestion plainly means nothing to the peasant, who is ignorant of the Jews and, indeed, suspects that they may simply be a branch of the Catholic faith. What matters, though, is not the truth or otherwise of Bernstein's suspicions but that, at least in his own mind, here is the tradition he thought dead. It is the impact on Bernstein that interests Miller. Suddenly he feels relaxed about his companion's quest, at peace with himself. Doubt, guilt, denial have been replaced by pride that, even unknowingly, this Jew – for that is what he is convinced he is – has survived. And if he has survived, then so has the past, so assiduously annihilated not only by the Nazis, who are never mentioned, but by those for whom the American experience was a rejection if not of heritage then of pride in the history of that heritage. He has, in effect, come to Europe, as unknowingly as the Italian peasant perhaps enacts the rituals of his faith, to reinvent the history whose spine he had thought broken: 'Suddenly ... he saw that his life had been covered with an unrecognized shame.'

When Appello finally discovers his family tomb, Bernstein no longer feels jealous or irrationally superior, crucially realizing that uncovering the past is something more than a sentimentality. When his friend grasps his wrist he does not recoil because there is no longer an 'implication of a hateful weakness'. 'They walked side by side down the steep street away from the church. The town was empty again. The air smelled of burning charcoal and olive oil. A few pale stars had come out. The shops were all shut. Bernstein thought of Mauro di Benedetto going down the winding, rocky road, hurrying against the setting of the sun.'

Simple fact is added to simple fact, in sentences that seem bleached of emotion, drained of interpretative comment beyond the fact that the adjectives reflect something of the struggle of an American Jew to discover himself: 'steep ... burning ... pale ... winding, rocky'. He has completed his own journey, a journey on which he did not know he had embarked. No wonder, then, that he invests the hurrying figure of Mauro di Benedetto with such meaning, as he makes his way home before nightfall because he comes from a people for whom this urgency, unbeknown to him, is flooded with meaning. And somewhere, beyond Bernstein, lies Arthur Miller aware, suddenly, of a sense of guilt, responsibility, connection, identity. Those who would later accuse him of denying or obscuring his Jewishness were simply ignorant of the frequency with which he circled it in both his published and his unpublished work, though shortly after his Italian trip he would explain something of his ambivalent attitude towards being seen primarily as a Jewish writer.

There were other aspects of his trip to Europe that struck Miller, beyond this stirring of ancestral memories, of an identity if not shunned then displaced. Italy, in particular, was a curiosity in another sense. It was a country in which the Communist Party still held a good deal of local power and yet which in some areas seemed happily to cede authority to the Church. Ideology performed here a graceful dance with pragmatism. Yet, at first glance, it all seemed beside the point. Power had shifted across the Atlantic. These were people performing in an empty theatre, or made to feel such by American authorities now concerned only to halt the communist menace wherever they encountered it, quite as if it were as monolithic as it proclaimed.

Meanwhile, the Mafia, casually employed by the Americans during the war, went about their business, the presence of Lucky Luciano being evidence of at least one thriving Italian-American connection. He had been exiled to Italy, having attracted the attention of Special Prosecutor Thomas E. Dewey, and Miller later wrote of his embarrassment at being taken up by Luciano after encountering his fellow Brooklynite in a Palermo restaurant. On the other hand, it had its advantages. Gasoline was in short supply and it seemed likely that Miller and Longhi would see little of the island. But nothing was in short supply for the Mafia.

On a tour organized by Luciano, using the gangster's green Lancia and accompanied by an armed bodyguard, they were taken to Siracusa where Miller saw the remains of the Greek theatre – a visit he would later recall for its reminder of a different version of theatre, one in which all the people of a community would meet to see public myths publicly enacted. Here was a theatre, first heard about from Professor Rowe in Michigan, not primarily concerned with private issues; one that managed to appeal to everyone without vulgarization. Here was a theatre in which past event and present fact were linked by an ineluctable logic that bred tragedy. He later recalled the last line of Ezra Pound's translation of Sophocles' *Ajax*, 'IT ALL COHERES!',[23] hearing in it a fundamental principle of his own drama but, beyond that, the justification of all art.

Back in America, in March 1948, he published an article in *Jewish Life* in which he attempted to explain his position, not as a Jewish writer but as a Jew who writes. The article reproduced a speech he had made at a dinner given in his honour by the American Committee of Jewish Writers, Artists and Scientists in New York on 24 November the previous year. It is not clear that he was telling its members exactly what they wished to hear.

The magazine was a product of the Freiheit Association, heavily influenced by the Communist Party, but he was less concerned here with exploring political issues than explaining his own attitude. In many ways it is a curious and even disturbing article, in which even as he tries to outline the nature of his relationship to his own Jewishness he acknowledges his distance from it, accepting a responsibility which he nonetheless would choose not to discharge. At a time when Jews had been forcibly reminded of their identity, he was conscious of a pressure to create a Jewish literary movement with writers addressing Jewish themes, history and political life. His own equivocal position is neatly captured by a pronominal uncertainty in his opening paragraph which refers to 'a new national feeling' having taken hold of so many of 'us', to which Jewish writers feel it 'their' duty to respond. He was, it seems, at the same time claiming inclusion and exclusion.

He had, he explained, 'graduated out of' any binding tie 'to what could be called Jewish life', like many other second- and third-generation immigrants and like many Jewish businessmen and workers of every kind. 'The cords which bind any people together to the degree that warrants their being called homogeneous nations or people have been so loosened and cut as to leave the Jewish writer with no other identity than his American identity.' He was aware that some would regard this as 'reprehensible'. However, it seemed to him that 'Western culture, western art and literature are much more highly developed, much more varied, and much more at home in America than are Hebrew culture, art and literature.' It was not that Jewish writers were deserting a highly unified culture of their own, since it 'was not a unified culture we left behind. Indeed,' he admitted, 'in my own experience it could hardly have been called a culture at all.'

It is hard to imagine that a Jewish committee of anything would have enjoyed being told this by the man it had gathered to celebrate, the more so since he went on to say that he 'did not yearn for some national home outside of America' – and this, moreover, in a speech reprinted in a magazine which on the same page announced the need to build the 'democratic unity of the American Jews' and support the efforts to consolidate a 'Jewish Palestine', albeit with the help of the Soviet Union, American progressive labour and a mass movement for Henry Wallace as President.

He knew 'of course' that he was Jewish but did not feel 'in any way set apart, in any way a minority, in any way a traditional Jew' until he left school and went to work. He had never chosen his friends on the basis of race or religion and, apart from the odd remark, never had his Jewishness dramatized to him. There were traces of Jewish religion and culture in his upbringing, he acknowledged, but the Friday night Sabbath ceremony was as close as he got to it, and even this had seemed to have no greater significance than saluting the flag.

He is, of course, being disingenuous. He makes no mention of his bar mitzvah, of his time in the synagogue, of his short-lived search for God. It simply does not form part of the logic he is intent on developing.

He insisted that, but for the Depression, 'Jewishness as a state of mind and anti-Semitism would have largely disappeared'. Unhappily, 'anti-Semitism has confused my generation on the matter of the Hebrew religion as separate from Jewish culture'. He then described something more of his own background, noting that his first play had, indeed, featured Jewish characters, though not because they were Jewish. He wrote about them not 'as Jews but as people', a phrase that is understandable enough but must have stirred a misgiving or two.

Now came a more interesting passage as he asked himself, 'Why didn't I go on writing about Jews?' His answer was that it was a consequence of the psychological shock administered by Hitler and what happened to the Jews. 'I felt,' he told his audience, 'for the first time in my life that I was in danger.' He described the fate of his first play, rejected by Jewish producers convinced that this was not a good time for a play about Jews, one, moreover, in which a Jew was a villain. 'I think I gave up the Jews as literary material,' he explained, 'because I was afraid that even an innocent allusion to the individual wrong-doing of an individual Jew would be inflamed by the atmosphere, ignited by the hatred I suddenly was aware of, and my love would be twisted into a weapon of persecution against Jews ... I turned away from the Jews as material for my work.'

Had he been asked while writing his first play to celebrate Jewish life, he would, he confessed, 'have been perfectly happy to do so. Now, however,

I have been insulted, I have been scorned, I have been threatened, I have heard of violence against Jews, and I have seen it. I have seen insanity in the streets and I have heard it dropping from the mouths of people I had thought were decent people. Instantly, therefore, and inevitably, when I confront the prospect of writing about Jewish life my mood is defensive, and combative. There is hardly a story or play I could write which would not have to contain justifications for behavior that in any other people need not be justified.

His point is that just as in the 1930s it was thought necessary to include strikes in socially aware works, so, if he were to deal with Jewish characters, he would, inevitably, have to engage with the question of anti-Semitism. Audiences, in turn, would be on the lookout for it. His logic is akin to that developed by James Baldwin in his essay 'Everybody's Protest Novel', in which he attacked the black writer Richard Wright for in effect allowing his novel to be determined by those he would denounce; or by Sartre in his essay on anti-Semitism in which he suggested that the Jew was allowing himself to be defined by the anti-Semite.

Miller's article ends, curiously, with a rededication to Jewishness and an end to his pronominal ambiguity: 'we ought to be able to create a gallery of Jewish characters so powerful in their reality, so hearty in their depictions, so deeply felt in their emotional lives' that an audience or reader would be able to reach back to the state in which he had found himself in 1935, when Jewish characters were part of 'the common pool of humanity'. The issue was not

> whether we are Jews who write, or Jewish writers. ... To face away from Jewish life when one has a story to tell is not to be more universal and less parochial; it is to refuse to do best what no one else can do at all; and equally important, to draw upon Jews for our works is to bring into the family of people – our people, our beloved and creative people, who have been edged away from the table to wait in the shadows like ghosts or pariahs ... we wrong ourselves and our own art, as well as our people, by drawing a curtain upon them.[24]

What are we to make of this? He gave the speech just two years after *Focus* in which he had, indeed, engaged with anti-Semitism, and just over two years after the end of the war. The shock of the Holocaust was still fresh. This was a time of great pressure for the creation of the state of Israel (the Zionist Organization of America had just announced 100,000 new members in the previous year). It was also, however, a time when New York intellectuals were making their presence felt in the culture, when Jewish writers and critics were laying claim to the society from which they had been excluded and distancing themselves from the religion, and to some large degree the values, of their parents. Already theirs were beginning to seem the legitimate voices of an American society in process of remaking itself. And though Miller was never among their number, he recognized the pressures being brought to bear. His speech to the Jewish Committee was his attempt to declare a certain independence while at the same time acknowledging a responsibility which in truth he forbore to assume.

At the start of his speech he rejected the notion of a duty to address himself to contemporary Jewish life. At the end he seems to embrace not the duty but the opportunity to do so. The fact that he would not choose to walk down that path – the short stories aside – not subsequently writing a play with an avowedly Jewish character until *Incident at Vichy* seventeen years later, is no longer explained by wartime sensitivities about exposing the Jews to persecution, while he would, with *Death of a Salesman*, be accused of precisely the conviction that the Jew was not an apt model for the universal that he decries in the article.

The Crucible and *A View from the Bridge* simply precluded the use of Jewish characters. In *Salesman*, so close to his own family's experience, he evidently decided against identifying them as Jews, perhaps precisely *because* the play was modelled so closely on his family, and perhaps because his first play had been rejected on the grounds of its ethnic specificity. The pressure to be loyal to a presumed responsibility, though, was strong and did not disappear with time. Nearly half a century later, David Mamet would regret Miller's failure to make Willy Loman Jewish when he worked, after all, in 'a Jewish industry', and this in a play in which no industry is mentioned. When, many years later, Warren Mitchell played the role of Willy Loman in the British National Theatre's production, Miller was astonished by his likeness to his Uncle Manny, the model for a man baffled by a sense of failure, in an endless competition whose purpose he cannot fathom.

After *Focus* it was impossible to say that he was unwilling to confront his Jewishness or to acknowledge the urgencies of the moment. In *Salesman*, though, that Jewishness was not the essence of the play and therefore not specified, though, equally, not denied. He did not, as he had said, feel any binding tie to Jewish life. By the same token, he acknowledged his connection to it and would continue a dialogue with his Jewishness throughout his life, searching for that sense of belonging that he nonetheless felt it impossible to realize.

Meanwhile, another, more public event punctuated the year. In May 1948, six months after Miller's speech and five after its publication, Jewish leaders declared the creation of the state of Israel. Eleven minutes later, America recognized it. Miller was one of the signatories of an advertisement paid for by the American Committee of Jewish Writers, Artists and Scientists, saluting the new Jewish state. The communist *Der Freiheit* reported him as a speaker at a rally at the polo grounds, New York, on 15 May, offering a 'salute to the Jewish state'. When the speakers pointed to the role played in the realization of the birth of the Jewish state by the Soviet Union, the paper reported that the audience 'responded with thunderous applause'. The report was duly noted in Miller's, FBI file.[25]

In fact, writing in 2002, Miller maintained:

[it] had absolutely not the slightest connection with any left-wing thing! It

was all the synagogues, and if there was ever a total Jewish community in this part of the country who appeared at anything it was at that. I hadn't seen so many people with yarmulkes since I was a child. My father was there with me. I remember that occasion because I spoke for a minute or two. I hadn't connected that many religious Jews with Israel because so many of them still said this can't be the real Israel because it's not being established by the Messiah. But a lot of them were there! Now that's why it was noteworthy to me.[26]

Five months earlier, on 30 December 1947, a dinner was held at the Hotel Commodore though, which did have a left-wing dimension to it. It took place under the banner 'American Soviet Friendship for a Jewish state in Palestine'. It was an unlikely event. The Soviet Union, after all, would soon be blockading Berlin (June, 1948). The guests awaited the arrival of Andrei Gromyko, the Soviet Union's representative at the United Nations. Once again, Miller delivered a speech, as did Dr Emanuel Neumann, president of the Zionist Organization of America. There was an air of expectation and hope. The Jews, who had emerged broken from the camps of Europe, who had been chased for centuries, been scapegoats, pariahs, were to have their own home. For all Miller's detachment from his Jewish roots, this was an historic moment. 'I thought it was pretty terrific that for the first time since the Roman period there would be a totally Jewish society: Jewish bus drivers, Jewish prostitutes, Jewish everything. Apart from that it would be a place where Jews could safely live.'[27]

Those who had been scattered were now restored, if not yet secure. The violin and the gun, he would write in a lengthy poem in July 1998, were the guarantee of survival, and survival with a purpose. Yet Miller was not a Zionist,

because I had the illusion that Arabs and Jews could live side by side. It never occurred to me that this was being set up as a clerical state, because, indeed, the Orthodox didn't recognize Israel. Everybody has forgotten that. They said this is not the reinstitution of the ancient state because that could only happen with the return of the Messiah, and no Messiah had returned. And, indeed, they didn't serve in the army. If not sneered at, then, they were only tolerated by the genuine Israelis who were busy building up an army, an agriculture, the usual accoutrements of a modern state. These others were ghetto Jews building up a ghetto inside the state of Israel. So what attracted me was that this was going to be a modern state not a racially exclusive state.

Staring back through fifty years of history, the drama of that evening at the Commodore had, to Miller, lost its force. The applause, he commented, had died away. For this was a drama in which the Jews were not the only characters and in which all were simultaneously both right and wrong. The hope felt by so many in 1948 had, it seemed to him, turned to a despair born out of competing cruelties sanctioned by the religion that had given birth to the state. 'I often feel a tug of pride whenever they [the Israelis] do something decent,' he explained in 2001, but this is balanced by 'this dreadful right-wing crap that they have indulged in for the last few years. Those settlements should never have been put out there in the first place.'[28]

The poem he wrote in 1998[29] to mark the fiftieth anniversary of Israel is a telling one in that it reflects not only Miller's shifting view, but that of a generation. Here was one more ideal, fracturing on a flawed human nature. Back in 1948 though it had seemed to mark the birth of a new hope – as did his support for a radical candidate for the presidency; for it was in that same year that Miller's name appeared on the list of those sponsoring a dinner to be held at the Hotel Astor in honour of Henry Wallace. Two years later, in a State Department loyalty investigation before the Senate, the document was duly flourished. He was also one of an 'initiating committee' of one hundred and fifty 'writers for Wallace'. The committee, under the auspices of the National Council for the Arts, Sciences, and Professions (cited as a communist front organization by HUAC), was to have its headquarters at the Iroquois Hotel and take an active part in the forthcoming presidential election. Henry Wallace, a third-party candidate for the presidency, would fall under the indirect influence of the Communist Party as the campaign developed.

The other writers registering their support included Lillian Hellman, Dashiell Hammett, Norman Mailer, Norman Rosten and Armand D'Usseau, about whom Miller would be questioned in his appearance before HUAC. On 19 October 1948 he was among five hundred to declare support for Wallace's candidacy. This time he was joined by Lee J. Cobb and John Huston. On the 28th he spoke at a rally in support of Howard Fast and Hanns Eisler (both of whom were blacklisted), brother to Gerhart. He was, it seems, determined to use his new fame to support radical causes of all kinds.

In November, he signed a petition attacking the withdrawal of tax-exempt status from the International Workers' Order (an organization that featured on the Attorney General's list, and yet another identified as a communist front). He was also among those who welcomed a visit by the so-called Red Dean, the Very Reverend Hewlett Johnson, Dean of Canterbury, known for his radicalism. In December, Miller appeared with Paul Robeson at the Central Needle Trades High School and, that same month, signed a statement released by the National Council of Arts and Sciences and Professions calling for the abolition of HUAC.

In 1982, he recalled a dinner at Lillian Hellman's house in the autumn or winter of 1948. The principal guests were two members of the Yugoslav delegation to the United Nations, who in the course of the meal explained the reason for their resistance to the Soviets: it was not a matter of ideology, but of nationalism. He offers a version of this occasion in *Timebends*, but there is a more elaborate account in an unpublished essay dated 22 August 1982.

It was an evening that stayed in his mind because it challenged his belief that nationalism and Marxism were incompatible. Like many others, he had assumed that the loyalties of the Yugoslavs, who had so attracted Mary Miller's sympathy even at the moment of giving birth, transcended nation. They were simply part of the worldwide brotherhood of communists. Now he found himself confronted with two people, wartime martyrs to the cause, who outlined their sufferings at the hands of what was in fact, it seemed, no less than Russian imperialism. He was not yet ready, though, to accept what would potentially invalidate much that he had believed.

As for Hellman, she could not accept the idea that a socialist state could be exploited, still less menaced, by a sister state. The heritage of the Left for the two previous decades had suggested that American values were irrelevant in a world being transformed, politically, socially, culturally, by socialism. She was no more willing than Miller to throw this away, not least because in both their cases it would mean not merely that they had been naive but that they had wasted their sympathies, their moral capital, on those happy to exploit their naivety. They had made themselves vulnerable in their own society for no good reason.

Writing in 1982, Miller is thinking his way back into the mentality of the Left in 40s America, as he and Hellman considered the meaning of these two earnest emissaries from a country in which, evidently, it was seriously thought that foreign writers might have influence over their political leaders. He was disturbed, but deferred a decision as to the truth of their remarks. Hellman was more peremptory, more inclined to draw conclusions quickly, though it seemed to him that this was less a product of certainty than its reverse. It appeared to Miller that a battle always went on inside her between an egregious self-concern and genuine commitments – and, perhaps surprisingly for a woman roundly attacked and in many ways imperious, she could, he thought, be compassionate. Two years later, on her death, he was more critical, regretting not asking whether she had ever felt remorse for all the help she had given the Russians and the cruelties for which they had been responsible.

In 1948 it was an accusation he could have directed at himself. Others certainly did, a few years later. But, unlike Hellman, he would acknowledge his sense of guilt and actively involve himself in working to release those imprisoned in the Soviet Union and elsewhere. The sin was not once to have believed but to have allowed belief to become a faith resistant not only to argument but to evidence. In truth it took a long while for Miller to bow to the weight of that evidence. It took Lillian Hellman a great deal longer, so bound up with her own psychology was the stance she had adopted as the moral conscience not so much of America as of her own deracinated class.

In April 1948, Miller left his Grace Court home in Brooklyn and drove to his new house in Roxbury. Before doing anything else he dug a vegetable patch, a habit he never lost, each year pitching himself into the uneven battle with nature for a bowlful of tomatoes and the lettuces he usually refused to eat but that rabbits and other creatures seemed partial to. The woods in Roxbury were full of animals: deer, foxes, skunks, raccoons. Happily, there were no snakes. For some reason no one could understand, a nearby ridge seemed to mark the extent of their wandering. It was here, in his newly constructed studio and with *All My Sons* still running back in New York, that, with only the first two lines of the new play clear in his head ('Willy' – 'It's all right. I came back'), he sat down to write what would become *Death of a Salesman*.

He had had a hard time building the cabin, especially raising the roof rafters on his own, but felt he could not start the play until it was ready. He had made a desk out of an old door and the place smelled of fresh wood. He started in the morning, went on through the day, then had dinner, before working until one or two o'clock in the morning. He later described the play as unveiling itself as if he were no more than a stenographer.

The first lines he had written in his notebook had no connection with what was to follow, except in so far as they focused on suicide. In two and a half lines he imagines two guards on top of the Empire State Building discussing who will jump, an echo, surely, of the 1930s. The next entry is an account of the night-time world outside his Roxbury window, as the insects brush against the screen. He finally began the play knowing only that it would end with a death, the death of the man who became Willy Loman. He later recalled the origin of the name.

In New York, he had stepped out of a bitterly cold winter, the coldest for years, into a 42nd Street movie theatre to see Fritz Lang's *The Testament of Dr Mabuse*, a film he had seen some years before. Here, in a virtually empty cinema, one more element of the forthcoming play slotted into place. He had already started sketching out his ideas for a drama about a family called Loman. Now, he heard the same name from the screen and realized where it had come from. As he explained in his autobiography, in the film a young detective on the track of a killer finds himself alone in an office, desperately trying to call through details of what he has discovered, whispering into the telephone, 'Hello? Hello! Lohmann!' before the light snaps out. In the next shot he is discovered alone in a mental asylum, grasping a non-existent telephone and repeating the same words. What the name Loman had meant to Miller, therefore, though purely on a subconscious level, was 'a terror-stricken man calling into the void for help that will never come'.

Salesman was not to be another Ibsenesque play. He wanted to move away from the realism he had thought necessary in *All My Sons*. He wished to open his drama up to the poetic impulse of his earlier work and that he had detected in Williams's *Streetcar*. It was not that *Salesman* was to be a poetic drama but that Willy's prosaic life was to be contained within a dream of possibility. Miller wanted to reach for an 'emergency speech'.[30] Here, after all, was the final day of a man's existence in which he tries to explain himself to himself, to embrace a world of illusions to which he desperately wishes to grant the sanction of reality. Willy Loman is not articulate. He struggles to understand the world through which he moves with a blend of hope and despair, the two alternating with a rhythm that defines him as clearly as the job that he believes is consonant with his life. Words buzz around his head, along with memories, as if they are always about to settle into some final form. And those who surround him, partly products of his troubled mind and partly standing apart, watch dismayed at the collapse of a man they never fully understand. They speak of him with an oblique affection, and even love, in a language which itself carries the impress of their concern and their awareness of his exemplary status. It is a language commensurate with the tragic role that Miller wished to confer on him. 'Attention, attention must be finally paid to such a person,' Willy's wife Linda famously remarks, and the very structure of the sentence reinforces its meaning.

The play was also to have an innovative form. With *Salesman* he determined to be more radical. He wanted to take his audience on an internal journey through the mind, memories, fears, anxieties of his central character, locating these in the context of those he encounters both in fact and in imagination. And to do this he chose to break open the supposed solidities of a home presented simultaneously as real and invented; he chose to see time as non-linear and explore the ironies generated by simultaneity. The new play was to be poetic and structurally experimental. *All My Sons* had had too many echoes to be seen as wholly original. It was powerful and deeply moving, but the debt to Ibsen and Chekhov was clear. Now, he was determined to go beyond.

The first half came quickly, completed in that single day and night. He found himself laughing out loud at Willy Loman's contradictions. It was composed in the writing, each scene generating the next. The second half took another six weeks. As he wrote, he felt that he was in a dialogue with Willy, who was out there somewhere in the woods. It was also another play that was not without its personal dimension. He understood all too well Willy Loman's sense of failure, relying on a use of humour, though, to maintain a sense of distance.

When he finished the play he read it to his wife and two friends. Mary cried, though, mysteriously to Miller, at a scene he regarded as comic. He then mailed it to Kazan who, like so many in subsequent years, saw in Willy Loman a portrait of his own salesman father. Two days later he telephoned to say that he not only wished to direct it but wanted to move ahead immediately with casting.

Miller's response was elation. His wife's was more restrained, and it is tempting to hear a suggestion of quiet reproach in his memory of that moment. Mary, he recalled, 'accepted the great news with a quiet pride, as though something more expressive would spoil me'.[31] There is a subtle difference between sensible restraint and a lack of real enthusiasm. Until *All My Sons* he and Mary had had some kind of equality. She, after all, had sustained him when success proved so elusive. Now he was being fêted, lured more and more into another world. They were no longer equals. Many years later, Mary Miller confessed that happiness had fled with the coming of fame.

The second person to read the new play was Jim Proctor, who went to Roxbury to do so and would later be in charge of publicity. He sat in the small studio where it had been written and came out two hours later, weeping and saying, 'Oh my God, Oh my God.' He would not be the last to see in it aspects of his own life, having, like the young Willy Loman, been abandoned by his father. For his part, Miller was beginning to realize the power of what he had created.

Kazan now sent the play to the producer Cheryl Crawford, who had worked with the Group Theatre and had recently broken with Harold Clurman. Her reaction was negative. She explained, 'I didn't care much for the title, *Death of a Salesman*, but what really bothered me was the flashbacks – I couldn't see how they would work out. And the main character struck me as pathetic rather than tragic. Who would want to see a play about an unhappy travelling salesman? Too depressing.'[32] This, after all, was a time of postwar boom, on the verge of the 1950s in which, the writer Herbert Gold recalled, the instructions given to television scriptwriters was to produce 'happy stories about happy people with happy problems'.[33] What, after all, could Willy Loman have to do with the new explosion of consumerism, the feel-good America now four years removed from the war and nearly a decade from the Depression?

Rebuffed by Crawford, Kazan passed it on to Kermit Bloomgarden (another friend from Group Theatre days) and Walter Fried, who agreed to produce but were equally afraid of the word 'death' in the title. They preferred 'Free and Clear'. Under Dramatists Guild rules, however, Miller had the last say. He was supported by Kazan.

The producers had difficulty financing the play, not least because of its innovative qualities. One backer, who had invested $1,000, cut this by half when he discovered how 'depressing' it was. In the end they raised $100,000, but actually staged it for half that amount. Shortly before opening, it had advance sales of a quarter of a million dollars and within a few months was booking nearly six months ahead.

Miller's notes for the staging of the play were transformed by the designer, Jo Mielziner, into a set that addressed some of the problems posed but not fully solved in the text. For the cast, Kazan again turned to actors familiar from his Group Theatre days. Lee J. Cobb had appeared in a road version of Odets's *Golden Boy* while Arthur Kennedy, who had played Chris Keller in *All My Sons*, was cast as Biff Loman. Also from *All My Sons* came Thomas Chalmers and Hope Cameron.

Cobb was cast against the script in that Willy Loman was described as a small man – closer to Dustin Hoffman, who played him in 1984. Other actors were auditioned, including Roman Bohnen and Ernest Truex, but in the end it was easier to adjust the text than settle for what was beginning to look like second-best. Whenever Miller talked about Cobb he emphasized the air of melancholy he exuded, a sense of disappointment that seemed to chime with that of a Willy Loman who feels that the best times are in the past and that he has missed his direction without quite knowing when or how. During rehearsals, however, Cobb seemed to be floundering: 'Dying a slow death.'[34] After two weeks, Kazan considered firing him. Then, rehearsing on the roof of the New Amsterdam Theatre, Cobb suddenly reduced those watching to tears, including Miller, who would cry more than once in subsequent productions.

If Lee Cobb made an unlikely Willy Loman, at least in the terms in which Miller had originally envisaged him, Mildred Dunnock made an even more unlikely Linda. She was, Miller later recalled, as 'thin as a rail, bird-like, a cultivated speech teacher out of a woman's college'. Having managed to get hold of a copy of the play, she turned up at Kazan's office and demanded to be auditioned. 'Of course she was impossible, and we told her so. She was simply out of the wrong corner of America for this play.' Several days later she reappeared, disguised now with padding to make herself appear less bird-like. Again she was rejected, but after a few weeks in which no other actress impressed, Kazan and Miller turned back to her: 'Kazan told her that we thought she was totally wrong for the part but that nobody else should play it.'

When rehearsals got under way her only weakness seemed to lie in her savouring of the language. Her delivery was precise but too external. Kazan suggested that she should deliver the lines at double speed and then at three times the speed. She did so. Then he told her to cut the speed in half. Now, as Miller recalled, she 'spoke ... in a nerved-up way, the words coming off her spine. The absence in her of self-pity made it all marvellous – it was Willy she was sorry for, not Linda.' It seemed to him that she had understood something of the play's tone and method:

[*Death of a Salesman*] had never had the kind of mental pace and rhythm of realism, but was a highly condensed, fiercely structured collapsing of time and place in order to deliver up a dense symbolic image of this man and his life. Because she was trained not only as an actress but as a student of literature and poetics, Millie quickly understood this. She knew how to make entrances in full emotional stride ... and she understood at once that her role was thematic rather than wholly psychological and 'real'. She created a style for the role by virtue of her understanding of its place in the whole scheme, which is flushed with expressionist overtness.[35]

The play's music was specially composed by Alex North (who had written the music for *A Streetcar Named Desire* and would provide the scores for *Spartacus, Antony and Cleopatra* and *The Agony and the Ecstasy*), more used to a laid-back California than a New York whose Athletic Club, where he stayed during rehearsals, required him to wear a tie. Miller first heard the score played on an upright piano in the basement of Kazan's brownstone on 74th Street, and was thrilled by its lyricism. Molly Kazan, renowned for her tin ear, was doubtful.

Miller travelled in by subway from Brooklyn each day for rehearsals at the New Amsterdam on 42nd Street. There were occasional rewrites and the set was modified. In particular the gas heater, reminder of Willy's suicidal tendencies, placed centre stage by Kazan, was removed as a too obvious reminder of what was implicit in much of the action.

In the years to come Miller would try to understand and explain the appeal of *Death of a Salesman*, a play that simultaneously appeared so specific to America and yet so exportable. Then, and later, he thought it lay partly in its form, its eclectic sources, and partly in its tragic nature. It was, it seemed to him, a democratic tragedy which elevated a discarded salesman to the centre not only of his universe, but of ours.

The play opened at the Locust Theatre in Philadelphia. Celebrities began to make their way there, as word spread. The play was, Miller explained to a *New York Times* reporter, about 'the significant commonplaces', the relationships between father and son, the individual and society. The theme was that every man 'has an image of himself that fails in one way or another to correspond with reality. It's the size of the discrepancy between illusion and reality that matters. The closer a man gets to knowing himself, the less likely he is to trip up on his own illusions.'[36] *Salesman*, he added, has 'more pity and less judgement' than *All My Sons*.

At first Lee J. Cobb, a Lear-like figure, had difficulty in managing the play's finale, indulging in what Miller has called 'aimless roaring'. With only hours to go before the first paying audiences, Kazan, largely to relax him, decided to take him across the street where Beethoven's Seventh was being performed. When, in 1999, Miller wrote a note for a recording of the same piece, he recalled sitting behind him at that concert and recognizing the relevance of the music to the performance they had been struggling to provoke:

> I recall being struck for the first time by the series of near-climaxes, each reined in until the final ingathering explosion. I leaned forward and whispered in Lee's ear, 'This is the last ten minutes.' He understood; as Willy, he had often yielded to the temptation of blowing all his forces well before his final climaxes. He was a terribly edgy horse, and sometimes, because he wanted every moment to count, nearly gave way to his own emotions rather than the controlled arc of the play.[37]

Many years later he recalled one particular contribution that Cobb made to the production. There is a moment when Willy Loman tries to discover the cause of his son's failure from Bernard, the son of his next-door-neighbour and now a successful lawyer. The actor playing Bernard offered him a cigarette from a solid-gold cigarette case. Cobb took not the cigarette but the case, and as they talked turned it over and over restlessly in his hands. To Miller, it was a brilliant gesture that 'silently embodies Bernard's success and his son's failure ... It seems so easy, but it is terribly hard to "not-see" something one is looking at, and to "not-think" what one is thinking, for the whole action is being done without the least deliberation, yet before our eyes.' It was, he thought, 'Lee's masterstroke, a little thing that shone forth his greatness'.[38]

When *Death of a Salesman* opened at the Morosco Theatre in New York, on 10 February 1949, there was a sense that something special had happened in the American theatre. On opening night, Irene Selznick, whose first venture this was as a producer, sent him a telegram: 'TONIGHT AT EIGHT AND THEN THE WORLD IS YOURS.'[39] 'Her Hollywood background may have been showing through, but she was far from wrong.

Miller celebrated the success of the play by treating himself to a new convertible, the one he was driving over Brooklyn Bridge when he spun and crashed into the Ford. His anxiety over the gap between himself and the common man seems to have stilled, though even now he told his *New York Times* interviewer in Philadelphia that he disliked living anywhere that cut him off from the life of the average family. He maintained, like Huck Finn stretching things a little, that he spent a few weeks every year working in a factory: 'Anyone who doesn't know what it means to stand in one place eight hours a day ... doesn't know what it's all about. It's the only way you can learn what makes men go into a gin mill after work and start fighting. You don't learn about those things in Sardis.'[40] Immediately after the opening, already acknowledging a second success, he sponsored a rally calling for an end to segregation and discrimination. Once again, success demanded a penance.

The *New York Times* review was telephoned through to the opening-night party from Sam Zolotow, a *Times* reporter. According to Miller, he was reading directly from Brooks Atkinson's review as it was being typed. It hailed 'a superb drama', a 'rich and memorable drama'. Kazan's direction was 'masterly' and Cobb's performance 'heroic'.[41] Other reviews were equally laudatory. The *New York Sun* found it a triumph, the *Post* the most important play of the year, and the *New York Journal* a potential Pulitzer Prize winner. It was not wrong. On 2 May, Western Union delivered a telegram to the Morosco Theatre. It read: 'IN THE ABSENCE OF AND ON BEHALF OF PRESIDENT EISENHOWER I HAVE THE HONOR TO ADVISE THAT UNI-VERSITY TRUSTEES HAVE AWARDED PULITZER PRIZE TO DEATH OF A SALESMAN FOR ORIGINAL AMERICAN PLAY.' It was signed by Albert C. Jacobs, Provost of Columbia University, and sent at 3.45 p.m. It arrived at the theatre fifty minutes later.

For the FBI, however, the play was 'a shrewd blow against [American] values' that seemed to substantiate reports from the National Commander of the Catholic War Veterans, whose organization had assembled a file that noted Miller's subversive nature as evidenced not merely in his plays but by his forthcoming attendance at a conference on the Bill of Rights, at which he would 'undoubtedly slander FBI officials.'[42] Meanwhile, the *Death of a Salesman* road company was picketed by 'patriots' in Cairo, Illinois, and finally forced to close down.

> It is evening, the order book has been put away, *homo vendens* [the man who sells] perhaps a commuter riding home on a train or a traveler, settling down in a motel at the edge of an unfamiliar town, closes his eyes for a moment, and in the mirror of darkness glimpses his human life. Who is he? How does he value himself? What is it about him that offends? . . . If *homo vendens* is a woman, she may study the clarity of her eyes or the shape of her waist. They are interchangeable, the man and the woman; they sell, and it is selling that defines them.
>
> They consider themselves useful. In the courtship of mind and matter, they are the dancing masters. It has always been so, since Eden, since Prometheus, coyote and crow. The man or the woman sees a blemish, an unexpected hair, sweat, colonies of bacteria growing in a bodily crease; could that be the offense? . . .
>
> They have . . . loved their children, buried their parents. What about them offends? It must be an error of judgement, they say to themselves, but in the revelations that come in the blink of an eye they read the signs of unhappiness. Something is wrong.
>
> *Homo vendens* bears the burden of the sadness of the age; he has no dignity.[43]

Death of a Salesman is not set during the Depression but it bears its mark, as does Willy Loman, a sixty-three-year-old salesman who stands baffled by his failure. Certainly in memory he returns to that period, as if personal and national fate were somehow intertwined, while in spirit, according to Miller, he also reaches back to the more expansive and confident, if empty, 1920s, when a President of the United States declared that the business of America was business.[44] And since he inhabits 'the greatest country in the world', a world of Manifest Destiny, where can the fault lie but in himself? If personal meaning, in this cheerleader society, lies in success, then failure must threaten identity itself. No wonder Willy shouts out his own name. He is listening for an echo. No wonder he searches desperately back through his life for evidence of the moment he took a wrong path; no wonder he looks to the next generation to give him back that life by achieving what has slipped so unaccountably through his own fingers.

Death of a Salesman had its origins in the short story/memoir that Miller wrote in 1932, at the age of seventeen (approximately the age of Biff Loman), when he worked briefly for his father's company, having just graduated from high school. It told of an ageing salesman who sells nothing, is abused by the buyers, and borrows his subway fare from the young narrator. He is a man, the story reveals, who displayed his emotions at the wrong times. More significantly, he is a man whom the young Miller describes as incomplete and who never belonged. For those who would later worry about the product Willy Loman sold, this man, like the Miller company, sells coats. For those who were to worry about his ethnic identity, the name of this ageing salesman is Schoenzeit, in all probability a Jewish name. The narrator is 'Arthur', and the account is based on an actual incident. It ends with the reported death of the salesman.

In a note scrawled on the manuscript Miller recalls that his mother had rediscovered it when *Salesman* was finally produced. The same note records that the real salesman, whom he had known only for a day, had subsequently thrown himself under a subway train.[45] It is, Miller has conceded, 'obviously the genesis of the play', but not the only genesis in that it also draws on 'Schleifer, Albert: 49', the short story he wrote in 1938. But, he has observed, *Death of a Salesman* also traced its roots closer to home.

Willy Loman, as noted earlier, was kin to his salesman uncle Manny Newman, a man who was 'a competitor, at all times, in all things, and at every moment. My brother and I he saw running neck and neck with his two sons in some race that never stopped in his mind.' The Newman household was one in which you 'dared not lose hope, and I would later think of it as a perfection of America for that reason ... It was a house ... trembling with resolutions and shouts of victories that had not yet taken place but surely would tomorrow.'[46] Manny's son Buddy, like Biff in Miller's play, was a sports hero and, like Happy Loman, a success with the girls, though, failing to study, he never made it to college. Manny's wife, meanwhile, 'bore the cross of reality for them all', supporting her husband, 'keeping up her calm, enthusiastic smile lest he feel he was not being appreciated'. It is not hard to see this woman honoured in the person of Linda Loman, Willy's loyal but sometimes bewildered wife, who is no less a victim than the husband she supports in his struggle for meaning and absolution.

Though Miller spent little time with Manny, 'he was so absurd, so completely isolated from the ordinary laws of gravity, so elaborate in his fantastic inventions ... so lyrically in love with fame and fortune and their inevitable descent on his family, that he possessed my imagination.' To drop by the Newman family home, Miller said, was 'to expect some kind of insinuation of my entire life's probable failure, even before I was sixteen'. Bernard, son of Willy's next-door neighbour, was to find himself treated in much the same way by the Lomans. Of another salesman friend of Manny, Miller writes:

> Like any traveling man, he had to my mind a kind of intrepid valor that withstood the inevitable putdowns, the scoreless attempts to sell. In a sense, these men lived like artists, like actors whose product is first of all themselves, forever imagining triumphs in a world that either ignores them or denies their presence altogether. But just often enough to keep the game going one of them makes it and swings to the moon on a thread of dreams unwinding out of himself.

Willy Loman himself is just such an actor, a vaudevillian, getting by 'on a smile and shoe shine', staging his life in an attempt to understand its plot and looking for the applause and success he believes his due. He wants, beyond anything, to be 'well-liked' – for without that, he fears, he will be nothing at all.

During the run of his first great success, *All My Sons*, Miller met Manny again. Rather than comment on the play his uncle answered a question he had not been asked: 'Buddy is doing very well.' The undeclared competition was still under way, as if time had stood still. The chance meeting made Miller long to write a play that would recreate the feeling that this encounter gave him, a play that would 'cut through time like a knife through a layer cake or a road through a mountain revealing its geologic layers, and instead of one incident in one time-frame succeeding another, display past and present concurrently, with neither one ever coming to a stop'. For in that one remark Manny brought together past hopes and present realities while betraying an anxiety that hinted at a counter-current to his apparent confidence.

Miller likened the structure of *Salesman* to a CAT scan, which simultaneously reveals inside and outside, as he did to geological strata, in which different times are present in the same instant; and the timescale in *Death of a Salesman* is, indeed, complex. The events on stage take place over twenty-four hours, a period which begins with a timid, dispirited and bewildered man entering a house once an expression of his hopes for the future. It is where he and his wife raised a family, that icon of the American way, and reached for the golden glitter of a dream. He is back from a journey he once saw as a version of those other journeys embedded in the national consciousness, in which the individual went forth to improve his lot and define himself in the face of a world ready to embrace him. But the world has changed. His idyllic house, set like a homestead against the natural world, is now hemmed in by others and his epic journey no more than a drummer's daily grind, travelling from store to store, ingratiating himself with buyers or, still more, with the secretaries who guard the buyers from him.

The play ends, after a succession of further humiliations, frustrated hopes and demeaning memories, when Willy Loman climbs back into his car, which itself is showing signs of debilitation, and attempts one last ride to glory, one last journey into the empyrean – finally, in his own eyes, rivalling his successful brother Ben by trading his life directly for the dream that lured him on.

Willy Loman sallies forth, a sad Quixote fighting the windmills of American possibility. He is a pioneer only in memory and ambition, never in the present, which he fills so full of past and future that it lacks all definition. He exists in the past of his reconstituted memories, and a future part-dream, part compromised hope. He is a man who knows pure despair. The person who assembles the instrument of his suicide is not a man who believes the lies he tells. He is a man who looks down the slope of his life towards a darkness that he fears will retrospectively flood that life with irony. He startles himself into action as his life insurance policy begins to run out. He is in the period of grace in more than one sense.

Death of a Salesman differs radically from the more traditionally constructed *All My Sons*, while still focusing on father–son relationships. It is technically innovative, with its near-instantaneous time shifts. It is also lyrical, as Miller allows Willy's dreams to shape themselves into broken arias.

Death of a Salesman begins with the sound of a flute, a sound that takes Willy back to his childhood when he had travelled with his father and brother in a wagon. It is a correlative of his longings. His father made and sold flutes. He was, in other words, a salesman, though one who, unlike Willy, made what he sold. It is, however, a tainted memory. The distant past is not as innocent as, in looking back, he would wish it to be. It represents betrayal, for his father had deserted the boys, as his brother Ben had deserted Willy, going in search first of that father and then of success at any price. Betrayal is thus as much part of his inheritance as is his drive for success, his belief in salesmanship as a kind of frontier adventure whose virtues should be passed on to his sons.

In the notebook he kept while writing the play[47] Miller saw Willy as waiting for his father's return, living a temporary life until the time when meaning would arrive along with the person who had abandoned him, as Vladimir and Estragon would await the arrival of Godot. That idea is no longer explicit in the text, but the notion of Willy leading a temporary life is. Meaning is deferred until some indefinite future. Meanwhile he is a salesman, travelling but never arriving, regretting that he has never followed his brother on his adventures in which wealth has seemingly been gifted to him as a reward less for effort than for ambition.

Before a word is spoken, something of Willy's character is established by the way in which he appears and walks across the stage. His exhaustion, Miller instructs, is apparent. He carries two large sample cases. This image has acquired iconographic force. It featured on the original poster, was echoed on the poster and programme of the National Theatre production in England in the early 1980s, and provided the startling opening image of the 1999 Broadway revival as Brian Dennehy, as Willy, stood, framed against a bright light, in what amounted to a quotation from that first production whose fiftieth anniversary it was celebrating.

Willy Loman is a travelling man who can no longer travel and hence, in his own mind, has lost his definition, his sense of himself. The suitcases are more than the tools of his trade, so that when, in the words of the stage direction, he 'lets his burden down' and sighs there is already clearly something more at stake than a man at the end of a day's work. As we will learn, he will never pick them up again.

The first word of the play, Linda's cry of 'Willy!', is uttered, we are told, with 'trepidation', while his reply, 'It's all right. I came back', is a contradiction in terms. If he has come back it is not all right. Likewise, his comment that 'nothing happened' is denied by his presence. Something has happened, and Linda's trepidation suggests that it is not a surprise. That first stage direction also encapsulates Linda's character, explains her loyalty, the root of her collaboration in the dreams that have so nearly evaporated. As Miller remarked, 'she more than loves him, she admires him, as though his mercurial nature, his temper, his massive dreams and little cruelties, served only as reminders of the turbulent longings within him, longings which she shares but lacks the temperament to utter and follow to their end'.[48]

In a speech he chose not to include in the final version, he has Linda remark of Willy that he had never meant to hurt her. He simply needed to be better than someone, and she had played that role. She believed herself to know every thought he had ever had. The irony of that, of course, and of Linda herself, is that in the end not only does she become complicit in the dreams that destroy Willy but there is a sense, we eventually discover, in which she does not know every thought he ever had. How else, at the end of the play, can she remind him that they have paid off the mortgage as if that were his definition of success? How else can she cry out, 'We're free!' at the very moment he has sacrificed his life in a demonstration that he is still in thrall to the destructive dream she has sustained, believing that thereby she sustained the man she loves?

Also, and intriguingly, Miller jots down a thought in his notebook which suggests another dimension to the relationship between Willy and Linda. Willy, he notes, resents Linda's unbroken, patient forgiveness, knowing that there must be great hidden hatred for him in her heart. This is *Death of a Salesman* as *The Iceman Cometh*.

The minimalism of the stage set is in part a function of a play that he determined should not be cluttered with the defining detail of realism, and in part a reflection of a family that has lived out its life in relative privation, a privation that can never be directly addressed. Miller toyed with the idea that Linda should be referred to as paying the family bills in person so as to save money on stamps, as his own family had done. He does have her mending her stockings, an action that becomes freighted with meaning as her husband simultaneously offers stockings as a gift to a woman with whom he attempts to boost his flagging morale. In his notebook it is possible to see the moment that plot development first occurred to Miller. Either, he suggests to himself, Biff should catch Willy with another woman, or a letter should be discovered. The difference, of course, is between action and reported action, and it is the former that gives the play its dynamic. The play, he later noted, is 'the materialization of Willy's mental processes'. When he steps over the wall line of the kitchen and the forestage, 'he is entering his own mind'.[49] Interestingly, in his notebook he played with the idea of beginning Act Two with what he called a '<u>real</u>' scene.

When Jo Mielziner received the script in September 1948, it called for three bare platforms and the minimum of furniture. The original stage direction spoke of a travel spot that would light 'a small area stage left. The Salesman is revealed. He takes out his keys and opens an invisible door.' It said of Willy Loman's house that 'it had once been surrounded by open country, but it was now hemmed in with apartment houses. Trees that used to shade the house against the open sky and hot summer sun now were for the most part dead or dying.'[50] Mielziner's job was to realize this in practical terms, but it is already clear from Miller's description that the set is offered as a metaphor, a visual marker of social and psychological change. It is not only the house that has lost its protection, witnessed the closing down of space; not only the trees that are withering away with the passage of time.

In Mielziner's hands the house itself became the key. What was needed was a solution, in terms of lighting and design, to the problem of a play that presented time as fluid. That solution fed back into the play, since the elimination of the need for scene changes (an achievement of Mielziner's design), or even breaks between scenes, meant that Miller could rewrite some sections. The play now flowed with the speed of Willy's mind, as Miller had wished, past and present coexisting without the blackouts he had presumed would be required.

Mielziner solved one problem – that of Biff and Happy's near-instantaneous move from upstairs bedroom in the present to backyard in the past – by building an elevator and deploying an element of theatre trickery. He later noted:

> the heads of the beds in the attic room were to face the audience; the pillows, in full view since there were to be no solid headboards, would be made of papier-mâché. A depression in each pillow would permit the heads of the boys to be concealed from the audience and they would lie under the blankets that had been stiffened to stay in place. We could then lower them and still retain the illusion of their being in bed.[51]

Miller's memory of this device was slightly different. The mechanism, he recalled, 'worked on a winch, was very heavy, and periodically got stuck, requiring whole fountains of improvisation to spew from Willy's mouth on the stage.'[52] On one occasion as the elevator rose there was a crunching sound and everyone stopped, terrified that this was the sound of crushing skulls. In fact it was the papier-mâché.

Nonetheless, the collapsing of the space between youthful hope and present bewilderment that this stage illusion made possible generates precisely the irony of which Willy is vaguely aware but which he is powerless to address, as it underscores the moral logic implicit in the connection between cause and effect as past actions are brought into immediate juxtaposition with present fact.

Other designers and directors have found different solutions, as they have to Mielziner's use of back-lit unbleached muslin, on which the surrounding tenement buildings were painted and which could therefore be made to appear and disappear at will. They have developed alternatives to his use of projection units that could surround the Loman house with trees whose spring leaves would stand as a reminder of the springtime of Willy's life, at least as recalled by a man determined to romanticize a past when, he likes to believe, all was well with his life. Fran Thompson, designer of London's National Theatre production in 1996, chose to create an open space with a tree at centre stage, but a tree whose trunk had been sawn through leaving a section missing, the tree being no more literal or substantial than Willy's memories.

With comparatively little in the way of an unfolding narrative (its con-clusion is, in essence, known from the beginning), *Death of a Salesman* becomes concerned with relationships. Miller 'wanted plenty of space in the play for people to confront each other with their feelings, rather than for people to advance the plot'.[53] This led to the open form of a play in which the stage operates partly as a field of distorted memories. In the National Theatre production, all characters remained on stage throughout, being animated when they moved into the forefront of Willy's troubled mind, or swung into view on a revolve. The space, in other words, was literal and charged with a kinetic energy.

Elia Kazan observed: 'The play takes place in an arena of people watching the events, sometimes internal and invisible, other times external and visible and sometimes *both*.'[54] The National Theatre production sought to realize this finding thereby a correlative for that sense of a 'dream' that Miller had specified in his stage directions. It is the essence of a dream that space and time are plastic, and so they are here. Past and present interact. The jump from reconstructed past to anxious present serves to underscore the extent to which hopes have been frustrated and ambitions blunted. The resulting gap breeds irony, regret, guilt, disillusionment.

In part Willy taunts himself by invoking an idyllic past in which he had the respect of his sons who were themselves carried forward by the promise of success, or by recalling betrayals which he believes destroyed that respect and blighted that promise. The irony is that Willy believed that he failed Biff by disillusioning him with the dream of success, when in fact he failed him by inculcating that dream so completely that even now, years later, each spring he feels a sense of inadequacy for failing to make a material success of his life.

The motor that drives the play is the relationship between father and son, the need by the former to pass on his false values if he is to retain a sense of his own significance, and the need of the latter to cut himself free. Biff returns not in search of success but in an attempt to save his father's life. The problem is that if he seeks to do so by bolstering Willy's illusions he will do so at the price of his own peace of mind. For Willy to survive, his son must stay, if he is to assuage his sense of guilt.

Miller has said of Willy Loman that 'he cannot bear reality, and since he can't do much to change it, he keeps changing his ideas of it'.[55] He is 'a bleeding mass of contradictions.'[56] And that fact does, indeed, provide something of the rhythm of his speeches as though he were conducting an argument with himself about the nature of the world he inhabits. At one moment Biff is a lazy bum, at the next his redemption is that he is never lazy. A car and a refrigerator are by turns reliable and junk. Willy is, in his own eyes, a successful salesman and a failure. It depends what story he is telling himself at the time, what psychic need such remarks are designed to serve.

Hope and disappointment coexists, then, and the wild oscillation between the two brings him close to breakdown. In a similar way he adjusts his memories, or 'day dreams', as Miller has called them, to serve present needs. These are not flashbacks, accurate accounts of past time, but constructions.

Thus, when he recalls his sons' schooldays he does so in order to insist on his and their success. His brother Ben, by the same token, is less a substantial fact than an embodiment of that ruthless drive and achievement which Willy lacks in his own life and half believes he should want.

In one sense the strain under which Willy finds himself erodes the boundary between the real and the imagined, so that he can no longer be sure which is which. His thoughts are as much present facts as are those people he encounters but whose lives remain a mystery to him. Like many other Miller characters, he has built his life on denial. Unable or unwilling to acknowledge the failure of his hopes, or responsibility for his actions, he embraces fantasies, elaborates excuses, develops strategies to neutralize his disappointment.

Willy Loman is not, however, a pure victim. As Miller has said, he is 'a little bantam with quick fists and the irreducible demand that life give him its meaning and significance and honor'.[57] The one thing he is not, Miller insists, is passive. Something in him knows that 'if he stands still he will be overwhelmed. These lies and evasions of his are his little swords with which he wards off the devils around him ... There is a nobility, in fact, in Willy's struggle. Maybe it comes from his refusal ever to relent, to give up'. And yet, of course, that energy is devoted to sustaining an illusion that is literally lethal. His nobility lies less in his struggle to uphold a dream that severs him from those who care for him than in his determination to leave his mark on the world, his desire to invest his name with substance, to make some meaning out of a life that seems to offer so little in return for his faith. Beyond that, as Miller has commented, 'People who are able to accept their frustrated lives do not change conditions ... [Willy's] activist nature is what leads mankind to progress ... you must look behind his ludicrousness to what he is actually confronting, and that is as serious a business as anyone can imagine'.

This claim is a large one. Willy, to Miller, is not a pathological case, and anyone who plays him as such makes a serious mistake. He is battling for his life, fighting to sustain a sense of himself that makes it worthwhile living at all in a world that seemingly offers ever less space for the individual. The irony he fails to acknowledge is that he believes that meaning lies less in himself and his relationship to those around him than in the false promises of a society no longer structured around genuine human needs. His vulnerability comes from the fact that he is a true believer. Like any believer he has doubts, but these seldom extend out into the world. America, after all, offers itself as utopia. He looks, therefore, within himself.

He is haunted by an act of adultery, with a woman in a Boston hotel room, that he believes deflected his son Biff from the success which would, retrospectively, have justified his own faith in the American way. But he is unaware of the more substantial flaw implicit in his failure to recognize the love of those around him, namely that offered by Linda, his next-door neighbour Charley and, most crucially, Biff himself. The fact that Willy has so completely internalized the values of his society that he judges himself by standards rooted in social myths rather than human necessities gives a clue to the sense of the tragic that Miller and others have seen in the play. But Miller has also said that he wanted to lay before America the corpse of a true believer. To that degree it is a social play. Tragedy: social play. For the critic Eric Bentley the two were incompatible. Either Willy Loman was a flawed individual, he argued, or he inhabited a flawed society.[58] It is a curious opposition. In fact, both are true as, of course, they are in *Oedipus* or *Hamlet*. The argument over the tragic status of *Death of a Salesman* is, finally, beside the point, but Miller's remark that 'tragedy ... is the consequence of man's total compulsion to evaluate himself'[59] does convey his conviction that tragedy concerns not only the self under ultimate pressure but the necessity for the protagonist, if not to justify his own existence, then to accept responsibility for his actions. This Willy cannot do. Denial becomes his mode of being.

Willy Loman's is a wholly recognizable dilemma. In Miller's words, he is 'trying to write his name on ice on a hot July afternoon ... he is trying to create meaning. It is that struggle which creates a high anxiety in people.' His problem is that he believes that meaning to inhere in the material world. He spends his life 'chasing after things which rust. For Willy, there is a God. He dies for that God. Willy is a real idealist. He believes it enough to give his life for it.'[60] He wants to leave a trace on the world, to mark his presence if not through his own life then through that of his sons. He dies with a final throw of the dice, a suspect bargain with his God – his life in exchange for a justification for that life. The irony is that those whose good opinion he thought necessary for his own definition fail to mark his passing. It is those who valued him for what he is who gather at his grave, the grave of a man who shouted out his name – 'I'm Willy Loman!' – but never knew who he was.

Where a tragic hero comes to self-knowledge, in *Death of a Salesman* Willy does not, and Miller came to feel that this might, indeed, have been a weakness: 'I feel that Willy Loman lacks sufficient insight into this situation, which would have made him a greater, more significant figure ... A point has to arrive where man sees what has happened to him.'[61] It is finally Biff who reaches this understanding, though his own choice of a rural life perhaps smacks a little of Huck Finn lighting out for the Territory, ahead of the rest. He is moving against history, that history encapsulated in a stage set that fades from rural past into urban present. Indeed in *The Misfits*, written only a few years after *Salesman*, we see what happens when the modern world catches up with such dreams, as wild horses are rounded up to be turned into dog food. It was also, of course, in such a world, as Willy remembers it, that he was abandoned by his father and brother and glimpsed for the first time the life of a salesman.

If Willy is not a pure victim then neither is his wife Linda, who, to Miller, is strong by virtue of concealing her strength. The critic Rhoda Koenig objects to Miller's treatment of women, 'of whom he knows two types. One is the wicked slut . . . The other . . . is a combination of good waitress and a slipper-bearing retriever.' Linda, in particular, is 'a dumb and useful doormat'.[62] It would be difficult to imagine a comment wider of the mark. As Miller was apt to remind actresses in rehearsal, Linda is tough. She is a fighter: 'They all think Linda is sort of a wet rag. The lines aren't that way. She's got great indignation and wrath!'[63] Her function is to 'keep Willy from wandering too close to the edge'. She 'affects a happiness with his positive moments, insinuates the truth when he cannot bear hearing it, always reaching a hand out as to a child who cannot walk without falling down'.[64] She 'has held this family together and she knows this very well. She has the intelligence to run a large office, if that had been her fate . . . After all, it is she who keeps the accounts, it is she who is marshaling the forces, such as they are, that might save Willy.'

Willy is prone to bully her, cut off her sentences, reconstruct her in memory to serve present purposes, but this is a woman who has sustained the family when Willy has allowed fantasy to replace truth, who has lived with the knowledge of his suicidal intent, who sees through her sons' bluster and demands their support. And if we are to take seriously an underlined sentence in his notebook which indicates that Linda had known of the woman in Boston and long since forgiven him, it is, perhaps, this unspoken forgiveness that intensifies Willy's guilt.

In part a product of Willy's own disordered mind, in part autonomous, Linda defines herself through him because she inhabits a world that offers her little but a supporting role; she is a committed observer incapable, finally, of arresting his march towards oblivion, but determined to grant him the dignity he has conspired in surrendering. That she fails to understand the true nature and depth of his illusions or to acknowledge the extent of her own implication in his human failings is a sign that she, too, is flawed, baffled by the conflicting demands of a society that speaks of spiritual satisfaction but celebrates the material.

Despite her practical common sense she, too, is persuaded that life begins once all debts are paid. It is she who uses the word 'free' at the end of a play in which most of the central characters have surrendered their freedom. Linda's strength, her love and her determination are not enough, finally, to hold Willy back from the grave. This does not make her a 'useful doormat', but a victim of Willy's desperate egotism and of a society that sees his restless search as fully justified and her tensile devotion as an irrelevance in the grand scheme of national enterprise.

To Miller there is a genuine love between Willy and his wife, a love with a history as well as a present reality. He has provided Linda with a back story. Addressing the actors Ving Ruocheng and Zhu Lin in the Chinese production in 1983, he explained that she had accompanied Willy on some of his winter trips, sitting beside him in the car to keep him company. She 'has walked miles to pay the gas and electric bills and save the postage',[65] an echo of his notebook entry nearly forty years earlier. Theirs 'was a love match . . . her family disapproved of him because he had no money or prospects and . . . she, in effect, had run off with him . . . they are still physically in love . . . she means it when she is to say, "Willy, darling, you're the handsomest man in the world."'[66]

Linda is practical, self-sacrificing, loving, strong in ways that have enabled her to survive disappointment and to sustain her husband. Her horizons, though, are limited by the suburban world in which she finds herself and by her desire for an untroubled life, as also, more strikingly, by her love for a man broken on the rack of time. Of Elizabeth Franz's performance in 1999 Miller has said: 'She has discovered in the role the basic underlying powerful protectiveness, which comes out as fury and that in the past, in every per-formance I know of, was simply washed out.'[67]

For Franz, the relationship between Linda and Willy was a sexual one. It was his last resort, the bedrock on which he could rest his sense of himself, except that he fails to understand the relationship for what it is. He is always looking outside himself and beyond the relationship that might save him. The lesson he had absorbed was that triumph had to be conspicuous, publicly validated by a society he sees only vaguely, as it is reflected in the windows of Filene's and Slattery's, the Boston stores where he hawks his wares and in whose size and importance he wishes to share. The casting of herself as Linda and Brian Dennehy as Willy seemed to underscore the losing battle being waged in this small suburban house: 'You look at Brian,' she remarked, 'a mammoth of a man disintegrating in front of your eyes. You realize there's no way you can help him.'[68]

Speaking at the time of the fiftieth anniversary of his play, Miller com-mented on the various qualities that different actors had contributed:

Lee Cobb had one thing; he was born sad . . . There was some majestic pathos in him that fit this role very well. George Scott had great power and enormous authority. So what you saw going down was a man who was losing his authority, which was very effective. Dustin Hoffman was a little different peek at it. I think his Willy started out looking more ordinary, but he grew as the part went on, and all the emotions were tucked into that little body he's got. He was a slightly dictatorial Willy, always ordering people around. And Dennehy is a combination of several necessary elements . . . he's got that

feeling of something of size, like something big being destroyed, which is
terribly important. And at the same time, he's got this naïveté, like when his
smile breaks out and he seems to be enjoying himself.[69]

In conversation with Mel Gussow at the time of the Dustin Hoffman
revival, he chose a different image. Willy Loman, he explained, 'is changing
direction, like a sailboat in the middle of a lake, with winds blowing in all
directions, and I associated that with a small man rather than a great big man
who makes slower turns. Willy's a sidestepper. He's a little puncher.'[70]

America has generated a seemingly inexhaustible supply of popular literature promising success as a product of personality, a matter of presentation
rather than substance, and Willy Loman plainly believes it all. The problem
is that failure is therefore logically to be traced to a flaw in the personality
rather than the system, and for that there is no cure. It also boasts a literature
of frontier endeavour, in which a man comes into possession of himself in the
process of his encounter with the world, and he, or his brother Ben, plainly
believes that, too.

Willy is a failed pioneer who blames himself for the fallibility which in
part defines him and for his inability to live what he thought his destiny.
Offered a vision of endless possibility, of frontiers breached in the name
of existential truth, he lives a life of quiet desperation, baffled by the space
that has opened up between ambition and fulfilment, between an expansive
national dream and the details of daily existence. Slowly, the vision that
holds the pieces of his life in place begins to fade. The axial lines of time
and space dissolve. A man for whom the future held the key to personal
and social meaning finds his mind flooded with fragments of the past as
though his world were going into reverse. Hope becomes a tainted nostalgia
as he recalls and relives moments of seeming triumph, invaded, now, by
an irony born of passing time. He re-experiences events and decisions
whose significance is hidden until they finally begin to form a pattern that
leaves him the product of his actions, this man who believed himself
outside the logic of causality.

The play is, as Miller has insisted, a love affair between Willy and Biff
and between both of them and America. Biff wants to save his father
(while at the same time freeing himself), as his father wishes to save him
from what he regards as a wasted life. Yet, to survive Biff must abandon
his father and his false values just as his father must embrace him if he is
to die for a purpose. To free himself is to destroy Willy. It is within that
tension that the play exists and has its being. Beyond that, meanwhile, is
the question of the redemption of America, itself seemingly, like Willy
Loman, dreaming the wrong dream.

*

For Mary McCarthy, a disturbing aspect of *Death of a Salesman* was that Linda and Willy Loman seemed to be Jewish, to judge by their speech cadences, but that no mention is made of this in the text. 'He could not be Jewish,' she said, 'because he had to be "America" . . . [meanwhile the] mother's voice [is] raised in the old Jewish rhythms . . . "Attention, attention must be finally paid to such a person" . . . ("Attention must be paid" is not a normal American locution; nor is "finally", placed where it is; nor is "such a person", used as she uses it.'[71]

Ironically, a road production of the play that opened in Boston starring Mary McCarthy's brother, Kevin, and a number of other Irish-American actors, was hailed as an Irish play. The fact is that Miller was not concerned with writing an ethnically specific play, while the speech pattern noted by McCarthy was an expression of his desire to avoid naturalistic dialogue. In fact, he wrote part of the play first in verse, as he was to do with *The Crucible*, in an effort to create a lyrical language that would draw attention to itself. He wished not to write in a Jewish idiom, or even a naturalistic prose, but 'to lift the experience into emergency speech of an unashamedly open kind rather than to proceed by the crabbed dramatic hints and pretexts of the "natural".'[72] The Lomans, he commented, 'are usually trying not to speak "commonly". In fact their rhetorical flourishes dot the play and are echoes of Willy's vision of himself and Biff transcending into something more classy in life, something like glory.'[73]

When Mel Gussow asked him whether the play became more Jewish in the 1984 production which featured Dustin Hoffman (whose own father, incidentally, was a salesman peremptorily fired in his sixties), Miller pointed out that Lee. J. Cobb had also been Jewish, though in a production featuring no other Jewish actors. Warren Mitchell had played Willy as Jewish in the National Theatre production, but the 'whole thing is absurd to me because it's played everywhere in the world, and this is not a consideration.'[74] Interestingly, his friend Harold Pinter went to see the play's London production in 1949 (with Paul Muni as Willy Loman) along with his parents:

> It was a very popular play with Jewish families. Jewish people took it very much to heart, the whole idea of selling and going down the drain, of life falling apart. It touched a real vein in the Jewish community in London. They were keen to see it and make it their own but at the same time not all of them approved of it because it was a question of defeat. They found it very worrying. It was understood by the Jewish community on its own terms. What his own understanding was is another matter.[75]

Like Miller, Pinter has been attacked, in his case by the *Jewish Chronicle*, for not making the characters in *The Homecoming* Jewish. His response: 'While there are obviously ingredients in my own play that could support the idea of it being about a Jewish family, the other elements outweigh that, I think. I think it's not restricted to Jewish culture and I think the same thing applies to *Death of a Salesman*. It has a much wider interest.' Just how wide would be evident from its 742 performances and its production in Communist China.

6

THE WALDORF

Miller confessed to doubts about *Death of a Salesman* and its initial production. His original conception had been that the play would be performed on a bare stage, and he still found the idea appealing. He wondered, too, whether he should himself have written the music, which at first he thought uneven. The very technical proficiency of Mielziner's set had smoothed over transitions that he had once thought might have a more jolting effect on the audience, making them judge rather than empathize. As the run extended, he also felt that Cobb was beginning to indulge himself, take pleasure in his ability to inspire a pity that had more to do with an unexamined sympathy than a tragic sensibility.

In the end, Cobb stayed with the production for only three months. He lost his voice and asked for a vacation to recover. The producers would not agree and he left, as Miller later remarked, to be a sheriff in Westerns. The London production, in July 1949, was also not without its troubles. There the part was played by Paul Muni, who recorded the whole role on to tape and then proceeded to imitate himself in what seemed to Miller to be a parody of 'the American salesman'. Kazan wrote to Miller from Hollywood explaining that every time he mentioned that Muni was playing the part people began to 'look sideways' at him. He wrote to Muni suggesting that he should stop trying to play a salesman and instead play a father.

For his part, Tennessee Williams noted Miller's success with something less than total enthusiasm, not least because people had hurried to send him copies of the play's notices:

> It is hard to analyze one's feelings about the triumphs of another artist: even though one may like the artist there is likely to be a touch of the invidious in your feelings which makes you feel cheap and shameful. I liked the play, when I read it, but I must say the great success of it is a surprise as I felt the retrospective scenes were flatly written and that the whole thing lacked the dynamism of his other play. It did, however, have a genuine warmth of

feeling. I think Gadge [Kazan] must deserve more credit than the notices give him.[1]

However, since he later remarked that one 'can never have too many copies of any good notice except a rave for Arthur Miller', this seems little more than an admission that he saw Miller as his chief rival. On 22 February 1949, Miller wrote a respectful letter to Eugene O'Neill expressing his admiration for the older playwright's work and inviting him to see *Death of a Salesman*. It was two months later before a typewritten reply came. He was, O'Neill explained, too sick to travel down from Boston. His tremor (he had a Parkinson's-like illness) had rendered him unfit for everything. He had, though, already placed his order for the book. The letter ends with a shaky signature, his tremor by then meaning that it could take minutes to sign his name.

Whatever doubts Miller or others might have had about the play or its productions, there was, finally, no arguing with its success. It became the first ever to receive all three drama prizes: the Pulitzer (which he claims never actually to have received, it being apparently lost somewhere in the vaults of the Pulitzer Committee), the New York Drama Critics' Circle Award and the Antoinette Perry Award (the Tony) for best play, best direction, best design and best supporting actor (Arthur Kennedy). It also won prizes from the Theatre Club and the American Newspaper Guild. The published version was the first play ever to be chosen as a Book-of-the-Month Club selection. By May, productions were scheduled for seven countries. Oddly, Miller was also named the outstanding spokesman for the selling profession by the National Council of Salesmen's Organizations, while the president of the Fuller Brush Company praised him for recognizing that the salesman was the real hero of American society. Success hardly comes more complete.

There were, though, some dissenting voices. The *Hudson Review* found the play devoid of merit, trite, thematically clumsy and offensive, while Joseph Wood Krutch in the *Nation* thought it unpoetic and unmemorable. Eric Bentley suggested that whatever strengths it might have were in part thanks to Elia Kazan, who had changed the nature of the principal characters – a claim which, when the original article was published in book form, led Miller's lawyers to demand its excision (Bentley had made similar claims about *A Streetcar Named Desire*, which led to another legal intervention). Miller and Kazan, in a letter to the *New York Herald Tribune*, declared Bentley's comments 'a lie', while, perhaps significantly, Kazan's wife favourably reviewed the Bentley book.

As late as 1975, more than a quarter of a century later, Stanley Kauffman, reviewing a production of the play starring George C. Scott, would declare: 'It's hard to believe that, centrally, Miller had anything more than muzzy anti-business, anti-technology impulses in his head.' It was 'a flabby, occasionally false work'.[2] Robert Brustein, over a decade later in his book *Who Needs Theatre?* described the play as a 'social realist melodrama' about a man who is a victim of 'a ruthless, venal and corrupt system'. It was, in his view, fatally flawed by 'Miller's failure to tell us what Willy Loman sells'. As he remarks elsewhere, at least we know what Hickey sells in *The Iceman Cometh*. Apparently knowing that Hickey sells hardware transforms our understanding of that play, though I doubt that many members of the audience either register that fact or see it as crucial.

While denouncing the 'fickle affections of his countrymen',[3] Brustein simultaneously attacks Miller for his social realism and his failure to offer naturalistic detail. Brustein, in particular, would prove difficult to please, as far as Miller was concerned, but it is interesting to note just how early in his career he would attract the hostility of American critics who thought they understood the connection between his assumed politics and his dramatic forms. In his 1965 book, *The Theatre of Revolt*, Brustein dismissed Miller as a 'secondary dramatist'. Along with O'Casey, he maintained, he confronted audiences 'less with works of art than political acts ... and it is by utilitarian rather than literary criteria that such acts and gestures should be judged'.[4] It was certainly not by literary criteria that some critics would judge it in 1949.

Driving home with his wife at three in the morning after the first night of *Death of a Salesman*, Miller listened to the reviews being read over the radio. They were positive; the negative ones would come later. This was the beginning of his real fame, and he quickly realized that it could change everything. *All My Sons* had brought him success but here was proof that he could sustain it, and with a play that was wholly original. The promising playwright had, overnight, been hailed as transforming the American theatre. And with success came a sense of power, as yet undefined and unfocused but real enough and potentially destabilizing. In particular, as noted earlier, it changed the nature of his relationship with Mary, who had also looked forward to this moment but surely not realized what it might mean in terms of her own life:

> as Mary and I drove home, I sensed in our silence some discomfort in my wife and friend over these struggling years. It never occurred to me that she might have felt anxious at being swamped by this rush of my fame, in need of reassurance. ... Some happiness was not with us that I wanted now. I had no idea what it might be, only knew the absence of it, its lack – so soon. In fact, the aphrodisiac of celebrity, still nameless, came and sat between us in the car.[5]

For Mary, speaking more than forty years after the event, this was an accurate summary of her feelings. Still bitter at the collapse of her marriage, she accused him of being self-centred, of looking for praise and subsequently turning away from her. In retrospect, she realized that there had indeed been a shift of power on that night. Their marriage had been born in one world, one of political and social enthusiasms, of ambitions that linked private hopes with utopian visions; it was required to mature in another. He had two lives, one at home in Brooklyn or up in Connecticut, another not so much in the everyday world of the theatre as in the virtual reality generated by success. It was that success which helped further to undermine an already strained marriage. Speaking in September 2001, Miller admitted:

> [there was] no doubt about it. I think that's what did it. Had I not succeeded, had I remained a radio writer, for example, I probably would have remained married. What happens is that you get another mistress, and that is your career, and you get this absolutely obsessive, crazy concentration on the work. You don't hear anything anymore. In all justice to her, she was talking to the wall. I was really obsessed with developing new kinds of plays and I didn't know how to do that and function in any other way. Even when I wasn't locked away in a room I was doing that my whole waking life. I was obsessed with writing. You do pay a terrible price. It's a total engagement with this art. Work occupies your whole brain. I equated it with my father. He had to get out the new spring line. One day I found myself saying, 'I have to get a new play ready for autumn.' And I suddenly realized I was talking as though I were in some business. But I felt an impulse to do that. Later I shook it off.

Once Mary had worked a regular day while he stayed at home earning an occasional fee for a radio play, but now: 'It was two kinds of life that were not in step.'

He would later write a brief ironic sketch called *Fame*, about the limitations of success. For the moment, though, it gave him something else – a power, which, as he later remarked, 'is always implicitly sexual'. *Death of a Salesman*, in part about the suspect nature of success, had gifted him success and thereby stripped him of the innocence that had allowed him to write it. There was, in other words, though it would have seemed absurd to think so at the time, a high price to be paid for that play. It lifted him out of his former life and exposed him to a world for which he was unprepared. He no longer stood on the same ground as he had so shortly before and he would come to feel that he no longer stood with quite the same moral certainty. He was in danger of becoming the thing he had warned against, like Biff Loman listening to the seductive applause of the crowd, even as he understood the loneliness that had sent Willy Loman into the arms of a woman in Boston. In truth, moral certainty was giving way to equivocation. In a verse written in his notebook a few years later he asked himself why he condemned private property when he desired it, why he mocked fame when he enjoyed it, why he claimed to seek anonymity when he revelled in recognition.

For Elia Kazan, the person most affected by *Death of a Salesman* was, indeed, its author:

> Nothing was the same for him once the play opened in New York. It even made Art reckless – albeit in a cautious way – with certain constraints on his personal life and curious about experiences that lay outside the bounds of his behavior up until that time. His eyes, to speak of externals, acquired a new flash and his carriage and movement a hint of something swashbuckling ... It was at this time that I had a first premonition of danger coming, that particular domestic peril which results when certain ties of restraint that a middle-class man has always lived within are snapped.[6]

As far as theatre was concerned, though, his success seemed to consolidate his position as, along with Tennessee Williams, he was hailed as the redemption of an otherwise faltering American drama. To Miller himself, *Streetcar* and *Salesman* represented less the beginning of something than the end. They displayed an unabashed compassion for their characters, a sense of pity for those who failed, driven back against the wall of their authenticity by a system that closed down their possibilities, by a modernity that left ever less space for the individual in search of a personal meaning that could be generalized to a society in need of redemption. The success of both plays revealed some surviving social instinct that seemed to him to die soon afterwards, as patriots of one breed or another arranged pickets, imposed censorship or called for acquiescence in the new orthodoxy. For the moment, though, he revelled in that success, assuming that it conferred on him at least a limited immunity. Just how limited he would quickly discover.

Somewhat to his embarrassment, Miller was suddenly extremely well off. *All My Sons* had brought him wealth, but the new play, swiftly made into a film, moved him into a new financial bracket, one he would previously have despised. The American Legion (which, since 1940, had been working with the FBI) might be picketing the road company of *Death of a Salesman*, but his income was soaring. As well as buying himself a new Studebaker convertible, designed by Raymond Lowey and to Miller the most beautiful car of its time, he also considered investing in property in Columbia Heights – four connected brownstones boarded up since the 1930s but now on offer for $40,000. The idea of being a landlord, though, re-ignited political feelings which, if not similarly boarded up, had at least deferred to other urgencies. He felt he would be crossing a line, committing a moral wrong, getting rich by doing nothing but sign his name to a piece of paper. He had also, surely, not forgotten that it was his father's belief in getting something for nothing that had destroyed the family hopes and come close to breaking a marriage. Investing in the brownstones was scarcely less immoral.

Later, he would wonder where such ideas came from. Was it, he asked himself, the residue of 1930s Marxism? After all, he reminded himself, the American Indians had had no sense of property and Christians might feel a similar twinge of guilt. Whatever the cause, the idea of becoming a landlord was a threat to his political beliefs, his sense of himself, and to his own freedom. Where, after all, was the poetry? In truth, though, he had already crossed over to the other side. He was, after all, the landlord of his Grace Court house.

He was to sell that property in 1952, not least because he disliked the man in the duplex below his own. Henry Davenport, President of the Brooklyn Savings Bank, used to dine formally with his wife every evening and throw occasional parties which lined the streets with limousines. Even so, he was not above calling his landlord, author of a Broadway hit play, asking him to fix minor plumbing problems. Only later did Miller discover that the new owner was the black intellectual and leader W.E.B. Dubois, who, given the racial situation, had to use an official in the La Guardia administration as cover, for fear that the sale might be blocked. He was the first African-American to move into Brooklyn Heights.

Money, no matter the occasional tremors of guilt it inspired, was no longer a problem. Travelling one day on a Madison Avenue bus he suddenly realized that he could have bought it, and several others, for cash. He was at risk of turning into what he had once despised. Six months in his Connecticut studio had earned him a small fortune. The trick, he thought, was to accept it all without compromising his essential values. He could keep his radical credentials burnished by using his new fame in the cause, if not of a radically reconstituted America, then at least in the name of the idea of that international unity that had once inflamed his imagination and which was now under assault.

His decision to do so can only have been confirmed by a sudden echo of the controversy that had flared at the end of the war over Ezra Pound, who was now awarded the Bollingen Prize for Poetry. Here, suddenly, was a reminder of wartime fascism as his fellow writers debated the morality of rewarding a man whose literary accomplishments had coexisted with a fierce anti-Semitism. Allen Tate, one of the judges, excused it, and Pound's wartime broadcasts, on the grounds that they had never influenced anyone and that his anti-Semitism would never be taken seriously by anyone but liberal intellectuals. Auden, another judge, explained that anti-Semites should be regarded as children who had yet to reach the age of consent and perhaps should not be permitted to read Pound's work. Awarding it a prize, though, was another matter. George Orwell, not a judge, announced that Pound's broadcasts from Italy had been 'disgusting', defending, as they had, the massacre of East European Jews and warning American Jews to expect a similar fate.

And so the battle rolled on. For one side it was a matter of ethics, for the other of aesthetics, but the fact is that for Miller it recalled precisely why the war had been necessary and why wartime solidarity should not be so casually abandoned in the name of Cold War necessities. Indeed that solidarity was, he felt, a defence now against the war for which some, at least, seemed to be preparing.

New York in the immediate postwar years was a flurry of Jewish intellectuals. Miller, though, was not one of them, if we mean by that a member of that coterie of like-minded sectarians who gathered around the various magazines that helped to define the cultural politics of the age. His emotional commitments to Russia, his longing for wartime solidarities, were such that he seems not to have registered that revulsion against Soviet repressions that characterized so many on the liberal Left.

He still tended to think of the *Partisan Review* crowd and others in the language of the 1930s. They were Trotskyites attacking the one working paradigm of a socialist society. Never really participating in the furious debates between the so-called Stalinist liberals and Trotskyite liberals, he nonetheless instinctively rejected the latter and found himself attacked by them. For him, the Trotskyites were, anyway, a minority. The circles in which he moved were pro-Soviet, as were the unions, though that was beginning to change. The Trotskyites 'were a New York literary phenomenon rather than anything else. I never heard of them as being active in unions or election politics'.[7] He had no desire to enter that literary world, still regarding it in some ways as antithetical to his own concerns.

His desire to retain his grasp on the immediate experiences of ordinary people was as strong as ever, as he wandered the waterfront, talking to those who laboured there. His engagement with broader political issues was an expression of the same anxiety. For the moment, though, he felt himself if not immune to, then empowered by, his new success which he determined to use to breathe life into a social unity once glimpsed but now threatened. He was also alarmed at the direction his society was taking. In an unpublished article he attacked the Mundt-Ferguson Bill of 1949 (see p. 292). It was, he suggested, akin to a Nuremberg Law. The piece was called 'Dangerous Thoughts', though whether this was a reference to the Bill or his own presumption in attacking it is unclear.[8]

One thing fame did not incline him to do was abandon his old beliefs. Indeed, if anything, his immediate response was to neutralize the vague feeling of guilt by rededicating himself, in public, to loyalties first forged more than a decade before. It was a decision whose consequences were both immediate – he was denounced as a fellow traveller – and long-lasting, in that enmities born now would pursue him down the years. The focus of his continuing commitment was a conference, famous at the time and still more so later when it came to be seen as a defining event in which political loyalties were declared, though not always openly, and hostilities provoked would take a long time to dissipate.

It was on 25 March 1949 that he attended the Cultural and Scientific Conference for World Peace, held at the Waldorf-Astoria Hotel on Park Avenue and 50th Street. Beyond its international focus, it was, in some ways, perhaps, designed as a positive response to the debacle of the Henry Wallace presidential campaign of the year before. Attendance at this conference would in later years come to be seen as an indicator of radicalism and earned several a place in FBI files.

The conference title was transparent for those who had followed the history of such events during the 1930s, while the organizers were part of a communist front organization and cited as such in a report of the House Un-American Activities Committee, a fact duly noted in Miller's FBI file.[9] It was, to a degree, a follow-up to the World Congress of Intellectuals (another communist front) held in Wrocław in August 1948, at which Aleksandr Fadeyev, also to feature at the Waldorf, had remarked: 'If hyenas could type and jackals use a fountain pen', they would write like T.S. Eliot, John Dos Passos, Jean-Paul Sartre and André Malraux.[10] While the British philosopher and science fiction writer Olaf Stapledon had demurred, his compatriot Professor J.B.S. Haldane had agreed, adding that the United States represented the main threat of war. This political dog's dinner should have been a warning to those who met so shortly afterwards in New York. Western press hostility, however, was inevitably discounted by those who saw it as further evidence of the new Cold War mentality.

The chairman, of the Waldorf Conference, the Harvard astronomer Harlow Shapley (whose telephone was duly tapped), had been at Wrocław, though he had reacted against the anti-American speeches he heard there and in that sense did not see the American conference as a direct follow-up. Indeed, he seems to have been quite independently minded, seeing it as a bid for international understanding as well as a peace conference. Nonetheless, it was patently part of a Soviet cultural offensive designed to show the solidarity of artists with the Soviet Union.

From Miller's point of view, it was an attempt by an admittedly strange admixture of liberals and harder-left individuals to resuscitate an alliance now threatened, if not shattered, by the Cold War. To quite what extent it was a piece of theatre, carefully scripted and rehearsed, he seems not to have realized. On the one hand there was the Cominform (Communist Information Bureau), on the other the fledgling CIA. Miller was in between. In Irving Howe's words, the Waldorf Conference was 'the last hurrah of the fellow-traveling intellectuals in the U.S'.[11] It was the scene of a battle between the left and the centre left, and the conflict was a bitter one.

It is worth recalling the wider context. In 1946 the Soviet Union had, for the first time, used its veto in the United Nations and refused to withdraw from Iranian territory occupied during the war. A Canadian spy ring had been exposed, and Churchill had made his speech about an iron curtain descending on Europe. In 1947 the Soviet Union opted out of the Marshall Plan and President Truman announced aid to Greece and Turkey to resist communism (the basis of the Truman doctrine). The same year the Attorney General issued his list of subversive organizations (p. 292). In 1948 the communist minority overthrew the coalition government in Czechoslovakia and the Berlin blockade began. War was beginning to look a distinct possibility. In the week prior to the conference the trial of eleven communists charged with planning to overthrow the government by force took place in New York, while Yale University banned Dmitri Shostakovich, who was to attend the Waldorf Conference, from speaking and playing. It was not a good moment to be seen to celebrate the Soviet Union and call for amity between that country and the United States.

In explaining his decision not only to attend but to play an active role in the Conference, Miller acknowledged the problems it was likely to bring him and admitted that, but for the success of *Death of a Salesman*, he might not even then have taken part. Success was a thrill but also a moral burden. The froth of show business repelled as well as attracted. Perhaps it was even the risk that in some way attracted him. Odets had carried his success off to Hollywood. Miller also could have chosen to cash in his talent for America's rewards, but for a decade and a half he had thought of himself in quite other terms, regarding a commitment to his craft as balanced by a commitment to political and social values not easily reconcilable with simple success. He had also watched bemused as the Soviet Union, only a few years before a gallant ally, was transformed into an ominous threat, and as fellow writers seemed to fall into line with the new orthodoxy. He attended and participated in the Conference because the organizers

[were] trying to prevent an outright Cold War. And there were issues left over from the war. What, for example, were we to do about the Nazis, many of whom were getting good jobs in American corporations and in American governmental organizations? My sympathies were with keeping our alliance with the Russians out of sheer gratitude, I suppose. It seems impossible now, but at the time it seemed as though we were genuinely generating a war spirit

in the United States and a kind of vindictive hatred was growing which I found alarming. So when they asked me to show up, along with some American scientists who were terribly worried about the whole thing, I decided to go up there ... the keel of the ship, as far as I was concerned, was fear of another war. I had met a pilot who had delivered fighter planes to the Russians during the war and he had told me that preparations were already under way for a new war. And that had astonished me and worried me. Only one out of a hundred Americans realized the contribution the Russians had made to the winning of the war.[12]

He would have been chilled, if not entirely surprised, to learn that, fifty years on, a poll of the American people revealed that only 49 per cent knew that the Soviet Union had fought on the American side in the war.

In 1949, Miller was not unaware of the implications of the step he was taking. There was, he admitted, 'no denying the probability of retribution against the conference participants as its opening day drew near'.[13] He was, though, unaware of the covert forces that would play their role in the unfolding events: 'I just thought that having been invited, if I turned it down I would be turning myself down, so I went.'[14] On the other hand, he knew all too well, as he observes in his autobiography, that:

It was dangerous to participate in that fateful attempt to rescue the wartime alliance with the Soviet Union in the face of the mounting pressures of the Cold War, and one knew it at the time. For me, however, the conference was an effort to continue a good tradition that was presently menaced. To be sure, the four years of our military alliance against the Axis powers were only a reprieve from a long-term hostility that had begun in 1917 with the Revolution itself and merely resumed when Hitler's armies were destroyed. But there was simply no question that without Soviet resistance Nazism would have conquered all of Europe as well as Britain, with the possibility of the United States being forced into a hands-off isolationism at best, or at worst an initially awkward but finally comfortable deal with fascism − or so I thought. Thus, the sharp postwar turn against the Soviets and in favor of a Germany unpurged of Nazis not only seemed ignoble but threatened another war that might indeed destroy Russia but bring down our own democracy as well. The air was growing with belligerence. I thought one must either speak out against it or forfeit something of honor and the right to complain in the future.[15]

There is no reference, in this account, to the Berlin airlift or the communist coup in Czechoslovakia, as there was not to be, either, in Lillian Hellman's memoir *Scoundrel Time* − a fact that, in the latter case, Irving Howe found astonishing since it was that, as much as anything else, that had led many who had accepted the Moscow trials and the Hitler–Stalin Pact finally to give up on communism.

As to the fate of the Jewish writers in the USSR, a subject of debate at the Conference, the Party, in America and Moscow, had done its best with smoke and mirrors to obscure that issue with a conscious campaign to win over Jewish support in the late 1930s, while it had been Soviet troops who had liberated some of the camps, and the appalling Soviet losses that had eventually secured victory.

On the eve of the Conference, *Life* magazine published a two-page spread of 'Dupes and Fellow Travelers', identifying, for those who might wish to know, those on the left who wished to sup with the Devil. Miller's picture was among them, as were those of Charlie Chaplin, Langston Hughes and Marlon Brando. Henry Luce personally supervised the piece in a magazine that, just six years earlier, had dedicated an entire issue to the Soviet Union, with Uncle Joe Stalin on the front cover.

The State Department also issued a statement, printed on the front page of the *New York Times*, that attacked the Conference as a sounding-board for communist propaganda, pointing out that the Soviet Union had rejected the idea of cultural exchanges with the United States. The *New York Daily Mirror* carried an article entitled 'Who Invited Them?', which named Miller as a signatory to a petition demanding that Stalin's agents in countries not behind the Iron Curtain should be admitted to the United States. In an article in *Commentary* magazine, William Barrett said of those who supported the Conference that they were suspicious of the State Department and preferred 'to risk being wrong with Stalin for fear of being right with Hearst'.[16]

In agreeing to chair a cultural session at the Conference – he introduced the Fine Arts panel speakers, including Shostakovich, Aaron Copland and Clifford Odets, on the Saturday afternoon – Miller was trying, as he had been after *All My Sons*, not so much to reclaim his radical credentials as to insist to others, but primarily to himself, that he had not sold out, that pre-war idealism had not been naive and that he retained a universal vision. Other participants in the Conference included Lillian Hellman, Dashiell Hammett and Leonard Bernstein. Somewhere, too, was William Sloane Coffin, the following year to join the CIA, but who, as Chaplain to Yale University, would work with Miller in the 1960s to oppose the Vietnam War and later preside over the marriage of Miller's daughter Rebecca to Daniel Day-Lewis. Along with these came representatives of the Soviet Union at a time when anyone with a Soviet passport was assumed to be a stooge or an agent.

Meanwhile, pickets, organized by the American Legion (which regarded the *New York Times* and the *Herald Tribune* as dangerously radical), the Catholic War Veterans and a scatter of other patriotic groups, gathered outside to protest against this new threat to the American way. Indeed, Miller recalled having to step between two nuns, praying for his soul and those of the other participants, in order to get into the building. The nuns aside, it was all fairly decorous. The 100,000 pickets predicted never appeared and the police easily outnumbered those who did, representatives of the veterans' groups, religious organizations and European émigrés shouting, 'Go back to Russia!'

The Conference itself was scarcely an exchange of views. It consisted largely of a series of statements, some sententious, others merely banal, interrupted by awkward questions from those who attended in order to expose Soviet villainies. Shostakovich, described by William Barrett as having the face of a boy, sensitive, unformed and immature – 'the face not of a happy boy, but one sickly, nervous, drab'[17] – read from a prepared text attacking 'bourgeois formalism' and 'reactionary modernism' and praising 'social realism'. In an astonishing mea culpa he acknowledged that his own works 'found response only among the narrow strata of sophisticated musicians, but failed to meet with approval among the broad masses of listeners'.[18] This was a reflection of the fact that, in a decree of the Central Committee of the Communist Party on 10 February 1948, he had been denounced for his 'formalism' and lost his post as composition teacher at the Moscow Conservatory. The president of the Association of Soviet Composers had said of his music, along with that of Stravinsky and Prokofiev, that it 'openly harks back to the primitive barbaric cultures of prehistoric society, and extols the eroticism, psychopathic mentality, sexual perversion, amorality, and shamelessness of the bourgeois hero of the twentieth century'.[19] He had been sent to the conference, it seems, largely to endorse his own humiliation, praising the very system that treated him with contempt.

Arthur Schlesinger Jr, in his key work *The Vital Center*, published in America in 1949, recalled Shostakovich's comments of the previous year: '"I know that the Party is right ... and that I must search and find concrete roads that will lead me toward a realistic Soviet people's art"', as he did Sergei Eisenstein's remark in that same year that a '"stern and timely warning of the Central Committee ... stopped us Soviet artists from further movement along the dangerous and fatal way which leads toward empty and non-ideological art for art's sake"'.[20] Shostakovich's self-immolation at the Waldorf Conference thus came as no surprise to Schlesinger, though it clearly did to Miller who, from Schlesinger's point of view, was either a willing agent or a naive dupe of the Party, and hence more dangerous than alien ideologists. 'We are restrained from outlawing the Communist Party,' Schlesinger lamented, 'and some people feel that it is somehow below the belt even to report on Communist Party activities or to identify its influence. Yet, given the nature of the Soviet drive against free society, given the frightful tyranny implicit in the principle *cuius regio, eius religio* [loosely, whoever rules decides], there is surely no alternative to paying exact and unfaltering attention to the Communists in our midst.'[21] One of these communists, by inclination if not formal membership, was Arthur Miller.

In truth, Shostakovich's *was* a humiliating performance, and it was duly attacked by those attending the session chaired by Miller, people like Nicolas Nabokov – a composer, and cousin to Vladimir – and Mary McCarthy, who wished to draw attention to Soviet oppression. The speeches were delivered in a room full of Marxists, Trotskyites, liberals and those who regarded all the above as legitimate targets.

The State Department, while denying visas to European delegates whose Party affiliation made their positions clear, had also recommended the need to 'discretely get in touch with reliable non-communist participants in New York to urge them to do what they can to assure objective debate and to expose Communist efforts at controlling the conference'.[22] Such reliable non-communist participants were duly identified. Mary McCarthy joined with journalist and critic Dwight Macdonald, Elizabeth Hardwick and her husband Robert Lowell, Arthur Schlesinger, Philip Rahv, editor of *Partisan Review*, and others, to infiltrate the Conference.

They acquired tickets and were summoned to what was called the 'anti-communist suite', room 1042 in the Waldorf (the bridal suite), by the editor of the *New Leader*, Sidney Hook, professor of philosophy at New York University and himself a Brooklynite. He had worked for a time in the Marx–Engels Institute in Moscow, had translated Lenin's *Materialism and Empiriocriticism* for the American Communist Party, and had been a Trotskyite before turning against the Party and becoming what it called a 'counter-revolutionary reptile' (later he would go on to campaign for Richard Nixon and endorse Ronald Reagan). Indeed, for seven years, according to the editor and critic Malcolm Cowley, who had seen his name in an FBI file, he had been informing for the FBI, though Hook denied the charge. Hook, who like many other former Trotskyites, including Irving Kristol, Melvin Lasky and Lionel Abel, would become a neoconservative in the 1980s and thereafter, was described by Arthur Schlesinger Jr as a 'short stocky man with a moustache and spectacles and a weakness for New York sarcastic humor'.[23] He also had a weakness for intrigue and a fair amount of Machiavellian deceit.

Formed only the weekend before the Waldorf Conference, the group called itself Americans for Intellectual Freedom (AIF), which quickly became the American Committee for Cultural Freedom (the ACCF), an offshoot of the anti-communist Congress for Cultural Freedom (CCF). These titles are not without a certain ironic humour since, unbeknown to many associated with it, the latter was funded by the CIA, then in process of launching a more complex and far-reaching plan to finance cultural agencies and co-opt intellectuals for Cold War purposes.

As late as 1983 William Phillips, co-editor of *Partisan Review*, who served on the executive committee of the ACCF, was still insisting that it had no links with the CIA: 'If we were funded by the CIA, why were we always broke?'[24] In fact, as a memo from Frank Wisner indicated (Wisner being a CIA man with a history of clandestine activity), 'the American Committee for Cultural Freedom ... was inspired if not put together by this Agency [the CIA]'.[25] Certainly, Sidney Hook was aware of it, as was the literary critic Diana Trilling. Ironically, the CIA soon became disillusioned with the zealotry of the anti-communists who, it came to believe, threatened both its strategy and the ostensible independence of its creature – as, equally ironically, it would be dismayed by the activities of Senator McCarthy, who was attacking some of the people it wished to use for its own propaganda purposes. In fact, many at this time cooperated with the CIA because it still had the patina of wartime intelligence about it and actually seemed more liberal than other wings of government.

The activities of the anti-Stalinists at the Waldorf Conference so impressed Frank Wisner at the Office of Policy Coordination (formed early in 1949 as a new division of the Agency) that he immediately began planning an event to counter the Cominform's next conference, to be held in Paris. With funds from the Economic Cooperation Administration (which administered the Marshall Plan), he arranged an International Day of Resistance to Dictatorship and War, and though it was far from successful he then devised a more elaborate plan for a conference in Berlin, to be staged by the Congress for Cultural Freedom, which relied on the acquiescence of American and European intellectuals, some of whom knew of the source of their funding, though others did not. One of those involved in planning the Berlin Conference was Ruth Eisler, Gerhart Eisler's sister, who had denounced her brother to HUAC.

Before the Waldorf Conference began, members of Americans for Intellectual Freedom began telephoning around, trying to persuade its sponsors to dissociate themselves from the event. So eager were they that they announced a list of defectors, a number of whom immediately denied the claim, a fact embarrassingly reported in the *New York Times*. Hook, however, was not easily embarrassed, which was just as well since his anti-Stalinism had in the past led to his being hissed as he walked through Washington Square. At the Waldorf he explained to the others who accompanied him how they could avoid being expelled from the hall, where he assumed they would encounter hostility: 'They were to bring umbrellas to bang on the floor when they were not recognized, and then tie themselves to their chairs.' Their mimeographed speeches would then be distributed to reporters by the AIF.[26]

This group had declared the conference 'a gathering of specially selected apologists for Russian communism – designed to provide a platform for attacks upon American and western democracy'.[27]

They did bring umbrellas and they did bang them on the floor, but they did not tie themselves to their chairs. Nor were they expelled. They were each granted two minutes to address the Conference, Dwight Macdonald using his time to list a number of Russian writers who were missing and ask the head of the Soviet delegation, Aleksandr Fadeyev – then Secretary General of the Union of Soviet Writers, later to go on a twelve-day drinking spree and shoot himself in the head after Khrushchev's secret speech to the 20th Party Congress – to account for them. Fadeyev was described by Dwight Macdonald as more like a plain-clothes detective than a writer.

Meanwhile, a young maverick called Norman Mailer was booed when, in a speech inspired by the ideas of the communist writer Jean Malaquais lasting only three minutes, he suggested that both societies were wedded to state capitalism (though Irving Howe, covering the event for *Partisan Review*, recalled the audience listening quietly). In fact, both were correct. Members of the audience had demanded that he speak and applauded him when he did so. The boos came when he announced his views on Russian capitalism. Lillian Hellman later recalled, 'I wasn't on the panel and was sitting in another room, reading or something, when somebody who worked on the committee came running in and said, "Guess what? Come quick. Norman Mailer is denouncing all of us!"'[28] The speech, she later assumed, was the reason Mailer was never called before HUAC. He was announcing that he was not a Stalinist but a Trotskyite.

Mailer, like Miller, had been a supporter of the third-party candidate Henry Wallace (whose nomination for the presidency had been seconded by the critic F.O. Matthiessen) in the November 1948 elections, and had even been tempted by the Communist Party. As he explained in an interview in February 2002, 'I was a somewhat reluctant member of that peace conference because I knew that my thinking was no longer the same as theirs. The booing was not that bad because I was one of their favourite people at the time and it hurt their feelings. I felt terrible getting up there and making that speech because I thought I was betraying them. And afterwards they argued with me for hours. It was not an ugly break; it was a lachrymose break.'[29]

In their speeches the Hook group sought to expose the repressive nature of the Soviet regime, while Mary McCarthy challenged Matthiessen, author of an influential study of nineteenth-century American authors, over his remarks that Emerson had been a natural predecessor of communism. Irving Howe later recalled the occasion in *A Margin of Hope*:

Dreadfully nervous this gifted, tragic figure seemed perversely intent on putting his cultivation to the service of the commissars. He spoke with a maddening simplicity, praising Melville for having made the hero of *Moby Dick* a 'common man' (what else could a nineteenth-century hero be?). Asked his opinion of Fadeyev's dismissal of the question about Soviet dissident writers, Matthiessen did not plead, as prudence might have led him to, ignorance about Russian literary life; no, he praised Fadeyev's answer as 'direct and forthright'.[30]

Matthiessen later committed suicide, his suicide note reading: 'As a Christian and a Socialist believing in international peace, I find myself terribly oppressed by the present tensions.'[31]

Nicolas Nabokov, who attended the conference hoping to subvert it, challenged a panel of musicians over a *Pravda* article attacking Western composers. A cowed Shostakovich, his hands trembling, his droning voice perhaps designed to subvert the nonsense he was required to speak, was forced to support that attack. Thirty years later, in his memoirs, he admitted:

> I still recall with horror my first trip to the USA. I wouldn't have gone at all if it hadn't been for intense pressure from administrative figures of all ranks and colours, from Stalin down. People sometimes say it must have been an interesting trip, look at the way I'm smiling in the photographs. That was the smile of a condemned man. I felt like a dead man. I answered all the idiotic questions in a daze, and thought, when I get back it's over for me. Stalin liked leading the Americans by the nose that way. He would show them a man – here he is, alive and well – and then kill him. Well, why say led by the nose? That's too strongly put. He only fooled those who wanted to be fooled. The Americans didn't give a damn about us, and in order to live and sleep soundly, they'll believe anything.[32]

One of those fooled was Arthur Miller, unaware, at the time, of the pressure being exerted on the composer he would later describe as 'small, frail, and myopic', standing 'as stiffly erect as a doll and without once raising his eyes from a bound treatise in his hand' as he 'read a *pro forma* statement affirming the peaceful intentions of the Soviets'.[33] This was the first time Miller had ever met a Soviet citizen. 'I didn't know what his situation was in Russia. I had no idea. I don't think anybody did. He was famous in Russia so he had to have some favour in Russia but he was totally incommunicado.'

There is an AP photograph of Miller alongside Shostakovich, Olaf Stapledon (detained for two and a half hours by the FBI before being allowed into the country), a tussle-haired Norman Mailer, cigarette in hand, and Aleksandr Fadeyev. All wear ties and suits, in Mailer's case seemingly a size

too small. It makes a curious picture. Miller appears to be listening to
Stapledon, who was to die a year later, on 6 September 1950. The others stare
blankly ahead, like suspects in a line-up or delegates at an undertakers'
convention.

Stapledon had attended the World Congress of Intellectuals held in
Wrocław and felt decidedly uncomfortable, even challenging Fadeyev's view
of Eliot's poetry, if not his politics, a defence which probably won him his
visa to attend the Waldorf Conference. It was to prove a disturbing experience,
beginning with the fact that coming from the austere world of postwar Britain
he was shocked by the extravagance of the hospitality. The opening banquet
boasted roast turkey, strawberries and what seemed an exotic dish, baked
Alaska. In Britain there was still rationing. They ate beneath a mural by the
socialist artist William Gropper in which peace was shown triumphant over
war. Stapledon was the only speaker from Western Europe to make his
way through the State Department defences. He was derided by Dwight
Macdonald and William Barrett and humiliated in a television confrontation
with Sidney Hook, though pleased with his twenty-five-dollar fee.

Miller chaired the arts panel for one session which, to his surprise, attracted
no more than twenty or thirty people (though there were a reported three
thousand delegates), some third of whom were hostile, including Nicolas
Nabokov, in later years a friend, and Mary McCarthy. Howard Fast, a staunch
communist until the 1950s, who also chaired the panel, later recalled McCarthy's questioning Fadeyev about what had happened to a number of Soviet
writers. He 'not only gave his word as a Soviet citizen that all the named writers
were alive and well, but he brilliantly ticked off the titles and description of
the work that each particular writer was engaged upon. He described where
they lived, when he had seen them, and even repeated details of their merry
reaction to the "capitalist slander" that they were being persecuted.'[34] Fast was
at the time convinced, and persuaded himself that Mary McCarthy might
also have been. Later, he learned that all those of whom Fadeyev had spoken
were either already dead from torture or firing squad, or were in prison, to
die later.

Meanwhile, into this turmoil at the Waldorf-Astoria stepped Clifford
Odets, once Miller's role model, a Marxist playwright turned Hollywood
screenwriter, a man who had felt so guilty about leaving the Group Theatre
that he sent them money to keep them going. His speech, Miller observes,
with more than a touch of puritanical accusation, leaped back over 'his ten
years of Hollywood luxury',[35] a luxury that included two houses, a Lincoln
Mercury and a Cadillac, to reinhabit the rhetoric of 1930s America: 'Why is
there this threat of war? . . . Why . . . are we so desperately reaching out, artist
to artist, philosopher to philosopher, why have our politicians failed to insist
that there cannot and must not be war between our countries? What is the

cause? Why this threat of war? ... MONEEY!' He repeated the last word four or five times. The absurdity of a now rich Hollywood screenwriter denouncing money was apparent to both those on the right and those on the left. His speech, indeed, was an embarrassing reminder of precisely the ideological simplicities that had lured so many to Marxism. He attacked American capitalism as a 'mad beast'.

Miller may have resisted Hollywood until then (though eighteen months later he would head west), but he was ever conscious of the apparent contradiction between his former commitments and his present condition. Odets was a disturbing image of this. He was, however, scarcely alone in his contradiction.

Here at the Conference for World Peace were American liberals underwriting an alliance which politicians of neither side wished to see. Jewish writers spoke out for a Soviet Union already persecuting Jewish writers, while those like Mary McCarthy who inquired into the plight of Soviet intellectuals, separate though they were from the newly emerging super-patriots, found themselves keeping strange company. Many of them, meanwhile, were, unbeknown to them, benefiting indirectly from CIA money, then beginning to pour into the magazines that published their work. The seemingly simple dynamics of the war had now given way to a sense of unreality. Miller remarked:

> It was becoming a surrealist world ... where no fact was as important as the
> intentions of the man who raised it. The State Department's whole China
> desk could be cleaned out, its experts disgraced for having *reported* home that
> Mao would undoubtedly win the Chinese Civil War. An old friend of mine
> would be fired from a television show (by a producer he had taught in college),
> not because he was believed to be a Communist but literally because he had
> nothing to recant, and having aroused the suspicion of the [American] Legion
> and other patriotic groups, his silence would enrage them further against the
> network.[36]

Nicolas Nabokov, later General Secretary of the Congress for Cultural Freedom, was not himself CIA but, according to Frances Stonor Saunders, was fully aware of the games being played. He 'wanted to be in the game. He didn't pass the test for employment by the US Government – so this was a kind of palliative.'[37]

Looking back forty years later on his own involvement in the Conference, Miller asked, 'And what of myself? If I was unsure of my own posture, why was I risking attack by chairing this session, something that I indeed sensed would do more to interfere with my freedom in the coming years than anything I had done until then?'[38] In part it was because 'whatever my misgivings about doctrinaire Marxism, it was beyond me at the time to join the anti-Soviet crusade, especially when it seemed to entail disowning and falsifying the American radical past.'

He was still not aware of the extent of Soviet repressions. 'Once you accepted that the Russian Revolution was necessary . . . you accepted a lot of other things with it, namely that they were going to suppress the counter-revolution. I've often regretted that I was amenable to all that. The Show Trials turned me off but to take a position against them put me in the lap of the State Department', which was precisely the dilemma of those who sought to sabotage the Waldorf Conference and who ended up in the lap of something potentially more sinister than the State Department. It was the State Department, after all, Miller recalled, 'who were denying people passports'. The Hitler–Stalin Pact had been 'a bitter pill to swallow' but to denounce it, even in retrospect, when the war was over, was impossible because the alternative was 'to slip into the abyss of denying the sacrifices of the people in the Second World War. Russia turned the Hitler machine back. I felt a loyalty to the forty million people who got killed there.'[39]

Among the devices proposed by Sidney Hook to derail the Conference, as noted above, was the establishment of Americans for Intellectual Freedom which included T.S. Eliot, André Malraux, Bertrand Russell, Igor Stravinsky and Albert Schweitzer – the last, as Frances Stonor Saunders has pointed out in her study of the CIA and the cultural Cold War, being named by both sides and apparently happy to be so.[40] They set out to intercept mail and alter official press releases. Hook's time as a communist had made him adept at manipulation. They issued their own press releases, identifying the communist loyalties of many of the speakers. It was also arranged that telegrams denouncing events would be sent, and cables from John Dos Passos and Thomas Mann duly arrived. They also had the support of the Hearst press.

On the Saturday afternoon, the Hook group staged a rival meeting at a building on 40th Street. Over the entrance was a large banner declaring 'FREEDOM HOUSE', itself, of course, not without its ironies, while on the other side of the street was a crowd of some five hundred, composed almost entirely of men, who listened to the proceedings via loudspeakers mounted on the balcony. Speakers included Hook and Arthur Schlesinger Jr.

The problem for Mary McCarthy and the others was that, with HUAC holding hearings, loyalty oaths proliferating and the Attorney General's list of subversive organizations inhibiting free speech, they risked associating themselves with a new conservatism, of which, in truth, Sidney Hook increasingly seemed an example. And indeed, FBI agents were reporting on those who attended. This was when Norman Mailer first earned his place in one of J. Edgar Hoover's filing cabinets. In the case of Howard Fast the agency went further, intimidating publishers into refusing his manuscripts. In an article in

Partisan Review in May 1949, Irving Howe would write an account of the Conference in which he described the 'untainted innocents who really thought the conference had some genuine relation to working for peace', observing that somehow 'the Stalinists always find new innocents, each batch on a lower cultural level'.[41] Miller was plainly one of the innocents, whatever his cultural level.

The Conference ended on 27 March with a rally 18,000 strong in Madison Square Gardens. Olaf Stapledon went on stage to declare that he was no communist but was happy to work with them in the cause of peace. The *Manchester Guardian*'s correspondent, Alistaire Cooke, dismissed the Cultural and Scientific Conference for World Peace as being 'as peaceful as Madison Square Garden is on championship night, as scientific as the jungle, and as cultural as a swarm of bacteria'.[42] The evening ended as Shostakovich played the second movement of his Fifth Symphony which now carried the subtitle: 'A Soviet Artist's Reply to Just Criticism'. After the Conference, Stapledon had wanted to see Clifford Odets's *The Big Knife* but tickets had already been bought for *Death of a Salesman*. He was impressed by what he took to be its attack on the American myth of the go-getter.

The fact was that by the time he attended the Conference Miller was already feeling uneasy at the company he was keeping. As he explained to me in 2003:

> I felt uncomfortable at the Waldorf Conference, to tell you the truth, because ... I was not prepared to dump these people [the Russians] who I thought had saved Europe and probably the Jewish population of Europe ... Without them I think there would have been a deal between Britain and the Germans. They would have had to have a deal. And the United States would have gone along, and there would have been support here for it, too. I couldn't forget all that. It was impossible. So I was caught in the middle. At the same time some of the left/communist positions made me very, very unhappy.

The *Life* magazine report of the Waldorf Conference, which ended with Fadeyev describing the Atlantic Pact as 'infamous', managed to imply that most of those involved were willing or unwilling, conscious or unconscious agents of a foreign power. The *New York Journal-American*, in an article transcribed for the benefit of Miller's FBI file, described the Conference as 'an emanation which rankled the noses of all save those traitors who have committed themselves to Russia's side in the cold war'. The 'come-all-ye of avowed Communists and their intellectual Fifth Column isolated the luminaries of the theatrical and artistic world who have now openly enlisted their talent in the revolutionary struggle'. The article's author Frank Conniff then highlighted Miller in particular, thereby underscoring the risk he was taking in associating himself with the Waldorf-Astoria conference:

The cultural clambake also blew the fuzz from several questions heretofore blurred. Let us take the case of Arthur Miller, who wrote 'Death of a Salesman', currently a hot ticket along Broadway. Some years ago Mr Miller gave birth to another epic of home front frustration entitled 'All My Sons'. For its dramatic finale, this somber study depended on the notion that an American industrialist would knowingly sell defective combat equipment to the armed forces.

That this implausible premise was accepted as a sound dramatic contrivance is an index either to the loose standards of contemporary criticism or the persuasive skill of Mr Miller's writing . . . One wondered about Arthur Miller at that time, but, as I say, the edges of his meaning remained blurred.

Mr Miller lifted the ideological curtain around his own identity a bit higher when 'Death of a Salesman' reached Broadway. Here was another grim picture of doom and frustration in an American family. The greatness of heart, the peaks of spiritual fineness achieved in America's long progress to eminence, found no reflection in Mr Miller's clinical probing of the decline and fall of his disillusioned drummer.

The essence of Mr Miller's intentions might still have remained shrouded had not the Communist cultural bash come along to bring the loose ends into focus. We now see him presiding happily at a panel where American capitalism is savagely blistered, beaming approval upon calls for the fuller participation of artists in the coming struggle, and nodding agreement with Soviet spokesmen who praised the political criticism of their Communist Party bosses.

Suddenly the data on Mr Miller began to add up into a recognizable pattern. Little wonder the reviewer of the Daily Worker expressed fervid hope that Mr Miller's next effort would truly be a 'revolutionary' drama . . . No, you won't find any overt Communist propaganda in 'Death of a Salesman'. But in its negative delineation of American life, extending the implications of Mr Miller's implausible war profiteer, the play strikes a shrewd blow against the values that have given our way of life its passion and validity.

The world being in the shape it is, you do not necessarily have the full meaning of 'Death of a Salesman' when the curtain clanks down at the Morosco. It remained for Mr Miller to clarify just exactly what he meant by both 'All My Sons' and 'Death of a Salesman' when he enlisted his talent and prestige in the cultural jam session at the Waldorf Astoria.[43]

Nor was Miller the only person to attract attention to himself. Walter Bernstein, a radio writer, found himself listed in the American Business Consultants' publication *Red Channels*. Prominent among his sins was attendance at the Waldorf Conference.

At *Commentary* William Barrett, echoing Irving Howe, remarked on the extent to which each year the Soviet Union 'harvests its new crop of innocents', one of whom, implicitly, was the author of *Death of a Salesman*.[44] Miller's FBI file noted a message of greetings to him from the Bakery and Confectionery Union hailing the Conference as a great success which helped the cause of peace, while insisting that the State Department had done everything in its power to sabotage it and brand the participants as communists on communist fellow travellers.

According to Miller, the reigning critic of the most prestigious literary magazine in New York would soon be warning his readers away from him and his works on the grounds that he had changed his name some time before to escape his Jewishness. The accusation was not so unlikely, in fact, given that the changing of names was far from uncommon, for Party or professional reasons. William Phillips of *Partisan Review*, whose pseudonym was Wallace Phelps, was the son of a man who changed his name from Litvinsky. Philip Rahv was born Ivan Greenberg. Irving Howe, whose pseudonyms included R. Fahan, R.F. Fangston and Theodore Dryden, was born Irving Horenstein. George Novack, one of whose pseudonyms was John Marshall, was born Yasef Novograbelski. Anti-Semitism exerted a pressure on identity in more than one way.

Miller's attendance at the Conference, he later conceded, 'did a great deal to destroy me'.[45] He was now regarded by the non-communist Left as no more than a Stalinist. William Barrett, again in *Commentary*, described those who had attended as Stalin's emissaries, while Robert Warshow later described Miller as 'a danger to culture'.[46] Louis Budenz, the ever-eager and serial testifier, happily identified him in 1950 as a 'concealed communist'. Increasingly, he was denounced by those whose politics were at odds with his own.

Here, for example, is part of a review of *Death of a Salesman* by Eleanor Clark, a Trotskyite, in fact married to one of Trotsky's secretaries, who had served with the Office of Strategic Services in Washington during the war. It was published in *Partisan Review* in June 1949. Having explained that *Salesman* was boring and 'stuffed full of gloom', a 'hodge-podge of dated materials and facile new ones', the product of a 'second-rate mind', she proceeds to underline its faulty politics:

> [It is] of course the capitalist system that has done Willy in; the scene in which he is brutally fired after some forty years with the firm comes straight from the party literature of the 'thirties, and the idea emerges lucidly enough through all the confused motivations of the play that it is our particular form of money economy that has bred the absurdly false values of both father and sons.

The play, she concludes, displays an 'intellectual muddle and a lack of candor that regardless of Mr Miller's conscious intent are the main earmark of contemporary fellow-traveling'.[47] The review, by a woman coincidentally raised in Miller's new hometown of Roxbury, Connecticut, appeared four months after the play had opened and three months after the Waldorf Conference.

Another minor consequence of the Conference was a hostility between Mary McCarthy and Lillian Hellman that would result in a $2.2 million libel suit, brought by Hellman over McCarthy's comments, on the *Dick Cavett Show*, about her lack of honesty. She famously remarked that Hellman had never said a true word and that that included 'and' and 'but'. The suit only failed when Hellman's death intervened. Perhaps it is to this moment, too, that McCarthy's hostility to Miller's plays can be traced.

Such were the passions of the ideological battles of the 1930s, for which the Waldorf Conference provided an epigraph. As Carol Brightman, McCarthy's biographer, echoing Irving Howe, remarked, it was 'the last hurrah for the idea that the ideological interests of the Soviet Union might be grafted on to the progressive traditions in American society',[48] but Brightman's comment conceals the extent to which the response to this last hurrah had been carefully orchestrated by American intelligence. When Nabokov gave a final Conference speech on 27 March 1949 he was enthusiastically embraced by Michael Josselson acting on behalf of his CIA chief Frank Wisner, a man who had a reputation for hiring German fascists after the war provided that they were sufficiently anti-communist – which, by definition, they were. Josselson himself had joined the Agency in autumn 1948 as head of its Berlin Station for Covert Action.[49]

The CIA was only two years old in 1949, indeed the Act that allowed it to disburse funds without accounting to Congress was passed that year. It was this Act that legitimized the payments made in relation to the Waldorf Conference. Cash had been handed to Nabokov (some $5,000), while the Agency secured the Hook suite in the Waldorf working through David Dubinsky of the Ladies' Garment Workers' Union. Dubinsky threatened to have the hotel closed down if the management refused to make the accommodation available. A similar threat led to the installation of ten telephone lines on a Sunday morning. Nor were Nabokov and Josselson strangers to one another. Nabokov already knew Josselson from Europe.

An Estonian Jew, Josselson had arrived in Berlin in the 1920s, emigrated to America in 1936 and then served in the intelligence section of the Psychological Warfare Division. After the war he stayed in Germany as a public affairs officer in which capacity he met Nabokov, a White Russian émigré.[50] Nabokov would later go to America, where he shared an apartment with Henri Cartier-Bresson, a dedicated communist who, as an outstanding photographer, would prove an inspiration for a young Austrian woman, Inge Morath, who became Miller's third wife. The encounter between Nabokov and Josselson at the Waldorf was anything but a coincidence.

Along with Josselson there was another enthusiast for Hook's activities, Melvin Lasky, American-born and, like Josselson, Jewish. He had known Hook in Berlin and now turned up at the Waldorf Conference. He was a staunch anti-Stalinist who had written for both *New Leader* and *Partisan Review* and had been embraced, when living in Germany, by General Lucius Clay. At his urging, Clay supported the establishment of a magazine, *Der Monat*, designed to advance American interests. It was financed by the CIA as was the British magazine *Encounter*, of which Lasky later became editor. *Encounter*, indeed, was almost wholly a product of American intelligence. Once again, Josselson was in the wings, as he would be when Richard Krygier, secretary of the Australian branch of the Congress for Cultural Freedom, founded *Quadrant* magazine, one of twenty such established by the Congress around the world. When Lasky (a cofounder of the CCF) showed signs of forgetting *Encounter*'s covert purpose, Josselson wrote a terse reminder: '[You say] that the Congress is in the publishing business to just give readers what they want to read ... Your theory is absurd ... You will remember that at our Executive Committee meeting everyone was in agreement that the period spent so far by *Encounter* in overcoming covert and overt resistance ... was time well spent, but now it [is] time to go one step further.'[51]

In a 1967 article Thomas W. Braden, who supervised the cultural war conducted by the CIA, published an article in which he announced: 'We ... placed one agent in a Europe-based organization of intellectuals called the Congress for Cultural Freedom [Michael Josselson]' and 'Another agent became an editor of *Encounter* [Melvin Lasky].'[52] The CIA had also, as Christopher Lasch has pointed out, infiltrated the National Student Association, the Institute of International Labor Research, the American Newspaper Guild, the American Friends of the Middle East and the National Council of Churches.[53]

The Cold War, as Frances Stonor Saunders has demonstrated, was by now being fought on a cultural front, with US and British government money going into a massive promotion of American and anti-communist writers (paradoxically, a government-financed theatre programme even included the works of Odets and Hellman). Thus it was that Arthur Koestler's revelation of Soviet crimes, *Darkness at Noon*, was actually distributed by the British Foreign Office, in a confidential deal concluded with the publisher Hamish Hamilton, himself a man with intelligence links, while in France the Communist Party swiftly bought up as many copies at it could to take them off the market.[54] Koestler himself, meanwhile, was also involved in the Foreign Office's propaganda wing and in 1948 toured America urging former radicals to rally to the anti-Soviet cause. This was the Koestler who had written a propaganda book financed by the Communist International in 1932 and

informed on a Soviet lover, but had become disillusioned by the show trials
and then by the Hitler–Stalin Pact.

Such was the complex and covert world into which Miller had wandered,
still clinging to the wartime idealism he had sought, but seldom found, when
writing his non-fiction book *Situation Normal*. In common with most people,
he had been unaware of the extent to which American and British diplomacy,
and intelligence agencies, had been dedicated during the war to suppressing
inconvenient truths about Stalin and the Soviet Union when it served their
purposes, and were now equally dedicated to the dismantling of the very myths
they had propagated. Writing later, he observed of the Waldorf Conference:

> Even now something dark and frightening shadows the memory of that
> meeting nearly forty years ago, where people sat as in a Saul Steinberg
> drawing, each of them with a balloon overhead containing absolutely inde-
> cipherable scribbles. There we were, a roomful of talented people and a few
> real geniuses, and in retrospect neither side was wholly right, neither the
> apologists for the Soviets nor the outraged Red-haters; to put it simply,
> politics is choices, and not infrequently there really aren't any to make; the
> chessboard allows no space for a move.[55]

The Waldorf Conference was seen as disastrous for the communists (a Polish
delegate, the poet Czeslaw Milosz, later defected), but as suggesting a possible
way forward for the Right. Indeed, planning immediately began for the Anti-
Waldorf-Astoria Congress in Berlin, to be sponsored by the Congress for
Cultural Freedom whose General Secretary was now Nabokov and which
was funded partly by money raided from Marshall Plan funds and partly by
the covert support of the CIA's Office for Policy Coordination, which bought
tickets for the American delegation through a series of other organizations.
Arthur Schlesinger Jr, who had been involved with the Office of Strategic
Services (the OSS), came to regard the Congress as 'an immensely powerful
instrument of political and intellectual warfare'.[56]

Again, Josselson and Lasky were involved, as was Hook. Held in June 1950
at the Titania Palace, it flew writers from America, including, surprisingly,
Tennessee Williams (who had an abbreviated FBI file of just seven pages)
and Carson McCullers, along with Arthur Schlesinger Jr. These joined with
Europeans, including Ignazio Silone, who had once run a network for the
Soviets and then one for Mussolini before being associated with the American
OSS.

The Congress was regarded as a great success by virtually all agencies of
government, from the CIA and the Defense Department to the Office of
the Presidency. The Waldorf Conference, far from breeding peace and
harmony had, in fact, played its part in prompting a cultural cold war which
would affect a generation of writers and intellectuals.

Thereafter, cultural front organizations proliferated. The CIA's Tom Braden explained: 'We had many foundations ... We would give them $20 million with which they would set up a foundation which would then offer its services to one or other of the specialist organizations.'[57] One such was the Farfield Foundation, whose president, Julius Fleishmann, a Broadway backer and philanthropist, was required to put none of his own money into the venture since it was funded directly by the CIA (the Farfield also funded the anti-communist American Jewish Committee whose magazine, *Commentary*, proved so critical of Miller). Ronald Reagan, meanwhile, was a spokesman for another front organization, the Crusade for Freedom, which reportedly brought ex-Nazis into America to join the anti-Soviet campaign. Slowly an elaborate and covert apparatus was put in place, laundering money through the Ford and Rockefeller Foundations. An outside director of the CIA, C.D. Johnson, even ended up on the board of the Lincoln Center, with which Miller was to have arguments, while a director of the Farfield Foundation became an advisory member of the National Endowment for the Arts, for which Miller would one day deliver the Jefferson Lecture in which he so successfully satirized politicians that the man who had invited him was summarily fired.

Another Farfield trustee, Cass Canfield, with close contacts in intelligence and chairman of the editorial board of Harper Brothers, the American publisher of *The God That Failed*, was later one of the founding members of the American National Theatre Academy (ANTA), along with another CIA friend Jock Whitney. ANTA has been described by Frances Stonor Saunders as 'the equivalent of the foreign affairs branch of American theatre.'[58]

For Miller, though, it was precisely the pressure to join the rest of his society in drifting to the right that led him to move in the other direction. Certainly he did, as he was later charged with doing, attend meetings with communist writers. He claimed that it was to do with a vision of the future, but it seems to have had as much to do with nostalgia. These meetings were not literal reunions but they offered a comforting sense of reaching back to principles that had once been embraced, if not by a whole generation, then at least by his closest friends and role models, and which, in an oblique form, had seemed justified by the solidarities provoked by war, even if he found the meetings themselves boring and mostly beside the point. One was devoted to a discussion of whether circumcision was a suitable subject for committed fiction.

In truth, he belonged more in the company of people like Joe Rauh and even Arthur Schlesinger Jr of Americans for Democratic Action (ADA) than in that of those who spoke for the communist Left at the Waldorf. He shared that sense of a flawed human nature pinpointed by Reinhold Niebuhr and Schlesinger. This, after all, lay behind the tragic sense of life that he felt inhered in his plays. He also shared their distrust of utopianism (*All My Sons* hints at but does not explore this) and their sense of the human will to power. Rauh would become a close friend, and Miller would later accept an analysis that accommodated both fascism and communism to totalitarianism of the kind outlined by Hannah Arendt, but for the moment he had too much emotional investment in the passions of the 1930s to acknowledge the betrayals at the heart of a dream. Over forty years later he was still bewildered by the persistence of his stance; but characteristically, he looked for the answer partly in history and partly in psychology. It was, he thought, partly the collapse of the family fortunes which played its role in convincing him that his father's approach had been selected against, partly a teenager's rejection of parental power.

In the end, though, the answer he settles on for his continuing loyalty is the impact of the Depression, Spain, the Second World War. But those, of course, were crucial events for others, too, for whom the Moscow trials, the Hitler–Stalin Pact and the trials in Czechoslovakia proved too much to bear. Even the Soviet Union's supposed rejection of anti-Semitism, loudly trumpeted, constantly betrayed, failed to persuade others to overlook its crimes. Miller may have read *Partisan Review*, but he had written for *New Masses* and those Jewish magazines affiliated to the Party. He did not want to surrender his enthusiasm. It gave ambition a social purpose. It offered rebellion a rational basis and naivety a name.

In the late 1940s, however, with the Waldorf Conference barely over, he was finally beginning to turn away from the ideas that had sustained him. The certainties pronounced by those still resolute in their Marxist loyalties simply failed to match his own growing uncertainties, which extended beyond the question of society and how it chose to organize itself. At home, for example, he felt increasingly uneasy. Faithful to a cause, he was no longer faithful, at least in his mind, to his wife. Perhaps his recreation of the old political camaraderie had something to do with his wish to recreate something else that seemed to be lost to him. His wife, still fiercely committed, approved of his involvement with the Waldorf Conference, but that commitment was no longer a sufficient bond between them and soon his political loyalties, too, would defer to new realities.

Arthur Koestler likens his time in the Party to Jacob's wooing of Rachel. 'I served the Communist Party,' he explained, 'for seven years – the length of time Jacob tended Laban's sheep to win Rachel, his daughter. When the time was up, the bride was led into his dark tent; only the next morning did he discover that his ardour had been spent not on the lovely Rachel but on the ugly Leah. I wonder,' he asked, 'whether he ever recovered from the shock of having slept with an illusion. I wonder whether afterwards he believed that he had ever believed in it.'[59] There were many who experienced such a morning after the night before and Miller was one of them. Soon after the Waldorf

Conference he realized that he had embraced an illusion; he, too, would eventually come to see just how ugly his true bride had been. Nonetheless, it was not possible to turn away from early passions without regret, or something more. The longer the relationship, he insisted – drawing, like Koestler, on the image of love betrayed – the greater the bitterness.

Two months after the Waldorf Conference, however, there was a first evidence of a change of mind. In May he sent a message to a meeting at the El Patio Theatre in Hollywood protesting against blacklisting by the Motion Picture Producers' Association and, in particular, Twentieth Century Fox's refusal to film a screenplay by Albert Maltz, one of the 'Hollywood Ten', among those subpoenaed by HUAC. That same month he wrote to the *Herald Tribune* protesting at their distortion of a remark he had made at a testimonial dinner for one Reverend Howard Melish. Miller had been reported as saying that 'the concept of intellectual honesty does not apply when peace is at stake'. He wrote indignantly correcting the report, in the process underlining his attitude to the Soviet Union in the aftermath of the Conference and in the context of the intensifying Cold War:

> No one need convince me that there are certain injustices and excesses which can be laid to the Soviet Union. I am advised by some, however, that it is incumbent upon me if my intellectual honesty is to be taken seriously, to be vocal if not vociferous upon these points.
>
> Although slightly beside the issue, I must say that it requires no great courage to launch an attack upon the Soviet Union in the atmosphere of 1949 America. I believe that inasmuch as the overwhelming preponderance of published comment wholly emphasizes and dwells upon the negative side of Soviet society, and the question of war and peace is now moot, the right role of the honest person is certainly not to add to that dangerous imbalance. I would be satisfied if the whole truth were told about the Soviet Union, and if it were materially possible for me to tell it, intellectual honesty would then be served completely. As it is I will not contribute to the distortion that now has such a grip on the public mind.
>
> In short, and I add this to make myself perfectly clear, intellectual honesty is not only a private imperative to which one submits in order to save one's soul. It has a broader collective reference, the public. Its aim is to create an impression of the whole truth as one sees it upon the public. Joining those who, from whatever motives, have attacked the Soviets irresponsibly until a kind of frenzy is now overtaking much of the popular consciousness, is not, in my opinion, a service either to intellectual honesty, the welfare of the American people, the Russian people, or to the cause of world peace.[60]

It is an interesting statement. Plainly, it could be seen as mere equivocation, conceding but refusing to identify or denounce Soviet repressions. Faced with a new orthodoxy, however, in which the Soviet Union was vilified and Americans required to affirm their loyalty by denying past commitments, he was unable to express such doubts as he felt. Even so, here, for the first time, is a public acceptance that this paradigm of a Marxist society was not without its flaws though he did not abandon his political gestures.

In September 1949, he was one of those protesting against an assault on Paul Robeson following an outdoor concert for the benefit of the Harlem chapter of the Civil Rights Congress at Peekskill. At the Paris Peace Conference in April that year, Robeson had been quoted as remarking that he would not fight for his country against the Soviet Union. On his return he had clarified his statement: 'We do not want to die in vain any more on foreign battlefields for Wall Street and the greedy supporters of domestic fascism. If we must die, let it be in Mississippi or Georgia! Let it be wherever we are lynched and deprived of our rights as human beings!'[61] A concert planned for Peekskill, in Westchester County, New York, in August had to be abandoned but was rescheduled for the following month. Twenty thousand attended, but afterwards members of the audience were attacked and beaten by an estimated one thousand protesting veterans. Miller put his name to a statement denouncing the 'lynch attack' on Robeson as a 'reenactment of the Nazi assault on cultural and human life'.[62]

The same month he signed a statement calling on the Supreme Court to reverse the convictions of screenwriters John Howard Lawson and Dalton Trumbo (both of whom had been convicted of contempt of Congress for refusing to cooperate with the House Un-American Activities Committee) and protesting against censorship. The following month he was still, it seems, happy to support the National Council of Arts, Sciences and Professions, appearing at the St Nicholas Arena on 66th Street for a protest against the conviction of eleven communist leaders under the Smith Act. His FBI file quotes from his speech: 'In all humility I think the time has come for the liberal, the progressive to look to his honor ... The Smith Act in this trial must be condemned ... Reaction has spoken ... Our time is now.' However, to the discomfort of the *Daily Worker*, Miller 'utilized the occasion for an attack on the Soviet Union. He distorted the position of the Soviet Union – in art as in other things, as one antagonistic to the artist.'[63] Miller, it appears, was beginning to change. The appeal was now to the liberal.

Barely six months on from the Waldorf Conference, the Soviet Union was now guilty of offences against the artist. His old loyalty was finally broken, although this did not diminish the FBI's interest in his affairs. The following year, its New Haven office was asked to verify details of Miller's Roxbury home, while the Washington office attempted to review the Catholic War Veterans file (in fact non-existent; it was a figment of the anti-communist newsletter *Counter-Attack*). The Cleveland office checked details of his 1940 marriage to Mary.

Miller's true subject, like Fitzgerald's, had always been the crack-up, the dislocation, of the social and moral world. He registered the slippages, the slide of certainties prised away from a language that once seemed so confident of its power to define. The dream that his parents had struggled to possess he had regarded with a deepening suspicion. Religion, national myths, seemed to exhaust themselves, so unrelated did they seem to experience. Growing up in a world in which those in political power had no leverage on an economic system in free fall, he looked for some validating principle, staging the drama of the individual's struggle for significance. Dealing in language, he had nonetheless proved vulnerable to rhetoric, presuming that a system that stood against fascism must draw from a pure well. Thirty years on, the Marxist ideal had foundered, mired in tyranny and collectivist thought. In Camus's words, a 'gigantic myth collapsed. A certain truth, that had long been disguised, burst upon the world.'[64] He and others, he realized, had, in the words of the British airman and writer Richard Hillary, been fighting a lie in the name of a half-truth.

The process of Miller's disaffection had gathered momentum with a meeting, later that year, at the home of an episcopalian minister in Brooklyn Heights who had been the president of the Russian war relief campaign. He was playing host to a number of Russian visitors, and to this moment Miller had never met a Russian, 'white, red or otherwise', besides those encountered at the Waldorf. They praised *Death of a Salesman* and said they would like to stage it in Russia, where, relieved of commercial pressures, they would be able to produce it with a different set for each scene. He pointed out the fallacy of such an approach, at odds, as it was, with the whole concept of the play, explaining that his choice of a single set had nothing to do with capitalism or the commercial pressures of Broadway:

> I then experienced a tone that I had never experienced before. They told me that I didn't know what I was talking about. I smelled a certain kind of arbitrary power there. It stuck in my head because I had never run into such a thing. I realized that if I were a Russian writer they would be telling me what I was supposed to be doing. And here they were not even in Russia and doing that. The whole meeting ended on a very tense note. There was nothing to be done about it because if they were going to steal the play they were going to steal the play, which is what they did anyway. So, when they did *Salesman* they made Charley into a clown because he was a capitalist. They didn't know what to do with him because he was a generous, sentimental capitalist. They distorted that whole part of the play and that alienated me from them. It was a gradual process. It became

more and more strange and foreign and less like the sentimental leftism that I attributed to it.[65]

He also recalled a comment made to him five years earlier when he was appearing on a radio station to promote *Focus*. A fellow guest had told him of the problem of anti-Semitism in Russia:

> At the time, the Soviet Union had the only constitution forbidding anti-Semitism ... You couldn't have anti-Semitism in Russia. He started to tell me about it and it really shook me. It hung over my head for some time. It was an entry point but one didn't see anything about it until later so that little by little, through one blow or another, I began to change. I guess I was clinging to the idea that this was a new society. It turned out to be older than any society.

He could, if he had wished, have read an account of anti-Semitism in the Soviet Union in an article written by Solomon M. Schwartz published in the same issue of *Commentary* that printed Barrett's account of the Waldorf Conference. But for the moment such voices seemed suspect in the context of anti-Soviet sentiment fomented by the State Department and the Hearst press; and, anyway, the evidence itself seemed fragmentary and unconvincing. In fact, even that article conceded that perhaps 'the only statement about the USSR that Americans – whether hostile or friendly – have been able to agree on is that "at least you can't deny that the Soviets put an end to anti-Semitism"'.[66] That, however, Schwartz maintained, had now changed. The evidence adduced spoke of the closing of Yiddish newspapers and the under-representation of Jews in elected bodies. The piece also recalled the Jewish victims of the show trials of the late 1930s, and spoke of 'the appearance for the first time of signs of anti-Jewish feeling in official government organs'.[67] But it offered less than a full case. It is not surprising, therefore, that Miller was not, as yet, willing to give such reports much weight.

These were, anyway, years of political naivety on both sides. In France, security forces stopped the car of Jacques Duclos, the Communist Party leader who in 1945 had denounced Earl Browder, the American Party leader. Finding two pigeons inside, they charged him with taking orders from Moscow by carrier pigeon. He was arrested. In fact the pigeons were to be the main course for the Duclos family evening meal. Miller reports his neighbours, in the early 1950s, erecting a shed from which to keep a twenty-four-hour watch for Russian bombers. Quite what they intended to do should they see any was not clear. Perhaps his own naivety, different in kind but none the less real, is itself best seen as a product of the times.

Miller was far from alone in his loyalties. Indeed there were many who sustained them far beyond 1949. In Britain, Doris Lessing would not finally abandon the Party until the mid-1950s, although, unlike Miller, she was a member. For her, she observed, looking back in 1997, 'The Party represented the purest of humankind's hopes for the future – *our* hopes – and could not be anything but pure.' She campaigned for the Rosenbergs, accused of espionage, though was vilified for doing so, and in 1950 was herself involved, at least as a footsoldier, in the proposed Sheffield Peace Conference of 1950: 'My job was to go around to houses and hand out leaflets, extolling this festival. I was met at every door with a sullen, cold rejection. The newspapers were saying that the festival was Soviet-inspired and -financed – and of course it was, but we indignantly denied it and believed our denials.'[68] In the end the conference never took place. The delegates were refused visas and the event was moved to Warsaw.

More parochially, but of longer-term personal significance, it was in 1949 that Miller first encountered a man whom he was to know until his death some three decades later and on whom he was to base one of his plays ('I Can't Remember Anything') – Alexander Calder, son of the creator of the arch in Washington Square and known to his friends as Sandy. Calder had settled in Roxbury in 1933, barely half a mile from where Miller would later live. The eighteenth-century colonial house, ice house and barn, together with eighteen acres, cost $3,500. Calder's increasing fame as an artist and sculptor meant that this small Connecticut farm would play host to artists from around the world, including André Masson and André Breton, along with writers and critics such as Malcolm Cowley. Miller's arrival, followed later by William Styron and Frank McCourt, Richard Widmark and Dustin Hoffman, would further turn this New England town into an unlikely artistic and intellectual centre.

Miller's first encounter with Calder had nothing to do with art. In the winter of 1949 he was at a garage in nearby Woodbury when Calder swung in, driving the open touring LaSalle he had bought in 1930, a car still bearing the evidence of a fire some time before. Its silencer was blown, the switches on its dashboard had been replaced by wires and its wheels were squeaking, not least because the spokes were made of wood. Miller, always fascinated by machinery, intervened, suggesting that the problem might be solved by soaking the wheels in water for a day and a half, though he felt obliged to tell him that he had once tried the same cure with a model T Ford he had co-owned and that had cost twelve dollars. Driving along he had been overtaken by a tyre and a rim, only gradually to realize that they came from his own car.

Calder and Miller were then the only two non-farmers in Roxbury, though not, it has to be said, for long. The Calders, Sandy and his wife Louisa, would later embrace Miller's stance on the Vietnam War and thus be joined by something more than friendship and commitment to one another's careers.

For the most part, though, they were simply neighbours who would share meals and memories, the more so since Calder had known Inge Morath, Miller's third wife, many years before in Paris. Calder was to give him a painting to mark the production of *The Creation of the World and Other Business* (in 1972) and, after a party at the Miller home, drew his portrait on the wall of the barn, an image later brought into the house. Their friendship was part of what made Miller feel increasingly at home in Roxbury, and for years to come he would express a sense of relief whenever he could escape the pressures of New York for the Connecticut hills.

If 1949 marked the year of *Death of a Salesman*, it was also, to Miller, the last postwar year (though this was by no means immediately apparent). Things were changing, in the theatre and beyond. As he was to observe, there had been a time when there was effectively only one theatre, Broadway, the brief success of the Group Theatre and the Federal Theatre notwithstanding. Whatever O'Neill and Odets might have said about its deficiencies, this was the audience that had once embraced equally the experiments of a Nobel laureate and the Ziegfeld Follies. And if both of those were now receding into the past there was still at least the illusion of a single audience to be addressed. In fact, after *Salesman*, he began to detect signs that the Broadway audience was changing, reflecting the growing conservatism in American society. Whereas in Britain the people voted for radicalism, rejecting the war leader Churchill in favour of a socialist government, in America the desire 'for normalcy' was powerful, if – as was quickly evident – threatened. Two years after Roosevelt's death, Congress had a Republican majority, and in 1948 Truman had barely crept back into power. As Miller was to say, 'An inner sense of direction, a moral compass, shuddered.'[69]

This was a time, too, as he later recalled, when psychoanalysis invited those who had seen disturbances in the political and moral world as a product of social injustice to reconsider their position and acknowledge that the real flaw perhaps lay in the self. Guilt, once discharged through social alliances with a liberated working class, could now be assuaged in the high-priced consulting rooms of those who spoke, for preference, with an Austrian accent even if they charged in US dollars. This was one reason why Marxism had treated psychoanalysis with such suspicion. It saw as psychosexual what the committed radical necessarily saw as socioeconomic.

Miller should, like many other former Marxists and fellow travellers, have thus treated it with suspicion. However, at the same time, there was surely something about its inner procedures that would have appealed to a man for whom the past did indeed hold the key to the present, and who had come genuinely to believe that there was a connection between private and public betrayals. Either way, he would spend two years, and a large amount of money, in analysis in a futile attempt to save his marriage. It failed in that objective but Miller did not entirely regret the experience, merely the time he gave to it. Vestiges certainly remained with him. At the very least he discovered in the methods and processes of analysis a useful analogue to dramatic structures.

Meanwhile, he turned back to his work, still convinced that it was possible to write socially conscious material – convinced, indeed, largely through his relationship with Elia Kazan, that he might receive the same kind of welcome in Hollywood that he had on Broadway. Earlier in 1949 he had let it be known that he was working on a 'pathetic comedy' about an Italian worker in the Red Hook section of Brooklyn. On 17 March, an old vaudeville star wrote to him hoping he might be cast in it, being Italian and knowing a thing or two about pathetic comedy. But the script Miller would write would be a long way away from comedy.

Back in 1947, Miller had trawled the bars in search of information, sensing a possible play, still wanting, too, to see the theatre as a place where public issues could be engaged. Beyond that, he had a commitment to the idea of tragedy and the notion of a man destroyed while challenging the modern gods of crime and big business appealed. This was a largely Italian community, the people he had worked with in the Brooklyn Navy Yard, and he felt he knew something of them. He had accordingly immersed himself in the waterfront world, watching the humiliating hiring process which gave the hiring boss absolute authority, favouring those who caused least trouble.

He had been appalled equally by this stark symbol of capitalist power and by the passive acceptance of it by the workers. The war might be over but effectively, on the waterfront, the Depression lingered on within sight of the Statue of Liberty whose symbolic freedoms he had celebrated as a radio dramatist. There were, though, those prepared to challenge the system.

He was approached by a man from the American Labor Party in Red Hook, Mitch Berenson, who was determined to oppose the corrupt union headed by Joseph Ryan, whose activities would later be exposed by the press and investigating committees. From him, and from Vincent Longhi, the lawyer who accompanied him, he learned more of the corruption infecting the docks, which required pay-offs to secure work, and of the systematized thefts conducted by the criminals who now ran the unions. At the top of the criminal empire was Tony Anastasia, whose brother Albert was the head of 'Murder, Inc.', itself later the subject of investigating committees. It was from Longhi that Miller learned part of the story that was to be the basis of *A View from the Bridge*, but at the time his interest lay in another direction.

He now turned back to his waterfront material and completed a movie script, which Elia Kazan agreed to direct. In October, Miller sent a copy to Paul O'Dwyer (a radical lawyer) asking him to check its accuracy with respect to the docks. He made a few suggestions, correcting what seemed to him to be certain Jewish usages attributed to the Italian workers and explaining further details of waterfront corruption. On the whole, though, he thought it 'a wonderful job'.

As yet they had no studio backing, but Kazan had Hollywood contacts through his work as director of the movie version of *A Streetcar Named Desire*. They decided, therefore, to head west and try their luck, intending to offer it first to Darryl Zanuck. Miller's early doubts about the movie industry seem temporarily to have been set on one side – amongst other things because here, he told himself, was a work that celebrated the working man.

It was not, to be sure, a good time for a socially conscious script. Here, meanwhile, was Arthur Miller, whose name was already associated with pro-Soviet opinions, suggesting that a significant and strategically important business was in the hands of the Mob and that the New York police were happy to tolerate corruption. Miller, though, was pleased with the new script, if not without reservations. As he would later say, 'It was a persuasive story ... but one I had not really lived and therefore did not quite trust.'[70]

On 8 January 1951 Kazan wired Darryl Zanuck: 'Arriving Monday. Will bring with me original screenplay by Arthur Miller that I want to do imme-diately. You will get first crack.' He also wired his agent, the head of the William Morris Agency, Abe Lastfogel: 'Arthur Miller and I will arrive on Monday on the Super Chief. Will bring re-written Miller script ready to go. I want to do it immediately. Give Zanuck first crack but doubt he'll do it. If he doesn't, I will move quickly in the direction you choose. This is the big push.'[71] In fact, neither man was confident. Kazan thought the script in part a 'half-ass job', while Miller had doubts that anyone would be interested. He was also depressed. According to Kazan,

> he was distraught and ill. The worst of it was he was unable to write. He was longing for something nameless, a condition I recognized from my own life. What did he want? It was not complicated: call it fun, a new experience, ease of mind and heart, relief from criticism, happiness. His life, he told me, seemed all conflict and tension, thwarted desires, stymied impulses, bewil-dering but unexpressed conflicts ... Above all, he had sex on his mind, constantly. He was starved for sexual relief.

Miller has said of his first marriage, 'I'd reached a time when it just leveled out. She wasn't doing anything terrible, my wife. It just had no spiritual center anymore. It was routine. And I was still young, and I wanted to do a lot more work, and also I was feeling a lot of self-blame, because I wasn't wholly committed to the life I was living. It seemed to me full of falsehood.'[72]

The trip to Hollywood was thus a matter of new beginnings, and not only in terms of his career. But something had already happened that had changed him. Six months before he climbed on board the westbound train, he had already strayed from his wife in search of a passion he had despaired of finding at home.

In his autobiography, Miller tries to be both honest and guarded about what was happening away from the public eye. The marriage, he suggests, had become empty. He had begun to feel trapped:

> I wanted to stop turning away from the power my work had won for me, and
> to engorge experience forbidden in a life of disciplined ambition, at the same
> time dreading the consequences – less to myself, perhaps, than to those I
> loved ... Cautiously at first, or so I fatuously thought, I let the mystery and
> blessing of womankind break like waves over my head once or twice, enough
> to shatter for me the last belief that social arrangements, including marriage,
> had something to do with inevitability.[73]

That last sentence hardly needs decoding. The confession comes in the middle of his description of the collapsing loyalties of the postwar world. It is as though he looks on the political world to buttress the collapse of other commitments. He finds it necessary to be absolute in one sphere precisely because he can no longer be so in another. Nonetheless, he was flirting with danger in terms of both politics and private life: 'the chaos within remained; a youth was rising from a long sleep to claim the feminine blessing that was the spring of his creativity, the infinite benediction of woman, a felicity in the deepest heart of man, as unmaterial, unrepayable, and needful as the sky'.

Those words were written forty years later, but they suggest that a citadel had been stormed. Faithfulness had become another word for repression, sexual licence an avenue to fulfilment. Behind the quasi-religious language is an implicit description of a marriage that had failed to offer genuine fulfilment. What he seemed to be claiming was that he had in some sense been deprived of his youth and was now retrospectively claiming it, while the eloquent language could hardly conceal that what he was confessing to were affairs with other women or, in fact, a very brief affair with one, and a flirtation with another, Monroe. The benediction was an entirely familiar one, the felicity enough to reinforce his new sense of power and autonomy to be balanced by a generalized feeling of love for his fellow man. No wonder, though, that one seemed the real goods and the other a kind of charade.

There were other contradictions in his life, too. Speaking of 1930s radicals, of which he was undeniably one, he has described the way in which he rejected family in favour of mankind but was 'compromised – when he found himself lifted up the economic ladder – in his effort to keep his alienation intact'. This would be precisely the confusion from which he would suffer when, indeed, he was lifted up the ladder. 'When he married,' he added, the 30s radical 'vowed never to reconstruct the burdensome household he had left

Arthur Miller and Bertolt Brecht, both of whom appeared before HUAC.

All My Sons (1947) directed by Elia Kazan. (from left) Arthur Kennedy, Karl Malden, Beth Merrill, Ed Begley and Lois Wheeler.

Arthur Miller in the studio he built himself and where he wrote *Death of a Salesman*.

The Waldorf Conference, 1949:
(from left) A.A. Fadeyev, Norman
Mailer, Dmitri Shostakovich,
Arthur Miller and Dr William
Olaf Stapledon.

Protestors at the Waldorf
Conference.

An anti-Communist handbill distributed to theatre-goers attending the Dublin production of *Death of a Salesman* in 1951.

Elia Kazan and Arthur Miller on the set of *Death of a Salesman*.

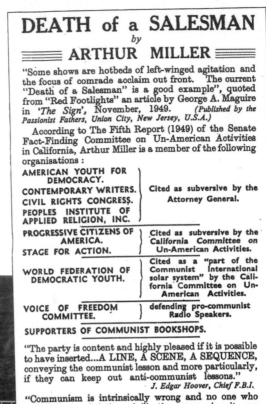

DEATH of a SALESMAN
by
═══ ARTHUR MILLER ═══

"Some shows are hotbeds of left-winged agitation and the focus of comrade acclaim out front. The current "Death of a Salesman" is a good example", quoted from "Red Footlights" an article by George A. Maguire in 'The Sign', November, 1949. *(Published by the Passionist Fathers, Union City, New Jersey, U.S.A.)*

According to The Fifth Report (1949) of the Senate Fact-Finding Committee on Un-American Activities in California, Arthur Miller is a member of the following organisations :

AMERICAN YOUTH FOR DEMOCRACY. CONTEMPORARY WRITERS. CIVIL RIGHTS CONGRESS. PEOPLES INSTITUTE OF APPLIED RELIGION, INC.	Cited as subversive by the Attorney General.
PROGRESSIVE CITIZENS OF AMERICA. STAGE FOR ACTION.	Cited as subversive by the California Committee on Un-American Activities.
WORLD FEDERATION OF DEMOCRATIC YOUTH.	Cited as a "part of the Communist International solar system" by the California Committee on Un-American Activities.
VOICE OF FREEDOM COMMITTEE.	defending pro-communist Radio Speakers.

SUPPORTERS OF COMMUNIST BOOKSHOPS.

"The party is content and highly pleased if it is possible to have inserted...A LINE, A SCENE, A SEQUENCE, conveying the communist lesson and more particularly, if they can keep out anti-communist lessons."
J. Edgar Hoover, *Chief F.B.I.*

"Communism is intrinsically wrong and no one who would save christian civilisation may give it any assistance in any undertaking whatever."
(Encyclical Letter DIVINI REDEMPTORIST on Atheistic Communism, Pope Pius XI.)

Issued by the Catholic Cinema & Theatre Patrons' Association, 85-86 Grafton St., Dublin

INDIANA

Lee J. Cobb, Mildred Dunnock, Arthur Kennedy and Cameron Mitchell in *Death of a Salesman*.

Arthur Kennedy, Lee J. Cobb and Cameron Mitchell in *Death of a Salesman*.

Joseph L. Rauh Jr and Arthur Miller appearing before the House Un-American Activities Committee, 1956.

Arthur Miller and Marilyn Monroe in New York, 1957, after his trial for contempt of Congress.

Madeleine Sherwood (second from left), Arthur Kennedy (far right) and Walter Hampden (second from right) in trial scene from Broadway production of Arthur Miller's play *The Crucible*.

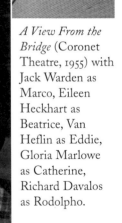

A View From the Bridge (Coronet Theatre, 1955) with Jack Warden as Marco, Eileen Heckhart as Beatrice, Van Heflin as Eddie, Gloria Marlowe as Catherine, Richard Davalos as Rodolpho.

Arthur Miller with Mary Ure and Anthony Quayle during rehearsals for the London production of *A View From the Bridge.*

behind, the pots and pans, the life of things. The god was the unillusioned life, the opposite of the American Way in nearly all respects. The people were under the pall of materialism, whipped on unto death in a pursuit of rust.'[74] That, of course, was Willy Loman with his faulty refrigerator and failing car, his faltering faith in the material in a play in which, in one draft, he urges his son to have faith in 'things'. But it was also, inevitably, Miller and Mary as the children – Robert and Jane – were born, as apartment was exchanged for house, as refrigerator and car became first necessities and then lifestyle accessories.

They were hardly the first to discover that a life of abnegation, which is easy enough to sustain as a student – when a glass of beer, sex and a cause seem entirely adequate – became more difficult with the arrival of the pram in the hall. He was hardly the first to find that success brings opportunities that make the pram no longer the principal urgency.

Miller was not the only one for whom desire was rivalling ideology. In the literary world, flirtations and affairs appeared to be epidemic: Mary McCarthy with Koestler, Sartre with the mysterious M, Camus with Patricia Blake, Simone de Beauvoir with Nelson Algren and Edmund Wilson with Mamaine Paget, who later married Koestler. The war had dissolved certain conventionalities and the puritanical backwash of ideology had largely disappeared along with the intensity of political convictions. There was now a certain ritualistic air, even a patina of nostalgia, to debates that had once seemed of central and overwhelming significance.

Writing in 1973, Miller observed: 'By 1949, a Thirties man would never know there had ever existed, only a few years before, a movement for social justice, loud and pervasive. By 1949 the word "society" had become suspect again.'[75] It would become suspect once more in the 1980s, when Miller staged his 1930s drama *The American Clock*. For the moment, though, he found himself deeply divided, still clinging to his earlier faith, while plainly denying it in terms of his values; still trying to breathe life into a marriage that linked him back to his student days, but at the same time beginning to revel in the new freedom he had begun to suspect might be his by right.

In *After the Fall* (1964), Quentin, the character modelled on Miller, recalls a moment in what seems to be 1950 when Louise, Miller's version of his wife, suggests that perhaps divorce might be the solution to their problems. She had found a note in his suit, which, to her, suggested an affair, and Miller had such an affair, albeit a brief one quickly disposed of. From his point of view, he had otherwise been working at the marriage, only to find himself continually on trial and sexually alienated. Quentin's comment, 'How much shame do you want me to feel? I hate what I did. But, I think I've explained it – I felt like nothing; I shouldn't have, but I did',[76] has its parallel in *The Crucible*, written only two years after the event referred to in *After the Fall*.

There is something undoubtedly authentic about the exchange between Quentin and Louise and, indeed, Miller took pride in the honesty with which he had presented his own relationship with Mary through these characters, admitting that she had had justice on her side and that, in retrospect, he was amazed that he should have written it so honestly:

> QUENTIN: You have turned your back on me in bed, Louise, I am not insane!
>
> LOUISE: Well, what do you expect? Silent, cold, you lay your hand on me?
>
> QUENTIN [*fallen*]: Well, I – I'm not very demonstrative, I guess. [*Slight pause. He throws himself on her compassion.*] Louise – I worry about you all day. And all night.
>
> LOUISE [*it is something, but not enough*]: Well, you've got a child; I'm sure that worries you.
>
> QUENTIN [*deeply hurt*]: Is that all?
>
> LOUISE [*with intense reasonableness*]: Look, Quentin, you want a woman to provide an – atmosphere, in which there are never any issues, and you'll fly around in a constant bath of praise —
>
> QUENTIN: Well, I wouldn't mind a little praise, what's wrong with praise?
>
> LOUISE: Quentin, I am not a praise machine! I am not a blur and I am not your mother! I am a separate person!

Mary once remarked that her husband had always wanted her to affirm that he was the new Shakespeare, and in 1991 she confirmed the accuracy of the portrait of her drawn in *After the Fall*.

Received at the time as a self-justifying play about his relationship with Monroe, in fact *After the Fall* is a startlingly honest account of key aspects of his life, its honesty a necessary component of its therapeutic function. In the play, becoming a separate person is not a virtue but a symptom of that dissolution of connectiveness that facilitates cruelty. He acknowledges the same fault in himself that he had once seen in his mother, who had withdrawn from her husband when failure came close to cutting the links that had connected them. Nonetheless, he did, like Quentin, accuse his wife of refusing responsibility for their failed relationship as if her desire to insist on her own innocence, and hence his ineradicable guilt, was at the root of their estrangement: 'If you would come to me and say that something, something important was your fault and that you were sorry, it would help ... Is it enough to prove a case, to even win it ... when we are dying?'

The final blow in the play comes when she refuses to sleep with him, leaving him to explain to their young daughter why he is sleeping on the couch. Whether a direct or oblique reference to his own marriage, Miller has said enough about the sexuality that flooded his life when his relationship with Monroe started, and the coldness of his relationship with Mary, to make this a plausible account of a dying marriage. Louise's observation of her husband that he has been 'trying to keep the home fires burning and see the world at the same time' seems an accurate portrayal of Miller in the early 1950s, and was subsequently confirmed as such by Mary. To Kazan, he 'had a roving eye and a bleeding heart'. He 'wanted to stay safe and secure inside his home, wanted to roam freely outside'.[77] As Louise/Mary observes, the breach between them had already lasted for three years and, as Quentin says, would last another three – not all desperate years, though: 'Suddenly, God knows why, she'd hold out her hand and I'd hold out mine, and laugh, laugh it all away.'[78]

Such moments between Miller and his wife, however, were increasingly rare, and in the end there no longer seemed anything worth saving and no way of saving it anyway. There was no real relationship, only civilities which he was accused of failing to acknowledge. Quentin's bitter prescription for saving a marriage is 'admit nothing, shave closely, remember birthdays, open car doors, pursue ... not with truth but attention. Be uncertain on your own time, in bed be absolute.'[79] In an unpublished screen treatment for a film of *After the Fall* that was never made, he says of the relationship between Quentin and Louise that it had foundered as a result of pride, intolerance and repressed hostility. Miller was drawn to try to repair the relationship, yet at the same time felt repelled. In 1950, he had met and had a brief affair with a young woman. Unsurprisingly, it led to a crisis. At the time, he appears to have convinced himself that he was doing little more than get something out of his system and that Mary might even understand the necessity. He confessed to his already deeply suspicious wife. The consequence of this admission was to drive them further apart and convince her that her long-standing suspicions now stood justified.

There is an unpublished short story that seems to bear on the situation. It begins with the central character returning home from the city at two o'clock in the morning. The woman he has just left made no demands. For his part he was not only seizing the moment, indulging a sensuality that seemed to him missing in his marriage, he was rebelling against conformity, knowing that art, too, had its roots in rebellion. Afraid that his wife may suspect the truth, he nonetheless feels oddly justified and liberated. He respects her but has never really loved her, not responded to her sensually. Now he convinces himself that his sexual adventure may actually improve their relationship. His affair has involved no real commitment, and for the first time he feels he may now be able to approach his wife without any barrier between them.

She is waiting for him, lying in bed, the ashtray full of cigarettes. She knows what has happened and asks why he has returned instead of divorcing her. Though he feels that in some perverse way he has engaged in his adulterous affair for her sake, that their relationship will now be able to continue, refreshed by his own reinvention as a sexually liberated man, in the face of her assertions to the contrary he comes to understand his inability to handle women. He acknowledges that he has been frightened of sexual women, even as he has desired them, and that in some senses his marriage has been evidence of that. He has been denying or suppressing his sexuality. For her part, his wife has seemed to lack not only allure but also a sense of egotism, which has begun to seem like a lack of femininity. Nor is this the first time she has spoken of divorce. Indeed, part of his animus against her derives from the casualness with which she proposes it – divorce, in his experience, being an alien concept. She has, in other words, already told him that she has no interest in continuing their relationship. They have in truth been living parallel lives, at times hardly speaking, that silence being a denial of their supposed relationship.

In this unpublished, untitled, undated piece, he spins a fiction that seems remarkably close to his own situation with Mary. After all, he had not once but twice tried to convince himself that his attractiveness to other women would be seen by her as testament to his value, and he would do so again with Marilyn Monroe. Looking to energize what seemed to him an inert marriage and his own substitution of respect for passion, he had confirmed her in her suspicions and left himself suddenly aware of what he had conspired in excluding from his life.

It was this affair that he acknowledged had marked the real end of their relationship, though it continued for some years. Mary now made it clear that but for the children she would leave him. He severed the relationship he had been conducting in New York and returned home. He felt simultaneously guilty and bitter. They tried to talk things out. What had been a marriage seems to have deteriorated into a series of negotiations.

Nor was it simply a matter of his infidelity that pushed them apart. He now found her views narrow, her judgements of people and issues peremptory. What had once seemed forthrightness and dogged commitment now increasingly seemed to him like an unyielding stubbornness. To his mind, she cut him off from experience. The following year, 1951, he met Marilyn Monroe, a woman who both admired and desired him, and expected the same in return. Mary, it seemed, did neither. She simply demanded he play out a required role.

It is hard to avoid the conclusion that he was trying to provoke a crisis. Supposedly working to resolve their differences, he seems to have done everything to confirm his wife's suspicions. Forty years later he wrote *The Ride Down Mount Morgan*, in which a man trying to sustain two relationships at the same time unconsciously precipitates a confrontation that will redefine his relationship to both women. Though this portrait seems to owe rather more to Kazan than to himself (in early drafts we learn that the protagonist had informed on friends to an investigating committee), it is tempting to hear an echo of his own dilemma in that of the protagonist, as he balances his relationship with a somewhat staid, unimaginative and dogmatic wife, on the one hand, and a younger, more sensuous woman on the other. If Miller had been attempting to precipitate a crisis, however, he lacked the will to see it through to its conclusion. But his relationship with Mary was about to come under even greater pressure as he accompanied Elia Kazan to Hollywood.

In the shadows, meanwhile, there were still those whose interest in him had nothing to do with his private life – indeed, to whom the very concept of a private life seemed alien. It was on 26 June 1950, even as he was conducting his brief liaison in New York City, that Louis Budenz, formerly managing editor of the *Daily Worker*, who had broken with the Party in 1945, had identified Miller as a 'concealed Communist' (defined as 'one who does not hold himself out as a Communist and who would deny membership of the Party').[80] No action, though, was taken, and Miller's file was closed again the following April 'in view of the fact that all apparent logical leads have been covered', though an anonymous letter denouncing him was received by the Bureau that August. The file was reopened in the December. It contains a note suggesting that if there was confirmation that he had been in the Party but had subsequently left he 'might be amenable to being interviewed by Bureau representatives'.[81] It is not clear whether this was to have been with a view to a hearing before HUAC, or whether he was to be approached as a possible informer. The suggestion was never followed up.

7

MARILYN

In the second year of the 1930s, a young child took part in an open-air service at the Hollywood Bowl, held by a fundamentalist church. All the girls, arranged in the shape of a cross, wore white dresses and a reversible cloak, one side black the other white. At the command, they were all to change from black to white, a sign that their sins had been washed away. Only one forgot. She was a black mark of sin against a white cloud of absolution. The one was a five-year-old called Norma Jean. In recounting the event to Miller twenty-five years later, she explained that she had been beaten for her failure and told that she stood condemned by Jesus.[1] She also recalled the colour of the cloaks as being white and scarlet. In memory, sin had become Technicolor.

Norma Jean Mortenson was born on 1 June 1926. Her twenty-four-year-old mother, Gladys Baker, was not married to Edward Mortenson, the Norwegian immigrant named on the birth certificate. He had disappeared on the birth of the child, apparently (though not actually) to die in a motorcycle accident three years later. Gladys's own last name was the result of a marriage contracted at the age of fifteen, and concluded when she accused her husband of profanity and violence and he described her as lewd and lascivious. Desertion seemed to be her fate. Much the same would prove true of her daughter who, at the age of two weeks, was placed with a foster family.

Gladys Baker was a film cutter, first at Columbia Pictures and then at RKO-Radio Pictures. Years later, her daughter would recall the smell of the glue used to edit lengths of film together. It was not a happy memory, but, then, she had few happy memories of her upbringing. Her maternal great-grandfather had committed suicide, her grandfather died of dementia in an institution and her mother spent time in a mental hospital. She herself lived in an orphanage, just one block from the RKO studios, from 1935 to 1937, and was parcelled out to families who offered her little affection. Later she would say that 'there were no kisses or promises in my life'.[2]

She watched as other children received the love she was denied: 'I never dreamed of anyone loving me as I saw other children loved ... I compromised by dreaming of my attracting someone's attention ... of having people look at me and say my name.' She had, she insisted, 'dreamed of . . . becoming so beautiful that people would turn to look at me when I passed'. By the time she wrote those words (though they come from a suspect autobiography, ghosted and edited), she had realized her dream but had already learned the price to be paid for achieving it. She claimed to have been sexually abused by a boarder in one of her foster homes and then disbelieved when she complained to the woman then playing the role of her mother. Later in life she would recount stories of other sexual assaults, as she would confess to offering herself casually as if that were the only way of succeeding or, like Blanche Dubois, of proving her reality.

The orphanage, a simple brick building with slatted shutters and a tree looped over the front porch, offered few luxuries. She earned five cents a month for washing dishes but one cent a week was deducted for Sunday School. She was moved from school to school. As she said later in a series of interviews conducted by George Belmont and Richard Merryman, she 'didn't like the world around me too much. It was kind of grey'.[3] She used to be taken to the movies at weekends and would frequently watch them through several times. At seven her favourite was Jean Harlow because she, like the young Marilyn, had white-blonde hair. She thought of Clark Gable as her father. At school, she remembered gathering other children around her and suggesting games – 'Now we're going to have a murder, and then a divorce.'

The world changed for her when she was eleven and began to develop physically. As she told Richard Merryman, 'I had a long walk to school – two to two and a half miles and every fellow in a car used to honk his horn. I would sit in a tree at eleven or twelve and boys would come by and I would say, "Can I ride your bike?" and they'd say, "Sure." I loved the wind. It caressed me.'

If she was raised in Hollywood and encouraged to think of herself as one day playing a part in it, she also found herself the victim of a series of foster parents whose religious fundamentalism instilled in her a sense of guilt and who thought of Hollywood and sex as the source and substance of sin. Since no one offered to adopt her, she also felt unwanted and unvalued. Every now and then her mother would reappear in her life and offer the semblance of normality, encouraging piano lessons, buying a house, only to break down and be carried off to a mental institution once again.

Despite her later tendency to dramatize these early years, it is not difficult to identify the roots of Marilyn's neuroses. Her desire for attention, for fame, for unquestioned admiration, can surely be traced to her experience of being abandoned and treated with disregard. Her desperate desire to be acknowledged, her need for relationships that would somehow combine paternal and sexual engagement, were the product of years in which she had no father and little in the way of love. As she explained to the biographer Maurice Zolotow,

'I know that I feel stronger if the people around me on the set love me, care for me, and hold good thoughts for me. It creates an aura of love, and I believe I give a better performance.'[4] Few actors expect an 'aura of love'. These days, a large trailer, personal trainer and Porsche will suffice. But for Marilyn the movie set seems to have become both a torture and a therapeutic site where she could command what she had previously lacked.

Her panic on finding herself in a mental hospital, following the end of her marriage to Miller, seems wholly explicable given her family's record of mental instability and the horror with which she recalled her mother being taken away screaming in an ambulance. Gladys Baker remained in the Norwalk Hospital for Mental Diseases until 1945, by which time her daughter was nineteen and married.

To Miller, too, it seemed that her problems had their origins in these early years:

> It was partly that she had a crazy mother . . . She was a paranoid schizophrenic who ended up spending half her life in an institution. The mother tried to kill herself three times and [Marilyn] was convinced that she was a worthless creature because she was illegitimate . . . It was a terribly mixed up situation, with the whole idea that she was worthless being at the bottom of it. And, of course, the religious side of it played an important role. They were fundamentalists – the mother was, all the people around her mother were. They believed in hellfire and damnation. Sex was bad, any self-displaying was evil; beauty itself was evil . . . She was guilty by looking in the mirror! She felt guilty because she was so attractive and beautiful. The Devil is always the handsomest creature in the cosmology, isn't he? Milton tells us that.[5]

As 'Marilyn Monroe' (Monroe being her mother's maiden name), she may have had a vested interest in dramatizing her early years, but she was undoubtedly deprived of love and attention until, with puberty, she recognized, without at first understanding it, the impact of her physical beauty. It gave her what she had craved, and she never regretted it, but at the same time there would always be the risk of it defining the terms on which other people encountered her. She determined to make her way into films, and quickly met with the demeaning process involved in catching the eye of those with the power to offer what she wanted. Having, by her own account, escaped the clutches of a movie mogul, she saw with some prescience that 'there was something special about me, and I knew what it was. I was the kind of girl they found dead in a hall bedroom with an empty bottle of sleeping pills in her hand'.[6] She retained very little from her early years. There was, indeed, very little to retain, beyond memories of emotional destitution and a piano her mother bought and which she later found in an auction room after it had been repossessed. She moved it into her Hollywood home, painting it white. Kazan recalled seeing it in her small apartment near that of her drama coach. She would not tell him who gave it to her. In 1956 it was shipped across the country to the house in Roxbury, Connecticut, that she and her new husband had bought and reconstructed in the expectation of a happy married life.

Norma Jean had married on 19 June 1942, three weeks past her sixteenth birthday. Her husband, Jim Dougherty, was working the night shift at Lockheed Aviation. Her current foster-mother Grace McKee (one of her mother's friends), who more than anyone had looked after her, had married a man younger than herself with three children. There is film of them all on a beach, Marilyn older than the other children and leading them in gymnastics. But Grace and the family were leaving the district. She had been instrumental in bringing about a marriage for Marilyn that was at least an alternative to returning to the orphanage. Marilyn felt little for the young man who was now her husband. The marriage was, though, a chance to draw a line across her childhood, to take her own life in her hands and, for a time, she had someone to look after her. They lived in a one-room furnished bungalow at 4524 Vista Del Monte Street, Sherman Oaks, Los Angeles.

In 1944, Dougherty enlisted in the US Merchant Marine while she worked as a fitter at Lockheed at a time when, on the other side of the country, Arthur Miller was working, also as a fitter, in the Brooklyn Navy Yard. It was at the Lockheed plant in 1944 that she was singled out by a young Army photographer (whose commanding officer was Ronald Reagan), taking morale-boosting shots of women war workers. This was effectively the beginning of her career, since these pictures led to a modelling job. This, in turn, led to a screen test and the first of a series of minor parts in the movies.

The marriage was not a success, any more than were those that were to follow. As she later explained, 'My marriage brought me neither happiness nor pain. My husband and I hardly spoke to each other. This wasn't because we were angry. We had nothing to say.'[7] She sued for divorce in Las Vegas, on the grounds of 'extreme mental cruelty', while her husband was still at sea. The decree was granted on 2 October 1946. All she had to show for her first marriage was her ex-husband's Ford coupé. By then, however, she was a cover girl. She quickly began to appear in a range of men's magazines from *Glamorous Models* and *Glance* to *Peek* and *US Camera*. The head of Monroe's modelling agency sent a note to both Hedda Hopper and Louella Parsons, Hollywood gossip columnists, who duly published it: 'Howard Hughes must be on the road to recovery. He turned over in his iron lung [he had been injured in an accident] and wanted to know more about Norma Jean, this month's cover girl on *Laff* Magazine.' The story was an invention, but it did her no harm.

Meanwhile, without an appointment, she had been to see Ben Lyon, head of casting at Twentieth Century Fox. Lyon, who had been an actor for twenty years, immediately arranged for her to have a Technicolor screen test. According to the cameraman Leon Shamroy, 'This girl had something I haven't seen since silent pictures. She had a kind of fantastic beauty, like Gloria Swanson, when a movie star had to look beautiful, and she got sex on a piece of film like Jean Harlow.'[8]

A contract was drawn up on 26 August 1946. Ben Lyon made it clear that she would have to change her name. An admirer of the singer-actress Marilyn Miller, he proposed 'Marilyn'. Though she preferred the name Jean, she agreed. The contract, which was to last six months, was with Twentieth Century Fox, where she found herself among other young hopefuls. As yet, she was merely one name among many, but her contract was renewed after six months. She was earning $150 a week. She eventually secured a part in an undistinguished film with an unappealing title, *Scudda Hoo! Scudda Hay!*, in which she was required to walk up to another character, say 'Hello', then walk on – the kind of role she characterized as 'walking ten feet to nowhere'.[9] Most of it ended on the cutting-room floor.

It was scarcely an auspicious beginning. She quickly realized how brutal Hollywood could be and how such young women as herself were regarded: 'A girl's virtue is much less important than her hair-do,' she explained. 'You're judged by how you look, not by what you are. Hollywood's a place where they'll pay you a thousand dollars for a kiss, and fifty cents for your soul. I know, because I turned down the first offer often enough and held out for the fifty cents.'[10] In August 1947, the studio failed to renew her option and she returned to modelling. The money quickly ran out, though she still invested in the occasional acting lesson or voice coaching.

While at Twentieth Century Fox she had studied at the Actors' Lab, established by Morris Carnovsky and others, and she continued with this now. Maurice Zolotow later suggested that something of the radical leanings of this group left its mark on her, though her sympathy for the damaged and the marginal plainly had its roots in her own experience. She was, after all, as much a child of the Depression as Miller. She certainly knew what it meant to have no money. Though Miller was later to say that he never knew her to finish a book (implying that this was because she quickly grasped its essentials), many have attested to her almost desperate desire to learn, and among the books she seems to have studied was the autobiography of the radical Lincoln Steffens. She worked with the group for nearly a year and read some of the plays for which the Group Theatre had been famous, including Clifford Odets's *Awake and Sing*, a work which moved her to tears. She also read the same writer's *Clash by Night*, later appearing in the film version. Her contact with Carnovsky and his wife, the actress Phoebe Brand, made her look beyond the Hollywood in which she had yet to make her mark:

All I could think of was this far, far away place called New York, where actors and directors did very different things than stand around all day arguing about a closeup or a camera angle. I had never seen a play, and I don't think I knew how to read one very well. But Phoebe Brand and her company somehow made it all very real. It seemed so exciting to me, and I wanted to be part of that life. But I'd never been out of California.[11]

Then, in March 1948, she was contracted at $125 a week for a further six months, this time by Columbia Pictures, as the result of a request to Columbia's Harry Cohn from Fox's Joe Schenk with whom, it seems, she had had a relationship, one of many in her rise to success. Schenk was sixty-nine. Again, the contract carried with it the chance of further training, this time with Natasha Lytess, a refugee from Nazi Germany who had worked with Max Reinhardt and whose husband, who had died in 1945, was the novelist Bruno Frank. It was partly on the recommendation of Lytess that she was offered the lead in *Ladies of the Chorus*, a story about a poor girl rising to success, one that plainly mirrored Marilyn's own aspirations if not yet her reality. It was a second-rate film but it gave her the chance to sing and dance. A review in *Motion Picture Herald*, in October that year, found that 'one of the brightest spots is Miss Monroe's singing. She is pretty, and with her pleasing voice and style, shows promise'.[12]

Nonetheless it seemed to lead nowhere, and once again she found herself out of contract and without enough money to run a car, essential if she was to attend auditions. It was at this stage, in May 1949, that she posed as a nude calendar girl for $50, a photograph that was to become an icon of the 1950s and beyond. As she observed later, 'I was at the Hollywood Studio Club. I couldn't stand it there. It was like the orphanage. I was behind on the rent. So I was asked to pose nude. I said, "No, I don't pose nude. Never." But I was behind on the rent so I called up and said, 'Are you sure I won't be recognized?"'[13] She insisted that the picture be shot at night.

It was in 1949, too, that she met a photographer, Milton Greene (real name Greenhaltz), with whom she would have an affair and who would later become her partner in Marilyn Monroe Productions, her attempt to gain control over her career.

Her breakthrough came with a walk-on or, rather, walk-off part in a Marx Brother's film, *Love Happy*, in which she was shot from the rear, hips swaying, and for which she was paid $50. The role, which she had heard about from someone she met at a lunch counter, called, as Groucho explained, for 'a young lady who can walk by me in such a manner as to arouse my elderly libido and cause smoke to issue from my ears'. She got the part and was warned by Harpo not to 'do any walking in any unpoliced area'.[14] The brief appearance attracted attention and she was used for the film's promotional tour, during which she claimed to have read Marcel Proust and Thomas Wolfe in her hotel room. The success of the tour also encouraged her agent, Johnny Hyde (original name Ivan Haidebura), executive vice-president of the Hollywood branch of the William Morris Agency, whom she had met at a New Year's Eve party, to secure a part for her that was to prove central to her career.

Hyde, fifty-three, a bare five feet five tall and with a red complexion, was the man who had discovered Lana Turner sitting on a drugstore stool. He had a habit of acquiring budding actresses as companions, often referring to them as 'tramps', but Marilyn was to become a virtual obsession. They began a relationship that was inherently unequal. He had the money and the power, but seems to have been totally vulnerable to her charms. Natasha Lytess later repeated a conversation in which Marilyn had confided to her: 'I knew nobody could help me like Johnny Hyde ... But I felt sorry for him, too, and he was crazy about me. I never lied to him, and I didn't think it was wrong to let him love me the way I did. The sex meant so much to him but not to me.'[15]

The part he now secured for her was in Twentieth Century Fox's *Asphalt Jungle*, directed by John Huston, who was also to direct her last film, *The Misfits*. It was the casting agent Lucille Ryman who first thought of her in relation to *The Asphalt Jungle* and drew her to the attention of Huston, but it was Hyde who concluded the deal. At this juncture Marilyn had some minor surgery to her nose and jaw, along with dental work. She was shaping herself for a career that she hoped was now gathering momentum. *The Asphalt Jungle*, released in 1950, proved to be her crucial breakthrough, though it was Twentieth Century Fox rather than Metro Goldwyn Meyer who picked her up for her next film, *All about Eve*, in which she played a minor role and for which she was paid $500.

Marilyn's impact on Johnny Hyde was such that he abandoned his wife and devoted all his energies to her, proposing marriage to her, and suggesting that she would become the beneficiary of a million-dollar estate. She refused:

> I sat in the theater with Johnny Hyde. He held my hand. We didn't say anything on the way home. He sat in my room beaming at me. It was as if *he* had made good on the screen, not me. It was not only because I was his client and his 'discovery'. His heart was happy for me. I could feel his unselfishness and his deep kindness. He not only knew me, he knew Norma Jean, too. He knew all the pain and all the desperate things in me. When he put his arms around me and said he loved me, I knew it was true. Nobody had ever loved me like that. I wished with all my heart that I could love him back.[16]

For her part, she had also been conducting an affair with the singing coach Frederick Karger. She plainly cared about Hyde, though, not least because he so evidently cared about her. On his death, on 20 December 1950, she attended his funeral in the face of appeals from his family. Years later, one of Hyde's sons recalled her repeatedly shouting out his father's name and she was plainly distressed. Natasha Lytess found her with a bottle of pills beside her, one of them between her lips. It may not have been the suicide attempt some later claimed – she seems simply to have fallen asleep when taking the pills – but she was clearly distressed. Whatever the truth of the alleged suicide attempt, Hyde's death was clearly upsetting her as she shot her new film, *As Young as You Feel*. Under control in front of the camera, she broke down in tears between scenes.

It was at this time that Miller and Kazan climbed aboard the *Super Chief* passenger train in New York, heading towards Los Angeles. It was something more than a business trip, though they had high hopes for the new waterfront screenplay, which seemed to combine social commitment with dramatic action. It was a chance to get away from New York, from the daily routine of writing and, in Miller's case, from his tense marital life. 'For a man of thirty-five,' he lamented, 'I seemed to have done nothing but work ... When, I wondered, does one cease to work and start to live?'[7] The answer, it seemed, was now. As the train waited in a siding at Albuquerque, he climbed down on to the track and sat on an abandoned beer box, while Kazan stayed in the compartment and read the script. He felt, he later recalled, the 'lure of another identity and of losing oneself in America. There was,' he confessed, 'something mistaken in my life. Maybe I had simply married too young.'

For Miller, Hollywood had always been the siren call he had resisted. When other young playwrights had been easily seduced, he had staked his future on the theatre. His work on *The Story of GI Joe* reinforced his scepticism about an industry that seemingly relegated writers to a subordinate role. Perhaps in some sense it was his success in the theatre, though, that now permitted him this indulgence, and the conviction, soon dispelled, that the integrity of a screenplay by a Pulitzer Prize winner would be respected. Beyond that, though, it was undoubtedly a trip that he thought might resolve some of his problems.

His earlier visit had been a brief one. Hollywood was now an entirely new experience. The journey from East to West Coast was more than a matter of geography. Hollywood seemed to operate according to different principles, to trade in a different currency. What he detected, above all, was power and sex. He was ready to deploy the power that had seemed to come with the success of *All My Sons* and *Death of a Salesman* in order to secure production of his screenplay. But here, he quickly realized, it could be traded for something else, something not so readily available in the east. He both relished and feared that power; was both drawn to it and resisted what it could buy.

For him, Hollywood represented a 'sexual damp' – a curious phrase, but a revealing one.

He and Kazan stayed at the house of Charles Feldman, a producer of the film version of *A Streetcar Named Desire*. Sitting beside a swimming pool, with a Filipino houseman bringing him everything he wanted, Miller now got a taste of what success could command. More used to being sequestered in his Brooklyn house, he found himself disoriented and seduced by an entirely new social world. Each night there were parties at which he met Hollywood names, but the parties were also attended by young single women, would-be stars, and there came a moment when he realized that these were, implicitly, on offer to him. He had, he said later, 'never before seen sex treated so casually as a reward of success'. It was to one of these parties, held in Miller's honour, that a young actress came, a woman 'almost ludicrously provocative', in a dress that was 'blatantly tight, declaring rather than insinuating that she had brought her body along and that it was the best one in the room'.

Morton Miller, Arthur Miller's cousin, later recalled her seductive, indeed indecent, approach to clothes.

> [Marilyn] was utterly lacking in self-consciousness about her blatantly revealing clothing. One night she turned up at a small gathering of the Strasbergs' in a skintight, see-through dress with a clear view of pubic hair. Another time, at a gathering of five of us at my house, she arrived, with Arthur, sewn into a rough-textured, brown-and-black, above-the-knee, tight-fitting skirt, black stockings, and black sweater that barely contained her. I noticed the popping eyes of the fifth person – Rabbi Goldberg [the man who in 1956 was to marry them].[18]

For the moment, though, the encounter with Marilyn still lay days ahead. The immediate issue was the fate of Miller's waterfront script. Writer and director were not unaware of the difficulties that faced them, but Miller was the author of two hit plays and Kazan's reputation was high after *Streetcar* and *Salesman*. They both had ambitions to do for Hollywood what they felt they had already done for the theatre – namely bring to it a moral seriousness, a sense of social significance. Kazan was contracted to Twentieth Century Fox but Fox had turned out to have no interest in the grim realism of *The Hook*, named partly after the waterfront area Red Hook and partly after the cargo hook used by the dock workers. (An earlier title, 'Shape-Up' was a reference to the demeaning hiring process to which the men were forced to submit.) This was to be a 'film about a dark cellar under the American Dream' – but what did Hollywood represent if not the Dream? For Darryl Zanuck at Fox the subject matter alone was enough to rule it out.

Miller, as noted earlier, had been guided in writing the script by Vincent

Longhi, whom he had shadowed when he was running for Congress. 'We spent weeks visiting locations,' he later explained, 'talking to workers, getting onto the ships with Kazan'. These were men who earned eight dollars a day but had to pay two dollars to the boss for the right to work at all. Only those raising two fingers to signal their acceptance of the deal were hired. Miller and Kazan thought they were addressing a significant social issue, but Hollywood at the time was not overly enthusiastic about significant social issues.

The surviving typescript of *The Hook*[19] is over-long (at 156 pages it would have run for over two and a half hours), and melodramatic, though perhaps hardly more so than *On the Waterfront* or than the Brooklyn piers themselves, where corruption and violence were, as it implied, endemic. It is also, revealingly, subtitled 'A Play for the Screen', and there are other reminders of its author's roots in the theatre. Scenes can appear over extended, language substituting for action, though that language has an authenticity that comes from Miller's intimate knowledge of those whose lives he portrays. It tells the story of Marty Ferrara, an Italian immigrant, who challenges the power of a corrupt union which, instead of representing its members, is the agent of the employers and the gangsters who run the waterfront. When they increase the work rate and a man is killed when steel is being loaded on to one of the ships, Marty challenges the union boss, Louis, only to find that his fellow longshoremen are at first afraid to back him; but he slowly gains their support.

It would be tempting to think that the chances of *The Hook* ever being made were slim but for the fact that a film based on essentially the same material and equally melodramatic was made, in 1954. *On the Waterfront*, directed by Elia Kazan, became one of the most successful films of the period, and a source of contention between Miller and Kazan not merely because of possible borrowings from the earlier script but also because it seemed to Miller – and, indeed, to Kazan – to be offered as a piece of self-justification by those who chose to betray their friends when called before the House Un-American Activities Committee. It is a film that presents the informer as hero.

Miller first met Marilyn Monroe on the Fox lot. She was walking with Cameron Mitchell (who, the previous year, had appeared in *Death of a Salesman*), when they came upon Kazan and Miller. Later, the two men watched her at work on the set of *As Young as You Feel*, a comedy based on a story by Paddy Chayefsky, starring Monty Woolley. It was a nightclub scene and she was required to walk across the floor in a black openwork lace dress, swaying her hips in a way that Miller would later insist was natural to her (her footprints on a beach, he explained, 'would be in a straight line, the heel descending exactly before the last toeprint, throwing her pelvis into motion').[20]

Others, less emotionally committed, spoke of her lowering the heel on one shoe to create the effect.

When the shot was over, she crossed to Kazan, who had met her once before with Johnny Hyde, tears in her eyes, still upset by the thought of Hyde's death. 'From where I stood, yards away,' Miller wrote in *Timebends*, 'I saw her in profile against a white light, with her hair coiled atop her head; she was weeping under a veil of black lace that she lifted now and then to dab her eyes. When we shook hands the shock of her body's motion sped through me.' Kazan's memory differed in certain respects. He recalled finding her in tears in the empty office of an adjoining sound stage and offering his sympathies, less a genuine gesture, it seems, than a stratagem of seduction since, in his experience, 'a genuine interest ... would produce results', prompting women to 'empty the secrets of their lives into a sympathetic ear'.[21]

In his autobiography, he affects to despise Johnny Hyde and those others in Hollywood who traded their power for sex – 'The scorn these men have for women is total!' – but it is clear that he was himself no less predatory, and Monroe had already sparked his interest even though he later blamed the Hollywood system for destroying her. She was, he explained, 'a simple, eager young woman who rode a bike to the classes she was taking, a decent-hearted kid whom Hollywood brought down, legs parted'.

His own 'genuine interest' and 'comfort', meanwhile, seemed to him to be paying off: 'I gave her comfort. She had a bomb inside her. Ignite her and she exploded.' While offering his analysis of the problems of a vulnerable young woman in Hollywood, he seems oblivious of his own exploitation of those problems. 'She deeply wanted reassurance of her worth, yet she respected the men who scorned her, because their estimate of her was her own.' It was an analysis that she would herself later confirm. As she remarked to the British journalist W.J. Weatherby,

> There was a whole period when I felt flattered if a man took an interest in me – any man! ... There would be times when I was with one of my husbands and I'd run into one of these Hollywood heels at a party and they'd paw me cheaply in front of everybody as if they were saying, *Oh, we had her.* I guess it's the classic situation of an ex-whore, though I was never a whore in that sense. I was never kept; I always kept myself. But there was a period when I responded too much to flattery and slept around too much, thinking it would help my career.[22]

The next day, and for no reason Miller could later recall, she accompanied him and Kazan to Harry Cohn's office at Columbia Pictures, where they were to discuss *The Hook*. Kazan suggests that he had taken her along as a 'mascot', pretending that she was his secretary and that she would be keeping notes of everything that was said. She sat in a corner wearing large horn-rimmed glasses, with a pad on her knee and a pencil poised. She was referred to by Kazan as Miss Bauer. Disturbingly, Cohn stared at her and said, 'I t'ink I know whose goils you were.'[23] As Miller recalls the interview, Cohn insisted: 'This picture won't make a dime ... I'll go in with yiz, pervided yiz don't take any money unless it makes money.' According to Kazan, Cohn's reaction to the script was: 'Burn it! ... Throw it in the ash can',[24] and it did still need work as is evident from the surviving typescript, in which a missing speech is replaced by a note saying, 'I'll fill it in. A.M.' Nonetheless, Cohn approved it, or so it seemed.

Miller was thrilled by what appeared to be a green light for his project, but he was also acutely aware of Monroe's presence. Afterwards, the three of them went to a local bookstore where Miller bought her a copy of *Death of a Salesman* and she thumbed through poetry books, her lips moving as she read. It was only a matter of hours since he had met her but already he found it difficult to keep his eyes off her.

It was at a party a few days later that the relationship between Miller and Monroe seems to have started. The party was thrown specially for him, and a number of young women were invited. The invitation list was not without interest. It read:

> Buffet for Arthur Miller
> 1. MONA KNOX
> 2. RUTH LEWIS
> 3. CHERYL CLARK
> 4. DIANE CASSIDY
> 5. KAZAN GIRL

Marilyn as yet clearly existed only in relation to Kazan, a man she had only recently met.

Miller recalled the evening, at which the two of them danced together: 'The eye sought in vain to find the least fault in the architecture of her form ... her perfection seeming to invite the inevitable wound that would make her more like others. And so it was a perfection that aroused a wish to defend it.' He remembered a comment made at the time by the actress Evelyn Keyes, ex-wife of John Huston: 'They'll eat her alive.'[25] It made him feel oddly protective towards her. The curious combination of sexuality and naivety that would carry on to the screen was disturbing and compelling in equal degrees. There could hardly be any greater contrast than that between this Hollywood starlet and his wife back in Brooklyn.

That Marilyn Monroe should prove so disturbing to Miller is not surprising; that she should have been attracted to him, not part of the Hollywood power system and with apparently little to offer in the way of advancement to her career, would be surprising only if she saw relationships purely in such

terms. In some ways the attraction seems to have come precisely from the
fact that he was outside the system. Certainly, she was to say of this encounter
that it 'was like running into a tree! You know, like a cool drink when you've
got a fever.'[26] She liked him not least because of his courtesy. She was to have
been accompanied to the party by Kazan, but he was preoccupied with another
young actress with whom, he explains in his autobiography, he became
intimate that same night, having just met her. Monroe offered to take a taxi
to the party but Miller insisted on collecting her himself. She was impressed.
To Kazan, this was evidence of 'how little these glamour girls expect of life'.

In fact it is not hard to see why she was impressed with Miller who, unlike
Kazan, did not make an immediate play for her – indeed who was, in effect,
to run away from her. The attraction was immediate. As Kazan recalled, 'I
could see that need had met need and the lovely light of desire was in their
eyes. I watched them dance; Art was a good dancer. And how happy she was
in his arms! Not only was he tall and handsome in a Lincolnesque way, but
he was a Pulitzer Prize playwright. All her doubts about her worth were being
satisfied in one package.'[27]

Miller talked to her into the early hours. He was impressed by her sensitivity
and her sense of reality; she responded to his gentleness. He spoke to her of
the theatre and suggested that she go east for actor training, insisting that she
could have a life in the theatre. No one had taken her seriously as an actress
before, and now a famous writer was suggesting that she had the talent to
succeed on Broadway. Later, she recalled the meeting and its impact on her.
'I didn't see him for about four years. I used to think he might see me in a
movie and I wanted to do my best because he had said he thought I ought to
act on the stage. People who were around and who heard him laughed, but
he said, "No, I'm very sincere."'[28] This was perhaps one reason why she later
enrolled at UCLA, taking a course on literature, turning up after her day at
the studio was over, sometimes falling asleep.

Meanwhile, the deal over *The Hook* quickly came undone. Despite the fact
that Cohn's own labour relations executive had praised the script, vouching
for its accuracy, this was not, it appeared, what Cohn himself wished to hear.
No sooner had it been accepted than a series of obstacles were put in the way.
Cohn notified Kazan that there might be problems and arranged a meeting
with Roy Brewer, head of the International Alliance of Theatrical and Stage
Employees, itself affiliated to the American Federation of Labor. Because the
script involved unions, he explained, it would be necessary to consult him.

Brewer claimed already to have read the script when it was submitted to
RKO, though there is no evidence of this. He recalled telling the studio that
they had not only a union problem but a communist one, since while the
Longshoremen's Union on the East Coast was violently anti-Soviet, Harry
Bridges, the pro-Soviet leader of the West Coast International Long-

shoremen's and Warehousemen's Union, had 'announced that he is going to file a petition to try to gain representation for the employees on the East coast waterfront and the picture could play an important role in convincing them to join with Bridges'.

Brewer also claimed that he had then called Harry Cohn to tell him that 'I was not going to stand by and see a Communist union take over the members in New York if I could help it.' The problem, he said, was one of timing. The script seemed to him deliberately designed to influence the outcome of forthcoming union elections: 'I told Cohn the reason for making the picture now and giving them the script for such extraordinary terms was an attempt to influence the East coast longshoremen, who had been traditionally anti-Communist.'

It is very difficult to take any of this seriously. Not only is he wrong about the 'extraordinary terms', the story is also at odds with his further account of his involvement with Columbia Pictures. Despite his earlier comments, Brewer affected to be surprised to be summoned and required to make suggestions for revisions.

Kazan's memory of the meeting is that after comments from Brewer about the need to expand the role of the narrator (there is none in Miller's 1951 script) he asked them, 'Have you thought of anything … for the anti-Communist gimmick?' – a somewhat mystifying comment since there were no communists in the screenplay. Brewer's own memory of the occasion is this:

> One day I had a call from the labor relations director that Cohn wanted to see me. I walked into his office and there was Kazan and Miller. I was supposed to tell them how I wanted the script changed. Well, I realized this was a pretty big order and one for which I was unprepared. They asked me what I objected to in the script … I got my inspiration … 'Well, maybe if we had the representatives of the *People's Worker* come down here' – that was a contraction of the *People's World* and the *Daily Worker* – 'and offer their services to help lick these gangsters, and this fellow would tell him, "Get off the waterfront! You're worse than the gangsters."'[29]

According to Kazan, 'Miller volunteered that we'd show that we were correcting our social evils in the American way, by the technique of democracy. This didn't satisfy Brewer. "Have a guy come in from the *People's Worker*," he urged, "and try to tie up with Marty and his gang. Marty could say … 'Nothing doing! We don't want anything to do with a communist sheet.' That would be a real way of showing he is not a Commie, because a Commie wouldn't say he is not a Commie, he'd lie about that, but he'd never disavow an official Communist paper. It's very important that you do this."'

Cohn asked whether, if such changes were made, the picture could go ahead. The reply was not encouraging. Brewer, warming to his task, indicated that there was 'a certain amount of danger in doing a picture of this particular type at this particular time'.³⁰ He would anyway, he added, need to confer with the head of the American Federation of Labor. Brewer's own position was clear, if not entirely rational:

> I don't believe Communists have any business writing our screenplays. If they were going to take dictation from a foreign country as to what to put in our screenplays so as to prejudice our interests against the enemy, they had no right there. Everybody that helped them should go kneel and pray for forgiveness ... The course of events [is] moving toward the basic line of the prophecies ... I believe the Bible is true ... Don't forget that the conflict right now is shaping up between the legitimate sons of Abraham and the illegitimate sons of Abraham. Did you realize that?³¹

The idea that the head of a major studio appeared willing to defer on details of script to a union leader of an apocalyptic turn of mind left Miller, in particular, shocked. In retrospect, however, it is by no means clear that Cohn ever had any intention of making the film. He wanted to retain Kazan's services for future films without being saddled with a socially worthy but in his view commercially worthless project. He needed, therefore, to appear receptive to *The Hook* while ensuring that it was never made.

Speaking to me in 2002, Miller remarked, 'Cohn didn't care about the movie one way or another. A film like this was impossible to conceive in Hollyood. It was a dark film about corruption. Indeed, when he showed the slightest interest in it Kazan and I were quite surprised. I remember he said, "This film isn't going to make a dime but I want you to direct it for me."'³² As to Brewer, he 'was a very good friend of the head of the New York waterfront union, a man named Joe Ryan who was a big shot in the AF of L ... Within about a year and a half from that point, Ryan went to prison for racketeering.'³³

The next day Miller left California, though not because of his problems with Brewer. He had planned to stay for only a few days but admitted later that he left when he did partly because he was in flight from his own feelings about Marilyn who, together with Kazan, saw him off at the airport: 'I desperately wanted her and decided I must leave ... or I would lose myself here.'³⁴ There was an air of panic about his departure, a sense of moral vertigo. After years of disciplined work, and in a marriage which seemed always to be bumping up against its own limitations, he had suddenly found himself in a world seemingly without limits. Here, fantasies could be realized; he could feel the ground shift beneath his feet. Just six months after ending the brief affair that had threatened his marriage, he could feel himself being swept away again. Duty did battle with desire.

Securely back in Brooklyn, he wrote after a few days offering to continue work on the script. Later he recalled a telephone call in which Kazan explained that it could go ahead if 'the bad guys in the story, the union crooks and their gangster protectors, should be Communists'. This seems an odd thing to have said since both Kazan and Brewer insisted that he had been present at the meeting at which this was proposed. He himself, however, was adamant that the proposal was passed on to him in the course of this telephone call, during which he was also told that Brewer had described allegations of union corruption as false, claiming that if the film were to be made all the projectionists across the country would go on strike.

In 2002, Miller confirmed his own account: 'That's the way it was. I met with Kazan, Harry Cohn and his labour relations man, and when I left for New York I considered that we had a deal. I was in New York when Kazan called and said that they wanted to make changes.'[35] He was also informed that the FBI regarded it as irresponsible to make such a film during the Korean War at a time when *matériel* had to pass through New York's docks. Three years earlier he had remarked, 'It might be asked why I did not fight to make this film despite these problems. The answer is that in the mid-1950s it was absolutely hopeless to find allies once the imputation of communism was laid upon a work or its author. In this particular case Brewer's suggested concoction was clearly a cover for gangsterism whose existence the federal government itself would soon prove independently of me.'[36]

Miller was as disturbed by his encounter with Marilyn as by the fate of *The Hook*. He felt like a man who had escaped the fire. Prompted by a telegram, supposedly from Cohn's secretary (Kazan thought it was from Marilyn), urging him to return to Hollywood, he wrote to Kazan ostensibly about the problems over *The Hook*, but in fact acknowledging the impact of Marilyn. For his part, Kazan recalled receiving a letter which, beyond enclosing a few pages of text revision, 'was going on in the most rapturous tone about certain feelings he'd been having, awake and asleep, dreams of longing'.[37] To Kazan it was a letter which, while implying that his family situation had deteriorated, was full of a new confidence: 'He was a young man again, in the grip of a first love, which was – happily – carrying him out of control. He didn't read like the constricted man I'd known.'

According to Kazan, Miller now made a series of telephone calls to Molly Kazan in which he expressed apprehension that problems with the script might have drawn attention to him and that he might be called in by HUAC to account for his earlier actions, most especially his involvement in the Waldorf Conference. Herself unenthusiastic about *The Hook*, she suggested that this was perhaps not a good time to proceed. For his part, Miller makes no reference to such calls. Then, as he attended a budget meeting over the film, which was supposedly not yet cancelled, Kazan received a call from Miller indicating that he intended to withdraw from the project. It was followed by a telegram,

> declaring that he was sick about it, but in the light of what was happening in the country he was convinced that we'd have no way of defending ourselves, and that there had been inquiries launched by Roy Brewer about him and me. Art spoke of certain evil men who'd gone on the attack because of Roy. He said he didn't believe that anything we had or could decently agree to would protect us or our work.

To Kazan, in other words, Miller was unaccountably running scared. He himself had been a Party member but Miller, as far as he was aware, had not. Why, then, was he breaking off the project?

The obvious reason was that a film which he had hoped would have something to say about the real situation on the waterfront was at risk of being turned into an attack on the Left. Always suspicious of Hollywood, he had also been offered further confirmation of the contempt with which writers were treated. Beyond that, there was another reason. Though he had for the moment run away not only from Marilyn but from his own feelings for her, he felt that something had happened that would change not only his personal life but also his writing. Certainly, he was no longer inclined to negotiate over a script that he thought would be compromised and which was 'a form of knowing rather than being and feeling'.[38]

Kazan went to report the news to Cohn, whose response was to explode with rage: 'I knew it ... Miller is a Communist ... I could tell just by looking at him ... He's still one of them.'[39] He sent a telegram to Brooklyn Heights declaring: 'ITS INTERESTING HOW THE MINUTE WE TRY TO MAKE THE SCRIPT PRO-AMERICAN YOU PULL OUT. HARRY COHN.' The film was dead.

Ironically, in March 1951, the liberal *New York Daily Compass* commissioned Miller to report on the Senate hearings on organized crime then being conducted by Senator Estes Kefauver, hearings which confirmed the essential premise of *The Hook*. As he wrote in his article:

> It is no accident that Anthony and Albert Anastasia were bred on the waterfront. If there is a heart, a nuclear center of the pervading evil glimpsed at by the Committee, it is the New York waterfront ... From the corner of Columbia and Union Streets in Brooklyn's Red Hook district come Al Capone, Frankie Yale and a dozen of the most murderous killers and racketeers. Here was the heart of Murder Incorporated. ... The workers are

traditionally barely literate and docile. They are 'organised' in a union which enforces the shape up, meaning that the worker is hired anew each morning, and his job is daily at the mercy of the hiring boss. The open invitation to favoritism in this system has broken the back of every rank and file movement in the unions – along with actual murder and beatings. Terror is born out of this hiring process.[40]

Here was the germ not only of *The Hook* but of *A View from the Bridge* whose opening speech echoes part of this article.

But Miller had other concerns. Marilyn had confronted him with a dimension of himself he had suppressed or at least hesitated to acknowledge. When she had accompanied him to the airport it was clear that for her, too, their encounter had been something more than a party flirtation. The farewell kiss, on his side, as he thought, a formal gesture, on hers seemed something more and that only served to heighten his guilt and alarm in equal measure.

Nearly four decades later, he could still recall what she was wearing as they said goodbye, as he did his own feelings:

She was in a beige skirt and a white satin blouse, and her hair hung down to her shoulders, parted on the right side, and the sight of her was something like pain, and I knew that I must flee or walk into a doom beyond all knowing ... [It] was not duty alone that called me; I had to escape her childish voracity, something like my own appetite for self-gratification, which had both created what art I had managed to make and disgusted me with its stain of irresponsibility. A retreat to the safety of morals, to be sure, but not necessarily to truthfulness. Flying homeward, her scent still on my hands, I knew my innocence was technical merely.[41]

At a time when life was

havoc, seizures of expansive love and despairing hate, of sudden hope and quick reversals of defeat ... I knew in my depths that I wanted to disarm myself before the sources of my art, which were not in wife alone nor in family alone but, again, in the sensuousness of a female blessing ... In some diminished sense it was sexual hunger, but one that had much to do with truthfulness to myself and my nature and even, by extension, to the people who came to my plays ... By now, even after only those few hours with Marilyn, she had taken on an imminence in my imagination, the vitality of a force one does not understand but that seems on the verge of lighting up a vast surrounding plain of darkness. I was struggling to keep my marriage and family together and at the same time to understand why I felt I had lost a sort of sanction that I had seemed to possess since earliest childhood ... I needed the benediction of something or someone, but all about me was mere mortality.

Speaking in the early 1990s, Mary Miller confessed that she knew something had happened on his trip west. He was restless, she recalled. She also recognized something of their relationship in the plays he subsequently wrote. Ahead, after all, lay *The Crucible* and *A View from the Bridge*, in both of which duty, social responsibility, rational commitment are challenged by a disturbing and destabilizing sexuality. In *The Crucible*, John Proctor is lured from his wife's side by a younger woman, while in *A View from the Bridge* a man sacrifices everything when he is swept away by feelings he can neither openly acknowledge nor act upon. Mary could see herself in the unyielding figure of Elizabeth Proctor, and something of her husband in John Proctor, disabled by his affair with a woman out to displace his wife. The sexual estrangement of Eddie Carbone and Beatrice, meanwhile, was an accurate reflection of her own relationship.

For his part, Miller had returned to Mary determined to try to breathe life back into a relationship whose fragility had become doubly clear to him. It was self-evident that she could never offer what Marilyn could. A dream was confronted by a familiar reality, possibility by the wholly known. Yet a part of him needed a sense of stability, nor was he ready to face the pain that a break-up would bring to his children. He had come close to the flame, and knew it had the power to burn.

Despite his swift departure from Hollywood, Miller had not entirely cut himself adrift from Marilyn. According to Kazan, he asked for her address, but the first approach came from her. He was, though, for a while, seemingly reconciled with his wife, to whom he dedicated his next play. But there were, he acknowledged, 'parched evenings when I was on the verge of turning my steering wheel west and jamming the pedal to the floor. But I wasn't the man who was able to do that either.'[42] He took to riding his bicycle aimlessly around Brooklyn, as he had in 1949 when he was 'looking for something real' or simply preparing for some imagined escape. He was scared, trying to 'reorder the mind with the unchanging vitality of ordinary life'.

At the same time, if he seemed to have made a decision in returning to Mary, their relationship would never be the same again, though they did now try to mend what had begun to seem irretrievably broken. A marriage born, in part, out of shared political loyalties had begun to founder, and not even a high-priced Freudian analyst, financed by the very success he had simultaneously sought and feared, could stop it. His marriage would now be characterized by a series of phased withdrawals, concealing the inevitability of defeat. He retreated into the privacy of his art, she into a reactive affront, slamming the door on intimacy.

At her insistence, they both continued with their analysis, conducted by Rudolph Loewenstein (one of those psychoanalysts driven out of Europe by Hitler) until 1949. Miller commented later, 'I doubt that I was acquainted with more than two or three people who had actually seen a psycho-analyst face-to-face. Psychiatry was for the critically ill or the idle rich grown desperate for something to do. Like divorce, it implied personal failure, a painful admission especially for liberals and radicals whose pride in their enlightenment was the counterpart of success for the Philistines.'[43]

Loewenstein had hidden in Vichy France during the war, before the Nazis occupied the whole country. Later he would tell Miller a story of a Jewish analyst arrested with false papers and saved by an unknown gentile, a story that would lead to his play *Incident at Vichy*. Loewenstein's work would have made him seem especially compatible to Miller, writing, as he did, on anti-Semitism, the frigidity of women and the nature of self-sacrifice.

The sessions took place every week over two years, at $25 a time. It was a costly exercise. What did he learn? 'I learned a lot but I would never advise anyone to do that because about eighty per cent of it is repetition. Whatever there is to be learned can be learned very quickly. I learned a lot about the oedipal stuff, but I knew that already. Most of it was a waste.' One of the things he had learned, it seemed to him, was that guilt had come close to disabling him. Beyond that, he came to see psychiatry's attempt to reconcile the individual with normative values as mistaken, and its intent to neutralize suffering as misguided. Suffering, he felt, often lay at the heart of creativity. And its utilitarian purpose – to save the marriage – undermined its value. It was a 'distorting premise'.[44]

Analysis, however, was in vogue, more especially among those with whom he now found himself associating. If Marx had for some been a substitute for religion, Freudian analysis offered a more American solution. It proposed a flawed human nature but offered redemption without the disadvantages of self-abnegation. Nor was there any embarrassing talk of the rich finding it difficult to enter the kingdom of heaven. Freudians charged at the door. You lay on a couch rather than kneeling in a pew but in return could see yourself at centre stage. Confession was a rite central to both, but Freudians required no penance beyond prompt payment of the bill, and were not likely to embarrass by invoking morality. Marx had offered a scientific approach to history and social action. Freudians offered a scientific account of the soul.

For Miller, there were various layers of guilt to be penetrated, not least the fact that a playwright who had been so engaged with the public world should now be indulging himself with explorations of his own psyche. It might be a fashionable step to take but there was also, potentially, an element of evasion in seeking this kind of help, even if it was the price to be paid for domestic harmony, if not happiness. Looking back, he suspected that, for a generation, psychoanalysis proved a kind of bolt-hole from past commitments and current dangers. The Right was resurgent; the Left was in retreat, in denial and in therapy. Miller recalls the writer Louis Untermeyer, dropped from the television show *What's My Line?* as a result of his attending the Waldorf Conference, closing his front door in fear and despair and not opening it for a year. Psychoanalysis, designed to open a door into the psyche, was perhaps also a way of slamming it on the increasingly dangerous world outside.

Analysis could be the debt paid for success as well as for a sense of failure. He was, after all, still not wholly reconciled with what he had become. He was feeling guilty for something more than infidelity. But he was also fascinated with the inner procedures of psychoanalysis. It was, after all, concerned with denial, the return of the repressed, the transformation of guilt into responsibility – all key aspects of his drama – and it is perhaps no wonder that some of his plays tend to replicate its methodology. Nonetheless, he found his visits something worse than an indulgence, something more than a penance.

He finally abandoned the sessions partly, at least, for fear that they would pry into those aspects of his life from which he derived his art. The price of knowing himself might be ceasing to know what to write about. He feared being 'bled white', provoked into an objectivity that could only damage a writer for whom the chaos of an instinctual life was the raw material of creativity. Invited to confess 'to having been a selfish bastard who had never known how to love',[45] he increasingly felt that the true selfishness lay in agonized sessions in which he became the protagonist of a drama in which he was author, actor and critic.

In the end, he chose his art over his marriage. For her part, Mary enrolled in courses at Vassar, perhaps in an attempt to balance the scales between herself and her husband, perhaps in an act of reinvention in the face of uncertainty. Marilyn was not the reason for their break-up. She was a symptom of it.

As Elia Kazan would remark, looking back on his and Miller's trip to Hollywood in January, 1951,

> within Art there is a serious conflict, even if he wasn't totally aware of it. On the one hand, I assume he must have felt he deserved punishment because he had hurt his wife – every time he looked at her he could see that. On the other hand, memory of pleasure is not easily forgotten. He respected the moral law, but he also found it constricting to a suddenly reawakened side of his nature: the life of the senses. His side trip into new territory had made him feel great ... I believe Mary Miller blamed her husband's moral 'deterioration' on me. I suppose I did give him a gentle shove down the slope into the jungle of turpitude. She said to me one day – and this is exact, because I wrote it down – 'Art is acquiring all of your bad habits and none of your good ones.' I wondered what she thought my good qualities were that Art was failing to acquire. I knew what she meant by my bad qualities.[46]

Meanwhile, Kazan and Marilyn (under the name Miss Bauer) exchanged letters, letters which on her side spoke obsessively about Miller: 'Try to cheer him up,' she wrote, 'Make him believe everything isn't hopeless.' For his part, Miller felt something approaching pride at having fled the west coast. Marilyn, however, having written directly to him, then flew from California, hoping for a meeting. She waited for him in her hotel, passing the time by having her hair done. He did not go. Kazan rushed over to console her: 'I knew how wounded she'd been because I'd seen how high her hopes were that morning. But my feelings, if not my sense of justice, were with Art. There is nothing more painful than pulling down a home where your children live.' Kazan's comment on the situation was that 'a Catholic upbringing stamps the concept of sin on its people. Art simply had to be punished – despite the fact that I believe Mary felt she had failed in the marriage too. It was obvious to me that another woman could now take Art away.'

Kazan hints, in his autobiography, at Miller's brief 1950 affair: one weekend, 'during a gathering of intellectuals for political deliberation, Art did something his wife Mary thought he should not have done. Considering the boredom that hangs like a fog over these events, perhaps his wife might have excused his "sin". But he told me Mary was unyielding. What astonished me was that Art appeared to agree with his wife.' Quite which wife, anywhere, would have seen boredom as a justification for infidelity is hard to guess. His affair, however, had been without meaning or future. Marilyn, by contrast, had turned his world around. To have walked away from her, as he tried to do, was in the end impossible, though it would still be several years before their affair became real.

It is not clear whether anyone was aware at this time or, indeed, later, of Miller's involvement in another film project. He had written the narration for a film by the Italian director Luigi Zampa called *Difficult Years (Anni Difficili)*. The title of this neo-realist film refers to the years Italy spent under the fascist dictatorship. The central figure is a government clerk who joins the Fascist Party simply to get a secure job. He accommodates himself to the system and, when the war is over, is accused of being a fanatical supporter. In fact his crime, like that of many, was not to speak up, to be one of those who acquiesces. It was a theme with obvious relevance to Miller who had, after all, spoken up for what he believed and was now paying the price.

The political problems Miller had encountered in Hollywood, meanwhile continued, though now in the context of the film version of *Death of a Salesman*, starring Fredric March. This ran into trouble even before it was released. He was asked by Columbia Pictures' publicity department, under pressure from the American Legion, to issue an anti-communist statement. He declined, only to discover that they planned to distribute a twenty-five-minute film along with *Salesman* in which the life of a salesman – 'Willy Loman with a diploma'[47] – was shown as fulfilling and socially valuable.

In the film, a suitably reputable man, wearing jacket and tie, and with a handkerchief discreetly appearing from his top pocket, stands at a lectern while behind him is a banner declaring: 'TRAINING FOR BUSINESS' and 'THE PRINCIPLES OF PROFESSIONAL SALESMEN'. Addressing a classroom full of equally well dressed people, he declares, 'No wonder poor Willy was such a failure. He simply didn't have it, the background, the training, the preparation. He was a product of an era that happily has long since passed.'[48] In other words, Willy Loman is aberrant and his plight no longer relevant. Miller threatened a lawsuit (though none too sure on what grounds), and the planned distribution was abandoned.

At the peak of his success Miller was fast becoming aware that 'powerful people had me in their sights and were only awaiting a clear shot'.[49] The American mood had shifted. As he later observed, in 1949 it was possible for *Death of a Salesman* to be seen as a portrait of American life, but in little more than a year the company filming it tried to distance themselves from him. In December 1950, the film was picketed in Hollywood by a group calling itself the Wage Earners' Committee. It was still being picketed by the American Legion two years later when it was shown in Washington. The Legion objected to Hollywood subsidizing 'folks like Arthur Miller'.[50] In Europe, meanwhile, *Salesman*, like *All My Sons* before it, was subject to the authority of the American Military Government where US bases were concerned, so that he had to rely on German-language productions in Zurich and Düsseldorf.

Miller disliked the film, particularly because March played the part of Willy as though he were clinically deranged. Thirty-five years later he was still inclined to see this as a deliberate attempt to defuse the social critique contained in the play in favour of an account of a pathological individual at odds with his society. His problems over the film, however, real and possibly imagined, were a reminder of his vulnerability.

When Sean O'Casey's *Cock-a-Doodle-Dandy* was threatened by the American Legion (which had a formal relationship with the FBI and was in receipt of confidential HUAC files), not because of the play itself but on account of its author's politics, Miller introduced a motion before the Dramatists' Guild to organize a counter-picket to that proposed by the Legion. It failed. Arthur Schwartz, writer of several popular musicals, insisted that he would resign if any Guild money were spent to protect the rights of a communist playwright. The inference was that he would take a lot of members with him.

Miller admitted that he was scared by the Guild's decision, not least because of the implications for any future play of his own. But if he was scared he was also, as he subsequently wrote, 'scared of being scared'.[51] The play never opened, the backers frightened off by the controversy, and O'Casey was effectively banned from a country which Miller regarded as psychologically on the brink of totalitarianism. A communist, it seemed, existed outside the law, as, increasingly, did those who defended or could be seen as associating with communists, or, indeed, former communists.

When *Salesman* was staged in Ireland in 1951 the Catholic Cinema and Patrons' Association distributed a handbill attacking Miller as a communist. Brenda Murphy has reproduced a copy of it in her book *Congressional Theatre*, a fascinating study of the impact of McCarthyism on stage, film and television. The flyer begins by quoting from an article in the Catholic journal the *Sign* of December 1949, which itself quotes from *Red Footlights*: 'Some shows,' it states, 'are hotbeds of left-wing agitation and the focus of comrade acclaim out front. The current "Death of a Salesman" is a good example.'[52] Quoting the Fifth Report (1949) of the California Senate Fact-Finding Committee on Un-American Activities, it then lists Miller's membership of a series of suspect organizations: American Youth for Democracy, Contemporary Writers, Civil Rights Congress, People's Institute of Applied Religion, Inc., Progressive Citizens of America, Stage for Action, World Federation of Democratic Youth, Voice of Freedom Committee, Supporters of Communist Bookshops.

The leaflet concludes with two *ex cathedra* pronouncements, one, logically enough, emanating from the Pope, and the other from J. Edgar Hoover. The latter is quoted as observing: 'The [Communist] party is content and highly pleased if it is possible to have inserted [in a play] ... A LINE, A SCENE, A SEQUENCE, conveying the communist lesson and more particularly, if they can keep out anti-communist lessons.' The Pope was more forthright: 'Communism is intrinsically wrong and no one who would save Christian civilization may give it any assistance in any undertaking whatever.'

For the moment such attacks added up to very little. Besides which, play-goers seemed to show little inclination to listen to moral zealots or political revanchists. But in a new play which reflected both what seemed to him to be the mood of the 1950s and his own troubled state of mind, Miller acknowledged that the public mood had changed and was changing. It concerned a group of scientists in the pay of commercial interests. Into this troubled world of competing loyalties comes the figure of Lorraine. Though he claims that she was 'modeled rather distantly on Marilyn', in fact his description of her makes the connection explicit: 'With her open sexuality, childlike and sublimely free of ties and expectations in a life she half senses is doomed, she moves instinctively to break the hold of respectability on the men.'[53] The scientists are already confused as to their social morality. One, he explains, retreats to a loveless and destructive marriage in fear of losing his social standing; another abandons his family for her, only to be abandoned in turn when her interests change. Like a blind, godlike force, with all its creative cruelty, her sexuality comes to seem the only truthful connection with some ultimate nature, everything that is life-giving and authentic. She flashes a ghastly illumination upon the social routinization to which they are all tied and which is killing their souls – but she has no security of her own and no faith, and her liberating promise is finally illusory.

Not so distantly modelled, it seems. These words were written more than three decades later, but they do offer an account both of his feelings about Marilyn, and of his awareness of her potential for liberation and destruction.

The draft play seems to have accurately caught his mood at that time. On one side was a utilitarian society, in which money was a value and individuals no more than producers or consumers. On the other were idealists, easily dislodged from their ideals or no longer able to see how they could be operative in the world. Mere pragmatism prevails. Sexuality, meanwhile, is spun off as some unrooted quality, liberating and destructive by turns. This was the space Miller occupied. Convention drew him one way, a liberated sexuality another. The certainties that had once fired his imagination were now obscured. Though he was repelled by the politics of postwar America, he could no longer convince himself that a world view based on the Depression, on Guernica, on progressive unions fighting for the brotherhood of man, adequately explained what he saw around him.

In talking about this period he repeatedly returned to the idea that his life had in some way become divided, that his social impulses had become separated from his personal needs, in particular his sexual needs. His was a society, he believed, in which sexuality was alienated from the individual and offered back in the form of gratuitous imagery. The erotic became detached from the social, as though the individual were no more than a fragmented self. His encounter with Marilyn had momentarily offered the possibility of closing such gaps in experience, forging a new, more unified sense of identity.

In his play, the scientists, who had once believed their skills to have the power to transform the world, settle for a compromise born less out of external pressures than out of their own seeming sophistication. Acknowledging that the world does not yield to the pressure of their idealism, they make those subtle adjustments which eventually turn into betrayal. Miller suspected himself of no less. His career was born out of a conviction that the theatre could play a central role in changing the world. His talent was to be at the service of mankind. A decade and more on, and Cold War revelations had exposed his political naivety and potentially gifted him a cynicism that had its own attraction, its own internal logic. Lorraine thus becomes simultaneously a reminder of a vivifying principle and a symbol of the social treachery of those once wedded to the ideal. He finally abandoned the play, not least because it seemed to be leading him towards an endorsement of that cynicism. He turned, instead, to *An Enemy of the People*, with its assertion of the rights of the nonconformist.

For all the unfocused rebellion of the 1950s, embodied in a James Dean, the power of conformity was strong. One of the most successful books of the day, Herman Wouk's *The Caine Mutiny*, took as its central theme a sentiment which, in the previous century, had led Queen Victoria to write in her private journal of the sinking of a ship as the result of a junior officer's failure to countermand his superior: 'To say, as many did, that juniors should disobey in the event of anything dangerous taking place, would never do.'[54] In *The Caine Mutiny* a manifestly psychotic and cowardly commander nearly wrecks his vessel, forcing a junior officer to relieve him of his command. The junior officer is called before a court martial but exonerated, thanks, in large part, to his defence counsel. At the celebratory party, however, the same counsel throws a glass of wine over his client. For the good of the system, he tells him, he should have followed orders.

The new orthodoxies of the 1950s were such that resistance implied a form of treachery, symbolic or actual. It was this mood that led Miller, at the urging of two actors themselves threatened with investigation, to stage his own version of Ibsen's *An Enemy of the People*, in which, with the support of the majority, a truth teller is denounced and driven out by demagogues.

Shortly after the production of *Death of a Salesman* Miller had been approached by Robert Lewis, a veteran of the Group Theatre, to write an adaptation of Ibsen's play for Fredric March and his wife, Florence Eldridge. He was enthusiastic in so far as here was a play about a man who stood up for what he believed, a man for whom truth mattered more than trimming one's sails to the wind of public opinion. He staged the play as an act of resistance, not least because it seemed to be a comment on conformity and denial. Dr Stockmann, whose scientific work has led to the creation of a spar – he has identified the beneficial qualities of the spring water in the provincial town where he lives – discovers that the water is polluted. By making his findings public, he believes he would be saving the town from embarrassment and perhaps more. The problem can be easily resolved, though it will require money to do so. To his evident surprise he is not greeted with enthusiasm. Even those on the political left, who might be assumed to support him, back off when it becomes evident that it may be necessary to raise taxes. The press proves pusillanimous and his own brother, the mayor, rejects him. At a public meeting he is shouted down and subsequently attacked.

It is true that Stockmann is himself presented as dangerously unbalanced, extreme in his social views and seemingly careless of the well-being of those closest to him, but he is right, and he is being silenced for the truth he would tell. This is not, however, another Ibsen play offered as a warning against those who believe they have special access to the truth. Stockmann is a flawed idealist of a kind to be found also in *The Wild Duck*, but that is not the core of the play. Though it is freighted with ironic comedy, there is a deal of bitterness in it and Miller picks up on this even while mitigating some of the more extreme aspects of the language and characterization. An admirer of Alexis de Tocqueville, Miller was responding to what he took to be Ibsen's comments on the tyranny of the majority, the ease with which political and social convictions are laid aside in the name of self-interest.

An Enemy of the People must have seemed an apt choice, presenting, as it does, the drama of a man who finds himself at odds with his society. Stockmann has shifted from hero to villain virtually overnight, just as Miller had found himself celebrated at the start of 1949 as a Pulitzer Prize winner and denounced at the end of it as a man who had consorted with the Devil at the Waldorf Conference.

Miller, of course, had been an admirer of Ibsen back at Michigan, and he responded now with enthusiasm. Ibsen had written the play in an angry mood. He attacked Right and Left alike and seemed to endorse a patrician distrust of the masses and a special status for the revolutionary artist. His previous play, *Ghosts*, had not been well reviewed and his mood had scarcely improved since then.

After the hostile response to *Ghosts* Ibsen had denounced those liberals who had tried to keep their distance from him, afraid to be tainted. This must have seemed familiar territory to Miller, assailed by those who sought to distinguish their own past Marxism and present liberalism from his own.

There is a Darwinian tinge to some of Stockmann's statements, and Miller was keen to mitigate this. Stockmann is in part a comic character, in so far as he is at first oblivious of the forces ranged against him, egoistic, blind to the human needs of those around him. His seeming faith in rationality is, ironically rooted in a largely irrational sense of his own messianic role and, indeed, he gathers twelve disciples around him. In Miller's hands, however, some of this is filtered out, standing as he does for a certain moral rectitude, and he remains uncowed by intimidation.

Miller's Stockmann was to be rather more balanced than Ibsen's. His nonconformist was to be more rational. He is still prone to overheated diatribes, but mainly operates at a lower temperature. Ibsen's play ends with a self-centred man, contemptuous of the masses. Miller's ends with a man determined to confront those who attack him.

The idea of staging the play also had the added piquancy that at that time the actors involved were suing *Counter-Attack*, the same magazine that had compiled a file on Miller. Along with *Red Channels*, it was closely allied with HUAC. *Counter-Attack* had identified March and Eldridge as communists (the case was settled out of court, though with the Marches contributing a statement of their anti-communism to the magazine), an accusation that had effectively put them on a blacklist denying them several roles in Hollywood. They saw in the figure of Ibsen's Stockmann someone who resisted such intimidation. The parallel was more than a little stretched, but for Miller it was a chance to say something about the erosion of free speech that increasingly threatened America. He adapted the play, he later explained, 'with the hope of illuminating what can happen when a righteous mob starts marching'.[55] It was also, he admitted, in part,

> a reflection of my own split, which I could not stop from widening, between the willed determination to keep my family together and fulfill my role as father and the corrosive suspicion that family, society, all 'roles', were just that – conventions that would pour me in concrete, forbidding my nature and vision their revolutionary changes. What I had repressed was indeed returning, and the self-accusations of insincerity that hounded me were deserved.[56]

It was a play, he noted, in which sexuality was expressly absent. Having looked to integrate two aspects of his self, he had opted instead to stage the conflict purely in social terms. Privately he yearned for a 'female blessing', confessing that in 'some diminished sense it was sexual hunger' that drove him. At the same time, he stressed that what he felt he needed above all was a commitment to truth. The play publicly proclaimed the virtue of such. In his private life, by contrast, he continued to dissemble. He accused himself time and again of lacking the courage to break free. The youthful iconoclast had confidently challenged political and religious orthodoxies. Now, as it seemed to him, he censored the truths that were his claim on the attention of his audience.

On one level, of course, he was a man edging towards middle age, revivified by the knowledge that he could attract not only a younger woman but a woman of uncommon beauty. Later rationalizations have the sound of post-facto justifications. Nonetheless, he felt suddenly ill at ease, confused: 'My life was havoc, seizures of expansive love and despairing hate, of sudden hope and quick reversals of defeat.' The price of sustaining his life as before was now a sense of guilt and dissatisfaction, a denial of that self which had suddenly been revealed. He felt inhibited, oppressed, and that sense of oppression had a focus in terms of his wife, who became the embodiment of those repressions that he had briefly come close to abandoning.

Separation from Marilyn, if anything, served to magnify the significance of their encounter. He had refused to follow his instincts and, in his private life, found himself sustaining values in which he no longer believed; in his public life, he instinctively sided with those, now harassed and persecuted, with whom he had once shared commitments which, in common with most of them, he no longer held. Marilyn represented freedom, and his wife that kind of inhibition he had once felt in the presence, literal or symbolic, of his mother. He continued with the details of domestic living but 'the ease of mutual trust had flown from us like a bird, and the new cage was as empty as the old where no bird sang'. The image is a telling one.

A photograph of Marilyn, taken by the actor Harold Lloyd at his estate in Los Angeles in 1952, shows her posing against a bookcase in which is to be seen a copy of the paperback version of *Death of a Salesman* and a hardback of Ibsen's *An Enemy of the People*. Was this chance, or was she the one who chose where the picture was to be taken? Was there a message for those with the eyes to see?

Miller, sitting in on rehearsals of *An Enemy of the People*, found Florence Eldridge's performance at odds with his sense of the character of Mrs Stock-mann. As Robert Lewis has recalled, 'She had a touch of the disease that afflicts the work of some talented American leading actresses: the need to be "sympathetic". Arthur sensed this wish of Florence to be loved by the audience. Blowing his top in the middle of a scene one day at a run-through, Arthur yelled up to Mrs March [Eldridge], "Why must you be so fucking noble?"'[57] Florence Eldridge immediately disappeared to her dressing room, followed by her husband, refusing to return until the playwright had apologized in front of the company. In the end a private apology sufficed.

Miller worked from a literal word-by-word translation, believing that

> there was a sufficient number of people like me out in that audience who were simply scared to speak or uncertain what to say about this situation and, I thought, would respond to this kind of work; and I turned out to be right and wrong. They rejected *An Enemy of the People*, but that was partly due to the woodenness of the production, and it *was* quite wooden, despite Fredric March playing the lead.[58]

In a 1983 article he described Fredric March's performance as 'brilliant'. Lewis thought it the best of his life. By 1995, Miller had modified this view. 'He played it like Jesus Christ,' he observed, 'terribly seriously, when the fact is that the character of Dr Stockmann is that of a semi-lunatic scientist who is really a very frantic kind of person.'[59] The critics, he explained, 'batted the play right back at my feet', partly, he thought, because at that time 'things artistic were supposed to deal with sentiments and aspirations, but never with society'.[60] Beyond its failure to move the audiences, what struck him most was the hostility he felt not so much towards the play or any deficiencies in his adaptation, as towards his desire to stage it at all, as if he were oblivious to the mood of the day, anxious to present the liberal or radical as a martyr instead of a threat.

In fact, reviews were not bad. *Newsweek* called March's performance more forceful than any then on view on Broadway, and it was not alone in this. It was the public that turned its back on the production, which closed in under five weeks. In inscribing a copy of the play to Robert Lewis, Miller wrote: 'The God of the Theatre is the old God – the last incarnation of Jehovah, and his ways are crazy, his wrath insane ... Whatever else is to be said, we bucked the time, and stood for Man – and that is more than a little to have done.'[61] A note in his FBI file recorded the date on which the play closed.

It ran for thirty-six performances. Ibsen, in the 1930s seen as a radical figure, was now unlikely Broadway fare, and a play seemingly attacking the general populace, let alone its leadership, was perhaps unlikely to prove compelling. In later years, though, it achieved its place in Miller's canon and was often the preferred text for productions of Ibsen's play. At the time, however, its reception seemed to confirm the difficulty not merely of addressing contemporary reality, albeit by way of an adaptation of a European classic, but of finding a language that could hope to capture Miller's increasing sense of unreality, a culture destroying its values in the name of those values.

Cold War hysteria was creating an environment that struck him as increasingly dangerous and surreal. In October 1951, *Collier's* magazine devoted an entire issue to a Third World War which was projected to break out the following year and include the nuclear bombing of New York, Philadelphia, Detroit and other cities. Writers including Arthur Koestler and J.B. Priestley were invited to invent a detailed scenario. Happily, the Soviets were to be vanquished, America's nuclear supremacy winning the day. Miller wrote an angry sixteen-page response, but broke off before finishing.

America's failure to beat communism in Korea, he noted, seemed not to have troubled those who sketched out their fantasies for *Collier's*. The campaign against Russia was apparently to be conducted with nuclear weapons that distinguished the friendly Soviet people from their leaders and resulted in Americans being welcomed with open arms. Thereafter, according to Priestley, Miller suggested, the Soviet stage would be free to stage *Guys and Dolls*, watched by all except the thirty-two million Russians who were to die in this projected war. Perhaps it is hardly surprising that Miller lost the will to continue with his response.

His experience with *An Enemy of the People*, though, and his awareness that he was now in the sights of people in search of those who resisted the new political orthodoxies, did not prevent him seizing on a story in which once again the individual confronts the state. It was a story that sent him from his home in Connecticut to a small town in Massachusetts and from the nineteenth century to the seventeenth. The town was Salem, the resulting play, *The Crucible*. He was looking for a new language that would resist the sly code in which people increasingly spoke, the degraded vocabulary of a state that seemed to him increasingly to lack words with the power and authority to resist a drift into unreality, cultural and political stasis. He found it in the seventeenth century, where words could be similarly co-opted but where there was also a blunt directness long since drained from American English.

The irrationalities at large in *The Crucible* reflected both the political situation in early 1950s America and, to a degree, his own experiences, for here was a world in which reason was overthrown by a passion that threatened the self no less than the institutions of society, from the family to the state. It was about a moral guilt that could be assuaged by confession, by a form of words that offered the consolation of reintegration into an unquestioned norm. And though there is no doubt that it was the immediate political situation that led him to drive north to Salem, he also acknowledged that within the 'story's lines of force' were elements that 'instinct warned ... me ... would not leave me untouched'.[62] Nor was he only speaking of the political reaction that he knew must greet such a play. He was 'moving inward as well as north', and not without anxiety.

Kazan had no doubts about the roots of the play, more especially since he was convinced that Miller's power as a playwright lay in his ability to draw on his own experience, recognizing in it the archetypal. 'If we are to judge solely from ... *The Crucible*, we would have to say that Art did think of himself as a sinner; the central character in it expresses contrition for a single act of infidelity. I had to guess that Art was publicly apologising to his wife for what he'd done.'[63] His protagonist John Proctor, standing up before society and confessing his dalliance with another woman, seemed to Kazan no more than a displaced account of Miller's own situation as he lived out in art what he could not confront in reality Of course, Kazan, more than anyone, had reason to stress the personal over the political, to see *The Crucible* as focusing on sexual rather than social betrayal, since it was he who would appear before the House Un-American Activities Committee and name those who had once shared his beliefs and knowingly offer them up for persecution. It was he who had dedicated himself to a series of extramarital affairs.

For Miller, the sexuality was not consciously a product of his own situation but of the evidence he found in Salem. The Devil, after all, was the focus of sexual imagery and the township alive with sexual tensions. Guilt, betrayal, denial were the stuff of the drama that had been played out in seventeenth-century Massachusetts, as in 1950s America. Nonetheless, John Proctor's dilemma was one that Miller perhaps understood more completely than he would once have done.

8

THE CRUCIBLE

On 14 June 1951, Senator Joseph McCarthy rose in the Senate and gave a speech in which he accused General George Marshall of being at the heart of a conspiracy to betray his country, and suggested that he had the President of the United States in his power. It was time, he insisted, to seek out the enemy within.

That night, Miller attended a small dinner in New York at which McCarthy's charges were taken entirely seriously by those present, a group of people which included the editor of the *Herald Tribune*, the second most important newspaper in the USA. He was astonished. He suddenly found himself living in a country he could barely understand but with a desperate desire to alert people to the danger. The vehicle he chose was a play.

The idea for *The Crucible* had been in Miller's mind since taking a course on American history at the University of Michigan:

> I never did anything about it because it was too absurd. Nobody could be made to believe that people in a small village in seventeeth-century Massachusetts would start killing each other over whether someone was a witch or not. But there were trials taking place in the United States in 1949–50 where I heard actual lines being spoken by American prosecutors which I vaguely remembered from reading about the witchcraft in 1692. At first it was simply unbelievable, but I went back into history and there it was. It was mind-boggling that the same material could have arisen some three hundred years later.[1]

It was, though, only when a copy of Marion Starkey's book, *The Devil in Massachusetts*, came into his hands that the precision of the parallels struck him. It seemed to him, suddenly, that the inner procedures of HUAC were remarkably close to those that had prevailed in Salem in 1692.

For a brief time, in Puritan New England, values had been reversed. The accuser was innocent, the accused assumed to be guilty and stripped of social power. Judicial processes were perverted, a new language deployed. Survival depended on submission and an acceptance of the paranoid vision. As the

1950s were ushered in, it seemed to Miller that he was witnessing a similar moral inversion.

Individuals now became Un-American, while, through the looking-glass, in the Soviet Union, they became un-people, as history was revised with the aid of an airbrush. Those no longer politically acceptable were dutifully de-created as, in the United States, bureaucrats, teachers, actors were swiftly written out of the American narrative – sometimes, as in Hollywood, resurfacing under aliases, so many celluloid golems haunting the American conscience. This was to be a decade in which the casting-out of devils was seen as a national responsibility, the penitent an image of reborn man.

Miller gathered whatever other books he could lay his hands on with a growing sense of fascination, discovering, beyond the politics of the events, a sexual dimension he had not anticipated. Salem was a community in which a suppressed sexuality had broken surface. The accusations levelled by pre-pubescent and pubescent girls, it seemed to him then, and still more later, were intimately involved in the social threat registered by the community. Only in retrospect, however, did he acknowledge the connection with his own life, confess, at least to himself, that beneath the worthiness of his social and political aims was an opportunity to explore that aspect of himself so recently released. He would come to feel a strong affinity with his protagonist John Proctor, who would emerge as the pivotal figure, a man trapped in a cold marriage and tempted by a young woman whose sexuality had set him afire.

It is curious to note, indeed, how often his image, paradigm, exemplary gesture of betrayal, was a sexual one. In *Salesman*, *The Crucible*, *A View from the Bridge* and *After the Fall* a breach of loyalty, a denial of the social contract, is associated with the most personal of deceits. He hinted at aspects of his own character that made this of more than metaphoric force, but his point was more fundamental. It was that a flawed social world is of a piece with a flawed private one (though in the Clinton years he was at pains to stress that sexual misdemeanours have no logical connection with political acuity or probity). The latter is at the root of an incapacitating guilt which seems to have the power to paralyse the will. And guilt seems to him a mechanism at work no less on the political level, a guilt which 'the Right found a way to exploit'. As he observed, 'A similar guilt seems to reside in all sorts of American dissidents, from Jehovah's Witnesses to homosexuals, no doubt because there is indeed an unacknowledged hostility in them toward the majority for whose cherished norms they feel contempt.'[2]

This seemed to him one possible reason for the paucity of plays addressing what he perceived as the deepening hysteria that was virtually a defining quality of the culture – that, and the difficulty of finding a convincing analogue that would give audiences a purchase on the mechanism of the process they had difficulty in seeing if only because they were so deeply involved in it. What he needed to do, he felt, as he reminded himself in a notebook entry,[3] was to find a link between public evil and private guilt, between witchcraft and adultery. He later remarked: '*The Crucible* was in part a reaction against some of the weeping surrounding *Salesman*. I wanted a more acerbic kind of a play. I wanted to create as much knowing as feeling ... they're weeping for John Proctor, but they're also seeing him. That's the ideal thing, what I've always tried to do, make them see and feel at the same time.'[4]

In both periods – 1690s, 1950s – the demands of social unity reinforced the authority of leaders and undermined the legitimacy of dissent. Miller's reaching back into that past, then, was not without its subversiveness, especially since he chose to enter a period sanctified by American myth as marking the foundation of the national spirit. Even in its origins, it appeared, American utopianism had become implicated in exclusionary politics, in an arrogation of power in the name of a national purity that could best be sustained by projecting guilt on to others. Words, as he observed, 'had gotten fearsome'.[5]

He now planned a trip to Salem, where he would consult the historical records. It was on the very eve of his visit, however, when he had just phoned to book his room in a Salem hotel, that he received a call from Elia Kazan asking to see him. It was to be during this meeting that his friend and director admitted that he had asked for a second hearing before HUAC, at which he intended to name names. That meeting, in turn, and its immediate aftermath, would remain with Miller for decades to come, as he struggled to come to terms with its implications in published and unpublished works.

When Kazan was first summoned by the Committee, receiving the subpoena at the Actors Studio at 1697 Broadway, he determined to resist its demand that he should identify those who had been fellow Party members in the 1930s. Appearing in January 1952, he answered all questions except those related to this subject. When he travelled to Hollywood for the Academy Awards in March a trade paper, the *Hollywood Reporter*, offered an account of his supposedly secret testimony. He met with Darryl Zanuck, who urged him to name names. He also met with Spyros Skouras, President of Twentieth Century Fox. *Streetcar* had been nominated for twelve Academy Awards. Kazan lost out, as did Brando. The award went to *An American in Paris*. Kazan had been warned. The previous night he had been with Marilyn Monroe. He had called her at three in the morning. That night they slept together, though she told him that she was now engaged to Joe DiMaggio. It was not a good twenty-four hours.

In March, Tennessee Williams wrote to Maria St Just from New Orleans, having just returned from the West coast:

A dreadful thing has happened about Gadg [Kazan]. It broke in one of the Hollywood columns that Gadg had once been a Communist, and almost immediately they put him in the deep freeze out there. It was timed exactly with our arrival for discussions with Warners about the new film script [*Baby Doll*]; consequently everything was stalled and obfuscated. They are waiting to see what happens next. There is even the possibility of a jail sentence if he persists in his determination not to reveal names of other party members when he was in it. This I think very admirable of him, and very brave, and all decent people ought to respect his sense of honor about it. But of course most of them don't! Of course Gadg is not a Communist now and I know has absolutely no present sympathy with the system, but the red hysteria has reached such a pitch that this disclosure may very well wreck his career as a motion-picture director. This also came at the same time as Gadg's first big failure on Broadway. The Dame [Irene Selznick]'s play, *Flight into Egypt* [by George Tabori].[6]

In April, however, and under renewed pressure, Kazan back-pedalled and asked to be heard again. He now named eight members of his Group Theatre cell, along with others. There was, to be sure, a price to be paid for refusing to cooperate with the Committee. In that same year Elizabeth Gurley Flynn refused to name names, to 'degrade or debase myself by becoming an informer', and served two thirty-day contempt sentences.[7] For Kazan, the stakes were higher. His Hollywood career was in the balance.

Larry Adler, the harmonica player, recalled meeting him at Sardi's restaurant shortly before his appearance. With two million dollars in the bank, he had assured him, nobody could make him talk. Adler, who had joined John Huston, Humphrey Bogart and others to form the Committee for the First Amendment, remembered the thrill with which he heard Kazan's words and the despair that followed when he capitulated. But he had also seen Bogart crumble, so he knew the pressures that could be brought to bear. Adler found his own concerts being cancelled, while disagreements with his wife over whether to resist the Committee or not led to the dissolution of his marriage. He ended up exiled in Britain.

Speaking to the editor and professor Victor Navasky, Kermit Bloomgarden, producer of *Death of a Salesman*, also recalled that 'any number of times in the course of the investigations Kazan would say he had been [in the Communist Party], he was not now, he wanted no part of the Communists, but if they wanted him to give names, he'd tell them where to get off. He told me that as late as six weeks before he testified.' When he decided to testify he talked to Bloomgarden again who later recalled:

He told me he'd been to Washington and met with J. Edgar Hoover and Spyros Skouras and they wanted him to give names and he was going to call the people whom he had to name. Gadg . . . wanted to know what I thought, and I said, 'Everyone must do what his conscience tells him to do.' He said, 'I've got to think of my kids.' And I said, 'This too shall pass, and then you'll be an informer in the eyes of your kids, think of that.'[8]

The two men did not speak again for fifteen years.

Bloomgarden called Miller and told him that he was ninety-nine per cent convinced that Kazan was going to name names. It was 2 April 1952. It seemed to Miller that he saw his wife Molly behind the decision, along with his desire to protect his career. Psychologically, here was a chance for Kazan to purge his sexual betrayals by displacing them on to a confession of political errors, and thus return to respectability. Here was a chance to come in from the cold.

Kazan then telephoned Miller several times and, finally getting through, asked to talk to him, though without explaining what their meeting would be about. For his part, Miller had been loath to pick up the phone, fearing confirmation of Bloomgarden's prediction. In the end he took the call and agreed to see him.

He drove to Kazan's Connecticut home, an hour out of New York, in his green Raymond Loewy-designed Studebaker convertible. It was, as he later recalled, November, and raining. In fact it must have been April. The trees, which he remembered as stripped of their leaves, were so not because it was autumn but because spring was late. When he arrived, he pulled into the driveway, shut off his engine and sat for a while, dreading what was to come, aware that his life was about to change.

When he went into the newly built house he was met by Molly Kazan, pale-faced, a tall New Englander with bobbed hair wearing a beige blouse and tan slacks. He had never found his relationship with her an easy one and she evidently felt much the same. He had always been perplexed as to why Kazan and Molly had married. In many ways they were opposites, as he and Mary had been. He was the immigrant, she the true American. He was the id, she the ego. He relied on her precisely for her conservatism, which attracted and repelled him to equal degrees.

Kazan was in his studio with Vivien Leigh, working, as Miller later assumed, on her role as Blanche in the forthcoming film version of *A Streetcar Named Desire*. In fact his memory was again faulty since the film had been released the previous year. It was shot between August and November 1950 and released by Warner Brothers in September 1951. Molly asked why he was going to Salem. He explained that he was researching a play about witchcraft. She said nothing. At that moment, Miller said later, he knew that Kazan planned to name names.

When Kazan and Leigh came in he was introduced to her and then Kazan invited him outside. The rain had stopped, though the sky was still grey and threatening another downpour. Miller later recalled sitting on a rock while Kazan explained his plans, having warned him at the outset that by the time he had finished Miller might not be his friend any more.

He explained that he had long since abandoned his radicalism and was now against both the Party and the Soviet Union. The Committee was right to be alarmed at what was a genuine conspiracy, and for his part he wished to live openly, making clear his stance and hence cooperating. What struck Miller was that he was prepared to name as communists those with whom he had worked in the Group Theatre many years earlier quite as if they were foreign agents and a genuine threat to the state. Miller knew well enough that they, too, would long since have abandoned their youthful radicalism, but what was at stake was a public act of betrayal that Kazan was presenting as a moral act. His guilt and embarrassment had somehow transmuted into rectitude, a heroic resistance to those radicals and fellow travellers who he knew would be appalled by what they would see as his treachery.

Kazan then told him that Spyros Skouras had indicated that unless he cooperated with the Committee he would have no career in films. Miller replied that he would still have the theatre, where the blacklist was less effective. There seemed nothing more to say. But another thought was in Miller's mind.

Had Kazan known that he had been involved with the Party, he would have offered his name up along with the rest. After a long silence, Miller told him that he was making a mistake. Kazan disagreed. They walked back to the house in silence.

This encounter would remain a key moment in Miller's life. About to leave for Salem, he was confronted with a friend seeking absolution for an act of betrayal. On the other hand, both men knew that they had themselves been betrayed by an idea, by a utopian proposition turned dystopic. If old loyalties were to be abandoned in favour of new ones, those old loyalties, they both knew, had been misplaced. In the name of what, then, was Kazan asked to sacrifice his career? To Miller, though, there was another loyalty, not merely to those who were to pay the price for this exorcism of the past, but to the past itself, his own past, his sense of who he had been and what had once been the driving force of his work. And beyond that, there was the more private betrayal that could make a moralistic stance less than convincing.

In the end, though, it was not loyalty to dead causes, whether private or public, that was at stake. It was a willingness to offer up others as the acknowledged cost not so much of expiation as of personal immunity. Kazan had persuaded himself that the price was worth paying, that a sinner who confesses not only his own sins but those of others thereby brings those others to salvation. Or perhaps not. In subsequent years, he was by no means clear as to his motives. He had bad dreams. As for Miller, his immediate reaction owed something to his awareness of his own vulnerability, if not to Kazan then to others who might recall his presence at communist meetings and offer him up as part of a secular ritual of exorcism.

Unsurprisingly, the conversation was remembered differently by the two men, but Miller recognized the dilemma of a man who seemed effectively to have turned his back on the theatre and committed himself to Hollywood, where careers could be more easily terminated. Miller, like Bloomgarden, recalls reassuring Kazan that times would change, suggesting that he would live to regret any actions he might take under pressure from the Committee. He was torn between pity for a friend and an awareness that that friend could be dangerous.

As he left, Molly walked him back to his car, wearing no coat despite the rain. Miller was still stunned, convinced that the Kazans were both now his enemies and that they would not hesitate to destroy him if it served their purpose. Above all, Molly wanted security and Miller represented those who might cause her to lose it. He opened the car door and got behind the wheel.

Molly was more his enemy than he had realized, having dismissed not only key aspects of *Death of a Salesman* but also, though unbeknown to him, the screenplay on which he had placed such reliance, describing *The Hook* as 'lousy'. Now, as he prepared to research a play that could only condemn her husband and thereby herself, he had become a threat. And she was not a woman to accept public condemnation. It was she, indeed, who would draft the public document that Kazan would release to explain his decision and defend his public stance.

As Miller turned on the engine, she leaned into the car and, bizarrely, asked him whether he knew that communists controlled the United Electrical Workers and that everyone was on her husband's side. He, she suggested, was stuck in the past. For his part, he told her he thought her husband would regret his action and that it was wrong. He drove off towards Salem leaving her in the rain. At the same time he felt that he was not well placed to advise anyone what to do, having, as it seemed to him, retreated too willingly into his work rather than openly challenge an errant power. He had a fear of being used, and a sense of disgust when he was so used – an odd feeling for a man who had in truth played a very public role, lending his name to a meteor shower of protests and statements while making speeches at public rallies, but the private admission of fear is revealing. If Kazan did not know the details of Miller's involvement with the Party, the playwright himself was all too aware of his own vulnerability.

Kazan's memory was that Miller understood his dilemma, while insisting that he was naive. Most significantly, he recalled being embraced by him and offered reassurance: 'Don't worry about what I'll think. Whatever you do will

be OK with me. Because I know your heart is in the right place.'⁹ The phrase
was so striking that Kazan claims to have noted it in his diary. A few months
later, according to Kazan, Miller refused to acknowledge him when they met.
Bloomgarden's memory, presumably based on a conversation with Miller
since he did not see Kazan at that time, was that 'Miller told him he would
regret it for the rest of his life and tried to talk him out of what he was going
to do. When he couldn't, Gadg went to Washington and Miller went right
up to Salem and wrote *The Crucible*.'¹⁰

In 1999, Miller recalled an interview given by Kazan (on WNBC's *Speaking
Freely*) in 1972 in which he claimed he had no fear of blacklisting by Hollywood
since he had the theatre to turn to. It was entirely at odds with his own
memory not only of Kazan telling him of Skouras's warning, but of Kazan's
own insistence, during their walk in the woods, that the theatre no longer
interested him. Miller's own account, as given in *Timebends*, he maintained,
had been accurate. In truth, Kazan had himself confessed to the pressure
from Skouras, noting in his diary that in a 'conversation with Art Miller, in
the woods back of my home, I mentioned that Skouras had implied I couldn't
work in pictures any more if I didn't name the other lefties in the Group'.¹¹ In
a 1999 interview, however, he flatly contradicted himself, stating that such an
idea was 'an outright lie. He never did that to anybody. He didn't put any
pressure on me to do anything. He couldn't have. I wasn't pressurable by those
people.'¹²

What is significant is less the differing memories of a traumatic moment
than the fact that the Committee's activities had the power to break friendships as well as end careers, that it co-opted individual consciences and offered
its own definitions of right behaviour. HUAC insisted that people deny the
substance of their own identities in so far as it required them to deny the
validity of their past. It made idealism, even a wrongheaded idealism, an
agent of its own politics. Its activities were also less an attempt to expose
history and its processes than to exact revenge on those who had shaped it.
The New Dealers who had rescued American capitalism were now its hidden
enemies. The State Department had plotted against the Constitution that its
employees were sworn to uphold. Artists had sought to divide a united nation
by promulgating class warfare.

Miller was not the only person Kazan consulted before offering his testimony. He met Lillian Hellman at the Plaza Hotel, explaining that he had
talked to Miller and told him that though naming names would be a blow to
his career he could manage without Hollywood. Miller, he said, had 'shown
understanding'. Her response was to call Kermit Bloomgarden from the
restaurant's pay phone and, on his advice, leave.

He chose to break the news to Clifford Odets, whom he also intended to
name, at another restaurant, The Lobster, off Broadway. He told him that

without his permission he would refuse to testify and abandon Hollywood for the theatre, only to discover that Odets also intended to testify. Paula Miller (later Mrs Lee Strasberg) made no objection to being named, while declaring that she could not do so herself. Her husband, however, suggested that he had no alternative. Kazan told one other person, 'who told me to go screw myself'.[13] As a result, he decided to go ahead, without consulting the others he would name, a fact that, several decades later, still left him feeling guilty. In 1988, he observed:

> in the body of my conviction, there appeared the worm of doubt. I still believed what I'd done was correct, but no matter that my reasons had been sincerely founded and carefully thought out, there was something indecent – that's how I felt it, as shame – in what I'd done and something murky in my motivations. What I'd done was correct, but was it right? What self-concerns were hidden in the fine talk, how powerful a role had my love of filmmaking, which I'd been discounting, played in what I'd done? I felt unresolved, alternately humiliated then resentful of those who criticized me.

He did not consult the others because he knew what their response would be. Speaking in 2002, Phoebe Carnovsky (wife of Morris, and recruited into the Party by Kazan as Phoebe Brand) explained that there were only two people she could never forgive – Hitler and Kazan. The news that she and her husband had been named came as a total shock:

> We were terrified ... we didn't know how far they would go, what measures they would take. We had been through the war, the whole Hitler thing, and we wondered whether it was going to happen all over again, that fascism. It was a dirty business. Our lives were changed completely. We had to leave California. The Actors' Lab came under pressure and had to be closed. We moved to New York. It was a terrible, terrible time.[14]

The Actors' Lab was where Marilyn Monroe had studied in her attempt to reinvent herself as a serious actress.

Phoebe Carnovsky was doubly angry because her husband had in fact not, she insisted, been a member of the Party. She had been, because in the 1930s 'I felt there was no hope and labour couldn't get anywhere. There had to be another way.' Now, suddenly, their lives had come close to being ruined. She despised Kazan: 'I have never spoken to him since, never wanted to have anything to do with him.'[15] When, nearly fifty years later, an Academy Award was offered to Kazan, she was fiercely opposed to it.

The Actors' Laboratory had already been the subject of an FBI investigation, goaded by Louella Parsons, the Hollywood gossip columnist who, like Walter Winchell, had a close relationship with the Bureau. In a 1949 radio broadcast she had revealed that 'the FBI is keeping very close watch on a certain little theatre group ... infested with Communists'.[16] Even so, it survived until Kazan's testimony effectively closed it down.

There are few references to Carnovsky in Kazan's autobiography, and those there are are dismissive. He was, he claimed, a 'self-righteous prig'.[17] Kazan does not take the opportunity to identify him there as a communist, though the actor Larry Parks had named him in his testimony in 1951, while Sterling Hayden had admitted attending Party meetings at Carnovsky's house, though always in his absence. Lee Cobb also remembered such meetings. The Carnovkys survived by forming their own theatre group and travelling the country, but they never forgot or forgave.

When the 1999 Academy Award was announced, Rod Steiger, who had appeared in *On the Waterfront*, stated that neither age nor ability could absolve Kazan of what he considered a crime. Miller was more forgiving, balancing his brilliance as a director against what he still insisted was his moral failure. At the award ceremony, many refused to applaud. The right wing, however, in the form of the Ayn Rand Institute and Charlton Heston ('sometimes the good guys win'), celebrated. The *Washington Post* and William Kristol's conservative *Weekly Standard* saw the occasion as a triumph for anti-communism and a belated rectification of an injustice. Forty-seven years on, the events of 1952 were not forgotten.

Another named by Kazan in that year was Tony Kraber. Even Lee Cobb was shocked: 'How could you name Tony Kraber – a selfless man, a Band-Aid if you scratch yourself? It didn't sit well.'[18] Dalton Trumbo was equally disgusted: 'He brought down people in the theatrical and film world who had much more to lose than he and much less ability to function than he. And that is not nice ... Why did he bother to kill Tony Kraber?' When Kraber was fired from CBS Kazan remarked, 'I believed then and do now that Communists should not be in positions of control in communications.'[19] Years later, he dreamed of visiting Kraber, and of there being no rancour between them:

> Then I half woke ... and I thought what a terrible thing I'd done: not the political aspect of it, because maybe that was correct; but it didn't matter now, correct or not; all that mattered was the human side of the thing. I said to myself, 'You hurt another human being, and friend of yours and his family, and no "political aspect" matters two shits' ... I felt ashamed. I knew my dream was expressing a regret and a wish ... How is the world better for what I did? It had just been a game of power and influence, and I'd been taken in and twisted my true self ... As for why I'd done it, I couldn't look at that any more.[20]

Whatever his later feelings, in 1952, and with Skouras's warning ringing in his ears, he had felt no such scruple.

In October 1953, Miller tried out some speeches for a play, eleven years later to emerge as *After the Fall*, in which he staged a conversation between what was clearly Kazan (here, as in that play, named Mickey) and one of those with whom he had met before making his disclosures. The Kazan figure offers a virtual paraphrase of his speech to Miller in the woods outside his Connecticut home, insisting to the man he is about to betray that his motives are pure. He replies by reminding Mickey of the reasons they had been radicals. It was businessmen who denounced Roosevelt as a communist, he insists, and who in Germany financed a fascism which in turn killed Americans. It is no more than a fragment, but says something about Miller's own state of mind as he underlines the integrity of feelings that may have been overtaken by events but had a history and a justification. Kazan, he implies, betrayed something more than other people. He betrayed values. He betrayed a personal and a public past.

Kazan remained something of a mystery to Miller. His testimony created a stir which that of Jerome Robbins or Lee J. Cobb did not. It was, Miller thought, because he seemed an exemplar of the Communist anti-Fascist resistance. He was one of the secular saints. What was odd about this was that though people thought of him as a militant, Miller himself had never been aware of any militant activities, simply being convinced of his militancy by his demeanour. There was no doubt in 1952, however, that an angel had fallen from the heavens.

There was, of course, more than a tincture of truth in the accusations that HUAC directed at those it summoned. There were agents, there were those whose faith in working-class solidarity blinkered them to the manipulations of those who worked covertly for the victory of an ideology. But the Committee had no real interest in history or fine distinctions. Whenever witnesses sought to reconstitute the historical circumstances that gave meaning to their actions they found themselves silenced, and those actions severed from their context. The crisis of capitalism, the urgencies of poverty, the logic of European conflicts, were not the point. What mattered was who had supped with the Devil and who might, by confession and testimony, give strength to those who wished to purge themselves and hence the land.

There were those, formerly of the Left, who readily embraced the concept of a necessary confession from what they presented as a liberal position. Thus, Leslie Fiedler – a former member of the Young Communist League and the Socialist Workers' Party, who wrote an article on the Rosenbergs for *Encounter* which shocked even its CIA paymasters – declared: 'The confession in itself is nothing, but without the confession . . . We will not be able to move forward from a liberalism of innocence to a liberalism of responsibility.'[21] The issue, as far as the CIA was concerned, was not the rights and wrongs of the Rosenberg case but that *Encounter* might have its cover blown, and certainly on reading this piece T.S. Eliot thought that its American sponsorship was beginning to show.

Confession could prove destructive not just for those whose names were so recklessly revealed. Kazan proved resilient; Odets did not. As Kazan observed, it 'hurt Clifford mortally. He was never the same after he testified. He gave away his identity when he did that ... It choked off the voice he'd had.'[22] Why did it not do the same for Kazan? In part, surely, because he had swiftly abandoned his radicalism; but in part, also, because his ambition was as unclouded by guilt as it was by political commitment.

On 10 April Kazan attended an Executive Hearing of HUAC, the details of which were released the following day. Before appearing, he was offered copies of the testimony of three friendly witnesses, Budd Schulberg, Edward Dmytryk and Richard Collins. In his prepared statement, Kazan declared: 'I have come to the conclusion that I did wrong to withhold these names before, because secrecy serves the Communists and is exactly what they want. The American people need the facts and all the facts about all aspects of Communism in order to deal with it wisely and effectively. It is,' he concluded, 'my obligation as a citizen to tell everything that I know.'[23] He then listed the Party members from his time with the Group Theatre. There were eight, including J. Edward Bromberg, Morris and Phoebe Carnovsky, Clifford Odets and Paula Miller.

Their function, he explained, had been to turn the Group Theatre into a communist mouthpiece, the same Group Theatre whose productions Arthur Miller had watched with such a sense of awe in the 1930s. Kazan recalled later: 'I used to go downtown to Twelfth Street, where their [the Communist Party's] headquarters were, get orders and go back like a good ritualized lefty and try to carry them out.'[24] He had directed plays that effectively denounced Roosevelt, including *The Young Go First*, which had stressed the inequities of the New Deal, and this despite his respect for the President. The Party also told him to seek to gain a toehold in Actors' Equity and demand that actors be paid for rehearsal time. This last objective, hardly a radical one, was achieved but the Party had failed in its greater purpose. Beyond that, he explained, he had worked with the League of Workers Theatres (later the New Theatre League) and the Theatre of Action. Again he named names.

The Party, Kazan continued, had failed to take over the Group Theatre because its other directors – Harold Clurman, Lee Strasberg and Cheryl Crawford – were not members and remained in control. He had himself left the Party, he explained, when he was instructed to apologize for political errors. While he might have signed statements or appeals, he no longer did so as a communist. He had also, he conceded, continued to support the Hollywood Ten as late as August 1950, but had become 'disgusted by the silence of the Ten' and by their 'contemptuous attitude'.[25] He did not, he maintained, attend the Waldorf Peace Conference, the conference that Miller had attended in 1949, and his invoking of this occasion, about which he was not questioned, may indeed have been designed precisely to put some space between him and the playwright with whom he was so closely associated. But then again, perhaps he felt constrained to make the point because his wife's name had appeared as a sponsor, though without her permission, he claimed.

Miller, meanwhile, had been in Salem, driving there from his encounter with Kazan. Reading the archive records of the witch-hunt, it seemed to him that the parallels were eerily precise. In both 1692 and 1952 confession and betrayal were the necessary price for inclusion in the body politic. The purging of supposed private guilt was a required public gesture. The Devil was abroad, and salvation lay in informing. Friends and neighbours were to offer one another up if their own innocence was to be affirmed.

Several days later, on his way back from Salem to New York, he turned on the car radio and heard news of Kazan's appearance before HUAC and the names he had offered. He felt numb and then angry. The reports were repeated every half-hour, but in his autobiography he claims not to have recognized the names Kazan mentioned. Since they were mostly members of the Group Theatre, this would seem to be a faulty memory. Miller's subsequent explanation, not very convincing, was that while he knew the names of the people identified by Kazan he had not known them personally.

He had begun sketching out *The Crucible* before travelling to Salem, uncertain, as yet, that it could be made to work:

> I was not at all sure I could write this play when I went up there. It represented formidable technical difficulties that I wasn't at all sure I could manage. There must have been three or four hundred people involved in this whole thing. Clearly I was going to have to symbolize enormous amounts of the story if it was to make sense. I wasn't sure I could do that. Then there was the question of the language. It couldn't be written in contemporary English but at the same time the little of it that I had read would be difficult to comprehend, a post-Elizabethan English. I thought I could help make up my mind as to what to do if I went up there and discovered the original documents, so that I could especially study the language.[26]

Looking back nearly a quarter of a century later, he was inclined to see the sense of betrayal he had felt in his interview with Kazan, and again as he listened on the car radio to the list of those he had effectively denounced, as explaining a basic theme of his work: betrayal and the need to discover a basis for the restoration of integrity.

The shock of Kazan's betrayal, he now felt, had come from the feelings of intimacy he had inspired in actors and friends, from his authority as a moral leader; and now from the fact that it was clear that, for all his rhetoric, he would never allow himself to be put at risk. Kazan could, Miller said, smell the Devil in any human soul and knew how to pander to whatever need he detected there. It was why so many felt betrayed. He had affected to understand them, as he had affected to understand the world, while in fact, it now seemed, he had merely played people for fools, staging planned retreats from commitments, private and public. Miller knew that Kazan had scented the footsteps of the Devil in his soul.

Speaking on television in 1988, in response to a question as to why he had decided to name names, Kazan replied, 'I thought it over very carefully. I went one way and swayed the other way. I differ from some of my friends in that I think Congress has an absolute right to investigate anything like that, like the Communist Party in this country. I don't agree with the phrase "witchhunt". I think it's baloney. It suggests that they are being hunted. They were there, in the State Department, in the unions.'[27]

Back in 1952, on 12 April, he publicly defended his stance with regard to the Committee by publishing an advertisement in the *New York Times*. He was not the only person to adopt this strategy. José Ferrer, in line for an Academy Award, also took out an advertisement asserting that he was not a communist and supporting the continued existence of the Committee. Edward G. Robinson declared that the tribunal was the only place an American citizen could hope to clear his name of false accusations. In his own advertisement, Kazan spoke of having been lured into the Party during the Depression, and confirmed his subsequent rejection of it. He then emphasized the current need for right-minded people to follow his lead in speaking out. The text, drafted by Molly, is extensive, but what follows conveys the essence of what is plainly offered as a justification rather than an apologia:

In the past weeks intolerable rumors about my political position have been circulating in New York and Hollywood. I want to make my stand clear:

I believe that Communist activities confront the people of this country with an unprecedented and exceptionally tough problem. That is, how to protect ourselves from a dangerous and alien conspiracy and still keep the free, open, healthy way of life that gives us self-respect. I believe that the American people can solve this problem wisely only if they have the facts about Communism. All the facts.

Now, I believe that any American who is in possession of such facts has the obligation to make them known, either to the public or to the appropriate Government agency.

Whatever hysteria exists – and there is some, particularly in Hollywood –

is inflamed by mystery, suspicion and secrecy. Hard and exact facts will cool it.

The facts I have are sixteen years out of date, but they supply a small piece of background to the graver picture of Communism today. I have placed these facts before the House Committee on Un-American Activities without reserve and I now place them before the public and before my co-workers in motion pictures and in the theatre.

Seventeen and a half years ago I was a twenty-four-year-old stage manager and bit actor, making $40 a week, when I worked. At that time nearly all of us felt menaced by two things: the depression and the ever growing power of Hitler.

The streets were full of unemployed and shaken men. I was taken in by the Hard Times version of what might be called the Communists' advertising or recruiting technique. They claimed to have a cure for depressions and a cure for Nazism and Fascism.

I joined the Communist Party late in the summer of 1934. I got out a year and a half later. I have no spy stories to tell, because I saw no spies. Nor did I understand, at that time, any opposition between American and Russian national interest. It was not even clear to me in 1936 that the American Communist Party was abjectly taking its orders from the Kremlin.

What I learned was the minimum that anyone must learn who puts his head in the noose of party 'discipline'. The Communists automatically violated the daily practices of democracy to which I was accustomed. They attempted to control thought and to suppress personal opinion. They tried to dictate personal conduct. They habitually distorted and disregarded and violated the truth. All this was crudely opposite to their claims of 'democracy' and the 'scientific approach'.

He had not, he explained, told the story earlier out of a misplaced belief that not to do so was to defend civil liberties, the right to hold and express unpopular views.

I have thought soberly about this. It is, simply, a lie. Secrecy serves the Communists. At the other pole, it serves those who are interested in silencing liberal voices. The employment of a lot of good liberals is threatened because they have allowed themselves to become associated with or silenced by the Communists. Liberals must speak out.

In one sense it is hard to fault Kazan's description of the Party and its methods. It was everything he said it was, though if he did not understand back then that it was abjectly taking orders from the Kremlin it is hard to know who he thought it was taking orders from. Certainly he himself, as he acknowledged, took his orders, abjectly or not, from the Party headquarters in New York and never questioned their legitimacy. However, he was going a step further. It was, it seems, not the Committee that was silencing liberals but the communists. If a liberal refused to name names out of fear of, or loyalty to, the communists, it was the fault not of the Committee but of those communists who as a consequence lost him his employment. As for himself, 'first hand experience of dictatorship and thought control' had left him, he said, with an abiding hatred of communist philosophy and methods. It also left him

> with the passionate conviction that we must never let the Communists get away with the pretense that they stand for the very things which they kill in their own countries.
>
> I am talking about free speech, a free press, the rights of property, the rights of labor, racial equality and, above all, individual rights. I value these things. I take them seriously. I value peace, too, when it is not bought at the price of fundamental decencies.
>
> I believe these things must be fought for wherever they are not fully honored and protected whenever they are threatened. The motion pictures I have made and the plays I have chosen to direct represent my convictions.
>
> I expect to continue to make the same kinds of pictures and to direct the same kinds of plays.[28]

The declaration stunned Miller. The Committee had become the fount of virtue and the communists simple villains. Kazan was washed clean by a simple act of betrayal represented as civic duty and thus sought re-entry into the ranks of the blessed – though surely, Miller thought, at the price of a self-hatred that would eventually corrode his sense of himself. He could not stand the idea of banishment and loss of power, a power which he exerted as a director but also in terms of sexual relationships in which his cruel disregard was part of the allure.

The nature of the disagreement between Miller and Kazan became a little clearer in an exchange of letters between Molly Kazan and Miller. Hers is dated 10 April, the day of her husband's testimony. This is crossed through and the 11th substituted, the day he published his paid advertisement. The typewritten letter itself, however, refers to the 12th, so it appears to be a communication that she hesitated to let go. It begins as a response to Miller's proposed new play but, in effect, is a defence of her husband's decision to become a friendly witness:

> Dear Artie,
>   I love you because facts disturb you.
>   Fact. There are no witches.
>   That is the peculiar and horrifying fact at the dead center of the Salem

story. It's the eerie vacuum at the middle of the storm. It's a Henry James story, if James had allowed violence. Several towns and a lot of villages suspended normal operation and went more or less mad for a year and a half while they denounced and persecuted and executed people for being witches. And there ain't no sucha thing. As you say in Bklyn.

Fact. There are Communists.

Fact. It is a little difficult to find out who they are.

Fact. You don't pretend that the analogy between witch-hunting and Communist-hunting can be stretched very far. But it is the analogy and nothing but the analogy which set you to looking up the history. (Speculation: it turned out not to be quite as good an analogy as you anticipated.) It's the analogy and nothing else which keeps the subject in your head. If you write about it, what you write will be taken as an analogy and nothing else.

You've got to write about anything you damned well want to.

Fact. A faulty and patchwork analogy isn't a taking-off point for a good, healthy, strong statement.

* * *

Why do you pick this?
Nothing's accident. S. Freud.

* * *

Has it anything to do with the fact that this is a subject that bypasses the hard questions? That it isolates the question of hysteria? You're against hysteria? So're 98% of the population. But by picking this subject, in vacuo (in Salem it really was an emotional phenomenon, deriving chiefly from another emotional phenomenon, Puritan repression, and the links to material things were secondary and slight) you really avoided examining today's facts. YOU avoid them.

You bypass every question that really troubles honest people. What caused hysteria? How much hysteria? What'll cool the hysteria? Exactly what facts are there to cause alarm? Do you want to imply that there's no fire at all under the smoke that's causing the panic?

* * *

God damn it, Artie. The last twelvemonth, more and more, you've gotten to feeling that you're in a corner – a little threatened corner, away from the mainstream of the people of this country.

I don't think that's where you belong.

I think that's what makes writing hard.

You're a tough-minded, sensitive, fact-minded, honest writer. Don't you trust the people? You think the truth has to be edited for them?

They'll take the truth from you, if it's the whole, nothing but.

In the end the people are going to settle the whole civil rights, free speech issue. Not the Committee – which at least is extracting a few facts, to some benefit, I think. I believe there ought to be more facts and more kinds of facts out in the open. Or how the hell can people make up their minds and act sensibly?

As of this morning – April 12 – with Gadg's story on the street – I'm not resentful of the whole episode. I'm relieved. It's good to have a sort of muzzle of silence lifted. I'm grateful, in spite of all the tension, etc., that in the highly imperfect working of this democracy, he got forced to a showdown – with himself

Basta.

With love --

Molly

Scrawled on the side was a further, handwritten, note in which she observed that the witch-hunt had been brought to a conclusion under a good if imperfect form of government.

In his lengthy reply, Miller offered a description of the historical circumstances of the Salem affair, reminding her that while there had indeed been no witches there had been few who would have claimed, or even believed, as much. What he was writing about in *The Crucible*, he explained, was precisely the hysteria that could seize a society, a paranoia fanned by self-interest.

He then turned more directly to the real substance of the letter, which had less to do with the accuracy of the analogy than with Kazan's action in naming names. He had, he insisted, told her husband that it would be morally wrong to act out of fear – which is what he had done, the statement he had made in the *New York Times* confirming as much. *The Crucible* was to examine such fear. Gadg, he asserted, had been closer to him than any other friend, hence the distress he now felt.

Kazan was inundated with hostile letters and phone calls. So alarming was it that his wife hired a bodyguard. His own secretary left him. However, not everyone was hostile. In May 1952, John Steinbeck wrote to his editor Pascal (Pat) Covici:

Have not heard from Kazan. But I understand there is a great fuss and feathers over his statement as opposed to Hellman's. One can never know what one could do until it happens. I wonder what I would do. Isn't that strange? I understand both Hellman and Kazan. Each one is right in different ways but I think Kazan's took more courage. It is very easy to be brave and very hard to be right. Lillian can settle snugly back in a kind of martyrdom but Kazan has to live alone with his decision. I hope I could have had the courage to do what he did.[29]

Nearly three years later, in February 1955, Miller received a note from Steinbeck hoping that there might be a reconciliation between the two men:

Dear Artie:

Gadg mourns your loss with unending sorrow. Isn't there something he could do, or you could do or I could do so that you two could be together again? It is wasteful that two such men should be apart. Please do something to mend this break. You must be sad about it too. I beg you to give it a chance. I beg you.

No one knows I am writing this. I feel I have to. And I am sure he would do anything to regain your friendship.

Miller later recalled: 'It was a very moving letter. Then I met him afterwards; in fact, I think we met that evening at George Kaufman's. And as soon as I walked in, he moved over to me and grabbed me and said, "I'm sorry I wrote that. I understand you feel as you do." And I said, "Why are you sorry?" That man was always so moved with everything.'[30]

In fact, Miller jotted down a reply to Steinbeck's letter, though whether he sent it or not is unclear. In this draft letter he offers another reason for his break with Kazan, one that says something else about their relationship which he had come to feel was inherently unequal. It was, he explained, better for him not to renew his relationship with Kazan, despite everything he had meant to him. Oddly, however, it is not his naming names that was at stake. He simply felt he no longer needed him in terms of his creative life. He had no need of reassurance. Indeed, he had come to feel that the director might have begun to have a deleterious impact on his work. He himself came from a long line of entrepreneurs, self-sufficient and resistant to the opinion of others. Going back to Kazan would be like going to an empty class reunion. They had both moved on and no longer shared either aesthetic or human values.

In fact, Kazan and Miller were reconciled, briefly, at the behest of Marilyn Monroe. Madeleine Sherwood, who played Abigail in *The Crucible*, recalled:

there was a big party at the Actors Studio and Marilyn Monroe and Arthur Miller were there. I saw Marilyn Monroe take Arthur's hand and she walked across the room at the Studio and she took Elia Kazan's hand and she put their two hands together. Then she took her two hands and put them like a cradle around their hands. There was silence in the room. The music stopped. Conversation stopped. She said, 'It was the most wonderful moment of my life when those two men accepted that I had put their hands together.'[31]

Later, in 1964, they would work together on *After the Fall*, but in fact the relationship was never restored and Kazan's rationalizations for his testimony left Miller bemused and indignant. It was an indignation that would last for fifty years. He would regularly debate with himself the reasons for Kazan's actions, even speculating whether first-generation immigrants might have been more inclined to break, as if they were anxious to stake their claim, as if they were in some sense un-American and were prepared to pay what they saw as the price of inclusion. The record of Jews in front of the Committee, he noted, was mixed.

At the time, however, the issue was more immediate and personal. On 25 April 1952 Miller received a call from his sister Joan asking if he would go to a meeting at the Actors Studio. They were in some shock after Kazan's appearance before the Committee and his subsequent defence of his actions, and wanted his views. He felt very doubtful about attending. The Actors Studio, of which he was not an admirer, was in large part Kazan's invention, while his own status at such a meeting was by no means clear. After all, he had neither been summoned by the Committee nor named by Kazan. The issue, though, struck him as central to his sense of society and to the art that both reflected and engaged that society, and so he decided to go.

He explained to the assembled actors that he thought Kazan had effectively introduced a blacklist into the theatre to parallel that in Hollywood, but he hesitated to advise them as to what action they should take. The Studio, he acknowledged, had been Kazan's spiritual and real property and he understood that they did not feel it could go on without him. Yet it was evident to him that a number of the actors no longer felt they could work with him. They were unclear as to whether to resign or demand the keys to the building. The decision, it seemed to him, was theirs and he told them so. May Reis, who had been Studio secretary for five years, resigned. Later she became secretary to Marilyn Monroe and Miller. Marlon Brando declared: 'I'll never work with that sonofabitch again',[32] while contriving to do so in *On the Waterfront*.

Kazan stayed away for several months. Later in 1952 he wrote to Cheryl Crawford:

> About the Studio, I've alternated and wavered. Some days I've felt like withdrawing finally and completely. But that has been seldom and only when I felt most sensitive to the rejection and bitterness growing out of my 'stand' and reaching me in rumbles and rumors. I don't want to do anything destructive. I want to do something good. On the other hand I can't – no one could – work with unfriendly people. There are some. How many I don't know. How it will go from now on, no one can guess. I don't feel anymore like working there this minute, than I did all spring when I stayed away. However one

must count on the future with confidence rather than vengeance and I know, irrespective of how active I am, the studio is tremendously important.[33]

The American Committee for Cultural Freedom, of which Schlesinger was a member, managed simultaneously to support the idea of informing while finding the word itself offensive. It preferred the idea of 'frank testimony', and suggested that patriots should value the safety of their fellow citizens sufficiently to provide information about former communists, as even the Left would surely believe they should provide information about former fascists. Elia Kazan was invited to join the ACCF after his HUAC appearance, his name appearing on its letterhead. This was the organization that attacked Miller for being insufficiently critical of the Soviet Union.

Following his cooperation with HUAC, the ACCF was now happy to assist Kazan. Thus, when hardline anti-communists attacked the Actors Studio (which he had founded), Sol Stein, formerly of the United States Information Service and now Executive Director of the ACCF, claimed that Kazan was fulfilling the 'proper role for anti-Communists in the theatre [which] is that of missionary to their politically backward brethren who have taken much too long a time in appreciating the fact that service to front groups in this country contributes to the power of the Soviet mammoth'. Those 'who sided with the Communists in the past', Stein suggested, 'ought to be given an opportunity to direct their energies into genuinely anti-Communist enterprizes and efforts, if that is in line with their present convictions'. Kazan should offer the 'political Johnny-come-latelies an opportunity for redemption in order that their talents might be enlisted against the common enemy'.[34]

Writing in the *Daily News* in 1955, Ed Sullivan, columnist and later presenter of one of America's favourite television programmes, wrote praising Kazan's actions and pointing out that, far from doing him any harm, his stand before the Committee had been followed by success. *On the Waterfront, East of Eden, Tea and Sympathy, Cat on a Hot Tin Roof*, had been

> four giant blows in freeing the movies and the Broadway Theatre of Communist influence. Kazan loosened the Commie grip on entertainment by demonstrating that denunciation of the party didn't lead to personal disaster in the movies or in the theatre. . . .
>
> Far from being destroyed, Kazan went on to his great triumphs. In another field, that of ballet, Jerome Robbins denounced the Commies. Recently his production of *Peter Pan* on TV played to the greatest single audience in history. . . .
>
> So this season should be forever remembered as a blue-ribbon event in the movies and in the legitimate theatre, a shining experience for those of us who in earlier years fought the Commie invasion of theatre to the best of our ability.[35]

The article was duly reported in Miller's FBI file, a surprising number of entries consisting of nothing more profound than such pre-digested scraps. Indeed, many of the items of political gossip circulated by Walter Winchell, or the Hollywood grandes dames Hedda Hopper and Louella Parsons, had originally been supplied by HUAC or the FBI (by 'blind memos'), only for their newspaper articles or broadcasts to be solemnly noted and added to the relevant file in an Escher-like closed loop. The journalists frequently reciprocated, providing the Bureau with information about supposed communists.

It was at this time that Miller and Tennessee Williams met for lunch. For Williams, as for Miller, Kazan's public actions were a product of his private psychology. His multiple affairs were born out of a hatred for his wife and a desire to degrade her. He kept a separate bank account for his dealings with other women and there was, Williams suggested, a connection between such behaviour and his political betrayals. When Miller sought to continue the conversation, however, Williams deflected it – perhaps, Miller thought, because his collaboration with Kazan was too important for him to prejudice, and perhaps because he did not want to be lured into commitment.

On the subject of HUAC Williams had an equally low opinion of Kazan, but refused to sign a condemnatory letter, and, indeed, did work with him, on *Camino Real*, less than a year after his HUAC appearance – both, as Kazan commented, feeling themselves outsiders, though for different reasons. It is an ironic remark since, of course, Kazan had specifically opted to side with the majority, to come in from the cold. As to the notion that there might be a reconciliation between himself and Kazan, Miller was wary, seeing this as likely to have more calculation than friendship about it.

Kazan later confessed that 'on a personal level . . . it's a shame that I named people . . . I don't say that what I did was entirely a good thing'. In a 1972 interview he admitted to thinking that 'there is something disgusting about . . . naming names . . . If I made a mistake, then that was a mistake that was honestly made . . . when I look back on it . . . humanly I feel some regrets.'[36] Interestingly, when in October 1953 Miller tried out dialogue for what would become the figure of Mickey in *After the Fall*, he allowed him to defend himself precisely along the lines identified by Kazan.

Back in May 1952, just a month after Kazan's testimony, Clifford Odets, Miller's model of the committed playwright in the 1930s, appeared before the Committee. Howard Fast had tried to persuade him to refuse. 'He kept crying,' recalled Fast, 'and I kept saying "You don't have to do it. Nothing will happen to you. All you do in Washington is tell them to go to hell." And he said, "They'll send me to prison." I said, "They don't want to send Clifford Odets to prison." I begged him. I pleaded with him. I couldn't get to him.'[37]

In many ways Odets's political career had followed a familiar pattern. He had joined the Party inspired by the Depression and his own family background of poverty (his mother had worked in a stocking factory at the age of eleven and died a broken woman at the age of forty-eight). He had left swiftly, though not quite as swiftly as he recalled to the Committee, because he resented the Party's attempt to impose discipline upon him. His FBI file dated back to 1935. He was as forgetful as most other witnesses with respect to documents he had signed, organizations he had supported. He did name names, for the most part those already identified by Kazan, but speculated casually about others so that, ironically, it was a Committee member who warned him against guesswork.

Asked about Hanns Eisler, who had written the music for his play *Night Music*, Odets said he was an entirely apolitical friend. Eisler himself, as Eric Bentley points out, did not regard this as a friendly gesture, suggesting that in his view Odets 'behaved deplorably' before the Committee. As a result he broke off relations with him.[38]

Odets did, however, point out the difficulty faced by writers called before the Committee and asked to account for their support for various organizations:

the lines of leftism, liberalism, in all of their shades and degrees, are constantly crossing like a jangled chord on a piano. It is almost impossible to pick out which note is which note. I have spoken out on what I thought were certain moral issues of the day, and I found myself frequently on platforms with Communists that I did not know about then but evidently are now known Communists. Many of these people have some very good tunes.[39]

Even as Miller was reeling from Kazan's decision, aware of his own vulnerability, he was himself under surveillance. His FBI file contains a report which makes it evident that his movements and associates were being noted: 'It was determined that on the night of [date removed] he met with several unidentified persons at 155 Willow Street, Brooklyn, NY, several of whom were surveilled after the meeting to residence at 11 Cranberry Street, 31 Grace Court and 1 Grace Court, all Brooklyn.' The report is dated 3 July 1952.[40] 155 Willow Street was the Millers' address; 31 Grace Court was the home of W.E.B. DuBois. HUAC was also closing in on another of his associates, an actor who had starred in one of his greatest successes.

Nearly a year later, in June 1953, six months after the opening of *The Crucible*, Lee J. Cobb was called before the Committee. He had prospered in Hollywood after his days with the Group Theatre and his appearance in *Death of a Salesman*. He possessed both a car and an aircraft, gifts from his studio. The actor and writer Alvah Bessie recalls going to him for help when he had been blacklisted. They had been friends since Bessie had praised his performance in Hemingway's *The Fifth Column*, which he had reviewed as an 'antifascist play'. He was, in Bessie's view, 'a dedicated Socialist' who displayed 'what seemed to be a profound understanding of Marxist philosophy', a man who not only 'combined theory and practice' but 'had guts.'[41] He had, for example, Bessie recalled, refused to play the part of a brutish and sadistic Soviet Army officer on the grounds that 'I could no more play such a role ... than I could be an anti-Semite ... and I'm a Jew. What's more, I consider the script un-American, fascistic, and dangerous to the peace and well-being of my fellow Americans.' This, however, was before the Waldorf meeting of 1947 which instituted the Hollywood blacklist.

Cobb refused the help Bessie now requested of him, on the grounds that he was 'not solvent'. As he left, Cobb called after him, 'You're a revolutionary, you know. Go on being a revolutionary. Go on being an example to me.'

Roy Brewer, head of the International Alliance of Theatrical and Stage Employees, who had helped to sabotage Miller's screenplay *The Hook* and was an officer of the curiously named Motion Picture Alliance for the Preservation of American Ideals, also interviewed Cobb. Though not the most reliable of witnesses, he remarked: 'The only one that really lied to us was Lee J. Cobb. He told us he never was in the Party. We didn't have the proof at the time, but later on we discovered he'd lied to us. He named names afterwards, but he lied first.'[42]

Called before the Committee, Cobb did indeed testify, duly offering up details of those in the Group Theatre who had been Party members, excusing himself on the grounds that he had been influenced by their seniority. He had, he told them, been a Party member from 1941 until 1946 (he was somewhat vague), with a two-year hiatus when he was serving in the military. When asked, he added another dozen and a half names, including fellow actor Lloyd Bridges and his own wife. He also explained that he had been part of John Howard Lawson's attempt to rewrite the principles of Stanislavsky in such a way as to reflect communist ideology, but admitted that, unsurprisingly, this had been a failure (true to form, the Committee asked who Stanislavsky might be). He had also been a sponsor of the Cultural and Scientific Conference for World Peace (the Waldorf Conference). Indeed, he had signed a number of the same petitions, appeals and protests as Miller. He concluded:

> I would like to thank you [the Committee] for the privilege of setting the record straight, not only for whatever subjective relief it affords me, but if belatedly this information can be of any value in the further strengthening of our Government and its efforts at home as well as abroad, it will serve in some small way to mitigate whatever feelings of guilt I might have for having waited this long. I did hope that, in my delay to speak earlier, others of the people I have mentioned might have availed themselves of this opportunity for themselves to do likewise. I think by this time I can reasonably assume

that those who have desired to do so have taken the opportunity to make their position clear, and I can only say that I am sorry for those who haven't and that more haven't done so.[43]

He was duly thanked, in his turn, for giving the Committee the benefit of his knowledge about the communist conspiracy, this being familiar code for the Committee's absolution, a sign to his employers that he had purged himself and could now be employed without risk.

Cobb later argued that he had had little choice:

In 1953, it was they who made the deal with me. I was pretty much worn down. I had no money. I couldn't borrow. I had the expenses of taking care of the children. You are reduced to the position where you either steal or gamble, and since I'm inclined more to gamble than steal, I gambled. If you gamble for stakes where you must win, it's suicidal. You lose. And that's what happened ... When Elia Kazan testified I was shocked. I was offended. I wasn't in as deep. I thought, if I were in his boots I'd die before they'd break me ... If I had not been in need, I'd have never cooperated.[44]

Miller was not surprised by Cobb's capitulation. He was, it seemed to him, a man who desired nothing more than support and praise. He had no inner resources. Despite this, when he cast *A View from the Bridge*, Miller urged the director, Martin Rift, himself something of a militant, to hire Cobb as Eddie Carbone. Cobb turned down the offer, afraid that association with Miller would destroy his career.

The Committee had thus called both the director of *Death of a Salesman* and its principal actor. Miller might well have had reason to expect a call himself, especially since *The Crucible*, which had only just closed, was taken to be a direct challenge to its methods. In fact it was three years before the summons came, not least, presumably, because there was no clear evidence that he had been a Party member and perhaps because to take action against him at that moment would have seemed too crude and direct a response to his play (though crudeness and directness were scarcely sins of omission as far as the Committee was concerned).

Kazan continued to defend his decision to appear before HUAC, while acknowledging a sense of guilt. As he later wrote, 'The sorrow that ate me most concerned my children, how in years to come they'd have to carry the burden of my "informing" and be ashamed. This worry never eased.'[45] However, he also observed that 'I am not a forgiving man. I do not ask for the forgiveness of my enemies, nor do I forgive them and the company they keep.' Though he confessed to shame he also continued to justify himself, not least through his work on one of the period's most successful films.

Marlon Brando had to be persuaded to appear in *On the Waterfront* (he replaced Frank Sinatra) because of his revulsion at Kazan's testimony. None-theless, he found a way of dealing with the resulting atmosphere of conflict. Part of the deal was that he should have a car at four o'clock every day to take him to his analyst. The film itself, bringing together as it did so many of those who had decided to inform, turned into a justification and validation of their separate decisions, while taking as its central concerns essentially the same issues as Miller's earlier waterfront script, *The Hook*. The breach between Miller and Kazan was further widened by the decision to go ahead with *On the Waterfront*, which, as noted earlier, Miller thought suspiciously close to his script. According to Kazan, Miller's contract lawyer John Wharton announced that if he made the film he would never again direct one of his client's plays. At the time it must have seemed a hollow threat, since there seemed no possibility of that in any case.

On the Waterfront (originally called 'Crime on the Waterfront' and 'The Golden Warriors'), written by Budd Schulberg, who was also a friendly witness before HUAC, was set not in Red Hook but Hoboken, New Jersey, and was based on the story of Tony Mike DiVicenzo, who had appeared before the Waterfront Crime Commission, established in August 1953, and named those responsible for the rackets and the violence. Schulberg claimed to have finished the script before meeting Kazan in 1952 and to know nothing of *The Hook*. For Kazan, DiVicenzo offered a direct parallel to his own situation. He, after all, like Kazan, 'told the truth as no one had before. He named names. When he did that he broke the hoodlum law of silence . . . He was a rat, a squealer, a stoolie. He was ostracized . . . Friends he'd known for years didn't talk to him.' At the same time Kazan acknowledged that Schulberg felt the parallel less sharply:

> His reaction to the loss of certain friends was not as bitter as my own; he had not experienced their blackballing as frequently and intensely as I had in the neighborhood known as Broadway. I believe Budd regarded our waterfront story with greater objectivity, an objectivity I appreciated. But I did see Tony Mike's story as my own, and that connection did lend the tone of irrefutable anger to the scenes I photographed and to my work with actors. When Brando [as the protagonist Terry Malloy] at the end, yells at Lee Cobb, the mob boss, 'I'm glad what I done – you hear me? – glad what I done!' that was me saying, with identical heat, that I was glad I'd testified as I had. I'd been snubbed by friends each and every day for months in my old show-business haunts, and I'd not forgotten nor would I forgive the men, old friends some of them, who'd snubbed me, so the scene in the film where Brando goes back to the waterfront to 'shape up' again for employment and is rejected by men with whom he'd worked day after day – that, too, was my story, now told to

all the world. So when critics say that I put my story and my feelings on the screen, to justify my informing, they are right. That transference of emotion from my own experience to the screen is the merit of those scenes.

Kazan stressed that he regarded the film's central concern as being with 'a man who has sinned and is redeemed'. When he asks himself how that could be, since 'Terry's act of self-redemption breaks the great childhood taboo: don't snitch on your friends. Don't call for the cop! Our hero is a "rat", or for intellectuals, an informer', he replies, 'But that didn't seem to bother anyone in the audience ... Which is proof that Budd Schulberg struck a deep human craving there: redemption for a sinner, rescue from damnation ... That a man can turn his fate around and by an act of good heart be saved at last.' The language is revealing. On the one hand, informing is the product of a good heart; on the other, it is a sin requiring redemption.

On the Waterfront was released in 1954, three years after Budd Schulberg had appeared before the Committee, two years after Kazan had done so and just a year after Lee J. Cobb (who also appeared in the film), thereby, according to the logic of the film as Kazan saw it, redeeming themselves for the sin of communism. Schulberg's appearance had come only shortly after Miller's screenplay was rejected, and though he conducted his own lengthy research for the film, it still appears to owe a good deal to *The Hook*. Indeed it was his experience with that earlier script that led Kazan to suggest the waterfront as a possible subject for collaboration with Schulberg, who had written a screenplay based on Malcolm Johnson's Pulitzer Prize-winning series, 'Crimes on the Waterfront', called *The Bottom of the River*.

The conflict at the heart of *On the Waterfront* is essentially that in Miller's script, as attempts are made to overthrow a corrupt local union boss who gets rich on the backs of his members. In both scripts men have to bribe their way into work and are threatened with violence if they oppose those who are supposed to represent them. A number of set-pieces echo those in *The Hook*, from a scene in which the men are hired and tokens are thrown on the ground for them to fight for, to the killing of a man in the hold as cargo crashes down on him, and a moment in which a truck comes close to killing the protagonist. It was such echoes as these that convinced Miller that Schulberg and Kazan were not merely using the film to justify their political beliefs, but also borrowing aspects of the script that he had carried with him on the *Super Chief* en route to Hollywood.

On the face of it, it is hard to see why Schulberg's script did not seem as unacceptable as Miller's. The union is still seen as corrupt. Perhaps what has changed is that the key figures involved had made their public declarations of loyalty and disavowed their communist past. The political world was also changing. By 1953 the Korean War was over. For his part, Kazan was determined to go ahead with the film if only to show his old comrades, 'those who'd attacked me so viciously, that there was an anti-Communist left, and that we were the true progressives as they were not'.

Contemplating the newspaper coverage of the Oscar he received for *On the Waterfront* and the photograph of himself receiving his honour Kazan commented, 'It wasn't pretty . . . I wasn't proud of it. But you can understand that I was tasting vengeance that night and enjoying it.' *On the Waterfront* 'was my own story; every day I worked on that film, I was telling the world where I stood and my critics to go fuck themselves. As for Art Miller, the film spoke to him and to Mr John Wharton. I would forgive them both – but not that year.'

Arthur Miller remained in analysis in the early 1950s, still trying to sort out his relationship with Mary, which continued to be the source of mutual pain. She made no move towards him, nor he towards her. He felt the object of her disdain. The effect of the tension, meanwhile, was that he also felt unable to work, as if to do so would widen the gap between them. He wanted to end the analysis, which was increasingly confusing him by prompting a self-inspection that seemed to lead nowhere, and yet, at the same time, felt the need for it. What worried him most was that he was being invited to see that in some way it was his success, his talent, that stood between him and his wife and that the solution was to sacrifice that talent to his marriage in order to allow a more equitable balance of power. In a similar way, his father had wanted him to join the family business, even when it was in a state of collapse. It had been presented to him as a moral duty. To write, therefore, had seemed a betrayal. But who, at first, do you write for, if not parents and then wife? Now he was being told that it was precisely his writing, and the success it generated, that stood between himself and Mary. No wonder he began to seem suspicious of analysis, no matter how much, financially and emotionally, he had committed to it. Later, it came as a surprise to discover that Mary had become equally suspicious of its value.

The self-doubt, though, did not last long. He was quickly back at work on what would become *The Crucible*, which he was still calling 'Spirits'. By 29 May 1952, he had finished the second act. Four months later the first draft was complete and Jed Harris hired as director. Everyone, except Mary, seemed impressed. For his own part, he thought it had a tremendous moral force but doubted whether he had penetrated the essence of the situation, or managed to sustain a sense of intimacy with distant events.

The Crucible was not, then, to be directed by Kazan, who claims to have learned of this fact from a headline in the *New York Post* declaring 'Kazan Slap at Reds Cost Him Miller Play.' Instead it was in the hands of a man whose great directing days, as it seemed to Miller, were behind him but who was looking to this play to re-establish some of his credit in the theatre. Harris was, Miller noted, nearly bald, had a sloping forehead, dark, deep-set brown eyes and the grin of a jackal. His head was set on a thick neck and powerful shoulders. He was a charmer of legendary cruelty, who could not even find a home in Hollywood, a place where cruelty could be confused with talent. Friendship with him was thought to be akin to mating with a shark.

Harris was obsessed with, but baffled by, class, believing that what he brought to productions was a refined taste. He even insisted on tipping toll-booth operators. According to Miller, he resisted casting Arthur Kennedy as John Proctor because 'he stands like some Wooster, Mass., Irishman – look at his feet.' The fact that Proctor had been a farmer seemed not to register. He preferred Robert Ryan, also Irish though with better feet, but Howard Hughes refused to release him from RKO to work 'in a communist play'.

Kennedy was grudgingly accepted but Harris's view of the actor's feet had not changed, and he continued to harass him throughout rehearsals, insisting that he should stand still – a style, Miller noted, that he called 'classical' but which amounted to the actors being required to face forwards rather than towards one another. The only actor to rebel was E.G. Marshall, who turned up to rehearsals with a bottle of whisky which he steadily drank and then threw into the balcony. Harris, whose own directing style involved sudden explosions of anger, thereafter treated him with respect. The result of Harris's whims was, in Miller's view, a production that was emptied of life. It seemed to him that Harris no longer believed in the audience.

It was curious cooperating with someone he did not trust. Both men had difficulty negotiating a workable relationship, not helped when Harris telephoned in to say that he was dying, ceding his role to the playwright, only to seize it back after a few hours. As a director he was, Miller recalled, threatening. It had taken some time to cast the role of Proctor, and Miller continued rewriting the fourth act, sensing a lack of feeling in it. He began to regret granting too much power to Harris and deliberately skipped several rehearsals.

The play opened for try-outs in Wilmington, Delaware, where *The Man Who Had All the Luck* had opened nine years earlier. Happily, it did not suffer the same fate. The audience was enthusiastic. Miller, though, was unhappy with the performance, which seemed to him cold and inert. When it arrived at the Martin Beck Theatre in New York, and despite a reported nineteen curtain calls, it scarcely seemed any warmer. Certainly Miller felt a chill go over the audience as they began to realize the pertinence of what they initially took to be an historical drama. At the end of the play he stood in the lobby, something he had never done before, but only a few walked up to him, and then with some trepidation. He knew the production's weaknesses, but the response was clearly not a matter of aesthetics. Some of those who had turned out to see the new Arthur Miller play plainly felt uncomfortable, even compromised, as they were invited to share the playright's evident revulsion for witch-hunting, the state's determination to see informing as evidence of innocence, and conformity to received opinion as the price of inclusion.

How to balance the curtain calls with his sense of the audience's alienation? By now he felt able to distinguish first-night rituals from genuine response. The applause, it seemed to him, was in part no more than a relieved lapse into conventional behaviour. He had watched and felt their response throughout the play and was in no doubt as to their sense of shock and alienation. It is tempting to feel that his own apprehension may have magnified his feeling of dismay, were it not for the brevity of the play's run.

In the end it extended to only 197 performances – not unrespectable, but a long way from the 328 of *All My Sons* and 742 of *Death of a Salesman*. Meanwhile, the revenge of the Right was not long in coming. When he was due to fly to Brussels in March 1954 for the opening of the French-language version of the play, he was refused renewal of his passport under regulations denying passports to persons believed to be supporting the communist movement, whether or not they were members of the Party. It would be five years before his passport was once again valid for travel.

It was a challenge he took up, speaking, in an address to the Newspaper Guild, against John Foster Dulles's refusal of passports for journalists wishing to travel to China: and, in a speech to the National Council of Arts, Sciences and Professions, regretting what seemed to him to be the self-censorship that led writers to ignore the business of blacklisting now affecting all aspects of American culture. Meanwhile, and quietly, E.G. Marshall, who had played the Reverend Hale, and Beatrice Straight who had played Elizabeth Proctor in *The Crucible*, were blacklisted.

Laurence Johnson, the owner of four grocery stores in Syracuse, New York, and hardly at the hub of American affairs, threatened to place signs in his stores alongside products advertised on television, indicating that the sponsors employed communists. That the reaction of this obscure individual should have succeeded in creating pressure for a blacklist, and that both actors lost television work, says almost as much as *The Crucible* itself about the times. Straight later cleared herself by paying $500 to a Catholic priest, apparently in a position of influence.[46] Meanwhile, rather than support its members' challenge to such treatment, the Federation of Television and Radio Artists decided in 1955 to support HUAC.

In 1692 nineteen men and women and two dogs were convicted of witchcraft and hanged in a small village in eastern Massachusetts. By the standards of our own time, if not of that, it was a minor event, a spasm of judicial violence concluded within a matter of months. The bodies were buried in shallow graves, or not at all as a further gesture that the convicted had forfeited participation not only in the community of man in this life, but in the community of saints in the next. Just how shallow those graves were is evident from the fact that the people buried there were not eradicated from history: their names remain with us to this day. In Arthur Miller's hands the ghosts of those who died have proved real enough, even if the witches they were presumed to be were little more than fantasies conjured by a mixture of fear, ambition, frustration, jealousy and perverted pride.

In 1957 the Massachusetts General Court passed a resolution stating that 'no disgrace or cause for distress' attached itself to the descendants of those indicted, tried and sentenced. Declaring the proceedings to be 'the result of popular hysterical fear of the Devil', the resolution noted that 'more civilized laws' had superseded those under which the accused had been tried. It did not, though, include by name all those who had suffered, and it was not until 1992 that these omissions were rectified in a further resolution of the Court. It had taken exactly three hundred years for the state to acknowledge its responsibility.

This was the long-delayed end of a story whose beginnings lay in the woods surrounding the village of Salem, when a number of young girls were discovered, with a West Indian slave called Tituba, dancing and invoking spirits. To deflect punishment from themselves they accused others; and those who listened, themselves insecure in their authority, acquiesced, partly because it served their interests to do so and partly because they inhabited a world in which witchcraft was a feature of their cosmology. Their universe was absolute, lacking in ambivalence. There was only one text to consult and that text reserved only one fate for witches.

Why should it have taken so long to acknowledge error? More significantly, why offer apology at all for an event so long in the past? Perhaps because the needs of justice and the necessity for sustaining the authority of the court have not always been coincident, and because there will always be those who defend the latter believing that by doing so they sustain the former. Perhaps because there are those who believe that authority is all of a piece and that to challenge it anywhere is to threaten it everywhere.

It was not the first such apology. In 1711 the then Governor of Massachusetts, acting on behalf of the General Court of the province, set his hand to a 'reversal of attainder', which offered restitution for this miscarriage of justice. In particular he granted £150 damages to John and Elizabeth Proctor. Elizabeth had survived, by virtue of the child she carried. Her husband was not so lucky. He was executed on 19 August 1692. His accusers were young girls, barely yet on the verge of puberty. Perversely, damages were paid not only to the victims but also to those like William Good, who was his wife's accuser, and Abigail Hobbs, a 'confessed witch' who became a hostile witness. The events, it seemed, were to be treated as a general calamity from which all suffered and in which the state was essentially innocent. Indeed the whole affair was ascribed to 'the Influence and Energy of the Evil Spirits so great at that time', a time which, despite the declared purpose of the document, was described as being 'Infested with a horrible Witchcraft'.

Samuel Parris had spent many years as a merchant in Barbados before moving to Boston in 1680 and thence to Salem, in 1688, as minister, bringing with him two slaves, Tituba and John Indian. There were factions that made his position less than satisfactory. He was vulnerable, therefore, when his own home seemed invaded by a mysterious force. His nine-year-old daughter Betty and eleven-year-old niece Abigail Williams, wishing to discover who they might marry, apparently with the help of an egg and a glass, became frightened and acted in a decidedly odd way.

Urged on by a neighbour, Tituba and John Indian baked a witch cake, consisting of the girls' urine and rye meal, urine cake being regarded as a reasonable device in such circumstances. And it was a touch more palatable than that prescribed for a distracted woman a few years earlier by a Salem doctor. His notebook contained the following recipe: 'Tak milk of a Nurse that gives suck to a male Child and also take a hee Catt and cut of one of his Ears or a peece of it and lett it blede into the milk and then lett the sick woman drink it. Do this three times.'[47] Once, you might think, would have been enough.

The urine cake was then fed to a dog in an effort to discover the witch. The dog's reaction can be imagined; the girls' reaction was to accuse Tituba of assault, in particular of pinching them, a familiar punishment for children in Puritan times. When Tituba confessed that her former Barbadian mistress had herself been a witch, the situation became more serious, not least when Abigail suggested that forty witches had met in Parris's house to commune with the Devil.

A key aspect of the events in Salem, and one stressed by Miller, was the sudden sense of licensed anarchy. Ministers, grey-haired senior citizens, public figures, saw their authority challenged and negated by the mere invoking of invisible forces. They thought to control and contain it, but instead found themselves no more than its agents and potentially its victims. For this anarchy was not only literally lethal, it was also seductively subversive, lubricious, Dionysian. The repressed was suddenly exposed; the unspeakable spoken.

Like a child with a rifle at large in an American school, the witch trials offered a momentary inversion of the natural order at the terrible price of an unexamined violence. The young girls who watched their elders go to the scaffold may have been inspired by a desire to deflect attention from themselves, but for a brief moment power arced from their accusing fingers and they became what they had never been, the centre of attention, the arbiters of value, the source of all authority. The Cultural Revolution in China offered the same momentary exultance, at the same cost, which was what made a later performance of the play in Shanghai such a painful and seemingly relevant experience.

But such children did no more than appropriate to themselves the arbitrary power claimed by their elders, and arguably with no greater legitimacy and no less lethal consequences. The accusing children may have inverted the power structure but they did not invent its inner procedures or modify its implacable foundation. Contained at the heart of their hysteria, then, was a paradigm of social power. The sheer arbitrariness of their actions was a reminder of both the processes and the substance of power, as of the reasons why it is sought by those who assure us that they exercise it only in the interests of others. It was a moment of paranoia, of hysteria, of insecurity transmuted into absoluteness, but it was also a moment in which seemingly random inhumanities could be seen to serve the interests of calculation, ambition and self-concern. It was, in short, a lesson in human behaviour and the ease with which human decencies are laid aside in the name of principle.

Miller saw this at work in the 1950s no less than in the 1690s. The unbending ideology of the Puritans, which had facilitated their survival, had, by degrees, become an orthodoxy that required unquestioning obedience. 'The tragedy of *The Crucible*,' he said, 'is the everlasting conflict between people so fanatically wedded to this orthodoxy that they could not cope with the evidence of their senses.'[48] He saw this same phenomenon when, for example, Communist China was presumed by the American administration not to exist, the island of Taiwan being promoted as the legitimate government, with a seat on the Security Council of the United Nations. It was not the real, but the *realpolitik*, that defined the world.

If the story of Salem and its witches had stayed in Miller's mind, it was only as one of those mysterious incidents from a past separated from us by more than time. Before he came upon Marion Starkey's *The Devil in Massachusetts*, it had never occurred to him that he would one day take the story as subject matter, partly because he had yet to formulate what he called 'an aesthetic idea of this tragedy'. Not the least fascinating aspect lay in the fact that Starkey recognized the dramatic potential of the events, claiming to have tried to 'uncover [in them] the classic dramatic form of the story itself' and adding, 'Here is real Greek tragedy' with 'a beginning, a middle and an end'.[49] Interestingly, in the notebook he started at this time Miller wrote that the story had to be seen as a tragedy; then when *The Crucible* opened in New York, in 1953, he remarked: 'Salem is one of the few dramas in history with a beginning, a middle and an end.' Starkey recognized, too, a truth that has always lain at the centre of Miller's approach to theatre and the public world that it shadows:

The human reality of what happens to millions is only for God to grasp; but what happens to individuals is another matter and within the range of mortal understanding. The Salem story has the virtue of being a highly individualized affair. Witches in the abstract were not hanged in Salem; but one by one were brought to the gallows such diverse personalities as a decent grandmother grown too hard of hearing to understand a crucial question from the jurors, a rakish, pipe-smoking female tramp, a plain farmer who thought only to save his wife from molestation, a lame old man whose toothless gums did not deny expression to a very salty vocabulary . . . And after you have studied their lives faithfully, a remarkable thing happens: you discover that if you really know the few, you are on your way to understanding the millions. By grasping the local, the parochial even, it is possible to make a beginning at understanding the universal.[50]

Starkey also acknowledged the wider implications of Salem, implications Miller would choose to amplify. For the witch-hunt was scarcely a product only of the distant past. 'It has been revived,' Starkey wrote, 'on a colossal scale by replacing the medieval idea of malefic witchcraft by a pseudo-scientific concept like "race", "nationality", and by substituting for theological dissension a whole complex of warring ideologies. Accordingly the story of 1692 is of far more than antiquarian interest; it is an allegory of our times.'[51]

It was as an allegory of our times, indeed, that Miller seized upon it, and though it was to be the McCarthyite witch-hunts of the House Un-American Activities Committee that seemed to offer the most direct analogy, he, like Starkey, saw other parallels in a war then only a few years behind them. For the Nazis, too, had their demons and deployed a systematic pseudo-science to identify those they regarded as tainted and impure.

But for the moment it was a more domestic danger that commanded his imagination. It was the maturation of the hysteria of the time, he explained, that 'pulled the trigger'. As he remarked to Elia Kazan, the Salem trials offered a persuasive parallel: 'It's all here ... every scene.' And certainly Miller's own account in his autobiography suggests that what had once struck him as an impenetrable mystery had now begun to make psychological and social sense:

At first I rejected the idea of a play on the subject ... But gradually, over weeks, a living connection between myself and Salem, and between Salem and Washington, was made in my mind – for whatever else they might be, I saw that the hearings in Washington were profoundly and even avowedly ritualistic ... The main point of the hearings, precisely as in seventeenth-century Salem, was that the accused make public confession, damn his confederates as well as his Devil master, and guarantee his sterling new allegiance by breaking disgusting old vows – whereupon he was let loose to rejoin the society of extremely decent people. In other words, the same spiritual nugget lay folded within both procedures – an act of contrition done not in solemn privacy but out in the public air.[52]

Kazan, as we have seen, objected that the parallel was a false one, since while witches manifestly did not exist, communists, equally manifestly, did. It was an objection later echoed by others, including the critic Eric Bentley, but not one accepted by Miller. For, as he has pointed out, not merely was Tituba in all probability practising voodoo on that night in 1692 but witchcraft was accepted as a fact by virtually every secular and religious authority. To that end he quotes the eighteenth-century British jurist Sir William Blackstone as insisting that it 'is a truth to which every nation in the world hath in its turn borne testimony', and John Wesley, founder of Methodism, as stating: 'The giving up of witchcraft is, in effect, giving up the Bible.' By the end of the seventeenth century, indeed, an estimated two hundred thousand people worldwide had been executed as witches. The question is not the reality or otherwise of witches, but the power of authority to define the nature of the real, and the desire, on the part of individuals and the state, to identify those whose purging will relieve a sense of anxiety and guilt.

What lay behind the procedures of both witch trial and political hearing was a familiar American need to assert a recoverable innocence, even if the only guarantee of such innocence lay in the displacement of guilt on to others. To sustain the integrity of their own names the accused were invited to offer the names of others, even though to do so would be to make them complicit in procedures they despised and hence to damage their sense of themselves.

Nor was the parallel a product of Miller's fanciful imagination. In 1948 Congressman George A. Dondero (who would later announce that all modern art was 'communistic'), in the House debate on the Mundt–Nixon bill – designed to 'protect the United States against Un-American and subversive activities' – observed that 'the world is dividing into two camps, freedom versus Communism, Christian civilization versus paganism'. More directly, Judge Irving Kaufman, who presided over the Rosenberg espionage trial in 1951, accused those before him of 'diabolical conspiracy' and 'denial of God'.

Clearly, the past had attractions for Miller because a rational analysis and dramatic presentation of the political realities of early 1950s America presented problems:

> The reason I think that I moved in that direction was that it was simply impossible any longer to discuss what was happening to us in contemporary terms. There had to be some distance, given the phenomena. We were all going slightly crazy trying to be honest and trying to see straight and trying to be safe. Sometimes there are conflicts in these three urges. I had known this story since my college years and I'd never understood why it was so

attractive to me. Now it suddenly made sense. It seemed to me that the hysteria in Salem had a certain inner procedure or several which we were duplicating once again, and that perhaps by revealing the nature of that procedure some light could be thrown on what we were doing to ourselves. And that's how that play came to be.[53]

Oddly, perhaps, Miller chooses to interpolate some ten pages of character notes and historical observations into his published text of the play, and though he was, understandably, later to play down parallels that might make the play seem time-bound, he used these interpolated comments to underscore the nature of the immediate parallel as well as its more general applicability. Thus, in a note which begins as a comment on the Reverend Hale, he observes:

> Like Reverend Hale and the others on this stage, we conceive the Devil as a necessary part of a respectable view of cosmology. Ours is a divided empire in which certain ideas and emotions and actions are of God, and their opposites are of Lucifer. It is as impossible for most men to conceive of a morality without sin as of an earth without 'sky'. Since 1692 a great but superficial change has wiped out God's beard and the Devil's horns, but the world is still gripped between two diametrically opposed absolutes ... At this writing, only England has held back before the temptations of contemporary diabolism. In the countries of the Communist ideology, all resistance of any import is linked to the totally malign capitalist succubi, and in America any man who is not a reactionary in his views is open to the charge of alliance with the Red hell ... A political policy is equated with moral right, and opposition to it with diabolical malevolence. Once such an equation is effectively made, society becomes a congeries of plots and counterplots, and the main role of government changes from that of the arbiter to that of the scourge of God.[54]

America, under pressure, tends to see the world in Manichaean terms. It was true in the 1950s and would be true again in 2001 when the attack was launched on the Twin Towers in New York, or in 2003 when a pre-emptive war was waged against Iraq on the grounds that it was part of an 'axis of evil'. Suddenly the powers of lightness were confronted with the powers of darkness, military tribunals were established and those who questioned past or present policies regarded as subverting the national will – a parallel, perhaps, not lost on those who watched Richard Eyre's forceful production of *The Crucible* on Broadway in 2002.

The hostility of the Kazans towards the project came from their recognition that Miller was about to insist on parallels that would link them to the persecutions of another day. In 1952, Kazan offered names: Harry Elion, John

Bonn, Alice Evans, Anne Howe. The irony lay in the fact that in doing so he, along with Clifford Odets and Lee J. Cobb, replicated the processes of the 1692 trials when the children cried out against Sarah Good, Bridget Bishop, George Jacobs, Martha Bellows, Alice Barrow. A climactic scene in *The Crucible* comes when John Proctor, on the point of trading his integrity for his life, finally refuses to pay the price, which is to offer the names of others to buy his life. 'I like not to spoil their names . . . I speak my own sins; I cannot judge another. I have no tongue for it.' He thus recovers his own name by refusing to name others: 'now I do think I see some shred of goodness in John Proctor'.[55] Kazan felt no such inhibition. Miller's reply, when asked to betray others three years later, was a virtual paraphrase of that which had been offered by Proctor: 'I am trying to, and I will, protect my sense of myself. I could not use the name of another person and bring trouble on him.'[56]

If *The Crucible* is concerned with power, its source, its manipulation, its language, it is also concerned with betrayal. The historic John Proctor and Abigail Williams were distant in age. Miller narrowed the age gap and ignited a sexual flame, one with echoes in his own life. Marilyn, eleven years his junior, was a compelling presence in his mind, if not in his life, while his own marriage seemed increasingly cold, precisely John Proctor's dilemma in the play. As he observed in a typescript note in September 1976, he had strayed from his wife and was suffering from a sense of guilt. His decision to write *The Crucible* may have been socially motivated but he admitted, at least to himself in this private note, that it was also deeply implicated in his own life, in a sexuality to which he was drawn even as it left him in a state of confusion. But his real concern in introducing this element – for which, oddly, given her age, he thought he might have sanction, since Abigail Williams had been dismissed from the Proctor household – lay once again in his desire to link the private to the public. Proctor is a flawed man tempted to betray not only in private but in public when he agrees to sign his name to a falsehood. The play is in part to do with his recovery under pressure as he reinvests his name with an integrity he had come so close to surrendering. He dies to sustain his idea of himself and of a society in which such a death may redeem a sense of truth and justice momentarily laid aside out of fear.

In the first typescript of the play the sexual tension that motivates Abigail is introduced early. As she looks down at Betty, seemingly unconscious on the bed after having spent the previous night dancing naked in the forest and conjuring spirits with Tituba, she is described as stretching the cloth of her gown against her body. She is, we are told, in the throes of a sensuous excitement and chants a verse in which she imagines herself in the arms of Proctor, who had been denied the marriage bed for seven months. Abigail has 'a sense for heat' and had felt him 'burning' in his loneliness. In that early draft Miller included a scene, subsequently dropped from most productions, in which Abigail and Proctor meet. Six months after the play opened, when Miller restaged it, he reinstated it. Proctor and Abigail come together the night before his wife is to appear in court. Abigail is dressed in a nightgown.

When Laurence Olivier directed a production in 1965 he hunted down the extra scene in a theatre magazine. In a letter to Miller dated 13 August 1964, he wrote: 'I was a wee bit disappointed when I read it because I suppose I had assumed that Abigail would have tried to seduce Proctor in this scene and only agree to clear Elizabeth [of a false charge of witchcraft] on this sort of bargain. Would there be anything in this note being struck in this scene?' He added, 'I have never thought that Abigail's line in Act 1, "I know how you clutched my back ... ", really indicated the extent of the thing that had occurred, which we learn from Elizabeth, and later from Proctor, is a complete act of sex. Do you think you might strengthen Abigail's line into meaning all that it should mean?' Miller did not alter the line and Olivier decided against including the forest scene, explaining to Miller: 'You don't need it. It's nice when you read the play. You get an expanded view of it. But it destroyed that certain marching tempo that starts to get into that play to that place ... thus scene stops the beat.'[57]

In the handwritten draft that preceded his first typed version, a draft partly set out in verse, Abigail confesses her desire, her passion being pitched against the cold judgement of Elizabeth Proctor who, at this early stage of the text, her husband half believes, may have set herself to destroy him.

In 1998, Miller saw evidence of a political conservatism rooted in a concern with sexuality that seemed all too familiar. This time it was not a young woman called Abigail Williams at the centre of events but one called Monica Lewinsky (with whom he appeared on the television programme *60 Minutes*, oddly admiring of someone he thought of as a twentieth-century courtesan). In the right-wing attacks on President Clinton he heard echoes of the hatred that seemed to him to recall the Salem ministers attacking the Devil while revelling, lubriciously, in a suddenly exposed sexuality. Exposure had a double significance. Suddenly things could be spoken aloud that had previously been sublimated, denied. The fascination with witchcraft, and the laying-out of the details of sexual encounter, both betokened a fear of women and the displacement on to them of male desire, otherwise cloaked in the guise of moral concern. The sanctimonious denunciation, it seemed to him, whether in Puritan New England or in the guise of a twentieth-century special prosecutor, barely concealed not only personal ambition but something more radical in the human sensibility. Monica Lewinsky and Abigail would have recognized one another; but so, too, he thought, would Kenneth Starr and the Puritan judges come together to explore the details of a supposed depravity. There was, in short, a parallel in the sexual element ... Witch-hunts are always spooked by women's horrifying sexuality awakened by the superstud Devil ... In Salem, witch-hunting ministers had the solemn duty to examine women's bodies for signs of 'the Devil's Marks' ... I thought of this wonderfully holy exercise when Congress were pawing through Kenneth Starr's fiercely exact report on the President's intimate meetings with Monica Lewinsky.

Hatred for Clinton, it seemed to him, amounted to a 'hellish fear of him as unclean'.[58] Sex, however, was to be only one element in a play in which betrayal broadened out until it became a civic and, indeed, religious duty. Miller was concerned to underscore the moral and social implications of betrayals presented as duty, as brother is set to spy on brother while the fields go untended. At the same time, he was aware that to deny witchcraft was to invite the charge of trying to conceal the conspiracy and discredit those who alone claimed to be able to save the community. The parallel with HUAC was too compelling to be ignored. The accuser becomes an agent of the state, his or her accusation assuming a presumptive right. Here was a tragedy, it seemed to him, precisely of Greek proportions, in which the fate of the state was invested in the drama of a man who embraces his own fate in order to sustain a principle which he had come so close to abrogating. John Proctor rediscovers his integrity and in doing so potentially redeems his society. Justice is not done, but the principle of justice is upheld.

In 2002, Miller looked back to the 1950s: 'We lived in a time,' he observed, 'distorted by obligatory and defensive patriotism, an atmosphere unimaginable anymore.'[59] It was a time when the urgencies of the moment seemed to justify the laying aside of the very values that were to have sustained the society, just as they had in Puritan New England. But the processes that he identifies were not unique to those moments, nor, it would turn out, unimaginable.

Critical responses to *The Crucible* did pick up on the parallels between Puritan New England and Joseph McCarthy's America, but when the daily reviewers gave way to the weekly ones, this became a principal concern and the play gave rise to the kind of general debate that few works inspire.

Walter Kerr, in the *New York Herald Tribune*, was one of those who did see a connection, conceding that the play offered 'an accurate reading of our own turbulent age', while thinking it unduly polemical.[60] However, he found the characters little more than a convenience, props to what he took to be Miller's central theme. For Brooks Atkinson, in the *New York Times* of 23 January 1953, it was a powerful drama but 'too conscious of its implications' while lacking in 'universality' – that word now seemingly purged of its Marxist connotations. There was, he suggested, too much excitement and not enough emotion. The comment about the lack of emotion echoed Miller's feeling that the production had been too cool. He tried to warm it up a little with an article in the *New York Times* two weeks after the opening in which he recounted his own visit to Salem, its name, he recalled, deriving from the Hebrew *Shalom*, meaning 'peace'. He wrote of his own research, of those who passed through the Salem Museum and of the individuals on whom he had based his play.

The *New York Post* reviewer, for the most part sidestepping the dramatic and theatrical qualities of the play, thought that Miller provided confusion rather than clarity. He found the parallels invalid and the play a 'loaded allegory'. Modern political hysteria, he argued, as opposed to that operating in Salem, was based on the despotic threat of communism: 'There *are* spies and saboteurs; there are accused agents who are guilty.' The events in Salem, he suggested, were soon over. The threat to America and the world persisted. He found a more legitimate parallel in a revival of Lillian Hellman's *The Children's Hour*, concerned as it was with the conviction of people by rumour and innuendo.

Unsurprisingly, Miller fared no better with the *New Leader*.[61] Here Joseph T. Shipley accused him of bad faith, suggesting that the play was a melodrama and a contrivance and that the real analogy for Salem lay in the communist states. Eric Bentley in the *New Republic* found the material 'magnificent for narrative, poetry, drama', though for stretches unengaging. The production was, he thought, inert, while the language strove for a poetry it did not achieve. His main concern, as with so many others, however, was with the parallel between seventeenth- and mid-twentieth-century America: 'It is true that people today are being persecuted on chimerical grounds. It is untrue in that communism is not, to put it mildly, merely a chimera.'[62]

He, too, accused Miller of melodrama, of creating a play in which the conflict is between the wholly guilty and the wholly innocent. By way of evidence he invoked a John Proctor who, while having weaknesses, has no faults, and is self-evidently innocent not only of the crime with which he is charged, but of a crime that cannot conceivably exist. In a later reprint of this article he included a further point, excised from the original, seeing the clash between Miller and Kazan, who directed *Salesman* but was not asked to direct *The Crucible*, as of a piece with this Manichaean view. Seen thus, Kazan is the guilty man and Jed Harris, who did direct the play, the innocent in a social melodrama which is of as much interest as the play itself.

In his book *What is Theatre?* Bentley headed the relevant chapter 'The Innocence of Arthur Miller', and observed that 'the analogy between "red-baiting" and "witch hunting"' could only seem complete ... to communists'. He did not, he insisted, accuse Miller of communism, which would 'fall into the trap of over-simplification which he himself has set'. What he did accuse him of being was 'a playwright of American liberal folklore' who wrote a 'drama of indignation'. While seemingly acquitting Miller of the crime of communism, however, he noted that John Proctor 'belongs to the right class (yeoman farmer)' and 'does the right kind of work (manual)',[63] while the play itself seemed to be a response to Kazan's admission of his own former communism and his naming of others similarly committed.

The case against Miller was put at even greater length by Robert Warshow in an article called 'The Liberal Conscience in "The Crucible", Arthur Miller and his Audience' in *Commentary* in March 1953, then reprinted in his book *The Immediate Experience* (1962) and distributed by the American Committee for Cultural Freedom as part of its anti-communist drive. Like Joseph Shipley, he believed that the play meant virtually the contrary of what it appeared to. The Salem trials, he suggested, 'were not political and had nothing to do with civil rights, unless it is a violation of civil rights to hang a murderer'.[64] Which murderer, you might ask? Like Bentley, he maintained that the crime of which Proctor was convicted was 'impossible'. The witches died because of 'metaphysical error'. Miller, he said, showed an 'almost contemptuous lack of interest' in the particularities of the trials; he falsified the historical details, for example changing Abigail's age, and this falsification Warshow found ironic in a play that denounced falsehood. In making this change, he suggested, Miller offered a motive for the actions that did not emerge out of a religious and psychological complexity, the adultery, like that in *Death of a Salesman*, proving an irrelevant distraction.

Once again, here was a critic claiming that the real parallel for Salem lay in the show trials of Eastern Europe, specifically Czechoslovakia; and again Elia Kazan is invoked, as is Lillian Hellman's *The Children's Hour*. Like the cries of 'Strike!' that had rung out at the end of Clifford Odets's *Waiting for Lefty*, the cries of 'Bravo' that Warshow heard at the end of Miller's play indicated nothing so much as an unquestioning sense of solidarity inspired less by rational analysis than by a desire for community in the face of a vaguely perceived threat.

Perhaps it is hardly surprising that reviews of the play should have been, on occasion, less a response to its dramatic strengths and weaknesses than extensions of the ongoing political battle that had made American reviews of work by Hellman and Miller, in particular, so difficult to decode. They would continue to be so as ideological arguments from the 1930s forward through the succeeding decades.

Oddly, or perhaps not, it was the British critic Harold Hobson who, in the *Sunday Times* of 14 November 1954, welcomed Miller's play precisely because it seemed to him, in the spirit of Lord Acton's comments on the duty of the historian, to be fair to the other side. It was left to him to point out that Miller did not claim that the evil the court set out to purge was nonexistent. As he recalls, the Reverend Parris is right in believing that his niece and her

friends have danced naked and invoked the Devil, along with Tituba. Miller
also, he points out, represents the justices as having an honest desire to do
right, albeit a desire finally subject to other perceived necessities. He might
have added that Proctor doubts the existence of witches only because he has
seen no evidence for them and does, of course, know the motive of at least
one of the accusers, Abigail.

What all these critics reveal is that Miller's play was received in large
degree less as simply a new play from one of America's two most successful
playwrights than as a contribution to a core political and moral debate. He
was praised, or more often criticized, for the exactness, or otherwise, of the
parallel he proposed. For some, he was a fellow traveller, an apologist for an
ideology that he hesitated to identify, preferring to restage a political debate
as a moral and philosophical disquisition. The history of his relationship with
Kazan was not only taken to explain the choice of Jed Harris as director but
seen as evidence of his desire to paint the world in primary colours, to stage
history as a battle between innocence and guilt. This was despite the fact that
in Proctor he created a character at odds with himself, guilty at the thought
of his betrayal of his wife and bemused by the conflict between the faith that
is the lingua franca of his community and the sturdy pragmatism of a man
who distrusts what he does not know through his senses. He might later
forget the one commandment that pins him to his own bad faith, but he is
not a man who wishes to challenge the heavens or even a venal minister.

There is, though, something a touch disturbing in Hobson's praise of *The
Crucible* as a 'fair play'. For though he also accepts that it is an exciting drama,
his praise has a watercolour quality to it. For Herbert Blau, by contrast, who
directed the play in San Francisco in 1954 and who wrote about it in his book
The Impossible Theater a dozen years later, there was something altogether too
rational about it. To demonstrate this he likens the figures of the Reverend
Hale and Deputy-Governor Danforth to Melville's Captain Vere and Claggart in *Billy Budd*. Moral equivocation and evil circle one another and,
between them sacrifice good. To him, Claggart was what Miller said he
wished he had made Danforth. Here, to Blau's mind, was a drama that cut
deeper, that did, indeed, accept the idea of a profound and practising evil,
while Miller was by implication too liberal, too rational – pejorative terms to
many, in both the 1950s and the 60s, though for different reasons – too
considered to allow the diabolic, ostensibly at the heart of the play, to reveal
itself. And Blau did, of course, here take his cue from Miller for whom the
Fall had always had a central significance.

There is, though, no parallel to Billy Budd himself, no innocent to be
sacrificed on the yard-arm, only a man who surprises himself into an integrity
he had thought beyond him, an integrity he believed he had sacrificed on the
altar of self-concern. And this is what Miller has to offer in place of Melville's

try-works in *Moby Dick*. There are elemental passions in Salem. Proctor feels them, as do those who think they track the Devil to his lair. Lives, after all, hang in the balance. But those passions are not quite those of opposing powers contending for the soul of man. The action was to have begun in the antinomian forest which exists still, not only in the interpolated scene in the original play and in the opening of the film, but in the minds of characters who know in their soul that they are fringed about by the Devil. Those who would take advantage of that fact, though, do so not because they do battle for fallen man but for their own reasons, just as in 1953 while there were communists at home and abroad the exploits of Joseph McCarthy had little to do with a genuine attempt to exorcise them.

Ironically, while he was being attacked from the Right and the Trotskyite Left, Miller was also in trouble with the Communist Party. On 28 January 1953 the *Daily Worker* review, duly included in his FBI file, had effectively accused him of racism: 'Miller ... has marred his otherwise strong portrayal of brave men and women in the struggle against bigotry and persecution by writing an extremely stereotyped role for one Negro member of the cast. It is a mark of chauvinism to present on the dramatic stage at this day, when the struggle for Negro rights is such a burning issue, a Negro woman as an Aunt Jemima type. And Miller has made this bad error.'[65]

America in the 1950s was charged with the electricity of the Cold War. It is the light from that charge which seemed to flicker around the stage in 1953, and which, if somewhat fitfully, illuminated much of the criticism of the play. Eventually, however, with the passage of time, another play emerged, no longer concerned with America's moment of crisis, no longer presenting a trial of values defined in terms of Cold War politics. That play is to do with the struggle by the individual to find his way back to himself, to accept responsibility for his own actions and those of others. It is a play that still arcs between past and present, but that present is ever changing. The Devil still tempts in the forest of the mind.

John Proctor stumbles on an integrity he thought he was prepared to barter in exchange for mere survival, astonished that he is capable, at last, of bringing himself into alignment with the man he wished he might be. *The Crucible* remains Miller's most produced play not because it says something about a forgotten politician or an era that has passed not so much into history as into legend. It is so because the pressure to conform is a constant, because power will always exert its presumptive rights to define the real, and because it is never enough to watch history pass by as if it were something other than the product of decisions made or deferred, as if the individual could indeed declare a separate peace and rest content and immune from the flawed institutions of flawed men and women.

*

On the night of Friday, 19 June 1953, first Julius and then Ethel Rosenberg were executed at a prison in Ossining in New York State. The announcement was made at 8.43 p.m. They had been found guilty of conspiracy to commit espionage; more specifically, they stood accused of passing nuclear secrets to the Soviet Union. The time of their execution, originally to have taken place late that night, had been brought forward to avoid the risk of delays taking their deaths into the Jewish Sabbath.

Julius, from the Lower East Side, had been radicalized when he went to City College in 1934, Arthur Miller's freshman year at Michigan. He had embraced the usual run of radical causes, been a supporter of the Loyalists in Spain and a union activist. Found guilty of espionage, the Rosenbergs spent two years on death row, proclaiming their innocence. In sentencing them, the judge had accused them of partial responsibility for the war in Korea and for those who might yet die in a Soviet nuclear attack. For many others, they were victims of a family feud – having been turned in by Ethel's brother – and an FBI conspiracy.

On 19 June, *The Crucible* was nearing the end of its run. Two of its stars, Arthur Kennedy and Beatrice Straight, were about to leave to make films. The performance took its usual course until the moment of John Proctor's execution, at which, instead of the usual applause, the audience rose to its feet and stood in silence. Some of the cast were bewildered until told by others that news of the Rosenbergs' deaths had circulated. We now know that the audience were wrong about the Rosenbergs, at least with respect to Julius. His innocence was spurious. Ethel, it seems, was innocent, a true victim of those who sought to use her as leverage against her husband. They were not, though, wrong about a play that was indeed seen as offering an analogue for that frenzy of accusation, betrayal and callous indifference to the fate of the accused which seemed, to its author, to have typified the previous few years.

From this moment, the production of *The Crucible* became, in Miller's words, 'an act of resistance' for the cast. As ticket sales fell away so Miller redirected it, with Maureen Stapleton as Elizabeth Proctor while E.G. Marshall, who had previously played the Reverend Hale, took over from Arthur Kennedy. Miller removed the sets, to save on the cost of stage-hands, and played it against a black background in an unchanging white light. The actors took little or no pay. It limped on for a few more weeks and finally closed:

> After the last curtain I came out on the stage and sat facing the actors and thanked them, and they thanked me, and then we just sat looking at one another. Somebody sobbed, and then somebody else, and suddenly the impacted frustration of the last months, plus the labor of over a year in

writing the play and revising it, all burst upwards into my head, and I had to walk into the darkness backstage and weep for a minute or two before returning to say goodbye.[66]

Despite its struggle to find audiences, *The Crucible* won the Antoinette Perry and the Donaldson Awards, though it did not win the Pulitzer Prize, which in 1953 went to William Inge's *Picnic*.

Less than two years later it was back, in an Off-Broadway production directed by Paul Libin. It ran for nearly two years. Indeed it was still running when Miller himself was called before HUAC. *The Crucible* went on to be his most successful play, long after Julius and Ethel Rosenberg, Joseph McCarthy and HUAC were forgotten, and in countries where American history and politics were of no more than marginal interest. In 2002 it was still triumphing on Broadway, this time with Liam Neeson as John Proctor, another Irishman whose feet would no doubt have disturbed Jed Harris.

In 1953, however, Madeleine Sherwood, who played Abigail, explained the immediate impact on herself of appearing in Miller's play: 'Your friends would cross the street so that they wouldn't have to say hello to you . . . good people.'[67] In that same year Miller attended a cocktail party at which he overheard a television producer assuring a circle of guests that he was free to hire any actor or produce any script he chose. There was, he assured them, no such thing as a blacklist. As Miller recalled in 1983:

> Since I had friends who had not been hired in over a year despite long careers in TV and radio, and two or three who had suffered mental illness as a result, and I knew of at least two suicides attributable to the despair generated by blacklisting, I walked over to the producer and offered him the rights to *The Crucible*. He laughed, assuring me and his listeners that he would of course be honored but his budget would never stand for what such rights would doubtless cost. So I offered them to him for a dollar. He went on laughing and I went on persisting, growing aware, however, that our little audience, many of them in television and the theatre, was turning against me for a display of bad manners. Leaving that party, I exchanged glances with people who I was certain shared my knowledge and views but who showed nothing in their faces.

It was an experience, he said, that would prove useful when he later found himself writing about the life of the artist in the Soviet Union, China and Eastern Europe, 'where what might be called a permanent state of McCarthyism' reigned, 'always warning artists – who, after all, are the eyes and voices of the society – that their souls ultimately belong to Daddy'.[68]

Writing in 1967, he remarked:

I believe that life does provide some sound analogies now and again, but I don't think they are any good on the stage. Before a play can be 'about' something else it has to be about itself ... The truth is that caught up as I was in opposition to McCarthyism the playwriting part of me was drawn to what I felt was a tragic process underlying the political manifestation ... When irrational terror takes to itself the fiat of moral goodness somebody has to die ... No man lives who has not got a panic button and when it is pressed by the clean white hand of moral duty, a certain murderous train is set in motion. Socially speaking this is what the play is 'about', and it is this which I believe makes it survive long after the political circumstances of its birth have evaporated in the public mind.[69]

Twenty-two years later, now long after the events that supposedly prompted the play, he speculated on the reasons for the play's longevity:

I have wondered if one of the reasons the play continues like this is its symbolic unleashing of the specter of order's fragility. When certainties evaporate with each dawn, the unknowable is always around the corner. We know how much depends on mere trust and good faith and a certain respect for the human person, and how easily breached these are. And we know as well how close to the edge we live and how weak we really are and how quickly swept by fear the mass of us can become ... It is also, I suppose, that the play reaffirms the ultimate power of courage and clarity of mind whose ultimate fruit is liberty.[70]

9

A VIEW FROM THE BRIDGE

The political situation in the early 1950s was increasingly oppressive. In New York City a park lavatory attendant was dismissed because he had been a member of the Communist Party. Sidney Hook, in an article entitled 'Can Our Teachers Be Trusted?', argued in favour of firing certain teachers, suggesting that schools and universities should have no room for 'a man who has sworn or pledged himself to follow a party line through thick and thin, and insofar abandoned his freedom to think, to choose and to act'.[1] Irving Kristol suggested that it was impossible to argue that 'there is no harm in having ... children taught the three R's by a Communist'. No doubt, he asserted, some people had become communists because of the Depression, labour conflicts or racial prejudice but, 'as Fitzjames Stephens remarked many decades ago, "It does not follow that because society caused a fault it is not to punish it. A man who breaks his own arm when he is drunk may have to cut it off when he is sober."'[2]

Teachers in schools and universities found themselves confronted with loyalty oaths (by 1952, they were required in thirty-three states), security vetting, and dismissal should they choose to belong to subversive organizations as defined by the Justice Department. Nearly twenty states banned teachers from membership of such 'progressive' organizations. As Richard Pells reminds us in his book *The Liberal Mind in a Conservative Age*:

> New York adopted the Feinberg Law, which ordered principals to file reports on the loyalty of their teachers and clerical staff with the superintendent of schools; the principals themselves were to be 'cleared' by assistant superintendents. Twenty-eight public and private colleges in California, including Stanford and Berkeley, agreed to install security officers (usually former FBI agents) who compiled information on the political beliefs and affiliations of professors for use by state officials engaged in purging education of all un-American (or at least un-Californian) impulses.[3]

HUAC and the Department of Defense demanded details of library books and curricula. In 1948 the Carswell Committee declared of the University of

Washington: [There] 'isn't a student who has attended this university who has not been taught subversive activities.'[4] The regents of the University of California voted to impose a private oath on its faculty. They were given a deadline of 30 April 1950, after which those refusing to cooperate would be fired. Many refused, some were fired. According to Griffin Fariello, 'By 1951, the UC system had lost 110 scholars – twenty-six fired, thirty-seven who resigned in protest, and forty-seven others who had refused appointments.'[5] Miller's own alma mater, the University of Michigan, was one of those institutions that fired faculty and in which informers operated.

In Mary McCarthy's opinion, Sidney Hook and Irving Kristol were missing the real target. While denouncing the withholding of passports from US citizens, she observed that 'the fellow-traveler is far more insidious to deal with than the Party member for the fellow-traveler invariably calls himself a "liberal" and points to some small difference he maintains with official Marxism to certify his claim to that title. Students,' she observed, 'are frequently taken in by him, to the point where they become fellow-travelers themselves while imagining they are liberals.'[6] Writing in *Commentary*, Irving Kristol asked:

> Did not the major segment of American liberalism, as a result of joining hands with the Communists in a Popular Front, go on record as denying the existence of Soviet concentration camps? Did it not give its blessing to the 'liquidation' of millions of Soviet 'kulaks'? Did it not apologize for the mass purges of 1936–38, and did it not solemnly approve the grotesque trials of the Old Bolsheviks? Did it not applaud the massacre of the Communist left by the GPU during the Spanish Civil War? ... a generation of earnest reformers who helped give this country a New Deal ... find themselves in retrospect stained with the guilt of having lent aid and company to Stalinist tyranny.[7]

The assault on communists, in other words, was in large degree a retrospective attack on the New Deal and those who had seemingly foisted it upon a vulnerable nation. As to those who denounced the firing of university teachers, he regarded them as hysterical or worse. Kristol also vigorously rejected accusations of an emergent conformism in American society.

For historian and biographer Carol Brightman, 'It was perhaps the first time since the French Revolution that the significant components of an intellectual community decided that it was no longer *de rigueur* to be adversarial; that you could support your country without cheapening intellectual and artistic integrity' – an observation supported, as Frances Stonor Saunders observes, by *Time* magazine's insistence that 'The Man of Protest has ... given way to the Man of Affirmation – and that happens to be the very role that the intellectuals played when the nation was new.'[8]

That new conformity had been underlined by a symposium in *Partisan*

Review in 1952, called 'Our Country and Our Culture', declaring that radicalism was a thing of the past, as was detachment, even alienation from American institutions. Now, it was argued, most writers wanted to be part of American life. Sidney Hook, once a Marxist, now seemed to embrace the Smith Act (see p. 281). Granville Hicks, who had once celebrated the radical tradition in American writing, now praised those responsible liberals who had come onside the American way. Mary McCarthy celebrated the collapse of class barriers in the new America, suggesting that inequities were rapidly disappearing. It was no longer necessary or desirable to attempt to change America. The time had come to accept it as it was and even rejoice in it. The old oppositional stance was no longer fashionable or, more dangerously, acceptable.

The authors of the article were not people who favoured Senator McCarthy, but those who appeared before HUAC reminded them of an era in which idealism had seemingly been tainted with betrayal or, at the very least, a wilful refusal to acknowledge the repressiveness of a Soviet Union which now, through its contrast with America, made the latter seem so clearly a paradigm of the desirable. Those, like Miller, who appeared to side with the accused, were a reminder of their own youthful naiveties and a threat to the consensus they had once shunned and now regarded as a legitimate basis for art and action. Even the American Civil Liberties Union began, with some urgency, to distance itself from communism – indeed, to develop an anti-communist stance. It had been particularly careful to tiptoe round the Rosenberg case and did the same with that of the China scholar Owen Lattimore, when he was charged with perjury. There was much watching of the back in the early 1950s, a marked disinclination to go over the top in the battle even for constitutional freedoms which now seemed tainted with sedition.

It is hard now to appreciate the extent and nature of the assaults Miller suffered in the 1940s and 50s from magazines such as *Partisan Review* (originally called 'Partisansky Review' by Edmund Wilson), *Commentary* (whose editor, Elliot Cohen, was an adviser on communism to the Luce publications), the *New Republic* (pro-Stalinist in the 1930s, liberal in the 1950s and thereafter) and even, though for less ideological reasons, the *New York Times*. He found himself increasingly identified, by many of those who would come to be known as the 'New York Intellectuals', as a Stalinist whose work was thereby suspect and whose political views were to be denounced.

On reading Alfred Kazin's *Starting Out in the Thirties*, Miller noted, with interest, that it appeared to be the critics who had become Trotskyites and the writers who became Stalinists. He liked Kazin's stress on the spiritual content of the Left and his recognition that criticism ultimately became a question of morals. Certainly, Miller was to be assailed for what was taken to be his failure of moral vision as much as for his faulty politics, though in truth

for the Trotskyites the two were indistinguishable. The book reinforced
Miller's conviction that the critical assaults he had suffered had begun with
the Trotskyite attacks that had followed the Waldorf Conference and effectively never ended. The break between the Stalinists and the Trotskyites
seemed to him, as to Kazin, to have had a major impact on the culture, and
certainly on him. He recalled Diana Trilling's assertion that in the 1950s no
one could have a play staged on Broadway who was not a Stalinist, a patent
absurdity which made him wonder how an intelligent woman could have
allowed herself to say such a thing.

The editors of *Commentary, New Leader* and *Partisan Review* were all on
the board of the American Committee for Cultural Freedom (ACCF), whose
function, according to Sidney Hook, was 'to expose Stalinism and Stalinist
liberals wherever you may find them'.[9] As Michael Herrington explained,
'When Irving Kristol was Executive Secretary of the ACCF, one learned to
expect from him silence on those issues that were agitating the whole intellectual and academic world, and enraged communiqués on the outrages
performed by people like Arthur Miller.'[10]

In the 1940s and 50s Miller's work was denounced by those whose politics
were at odds with his own, hence the curious assault on *Death of a Salesman*
by the Trotskyite Eleanor Clark and the attack on *The Crucible* by Robert
Warshow, like Miller a graduate of the University of Michigan, though of
the class of 1946 and hence free of the Marxist incubus. *The Crucible*, Warshow
maintained, 'was written to say something about Alger Hiss and Owen
Lattimore, Julius and Ethel Rosenberg, Senator McCarthy, the actors who
had lost their jobs on radio and television'. It offered 'a revealing glimpse of
the way the Communists and their fellow-travelers have come to regard
themselves'.[11] The play was the product of a man who believed in the 'astonishing phenomenon' of communist innocence. This was the review that
the ACCF reprinted so as to ensure a distribution beyond the confines of
Commentary, a gesture that underscores the political nature of the attack on
Miller.

The fact that some of those writing for these magazines were linked to the
CIA does not mean that they were obeying Agency orders. Warshow, for
example, was an insightful movie critic, working for both *Commentary* and
Partisan Review. They were, however, employed by magazines whose policies
were clear enough, even if their funding and intelligence connections were
not.

Like Herrington, Irving Howe noted that 'on most issues agitating the
intellectual and academic world, the ACCF kept silent, refusing to defend
Communists under investigation or attack, though it could rage against people
like Arthur Miller and Bertrand Russell for exaggerating the dangers to civil

liberties'.[12] The future editor in chief of *Commentary*, Norman Podhoretz, outlined the literary politics of the time:

> Magazines like *Partisan Review, Commentary*, and *Encounter* ... were against radicalism ... The reason the anti-Communism of those liberals has to be stressed is that – to complicate matters still further – there were also liberals in America who were not anti-Communist ... They weren't Communists themselves, but they were generally sympathetic to the Communists. These liberals – fellow travelers, they were called – thought the Communists were on the same side.[13]

One of the fellow travellers he had in mind was Arthur Miller.

Partisan Review and *Commentary* had a clear political stance and that informed their attitude to writers who seemed to them at odds with their ideological position. As Irving Howe remarked in the mid-1960s, 'Far worse than anything one could say about *Partisan Review* was the approach of the writers grouped around *Commentary*. Their major stress during the fifties was not upon the struggle against McCarthyism, though of course "they too disliked it". What really stirred their blood was doing battle with the "anti-anti-communists", the few remaining (in Sidney Hook's phrase) "kneejerk liberals".' They were 'more deeply preoccupied, or preoccupied at deeper levels, with the dangers to freedom stemming from people like ... Arthur Miller than the dangers from people like Senator McCarthy'.[14] The country may have worried about McCarthy, but *Commentary* 'worried about who profited from the struggle against McCarthy'.[15] James Rorty, writing in that journal, while granting credit to McCarthy, thought him insufficiently anti-communist and, in his demagogic incompetence, harming the anti-communist cause.

Nathan Abrams in his thesis 'Struggling for Freedom' quotes a confidential internal memorandum which suggested that *Commentary* should 'publish appropriate articles dealing with the dangers of Communism to the security of the Jews and Americans'.[16] According to Podhoretz, *Commentary* 'could always be trusted to tell its readers what was right for American society more frequently than what was wrong'.[17]

Miller was clearly one of the knee-jerk liberals, the anti-anti-communists Sidney Hook despised. He was thus deeply suspect, and it is necessary to bear this in mind when reading some of the reviews of his work that reflect less aesthetic than political judgements. It explains, too, why to some of his critics it appeared important to bring his work into alignment with assumptions about his politics. Being of the Left, he must be a realist, thus lacking the true radical's commitment to modernism, a commitment that, in 1949, had led to the award of the Bollinger Prize for Poetry to Ezra Pound. Why Pound, an anti-Semite, convicted of treason for his broadcasts from wartime

Italy? Because, according to Richard Elliman, 'he represented the ultimate in the mandarin culture they were trying to preserve and promote',[18] the 'they' being T.S. Eliot, W.H. Auden, Allen Tate and Robert Lowell. They were enthusiasts for modernism if not for the modern; enthusiasts, too, for a conservative model of culture. For them, aesthetics took primacy over ethics, myth over history.

For Miller, the politics of modernism were not beside the point, since that politics had sustained a view inimical to the values which his art determinedly embodied. But in contrast to the art and literature promoted by the Soviet Union, it seemed, America was to take its stand on modernism, and Frances Stonor Saunders has made a convincing case for the CIA's promotion of abstract expressionism in particular, though there are those who think this view exaggerated. If the Soviet Union was selling socialist realism, then America would seek to market its cultural primacy by stressing the opposite. America was to stand for the new. Suddenly the abstract expressionists, little known and relatively poor, found their work being sent to international exhibitions with help from a benign if none too easily identifiable source.

Interestingly, *Partisan Review* took a leading role in promoting their cause. A similar point had been made, nearly twenty years earlier, by a French art historian, Serge Gilbaut, in *How New York Stole the Idea of Modern Art*. Abstract expressionism, according to Gilbaut, became 'a symbol of the fragility of freedom in the battle waged by the liberals to protect the vital center'. Jackson Pollock thus became 'a liberal warrior in the Cold War'.[19] Arthur Schlesinger Jr's observation that Pollock was apolitical and Harry Truman a hater of abstract expressionism, of course, hardly proves anything. The CIA, if indeed active, consulted neither.

For all his own theatrical experiments, there was a reason for Miller's resistance to modernism, though, in truth, his concern with a double consciousness, a tension – in his case, between a Jewish and an American heritage – was entirely compatible with it. Theodore Adorno once observed that Kafka's modernism was marked by the 'dawning awareness of the approaching paralysis of politics',[20] and it was precisely such a paralysis, as fact and as metaphor, that alarmed Miller. Daniel Bell, an officer of the ACCF, was to propose an end to ideology and Miller saw in such a proposal precisely that acquiescence in process, that shrug of resignation in the face of collapsing systems of thought, that alarmed him, though in later years he would come to embrace such an idea, in part by way of Hannah Arendt's observations on totalitarianism.

Modernism's refractive world seemed to him to draw much of its energy from decay, to pitch art against dissolution, and to render political convictions as mere ironies. He was interested in reproducing the strained consciousness of Willy Loman, who himself embodied what seemed to him to be a paralysis not of politics but of the will and imagination, but he was not concerned to celebrate the energy released by collapsing certainties, though acutely aware of such a collapse. It was why he had initially been drawn to Marxism, which refused such paralysis when the democracies were impotent. It was why even now he still clung to a version of life in which the invention of purpose and form was not displaced on to art whose coherences offered a mocking commentary on social and political dissolution.

For Miller, it was precisely such fragmentation that was the problem, though, in fact, his work was to bear the marks of modernism to a far greater degree than he was prepared to acknowledge, from the stream of consciousness stories written before his success as a playwright, through to plays which explore the social construction of reality, the shifting perspectives that are a product of memory and desire.

For those critics of the liberal centre right, Miller's plays of the 1940s and 50s were frequently seen as assaults on American values, barely enciphered invocations of a politically discredited communalism – hence the suspect title *All My Sons* and the supposedly false analogies of *The Crucible* which Sartre was so easily to transform into a Marxist fable. Miller's own admitted failure to condemn Soviet treatment of the Jews and writers as early as he might have done also attracted the opprobrium of those who thought he was therefore in some way complicit, even seeking to suppress his own ethnicity as though thereby the better to burrow into the national subconscious. It is surprising how many of his fiercest critics were Jewish. The bitterness engendered by this conflict was clear enough in the 1940s and 50s, but its residue was equally detectable in the subsequent decades.

In the early 1970s, the critic Malcolm Cowley warned him that the Trot-skyites had been plotting against him from the beginning and, looking back from 2001, Miller regarded the attacks launched on him by this group, whom the journalist and historian Isaac Deutscher called 'literary Trotskisants', as being of crucial importance. At the time he was unaware of the details of their political allegiances. Later, it seemed to him that they had been instrumental in shaping the reception of his plays in the United States. A number of them were key arbiters of the literary scene, influencing not only the New York cultural world but academe too.

In July 2000, right-wing Professor Emeritus Ronald Radosh launched an attack on Miller in the equally right-wing *Front Page* magazine, edited by David Horowitz, former editor of the radical left *Ramparts* magazine, now himself a convert to the radical right. What Radosh objected to was what seemed to him to be Miller's naivety, amounting to 'gross ignorance', in continuing to see the history of the 1950s as one in which a liberal left was assaulted by vindictive right-wingers who, for a while, had the national ear. The playwright, it seemed to him, might have had some reason for his stance in mid-century America, but by the turn of the millennium historians had exposed the true extent of communist subversion in America. The opening of Soviet archives had finally resolved issues over which there had earlier, perhaps, been some legitimate debate. The fact was that there had been extensive and effective Soviet spy networks, and many of those sanctified as victims had in fact been deeply implicated in subversion, their denials being merely a tactic demanded by their masters. Miller had failed to notice this 'drift in the zeitgeist', and continued to perpetuate his paranoid vision. There had, after all, been a conspiracy, organized from Moscow. America had been at risk. Hence, Miller's acknowledgement of the existence of communists, but refusal to grant that they were actual or putative traitors, showed that he remained trapped in a mindset now patently fifty years out of date.

In particular, Radosh objected to Miller's continued invocation, in his Massey Lecture at Harvard entitled '*The Crucible* in History' (published in 2000), of Harry Bridges, leader of the West Coast Longshoremen' Union, and William Remington, a one-time employee of the Tennessee Valley Authority (like Miller, represented by Joseph Rauh Jr when, in his case, charged with perjury), sentenced to jail and murdered by an inmate. The former, Radosh explained, had now been revealed as a communist and the latter shown to have handed over classified War Production Board material. However, Miller's reference to Bridges merely says that he was the idol of West Coast longshoremen and was driven back to his native Australia as an 'unadmitted communist'. His reference to Remington, is as follows: 'at least one [person], a man named William Remington, was murdered by an inmate hoping to shorten his sentence for having killed a communist'.[21] He was in fact so murdered.

Remington was described by Griffin Fariello in his book *Red Scare* as a 'hapless government employee whose 1936 undergraduate sabbatical as a messenger boy for the Tennessee Valley Authority included roommates who were, or may have been, communist'.[22] He certainly shared an address with a local Communist Party branch. He worked in the commerce department and was trained as an economist. He was accused, on *Meet the Press*, of being a communist by Elizabeth Bentley, known as the 'Blonde Spy Queen', who had been an FBI informer within the Party from 1945 to 1947. She accused Remington of passing her government documents for the Russians during the war. He sued Bentley, NBC and the programme's sponsor, General Foods, for $100,000, settling out of court for just under a tenth of that.

Rauh (who was to die on 3 September 1992) appealed against his conviction before the Loyalty Board, and won when Bentley failed to appear to justify her accusations. Remington was, however, fired on the grounds that he was spending too much time defending himself. He was then indicted for perjury by the Grand Jury for insisting that he had not been a Party member, the foreman of the jury co-writing a book with Bentley at the time. He was convicted, a conviction reversed on appeal. He was then indicted for statements he had made on the stand. He was convicted again and sent to prison in Lewisburg, where he was murdered by three car thieves on 22 November 1954, one reported as saying, 'I'm going to get me a Commie.' According to Rauh, the 'Remington case is the best illustration of how bad the climate had become. It shows the degree of government wrongdoing.'[23] Miller, however, makes no comment on it beyond noting Remington's murder.

Nothing here, then, suggests that Miller wilfully misrepresented these two men, or the period. He had frequently described the curious mix of dedicated communists, fellow travellers and unaffiliated liberals which constituted that group of individuals who had discovered their radical faith in the 1930s, and in most cases modified and in many cases abandoned it in the 1940s and 50s. He admitted his own naivety with respect to the Soviet Union. What he had not done – as, plainly, Radosh wished he had – was to rewrite his personal history, revise the sense of impotence and oppression he had felt, abandon his contempt for the Right's disregard of constitutional rights, or reject those who sought to precipitate a degree of economic and social justice.

Radosh accused Miller of being a 'Communist dupe', anxious to exonerate all those accused in the 1950s, and, by his continued concern with that decade, evidencing the hysteria of which he accused others. He conceded that some were unjustly accused and that civil liberties were violated but asked, 'Does Miller really believe that America was "delivered into the hands" of the equivalent of today's far right and that to doubt this "could cost you"?'[24] Well, yes, I rather fancy he did – not least, perhaps, because, even fifty years on, there were a sufficient number still alive to attest to the fact.

For Radosh, Miller was doing no more, in his account of the 1950s, than defend his own illusions. Would he, Radosh asks, have allowed a former Nazi not to name his old associates? – an echo of a line of questioning developed by HUAC itself. Why, he asks, is Miller not content with his own country? Fifty years on, Miller was still being urged to put his shoulder to the national wheel. Suddenly, he becomes a 'great playwright' who has only to acknowledge that America is 'the last great hope', just as HUAC had expressed the wish that he would devote his 'magnificent talents' to a more positive portrait of his country. Perhaps one reason for his continued concern with the 1950s was that there remained those, like Radosh, who, in their values and language, recalled just what it was that made that time so disturbing.

We do now know more about the 1950s than we once did. Some ambiguities have been resolved. A number of spies have been exposed, some resolute liars revealed for what they were. But, communists or not, Kazan was not a Soviet spy, nor was Lee J. Cobb or Clifford Odets, neither were the Hollywood Ten, nor were the majority of those hounded from their jobs and, sometimes, out of the country. That Julius Rosenberg and Alger Hiss were the agents the state assumed them to be (though in 2001 the chief prosecution witness, David Greenglass, confessed to lying at the Rosenberg trial) does not make all those summoned before the Committee mere agents of the Comintern. Nor does it render void the sense of threat and oppression felt by so many who discovered that they had no right to make statements, call witnesses or cross-examine their accusers, and who often found that they had been under surveillance or the victims of informers, only to be attacked as subversive for suggesting as much. Though they could employ lawyers, as Miller did Rauh, those lawyers were forbidden to speak, being allowed only for purposes of consultation; hence those curious whispered conversations, one hand over the microphone.

For Ronald Radosh, *The Crucible* simply gets it wrong. The passage of time has invalidated its assumptions. But the fact is that it does not, as Radosh claims, say that the accused are innocent because they are accused, or that the only enemy is the informer (echoes of Eric Bentley's complaint). Tituba conjures, as had others in a Salem riven with discord, in which rumour was taken for truth, before ever Abigail Williams set the deadly game in progress.

The Crucible is set at an historical moment when menace and uncertainty were in the air. At such a moment there were those who offered themselves as experts in identifying the Devil and his disciples and had few scruples in bringing them to book. It was this world, these people, these procedures, this suspension of the normal processes of justice, this contempt for the society they thought themselves intent on preserving, that Miller set out to capture. No new data have invalidated either the play, or Miller's description of what it was to find yourself accused of believing what others decided you had no right to believe. No new data have retrospectively justified demands for betrayal as the price of citizenship. When America found itself under attack in 2001, the resulting Patriot Act required librarians to inform on those who borrowed books. They refused.

For *Partisan Review*, itself secretly funded by Henry Luce, America was now the cultural leader of the West, while Leslie Fiedler, publishing in *Encounter*, sought to suggest that it was communism and not McCarthyism that should be engaging the attention of intellectuals. In 1952 Sidney Hook, deeply involved with the CIA's campaign, approached the US government for financial support for *Partisan Review* on the grounds that it had been so effective in 'combating communist ideology abroad, particularly among intellectuals'.[25] It did, in fact, receive CIA funds via the ACCF, whose members included Whittaker Chambers (whose evidence led to the indictment of Alger Hiss) and Arthur Schlesinger Jr, the latter resigning in 1955 when he thought its anti-communism was becoming 'obsessive'.[26]

Thus, while *Death of a Salesman* was being banned from American military establishments in Europe and its author deprived of his passport, US dollars were fighting a cultural war sometimes known to the recipients of its largesse, but more often not. Indeed when Miller attacked McCarthyism, a letter was sent to the *New York Times* by *Commentary* magazine's Irving Kristol, attacking his 'absurdities'. Kristol, as executive director of the ACCF, was effectively in the pay of the CIA. This was the man who, in 1953, remarked that 'there is one thing the American people know about Senator McCarthy; he, like them, is unequivocally anti-Communist'.[27]

A year earlier, in *Commentary*, he had attacked those who, like Miller, sought to defend the civil liberties of communists:

> If a liberal wishes to defend the civil liberties of Communists or of Communist fellow-travelers, he must enter the court of American opinion with clean hands and a clear mind. He must show that he knows the existence of an organized subversive movement such as Communism is a threat to the consensus on which civil society and its liberties are based. He must bluntly acknowledge Communists and fellow-travelers to be what they are, and then, if he so desires, defend the expediency in particular circumstances of allowing them the right to be what they are. He must speak as one of *us*, defending *their* liberties. To the extent that he insists that they are on our side, that we can defend our liberties only by uncritically defending theirs, he will be taken as speaking as one of them.[28]

There was no doubting where this put Arthur Miller. He had, according to Kristol, never been in the business of defending freedom. Indeed, by this definition he had never been a liberal of any description or in a position to argue about rights of any kind. He had been one of *them*.

Meanwhile, Mary McCarthy – who had herself flirted with Trotskyism, and whom Alfred Kazin characterized as being 'stimulated to literary production by the habit of seeing other people as fools', turning 'the very outrageousness of her judgements into a social virtue'[29] – while conceding that *Death of a Salesman* was a 'strong and original conception', regarded it as 'enfeebled' by its author's 'insistence on universality' (the Trotskyite Eleanor Clark uses the same word) and by his 'eagerness to preach', which gave the play a 'canting tone'. While attacking him as a realist – an increasingly common if bewilderingly inappropriate designation – she claimed that 'throughout Miller's long practice as a realist, there is not only a naive searching for another dimension but an evident hatred and contempt for reality'.[30] Willy Loman was 'a Human Being without being anyone, a sort of suffering Statistic'.[31] This was the Mary McCarthy with whom he had crossed ideological swords at the Waldorf Conference, and one of those for whom radicalism had been wedded to an enthusiasm for modernism, though she was unequivocal in her contempt for Senator McCarthy as well as in her support for those, like Miller, harassed over passports and subjected to the bad theatre and worse morality of HUAC.

To be fair, she was in fact catholic in her attacks on American playwrights. She denounced the 'oily virtuosity' of Hellman and Odets (both of whom had appeared at the Waldorf Conference), but she also deplored O'Neill as a man who 'cannot write', who demonstrated a suspect sentimentality wedded to a fear of sex. Despite the 'barber shop harmony'[32] of his work, however, she was fascinated enough with him to circle around his work like a bat sending out high-pitched shrieks in the hope that some kind of echo would come back. The redemption lay in Europe, certainly not in Tennessee Williams, whose *A Streetcar Named Desire* she dismissed in a review in which she unaccountably referred to Stanley Kowalski as Joe.

For Kazin, her authority came from a blend of intellectual authority and condescension. Hers was a criticism that raised gossip to the status of art. As he observed, '*The Partisan Review* group was interested in the people around them to the point of ecstasy.' What he says of McCarthy would apply to a number of America's intellectuals. They treated the creative imagination with suspicion 'except it came from the Continent, and thus could serve as an analogy for their kind of intelligence'.[33] And that phenomenon would characterize several of Miller's critics from the 1960s onwards, who continued to dismiss him as an incorrigible realist at odds with the severe truths being staged by the European theatre or an American avant garde influenced by European theorists, in particular Antonin Artaud and Jerzy Grotowski.

McCarthy was not alone in her scepticism. Eric Bentley attacked *All My Sons* as sentimental melodrama. *Death of a Salesman*, he suggested, was admired by those who liked bad poetry, it being marked by 'a false rhetorical mode of speech heard only on Broadway'.[34] *The Crucible*, meanwhile, was a play in which 'the accuser is always considered holy, the accused guilty', and which was admired less for its dramatic qualities than its political stance. Miller was 'strikingly characteristic of that large wing of the liberal movement which has been overpowered by communism'. *The Crucible*, in his judgement, was 'a play for people who think that pleading the Fifth Amendment is not only a white badge of purity but also a red badge of courage'. It represented 'a type of liberalism that has been dangerous and is now obsolescent'.[35] Interestingly, when Miller and Tennessee Williams threatened a libel suit over passages in Bentley's *The Dramatic Event*, the ACCF, which contrived to see Miller as an unrepentant Stalinist, offered Bentley support on the grounds that the action threatened cultural freedom and Miller had never been in favour of a free society.[36] When Bentley showed signs of softening, Sidney Hook complained of him:

At the time of Arthur Miller's interrogation by a Congressional committee, Bentley published a strong criticism of Miller and other former members of the Communist Party for refusing to speak truthfully about the character of their involvements. At the time he sent me personal letters, thanking me for the enlightenment he owed to my writings. When the political climate changed, Bentley was running with a new set of hounds. In his *Thirty Years of Treason*, he ... staunchly defended those interrogated by the Congressional committees.[37]

Such was the complicated and changing ideological background to literary criticism and theatrical reviews in the 1940s and 1950s when the anti-Stalinist Left took rather more pleasure in attacking those who had once shared their enthusiasm for communism than they did in attacking a Right for which they also had contempt. The word 'realist', in the mouths of some of these critics, was less a description of a style than code for writers they presumed to be in thrall to the Party, and hence the Party line, just as the word 'universalist', which occurs in a number of reviews, frequently hints at an aesthetic counterpart to political convictions.

By no means all reviews, of course, were products of these political infights, but there is a sense in which Miller suffered collateral damage and in which reviewers were responding to the current *Weltanschauung*. The echo of these early reviews continued to reverberate in subsequent decades. Susan Sontag, Robert Brustein, Richard Gilman, Philip Rahv, along with Walter Kerr, John Simon and others sustained an attack on him through the 1960s, 70s, 80s and 90s. In 1984, the American Gerald Bordman would sum up his achievement in *The Oxford Companion to American Theatre* in a devastatingly reductive sentence: 'Miller was a firmly committed leftist, whose political philosophizing sometimes got the better of his dramaturgy.'[38] Note the tense – *was*. Note the year – 1984. In 2003, plainly oblivious to this entry, Oxford University Press wrote to Miller soliciting an endorsement of the book. The endorsement was not forthcoming.

Miller, meanwhile, suffered further damage from a militant anti-communism. In the first months of 1953, the State Department prohibited use of works written by those designated not only communists but 'controversial persons ... fellow travellers, and so forth'. The 'and so forth' suggests something less than scrupulous about the definition. Miller was still, in the view of those on the right, a fellow traveller; and his work, in the State Department phrase, 'detrimental to US objectives'. As a result, his books were removed from overseas libraries.

In 1953 Senator McCarthy was at the peak of his power, though the following spring, when he made the serious error of taking on the US Army, began his swift downward spiral. Elsewhere, things seemed to be moving in

America's direction. In March, Stalin died, while the Korean War ended in July. For his part, more than a year after Kazan's appearance before HUAC, Miller was still concerned with the implications of his naming of names, still trying to understand what had led his erstwhile friend to inform. In the June he jotted down ideas for what seems to have been a possible play, with the title 'The End in View', in which he explored the possibility that Kazan had persuaded himself that there was a certain honour in informing. Guilty first at becoming successful, when success itself had seemed a form of betrayal, he had joined the Party, only to feel guilty at his own surrender to its dictates. To inform was thus to purge himself of that guilt and assert his control over his own life, albeit at the price of controlling others.

The play, if such it was, went nowhere and Miller's response to the times was now to turn to other work, that same year directing a production of *All My Sons* in Arden, Delaware, with his sister Joan. He then taught a playwrighting class at the Dramatic Workshop in New York, where one of his students was Tony Lo Bianco, who was in 1982 to star in a Broadway revival of *A View from the Bridge*. Miller's success as a director led to offers to direct other people's plays, which he refused. In subsequent years he lost his enthusiasm for directing, though still staging several of his own works, then later recovered it if only because it was a means of protecting his work from those whose deficiencies he thought could damage his reputation. He had, after all, been disappointed with a number of the first productions of his plays in America.

Writing to his former teacher Kenneth Rowe on 27 December 1953, Miller explained that he was anxious to start a new play, on which, in truth, he had been working for more than three years before breaking off to write *The Crucible*. He planned to finish it by the spring. His idea was to assemble a group of actors and even technical staff and then invite them all to Connecticut for two weeks the following summer in order to discuss it. In a letter of March 1954, he again indicated that he had been working on the play, which was to be about a man's salvation. Perhaps his next one, he suggested, would be a comedy. Nothing, however, came of this play either, and comedy made way for farce as the theatre became caught up with national politics and he was publicly identified as a subversive.

By December 1953, *The Crucible* had premieres in Amsterdam and Oslo and was scheduled for France, Germany and Denmark. The Belgian Jacques Huisman directed a production at the Théâtre National de Belgique. He had previously been responsible, with the help of Peter Brook, for the French-language premiere of *Death of a Salesman*. *The Crucible* now opened under the title *La Chasse aux Sorcières* ('The Witch-hunt'; in Paris changed to *Les Sorcières de Salem)* in January 1954. Huisman himself gave it its title; having no doubt as to its central thrust or its relevance beyond the boundaries of the United States. 'In a country like ours,' he commented, 'which had to suffer from the Spanish Inquisition, the parallels were immediately apparent ... Here was a play recognizably about freedom of conscience and the dark forces that attempt to repress that fundamental right. But nobody could suspect that by making explicit the original mysterious title I was about to create trouble for Miller.'[39] It was not the title, though, that precipitated that trouble, American bureaucrats not being renowned for their interest in foreign-language productions of American plays. When his application for renewal of his passport to attend the Belgian premiere was refused, it was for more domestic reasons.

On the first day of March 1954, Miller received a Western Union telegram: 'IF POSSIBLE FOR YOU [WE] ARE OFFERING FREE TRANSPORTATION FOR BRUSSELS PREMIERE CRUCIBLE.' The cable was signed by the Association Belgo-Américaine. Unfortunately, his passport was out of date. Accompanied to the Wall Street passport office by Montgomery Clift (then appearing in a production of *The Seagull*), he submitted the necessary form before cabling his acceptance of the invitation. It was Monday. He was scheduled to fly on the Friday.

When his passport was not forthcoming he cabled Brussels offering to fly out a few days later, 'DUE NORMAL PASSPORT DELAY'. The delay, though, was anything but normal. Unbeknown to him, his passport was effectively being withdrawn. He contacted his lawyer, who called a Washington friend, Joseph L. Rauh Jr, the man who two years later would appear at his side when he was called before HUAC. He, in turn, contacted the head of the Passport Bureau, one Mrs Ruth Shipley, and was told that it was 'not in the national interest' for Miller to leave the country. It was a stark reminder of his new vulnerability.

On 7 March, two days after the denial of his passport, Miller wrote to Ruth Shipley from his Willow Street address. He now withdrew his request, rehearsing for her benefit the timetable of his application, and the fact that the delay had made his trip impossible. She had, he insisted, misjudged him, and the best interests of the country. He pointed out that in his two European trips since 1947 he had given many interviews abroad, none of which expressed anything but a commitment to his country. He then recalled the performances of *The Crucible* that had already taken place in Berlin, Munich, Amsterdam and Copenhagen, and the positive response the play had provoked, a response that could only imply that its author was a credit to his country. This was especially so in the light of current anti-American propaganda. Whatever his private dossier might say, he went on, he was an American who wrote American plays and those plays were widely respected throughout Europe. He was neither pleading for a passport nor requesting one. Neither was he acting on lawyer's advice but merely expressing his disquiet as a citizen at an unfair and mistaken act.

His lawyers, Paul, Weiss, Rifkind, Wharton & Garrison, perhaps unsurprisingly, thought the letter ill-advised, not least because they had themselves not advised it. Accordingly, they quickly sent their own letter to Mrs Shipley, underscoring that their client's letter had indeed been sent without legal advice and that as a result he had referred to the denial of his passport, a phrase which they believed to be based on a mistaken assumption. They noted that in a telephone conversation in which she had outlined some of the material in her file, she had indicated that no final decision had yet been made. They were plainly trying to keep the door open for subsequent applications. Mrs Shipley replied to Miller's letter, noting his withdrawal of his application and returning his nine-dollar application fee.

Following a press release by the State Department, the newspapers were full of reports of the withdrawn passport. They observed that the action was taken under regulations denying passports to persons believed to be supporting the communist movement whether or not they were members of the Party. Miller was quoted in the press as likening his plight to that of John Proctor in his own play.

On 30 March, he issued a press release in which he attempted to defend himself against the State Department's accusations, declaring his loyalty and patriotism, while launching an attack on those persecuting him. Certainly the tone of his letter to Mrs Shipley, in which he had thanked her for her prompt attention and which had concluded 'Very sincerely yours', had now given way to a much more aggressive stance, not least because of his irritation at the State Department's decision to make its case public. His press release ran:

That I am supporting the Communist cause is not true. That I am opposed to much of what passes for American domestic and foreign policy is certainly true. However, in this particular instance the issue would seem to be whether, in the struggle for men's minds, the presence on foreign soil of one, Arthur Miller, is likely to damage the prestige or interests of the United States.

'The Crucible' deals with a hunt for witches in Salem, Massachusetts, some two hundred and fifty years ago. So I am rather an expert on witch hunts. I fully understand how deeply terrified perfectly fine people can become. I also know that they often live long enough to feel thoroughly ashamed of themselves after the terror has burned itself out. I know, too, that while the only defense against such phenomena is to repeat the simple truth, it is in the nature of the thing that the truth is the very last thing to appear believable until its time once again has come. The State Department, and all those who agree with its action, will excuse me, therefore, if I do not fall into a cold sweat or dead faint.

Quite the contrary; I know that I love this nation. I know that I could not function for three months under any kind of dictatorship. I know that my works are a credit to this nation, and I dare say they will endure longer than the McCarran Act (more properly the Internal Security Act of 1950 which called for the regulation of all subversives). It is even possible that through my plays, which have been produced in every theatre in Europe, I have made more friends for American culture than the State Department. Certainly I have made fewer enemies, but that isn't very difficult.

I only hope that the people abroad who admire this country will not assume from this action, as I know they have from the many similar passport denials in the past, that freedom is dying in America. It is not. It is only looking around for its friends, and it is finding many. And now, with the permission of the State Department, which gratuitously issued its statement, I should like to be left in peace to finish my new play, which, I may add, they will not like either.

Interestingly, on 1 April, Tennessee Williams, who had been unwilling to condemn Elia Kazan, now wrote to the State Department to protest against the treatment of his fellow writer:

Dear Sirs,

I feel obliged to tell you how shocked I am by the news that Arthur Miller, a fellow playwright, has been refused a passport to attend the opening of a play of his in Brussels.

I know only the circumstances of the case that have been reported in the papers, but since I have been spending summers abroad since 1948, I am in a position to tell you that Mr Miller and his work occupy the very highest critical and popular position in the esteem of Western Europe, and this action can only serve to implement the Communist propaganda, which holds that our country is persecuting its finest artists and renouncing the principles of freedom on which our ancestors founded it.

I would like to add that there is nothing in Arthur Miller's work, or my personal acquaintance with him, that suggests to me the possibility that he is helpful or sympathetic to the Communist or any other subversive cause. I have seen all his theatrical works. Not one of them contains anything but the most profound human sympathy and nobility of spirit that the American theatre has shown in our time and perhaps in any time before. He is one man that I could never suspect of telling a lie, and he has categorically stated that he has *not* supported Communism or been a Communist.

I don't think you have properly estimated the enormous injury that an action of this kind can do our country, even in the minds of those who are still prejudiced in our favor in Western Europe.

Yours respectfully,

Tennessee Williams

There is no evidence that Mrs Shipley ever saw this letter from a man who was then, with Miller, the best-known American playwright both at home and abroad. Either way, it had no effect. Miller did not go to Belgium. Two years later, Huisman himself found it difficult to obtain a visa to go to the United States. As he remarked, 'the witches were still haunting us'.[40]

On the same day that Williams wrote to the State Department, the American Civil Liberties Union sent Miller a letter noting its concern over what had happened and indicating that its representatives would be having a meeting with Mrs Shipley. The meeting, assuming it to have taken place, led nowhere.

Ironically, in the middle of this controversy, Miller received a telegram from Eric Bentley (who had been so dismissive of the analogy at the heart of *The Crucible*) asking him for a statement of his political views. He drafted, but never sent, a two-page letter, fired by his irritation at his treatment by the Passport Office, in which he pointed out that his political views should have been apparent from his plays, which contained a map of his mind and heart. He knew of few people, he explained, who had reacted so publicly to the issues of the moment in the most public of places – the theatre. He felt indignant that in order to secure his passport he was expected to assemble a dossier of his anti-left views and the hostility towards him of communist journals. He was, after all, a playwright and not a politician.

When he did reply to Bentley, a month later, he did so briefly, stating that a recitation of his own views would, he believed, be inadequate since he had learned in the interim that Mrs Shipley had been refusing passports for reasons having nothing to do with politics and everything to do with morality, taking against those who had committed adultery or offended against another of the Ten Commandments. He thought the issue best dealt with by a journalist. As for himself, he wished to get back to his play, which he thought his best answer.

The whole incident was a distraction but it laid the foundation for his appearance before HUAC, as it also, of course, established him in the public mind as a man judged sufficiently subversive not to warrant the full rights of a citizen. Certainly, he was feeling a growing tension between himself and the American society he sought to address but which increasingly seemed not only at a tangent to his own values and concerns but determined to harass him. The attacks were plainly beginning to get under his skin. He was, after all, a playwright. He did not run for public office. Nothing he did could affect the economic or military life of the country. He knew, and resented the fact, that he could escape his problems by the simple expedient of confessing his guilt and offering up the names of friends and associates. The mere notion that with such a gesture he could supposedly purge decades-long villainy was evidence enough of the absurdity in which he felt himself trapped. Meanwhile, to capitulate would be to undermine not only his personal integrity but the whole foundation of his art. He was not willing to become a patriot, as defined by the new dispensation, by denying who he was.

Nor was he wrong to feel himself threatened. In August 1954, his FBI file indicates inquiries to check his whereabouts, inquiries that extended to his postman. The following month, an agent checked with the Roxbury Post Office to see if he was at his Connecticut address.

By now, Miller was in a state of some despair about both his personal life and his career. In September 1953, he had written notes for what a handwritten comment indicates was to be an introduction to a play marked 'an early draft of *After the Fall*', an introduction which in fact seems to offer a remarkable insight into his relationship with Mary and his increasing need to break away. It addresses the relationship between men and women but seems so close to his own domestic situation that it is difficult to believe it is anything but a contemplation of the latter. Marilyn may still have been on the other side of the continent, but, on the basis of this document, he was surely preparing himself to turn in her direction.

In the play as outlined, the man is married to a woman who is morally pre scriptive and sexually remote. Love has taken second place to a battle for power. This was, in fact, precisely the relation he saw himself as having with Mary, the severity of whose moral judgements he in part accepted even while acknow-ledging that it destroyed their relationship. Having been guilty of an indis-cretion the man invites suspicion whenever he expresses a sexual interest in her, not least because her own confidence in her attractiveness has been eroded.

The strained prose that characterizes this draft introduction is surely his attempt to theorize what had gone wrong between himself and Mary. He conceded the moral force of her position, but they were now sexually estranged, mostly because her severity drained him of desire. In the notes for his proposed play he observed that she was prone to insist on monogamy precisely because she now feared that he would violate it. The result is that the wife becomes his conscience and he becomes impotent both within the marriage and beyond it. His desire for another woman thus becomes expres-sive of his need to re-establish himself as a free individual. In turning to another woman, the draft text suggests, it is easy for the man to convince himself that in some way the affair is not only unthreatening as far as his marriage is concerned, but might be seen as in some way strengthening it, since in restoring him to himself it will reinvigorate his relationship with his wife. This is precisely what Miller persuaded himself was true in his own case, and he came close to saying so to Mary.

In 1954, he wrote a two-page lament about marriage itself. It is a curious aria, a contemplation of the seeming arbitrariness of relationships and the inevitability of betrayal. It seems to him that marriage is a chance meeting of strangers who in some fundamental way remain strangers and may become enemies. In seeking to understand it, he tracks the factitious romanticism that attaches itself to the relationship back to the first, primal, relationship – that between mother and child.

By the end of that year he was in despair of both the public and the private world. He felt alienated from his work and saw nothing but the collapse of social and moral values in the world beyond it. Certainly, in the play he was then writing, he accused himself of doing little more than give shape to oblivion. It was to be a play about life as an inevitable defeat. There is a passage, not ascribed to any character, that reads like a personal statement in which he confesses to feeling exiled from love and life, unable to commit himself. One of the characters in this abortive play is clearly based on Marilyn. When she re-entered his life, she would dispel this sense of despair. For a time, though, he was at his lowest point, if not suicidal then trying to reconcile himself to an existence in which he no longer believed.

All the confidence that had driven him since leaving college, that had enabled him to challenge the presumptions of his culture, seemed to have drained away. His marriage was no more than a negotiated truce. Marilyn was the temptation to which he felt he could not succumb. His political certainties lay in ruins. He was the target of those who seemed to have a legitimacy conferred not simply by the state but by his awareness of his own false loyalties. He had, he feared, lost his audience and with it his connection to his art. His response, as far as the theatre was concerned, was to turn back to his own past and to a time when he had had a clear sense of his own ambition. It was also to explore the notion of betrayal.

His next plays were the result of an invitation from Martin Ritt, a graduate of the Group Theatre. A production of Odets's *The Flowering Peach* was coming to its close and Robert Whitehead, with whom Miller would later work at the Lincoln Center, had offered the theatre for Sunday night performances. Ritt turned to Miller who, in two weeks, wrote *A Memory of Two Mondays*, originally subtitled, 'An Improvisation of a Bygone Year'. The play is set in the autoparts warehouse where he had worked to earn enough money to go to university. 'I chose the material,' he explained, 'out of a need to touch again a reality I could understand, unlike the booming, inane America of the present.'[41] 'I think,' he added, 'you have to remind yourself constantly that other people have to stand in line and of the immense difficulty of life for so many people.'[42] More nostalgic than polemical, the piece nonetheless revealed its author's fascination with the processes of work, if also a certain distance from the working man he might once have wished to celebrate.

In fact it was based closely on an unpublished memoir called 'Two Years', written a decade earlier. In this, he had changed the names of his fellow workers while retaining his own, but otherwise described events at the warehouse much as they had occurred and much as they would subsequently appear in the play. So there was material to hand when the commission came. The play, which requires a cast of fourteen, is set in the shipping room of the warehouse. The public face of the building, the front office, switchboard, customer counter, are invisible. Like O'Neill in *The Hairy Ape*, he is interested in those who keep the system running, out of mind, invisible.

This is a workplace stripped of everything but the utilitarian. The lives of those who work here are similarly stripped down to essentials, a series of overlapping stories as condensed and exemplary as those in *The Iceman Cometh*. This is where they work. They live elsewhere, but the fact that we learn little of those other lives suggests that they offer no more fulfilment than the dull routine of the warehouse itself, the more so when compared to the student (plainly Miller) who is working alongside them, earning money to go to university. They have no ambition beyond a brief affair, a new car. Meanwhile, next door, invisible until the windows are cleaned, is a brothel, and the implication seems to be that there is a connection between warehouse and whorehouse, each demanding a suspect trade of self for cash.

The place, Miller insists, 'must seem dirty and unmanageably chaotic, but since it is seen in this play with two separate visions it is also romantic. It is a little world, a home to which, unbelievably perhaps, these people like to come every Monday morning.'[43] Whose 'romantic' vision is this, though, but Miller's, as he looks back partly with nostalgia, partly with a sense of frustration and even irritation at those who, unlike Eddie Carbone in *A View from the Bridge*, have settled for half? Though not acknowledged, the play seems to take place in 1933–4, Miller's time at the Chadick-Delamater company. Hitler has taken over the German government. At home, times are bad. But in the workroom little of this seems to penetrate, except as depressing messages of drunken evenings, dying and estranged wives, failed lives.

A Memory of Two Mondays is not without its comic set-pieces as well as its melodramatic tussles with fate. Stylistically it is for the most part realistic, except that as time passes the set is flooded with light and the prose is transformed, for a while, into verse. Indeed, the play offers a verse soliloquy in which the student, Bert (an echo of Miller's name, Art), laments those who will stay as he moves on. At the same time, another character, an Irish immigrant, slowly loses his own access to poetry. His life turns into prose as he settles into a world of dull routine.

On 19 June 1962, Miller wrote to the Italian director Giorgio Strehler, who had just staged a production of *A Memory of Two Mondays*. On the basis of reviews and photographs it appeared to him to offer something absent from the original production – namely, a sense of the poetry underlying the apparent realism. The play now stood vindicated. He recalled that in its first appearance, along with *A View from the Bridge*, reviewers had largely ignored a work which he insisted was closer to him than almost anything else he had written. The problem, as he later thought, was that he had chosen to present the play to the American public when 'the stock market was on the rise and the dollar was the only legitimate money in the world and a play about workers was the last thing anybody wanted to think about'.[44]

For Ritt, though, the play needed a companion piece, and suddenly 'the Italian play', picked up and put down so many times, had seemingly found its moment. As early as 1948, when his notebook was full of dialogue for *Death of a Salesman*, he had jotted down a note to write the Italian play, recalling the story of a man who ratted on two immigrants, and observing that the secret of Greek drama was the vendetta, something comprehensible to Jews. Red Hook, where *A View from the Bridge* would be set, was full of Greek tragedies, he told himself. On 16 November 1948, he had even sketched a stage set for what he was calling 'An Italian Tragedy'. It consisted of a series of tenement buildings. He got no further. Since all that was needed now was a one-act play, all the difficulties with which he had been wrestling fell away.

He finished *A View from the Bridge* in ten days, not quite such a feat, perhaps, in that it already existed as a previously unknown and unpublished short story, two drafts of which have survived. Here, Eddie Carbone is Jerry Mangone, himself an immigrant from Italy who had never spoken English until he was in his teens. His niece is called Flora. Her father, we are told, had been killed unloading coffee from a lighter. When she was twelve, Mangone had told her dying mother that he would take care of her daughter until she was married. This, then, is the back story of *A View from the Bridge*. Mangone is protective of Flora as she grows, not letting her cross the bridge to Manhattan with her girlfriends when they go to hear Frank Sinatra. If she wants to go to a film he accompanies her, and it has to be in the Brooklyn Paramount rather than the Manhattan Paramount, as if it carries fewer risks. He hardly notices his own two children.

The plot largely follows the story familiar from the play. Two cousins arrive as illegal immigrants and disturb a relationship between uncle and niece that is charged with something more than a family affection (one of Miller's own cousins had married her uncle, a marriage which seemed to have a touch of doom about it). Jerry kisses the younger one on the mouth, as Eddie would in the play, and knocks him down in a boxing lesson, challenging him as if he were a rival. There is, however, no sexual encounter between the young immigrant and Flora, though Jerry does inform the authorities of the two cousins presence and the story spells out in detail the profundity of the crime involved in such a betrayal.

In doing so it underscores, as the play would not, the political implications of the story. Whatever its origins, at least in this early version it was clearly offered as a parable for the betrayals precipitated by HUAC. Though the title – 'Tales Private and Public' – is crossed through, it remains legible and underscores not merely the thrust of this story but in some senses the essence of his work. It tells us that the one unforgivable crime is informing, this being worse than murder in that it lacks passion, worse than theft since theft is a product of need. Informing, the story insists, is a betrayal of human connectiveness at a time when many immigrants had precisely been fleeing from oppressive governments for which the informer had been a primary agent – plainly a conscious attempt by Miller to link the story to the contemporary situation in America, something not spelled out in *A View from the Bridge.*

The marriage between Flora and the young immigrant follows rather than precedes his imprisonment, being a device to secure his freedom. The story ends before the encounter which in the play would take Eddie Carbone's life.

There is a lawyer in the story as in the play, but we learn more of him. He is also an immigrant, son of a wealthy Milanese family who had banished him for his socialist views. He had worked as a longshoreman and organized two local branches of the union, which in turn threw him out because of his radicalism. The priests had warned against him and nuns had hanged him in effigy. He had made speeches at election time. It is he who seeks out Jerry to warn him of what he is afraid will happen.

In the play, put together so quickly, Miller stripped out the past and pressed the action to its logical, and for him tragic, conclusion. Short story became short play with its politics no longer spelled out but implicit in the story of a man who betrays others in order to protect his sense of himself.

In *A View from the Bridge* a longshoreman Eddie Carbone, married to Beatrice is – though he can never acknowledge it – in love with his niece Catherine. Her new sexual maturity disturbs him, not least because it might give a name to his own feelings for her. He resists the evidence of that maturity, struggling to keep her a child. In other words, a crisis is already at hand. It is precipitated when two of his wife's relatives – Marco and Rodolpho – illegal immigrants, arrive and stay with them. When Rodolpho seemingly falls in love with Catherine, Eddie's world begins to fall apart. Desperate to keep her, he consults a lawyer, Alfieri, who can advise him to do nothing but allow nature to take its course. In despair, he places a call to the Immigration Service, breaking a fundamental code of his community in order to preserve her innocence and hence, as he sees it, his own. When Marco kills him in revenge he dies, as he believes, an innocent man with a clean name, innocent not of informing but of an offence he dare not name. He dies, too, to uphold the very system of moral justice against which he has offended.

Plans for Sunday evening performances, though, now fell through as a result of the premature closing of *The Flowering Peach*. The actors had been keen on the venture, cross-casting between the two plays, and playing in the same unfashionable theatre. Now, Broadway emerged as a possible home. The two plays duly opened in September 1955 at the Coronet Theatre. They were designed by Boris Aronson, who would later work on Miller's Lincoln Center plays in the early 1960s and on *The Price* in 1968. In the mornings Miller, his mind awhirl with a mixture of guilt and elation at his private life, would study Aronson's constantly changing set designs on his way to his Central Park West apartment. In the afternoons he would often slip away to see Marilyn, who had come east and with whom he was having the affair he had so long resisted.

For Brooks Atkinson, writing in the *New York Times*, *A Memory of Two Mondays* was swamped with detail and overwritten, but *A View from the Bridge* seemed potentially to have the stuff of tragedy. To him, everything about the play rang true. Unsurprisingly, given the research that had gone into it, in Italy no less than in Brooklyn, Miller seemed to understand the people, their language and their attitudes. It fell short of tragedy, Atkinson felt, because its author had entered the story too late, before we know enough about the central character. The two women he also thought underwritten, something with which Miller would come to agree, expanding their roles for the two-act version he prepared for the London production. Unusually, Atkinson had had an early sight of the text, which he considered more substantial than the play as staged. Thus it seemed to him that Van Heflin was so concerned with Eddie's inarticulate speech that he badly underplayed. Eileen Heckart played Eddie's wife Beatrice as a neurotic.

In an article in the *New York Times*, Miller explained the difficulty he had experienced with casting, especially with respect to the role of the niece, Catherine:

> To find her the several acting schools in the city were ransacked, agents were enlisted for the search. Finally, high schools were canvassed. Toward the end, I found myself in danger of arrest as I wandered in and out of side streets looking at girls, looking for the bloom of youth ... After a while it began to seem as though they were all the same girls. More precisely, that they were all two versions of the same girl. One was what I came to think of as the Westchester girl, who is built for swimming, and the other is the anti-Westchester or Actors Studio girl.

The first is neatly groomed, walks and sits confidently, reads in a well-modulated voice, is unable to smile freely, and cannot laugh. The second, being better trained, is more likely to clump onto the stage strategically relaxing herself; she is willing to reveal her excitement and ambition, she tries to create some rudimentary attitude toward what she is reading, but she gets so involved in her interpretation that all the jokes go by unnoticed.[45]

The mood of studied irony suggests a gap between himself and the production that was real enough. His mind was, indeed, elsewhere. The result, he later confessed, was unsatisfactory. J. Carrol Naish, as Alfieri the narrator, was no better than Van Heflin. He 'scrambled his lines like a juggler who keeps dropping his Indian clubs'.[46] The director, too, on his first production, lacked conviction, but Miller blamed himself for lacking real interest. And in Van Heflin he had accepted as an Italian longshoreman an actor out of Oklahoma for whom the language of the Italian community seemed wholly foreign. He should anyway, he thought not have succumbed to the idea of a Broadway production.

In fact the reviews were mixed, and the double bill ran for 149 performances. He was disappointed and disoriented, and unbeknown to him on the verge of what was to turn into a nine-year absence from the theatre. At that time, he observed later, he 'feared dislocation for people of [his] generation'. He had 'lost any orientation, politically, socially ... I could not think of myself any longer as being allied with some working class or with the oppressed, because the oppressed were being middle-class ... I knew it was not true, but I did not know what was true.'[47]

Miller has said that *A View from the Bridge* was influenced by his visit to Sicily after the war and by time spent in the ruined Greek theatre at Siracusa. It was here, after all, that citizens had witnessed the great tragedies. He had known the story that was to become *A View from the Bridge* since 1947 when he was researching material for *The Hook* – indeed, in some of its essentials, since his time in the Brooklyn Navy Yard. Wandering the waterfront ten blocks from his house in the small hours, 'a desert beyond the law', and visiting longshoremen in their homes, he grew to know their families, their language with its 'mangled Sicilian-English bravura', and the 'untrammeled emotions' that would move to the centre of his play. He derived the central plot from Vincent Longhi – like the Alfieri who was to narrate *A View from the Bridge*, a lawyer. He recalled 'a longshoreman who had ratted to the Immigration Bureau on two brothers, his own relatives, who were living illegally in his very home, in order to break an engagement between one of them and his niece. The squealer was disgraced, and no one knew where he had gone off to, and some whispered that he had been murdered by one of the brothers.'[48]

At the time, the story meant nothing to him. He was interested in the contending power systems on the waterfront, looking for an authentic hero in an age that no longer seemed to find space for such. He later remarked that it had, anyway, seemed too complete, too fully formed, to be transferred to the stage. What could he possibly add to what seemed a classical story from another place and another age? Then, in the mid-1950s, that completeness began to seem appealing, as did the passion which set it in motion. The act of betrayal at its heart now had a clear political correlative. Beyond that, 'I saw that the reason I had not written it was that as a whole its meaning escaped me. I could not fit it into myself. It existed apart from me and seemed not to express anything within me.'[49]

He made those comments in 1960, suggesting that he wrote the play, partly at least, in order to discover what connection there might be between himself and this story of sexual guilt and betrayal. Many years later, in 1987, he hinted at a reason for the sudden relevance of this play in which, as in *The Crucible*, an older man, in a cold marriage, feels a passionate and destabilizing love for a younger woman. Speaking of attending rehearsals for the play, even as his relationship with Marilyn Monroe was at its most intense, he alluded to his sense that 'I was turning against myself, struggling to put my life behind me, order and disorder at war in me, in a kind of parallel of the stress between the play's formal, cool classicism and the turmoil of incestuous desire and betrayal within it.'[50]

This is, indeed, a description of the tensions within the play. Later still, he recalled another personal dimension to the story that he suspected had also allowed him to see its relevance to his own life, albeit subconsciously. While acknowledging that in literal terms the incestuous motif was more apparent than real, given that this is an unconsummated relationship between uncle and niece, he said: 'For years I unthinkingly thought of Catherine as his daughter ... there was no incestuous feeling, but in my mind there was. And this incestuous line, of which I was not conscious when I was writing, emerged one day in a later production when I suddenly saw relationships in my own family that were reflected on the stage.'[51] The relationship he had in mind was that between his father and his sister.

For several reasons, then, this story of a longshoreman's love for his niece, of his betrayal of others in order to remain loyal to his own feelings, now seemed to him to address personal and social issues of immediate relevance, even if he chose to locate these less against the background of an intrusive political reality than in an ancient world in which tragedy had been a central means by which a society addressed its conflicting necessities.

The scholar A. Robert Martin wrote to Miller pointing out the regularity with which he included lawyers in his work and asking, in particular, how he saw them as functioning. In replying on 30 May 1963, Miller explained that in *Death of a Salesman* the lawyer, Bernard, had been dispassionately studious of the facts, offering a detached mercy to Willy Loman. He represented the middle way. Willy Loman, by contrast, flirted with ecstasy and death. His attitude to justice in *A View from the Bridge* and its role in the death of Eddie Carbone, he explained, was different. Both Alfieri and Eddie are concerned with justice but they interpret it differently. Alfieri associates it with the law, even as his sympathies reach out to a man for whom the law offers no answer. For Eddie, justice is more transcendental. At some level he is aware of what he has done, of his breach of a fundamental trust, but it serves a higher purpose. He is about the business of rectifying what he sees as a flaw, a radical disorder in experience, and is prepared to pay the price that all tragic protagonists pay. He dies to set things right, to redeem himself in his own eyes, and in dying he upholds the law whose inadequacies he acknowledges.

Part of the subtlety of *A View from the Bridge* lies in Miller's ability to stage the passions of an inarticulate man. Eddie is not reticent. He blocks off the avenue to expression. He is convinced that what is not said does not exist. Despite his apparent forthrightness, he lives by indirection. When he visits the lawyer Alfieri he does so to seek confirmation for his sense of alarm, his feeling that there is something manifestly wrong with Rodolpho. What emerge are contradictory accusations. He is gay but also a sexual threat to Catherine. Eddie's own real feelings, meanwhile, must remain clouded.

Under pressure, he displaces those feelings on to action. He stages a boxing lesson with Rodolpho in which he strikes his implicit rival, desperate to humiliate him in front of his niece. Eddie kisses him on the mouth (an action which so alarmed Britain's censor, the Lord Chamberlain, that he banned the play from the public stage) for the same reason. Rodolpho is baffled by these actions but Marco understands and responds in kind, raising a chair above Eddie's head in a game which becomes a threat. Catherine and Rodolpho dance together in front of Eddie. He twists a newspaper in his hands, a dime is dropped in a pay-phone, men play street games with coins. Eddie moves in a physical world. He distrusts language, which can too easily betray him – which does, indeed, betray him and others. He wants to move things on to his own level but betrayal awaits him there, too.

In the end he is trapped in the logic of his own feelings, obliged to defend a sense of himself that is no longer congruent with his actions. He dies rather than acknowledge that he has lost everything he values – Catherine, Beatrice, his name. In the one-act version written for New York he dies with Catherine's name on his lips; in the two-act version written for the London opening, it is Beatrice's name. It is a crucial difference, the latter ending suggesting that he had finally abandoned his obsession, the former that he had not. Miller expanded the play at the suggestion of his British director, Peter Brook, in a production that more clearly invoked the Red Hook community. Lower wage rates meant that Brook could employ more actors, while the set provided a backdrop of the tenement buildings which constituted the community Eddie betrays and which Miller had first sketched in his notebook back in 1948.

It was the simplicity of the story, its unrelenting and unswerving nature, that appealed. In a context in which it seemed to him that the American theatre was retreating into what he called 'psycho-sexual romanticism',[52] celebrating the fragile individual, the victim, a theatre of 'tender emotions' and 'mere sympathy' – he was thinking, presumably, of Tennessee Williams, Carson McCullers, William Inge and Robert Anderson – he looked to create something altogether more disturbing. At a moment, he suggested, 'when great events both at home and abroad cried out for recognition and analytic inspection',[53] it was necessary to create a theatre that inspired such.

At first blush the reference to great events at home and abroad seems odd in the context of a play whose passions were to be presented as timeless, a play, moreover, in which psychosexual tensions were, whatever he said, undeniably central. But, as he observed:

> there is a political side to it, too, because we were in the middle of the McCarthy period ... The idea of a person who informs on his former associates and friends was in the air ... So that's in the play, too ... It is an attempt to look at informants informing as a tragic act, as an act which finally is unavoidable. ... what the play is pointing out is that there is an ancient, immemorial ache in the event of informing on someone. Though it has something to do with the external circumstances, they don't control it. The ancient ache controls it. And it's beyond rationality, I think; and that's why it's a tragic circumstance.[54]

He said this some thirty years after the play opened. At the time he took a rather different line. Stung by a piece of gossip published by Murray Kempton in the *New York Post* in January 1956 and inserted into an article about Sean O'Casey, to the effect that he had sent a copy of the play to Kazan so that he would know what he thought of stool-pigeons, he sent an angry letter of rebuttal:

> I never offered Kazan 'A View from the Bridge', and if I had, and he had accepted the job of directing it, I cannot conceive a more boorish act than Kempton ascribes to me, namely to then refuse him the project. I don't have time or the inclination for such idiocy and I am amazed that he could have judged me such a stupid man as to do such a thing ... I did offer the leading role to Lee Cobb, but for reasons that have nothing to do with politics it was impossible to arrange his appearance in the play ... I will offer Kazan a play

of mine to direct when I have one which I believe would be best served by his kind of talent. And I am sure he will accept or reject the job on the merits.

The play, he went on was anyway 'not about a political informer. When I write a play about a political informer he will be called a political informer. The situation in the present play is not analogous, is not even pertinent to that kind of dilemma.' In accepting gossip about the play and about his attitude to Kazan, Kempton, he suggested, had 'fallen prey to the wish-fulfilment assertions of Left dogmatists who join with the Right in finding secret plots, angles, and smirking analogies wherever it serves them to do so.'[55]

He was, at the very least, disingenuous about Cobb's reason for declining the part. In fact he refused because he was afraid to put his film career in jeopardy. Association with Miller had become a risky business. He was also being disingenuous with respect to the relevance of the theme to contemporary events, though *A View from the Bridge* is clearly not 'about a political informer'. Understandably, though, he was indignant about the reductive view of the play and the distracting gossip so casually recycled by a man who could, as Miller suggested to him, have simply picked up a telephone and checked.

Publicly, Kempton recanted: 'Mr Miller is the only proper witness in this matter, and it is my duty to apologize for the circulation of the story he denies', while referring to Eric Bentley's review in the *New Republic* which had made the connection between *A View from the Bridge* and HUAC. Privately, though, he sent him a letter in which he explained himself at greater length:

> Here are a few observations which I hope you will accept as in the friendliest spirit of which I am capable. They do not really seem to me to belong to public debate, because they are too easily misunderstood in times like these. Let me, if you don't mind my saying so, be wrong on the side of the victims and not their oppressors ...
>
> I confess and would confess publicly an enormous admiration for your posture in times like these. It has been a lonely one and has cost you many things which I don't believe are really worth much, but certainly seemed to Elia Kazan worth at least the price of pride. You have, after all, said what you thought of Kazan and in a good many places; it would be hard for me not to have heard at least the echoes – and not just from my Communist friends – even on the fringes of your world.
>
> I know that living in the real world is an enormous problem. I haven't solved it well. It is not so much the Communist who is forced to use Aesopian language in a society like ours, it is the artist who must get his work produced ... I have met my problem, badly perhaps, by being with Hellman against Odets and – even though you may not wish it – by being with you against

Kazan, because my only test of a man is how he acts in his time of trouble.

I hate to tell a man I do not believe what he says, but I can't really believe that you offered a part in a play of yours to Lee Cobb ... If a man does not stand with victims, he can find better company but it won't be mine.

It seems to me that Broadway is a street of disorderly houses, tenanted in a few cases with respectable people and in others with chippies. Mr Bloomgarden [the play's producer] is stuck with being a landlord; you are one of his tenants and Kazan is another. I cannot, so great is my admiration for your character, find it in my heart to complain if there are problems with the lease.

I shall await with patience the first play of yours that Kazan directs and I hope with all my heart that you feel no compulsion to prove me wrong in my private assumption that it will never be.

I wish there were a theatre for you as there is a column for me; it would be better used. Someday I think, when all the nonsense of the last 20 years is gone, we shall have what Europe has always had, and men can quarrel openly with one another as Sartre and Camus quarrel and as O'Casey and Yeats quarrelled, as, if you please, Silone and Togliatti quarrel and we shall have dialogue as we have not had it this century, and then discussion of the relations between artists will not be gossip but, what it should be, part of the reality of criticism.[56]

He was to be disappointed with respect to Kazan, though it would be eight years before he did direct a new Miller play. Since it would also prove to be his next play, however, Miller was plainly not dedicated to slamming the door. His reply to Kempton, dated 12 January, is altogether more conciliatory and informative. In particular, he now privately explained the situation with respect to Lee Cobb. Indeed, in a five-page letter to this journalist he was more forthcoming than he had been in public. It was a confidential letter, and Kempton respected its confidentiality.

In it, Miller said that since Kempton had been so understanding he was prepared to explain the situation further. He had, he confirmed, approached Cobb because he thought him the best actor for the part. The reason he was not cast was that Cobb, and not he, had begun to worry about a possible reaction by the American Legion. He had sounded so nervous in the course of their conversation that, Miller confessed, he had begun to fear that he might break down in the middle of rehearsals. For his own part, Miller insisted, he had had no such fears, nor was he concerned about any blacklist. Indeed, he presumed that if Cobb was attacked from the Right, he would also be attacked from the Left, as Miller himself had been by Eric Bentley and *Commentary* (if also by Ed Sullivan and the *Tablet*). He had offered the part to Cobb because not to have done so would have been to capitulate to the very forces he opposed. He had no interest in actors' politics.

The situation with respect to Kazan, he went on, was rather different in so far as a director works in some regard as a writer's representative. The reason he had not been invited to direct either *The Crucible* or *A View from the Bridge* was in part, he presumed, obvious; but he did not, he stressed, regard all informers in the same light. Besides, his view of Kazan was his business and he was distressed when he heard accounts of conversations that had in fact never taken place. He was happy to express himself through his plays and, at least for the moment, to remain silent with respect to his erstwhile director. Over the years he would shift his ground somewhat. Believing that Budd Schulberg's *On the Waterfront* had been a 'terrible misuse' of the theme of informing, he nonetheless admitted that he had himself been concerned to throw some light on the subject.

The surprise is that though his informer, Eddie, does breach the social contract, step outside the boundaries not merely of propriety but of the morally permissible – in his desire for his niece and in his act of informing – he thereby compels something more than pity, from Miller no less than from his audience, living as he does with an intensity, a fierce commitment to his passions, that has a perverse integrity of its own. What might so easily have turned into a tract, a self-righteous denunciation of the informer, becomes something quite other, and Miller's offer of the part to Lee J. Cobb was no ironic gesture, though it was made in the conviction that he would understand the true anguish of this man.

Miller's response to Kempton was in all probability heightened by the fact that in December 1955, in the *New Republic*, Eric Bentley had launched an attack both on *A View from the Bridge*, which he compared to *On the Waterfront* and Whittaker Chambers' book *Witness*, and on an accompanying preface to the published version. Bentley ironically praised him for seeming to move away from his 'Stalinism'. He remarked:

> It will surprise no one that, in the movie, the act of informing is virtuous, whereas in the play [*A View from the Bridge*] it is evil. What is surprising, or at any rate appalling, is that both stories seem to have been created in the first place for no other purpose but to point up this virtue and that evil, respectively ... In *Witness*, informing is dramatic because Whittaker Chambers has so much to say on both sides: he senses the infamy of the act *and* (under certain circumstances) its ultimate rightness. Both Kazan and Miller come to the informer because (to put it mildly) it is one of the great issues of the day. What a pity, then, that both empty it of all content and give us, instead of the conflict that life offers and dramatic art demands, mere melodramatic preachment. At that, I insult the fine arts of melodrama and preaching, for these works lack the verve and unpretentiousness of true melodrama, just as they lack the purity and profundity of good preaching.[57]

Then, writing of Miller's preface to the play:

> One detects a positive element in the new preface in the shape of an effort to transcend the outlook on which this author was, so to speak, raised. The only simple word for the outlook is 'Stalinism', yet it should only be used if we understand that its adherents weren't usually Communists but only progressives whose feelings were hurt if anyone said anything against Russia. This form of progressivism has lingered in the theatre long after being discredited in other sections of the community. But, if the new preface is any indication, Mr Miller is no longer helping it to linger.

Bentley moves effortlessly from critical contempt to condescension, seeing the play, and Miller's comments about it, purely in terms of what he takes to be its politics. In the same spirit, and in the same review, he recommended Robert Warshow as the best guide to Miller's work. His own critical acuity, however, is somewhat undermined as he identifies Eddie Carbone as Catherine's father and suggests that the play is in part about homosexuality, Miller having 'inherited' this theme from Tennessee Williams's *Cat on a Hot Tin Roof* (which had opened six months earlier).

Miller regarded *A View from the Bridge* as having got off to a false start. Certainly it failed to find the kind of audience he had grown used to in the late 1940s, though Brooks Atkinson in the *New York Times* praised it as having 'power and substance'.[58] It was a work, he stated, in which Miller understood 'the full tragic significance' of his stark drama. Praising him for 'scrupulously' underwriting the narrative, however, he then suggested that this might in fact be a weakness in that our knowledge of its central character is too limited to make him a fully realized tragic figure.

The play was originally to have been called 'Under the Sea', a reference to the term used for illegal immigrants – 'submarines'. The final typescript of the one-act play is dated 28 February 1955 and is set out in verse, in part an acknowledgement of his concern to write a modern equivalent of Greek drama. The verse is also designed to resist the pull of realism, to offer a sense of distance. Miller wishes simultaneously to earth the play in a tangible environment, a recognizable psychology and social milieu, and to lift it above a concern with mere representation. There was to be nothing of Archibald McLeish about it, a writer whose verse signalled its poetic status with a language detached from those who spoke it. For Miller, the verse is rooted in the language of the speaker, carried by the rhythms and nuances of character. This is a muscular verse drama, so close to prose that when he decided to transfer it from one into the other he did so by no more than a realignment of lines, as he had done in *The Crucible*.

*

In an essay 'On Social Plays', with which he chose to preface *A Memory of Two Mondays* and the one-act version of *A View from the Bridge*, he explained his conviction that

> [you] cannot speak in verse of picayune matters ... without sounding over-blown and ridiculous ... Verse reaches always toward the general statement, the wide image, the universal moment, and it must be based upon wide concepts – it must speak not merely of men but of Man. The language of dramatic verse is the language of a people profoundly at one with itself; it is the most public of public speech. The language of prose is the language of private life, the kind of private life men retreat to when they are at odds with the world they have made or been heirs to.[59]

The play was to be social, not primarily in its concern with public issues but in its acknowledgement that the central question facing anyone is How are we to live? – a question that must, of necessity, transcend the individual. Miller quite deliberately set out to construct in Eddie Carbone a tragic character who stepped outside the protective limits of convention and placed his soul in jeopardy. Verse was one way to give significance to an inarticulate longshoreman living in twentieth-century Red Hook, Brooklyn, and not ancient Sicily. Another was to create a chorus in the form of a narrator, a figure who would identify the connective tissue linking Brooklyn and Sicily, the present with the past, this man with all men.

When Miller first heard the story in Brooklyn he felt it had mythic origins and tried to locate the Greek myth from which he presumed it to have derived. There must, he felt, have been an ur-story, but, lacking that, he wished to convey that sense to his audience. He set about doing so by reference not merely to the Italy from which his two illegal immigrants have come but to another Italy in which historic and mythic figures played out their own rituals. He wished

> to write an extremely direct work in the way that Greek dramas also tell their story quickly. They tell us what is at stake. They don't waste much time. Sometimes a narrator, or what we would call a narrator, comes forward and tells us that the king is coming toward the city and his wife is in bed with three other guys. So something has got to happen here. In *A View from the Bridge* I wanted to eliminate all the usual stage machinery of playwrighting which spends the first act in a rather long and involved explanation of where we are. So I introduced a narrator who could set up what I would call the moral situation.[60]

This stripping out of the superfluous was what prompted Brooks Atkinson to complain about a lack of flesh, but it was what Miller found compelling. The narrator who steps forward is a lawyer, but the irony is that in the drama that he sets in motion the law has no role. Eddie Carbone is in peril precisely because he obeys other laws than those laid down by the tribe. As Miller observed, the law is helpless, has nothing to say, because

> Eddie Carbone ... is obeying an ancient law which predates the laws we know. That's one of the points of the play, and the reason for the title. It takes place beneath the traffic on Brooklyn Bridge, and the modern society we live in; down in a little neighbourhood an ancient tragedy is being worked out. ... it always struck me oddly that here is this commuter traffic going over it night and day, people going out to nice neighbourhoods somewhere else, passing over the area where this Greek drama was taking place and no one ever thought about it. ... so it was a view of our culture, which is up on the bridge, down into their culture.[61]

Reviewers of *A View from the Bridge*, meanwhile, were not the only ones to focus on the play. On 30 September 1955, FBI informant T-7 reported on it. He was plainly close to the production but also favourably disposed to Miller:

> The informant stated that about one thousand people had read for ARTHUR MILLER'S playlets including 'A VIEW FROM THE BRIDGE', and that he understood several Communists had been turned down. He said it would probably be coincidental if the cast turned out to be predominantly Communist. The informant described ARTHUR MILLER as 'left-oriented' and said MILLER had lost his sympathy for the Communist Party when the Party attacked him for giving derogatory notices to a Negro production which the Communist Party wanted praised. The informant stated MILLER's plays, though occasionally supported by the Communist Party, did not follow Marxist ideology. He said MILLER is very intelligent in his attitude and his interpretations are strictly his own.[62]

The eyes of the FBI clearly remained on Miller but the report is less than convincing. He had written a number of reviews for *New Masses* in 1945 (though he was not responsible for the reviews of various African-American plays which appeared under the name of Matt Wayne), but his sympathy for the Party continued beyond this and he had, of course, considered a former Communist for the part of Eddie Carbone. On the other hand, if the idea of auditioning a thousand actors makes A *View from the Bridge* sound like the search for Scarlett O'Hara in *Gone with the Wind*, Miller himself put the figure at fifteen hundred.

The double bill of *A Memory of Two Mondays* and *A View from the Bridge* had a limited run despite the fact that this was being hailed as a boom year on Broadway, though in a piece he wrote for the first volume of *International Theatre Annual* entitled 'Concerning the Boom' Miller was dismissive of the idea of a theatrical revival. In his view only three plays merited consideration:

Thornton Wilder's *Matchmaker*, Enid Bagnold's *The Chalk Garden* and Norman Rosten's adaptation of Joyce Cary's *Mister Johnson*, though he was not overly impressed by the first of these while the second, he noted, had been rejected by the critics. His comments on Rosten's work have the air of a token support for a friend whose play had been 'decisively defeated' by those same critics and who would go on to write the screenplay for *A View from the Bridge*. It was a season, he suggested, in which another work was a 'slapped together' piece which had begun as an Actors' Studio exercise (Michael V. Gazzo's *A Hatful of Rain*), when O'Casey's *Red Roses for Me* was rejected by critics, and when the previous season's *Cat on a Hot Tin Roof* (which won a Pulitzer Prize) was still running, in Miller's opinion, not because of its virtues but its sensationalism. Though he affected to sense the emergence of new writers, he could name none, and this whole piece has the air of a man increasingly at odds with the only theatre available to him. It has the air, too, perhaps, of a man who feels the need for a radical break.

Audiences and critics alike seemed, to him, incapable of responding to serious work. He was used to achieving runs of a year or even two (he was conveniently forgetting the initial production of *The Crucible*), so to close after three months was, he confessed, a shock. Political harassment aside, there seemed to him to be a coarsening in audience response. They hungered for realism, hence the success of *A Hatful of Rain*, or for sensation. There was no acting company; there was no enthusiasm for new approaches. Theatres demanded 40 or 50 per cent of the gross; ticket prices continued to rise; the names of authors disappeared from advertising material, the star and director taking prominence. Ironically, it seemed to him that the most significant dramatic event had not taken place on the American stage at all. It was, he suggested in 'Concerning the Boom', the publication of Eugene O'Neill's *Long Day's Journey into Night* – 'as true as an oak board' and produced only once, and that in Sweden: 'I have not heard that there is a line of producers clamouring for it here.'[63]

In part, it seemed to him that O'Neill had worked against the American grain. Like Miller himself, he had been concerned to dramatize a tragic sense of life, at odds in some respects with American melioristic philosophy and now with mid-century boosterism. From *The Golden Years* onwards Miller had tried to create a series of tragedies, only to see them described and alternately embraced or rejected as social plays. To resist such a reading he had written essays in which he set out his understanding of tragedy, thus inadvertently saddling generations of students with examination questions that would breed more resentment than enlightenment.

It is tempting to see, in his fascination with tragedy, a counter-current to his Marxism, for which the tragic mode, with its stress on the fate of the individual, on a flawed human nature, on a power and authority authenticated by rank and stature, was deeply suspect, though in 1934 Philip Rahv had suggested that it had a basis in the heroic struggle of the working class. For Miller, though, it was a form that had always proposed a symbiosis between the private and the public. Yet there is, perhaps, an echo of his political loyalties in his desire to create a tragedy of the common man. He still, it seems, felt the need to tip his hat in the direction of at least a democracy of the spirit.

In part he was reflecting a wider debate in the liberal community. In reaction against Marxist utopianism and in the shadow of the camps, there were those, like Reinhold Niebuhr and Arthur Schlesinger Jr (both members of Americans for Democratic Action), who stressed the flawed nature of human beings and, though politically at odds with them, Miller was drawn to such a conclusion. Hemingway spoke of the mechanistic nature of death and violence in the First World War as annihilating tragedy. The prevailing mode was irony. How much more so was this true of a war in which human beings' were reduced to numbers, stripped, gassed, incinerated, rendered into ash? The renovation of tragedy was thus of something more than antiquarian interest. It was an assertion of value, a refusal of an incapacitating and despairing irony.

Miller insisted that the cast of his mind was tragic. It was a statement that did much to explain his approach to drama, his attitude to language, his thematic concerns. Particularly in the first decade of his public career, he seemed to see drama as in some way reconstituting values threatened alike by history, by capitalism and even by an art which increasingly seemed to offer irony as a correlative to, and product of, metaphysical and social anomie.

The tragic, to his mind, conferred significance on what he was inclined to capitalize as Man. It proposed transcendent values rather than pragmatic improvisations. It contained and expressed the private and the public as if they were, indeed, organically related. His early interest in verse suggested a desire to reach back to older traditions, as if there had been no break in aesthetic or moral continuity. His fascination with betrayal as a central theme linked his work, in his own mind, to Shakespearean tragedies in which that had been a key component.

He reacted against that European theatre which had emerged from the war registering the shock of that war in terms of reified characters, echoic language, and despair rendered as a kind of vaudeville. In other words, he rejected the absurd. Here, in short, was a man who not only wrote plays but, unusually for America, had a theory of drama. He chose to explain his values and his attitude to the component elements of his drama in articles written for mainstream publications, quite as if he thought the theatre was still a place in which it was possible to debate the state of the culture and the culture of the state, the future shape of his society and the nature of Man in a time of postwar angst and nuclear threat.

He retained a curious assurance, a forward-leaning vision of human possibility. The ideology of the 1930s might have gone, but its spirit remained. 'Time is moving,' he announced, 'there is a world to make, a civilization to create that will move toward the only goal the humanistic, democratic mind can ever accept with honor. It is a world in which the human being can live as a naturally political, naturally private, naturally engaged person, a world in which once again a true tragic victory may be scored.'[64] This statement, made at the age of forty, takes a little unpacking in that it seems to echo a spirit of American positivism, while couching this in terms of what he chose to call a 'tragic victory'.

In many ways the commitments of his youth were still in play but he sought to see in his analysis of industrial alienation a more profound disruption in our view of the self, with neither capitalism nor communism offering to heal a wound much deeper than either was prepared to acknowledge. Thus he observed that 'where men live, as they do under any industrialized system, as integers who have no weight, no *person*, excepting as either customers, draftees, machine tenderers, ideologists, or whatever, it is unlikely (and in my view impossible) that a dramatic picture of them can really overcome the public knowledge of their nature in real life. In such a society, be it communistic or capitalistic, man is not tragic, but pathetic.'[65] This was what he was setting his face against.

Both systems, in his view, broke the connection between the individual and the community, eroded the integrity of the self and, ultimately, human meaning. 'The deep moral uneasiness among us, the vast sense of being only tenuously joined to the rest of our fellows, is caused, in my view, by the fact that the person has value as he fits into the pattern of efficiency, and for that alone.' Miller's tragic drama was designed to re-invest the individual with meaning, to reassert a unity of being. But he dealt not with the conventional characters of tragedy but with those who inhabit the new suburbia, the lower-middle-class houses of Brooklyn, the waterfront. He sent his tragic hero on a quest not for a climactic battle with powers earthly and supernatural but for an appointment with the buyer at Filenes store in Boston. That hero surrenders his life not in Athens but in Red Hook, the gullet of New York.

The end of Miller's marriage, when it came, was not without bitterness. He simply walked out, but insists that 'she was ready to go herself'. Nevertheless, 'it collapsed because of me, because of my involvement with Marilyn. But it would have happened anyway'. Half a century on, he was ready to accept his responsibility for Mary's suffering whereas at the time he had not been, thinking himself on the brink of a new life in which he would have everything he desired. For all his later acknowledgement of responsibility, he had found it impossible to live with Mary's sustained disapproval. By contrast, after all the recriminations and analysis, the unsatisfied desires, here, suddenly, was Marilyn, a woman who 'instead of being judgemental ... just took each moment for what it was, or seemed to at that point. As she matured, of course ... she became quite the opposite as a kind of paranoia took over, which had nothing to do with me. It was part of her mental development. She began to suspect everybody of exploiting or damaging her.' She 'was as judgemental as anybody else. It was just that I didn't know it then.'[66]

In the unpublished short story in which he tries to capture something of his relationship with Mary, he says of the protagonist Rufus Solomon that he had left his first wife because she had come to know him too well, because he had mistakenly believed in confronting the truth of their relationship and his behaviour. This was his version of those occasions on which he had felt compelled to reveal to Mary the truth of his feelings – for a young widow in wartime Washington, for a woman in New York, for a distant filmstar – quite as if truth could purge pain of its substance or perhaps because pain might be the source of a redemptive and reanimating shock. Confession was to be followed by forgiveness and immunity from punishment. But neither his character nor Miller himself found forgiveness, nor did they go unpunished. And neither, clearly, did Solomon's or Miller's wife find meaning or satisfaction in their husband's achievements or, in Mary's case, a sense of the value ascribed to her husband by the attention of other women.

In some ways the best account of his disintegrating marriage comes not from this fragmentary story, from his autobiography or those rare interviews in which he has guardedly talked about it, but from *The Best Comedians*, an unpublished novel that he dates to 1956 though it was probably begun in 1953 or 1954, and which was prompted by a street encounter with a Columbia University student from Argentina who had accosted him seemingly to discuss *The Crucible*. In this novel he explores his relationship with Mary in some detail, in the context of a work in which a playwright called Dan Weller is suddenly presented with a moral demand from a stranger. A novel about responsibility and guilt, it is in some ways reminiscent of Saul Bellow's *The Victim*, but, beyond its account of an encounter between a writer and an increasingly deranged individual, it also offers a frank insight into Miller's own life. In fact, it seems almost an exercise in self-analysis, a way of confronting the moral confusion he was suffering. In the end, as the protagonist finally rejects the feeling of obligation that has threatened his own sanity, it seems to stand as Miller's justification for abandoning the woman to whom, like Weller he had been married for sixteen years.

The Best Comedians tells the story of a student from Argentina, Jesus Rojas, who attaches himself to Weller, convinced by the moral concerns of the author's work that Weller will be able to help him. Weller does his best to evade what clearly seems to be a deranged young man but Rojas persists, even following him to his home in the country, as the real student had followed Miller to Roxbury. Weller recognizes a mixture of threat and reproach in Rojas's attitude but finds it impossible simply to dismiss him. It is not just that he is so persistent but that, no matter how irrationally, in some way Weller acknowledges responsibility for him, stranger or not. He admits to himself that somehow he has, indeed, presented himself as an exemplary figure, an absurd pretension but one that appears to incur responsibilities, even, it seems, to a confused and increasingly threatening young man.

Rojas claims that his aunt wishes to kill him and is the source of a mystical power, forcing him to injure himself. Recognizing a psychotic case best dealt with by a psychiatrist, Weller nonetheless feels a sense of obligation because he believes that Rojas has detected something in his work that others do not see, a quality that makes him vulnerable to this approach.

It is tempting to feel that there is something of Miller's sense of his own work in his description of Weller's, as well as an echo of his own name. Weller explains that he is thought of as a realistic writer, and has appeared to accept that designation when his real desire is to transcend the real. Known for his commitment to justice, he is afraid to offer evidence of an interest in transcendence. Though Miller scarcely saw himself as a mystic, the word used of Weller, he did, as noted earlier, resist the description of himself as a simple realist and was searching for something beyond the social and moral concerns that had seemed to define him. Eventually Rojas, after a brief session with a psychiatrist and continued efforts to impose on Weller, takes to his bed and fades away; and though Weller comes to see him for a last time he finally abandons him as the only way to continue with his own life. He thus frees himself from his sense of obligation.

A central concern of the novel is Weller's failing marriage which both makes him a poor moral adviser and a man who needs to escape a woman whose influence has become corrosive. When Weller goes home, the atmosphere between himself and his wife Kate is wholly destructive. He acknowledges that he was the first to offend when he returned from the city after an adulterous encounter, as Miller had done. He continues to feel culpable and she to remind him of that culpability but, that transgression aside, there is an unequal balance of power in the marriage. In the novel, as in life, he is the famous playwright, she the embittered wife. He resists the idea that there is a power struggle between them but acknowledges that she is weak, he powerful, not least because of his public reputation. He admits to feeling detached from her, but has resisted the idea of leaving her, in part for fear of his parents' disapproval and in part because he still has memories of those parents arguing, as Miller's parents had done.

There has, he has told her, been only one such lapse, knowing this to be a lie. He has, though, found no forgiveness. For her, infidelity is a sickness. People do not behave that way in Indiana. Or Ohio, one is tempted to say, since, again, this all has an authentic ring to it when applied to the relationship between Miller and Mary, who, like Weller's wife, also found her husband's friends unacceptable.

Both Weller and Kate, like Miller and Mary, have been in analysis, though Weller has resisted it. He even briefly restored their relationship, as Miller had his with Mary. Weller's wife thinks that her husband ignores her, failing to pay her the respect and attention she, like Mary, thinks her due. She no longer responds to his work as once she did and constantly recalls the occasion when he confessed to meeting a woman he was tempted to sleep with. In the novel, as in life, it is this that has poisoned a relationship which, lacking in passion, has limped on for ten years and more, she finally admitting the futility of it at the moment he decides to end it.

His mother, Kate believes, ruined him – equally Mary's view of Augusta Miller. Meanwhile, Kate herself is presented as inflexible. In her view, her husband is guilty, she innocent if unforgiving. His confession has earned no absolution. There must, Weller tells himself, be a woman to whom he can turn and who would be genuinely interested in him. In Miller's case, of course, there was, and he spoke in precisely these terms about his relationship with Marilyn. Weller asks himself whether he has ever really loved Kate, confessing that he never wanted to marry, merely deferred to her on the eve of their marriage when she burst into tears, convinced that he did not love her. Again, these are very precise echoes of Miller's own memories and later confessions.

The marriage in *The Best Comedians* seems to have reached a point at which the only way the protagonist can make his wife feel secure and wanted is for him to abandon his ambitions, retreat from the world. In a novel that itself seems to be an extended piece of self-analysis, he speaks at length to his psychoanalyst, insisting that to submit to her desire for a purely domestic life – a domestic life that she herself resents – would be to surrender not only power but his art. The problem is that she lacks abilities of her own and is therefore jealous of his. Only by laying aside his work, therefore, can they meet as equals. For her part, she withholds praise or even interest in his work, since it is that very work which threatens their relationship and which has opened up a wider world in which he is open to temptation. The irony is that love, apparently, can only thrive if he surrenders what matters most to him. This is the ironic comedy of the title.

Feeling increasingly trapped, he acknowledges that his primary fear is that he cannot imagine how salvation will arrive. In the novel we never learn. In Miller's case it was to be Monroe. Weller decides to abandon any sense of obligation he feels. Miller did no less. He ended his marriage and, to be sure, his doom vanished, if only for a short time. As far as writing was concerned, though – this self-referring fiction aside, a fiction never to be offered to the public – that seemed as far beyond him, for the moment, as it seemed for his protagonist.

A man and a woman marry, says Weller, because they believe they love one another. Then they discover that there was more to the contract than love. One or the other will do something the other regards as unforgivable, and then the marriage either ends or becomes nothing more than a front. For the writer to live with falsehood incapacitates his ability to tell the truth in his writing. Miller, like his protagonist, had come to feel that he was living a lie and that this not only destroyed the marriage but contaminated his art. With Marilyn he believed he had potentially found a way to bring his life into alignment with his artistic needs. As is apparent from *The Best Comedians*, and from comments in interview, however, it was not the relationship with Monroe that destroyed the marriage. If we are to believe him, it began the moment he entered into that marriage without love.

The novel ends as Weller deserts the young man who has been harassing him, leaving him, as Rojas insists, alone in the world. It is an action that recapitulates Miller's response to his marriage as, finally, he and Mary decided to separate – she to raise their two children alone, he to go to a woman who seemed the opposite of everything he had experienced for at least two-thirds of his marriage.

If Miller seems to shift the blame on to his wife in *The Best Connections*, he later confessed to his own complicity, recalling, for example, a visit with Mary to the composer Elmer Bernstein's apartment to discuss the possibility of a collaboration between the two of them. He had just finished *A View from the Bridge*, and Mary began to tell Bernstein its story. 'I was very resentful that she had presumed to do that, which was beastly of me, because she was being proud of me. But such was my absolute need to control my work that I didn't want anybody talking about it until I was ready to release it. That will give you some idea of how violent my self-absorption was. She had a tough row to hoe. Imagine living with a guy like that. I wouldn't want to be a woman or anybody in that position.'[67]

Marilyn, meanwhile, after her first encounter with Miller, had been suffi-ciently inspired in February 1951 to sign up for a University of California extension course in literature and art. He sent her a reading list. A recurring theme of Monroe stories is of a young woman desperate to educate herself, though few were willing to take her seriously. Anthony Summers, in his book *Goddess: The Secret Lives of Marilyn Monroe*, recalls a comment by Jack Paar, who acted with her in *Love Nest*. During the shooting, she carried a volume of Rilke's poems and was apparently reading Marcel Proust. For Paar, though, behind what he took to be a façade 'was only a frightened waitress in a diner'.[68] But the hunger to improve herself was real enough, and it applied to her acting efforts no less than to her sometimes naive enthusiasm for literature. Condescended to by movie moguls, seen as a commodity, she seems to have genuinely worked at a regimen of self-improvement. Now, though, she had an added incentive. She had fallen for a writer.

For Elia Kazan, there was little substance to her literary ambitions, which were anyway irrelevant to her career. She 'had little education and no knowledge except the knowledge of her own experience; of that she had a great deal, and for an actor, that is the important kind of knowledge. For her, I found, everything was either completely meaningless or completely personal. She had no interest in abstract, formal or impersonal concepts but was passionately devoted to her own life's experiences. What she needed above all was to have her own self-worth affirmed.'[69]

For all her ambition to be treated as a serious actress, however, in 1951 she was voted 'Miss Cheesecake' by American troops in Germany and won the Henrietta Award as Most Promising Personality of the Year, an award which took the form of a nude statuette of a woman which Marilyn was pictured grasping. A new contract with Twentieth Century Fox was finally forthcoming in May that year at a salary of $500 a week, rising by stages over seven years to $3,500. Natasha Lytess was to be employed at the same amount. In the September *Collier's* magazine published an article entitled 'Hollywood's 1951 Model Blonde'. Fan mail began to appear at the rate of two thousand a week.

In autumn 1951 she took acting lessons from Natasha Lytess and Michael Chekhov, nephew of the playwright and author of *To the Actor: On the Technique of Acting*. He had been associated with the Moscow Art Theatre and, in America, taught Anthony Quinn among others. She played Cordelia to Chekhov's Lear, placing the kind of absolute faith in his and Lytess's judgements that she was to place, when she moved to the East Coast in 1955, in Lee Strasberg and his wife Paula's. She always required reassurance about her performances, but in time reassurance devolved into the kind of shameless flattery in which Paula Strasberg specialized. When shooting scenes she would always look first to her acting coach rather than the director. 'I want to be an artist,' she insisted, 'not an erotic freak. I don't want to be sold to the public as a celluloid aphrodisiac. It was all right for the first few years. But now it's different.'[70]

Chekhov advised her to read *Death of a Salesman*, praising Miller as the creator of a genuine tragedy. He could hardly have said anything more likely to win her loyalty to him and his methods. Miller might be three thousand miles away but she still felt his influence. Perhaps it was his very remoteness, the fact that he had fled her, that made him seem all the more desirable.

Surrounded by men who thought nothing of their casual affairs, she found herself compelled by a man who had treated her with respect and retreated before what she was sure was his own passion.

However, the sudden appearance, the following year, of the nude calendar scarcely undermined her role as a celluloid aphrodisiac, a role which, in certain moods, she was quite happy to propagate. The calendar was banned in Pennsylvania and Georgia and would later be banned from the US postal service as obscene. But although Monroe cooperated with this kind of publicity and was largely content with the roles that gave her ever greater exposure, she always had the ambition to be something more than this, to use her fast-developing fame to negotiate control over her career. That very ambition, indeed, and the almost obsessive way in which she struggled to follow the precepts of Lytess, Chekhov and later Lee Strasberg, was also a symptom of the self-doubt that could make the film set such a painful place to be. She frequently vomited before performing, and desperately looked for confirmation of a talent she was fearful she might not possess.

In terms of her personal life, she had an affair with Kazan, who had stayed in California to direct *Viva Zapata* and who stood ready, he explained, to yield to Miller should he return. It was a curious relationship. He claimed that whenever the two made love he was confronted with a photograph of Miller on the bedside table, and that she liked nothing better than to talk about the man who had now returned to his wife, even while explaining how unhappy that relationship was. According to Lytess, whatever Marilyn's attitude to Kazan, she had fallen in love with Miller: 'She fell in love with him and he fell in love with her, no doubt about it ... she told me excitedly that this was the sort of man she could love forever.'[71] She wrote to him observing, somewhat oddly, that most people admire their father, as if she wished to claim him in a dual role as lover and parent. He replied: 'Bewitch them with this image they ask for but I hope and almost pray you won't be hurt in this game.'[72] Then, more coolly, he recommended that she should buy a copy of Carl Sandburg's biography of Abraham Lincoln. She rushed out and bought both the book and a portrait of Lincoln.

It is difficult to know what to make of Kazan's own account in an auto-biography that is alternately perceptive and self-justifying. His treatment of Monroe seems to have been casual to the point of callousness. While denouncing the uses to which others put her, he seems to have seen her as nothing more than a sexual convenience. When he left her, he told Miller that he had 'assigned' her to a friend. In her novelized version of Monroe's life, Joyce Carol Oates imagines a scene in which Miller requires his then wife to detail her relationship with Kazan. She is understandably evasive.

Once again Monroe was turning to someone who was not only successful but also politically and culturally sophisticated. Within a very short time, however, she herself was successful, her reputation as America's leading glamour girl firmly established and endorsed by *Life* magazine. She had become the hottest female star in Hollywood, and in *Clash by Night* and *Don't Bother to Knock* began to demonstrate something of her acting skills. Fox renewed her option, now paying her $750 a week.

She now began a relationship with Joe DiMaggio, son of Sicilian immigrants and America's most famous baseball player. He remained obsessed with her for the rest of her life and beyond. Theirs was a curious courtship and marriage. DiMaggio seems to have had little to offer beyond a dog-like devotion. He was certainly baffled by her interest in the arts, her desire to visit museums, her apparent love of poetry. If he genuinely loved her he was also extremely jealous, uncomfortable with the very public image that had initially attracted him. His jealousy was such that she seems to have felt uneasy at times in his presence, and he was occasionally violent towards her.

She met him in 1952, a year after his retirement from the New York Yankees and the same year that she confessed to being the nude calendar girl. He was not amused. At the time she was making *Niagara*. The deeply puritanical DiMaggio objected to aspects of the film and was never comfortable with the sexuality she so openly displayed, a sexuality also evident in her next film, *Gentlemen Prefer Blondes*, in which she co-starred with Jane Russell and sang 'Diamonds Are a Girl's Best friend' (earning $500 a week to Russell's $200,000 for the film). To Joe's complaints she replied, 'What do you want me to do – hide in a basement?'[73] In the end, for publicity purposes she continued to wear her usual revealing outfits, but in private she settled for a rather more demure look. They married two years later. She wore a high-necked suit in deference to DiMaggio. Bizarrely, on returning from her honeymoon she confided to a friend that she was planning marriage to someone else, the man whose photograph had stood on her bedside table – Arthur Miller.

Marilyn's marriage to Joe DiMaggio, which took place in City Hall, San Francisco, on 14 January 1954, lasted only nine months. It began to founder virtually the day it was contracted. He looked for an Italian household in which he determined his wife's future. She had her own agenda. In her divorce petition she claimed he had prevented her from seeing her friends and had remained silent for days at a time. He refused to go with her to premieres, including that of *How to Marry a Millionaire*, only the second Cinemascope production (the first, by contrast, being *The Robe* with its biblical theme). When he briefly attended the filming of *There's No Business Like Show Business*, in 1954, he refused to pose with his wife, settling for Irving Berlin instead while explaining that he had only come to listen to Ethel Merman. The tension between them was such that Marilyn was increasingly resorting to sedatives. Natasha Lytess remembered that Marilyn 'called me at two or three in the morning that spring when DiMaggio was being so filthy to her, when he beat her. She couldn't stand being treated that way.'[74]

That same year, she flew to Korea to entertain the American troops. DiMaggio accompanied her as far as Tokyo. He was not happy with the trip and left her to complete it on her own. She arrived by helicopter to perform on an outdoor stage in front of thousands of men. She was far from confident:

> It was cold and starting to snow. I was backstage in dungarees. Out front the show was on ... An officer came backstage: 'You'll have to go on ahead of schedule. I don't think we can hold them any longer. They're throwing rocks at the stage.' The noise I'd been hearing was my name being yelled by the soldiers. I changed quickly into my silk gown. It had a low neckline and no sleeves. I felt worried all of a sudden about my material, not the Gershwin song but the other I was going to sing – 'Diamonds Are a Girl's Best Friend'. It seemed like the wrong thing to say to soldiers in Korea, earning only soldiers' pay. Then I remembered the dance I would do after the song. It was a cute dance. I knew they would like it ... for the first time I felt like a movie star.[75]

With the conclusion of *There's No Business Like Show Business*, she moved directly to her next project *The Seven Year Itch*, flying to New York for the exterior shots in the September. DiMaggio refused to accompany her at all this time, following on behind. It was in New York that she shot a scene in which, famously, she stood over a subway grating as her skirt blew up around her. It was filmed outside the Trans Lux Theatre on Lexington Avenue at half past two in the morning in front of a crowd of four thousand people. It was a scene not only disliked by DiMaggio, who was in that crowd, but also denounced by sections of the press, the Catholic *America* seeing it as subverting a free society and the *Daily Worker* as eroding the moral basis of American democracy. The scene outraged DiMaggio and the two argued in public. That night he hit her. America's ideal marriage was falling apart.

Not only would that moment provide the film's central image but, the following year, a lifesize cut-out of Marilyn, skirt flying, stood outside a movie theatre that Miller passed each day on his way to the rehearsals of *A View from the Bridge*. By then Marilyn was in New York again, this time for the affair with Miller that would ultimately result in their marriage.

The filming ended with a party at Romanoffs in Beverly Hills where, with a cut-out of the skirt scene on display, she was fêted by the Hollywood greats, including the man she had admired as a child and with whom she would make her and his last film: Clark Gable. She asked for the autograph she had been wanting since she was twelve. As she had as a starlet, she wore a dress from the Twentieth Century Fox wardrobe.

Despite their arguments, though, Marilyn and DiMaggio were still appearing in public together, and she assured everyone, especially the press, that all was well. She returned to Hollywood on 15 September. There the two continued to fight. It was clear to her that their marriage was incompatible with her ambitions as an actress. By 1 October she had decided on divorce and on the 27th, following an eight-minute hearing, she was granted it on the grounds of mental cruelty, though DiMaggio, then and later, still believed he could repair their broken relationship. The complaint specified: 'The defendant caused her grievous mental suffering and anguish, all of which acts and conduct were without fault of the plaintiff.'[76]

Appearing before a Superior Court judge, she explained: 'I hoped to have out of my marriage, love, warmth, affection, and understanding. But the relationship turned out to be one of coldness and indifference.' She said later: 'He didn't talk to me. He was cold. He was indifferent to me as a human being and an artist. He didn't want me to have friends of my own. He didn't want me to do any work. He really watched television instead of talking to me.' Fox's spokesman, Roy Craft, offered a less than flattering response to DiMaggio's supposed sensitivity to Monroe's reputation and sexual image: 'Marilyn had a flamboyant reputation when they got married . . . If you build a home behind a slaughter house, you don't complain when you hear the pigs squealing.'

The edge of contempt was never far away in Hollywood's response to an actress who was simultaneously a superstar and the object of condescension. However, in Hollywood nothing mattered but the product. Everything else was smoke. As Marilyn herself observed, 'they took it, they grabbed it, they ran'. Private lives were significant only in so far as they damaged or enhanced the product. The studio issued a statement, indicating that the reason for the divorce was 'incompatibility resulting from the conflicting demands of their careers'.[77] For once, a press release was not far from the truth. For his part, DiMaggio explained that the break was for 'business reasons'. There was to be no property settlement.

He had not, however, given up. In early November, a private detective he had hired to follow her reported that she had been visiting the same address on several occasions and that she was there even as he telephoned in his report. DiMaggio, accompanied by Frank Sinatra, arrived and a number of men, summoned by the detective, broke into the apartment. It was the wrong one. Marilyn escaped. The surprised and shocked woman whose door had been broken down was later paid off when she initiated a court case. At the same time, and despite her statements, Marilyn continued to see DiMaggio, who was, in fact, to stay loyal to her over the years whenever she got into trouble. The man who was patently incompatible as a husband, who had broken her finger by slamming a case shut on it in Japan when she was on her way to Korea, would still function as a friend, and Miller himself always thought there was a dignity about him. There had always, he thought, been a residual attraction between his wife and the baseball player. He had simply wanted to make her into a housewife and never understood that of all the roles she was required to play that was the one she was least qualified, or inclined, to perform.

Monroe now made a decisive break. *The Seven Year Itch* finished shooting on 5 November 1954 as Milton Greene arrived in Los Angeles and revived the idea of creating Marilyn Monroe Productions. In December she flew from Los Angeles to New York announcing, 'In leaving Hollywood and coming to New York, I feel I can be more myself. After all, if I can't be myself, what's the good of being anything at all?'[78] From there she headed to Connecticut where she stayed with Greene and his wife. Greene, a freelance photographer, who also worked for *Look* magazine, had talked with her about the possibility of forming a production company that would free her of a financially and artistically disadvantageous contract with Fox. She had increasingly felt exploited on both counts and was looking for a decisive break that would enable her to move her career in a new direction. Marilyn Monroe Productions was duly announced in January 1955.

In March, the Greene house was the location for a CBS *Person to Person* interview of Marilyn by Edward R. Murrow. Asked why she had set up her own production company, she replied that it was 'primarily to contribute to help making good pictures ... It's not that I object to doing musicals and comedies – in fact, I rather enjoy them – but I'd like to do dramatic parts, too.'[79] Then, in April, she subleased an apartment in the Waldorf Astoria Towers. Finance for the new project came from Greene, who owned almost half of Marilyn Monroe Productions and whom Miller would later challenge over the arrangement. The money went not only on the apartment but also on psychoanalysts and beauticians, including her personal hairdresser on a salary of $125 a week.

Now based in New York, at the suggestion of Cheryl Crawford, one of its founders, she enrolled in the Actors Studio, whose alumni included many of the most famous names in the American theatre and cinema. She had first made the acquaintance of Paula Strasberg in Hollywood when she was visiting her actress daughter, Susan Strasberg. She now effectively became the Strasbergs' protégée, and a relationship began that Miller was not alone in regarding as personally destructive, whatever it may have done for her confidence as an actress. Even Susan remarked: 'Our household ... revolved around my father, his moods, his needs, his expectations and his neuroses. He was teaching people how to act, but that was nothing compared to the drama in our house ... Our entire family were intimate strangers.'[80]

The Belgian director Jacques Huisman remarked of Lee Strasberg, whom Miller called a 'talmudic destroyer':

I saw him in New York work on Marilyn Monroe. He was directing her in a scene from Anouilh's *Colombe*. His sole aim was to reduce her to tears in front of forty or fifty voyeurs who attended the course. It was scandalous and totally useless: he was not a teacher but a guru and the attendants were disciples not pupils. I have known many of those acting instructors who entertain very intimate relationships with their pupils; they are part priest and part doctor, dominating and doping those who come to them for advice or instruction.[81]

It was perhaps in some sense the equality granted to all members of the Studio that appealed. Here she could lay aside her fame. She was also desperate to learn. This was to be a route to those roles she had long wished to play, roles that would liberate her finally from her glamour-girl reputation. She attended private classes of the Actors Studio at the Malin Studios and at first presented her work there, including the part of Lorna from Odets's *Golden Boy*, Blanche from *A Streetcar Named Desire* and Holly Golightly from *Breakfast at Tiffany's*.

For many months she worked at exercises alongside such actors as Kevin McCarthy (who had appeared in the Boston production of *Death of a Salesman*) and Eli Wallach (who was, like McCarthy, later to appear with her in *The Misfits*). She was part of the Strasberg household, which perhaps explains her later over-reliance on Paula, who became both professional guide and substitute mother. As an indication of the significance she gave to the relationship, on her death Marilyn left 60 per cent of her estate to Lee Strasberg, along with her personal possessions, including the rights to *The Prince and the Showgirl*, the first venture of Marilyn Monroe Productions. She had earlier donated ten thousand dollars to allow him to undertake a research trip to Japan. It was Strasberg who delivered the eulogy at her funeral. It was also at this moment that she entered into analysis, with Dr Margaret Hohenberg, the first of a number of psychoanalysts who would attempt to understand what simultaneously drove and disturbed a woman whose public success concealed a deepening anxiety.

Norman Rosten recalled her first visit to Brooklyn. She had persuaded the photographer Sam Shaw, who had known her back in California, to take her across the Brooklyn Bridge, she wearing an ankle-length camel-hair coat given to her by her former agent Johnny Hyde. It was an odd request, but this was where she knew Miller lived, where she had sent the letters that had provoked Mary's suspicions. When it started to rain, Shaw called Rosten, a friend, and the two went to the Rostens' mid-nineteenth-century brownstone walk-up. Neither of the Rostens recognized her. Hedda gave her a change of stockings and some coffee. It was the beginning of a relationship that would last, on and off, for eight years. The Rostens were among those she called the night before her death. There is no indication that when she met them she realized they were also friends of the man she was so anxious to see.

Miller initially knew nothing of Marilyn's arrival in New York beyond what he read in the newspapers. They met at a New York party and later he asked Paula Strasberg for her telephone number. They encountered one another next at Norman Rosten's house, joining in some of the regular poetry evenings which he and Hedda held in their Brooklyn Heights home. Marilyn read the work of other poets while writing her own. She attended concerts and galleries as she retooled herself for a new life, consciously turning her back on Hollywood and the role she had collaborated in creating. Now she was to be a serious actress controlling her own destiny.

Although his grasp on the American public seemed to have loosened, for Marilyn Miller was the embodiment of that very artistic seriousness, that moral concern, which she liked to believe now motivated her. In an exchange at the Actors Studio about Kafka's *The Trial*, she quoted Miller as her authority for believing that it was in part about Jewish guilt. Strasberg might be her acting guru, but she now had an intellectual teacher who was broadening her sense of cultural values. The move from DiMaggio to Miller was to be a sign of her exchange of mere fame for integrity, of glamour for a concerned commitment to aesthetic and ethical probity. In truth, they were simply drawn to one another out of mutual need and genuine affection. Each seemed to answer the psychological and emotional needs of the other.

Miller now began to meet her at the Rosten apartment as Gatsby had met Daisy Buchanan at Nick Carraway's, though this time it was the man who was married and the woman who was free. And it is tempting to see his response to her as being not so very different from that of Gatsby, who had renewed his acquaintance with Daisy after several years. She, after all, was in part a fantasy, the embodiment of a dream, a woman with a past that could be wished away. Her power lay partly in the fact that she was a projection, an idea, somehow combining innocence and experience. Fitzgerald speaks of the 'colossal vitality' of Gatsby's illusion that had gone beyond the actual Daisy, 'beyond her, beyond everything'. Miller was Gatsby about to 'wed his unutterable visions'[82] to the 'perishable breath' of a woman who could never approximate to a fantasy generated out of need, no matter that he later claimed to have seen beyond the image to the substance. But the reverse was also true. As Miller admitted, 'I, too, was being idealized beyond all human weakness.'[83]

In a way, then, Marilyn also played the role of Gatsby. It was she, after all, who had invented herself, changed her name, clawed her way up from obscurity by means which perhaps bore little inspection. It was she who sprang from her Platonic conception of herself and was in 'the service of a vast, vulgar, and meretricious beauty'. Reverse the gender, and you perhaps have a clue to one dimension of Monroe when Fitzgerald says of the young Gatsby, a product of shiftless and unsuccessful parents, that 'He knew women early, and since they spoiled him he became contemptuous of them.'[84] This man, who early had a 'hint of the unreality of reality, a promise that the rock of the world was founded securely on a fairy's wing', perhaps had a parallel in a woman whose function was to spin the illusions that at times she came close to believing.

Daisy was drawn to Gatsby because, as he explains, 'She thought I knew a lot because I knew different things from her.' At least part of Miller's attraction for Monroe seems to have lain in a similar conviction. For him, meanwhile, she was the green light across the bay, an ambiguous and deceptive innocence, a redemption, a dream that 'must have seemed so close that he could hardly fail to grasp it'. For in a sense that is what Marilyn had become for America – not a crude sexuality, but an image, a symbol, a dream of possibility, of the unattainable. The irony on which Fitzgerald's book turns, however, is that dream and substance cannot coexist, and so both Miller and Marilyn were to discover.

In June 1955, *The Seven Year Itch* had its premiere in New York. Joe DiMaggio, still looking for a reconciliation, accompanied Marilyn, only to become involved in an argument with his ex-wife at the party that was to mark both the premiere and her twenty-ninth birthday. By now, though, she was launched on her relationship with Miller. Throughout the summer and autumn of 1955 they met regularly, unknown to almost everybody, though DiMaggio seems to have heard rumours of it and went to the Waldorf to challenge her. In an interview in July that year she mentioned that she was thinking of buying a house in Brooklyn. The interviewer noted an English bicycle by the kitchen on which, she explained, she cycled in Central Park and on Ocean Parkway in Brooklyn. What she did not reveal was that the man who cycled with her was Arthur Miller. Among those in on the secret were the Greenes in Connecticut, and the Rostens, whose summer resort was in Port Jefferson on Long Island. It was while she was staying at their beach house that Marilyn, a poor swimmer, found herself in trouble. Several decades later, Miller expressed his bitterness at Rosten's failure to help her when she was so clearly in danger of drowning.

They continued to conduct the affair in secret. When he and Marilyn wanted to go to a party together Eli Wallach would chaperone her. His sister remembers that none of the family suspected. Even Marilyn's assistant was kept in the dark.

Miller now surrendered to the forces he had previously resisted, seeing in her someone desperate to change her life and thereby evidence that such a change was possible. As he later told a *Time* magazine reporter, 'Instead of becoming a disbeliever in life, which she had every reason to become, she kept her ability to feel and search for a genuine human relationship. She has stopped wanting to throw herself away. She was preached to so much that she was a bad girl, not worth anything, that she developed an enormous self-destructiveness. She's coming out of it now.'[85]

Robert Whitehead, the producer of Miller's plays from *A View from the Bridge* through to *Broken Glass*, spent time with Miller and Marilyn in the spring of 1955. As he explained:

> We were having a lot of lunches together, at Child's in Times Square ... But I didn't realize at first he was going around with her. One day Arthur said to me, 'You gotta get a bicycle, Bob. It's the only way to get around New York.' I thought it was a little odd. Then, a month later, I read in the papers, 'Marilyn Monroe has been seen riding a bicycle around the city.' I thought it was kind of exciting that they were having an affair ... But I was kind of surprised when he married her. I was doubtful about the connection. Arthur was an immense force, the leading intellectual in the world at that moment. She'd had the leading baseball player in the world, so I guess he was next. I guess Arthur thought, I'm going to take this extraordinary child of nature and lead her to the light of day. And then he discovered you can't play God.[86]

He was not entirely wrong about the messianic impulse, but it was also a relationship that turned on mutual self interest. 'I began to dream,' Miller said, 'that with her I could do what seemed to me would be the most wonderful thing of all – have my work, and all that implied, and someone I just simply adored. I thought I could solve it all with this marriage.' At the same time, 'she was simply overwhelming. As I guess I was to her, for a while.'

The dying fall of that sentence comes from the fact that he was looking back on the relationship from the distance of 1991. At the time she was a 'kind of phenomenon ... there wasn't a conventional bone in her body', but then the 'devils weren't as obvious. She was a creative force. It was wonderful to be around her. Until she got ill.'[87] Again, the dying fall. At the time, though, everything seemed promise. The dull routine of married life was suddenly broken open by a woman who represented everything he had never encountered before. And there was always the seductive idea, as Whitehead had suggested, of leading her to the light, healing the wounds that Miller detected but which he thought would be amenable to the grace of love.

Nor, surely, is it irrelevant that in October 1955 Miller would be forty. There was a sense that this was his last chance for happiness, for that sensuality denied him at home. In the public world he had been harassed by the Left and the Right after *The Crucible* in 1953, refused a passport in 1954, publicly denounced by the press, and would be fired from a film project in 1955. Privately, though, he was courting America's most famous woman. What a kick in the eye for all his enemies. What a boost for the ego of a man whose private life had hitherto been a painful charade. What did anything matter now that he was, as he told himself, in love – and surely for the first time, if we recall all those equivocal statements about his relationship with Mary going back to the time of the marriage itself. He was briefly an adolescent again, with all the accompanying reckless unconcern for consequences. He had a secret, and if there were few with whom he was content to share it, he was awaiting the right moment to lay his ace on the table. Marilyn also had a secret. She was taking both sleeping pills and tranquillizers and finding it difficult to function without them, often washing them down with glasses of champagne.

Marilyn's new deal with Twentieth Century Fox, finally concluded at the end of 1955, gave her both more money and greater control. She was not turning her back on Hollywood, merely determined that she would work on her own terms and with freedom to develop her own projects. The first such for Fox was to be *Bus Stop*, while the first Marilyn Monroe Productions film was to be Terrence Rattigan's *The Sleeping Prince*, which she bought, on the advice of Greene, without reading the play.

She approached Laurence Olivier, who had starred in the West End production. She was to take the part originally played by Olivier's wife, Vivien Leigh. In February 1956 Olivier, intrigued, flew to New York to discuss the proposal, meeting her in the Sutton Place apartment to which she had now moved. Noël Coward's ironic response to the idea was to say, '*Il faut vivre*',[88] though, unbeknown to Olivier, he was at the time having discussions with Paramount about the possibility of appearing in a musical version of the same play himself. He wrote in his diary, 'Larry is going to make a movie of The Sleeping Prince with Marilyn Monroe, which might conceivably drive him round the bend.'[89] He was not wrong. But for the moment the idea of making a film with the world's most famous sex symbol appealed to Olivier, not least because his own marital problems had made him restless. He too was, at least temporarily, overwhelmed by Monroe, despite being kept waiting for two hours as she struggled to decide which dress would most impress what she thought of at the time as one of the world's great actors: 'She was adorable,' recalled Olivier, 'so witty, such incredible fun and more physically attractive than anyone I could have imagined, apart from herself on the screen.'[90]

At a press conference to announce the project he offered a description of her contrasting qualities: 'Marilyn is a brilliant comedienne, which means she is a fine actress. She has the extremely cunning gift of being able to suggest one minute that she is the naughtiest little thing, and the next minute that she is beautifully dumb and innocent. The effect on the audience is that they are gently titillated to a sense of excitement in not knowing which is which.' The description, accurate enough, was also a reflection of his own response: 'By the end of the day one thing was clear to me: I was going to fall most shatteringly in love with Marilyn ... it was inescapable.' In the end it proved highly escapable, as he encountered the other Marilyn Monroe, the one who infuriated directors and frustrated her fellow actors.

That same month, Marilyn made her will (later to be changed several times). The presumed estate was $200,000. Now it was to go to Miller.

Her work with the Actors Studio was giving her greater confidence in her own abilities, and her relationship with Miller was plainly something more than a passing affair. Marilyn, he said later, 'had finally moved into my life, and the resulting mixture of despair for my marriage and astonishment with her' left little room for the casting of *A View from the Bridge*, which was his immediate task. 'I was alternately soaring and anxious that I might be slipping into a new life not my own. My will seemed to have evaporated.'[91] Here he was, after all, staging a play in which the desire of an older man for a younger woman carried the stain of betrayal and was touched with ambivalence in that it seemed to confuse two roles. The eleven-year gap between himself and Marilyn was scarcely substantial, but it seems clear that if she was looking for a lover she was also, looking for a father and, indeed, called him 'Papa'. The role in which she cast him was that of teacher, guide, protector. For him she was a kind of child whom he wished simultaneously to protect and to embrace as a wife. The unreality of this drama they played out was what would lead to disaster.

Robert Lewis, a former actor turned producer, who directed Norman Rosten's dramatization of Joyce Cary's *Mister Johnson* in 1956, recalled readings of the play as he tried to raise money from wealthy backers:

> Earle Hyman would read the title role he was to assume, and I read all the other parts. Marilyn Monroe, a good friend of Norman Rosten's, would always enter and slither across through the room, after we were well into the first act, and settle down close to where Earle and I were acting our hearts out. Not many eyes were trained on us after Marilyn arrived, but we didn't mind too much, as she was the best shill for prospective buyers one could wish for.
>
> Later we'd go back to Norman Rosten's Brooklyn house for some food. Arthur Miller, a Brooklynite friend of Norman's, would be there carrying forward his courtship of Marilyn. After dinner, we helped with the dishes. I washed and Marilyn dried. Although she had a way with a dish towel, this talent figured only marginally in Arthur's ultimate wiving of Marilyn.[92]

The very domesticity was simultaneously part of the courtship, a glimpse at a shared life, and another source of guilt, since it was that domesticity he was betraying in pursuing her at all. He found himself momentarily paralysed: 'I no longer knew what I wanted – certainly not the end of my marriage, but the thought of putting Marilyn out of my life was unbearable. My world seemed to be colliding with itself, the past exploding under my feet.'[93] On the other hand there was duty, and a not inconsiderable social pressure of the kind that was to keep Sylvia Gellburg married in *Broken Glass*.

It was hard to imagine what marriage to Monroe might mean. Ultimately her career lay on the West Coast, his on the East. He had resisted the blandishments of those who had earlier urged him to turn his skills to screenwriting, feeling, in common with a number of those on the left, that Hollywood represented the very values against which he was in revolt. His experience with *The Hook*, that he had hoped might tell a socially responsible truth, had merely confirmed such suspicions. Meanwhile, for all her attempts at domestication during her time in New York, and her serious efforts to master her craft as an actress, there can have been little doubt that Marilyn would continue her career in films, no matter how much she insisted that marriage, should it come, would find her content with domesticity. She did, to be sure, stage a dinner party for Miller, with, as guests, the very few people who were aware of their relationship; she worked desperately to get the details right, but it was a role that she approached with the same nervousness with which she performed in front of a camera.

For Miller's cousin Morton, who, in common with the rest of the family, knew nothing of his relationship with Marilyn, the key moment was the Broadway opening of *A View from the Bridge* and *A Memory of Two Mondays*: 'There was a stir in the audience as Marilyn, bosomy in a strikingly tight gown, walked down the aisle to her seat. It struck me that her blatant appearance at the opening of these plays was the first public signal that Arthur's marriage to Mary was nearing its end.'[94] James Longhi was also in the audience. Miller came up to him and said, 'Jim, the kids are alright. It was only later,' he recalled, 'that I realized that the rumours about him were true.'[95]

To say that there was a degree of denial on the part of both Miller and Marilyn, that they failed to think beyond the moment, is to say no more than that their relationship was like many another. The problem was that they were not ordinary citizens. She was fully aware of the pressures the inevitable publicity would bring; Miller, perhaps surprisingly, was not.

Miller also had other problems to deal with at this time. In particular, he was having difficulties with the New York City Council, sponsors of a film on juvenile delinquency he had been commissioned to write. The film, a full-length feature to be shown in first-run cinemas, was to be made by Combined Artists Incorporated, an independent film company. It was scheduled for shooting between the casting of *A Memory of Two Mondays* and *A View from the Bridge* in the spring of 1955 and their opening in the autumn. He researched the project in the Bay Ridge area of Brooklyn with Vincent Riccio, a social worker, throughout the summer before eventually seeing it snatched away from him in a campaign involving the New York press and, covertly, the FBI and HUAC.

The Scripps Howard news service reporter Frederick Woltman attacked him, invoking his involvement with the Waldorf Peace Conference as evidence of his dangerous radicalism. The *New York World Telegram and Sun* duly published Woltman's article and a few days later the newspaper began to campaign for Miller's dismissal from the project, suggesting that HUAC was investigating him and intended to call him as a witness in November. HUAC even sent a representative, Mrs Dolores Scotti, to warn city officials that he was likely to be the subject of investigation for suspected communist allegiances. Jim McCarthy, Chief of Street Operations for the Youth Board, received an hour-long call from her – he was trusted, he presumed, because of his name and the fact that he had attended Notre Dame University, Indiana (the FBI had a fondness for recruiting Catholics, by definition anti-communist). He reported the call to Miller. Mrs Scotti had, he explained, been trying to place him in the Party. HUAC, it seemed, did not as yet have enough to call him in.

In November 1955, he was summoned before the Youth Board and questioned about his earlier passport application and an oath he had signed in connection with that application. This was to be a subject taken up the following year by HUAC at which time he indicated that he had categorically denied being a supporter of 'the Communist cause or contributing to it or . . . under its discipline or domination', adding that 'in my application at about the same time for renewal of my passport, I had signed under the penalties of perjury . . . that I was not a member of any subversive organization'.[96] In fact, as he would discover, his memory on this detail was faulty.

The Youth Board's subcommittee responsible for the delinquency project voted unanimously to continue with both the film and its scriptwriter, but the Board of Estimate, which also had to approve the contract, was now sensitive to the public attacks. New York's Corporation Counsel, as Walter Goodman pointed out in a *New Republic* article in December, decided that a re-vote of the Youth Board would be necessary, this time augmented by other New York City department heads, who duly appointed a subcommittee to handle the affair. What had begun as a worthy and profit-making venture (the City stood to take 5 per cent of the profits) had suddenly become a major issue. Miller submitted an eight-page document to the chairman of the subcommittee, Judge Nathaniel Kaplan.

The project, he insisted, was not money-making as far as he was concerned. He had undertaken it because he believed the issue of delinquency was an important one and that the film might do something to address the subject. He noted that the attack on him had come from a single newspaper and that he was being required to disavow his personal political faith and to declare his loyalty when anyone who knew his work would understand his commitment to democracy. He was, he reminded the subcommittee, on record as denying his support for communism. His plays had constituted what he called a biography of his awareness of the world. The issue, it seemed to him, was a clear one. Would American writers have to be regarded as politically reliable before being allowed to write? He could only proceed with the project, he insisted, if he was allowed to do so without violating his conscience or his sense of himself. On 6 December Miller appeared before the new subcommittee: 'I told the Board ... that I was not going to genuflect to any newspaperman or howling mob; I was not going to change my writing for anyone. My attitudes on dictatorship, Nazi and Communist, had been established by many essays ... I was not going to submit myself to any political means test to practice the profession of letters in the United States.'[97]

This frontal assault seemed to carry the day, the subcommittee voting five to one to continue with the project. This was not, though, the answer that city officials wanted. The mayor's Investigations Commissioner now became involved, not least because of charges made by the American Legion and the Catholic War Veterans that Miller was connected with subversive groups. He was, of course, entirely familiar with both organizations, which had already worked to get his plays banned, but complaints also came from AWARE, a private anti-communist organization. According to Judge Kaplan, a justice of the Domestic Relations Court, only the American Civil Liberties Union had come out in support of the project and Miller's involvement. Board officials indicated that Investigations Commissioner Charles H. Tenney, appointed by Mayor Wagner, had assured them that Miller had indeed sponsored or been associated with subversive groups. Though the Investigations Commissioner had found no evidence of a continuing relationship the Board now voted eleven to nine to overrule their own subcommittee, seven of the eight city commissioners registering negative votes. As one remarked, 'I'm not calling him a Communist ... My objection is he refuses to repent.'[98]

On 30 November 1956, a ninety-five-page summary report on his activities was compiled by the FBI. One of the items, dated June 1955, referred to a move to suppress a production of the 'Communist-line play' *Death of a Salesman* by the Texas Western College at El Paso, to be derailed by persuading an alumnus to object. The same file, however, also contains notes on his New York film project. These include details derived from a *New York World Telegram and Sun* article headed 'City Crime Film Off in Red-Taint Battle', and information on an approach by the Board of Estimate to Combined Artists to check out Miller's activity in communist-front organizations. At the bottom of the page J. Edgar Hoover comments: 'Some interesting items'.

At no stage did anyone challenge the twenty-five-page treatment he had produced for the proposed film. As the *World Telegram* editorial explained on 8 December, 'The question is not whether Mr Miller is talented – or whether he could write an unbiased script on the work of the Youth Board. It is simply whether the city should enhance the playwright's prestige and diminish its own by indirectly hiring a man with such a questionable political background.'[99] It now suggested that perhaps the film could be made but with Miller's name removed from the credits.

The project, however, was dead. Miller's final, and somewhat bitter, remark was: 'I had hoped to make not merely a drama but a civilizing work of art. The majority of the Youth Board has now decided that this picture shall not be made. So be it. Now let us see whether fanaticism can do what it never could do in the history of the world; let it perform a creative act; let it take its club in hand and write what it has just destroyed.'[100] In fact there is some doubt as to whether the film would have been particularly effective. Certainly the version he chose to describe in an article published in 1958 seemed a touch naive.

The New York City Youth Board, which had originally commissioned the script, was an arm of the mayor's office and an experimental unit that sent its men out into the field to get to know individual gang members. Miller's aim had been to work from the inside to address what then appeared to be a major problem. He spent two months in Brooklyn with the street gangs, attending their meetings, questioning them, observing their violence. His job was to shape his experience into a workable film, which he did by featuring two central characters, one a Youth Board worker, the other a gang leader, and even in his brief synopsis it is possible to see how this film was to relate to fundamental Miller themes. For his analysis of these alienated teenagers was that they had 'never made contact with civilized values', that they were 'boys without a concept of the father, as the father is normally conceived, boys without an inkling of the idea of social obligation, personal duty or even rudimentary honor'.[101]

The rescued gang leader, whom we are to first encounter with an iron bar in his hand leading his gang in a street fight, will end up as himself a Youth Board worker. The film tells the story of Jerry Bone, who slowly works to get himself accepted by the gangs, who uses his influence with the police but refuses to bend the law. It is about the redemption of more than a gang leader. Covering a period of four years, it is designed to show the utility of addressing the problem of delinquency by example. As Miller explained, 'Outwardly, the suspense, the progression of the story will be generated by two impending possibilities. Having drawn them away from gang-fighting and marauding, Bone will never know when, without a moment's notice to him, they will resume it ... The overhanging question will be, quite simply, whether and how each of these boys, with whom we shall have sympathy, will "make it".'

There is a curious air of naivety about many elements of the script – friendly cops, dances in which the gangs join together (though *West Side Story*, which opened in 1957, features just such a scene), a camping trip, a visit to a church. It was designedly an optimistic film. 'These are children,' he states, 'who have never known life excepting as a worthless thing; they have been told from birth that they are nothing, that their parents are nothing, that their hopes are nothing. The group in this picture will end, by and large, with a discovery of their innate worth ... That is what the picture is about.' Those who voted against continuance of the picture did so not because of any implausibility of plot, however, but because they feared association with a supposed subversive. For Miller, it was one more problem in a troubled period, and so much wasted effort.

Victor Navasky and Brenda Murphy, in their books *Naming Names* and *Congressional Theatre*, have drawn attention to an interesting footnote to Miller's problems with the Youth Board, details of which are also to be found in Jeff Kisseloffs *On The Box: An Oral History of Television 1920-1961*. On 18 January 1964 a television series called *The Defenders*, starring E.G. Marshall and Robert Reed as a father–son on defence team, aired an episode called 'Blacklist'. Written by Ernest Kinoy, it was in part based on Miller's experiences with the Youth Board, though, for Marshall, himself blacklisted, it had a special interest. It featured an actor who had been blacklisted for his association with Spanish War Relief in the 1930s and for opposing HUAC in the 1940s. In the film he is hired to make a documentary about the city's youth plan. The actor, Joe Larch, has been reduced to working as a clerk in a shoe store, but when his break comes two women from the National Security Vanguard League distribute flyers warning of his radical past. The papers pick up the story, as they had with Miller, and the mayor comes under pressure.

The attorney played by Marshall tries to treat with the Vanguard League but is rebuffed, with the warning that he may himself be corrupted by his client unless that client can be cleared by a friendly agency with which they happen to be in contact, itself a standard ploy of the time. The mayor evades responsibility, Larch is eventually fired and the project is abandoned. The liberal lawyers discover the limitations of the law, which has no power against anything as diffuse as a blacklist. The show won an Emmy for its writer and the actor who played Joe Larch. Ironically, the actor originally scheduled for the show could not be used as CBS was itself still blacklisting him at the time.[102]

There is another piece of fiction, or what Miller chose to call 'history in fiction', which came out of this experience. Called 'Scenes from History', it is a story of the gangs and of the drugs that had begun to appear in the neighbourhood. At its heart is a social worker, originally inspired to take on his job in the 1930s as a result of reading John Strachey's *The Coming Struggle for Power* (1933), a book which had also caught Miller's eye while at university. The social worker had never joined the Party but had been attracted to its apparent commitment to the poor. Now 'escaped from one deception', he finds himself involved in another, as the capitalist society he serves encourages him to placate rather than address the needs of the unemployed. The story, which effectively opens with the death by heroin of one of the supposed delinquents, is unfinished and was never published.

Looking back in 1962 on his work with the gangs Miller saw them as symptoms of a time when people – not the gang members but those who regarded them with a mixture of suspicion and fear – 'no longer seem to know why they are alive; existence is simply a string of near-experiences marked off by periods of stupefying spiritual and psychological stasis'. Far from being rebels, the delinquents themselves were 'pack hounds', conformists in a failed society. The 1930s, by contrast, he recalled as a time 'when you could not get a job, when all the studying you might do would get you a chance, at best, to sell ties in Macy's'. Then, delinquency consisted in 'joining demonstrations of the unemployed, pouring onto campuses to scream against some injustice by college administrations, and adopting to one degree or another a Socialist ideology'. This, he insisted, had been more dangerous to capitalism but more constructive, because it was 'still bent upon instituting human values' in its place.

What Miller saw in mid-century America was a struggle for the good life with no idea of what that might encompass beyond a satisfaction of artificial needs, for the 'good life itself is not the struggle for meaning, nor the quest for union with the past, with God, with man'. It is 'the life of ceaseless entertainment, effortless joys, the air-conditioned dust-free languor beyond the Musselman's most supine dream. Freedom is, after all, comfort; sexuality is a photograph. The enemy of it all is the real.' The delinquents were thus neither existential rebels nor threats to anything as definite as a social life in which anyone could have confidence or to which they could wish to declare their loyalty. They were caught in 'indefiniteness', an 'unreality, its boring hum'. Their spasms of violence were no more than attempts 'to feel a real pain, a genuine consequence', a desire to 'butt' against the 'rubber walls' of a culture with little to offer beyond its own conformities, its own illusory and self-negating virtues.

Those who vetoed the film project believing Miller to be a subversive were not entirely wrong. They simply failed to understand the nature of his subversion. The man who researched and planned the film was no longer a Marxist, but he *was* the man who became a Marxist because he saw a society seemingly content to drift on the winds of its own irrelevance, dedicating itself to the recovery of a dream at odds, in crucial respects, with human necessities. That society had not changed simply because it had exchanged the rigours of Depression for the flaccid pleasures of economic boom. The enemy within, to Miller, was neither the delinquent nor the political rebel but conformity and the 'seemingly universal sense of life's pointlessness, the absence of any apparent aim to it at all'.[103]

Nor were problems with the film the only thing bringing him to national attention at this time. In January and February 1956 he had received invitations from the American Committee for Cultural Freedom, the American Committee for Liberation from Bolshevism, and the Union of Soviet Writers, in the case of the last to celebrate the seventy-fifth anniversary of the death of Dostoevsky. In response he attacked the Soviet Union for 'cultural barbarism' and the United States for depriving him of his freedom and for the lack of support he had received from his fellow writers. 'In neither the Soviet Union nor in the United States today,' he asserted, 'could a man with his [Dostoevsky's] views have long survived without punitive condemnation, which in the Soviet Union could mean outright suppression if not worse, and in the United States an official but, nevertheless, powerful process of social and economic ostracism.'[104]

The ACCF was not amused by the parallel and requested Radio Liberation to broadcast its rebuttal of Miller's views, while a member of its executive committee, James Farrell, wrote a letter to the *New York Times* attacking what he saw as Miller's gratuitous exaggeration. From this, and from the response to his involvement in the juvenile delinqency film, it was clear that he was now very much on the firing line. HUAC, in particular, after ignoring him for so long, was beginning to close in.

In March 1956, the FBI was approached by an official of HUAC who 'desired to know "whether the Bureau could advise him in confidence if Arthur Miller could be placed inside the CP by a former informant of the FBI who would be willing to testify before the HCUA [its preferred acronym]"'. The file then notes, 'It was recommended that [name deleted] be informed that the Bureau could be of assistance to him concerning Miller.' On 19 March, the recommendation was endorsed: 'Yes, H[oover]'.[105]

In the face of the collapse of the youth project, and his domestic problems, Marilyn was, 'a whirling light to me then, all paradox and enticing mystery, street-tough one moment, then lifted by a lyrical and poetic sensitivity that few retain past adolescence'.[106] For her, he was not only an intellectual guide but a sympathetic and caring person. When Michael Chekhov died, she asked Miller to read to her from *The Brothers Karamazov*, a favourite book and one which Chekhov had suggested might provide a suitable role for her, that of Grushenka. Miller now agreed to the possibility of writing a screenplay of the novel.

To the forty-year-old Miller, there was nothing judgemental about Marilyn. To be with her 'was to be accepted'. She may have lacked the ability to protect herself from those who sought to compromise and exploit her, but to Miller this was evidence of a naivety that contrasted with the cruelty of those she encountered, the men who failed to see beyond her looks. He recognized her narcissism, her awareness of her physical beauty, but acknowledged, too, that this coexisted not merely with an occasionally disabling sense of inferiority but also with her yearning to be recognized for something other than her appearance. He claims to have had no illusions about her past: 'What I did not know about her life was easy to guess.'

Much of their time was spent in her room, at the Waldorf Towers or, later, at 2 Sutton Place. When she could not see him, she would take a taxi across the Brooklyn Bridge and get out on the Esplanade on the edge of Brooklyn Heights and walk, though careful not to go near his Willow Street house. He did feel guilty as he visited her in her Waldorf Towers room (there was a separate entrance on 50th Street and an elevator exclusively for the use of residents and their guests), but what was that beside someone who promised to break open his staid existence? For her part, she responded not merely to him but to his social and political ideas, so much in contrast to what she heard in Hollywood. Here was a man who seemed to care about those on the street, who wrote about those who found it difficult to articulate their passions. His work on juvenile delinquents, his plays about the autoparts warehouse and those who worked the docks, his contempt for those politicians who threatened artists and writers, all suggested a man who might understand someone like her, born on the wrong side of the tracks and ruled, at times, by necessities she would rather not confront. Such people, after all, constituted her audience, and whatever her antics on a movie set she was almost invariably responsive to those she encountered on the street.

'From life on the streets,' Miller remarked, 'to Marilyn high in the Waldorf Tower was a cosmic leap, but not such a discontinuity as it would seem.' He also recognized in her fight for respect – from the studios, from producers and directors – that need to be acknowledged that he had witnessed in Brooklyn as teenagers struggled to make a mark in a world that seemed to have no space for them.

They could hardly have been unaware of how different they were. As he remarked in *Timebends*, 'it was obviously a wrong fit'. Both, though, were at a moment in their lives when they wished to make a break with the past. Both had to believe in the possibility of change so that the very dissonances, the discontinuities, paradoxically seemed evidence of what they sought. Opposites as they were, they seemed to offer each other the radical transformation they desired. And yet neither could really imagine the marriage that somehow seemed implied by the affair they were conducting.

In the privacy of her Waldorf Towers room, she tried out some scenes from O'Neill's *Anna Christie* with him, exercises for the Actors Studio, but even now she seemed to lack conviction, as if she could not quite believe in the new life she was determined to lead, the new stage in her career she was so anxious to bring about. And one wonders why Strasberg chose this particular part for her to work on, that of a desperate prostitute. He had earlier suggested a scene from Noël Coward's *Fallen Angels*. Nonetheless, her performance, in February 1956, with the aid of coffee laced with Jack Daniels, seems to have been impressive. An initially sceptical Kim Stanley recalled that it was 'just wonderful. She *was* wonderful. We were taught never to clap at the Actors Studio – it was like we were in church – and it was the first time I'd ever heard applause there. Some of us went to her privately and apologized.'[107] Maureen Stapleton, with whom she performed, had suggested that she could have a copy of the text on stage if she was having difficulty with the lines but she felt 'If I do that now, I'll do it for the rest of my life.'[108] She was word-perfect. For Strasberg, she was 'phenomenal'.

Miller and Marilyn continued to cycle together, through Brooklyn and out to Coney Island, behaving like the teenagers they were not. He was introducing her to his world, showing her the places he had known as a boy. She joined him in Boston for a day, where *A View from the Bridge* was having its out-of-town try-out. Together they went to the cinema to see Paddy Chayefsky's *Marty*, featuring Betsy Blair, herself a victim of blacklisting.

Finally, in January 1956, the columnist Earl Wilson broke the story of Miller's impending divorce, and in February Walter Winchell used his broadcast to announce 'the fact that America's best-known blonde moving picture star is now the darling of the left-wing intelligentsia, several of whom are listed as red fronters. I do not think she realizes it.' Miller's FBI file duly noted the remarks and added, 'It was commented that this possibly referred to Marilyn Monroe, for a recent news article (unidentified) concerning the divorce action between Arthur Asher Miller and his wife reflected the rumor that Marilyn Monroe was linked romantically with Miller, however on interview by newsman, both admitted friendship but denied any romantic ties.'[109] The FBI had started to track Marilyn.

In spring, Miller took himself off to Pyramid Lake in Nevada, to wait out the six weeks' residency required to obtain a divorce – divorce being, as he later suggested, 'an optimistic reaching for authenticity, a rebellion against waste'.[110] A New York divorce would have required a finding of adultery, and everyone involved wanted to avoid this. Nevada was a popular option, and Miller found himself living in a lakeside cottage next to Saul Bellow, who was there on a similar errand. On 20 May Walter Winchell announced on air: 'The House Committee on Un-American Activities is going after the Broadway Commies again. Proceedings are on the way. One of Marilyn

Arthur Miller and Marilyn Monroe with Simone Signoret and Yves Montand during the making of *Let's Make Love*.

John Huston, Marilyn Monroe and Arthur Miller while shooting *The Misfits*.

The cast, writer and director of *The Misfits*: (clockwise from bottom) Montgomery Clift as Perce Howland, Eli Wallach as Guido, screenwriter Arthur Miller, director John Huston, Clark Gable as Gay Langland, and Marilyn Monroe as Roslyn Taber.

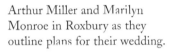

Arthur Miller and Marilyn Monroe in Roxbury as they outline plans for their wedding.

Isadore and Augusta Miller with Arthur Miller and Marilyn Monroe, shortly before their marriage.

Marilyn Monroe in Roxbury following the fatal accident of Mara Scherbatoff of *Paris Match*.

Marilyn Monroe with Arthur
Miller rehearsing between
scenes of *The Misfits.*

Miller and a literally and
symbolically absent
Marilyn Monroe.

Marilyn Monroe
and Arthur Miller
after their civil
wedding ceremony
in White Plains,
NY, on 20 June
1956.

The second
wedding, 3 July
1956.

Arthur Miller and Marilyn Monroe with
Laurence Olivier and Vivien Leigh, July 1960.

The Roxbury house, which Miller bought with Marilyn Monroe and lived in for the rest of his life.

Inge Morath and Arthur Miller on the day of their wedding.

Monroe's new romances, a long-time pro-lefto, will be asked to testify.'"""

In February, Marilyn had returned to Hollywood to make *Bus Stop*. Her mood was strikingly different. There was a new confidence. She broke off relations with Natasha Lytess, not least because she had a new drama coach in the person of Lee Strasberg – or, rather, his intermediary, Paula, who was paid $1,500 a week for her services. Miller, meanwhile, was to return to the University of Michigan to receive an honorary degree when news of his marriage break-up reached Professor Rowe, who wrote to him at Sutcliffe Star Route, Reno: 'Helen and I are very sad for the news of yours and Mary's marriage which we learned from Norman today. I tried to telephone you and when the operator did not have your unlisted number I called Norman for it. He told me of your being in Reno.'

On 22 May, Miller replied (there was a tri-weekly mail pick-up), attempting an explanation. He told him that he and Mary had been separated since the previous December but that they had drifted apart much earlier. He also repeated the point he had made with respect to the figure of Weller in *The Best Comedians*, namely, that it had become impossible for him to write truthfully while living a lie. The children, he added, were relieved of a burden and were happier than he had feared. He was by now five weeks into his stay on Pyramid Lake, a desolate place relieved only by the company of his neighbour Bellow, a man who once observed that to be close to Marilyn was like holding on to an electric wire and not being able to let go. As to his work, Miller informed Rowe that he had been writing a novel, in effect a dry run for a play which he thought so challenging that it might lead him straight to jail. He had been working on it since 1951. It was to be a study of several couples seen in the context of contemporary America. He was aiming to complete it by the autumn, but now doubted he would manage it.

In the end nothing came of either novel or play, as first the House Un-American Activities Committee and then marriage to Marilyn Monroe, and its unexpected exigencies, drove such thoughts from his mind. Indeed, though he did not realize it at the time, he was about to lay his career aside to support hers.

Looking back in 2003, he recalled another detail of his time in Nevada. 'There was,' he remembered,

> a guy who had his house on stilts. In the desert. And that was a very curious thing, looking at this house raised up about ten feet above the ground. I wondered, was he waiting for a flood? Well, it turned out he had a hole in the ground under that house, and there was a silver mine down at the bottom of this hole. He would periodically go down and dig himself out some silver. That was his bank. And I think that's like a writer. He's living on the top of that hole. He goes down there and sees if he can chop out some silver.""

Miller had himself always mined his own experience for his art, as he would when he wrote the screenplay inspired by his stay in Nevada, *The Misfits*. Meanwhile, as he waited out time there, so he continued his affair with Monroe, now back in Hollywood and shooting *Bus Stop*, by telephone. Since the cottages lacked this amenity it required him to take his calls at a nearby motel phone booth, he answering to Mr Leslie, Marilyn to Mrs Leslie, names taken from Vina Delmar's novel *About Mr Leslie*, which concerns a singer who lives with a married man for a period every year. Such calls were a secret, though one she shared with Eileen Heckart, who had just finished playing Beatrice in *A View from the Bridge* in New York: 'He calls me on the phone every night. Nobody knows he calls me on the phone. It's a secret.'[113]

Miller later remembered one conversation in which she called, distressed at being described as vulgar by Joshua Logan, director of *Bus Stop*. It was the first time she 'had sounded so unguardedly terrified'.[114] It was the moment he grasped the extent to which she had come to depend on him, as once she had on Milton Greene, who, she now felt, was failing to intervene on her behalf with Logan. Perhaps it should have been a warning sign of what was to come, but for the moment it seemed no more than evidence of her trust in him and their mutual future if, more worryingly, of what might be her suicidal tendencies. So distressing was this thought, and his sense of his own inability to intervene, that he remembered fainting briefly, before recovering to continue a conversation in which she seemed on the point of relinquishing her career in favour of domesticity.

'I don't want this anymore, Papa,' he recalled her saying, '. . . I want to live with you in the country and be a good wife', though even now she envisaged the possibility of being wooed back, albeit only for 'a wonderful picture'. The effect of the conversation was a new level of commitment. Suddenly, the 'anguish of this past year, the guilty parting with children and the wrenching up of roots, seemed now the necessary price for what might truly be waiting just ahead, a creative life with undivided soul'.

It is interesting to note that this recollected emotion turns as much on the impact on his career as on the new domestic life being plotted by a filmstar who had called to complain about her treatment by a director. It was a relationship, it seems, that not only promised to heal an inner conflict but also bridged a gap between his emotional and intellectual self that in turn would have an impact on his writing. Until now, he had written out of guilt, pain and confusion. Now those burdens were, as he presumed, to be lifted.

Once a week, and in breach of the residency rule which applied to those seeking divorce in the state of Nevada, Miller flew to Los Angeles to see Marilyn (at the Chateau Marmont Hotel), who was now feeling more relaxed about the film, though increasingly dependent on Paula Strasberg. In the years that followed, Strasberg became a fixture on Monroe films, intensely disliked by directors and, eventually, by Miller. Here, too, was a warning of Marilyn's dependency, her tendency to idealize those on whom, for a while at least, she relied. She was already terrified he would leave her, discover aspects of her past she would rather conceal. Indeed, he would recall her embarrassment when they passed a man twice her age with whom she had clearly had a relationship. She deflected his question and they went on their way to their hotel room, the incident not forgotten but part of the past both conspired to deny.

If Miller thought he could keep his plans secret, he was quickly disabused. A television camera crew arrived at his Nevada hideout to question him. Nor were they the only ones in pursuit. In June 1955, an internal FBI memo NY 100-57673 had stated: 'Subject is not being recommended for an interview under the regular interview program even though he was a member of the CP in 1946 and 1947, because of his position as a well known writer ... In view of subject's limited activity with the CP and his position in the business world, it is felt that an interview would result in embarrassment for the Bureau.' On 27 March 1956, however, two months after his relationship with Marilyn became public knowledge, an extensive memo to L.B. Nichols (Deputy Director of the FBI) listed all the 'communist type' organizations he had belonged to, speeches he had made, documents he had signed. It repeated the earlier assertion that his real name was Anton and listed his personal, academic and professional details. Two months later, on 29 May, a memo from Nichols to Clyde Tolson noted:

> Dick Arens, of the House Committee on Un-American Activities (HCUA) telephoned shortly after 5.00 pm tonight advising that the committee would like to have Arthur Miller, author of 'All My Sons' and 'Death of a Salesman', appear before the committee on 6-12-56, 6-13-56, or 6-14-56. Arens stated the committee knows he was a member of the party in 1943 but is unable to find a live witness that can put him in the Party. Arens enquired as to whether we could help him on furnishing a photostat of Miller's Communist Party (CP) card. We do not have a photostat of any CP membership card on Miller according to File Review, although main file on Miller reflects he was a member of CP in 1945, 1946 and 1947.[115]

The absence of such evidence was plainly irritating, but an investigator from HUAC, William Wheeler, now arrived in Reno to serve a subpoena. It was handed to Miller in an elevator of the First National Bank Building on 1st Street on 8 June, commanding him to appear in Washington on the 14th, though not before a total stranger advised him to resist. In town to conclude a cattle deal, a rancher approached him: 'I hope you're not going to tell those bastards anything.'[116] The man, Carl Royce, had, it turned out, served in the Aleutians with Dashiell Hammett, Lillian Hellman's lover, who had himself served time for refusing to divulge the names of contributors to the bail fund of the Civil Rights Congress, names which, in fact, he did not know. Royce now offered to shelter Miller on his Texas ranch, as he had Hammett for a time. It was too late, though Miller's attorney, Lloyd Garrison, successfully sought a week's delay.

On 10 June, Walter Winchell announced: 'Playwright Arthur Miller reported next husband of Marilyn Monroe will get his marital freedom tomorrow. Next stop trouble. The House Un-American Committee subpoena for Arthur Miller will check into his entire inner circle, which also happens to be the inner circle of Miss Monroe, all former communist sympathizers.'[117] By 13 June, the FBI had assembled a dossier, drawn from its files and stretching back a decade. It noted Miller's attendance at a closed Party meeting in the autumn of 1946, described as a seminar for playwrights and writers in the Communist Party. It also noted a 'pretext telephone call' conducted on 28 February 1950, designed to establish his whereabouts. Otherwise, it drew heavily on published material, especially the *Daily Worker*, a favourite Bureau source. A list of informants is blacked out, as are the names of individuals still to be contacted.

Miller's time in Nevada was not wasted. While there, he encountered two cowboys who hunted wild mustangs with the help of an ancient aircraft. On one occasion he and they came upon an abandoned house used as temporary accommodation by other cowboys looking for a night's sleep. The place was full of Western magazines, recounting movie versions of Western life. As with the original nineteenth-century cowboys, who had read the dime novels purporting to describe their lives, they looked to the movies for validation. Ironically, given their enthusiasm for Hollywood, it was these horse hunters who were to be the models for *The Misfits*, filmed in this same location five years later.

For Morton Miller, confirmation that Marilyn was in line to become Mary's successor finally came when he received a letter from his cousin saying, 'When I return east, Morton, the shit will hit the fan.'[118] Years later, in *The Ride Down Mount Morgan*, the central character, who had lived two separate lives with two women, confesses: 'If you try to live according to your real desires, you have to end up looking like a shit'. Miller acknowledged the relevance to his own life: 'I guess it's any time where you overthrow your obligations in order not to suffocate.'[119] Questioned by *Time* magazine about his marital intentions, Miller prevaricated. The $35,000 he had received for *A View from the Bridge*, which had just closed, was, he suggested, insufficient to support two families. It was somewhat disingenuous, to say the least, as was Marilyn's response. When asked if she was having an affair with Miller, Marilyn had replied, 'How could I? – he's a married man.'[120]

The divorce completed, on 11 June 1956 he returned to New York. In changing her will a week later, to leave most of her property to Miller, Monroe arranged for one-eighth to go in support of her estranged mother. She also inquired about securing the film rights to Miller's plays but declined the idea of a pre-nuptial agreement.

When he separated from his wife Miller had taken up temporary residence in an elegant West Side brownstone. It was there that Marilyn would visit him when she flew to New York. When she was in Hollywood she would telephone him, according to his cousin Morton, without regard for the three-hour time difference between West and East Coasts: 'Arthur could be seen and heard, at improbable hours, rushing upstairs, three, four steps at a time, to reach a phone lest Marilyn ring off.'[121] When she finally returned to New York they met in her Sutton Place apartment and eventually he took her to meet his parents at his old home on East 3rd Street in Brooklyn. For all that the separation from Mary had shocked them, they seemed to take to Marilyn, though in truth there was an unstated tension between her and Augusta Miller. Isidore, by contrast, was charmed. This was the family, she told them, she had been looking for.

Marilyn, however, was now coming under pressure from Hollywood. As she was later to remark, 'Some of those bastards in Hollywood wanted me to drop Arthur, said it would ruin my career. They're born cowards and want you to be like them.'[122] One of those bastards was Spyros Skouras, president of Twentieth Century Fox, who visited Miller and Marilyn on the eve of the HUAC hearing. When Skouras had called from the West Coast Miller had been disinclined to see him, but Marilyn asked him not to refuse. Despite the fact that she resented her treatment at the company's hands, she responded to Skouras's repeated assurances that he regarded her as his daughter. As to Miller, 'I was encouraged when she felt warmly toward him; we were to be married soon, and I found myself welcoming any of her feelings that were at all positive and unworried. In any case, it would be up to me how to respond ... and about that I had no uncertainty, although his coming increased my uneasiness that my public condemnation might harm her career.'[123]

When Skouras arrived, he asked Miller to use the hearings to make clear his differences from those on the left, reminding him of Stalin's baleful impact in the Greek civil war. For his part, no matter what his views of communism now were, Miller was still unwilling to follow Odets and Kazan down the path of informing. There was no meeting of minds. Something of the tone of the encounter can be gauged from an exchange of letters between the two men the following year.

On 5 January 1957, while he was on holiday in Jamaica, Miller wrote to Skouras. By then, he was waiting to hear the outcome of an indictment for contempt. In the letter he insisted that he was an anti-communist, not least because he was unwilling to submit to any dictates. He recalled that even when

poor he had resisted the blandishments of Hollywood, while his experience
working on *The Story of GI Joe* had further disillusioned him. In the privacy
of this letter, though, he was willing to go further, not only stressing the
essentially American nature of his plays but suggesting that were communism
ever to take over America, he would be one of the first victims precisely
because of that fact. Tears, he said, had come to Marilyn's eyes because of the
depth of his love for his country. He had, he said, never returned from trips
abroad without wishing to kiss the American earth, this being a country like
no other, a light for the world. His job as a writer was not to blow the trumpet
for that country but to sandblast away those illusions, of Left and Right alike,
that threatened it.

He could not agree to name names, he explained, perhaps partly from
stubbornness – the kind of stubbornness that had kept him writing plays
when he could persuade no one to produce them – but also because he saw it
as a question of honour. If he felt that government or people would be any
safer for his turning informer, he would do so. But the government already
knew the names of those he could name. He did not, he went on, want
communists protected. He was taking the stand not to protect others, but to
protect his sense of himself.

Here, as elsewhere, he was prone to go overboard in his emphasis on his
patriotism. So many attacks seem to have prompted a reactive hyperbole. The
thought of Marilyn Monroe in tears at his patriotism or of him offering a
papal kiss to an airport tarmac is a little difficult to conjure up. But he knew
his audience, or thought he did. Skouras was a businessman protecting his
investment. He was also, though, prone to sentimentality and effusiveness.
In his reply, sent from his New York office to Miller's new East 57th Street
apartment, Skouras explained:

> From the first time I talked to you over the phone, and also when I had seen
> you personally, there has never been any doubt in my mind that you are anti-
> communist. When Marilyn talked to me about you, I felt exactly as she did
> concerning your beliefs . . .
>
> I think it is quite admirable to hold fast to a conviction and even pride,
> but they should never be held on to at the expense of patriotism and the best
> interest of humanity.
>
> Of course, I do not want to offend you, but I do feel that your attitude is
> due to pride. You were not asked to reveal any names because they know the
> identity of the persons, but merely to comply with their request as a small
> sacrifice on your part. This possibly could have been done in Executive
> Session.
>
> Your anti-communistic spirit and feeling is so well expressed in your many
> works, and your acts clearly indicate that communism is not for the likes of

you and me. The recent events in Poland and the unequalled barbarism practiced on innocent Hungarians, who had looked to the Russians as their protectors and liberators, have produced revulsions in men's minds unequalled in our time. What would seem a compelling motive or principle at one time, can be by pressure of events rendered invalid at another time. It is very difficult for one to be a judge in his own case.

Admiring you as much as I do, I say to you unhesitatingly that by your attitude you are not placing your country above everything. Even these congressmen recognize your genius and surely respect you as a decent and fine human being. But they too have a duty to perform ...

There is one subject on which you and I will completely agree upon and that is Marilyn ... It would be a blessing to you both if you would, upon reexamination of this situation, take the position that I would take if I were in your place.

You are both deserving of serene happiness, which I am fearful is going to be difficult for you to enjoy if you do not bring yourself to view this matter not merely as an artist and a gentleman who feels it is not good manners to speak up, but as a patriot who will give the benefit of the doubt to those in authority who are attempting to protect our common country ...

Since you say it may be stubbornness or perhaps you are mistaken, why don't you put an end to this unfortunate situation, so that you and your wife may find the happiness you so richly deserve, and thus render to the world so much of your talent and brilliance.

I know in my heart that if you make this very small sacrifice you will bring a happy conclusion to this unfortunate situation. And I appeal to you as a friend of Marilyn and also a good friend of yours to put an end to this unfortunate situation because you are too valuable a person to be wasting your time on a principle, regardless of how lofty you may feel it to be.

There were two further letters, one in May 1957 and the other in August 1958. In the first he was still urging Miller, even at this late stage, to change his mind and name names: 'the important thing is to get it over with as soon as possible and clear the atmosphere for your sake and Marilyn's because I fear that unless you do so, it may do irreparable harm to you in the future'. Although, he said, he agreed with Miller's philosophy, he felt 'worried about your adamant attitude in view of my anxiety about its detrimental effect on you and those whom you love'.

The letter that Skouras would send to Miller at his Roxbury address on 8 August 1958 was a brief one. It congratulated him on his acquittal by the US Court of Appeals on the charge of contempt of Congress. It was a gracious concession that he had been wrong:

I am delighted with this outcome to your long ordeal and I certainly admire the courage and perseverance with which you met it and I cheerfully concede that I was wrong in my advice to you.

Surely this outcome is a great relief and a source of happiness to both you and Marilyn. But please don't tell Marilyn that I am congratulating you because, although I count her a friend and admire her greatly, I am peeved at her as an artist.

For the moment, though, back in 1956, Miller prepared to go to Washington, sure of what he would not say before the Committee but uncertain what the result would be. He sat at Penn Station in New York, waiting for the Washington train with his mother and Marilyn. As he said in his autobiography:

> All I could think of was the waste my trip implied. It was all for absolutely nothing, except that it would cost tens of thousands of dollars in legal fees even after a great part of them were forgiven by my lawyers ... Marilyn was gallantly trying not to seem unhappy, and since I was trying for her sake to maintain an even mood, neither of us could express anything we were really feeling, in particular our failure to find an hour's peace since deciding to make a life together.[124]

Marilyn held her mink coat across her face as the train drew out, for fear of being recognized, a reminder that the life he was about to enter was to be lived publicly, when what he needed for his work was privacy. HUAC, and marriage to Marilyn, were about to transform his life radically and to an extent that he could barely imagine.

Once in Washington, he conferred with his lawyer Joseph Rauh Jr, who, famously, passed on an offer from Francis Walter, chairman of the Committee, to waive the hearing if Monroe would pose for a photograph with him. As Miller later remarked, 'that's how dangerous he really thought I was. When I heard this, I said no. He then got back on his horse and acted as though I really was a danger to the country. They were headline hunters, that's all. They'd made their livings by scaring the great unwashed who would then be caused to run round in circles looking to them for salvation.'[125] When Marilyn joined him in Washington, Joe Rauh remarked, 'She had no desire to do anything but support her husband ... and she asked questions about the case every day and every evening. She had no movie commitments and seemed not a bit conflicted about it.' When the men went to the hearings, however, somewhat ominously perhaps, she 'picked books off our shelves − and every one she chose had something to do with psychiatry'.[126] Her opinion of the Committee was unequivocal: 'The bastards, I won't let them do it to him. He's got to tell them to go fuck themselves, only he can do it in better language.'[127]

It was before the Committee that he announced his impending marriage, apparently to the surprise of Marilyn. In answer to a question about his planned travel to Europe, he replied: 'I have a production, which is in the talking stage in England, of *A View from the Bridge*, and I will be there with the woman who will then be my wife.'[128] Back in New York Marilyn called the Rostens: 'Have you heard?' she said. 'He announced it before the whole world! He told the whole world he was marrying Marilyn Monroe. Me! Can you believe it? You know he never really asked *me to marry* him!'[129] Given the redrafting of her will and her rejection of a pre-nuptial agreement, this has the air of a theatrical pose.

She immediately came under siege at her apartment in Sutton Place, as reporters rushed to interview her. Other residents feared they constituted a fire hazard and threatened to call the police. An improvised press conference took place as Miller made his way back from Washington. Asked who had proposed to whom she replied, 'I guess he sort of initiated it ... It was simultaneous.' Asked about the testimony that her husband-to-be had offered to the Committee: 'I don't know much about politics. I'll have to talk with him and I think he's very tired. He's had quite a day.'[130]

Already there were rumours that he would be cited for contempt for his refusal to name former friends, though Drew Pearson, in his radio programme, thought that he would escape unscathed: 'I predict that Arthur Miller will not be cited for contempt ... Francis Walter of Pennsylvania, chairman of the HCUA, is considered a tough congressman but even he has a spark of romance in his soul. In the rush of adjournment Congress will follow the old Emerson axiom that "All the world loves a lover" and will not prosecute Marilyn's husband.'[131] He was almost right about Emerson ('All Mankind love a lover'); he was a long way from being right about Congressman Walter.

10

HUAC

Before his appearance in front of HUAC Miller had another problem to attend to. He still had no passport. How, then, was he to accompany Marilyn to England? When his request for its renewal had been denied two years earlier, the State Department had issued a statement declaring that the application had been refused under regulations denying passports to those 'believed to be' supporting the communist movement, a phrase seemingly requiring little in the way of evidence. In December 1955, however, in response to an inquiry from a Michigan State University academic, Ken Macrorie, the Department of State took a slightly different line, suggesting that 'When his attorney was told that the request must be sent to Washington for consideration, Mr Miller withdrew his application.' So he had, of course, though his lawyer had swiftly sent a clarifying letter. The fact is that the Department now seemed at pains to suggest that he had not been refused a passport. Bureaucratic obfuscation, or policy change? It was unclear. Ken Macrorie forwarded his correspondence to Miller.

Mrs Shipley's previous refusal to renew the passport had left him a prisoner in his own country. Now the idea of being separated from Marilyn, off to England to film *The Prince and the Showgirl*, seemed insupportable, but he was unclear as to how to reverse the earlier decision. On the advice of his lawyers, he prepared a statement – 'Memorandum on Arthur Miller and Politics' – to accompany his request for renewal of his passport which, technically, had, indeed, not been withdrawn. The surviving document is liberally annotated by his lawyers. In particular, a handwritten note insists that it should be a factual account rather than an argumentative brief. It urged Miller to work on the details. Nonetheless, it already offered what was in effect an elaborate summary of his own sense of his shifting political views.

In it he confessed to attending four or five meetings of writers held under the auspices of the Communist Party. He then explains that he is unable to confirm whether or not he was an enrolled member. The lawyers square-bracket this statement, suggesting its deletion. He insists that he cannot recall whether or not he paid the subscription, but that he assumes he did. Again the lawyers square-bracket this, since it might be construed as admitting to membership of the Party, the very thing he had denied and which he would continue to deny in subsequent years. He then points out that he left the group, feeling that it was not a happy fit with his views. He had joined initially, he says, believing himself to be a Marxist. As part of the process he wrote a brief account of his own political beliefs. This expressed the view that capitalism was in terminal decline and that any work that he wrote which represented life truthfully must by definition be Marxist. He was disabused of this belief by the group, who explained that if he was a true Marxist he had to embrace Marxist notions of the capitalist world. This, in turn, implied that he would need to embrace the Party line. This he could not do and hence left.

Does this document constitute a confession of Party membership, the point that HUAC had been so desperate to prove? The lawyers, plainly, were anxious to excise any possible admission of membership of the Party, its agencies or affiliates. Miller himself seemed a deal less certain. He did, after all, and by his own admission, attend the meetings as a self-identified Marxist, and even taking his account as an accurate description of his experience of them there is no reason to suppose that he originally attended as a sceptic. Party membership is plainly not the same as attendance at Marxist study groups, but in the America of the mid-1950s such a distinction was liable to be too fine for the minds of those who went trawling with wide-meshed nets. In truth, it was not a distinction that mattered overmuch to those whose commitments might or might not require the validation of formal Party membership. Nonetheless, this document is the closest Miller came to acknowledging that he might have been a signed-up member.

It is certainly somewhat difficult to credit his pose of the naive writer to whom it is suddenly revealed that Marxist literature was not simply a matter of the truthful depiction of life. This, after all, was a man who had read Marx, Lenin and Engels, if not very assiduously. He did not, as others would do before HUAC, describe himself as a dupe of communists, but there is a sense in which he was constructing this figure of the innocent abroad, suddenly made aware of his misreading of ideology and the writer's role.

He was conscious, though, that Miss Shipley's dossier contained rather more than suggestions that he had attended writers' discussion groups. The meetings may have been private affairs, at least in intent, but his signature on statements, petitions and manifestos was not. Accordingly, Miller's memorandum then addressed this issue, one that would soon resurface in the Washington hearings to which he was summoned. He acknowledged that he had lent his name to various causes and organizations but claimed not to have joined anything, at least to his knowledge. The lawyers marked this last phrase for deletion. He had subsequently become aware, he went on, that his name had been used by those who, if they were now to come to power, would destroy him. As a result, he no longer joined in such campaigns. He knew, however, that his name had continued to appear, but stressed that it did so without his knowledge or approval, though there were some organizations that he continued to support. Then, as if acknowledging that he might seem to be too accommodating, he insisted that he would continue making known his opposition to a right wing that seemed intent on destroying liberal values and hence the overseas reputation of the United States.

The memorandum continues for another three pages – too long, a lawyer's hand-written note observes. It explains his reasons for wishing to go to Europe, which include the production of *A View from the Bridge* in England, so long as the Lord Chamberlain could be persuaded not to impose changes or suppressions, and a lecture in Germany, the invitation to which was to be enclosed (it came from Hans Schalla, who had directed both *Salesman* and *The Crucible*). There was also, he continued, to be a French film of *The Crucible* – an ironic reminder, of course, of the French-language production of the same play, in Belgium, that had led to the earlier refusal to renew his passport.

He had, he pointed out received many invitations from Germany, but his agents there had dissuaded theatres from offering invitations to him since the refusal by the American government to allow him to go would undeniably have caused embarrassment. This passage, too, is marked for deletion by his lawyers, no doubt anxious not to offend those whose help he was requesting. They left in, however, the patently calculated remark that he believed his presence in Europe would give the lie to communist assertions that American writers were little more than victims of an oppressive regime. Finally, he added, no doubt in an attempt to melt the hitherto icy heart of Mrs Shipley, that he wished to go to Europe because a young woman in whom he had more than a professional interest would be making a film in London and he wished to be close to her. Plainly, his subsequent statement at the HUAC hearings was not the spontaneous remark it seemed. It was a gesture already rehearsed for the benefit of Mrs Shipley.

Nor was it quite 'finally', since the document continues for another page and a half as he reiterates that he follows no Party line, accepts no Party discipline and is opposed to all totalitarian concepts. Failure to permit his travel to Europe, he maintains, would be injurious to American interests because it would undermine assertions about American freedom while confirming the seemingly popular notion of American philistinism. He had, he said, been under pressure – and not only or even mainly from communist newspapers – to express an anti-American position as a result of the previous denial of his passport, but had refused to do so. Continued refusal of his passport, however, was, he believed, contributing to a negative view of

America not least because reviews of his work tended to be accompanied by reminders of the ban on his travel.

The tone of the document says a great deal about Miller's state of mind at this time, and even more about the nature of mid-century American society. The memorandum, after all, was designed to secure what should have been his right as a US citizen, the right to free movement. The curious mixture of rational argument and confessional was also to typify his evidence before HUAC, and illuminates something of the difficulty of someone seeking to defend his right to go about his business in a country then presenting itself abroad as a beacon of freedom.

The passport was, eventually, forthcoming, but before he was able to take his trip to England he had another hurdle to clear, that of a summons to appear before HUAC.

For many years Arthur Miller had the reputation of a secular saint for those on the left. Had he not, after all, refused to betray his friends, challenged the right of a congressional committee to summon him to account, refused to capitulate to the jingoistic rhetoric of the age? He, himself, though, consistently played down the significance of his appearance before HUAC. Working in the theatre, he explained, he was less vulnerable than those employed in television or film. The heyday of McCarthyism had anyway passed before he was called before the Committee, and the bullying tactics of the earlier years had given way to a softer approach. He had, he felt, at least a limited immunity that had not extended, for example, to Elia Kazan, whose ambitions lay in Hollywood.

HUAC had pursued Hollywood stars, employed by an industry whose products were distributed nationwide and controlled by a limited number of corporations potentially vulnerable to pressure, but, as Miller said in 1995, 'Who the hell in Indianapolis gave a damn about what was happening in a theatre that nobody was going to see anyway? . . . There was no national pay-dirt here for a politician.' A Broadway play, meanwhile, could be financed by two or three dozen people. Although from time to time hearings were held in New York, they came to nothing.

Beyond his refusal to offer the names of those with whom he had attended Communist Party meetings, Miller was, if not wholly cooperative, at least prepared to play the game to the extent of declaring his patriotism – and perhaps, as already suggested, in rather too effusive terms. Indeed, on rereading his testimony he admitted that it made painful reading, and that he had given them too much and failed to challenge the relevance of their questions to the issue of the use of passports to further the aims of communism which was supposedly the justification for the hearings. Instead he chose to dance with them, and the dance was not at all times an elegant one.

He was, of course, never up against McCarthy, who chaired a committee of the Senate and not the House and had, anyway, been effectively destroyed in 1954 when he was censured by the Senate. Indeed, Miller recalled watching Ed Murrow's earlier attack on him on CBS television in 1953. Having no television set of his own he watched in the Rostens' Brooklyn Heights apartment – Rosten believing himself the victim of blacklisting by television and radio – along with a relative of two people who had fought for the Loyalist cause in Spain. 'Oddly enough,' Miller said later, 'it was hardly ten minutes into the program when one knew it was the end of McCarthy, not altogether for reasons of content but more because he was so obviously handling subjects of great moment with mere quips, empty-sounding jibes, lumpy witticisms.'[2]

Three weeks later, McCarthy was given a right to reply and Miller went round to the Rostens' to watch, Hedda smoking Camel cigarettes and coughing at key moments. Later, he remembered how frightened they had been as McCarthy insisted that Murrow was supposedly in league with the communist Chinese. He tried to smear Murrow as a member of a terrorist organization – the Industrial Workers of the World (famous, during the 1930s, as the 'Wobblies') – and a transmitter of communist propaganda through the American Civil Liberties Union. Murrow had never been a member of the IWW while the ACLU, to which he *had* belonged, had not, as McCarthy had claimed, been a listed organization, a fact pointed out by Murrow in a subsequent broadcast.

With McCarthy's fall, something of the sting had gone out of both the Senate Committee and HUAC. Nor was Miller unique in refusing to name names. The folk singer Pete Seeger, for example, also refused, obligingly offering to sing a song instead. Today, anyone reading the transcript of Miller's hearing will discover that he was treated if not with deference then with a certain amount of respect. The prevailing tone was less hectoring than reproachful. His own replies were careful but for the most part not hostile. There was, as he explained, a certain ritual to appearances before the Committee, and that ritual was duly enacted. When he left the room it was with a curious speech from the Committee chairman that seemed to celebrate his achievements as a writer and merely urged him to put his shoulder more clearly to the wheel of national endeavour. It was almost as if there was no longer any question of punishing him.

In one sense his appearance before the Committee seemed inevitable. The FBI had been tailing him for years, noting his associates, receiving reports of his foreign visits cabled from local embassies. The Bureau would make telephone calls (apparent wrong numbers or supposed commercial inquiries) to establish his movements. Soon both the Connecticut and New York offices were investigating him. Yet, in a sense, his appearance before HUAC was almost certainly connected with his new relationship with Marilyn Monroe. He had not been garnered in with Lee. J Cobb and Kazan, or with Clifford Odets. Nor had he when he staged *An Enemy of the People* and *The Crucible*, both of which could have been seen by the Committee as provocations. In 1954, the American Legion had asked the FBI to take action against him but the following year the Bureau declined, even though it believed him to have been a member of the Party in 1946 and 1947 and contrived to interview him on the pretext of clearing someone else. He had, of course, been dismissed from his role as scriptwriter for the film on juvenile delinquency, but that proved nothing in itself beyond his vulnerability to behind-the-scenes political manipulation. Things, however, began to change in 1956.

In February, Walter Winchell, a direct conduit for information from the FBI, and an 'auxiliary agent', leaked a story given to him by Hoover suggesting that Marilyn was associated with 'red fronters'. In May, and more ominously, he published further leaked information, again linking Miller, by implication if not name, to Monroe. Then, on 29 May, Richard Arens, staff director of HUAC, called Clyde Tolson to say that Miller would be appearing before the Committee sometime in mid-June.

When the Committee summoned Miller, it had no evidence of Party membership, normally the sine qua non for calling someone, though later an unsigned and typed application would surface. Thus, that the hearing went ahead seems to say less about Miller's perceived threat, still less about the Committee's ability to pin anything on him beyond having lent his signature to the usual list of left-wing causes, than it does about the Committee's increasingly desperate need for publicity.[3]

It is not for nothing that Walter Goodman chooses to preface his study of the House Un-American Activities Committee with a quotation from H.L. Mencken, always a man with an eye for the self-advertiser, the fraudster, the politician as confidence trickster:

> The United States, to my eye, is incomparably the greatest show on earth. It is a show which avoids diligently all the kinds of clowning which tire me most quickly – for example, royal ceremonials, the tedious hocus pocus of haute politique, the taking of politics seriously – and lays chief stress upon the kinds which delight me unceasingly – for example, the ribald combats of demagogues, the exquisitely ingenious operations of master rogues, the pursuit of witches and heretics, the desperate struggles of inferior men to claw their way into Heaven.[4]

There was, indeed, a plethora of rogues and villains associated with HUAC, and not a little irony in the fact that a Committee that was, in part, the creation of a Jewish Congressman would go on to be anti-Semitic. And surely Mencken would have taken delight in a formally constituted

Committee of Congress deciding to give a platform to Ginger Rogers's mother, who proudly proclaimed that she had prevented her daughter, in an MGM film, from delivering the line 'Share and share alike – that's democracy', on the grounds that it was communistic, and whose hubris would extend to subpoenaing former President of the United States, Harry Truman.

At the same time there were many who did not get the joke, people for whom the Committee's Orwellian newspeak title offered ironies that were hard to appreciate as their careers were ruined and their lives destroyed. In 1947 J. Edgar Hoover had set nineteen field offices to investigate the activities of the National Lawyers' Guild (whose members at one stage included not only Thurgood Marshall (grandson of a slave and later to become a Supreme Court Judge) but even HUAC chairman Francis Walter. In 1949, the Guild produced a report on the FBI's surveillance practices. The Bureau responded in kind. In 1953, the Attorney General proposed listing the Guild as a subversive organization on the grounds that it had become a mouthpiece for the Communist Party. It was in fact the main expression of the Popular Front in the legal profession,[5] incorporating liberals and communists (its executive secretary was a Party member), and was unpopular with the Attorney General because of its willingness to defend those charged under the Smith Act. The FBI, though, took this as justification for illegal break-ins, fishing expeditions to uncover evidence against not only the organization but its clients. Due process, and the freedoms and protection required by the justice system, were, it seems, in temporary abeyance. One of those supporting the Guild and attacking the Bureau was Joseph Rauh Jr, Miller's attorney.

The original impetus for the Committee had come from Samuel Dickstein from New York, a member of the House of Representatives. His concern lay largely with American fascists, of whom he claimed, with no more evidence than Senator McCarthy would later deploy, that there were fifty thousand in Connecticut alone. Following the stock market crash, though, there were those more concerned with communist subversion. Key among these was Martin Dies from Texas, who had put forward bills to deport alien communists. Dickstein associated himself with this because of his alarm at religious persecution in Russia. In 1934 Dickstein, with John McCormack of Massachusetts (later Speaker of the House), had begun hearings about fascist influence. In January 1937 he introduced a resolution that proposed the investigation of all organizations

> found operating in the United States for the purpose of diffusing within the United States slanderous or libelous un-American propaganda of religious, racial or subversive political prejudices which tends to incite the use of force

and violence or which tends to incite libelous attacks upon the President of the United States or other officers of the Federal Government, whether such propaganda appears to be of foreign or domestic origin.[6]

Interestingly, the resolution found no support, but Martin Dies later put forward his own version of it. Events abroad – including the German move into Austria and the Sudeten crisis – together with developments at home having to do with fascists and the activities of the German-American Bund, along with the involvement of communists in the trades union movement, finally secured its approval in May 1938. This followed guarantees that the Committee would not be chaired by a foreign-born Jew.

The Committee held its first hearings on 12 August that year. Its chairman, Martin Dies, was plainly himself not lacking in irony when he announced that it would conduct itself at all times on a dignified plane, that it would maintain a judicial attitude and have no preconceived views of the truth. It would, he said, be fair and impartial, treat every witness with courtesy, and permit neither character assassination nor the smearing of the innocent. In investigating un-American activities, he continued, 'it must be borne in mind that because we do not agree with opinions or philosophies of others, does not make such opinions or philosophies un-American'.[7]

It was as though he was choosing to list in advance every vice that would be exhibited by the Committee by denying the possibility of it ever embracing them. For in fact it quickly abandoned dignity, fairness, impartiality and a judicial attitude and readily embraced character assassination while identifying what it regarded as alien philosophies as, by definition, un-American. Nearly thirty years later, Alvah Bessie (author of such screenplays as *The Very Thought of You* and *Hotel Berlin*, along with a book about the Spanish Civil War, *Men in Battle*), himself a communist, listed a series of suicides and wrecked lives that resulted from the activities of a Committee that increasingly chose to investigate those who had served in Roosevelt's administration, or who worked in the theatre and cinema and whose public visibility thereby guaranteed publicity for those hungry for such. As Ellen Schrecker has pointed out, Dies's attacks on the Congress of Industrial Organizations (CIO) 'ensured the backing of businessmen and AFL [American Federation of Labor] leaders alike'.[8] Henry Ford even offered to supply automobiles to HUAC and its staff.

Oddly, perhaps, HUAC's first target was the Federal Theatre, an organization for which Miller briefly worked. It recommended itself for assault on four counts: there were communists in its ranks; it had few friends in Congress; its Living Newspaper productions exposed shortcomings in the social and political system; it was a product of the New Deal. But when Hallie Flanagan, its National Director, appeared before the Committee in 1938, she gave as good as she got. She was faced by charges, brought by a disaffected employee, that the Theatre was an instrument of communist propaganda, and in that context was asked to explain articles she had written, in *Theatre Guild* magazine, in which she had described the burgeoning workers' theatre movement. She was required to justify trips to Russia she had taken on a grant from the Guggenheim Foundation. These, it was implied, were indicators of a bias in the theatre she now directed.

She had little difficulty in defending her actions. Then, when she was questioned about the productions for which she had been responsible, it became clear that her questioners regarded some, at least, as indicative of a disturbing hostility towards capitalism. She was asked, in particular, whether she would stage plays that called for the state ownership of power – in relation to the Living Newspaper production called *Power* – and if that, then, state ownership of everything. Was hers not indeed a workers' theatre, attempting to raise working-class consciousness and hence dividing an otherwise united country, and using federal funds to do so?

Hallie Flanagan's footwork was adroit, but this did not prevent the destruction of her theatre by Congress the following year. What she did not have to face, as many subsequent witnesses did, was accusations of communism and requests to name those who had been members of the Party. But the gloves quickly came off. Many found themselves in the unenviable position of being asked to explain commitments they no longer held and to defend people with whom they no longer felt they had much in common. And the price of failing to cooperate was considerable. Nor was private testimony a protection, since many found their transcripts of supposedly privileged depositions released to the media. In time, a mere rumour that investigators were interested in an actor, a writer, a director, was enough to see job prospects disappear. An estimated ten to twelve thousand lost their jobs.[9]

Joan Copeland, Miller's actress sister, recalled an incident when her brother was called before the Committee:

> I was doing quite a bit of work in television at the time, and radio, too. Suddenly, the work fell off very sharply, and I didn't know why. You couldn't get an answer, of course. Nobody would tell you why. People who had been hiring me regularly and who you felt were your friends and dependable employers, directors, etc., were saying, 'There's not much going on in the business. It's a slow season.' It wasn't until one day I went up to a big ad agency and I was up for a role in a big television show that I found out. The director was there and the writer and the sponsors and they said, 'We are so delighted, Miss Copeland, that you should be doing this. It's a wonderful role for you and you are the only one we can think of who can do it.' Very flattering. They said, 'We will probably start

rehearsing in about ten days.' The interview was over and one of the gentlemen – the director or a sponsor – walked me to the elevator and while we were waiting for it he said, 'Wait a minute, are you related to ...' I said, 'Arthur Miller'. And he said, 'Oh, yes. Well, it was nice to meet you.' And that was when I knew, because I never heard from them again ... I felt very badly for the position Arthur was in and fortunately I was married and my husband made a living so I was not out on the street. I wasn't destitute. But I was angry at them.[10]

Her experience was scarcely unique. In 1950, the actress Jean Muir found herself dropped from the popular television series *The Aldrich Family* after her name had appeared as a suspect communist sympathizer in *Red Channels*, one of a number of such publications which purported to monitor the politics of American citizens. Her listing resulted in calls to NBC and though she was cleared, the sponsor, General Foods, refused to see her reinstated because she was now regarded as 'controversial'.

The actress Mildred Dunnock found herself listed in *Red Channels* as a communist sympathizer because of her friendship with Miller and Kazan. When jobs ceased to be offered, her banker husband forced a withdrawal of the identification: 'It gave me an emotional understanding of being accused,' she explained, 'I felt contaminated, I felt I had leprosy. I felt I had incriminated my husband, a conventional man.'[11] Norman Rosten was listed, but due to a confusion an actor called Norman Rose found himself paying the price as he was dropped from a CBS science fiction series, seemingly by those whose reading skills were as suspect as their politics.

A whole raft of organizations became involved in listing suspect people, including one all too familiar to Miller – the American Legion. Others offered to research potential employees, for cash, and even to facilitate the purging of guilt should it materialize. It was like the medieval sale of pardons and indulgences. The Committee itself was, at least by 1950, more discriminating. For the most part it summoned only those whose communist affiliations could be established from at least two sources.

In 1947, the Committee turned its attentions to Hollywood. It did so largely because of the publicity value of bringing some of the country's most famous names to Washington. It is tempting also to feel that there were anti-Semitic sentiments at work, since this was an industry pioneered by Jews, and in which Jews played a significant role as directors, writers, actors, composers. As Victor Navasky reminds us, a large percentage of those who ran Hollywood were, indeed, Yiddish-speaking: Sam Goldwyn, Louis B. Mayer, William Fox, the Warner brothers, the Selznicks. For a time, a leading member of

the Committee was the anti-Semitic John Rankin. Walter Goodman has
suggested:

> The source of Rankin's animus against Hollywood – and he made no par-
> ticular effort to conceal it – was the large number of Jews eminent in the film
> industry. 'I have no quarrel with any man about his religion,' he explained
> after a Committee investigator was reported to have warned some liberal
> Jews to 'watch their steps lest the fate of Germany's Jews overtake them'. In
> Rankin's mind, to call a Jew a Communist was a tautology ... In the halls of
> Congress he called Walter Winchell 'a little slime-mongering kike'.[12]

When nineteen Hollywood figures were subpoenaed, ten were Jews while
of those who went ahead to Washington, and were known as 'the Hollywood
Ten', six were Jews. HUAC was in search of communists, but also, it seems,
something else. After all, were not a number of the spies that had been
unearthed – the Rosenbergs, Morton Sobell and others – also Jews? The logic
seemed undeniable: communist, Jewish, traitor. On the other hand, the
prosecutor in the Rosenberg case was also Jewish, as was the judge, and
the Jewish community was itself increasingly concerned to disentangle the
connection between Jewishness and radicalism.

In *Inquisition in Eden* Alvah Bessie, one of the Ten, recalls that the Committee had first shown interest in Hollywood back in 1938 when its chief
investigator was Edward F. Sullivan. Sullivan had, Bessie claimed, been
associated with the Nazi-inspired Ukrainian fascist movement in the USA,
and had addressed a meeting of the German-American Bund, some of whose
members were uniformed American storm troopers. He had also, reportedly,
been a labour spy. For Bessie, who had fought in the Spanish Civil War, what
the Committee was really interested in was raking over the coals of that war
on the assumption that supporters of the Republican cause were necessarily
subversives and un-American.

The assault on Hollywood began, indirectly, with Gerhart Eisler, supposedly a refugee from Nazi Germany. As it turned out, though he had denied
it on entry, he had been a member of the Party while in Germany and hence
the Committee had an ideal target. Miller, it will be recalled, signed a petition
in his support. The link to Hollywood came through his brother Hanns, also
a communist – though he, too, had denied it at the time – who had come to
America during the war with help from Eleanor Roosevelt. He was a composer
who created scores for the screen (and was to have been involved in the
proposed Los Angeles production of *The Man Who Had All the Luck*), but an
attack on him could also be seen as an attack on her and, through her, on her
husband and hence the New Deal, radical Jews and Hollywood itself. It was
not exactly a causal chain but – in a phrase that became increasingly familiar –
a case of guilt by association.

From there the Committee moved to bigger fish, some of them decidedly cooperative ones. The Hollywood moguls quickly distanced themselves from what they saw as trouble. Thus Jack Warner, head of Warner Brothers, explained his willingness to identify suspected communists and fire anyone with communist sympathies. Warner, indeed, supplied a list of names, some of whom had never been communists. He later admitted to getting 'carried away'. He even offered to establish a fund that would ship back to Russia anyone who did not like America. This was the Warner who remarked to HUAC that 'Arthur Miller and Elia Kazan worked on Broadway where they practised some sort of subversion.'[3]

Walt Disney supported the Committee, while the redoubtable Mrs Rogers, mother to Ginger, claimed to have successfully stopped her daughter playing in Theodore Dreiser's *Sister Carrie*, which, she felt, presented an unfavourable view of capitalism. Ronald Reagan, meanwhile, spoke of communist activity in the Screenwriters' Guild. And some people took to the business of informing with more enthusiasm than taste. Thus Sterling Hayden, whose film *The Asphalt Jungle* starring Marilyn Monroe had been a hit in 1950, named his former mistress, while Clifford Odets named J. Edward Bromberg, despite blaming the Committee for his premature death and delivering the eulogy at his funeral. Bromberg died at the age of forty-seven, Odets was not the only one who thought it a direct result of HUAC's harassment. The actress Lee Grant went to his memorial service and suggested as much in public. The next day she was blacklisted and did no more work in film or television for ten years. Madeleine Sherwood, who had played Abigail in the Broadway production of *The Crucible*, attended her first union meeting immediately afterwards; she later said, 'I stood up and said I don't understand why this is happening to Lee Grant. She is such a wonderful actress. And I felt someone pulling me down. They pulled me down and sat me in my chair and said, "Are you crazy? Shut up. Do you want to be in *Red Channels*?" The next day I was.'

There were undoubtedly former and present members of the Party in Hollywood, including the screenwriter John Howard Lawson (author of *Processional*), Ring Lardner Jr, the director Edward Dmytryk (who later, like Kazan, went on to name names) and Alvah Bessie. The Party, indeed, had targeted the industry. The question was whether this should be a reason for people losing their jobs, whether it should even be seen as illegal.

The hearings were chaired by J. Parnell Thomas, who the following year was convicted of taking bribes and found himself in the same jail in Danbury, Connecticut, as Ring Lardner, another of the Hollywood Ten, by then serving time for contempt. Just a few miles away in Roxbury, Arthur Miller was writing *Death of a Salesman*, still eight years from his own appearance before the Committee.

The lines were now drawn. What ensued was unedifying on both sides, with Committee members and actors haranguing each other. As Walter Goodman has pointed out, Eric Johnson, president of the Motion Picture Producers' Association, while denouncing the Committee for the way in which individuals were 'condemned without a hearing or a chance to speak in self-defense; slandered and libeled by hostile witnesses not subject to cross-examination and immune from subsequent suit of prosecution',[14] suggested to his fellow producers that they should refuse to employ proven communists. Then, in November, 1947, at a meeting at the Waldorf-Astoria Hotel in New York, motion picture executives agreed to drop the 'Ten' unless or until they declared that they were not communists. The blacklist was born. Eventually it would reach out to the most unlikely people, including the author of the lyrics of *The Wizard of Oz* – though he was also responsible for the Depression song, 'Buddy, Can You Spare a Dime', and hence vulnerable to those who now saw the Depression as having been commandeered by subversives.

Back in Hollywood, five hundred people formed the Committee for the First Amendment. It was created at Lucy's restaurant, across the street from the Paramount and RKO studios, and its first meeting was held at the home of Ira Gershwin. Among its more junior members were two young scriptwriters, Ben and Norma Barzman. They later recalled an occasion when they were sitting on the lawn of 1290 Sunset Plaza in Beverly Hills when an old Cadillac convertible drew up outside: 'The driver, a strikingly beautiful blonde, braked and got out of the car. She was on her way to a party at Minnellis.' She accepted a gin and tonic and then explained why she had dropped by: 'I guess I have to tell you: there's a deputy sheriffs car at the bottom of your hill and the guys are stopping every car that's going up and asking if they're going to 1290.'[15] The house, they had explained, was under surveillance because of the subversive meetings that were going on there.

That night the Barzmans had been scheduled to host a meeting of the committee but it had been cancelled at the last moment because Humphrey Bogart had called to say that he was resigning under pressure from Warner Brothers. As the girl left, Norma Barzman went inside to call her mother only to hear a tape-recording of a call she had made several days earlier. Two years later she and her husband fled the country with their children rather than give evidence against their friends. By coincidence, the blonde girl who had warned them was also called Norma, though she would later be better known as Marilyn Monroe.

Supporters of the Committee for the First Amendment included most of Hollywood's stars, so that it appeared for a while that there would be a robust response. As it turned out it fell a long way short of robust. Among those who supported the Hollywood Ten were Edward G. Robinson (who had appeared in one of Miller's radio plays) and Bogart, along with John Huston, who would later direct Miller's *The Misfits*. In fact, it was he, along with writer Philip Dunne and director William Wyler, who wrote most of the publicity for the Committee for the First Amendment.

Bogart swiftly clarified his situation, confessing that his trip to Washington in their support had been 'ill-advised, even foolish', and that he detested communism 'just as any other decent American does'.[16] In 1952, the year in which Charlie Chaplin was refused re-entry to the United States for his supposed communism, Edward G. Robinson was ready to say that he had been duped by 'sinister forces' and to offer the names of those responsible. A third supporter of the Ten, however, took a different line. Huston, along with Dunne and Wyler, continued to lobby against the blacklist that now began to operate; but opposition quickly shrivelled.

At the Waldorf-Astoria meeting in 1947 Hollywood producers drafted a policy statement which outlined their willingness to capitulate to HUAC. This dissociated them from the action of the Hollywood Ten and stated that they would discharge or suspend without compensation those who refused to declare under oath that they were not communists, that they would never knowingly hire communists and would invite the Hollywood talent guilds to work with them to eliminate 'subversives'. They called for Congress to enact legislation to outlaw 'disloyal elements', and declared their conviction that nothing subversive had ever appeared in any film for which they had responsibility. One talent association that did work with them was the Screen Actors' Guild, which, with an adroit reversal of responsibility, announced that 'if any actor by his own actions ... has so offended American public opinion that he has made himself unsaleable at the box office, the Guild cannot and would not want to force any employer to hire him'.[17]

Arthur Schlesinger Jr's *The Vital Center*, observed that:

> Like [Albert] Maltz, John Howard Lawson, Alvah Bessie and Dalton Trumbo, the fellow-traveling, ex-proletarian writers go to Hollywood and become film hacks ... Until, that is, they refused to own up to their political beliefs before a committee of Congress – in response to which the film industry, rearing itself up in an unwonted spasm of moral nobility, turned them out into the storm. I do not wish to imply approval of the questions asked by the Un-American Activities Committee. I suspect, however, that if the Committee had been asking witnesses whether they were members of the Ku Klux Klan, the Silver Shirts or the Trotskyites, Mr Lawson and his friends would be overflowing with indignation at the refusal to answer.[18]

Irving Kristol, looking back from 1952 in *Commentary*, attacked those

> martyrs whose testament is – 'I refuse to answer on the grounds that it might incriminate me.' These 'intellectuals' of Hollywood and radio who are

outraged at a Congressman's insistence that they say what they actually believe, and who wail that they are in danger of being excluded from well-paying jobs ... Are these the American rebels of today? Oddly enough, the majority of American liberals seem to think so: they have been moved to indignation by the questions, but never moved to disgust by the answers. [Instead, appeared] erudite essays on the 'right to a job' that would have corroborated [the philosopher/psychologist] William James in his mournful conviction that 'the prevalent fear of poverty among our educated classes is the worst moral disease from which our civilization suffers'.[19]

In 1951, the year Miller had his run-in with Columbia Pictures and Roy Brewer of the American Federation of Labor, who now headed the Motion Picture Industry Council which brought together producers and unions, Hollywood was back in the firing line. Brewer had originally been called in to sort out the International Alliance of Theatrical and Stage Employees, which had been infiltrated by the Mob. He became an avid anti-communist and a fixer who would advise people on how to clear themselves, but, in Miller's case advising Harry Cohn of Columbia that the script of *The Hook* was 'fallacious'. No AF of L union, he insisted, 'could conceivably tolerate racketeering', and 'no writer loyal to the United States would have conceived such a script, whose effect would only be to create turmoil on the New York docks across which flowed the supplies for our armies in Korea'.[20]

The executives of the Motion Picture Industry Council now praised the Committee for its work and urged it to be more ruthless in its pursuit of communists in all walks of life. The Screenwriters' Guild, still under the aegis of Ronald Reagan, backed away from confrontation, while Actors' Equity announced that those involved in 'the international Communist Party conspiracy' were not welcome in its ranks. Reagan had appeared before the Committee in 1947 to report that a 'small clique' had been suspected of 'more or less following the tactics that we associate with the Communist Party',[21] not exactly a precise identification of the enemy within, though interestingly at that time he opposed the outlawing of the Communist Party for its political ideology.

HUAC's pursuit of Hollywood was facilitated by the FBI's illegal wire-tapping of a lawyer working for one of the Hollywood Ten. When, a few years later, information alone proved insufficient, COINTELPRO (the Counterfeit Intelligence Program), a black propaganda unit established in 1956, faked documents and spread false rumours.

The odds were considerably raised by the outbreak of the Korean War. Actors' Equity now became even more forthright: 'This country is engaged in a war with Communism. Eighty-seven thousand casualties leave little room for witnesses to stand on the First and Fifth Amendments; and for those who do we have no sympathy.'[22] The First Amendment guaranteed freedom of speech, the Fifth protected against self-incrimination. Both, in the view of Equity, were dispensable. For his part, though, Miller was dismayed by those screenwriters who hastened to state that they had never allowed social issues to penetrate their work, as if this were a virtue to be claimed or a legitimate defence to be mounted. He was equally distressed by a press that seemed willing to accept the premise that the most vacuous of Hollywood movies had been carriers of the communist virus. HUAC seemed to exist in an alternative universe in which paranoia was presented as entirely rational.

By 1956, the Soviet Union could plainly no longer be seen as the home of progressive values, but those summoned before the Committee were asked not simply to disavow any allegiance to the ideology of a foreign power in the present but to confess to past sins, to deny their own youthful idealism. Proof of their repentance lay in the identification of fellow sinners. The dilemma was a real one. As Miller said, 'a perpetual night of confusion was descending',[23] and that confusion existed too within his own mind.

Where once he had placed his faith in the trades union movement, now he saw it corrupted by gangsters and at the heart of a new reactionary politics. The working class he had idealized was now seemingly content with a material dream, citizens of a country complacent about its world dominance even while paranoid about external threats. He saw clearly enough the repressions of Eastern Europe but found himself in a society whose values seemed profoundly at odds with his own. Summing up his feelings at that time, he said: 'I was all alone, as so many felt who could not quite make it aboard the American Century, that train one sensed was bound for nowhere, its tracks ending in the desert where the vast pauperized majority of mankind lived.'

It was precisely this feeling that led him to accept an invitation from Jack Goodman, a senior editor at Simon & Schuster, to join a group of fellow writers who would meet once a week and discuss the growing illiberalism, countering it by publishing articles. None of these, though, were to appear in print. Goodman was called before HUAC, and it became obvious that an informer had been placed in this small circle of supposedly like-minded people. It began to be difficult for people to exercise their responsibilities with integrity or without fear of betrayal. Miller explains in *Timebends*:

> Everywhere teachers were being fired for their associations or ideas, real or alleged, as were scientists, diplomats, postmen, actors, directors, writers – as though the 'real' America was rising up against all that was not simple to understand, all that was or seemed foreign, all that implied something slightly less reassuring than that America stood innocent and pure in a vile and sinister world beyond the borders. And from this there was no appeal.

For Miller, pressure from the right had driven him to the left, and for longer than might otherwise have been the case. By the time he appeared before the Committee his Marxist days lay more than half a dozen years in the past, but like so many others he was now to be required to disavow not only his old beliefs but those who had once shared his faith in a transforming ideology.

He was not the only playwright who found himself simultaneously confronting the Committee and his own former self. In May 1952, Lillian Hellman (whom Miller later called a 'monument to classy monomania', and whose 603-page FBI file described her as a 'Jew communist') was required to appear, and though she would become the focus of considerable controversy, Miller's later testimony echoed the words of a letter that she sent to the Committee in which she offered to waive her Fifth Amendment right against self-incrimination if they would not press her to name other people. The Committee refused to accept it but Joe Rauh, her attorney, handed out copies to the press and it was read into the public record.

It was Rauh, in fact, who, according to Miller, wrote the letter, Hellman adding only a single line, though that the most frequently quoted: 'I cannot and will not cut my conscience ...' The letter read:

> I am most willing to answer all questions about myself. I have nothing to hide from the Committee and there is nothing in my life of which I am ashamed. I have been advised by counsel that under the Fifth Amendment I have a constitutional privilege to decline to answer any questions about my political opinions, activities, and associations, on the grounds of self-incrimination. I do not wish to claim this privilege. I am ready and willing to testify before the representatives of our Government as to my own opinions and my own actions, regardless of any risks or consequences to myself.
>
> But I am advised by counsel that if I answer the Committee's questions about myself, I must also answer questions about other people and that if I refuse to do so I may be cited for contempt ... I am not willing, now or in the future, to bring bad trouble to people who, in my past association with them, were completely innocent of any talk or any action that was disloyal or subversive. I do not like subversion or disloyalty in any form, and if I had ever seen any, I would have considered it my duty to have reported it to the proper authorities. But to hurt innocent people whom I knew many years ago in order to save myself is, to me, inhuman and indecent and dishonorable. I cannot and will not cut my conscience to fit this year's fashions, even though I long ago came to the conclusion that I was not a political person and could have no comfortable place in any particular group.[24]

It was, as she admitted, a carefully calculated letter, with what she clearly felt to be the necessary concession to loyalty and rejection of subversion, a letter whose statement of principle coexisted with a somewhat disingenuous assertion of her apolitical nature which is difficult to square with her actions. Unsurprisingly, Kazan took a jaundiced view. She was so pleased with her testimony, he said, and the reaction to it, that she made a pressbook to hand out to reporters which she 'kept on a table by her front door, for visitors to see, a book of congratulatory letters and telephone messages'. Hellman, he suggested, 'spent her last fifteen years canonizing herself'.[25]

Technically, the Fifth Amendment is designed to protect against self-incrimination, so that its extension to protect the interests of others was, strictly speaking, without legal point. Also, as Eric Bentley has pointed out, the Supreme Court had ruled that 'disclosure of a fact waives the privilege as to details'.[26] When she was persuaded, therefore, to say that she had not been a member of the Party two years earlier but refused to answer, when asked, whether she had been a member three years previously, she was entering a legal morass – a fact appreciated by her lawyer who was, at that moment, kicking her vigorously under the table. Perhaps the most important significance of her testimony was that she was not cited for contempt. You could, it seemed, challenge the Committee and survive and, according to Saul Bellow, Miller admired her approach. Thereafter, she took to attacking those who chose not to challenge it, or at least not to do so in a way of which she could approve.

Quite the most robust response to the Committee came from Paul Robeson, called before it on 12 June 1956, just over a week before Miller's appearance, and it is worth dwelling on his exchanges with the Committee in so far as they suggest what an aggressive approach could achieve. Ostensibly, as in Miller's case, he was summoned in relation to inquiries into the use of travel documents 'in furtherance of the objectives of the Communist conspiracy'. The fig leaf with which the Committee attempted to cover its probing of political loyalties lay in the possibility of legislation with respect to the release and use of passports, the legitimacy of the Committee's inquiries depending on the existence of proposed legislation.

From the start, Robeson treated the Committee with unconcealed contempt. While repeatedly claiming the Fifth Amendment, he plainly revelled in the exchanges between himself and the Committee and took pleasure both in denouncing its activities and in attacking its individual members. Thus, he identified the chairman, Francis E. Walter, as the author of a bill to 'keep all kinds of decent people out of the country', including 'colored people like myself'. It was, he suggested, 'just the Teutonic Anglo-Saxon stock that you would let come in'. Indeed he used the Committee as a forum to denounce American racism. His own father, he recounted, had been a slave, while 'I stand here struggling for the rights of my people to be full citizens in this country. And they are not. They are not in Mississippi. And they are not in Montgomery, Alabama. And they are not in Washington. They are nowhere, and that is why I am here today. You want to shut up every Negro who has the courage to stand up and fight for the rights of his people, for the rights of workers.' His interrogators had a hard time stopping him. The response of the chairman was 'Now just a minute', to which Robeson, indicating the whole procedure, replied, 'All of this is nonsense.'

There was nothing here of that half-apologetic tone to be heard even from Hellman and Miller. This was a determined and systematic attempt at counterattack. Asked why he had not stayed in the Soviet Union if he found it so congenial, he replied:

> Because my father was a slave, and my people died to build this country, and I am going to stay here, and have a part of it just like you. And no Fascist-minded people will drive me from it. Is that clear? I am for peace with the Soviet Union, and I am at peace with China, and I am not for peace or friendship with the Fascist Franco, and I am not for peace with Fascist Nazi Germans. I am for peace with decent people.

Reminded that he was present that day because he had been promoting the communist cause, he replied, 'I am here because I am opposing the neo-Fascist cause which I see arising in these committees.'

His area of vulnerability appeared to be his support for Stalin (he had won the Stalin Peace Prize in 1952), who had just been attacked by Khrushchev at the 20th Party Congress. If he cared about slavery, he was asked, why did he care nothing about the slave labour camps so recently exposed to public view? Even here, though, and unlike Miller, he did not miss a beat, not least because it was extremely unwise of Richard Arens, in particular, to allow him once again to pursue his assault on American racism:

> Whatever has happened to Stalin, gentlemen, is a question for the Soviet Union, and I would not argue with a representative of the people who, in building America, wasted sixty to a hundred million lives of my people, black people drawn from Africa on the plantations. You are responsible, and your forebears, for sixty million to one hundred million black people dying in the slave ships and on the plantations, and don't you ask me about anybody, please. . . . The slaves I see are still in a kind of semiserfdom. I am interested in the place I am, and in the country that can do something about it.

His one false step, and a breath-taking one, was in his elaboration of this answer, when he said: 'As far as I know, about the slave camps, they were Fascist prisoners who had murdered millions of the Jewish people, and who would have wiped out millions of the Negro people, could they have gotten hold of them.' When Arens continued to press him he reverted to familiar territory: 'I have told you, mister, that I would not discuss anything with the people who have murdered sixty million of my people, and I will not discuss

Stalin with you. . . . Nothing could be built more on slavery than this society, I assure you.' Others tried to bluster with the Committee, but none quite so plainly got under the skin of its members or performed such an effective end-run.

When any Committee member spoke, he demanded to know their names and positions. He would refer to them as 'gentlemen', 'mister', and, perhaps most disturbingly, 'brother'. He would laugh at their questions:

MR SCHERER: Mr Chairman, this is not a laughing matter.

MR ROBESON: It is a laughing matter to me, this is really complete nonsense.

Asked questions he regarded as absurd, he replied, 'Oh, *please*', or 'This is really ridiculous.' Told to pay attention to his questioners – 'I usually listen, but you know people wander around in such fancy places.' Asked to speak up, he replied that he had invoked the Fifth Amendment 'very loudly', and had awards for diction. When they started inquiring into his beliefs, statements, friendships, he disingenuously replied, 'Gentlemen, I thought I was here about some passports.' Questioned about an individual who had denounced the black Ralph Bunch – 'He was dismissed from the FBI. He must be a pretty low character when he could be dismissed from that.'

When it was put to him that he was on record as belonging to 'the American resistance movement which fights against American imperialism, just as the resistance movement fought against Hitler', rather than retreating to forgetfulness or wordplay he replied, 'Just like Frederick Douglass and Harriet Tubman were underground railroaders, and fighting for our freedom, you bet your life.' Pressed to confirm having said that he loved the Soviet Union more than any other country because there he felt a real man, he replied, 'In Russia I felt for the first time like a full human being. No color prejudice like in Washington. It was the first time I felt like a human being. Where I did not feel the pressure of color as I feel [it] in this Committee today.'

Robeson was not, like so many others, a man who had abandoned his faith or felt equivocal about his earlier commitments – in large part, no doubt, because they made complete sense in terms of his experience of American racism. His Marxism was never simply a commitment to an abstract idea of Man. The games he played with the Committee, designed to strip it of the moral authority to which it laid claim, were not simply a tactic, though as such they were remarkably effective. They arose out of a genuine contempt for those who defended a notion of Americanism that had no difficulty with racism, only with those who sought to fight it, along with poverty and imperialism. Appearing in Washington, at the centre of power, he confronted the Committee members with their own history.

He did not, as did others, retreat from his statements about the need for peace, which in the curious code of Cold War America meant that you were a dupe of foreign powers. Instead he rededicated himself to that necessity, 'if committees like yours do not upset the applecart and destroy all of humanity'. When he was told he had learned his Marxism in Russia, he insisted that, on the contrary, he had learned it in Britain, having gone to Republican Spain with Lord Attlee to visit the Attlee Battalion, and being friendly with many members of the Labour Party. Unsurprisingly, the response to this was 'We have nothing to do with that.'

When the chairman, in some desperation, declared the hearing adjourned, this is how the exchange went:

> MR ROBESON: ... you are the nonpatriots, and you are the un-Americans, and you ought to be ashamed of yourselves.
> THE CHAIRMAN: Just a minute, the hearing is now adjourned.
> MR ROBESON: I should think it would be.
> THE CHAIRMAN: I have endured all of this that I can.
> MR ROBESON: Can I read my statement?
> THE CHAIRMAN: No, you cannot read it. The meeting is adjourned.
> MR ROBESON: I think it should be, and you should adjourn this forever, that is what I would say.

Living, as we do, in an age deeply suspicious of grand ideological narratives, it is sometimes difficult to understand the passionate loyalties of another time. Walls have fallen, monolithic systems collapsed. Capitalism seems everywhere triumphant. We are individuals linked, if at all, by the ethics and objectives of the market-place. Nineteenth-century liberalism has been reborn as twentieth- and twenty-first-century conservatism. Fragmentation has come to seem if not a virtue, then inevitable. Nationalisms, fundamentalist creeds, tribalisms, assert their presumptive rights. Multiculturalism, gender and ethnic identity, sexual preference – all reassemble the world into a tessellated reality. How can it ever have been otherwise?

Miller recalled his own bone-deep convictions and those of others like Ring Lardner Jr, one-time communist, who had been imprisoned for contempt of Congress for refusing to answer questions posed by the House Un-American Activities Committee. He had borne his imprisonment with quiet courage, strengthened by his convictions, only later to be disillusioned following a trip to Moscow. How, though, could people understand this man's life, Miller asked, if they never knew the passions that once drove him? It was this that made history seem so impenetrable and that opened a gulf between the generations. Passion was no less a fact than any other detail of a vanished period.

Miller spoke of hearing survivors of the 1930s, astonished that they could have said the things they said, believed what they believed. But these were not some others, mysteriously in thrall to ideas long since redundant. This was himself from the age of seventeen to thirty-five. When he says that 'a faith exploded is as unreasonable to the heart in its original intensity as a lost love',[27] it is a personal confession. He is identifying the problem of explaining himself to himself as much as to those who stare back through time as if old men were never young and yesterday had no authenticity.

And not the least of the reasons for this is that we change incrementally until at last that former self is so many steps away as to seem in a place no longer dense with reality. Memory is the sense the present chooses to make of the past, not the thing itself. *Death of a Salesman* turns this truth into dramatic form as a man looks back to his youth and sees the brightness of a light that now blinds rather than lights his way. In play after play Miller and his characters turn to the past in search of the moment when the blight came on the rose. Now, at least in his own mind, he was doing no less, years after the Marxist utopia had been revealed as a chimera, aware that a loss of innocence is an archetypal experience. In April 1985, he would jot down a poem in which he spoke of the human desire for Eden and of the Marxist betrayal of innocence.

Aware of the contradictions in his own life and career, Miller now prepared for the absolutes generated by confrontational hearings. The Communist Party that had once appeared the logical product of historic process now seemed at best an irrelevance. He had never felt that sense of shock that turned others into crusading zealots or that broke their faith in themselves and the possibility of social change. He had had his commitments but never, or so he claimed, joined the Party, and therefore never felt the sharp pain of apostasy. He carried no mortal wounds and knew few who did. The activities of the Committee, however, he held in contempt, and everything he had written suggested that the breaking of faith with friends was unthinkable. On the other hand, he had no desire to seem to support Russian communism. It would be another four months before tanks would roll into Hungary to suppress the uprising there, but he had no illusions about the power he had once seen as offering hope.

But that was not what was at issue before the Committee. Their eyes were on the past, in so far as they were seeking to rewrite it so that those of radical and liberal opinion became explicit or implicit traitors. What HUAC desperately needed in the mid-1950s was what Margaret Thatcher, in a different context, would later call the oxygen of publicity. Miller and Monroe were to be the vaudeville act that would do the trick, and though they could hardly subpoena her they could profit from Miller's new association with her. He later remarked:

An artist, an actor, a writer, gets an audience voluntarily to come to his plays or read his books or whatever, and the HUAC committees have to break their necks to get a line in the press or else they have to pay for ads in order to get into the press. That was a big job; that was almost all the committee were doing all the time – trying to get in the papers!

The FBI and the committee were very publicity conscious. They were adept at using the press when they were hungry ... anybody who was around the left knew that the real left guys were never bothered! Because they weren't famous, because they weren't known – so what the hell was the point of it? Why waste a day grilling some janitor from some union which was a Communist union if you can talk to someone who can get on the front page of the *Daily News?* And with their picture.[28]

The *Daily News* had little interest in playwrights. America's sex symbol was another matter. A red in bed with America's snow queen was irresistible.

Before the hearings began, Miller issued a statement to the press. He knew that, once before the Committee, he would have limited room for manoeuvre. In particular, unlike those charged under the Smith Act, it was impossible to sue for libel since HUAC proceedings were privileged. 'To my knowledge,' he stated,

> I have never broken any law. No one accuses me of espionage, aiding a foreign power, or acting in any way inimical to the interests of the United States. No one accuses me of breaking any law or intending or conspiring to do so.
>
> Why, then, am I subpoenaed by a committee of Congress to testify upon political matters? What legislation could conceivably be written as a result of a playwright's retailing his political and ethical views under order of a government body? Obviously, none ...
>
> The reason I have been called before this committee is, I believe, that my private opinions are anathema to those of the self-appointed vigilante groups such as the Catholic War Veterans, American Legion, and the publication Counterattack. For myself, I not only admit that these people stand for things I abhor, but I declare this fact most proudly and emphatically.

He proceeded to lay out his political stall in considerable detail, offering nothing in the way of compromise:

> I believe a new war would be a catastrophe for all humanity; these people believe it is a necessary crusade. I believe Roosevelt was a great and good man most of the time; they believe him a devil and a near-Communist. I believe the public schools must be kept out of the hands of the Catholic Church; they believe the Church ought to be permitted to expand its influence in public schools, and they are actively hounding teachers who oppose their viewpoint and their plans. I believe in militant trade unionism; they have always lent their men to the destruction of unionism. I believe in government-

supported housing, and free medicine for all. They call this communism and even anti-Christian. I believe that the power of super-monopoly, which is now in control of America's basic industry, must be curbed and controlled for the protection of the vast majority; they believe business is holy and that open lust for private profit is equivalent to Americanism itself . . .

If Arthur Miller is now a disgraced person; if my past and present antagonism to jingoism, monopoly capitalism, and the brick-headed reaction of veterans' groups and the lunatic political fringe – if this makes me unfit to speak through my plays to the People, then I leave it to history as to who is 'American' and who her enemy . . . I shall hold to an image of man free of irrational fears, conscious of his power to create goodness, and in control of machines that now enslave him. If that quest is now prohibited in America as treasonable then I belong in jail, for I will go on with it. I give fair warning. I will go on with it until the end.

This is not the statement of a man preparing to equivocate. It is the statement of a man spoiling for a fight. In the end, however, he was a deal less aggressive than this press release suggested.

The hearing took place in the Caucus Room of the Old House Office Building on 21 June 1956, just a year after Miller published 'A Modest Proposal for the Pacification of the Public Temper' in the *Nation*. In this he had developed a Swiftian proposal that, in view of the presumption of treasonable activities then current, every American citizen should, on attaining the age of eighteen, present him or herself for arrest as a 'conceptual traitor' (not guilty of subversion but not actively furthering the Defense of the Nation); as an 'action traitor' (anyone summoned to testify before any Committee of Congress); or as an 'unclassified person' (someone who is neither a conceptual nor an action traitor but who might be insane or a member of the FBI). Those in this last category would be automatically released, though subject to reclassification.

The hearing consisted of a not-so-Socratic dialogue between Miller and the chairman Francis Walter or the chief counsel, Richard Arens. Miller wore a dark suit and patterned tie. He sat drinking occasionally from a plastic cup of water. Beside him was his lawyer, the bespectacled Joe Rauh, with light suit and bow-tie. The tone was no longer that of the early days. There was no repeated banging of the gavel, no shouting out of statements, no invoking of First or Fifth Amendments, no crude bullying. The wider context had changed. The Korean War was over, Stalin was dead, a more emollient leader following him in the person of Khrushchev. By 1955, Hoover estimated, there were only 22,600 members of the American Communist Party (down from 80,000 eleven years earlier), an incredible third of whom were FBI agents.[29]

The hearing, like that of Paul Robeson, was ostensibly concerned with the question of the issuance and withholding of US passports and did, indeed, begin with questions about his previous passport applications, echoing those asked by the Youth Board when he was fired from the film project on juvenile delinquency. But there was a subtext.

A Court of Appeals decision had stripped the State Department's Passport Office of some of its powers, those it had invoked against Miller in 1953. Walter had himself introduced a bill that would return to the Secretary of State powers to strip communists and others of passports while denying access to the evidence on which such decisions were made. Pending passage of this, he called upon Secretary John Foster Dulles to deny passports to any suspected people. Thus he sought to call before the Committee those who were part of a 'skillfully organized Communist passport conspiracy by which Party members and fellow travelers are enlisted to travel abroad in the service of Soviet propaganda and subversion'.[30]

The questioning started with inquiries about Miller's passport renewal ten years earlier and his attempted renewal on the occasion of his planned visit to Belgium in 1954. He had, as we have seen, recently applied again, in connection with his forthcoming visit to England. But the questions were merely setting the stage for an examination of his experience with the New York Youth Board, in which the Committee had been indirectly involved.

At the time, he was reminded by Arens, he had recalled issuing a statement in which he 'categorically denied' that he was 'supporting the Communist cause or contributing to it or was under its discipline or domination', and that in signing a passport renewal application he had also signed, 'under the penalties of perjury', a statement declaring that he was not 'a member of any subversive organization'.[31] In fact, there had been no such oath on the application form, which Miller plainly now knew, not least because he had just had to sign one. Thus, to Arens's evident confusion, he apologized for the misstatement, while insisting that he would have signed one had there been such a thing.

It was not a good start. It opened the door to other hypothetical questions. Would he, then, have taken an oath that he had never contributed to the communist cause? He replied that he might have 'contributed a dollar or two' to organizations but had 'none in mind', though, pressed, he came up with the Joint Anti-Fascist Committee whose Republican sympathies during and after the Spanish Civil War had attracted his support.

Both sides, at this point, were merely treading water.

The problem was that Miller had contributed to so many causes, and signed so many protests, that he had genuinely forgotten many of them. As he remarked in 2001, 'I didn't remember them, any more than now I would remember invitations to speak, which I get every day of the week. In those days I got a petition every day of the week. I still get petitions, though not always political. If you said, "Did you sign this?" I more than likely did. I said to Arens, "Let's assume I signed all of them."[32] He did confess to supporting 'a number of things I would not now', adding, 'I would not support now a cause or a movement which was dominated by Communists.'[33] Nonetheless, and though it hardly contradicted his statement, he did seem equivocal when faced with evidence of his former allegiances. Thus, when Arens, drawing on the pile of papers in front of him, confronted him with a statement of the Civil Rights Congress in support of the right of the Communist Party to remain a legally constituted political party, instead of justifying or qualifying it, he simply replied that he had no memory of it: 'These things were coming across my desk.'

This is undoubtedly true, but the effect of his accumulating memory deficit began to create the impression not only of someone who signed whatever was put in front of him, but also of someone whose political gestures quickly faded from mind. So, asked to confirm that he had put his name to a protest in the *Washington Post* attacking punitive measures directed against the Communist Party, he replied, 'I see my name here. I would not deny I might have signed it.' Asked if he had signed a statement of protest at the prosecution of Gerhart Eisler, he denied any memory of it; then, confronted with a copy of the document, said that while he might have signed documents he was not their sponsor – a distinction, it might be thought, without a difference. But then, most of these questions were themselves irrelevant. What Arens was doing was trying to show a pattern of behaviour that would make his later charges, and his later demands for information, seem more plausible.

Miller's defence was that what he had done 'met the mood of the time that I was living in', which was true enough, but left him in the difficult position of seeming to disavow personal responsibility, as if he did no more than swim with the tide. Speaking in 2001, he explained that he had signed petitions, many of which had been set up by front organizations of the Communist Party, because they were in support of good causes. 'Sometimes I didn't know if these were the product of front organizations, but sometimes I would suspect that they were but to hell with it! – if it was for a good cause I would sign the damn thing. But when I got before the House Un-American Activities Committee they had about eight hundred of them!'

The next questions moved closer to home, at least closer to Arens's home: HUAC itself. 'Did you sign statements or lend your name, prestige and influence toward a movement to abolish the Committee on Un-American Activities?' Miller replied: 'I have no memory of that.' Had he been a speaker at a rally to attack HUAC at the Manhattan Center? 'I am not clear whether I was a speaker or not.' And so it continued. His somewhat defensive remark, 'I know very little about anything except my work and my field',[34] added to what seemed the emerging portrait of a man who had given scant attention to what he signed or to the public positions he had adopted. In fact, of course, since he had been attending Communist Party meetings throughout 1947, he can scarcely have been quite as detached and unaware as he now seemed.

Writing more than thirty years later, Miller described his growing sense of despair, not only at the process to which he was now subjected but at the implication of his own past behaviour:

> I remember feeling, as I glanced at one after another of the protests he handed me for identification, how fatuous it had all been. I remember thinking that my influence on my own history had been nil. The simple truth was that I myself could barely recall a great many of the organizations or causes to which I had given my support. And perhaps the worst of it all was that while these were 'facts' Arens was establishing about my life as a sympathizer, it would have been impossible under the circumstances to tell the larger truth.[35]

That larger truth had to do with plotting the chart of his own betrayed hopes, the convictions that, for a while, had structured his life, shaped his art and determined his responses. He had, after all, believed wholeheartedly in Marxism as 'the hope of mankind and of the survival of reason itself'. And this was the core of his dilemma. He had once been an unequivocal believer and had supported whatever causes seemed to serve that belief, because 'I had probably ... made up my mind that day or week that the only way to stand against fascism abroad or at home was to do what so many others of my generation also thought necessary'.

Arens now shifted his ground, introducing into the record the article Miller had written in 1945 denouncing Ezra Pound. Miller was to recall the questioning as petering out in the face of his statement that he was a Jew and that Pound had been in favour of burning Jews, as if Arens was taken aback by quite such a direct response. The episode, he said, 'cleared the air'. But in fact the question was only a pretext for the follow-up inquiry. Why, Arens wished to know, had he been willing to denounce Pound for his anti-Semitism why had he not issued a denunciation of the Soviet Union?

This won a confession from Miller: 'I am sorry to say that there was none. I am sorry to say something worse: that I was not shocked ... I am ashamed to say that I should have, and I did feel I was not completely ignorant of this. It isn't a matter of Khrushchev. I knew this before Khrushchev.'[36] What, then, asked Arens, of his attitude to communism in the United States? Why, in particular, had he defended 'twelve accused Communist traitors' convicted under the Smith Act (which made it an offence to conspire to overthrow the Government of the United States by force and violence)?

By this point Miller had recovered something of his equanimity. Defence turned to attack. 'I am opposed to the Smith Act,' he stated, and to anyone being penalized for advocacy; here he invoked the right and, implicitly, the responsibility, of authors to advocate: 'You can go from *War and Peace* through all the great novels of our time and they are all advocating something.'[37] It was not quite what Arens had in mind, as Miller doubtless realized, but the effect was to sow confusion as he continued to speak of literature and they of the overthrowing of the American government.

'If advocacy of itself becomes a crime or can be penalized without overt action,' he went on, 'we are smack in the middle of literature, and I don't see how it can be avoided.'[38] Given that he had just been asked by another Committee member who Ezra Pound might be – as in earlier hearings a witness had been quizzed about the communist leanings of Christopher Marlowe – he was seeking safety by deflecting the discussion on to his own territory. 'Let us leave literature out of that,' pleaded a Committee member. When another asked if he believed that 'freedom of literature is absolute', he replied, 'The absolutes are not absolute', showing, if nothing else, that he could be as at home in the mysterious linguistic black hole the Committee had created as anyone. This was not so much a dialogue as parallel mono-logues, though Miller's reference to advocacy had its roots in a dispute about the meaning of the concept of 'clear and present danger'. As 'the people's attorney' Louis D. Justice Brandeis had remarked, 'The wide difference between advocacy and incitement, between preparation and attempt, between assembly and conspiracy, must be borne in mind.'[39]

Desperate for some solid ground, another Committee member now asked him if he regarded his magazine articles as literature. By now, though, Miller was becoming fluent in newspeak. 'No, sir,' he answered, 'you are importing.' Urged to clarify, he said, 'You fail to draw a line between advocacy and essence.'[40] Understandably, his questioners changed tack, returning to familiar ground. Had he attended a conference that had suggested that the FBI used paid informants and penetrated political meetings and labour organizations, acting as 'peeping Toms'? It was an odd question, given that this *was* the modus operandi of the FBI and that Miller himself, as they well knew, had an extensive FBI file. Miller, while not denying this, had no memory of doing so, but regretted signing any document that came out of a meeting which also advocated denying civil liberties to Trotskyites.

He had, he explained, suffered at that time from 'a general lapse of interest in what was going on', which might have seemed true, given the fact that the event concerned took place in June 1949, shortly before the New York opening of *Death of a Salesman*, were it not for the fact that he plainly did find time in 1949 for all manner of political statements, as well as for the Waldorf Conference, about which he was also to be questioned. Asked about involve-ment in the World Congress for Peace, held in Paris, he replied, with an evident sense of relief, 'It is the only one that I actually believe I had nothing to do with', as indeed he had not. This had been another Cominform event, complete with the usual suspects – Howard Fast, Paul Robeson, Louis Aragon – accompanied by a CIA-sponsored counter-event, with Sidney Hook again to the fore.

Now he was pressed on the subject of Elia Kazan. Had he criticized him as a 'renegade intellectual ... an informer'? Miller denied making any such statements – denied, in fact, knowing precisely what his testimony might have been. His break with Kazan, he insisted, might have involved other issues of no political interest and no interest to the Committee, and he had no inclination to talk about private matters.

This was surely a curious piece of sophistry. He knew exactly what Kazan's testimony had been and had, indeed, broken with him because of aspects of it. But the Committee backed off and instead invoked a series of conferences, protests and sponsorships in which he had allegedly involved himself. This, in turn, provoked a statement from Miller in which he asserted his essential loyalty to the United States, as evidenced by his refusal to cooperate with the foreign press when they sought to interview him, particularly after the denial of a passport to go and see the Belgian premiere of *The Crucible*: 'Whatever I may have supported and however it looks, I do draw a line between criticism of the United States in the United States and before foreigners. I believe I am a good representative of this country abroad.' He would not now participate, he went on, and had not for 'the last few years ... in anything affecting international relations' or 'anything that was a Communist front of any kind'. The former remark might seem a strange one, and went beyond anything demanded by the Committee, but 'international relations', in the context of the hearings, plainly stood as code for activities bearing on communist countries, as was apparent from the fact that the remark came in response to suggestions that in May 1949 he had supported a China Welfare Appeal.

One odd dimension of the interrogation to this point was that at no time had anyone mentioned Miller's work as a playwright, despite the fact that it was supposedly his reputation in this regard that had brought him to the attention of the Committee. After all, he could scarcely be said to have been summoned because of his relationship with a filmstar. But now, for the first time, one of his plays was introduced into the record by his interrogators. This was not, though, as yet, *The Crucible* or *A View from the Bridge*, but the work he had co-authored with Norman Rosten in 1939, *Listen My Children*, when working for the Federal Theatre. Miller had evidently all but forgotten it; Arens flourished a handwritten version he had secured from the Library of Congress.

Listen My Children was based on a sketch Miller had written and that was subsequently amplified with Rosten. The Committee's interest stemmed from two facts: one was that in 1936, when Rosten was a student, he had been a member of the Young Communist League (and was so identified in the *Daily Worker* in December of that year); the other was that the play opens with a satirical attack on an investigating committee. Arens read the opening stage direction:

> Curtain slowly opens. The committee members are engaged in activity of an extraordinary variety, amid an equally extraordinary environment. Profuse bunting over the walls. There are several huge clocks ticking ominously. Also a metronome which is continuously being adjusted for tempo change. Secretary, at desk, pounds typewriter and, as alarm clock rings, she feeds the committee men spoonsful of castor oil . . . In center of room, in rocker, sits a man. He is securely tied to a chair, with a gag in his mouth and a bandage tied over his eyes. Water, coming from a pipe near ceiling, trickles on his head. Nearby is a charcoal stove holding branding irons. Two bloodhounds are tied in the corner of the room.

It has to be said that the Committee were not inclined to take this over-seriously. The chairman declared it 'corny', while Miller himself hastened to point out that the script was not in his handwriting and that he had not been responsible for that scene. He had, though, been responsible for *You're Next*, also an attack on the Committee, and advertised as playing at the Communist Party Congress as late as 1947, the year of *All My Sons*. He accepted responsibility for the play but not for those who chose to produce it: 'I take no more responsibility for who plays my plays than General Motors can take for who rides in their Chevrolets' – not, of course, strictly true since his permission was required for all productions of his work, but there is nothing like invoking a major American corporation for stilling the wandering heart of a congressional committee.

You're Next, an eight-page sketch, concerns a barber called Jerry Marble who is a supporter of a pro-labor candidate against an anti-labor judge. Not only does he have a photograph of that candidate in his window, but he also collects money for Republican Spain and Yugoslav refugees. A friendly lawyer warns him that HUAC (whose John Rankin had been the instigator of the new Committee in 1945 and who is named in Miller's text) is investigating the Spanish Relief Committee. He urges him to remove his collecting cans from the counter or risk being branded a communist by the press. Marble, grudgingly, complies.

All the other shopkeepers also remove the candidate's photograph but are still branded communists in the newspaper, as they are by those offering themselves as witnesses against them in Washington. When another shopkeeper tries to enlist Marble's support he refuses it on the grounds that the man had denied credit to striking workers. Realizing that a fundamental principle is at stake, he replaces the collecting cans, announces that he is opposed to fascism and is happy for the Committee to know as much. He ejects the other shopkeeper and persuades a paper boy to shout out the slogan, 'Beware, Rankin Threatens Liberty!' in the mode of Clifford Odets's *Waiting for Lefty.*

You're Next, a favourite with radical groups – it featured in a May Day rally in Philadelphia and at a mass rally in New York demanding the abolition of HUAC, both in May 1946 – is an agit-prop piece, with little to recommend it. Perhaps surprisingly, even as an all-out attack on the Committee it generated little interest during the hearing, not least because the Committee did not have a copy, merely a photostat of a *Daily Worker* announcement of its premiere. Beyond that, Rankin had himself not been particularly popular with the Committee and now represented something of an irrelevance. The brief questioning about the play, therefore, concentrated on the degree to which it followed the Party line and whether its performance had been personally sanctioned by Miller. His reply, 'Nothing in my life was ever written to follow a line', was true enough in general, but disingenuous, since *You're Next* coincided with the Party line in certain respects. The whole exchange took no more than a minute, despite the fact that this was the clearest example of his attack on the Committee and everything it stood for.

It was at this stage that, albeit perfunctorily, the question of his other plays arose, though, in the case of *All My Sons*, only indirectly in that he was asked if he had agreed to donate its Polish royalties to the League of Women in Poland, an organization that they identified, hardly surprisingly, as communist. Not unreasonably, he replied that it was impossible to derive royalties from Poland (its currency, of course, being non-negotiable) and hence he had agreed to donate them to a relief drive for Polish children.

Now they came to *The Crucible*. Once again, surprisingly, the questioning was peremptory; it lasted less than thirty seconds. Arens asked the playwright, 'Are you cognizant of the fact that your play *The Crucible*, with respect to witch hunts in 1692, was the case history [*sic*] of a series of articles in the Communist press drawing parallels to the investigations of Communists and other subversives by Congressional Committees?' Miller replied, 'The comparison is inevitable, sir.' Though Miller himself subsequently, and briefly, invoked the play, that was the full extent of the examination of *The Crucible*. *A View from the Bridge* was mentioned only in the context of his then current attempt to renew his passport to visit England for its staging there 'with the woman who will then be my wife', a revelation that seems to have shocked Monroe, though, half a century later, Miller remarked that if that was so then she must have forgotten the script.

The questioning now reverted to his membership, or otherwise, of the

Communist Party. He confessed to signing 'some form or other' when attending a Marxist study course in 1939 or 1940, but no such form was produced
by the Committee. A few minutes later, asked once again whether he had
made an application to join the Party, he shifted from 'I have no memory of
such a thing' to 'I would deny it.' The Committee was obviously lacking the
necessary evidence, despite its allusion to Sue Warren who had supposedly
proposed him for membership.

They were now approaching the central issue of the hearing. In truth they
had no interest in whether *The Crucible* was or was not an attack on the
Committee, nor in sketches he might have written for the Federal Theatre,
now seven years dead. The central question was whether Miller would or
would not name those present at the 'four or five' meetings he had attended.
Would he, in short, follow Kazan's path by acknowledging not only his own
past errors but those of others, enabling them to be brought before the
Committee where they, in turn, could purge their sins? Referring to the
meetings Miller had confessed to attending in 1947, Arens asked: 'Can you
tell us who was there when you walked into the room?' This was the moment
that Miller, and everyone else, had been waiting for. He replied:

> Mr Chairman, I understand the philosophy behind this question and I want
> you to understand mine. When I say this I want you to understand that I am
> not protecting the Communists or the Communist Party. I am trying to, and
> I will, protect my sense of myself. I could not use the name of another person
> and bring trouble on him ... I take the responsibility for everything I have
> ever done, but I cannot take responsibility for another human being.

It was, as noted earlier, a direct echo of John Proctor's speech in *The Crucible*.
He was not, though, to be allowed such a refusal and was instructed by the
chairman to reply. He asked that the question be deferred until the end of
the hearing and proceeded to outline his attitude to Marxism:

> I decided in the course of these meetings that I had finally to find out what
> my views really were in relation to theirs, and I decided that I would write a
> paper in which, for the first time in my life, I would set forth my views on
> art, on the relation of art to politics, on the relation of the artist to politics,
> which are subjects that are very important to me. And I did so, and I read
> this paper to the group and I discovered, as I read it and certainly by the time
> I had finished with it, that I had no real basis in common either philosophically
> or, most important to me, as a dramatist. The most important thing to me
> in the world is my work, and I was resolved that, if I found that I was in fact
> a Marxist, I would declare it, and that, if I did not, I would say that I was
> not, and I wrote a paper, and I would like to give you the brunt of it so that
> you may know me.

Not the least remarkable aspect of Miller's appearance before the Committee was the silence in which its members sat and listened to these words. Previous attempts, by a whole range of witnesses, to explain themselves, to identify their philosophies, had either been rapidly silenced by a pounding gavel or ruled irrelevant. Now the chairman merely asked if Miller had the paper with him. Unfortunately, although he thought it 'the best essay I ever wrote', he had been unable to find it. Nonetheless, he offered a précis and, once again, the Committee listened. Great art, Miller explained,

> like science, attempts to see the present remorselessly and truthfully ... if Marxism is what it claims to be, a science of society, it must be devoted to the objective facts more than all the philosophies that it attacks as being untruthful; therefore, the first job of a Marxist writer is to tell the truth, and, if the truth is opposed to what he thinks it ought to be, he must still tell it, because that is the stretching and straining that every science and every art that is worth its salt must go through. I found that there was a dumb silence because it seemed not only that it [his position] was non-Marxist, which it was, but that it was a perfectly idealistic position – namely, that, first of all, the artist is capable of seeing the facts, and, secondly, what are you going to do when you see the facts and they are really opposed to the line? The real Marxist writer has to turn those facts around to fit that line. I could never do that. I have not done it.

He continued for another five minutes, speaking of the reception of *All My Sons* by a Communist Party whose political line changed while he was writing it, and of *Death of a Salesman*, which had fallen foul of a similar ideological reception. At the end of his speech, which he had delivered uninterrupted, there were no comments forthcoming. Instead, he was immediately reminded by a Committee member that he had yet to answer the question about the names of those present at the meetings he had attended. He was now instructed to answer, and warned that if he did not he would be placing himself in contempt.

The remarks he had just made were plainly seen as little more than a delaying tactic. The more interesting question was why he made them. Was it merely tactical, a filibuster, or was he in some way using the occasion to think aloud, to place on record a genuine account of his changing views. He had, after all, by his own account, delivered the speech of which he had just offered a précis to meetings that took place in 1947, meetings of the Communist Party. But two years later he had still been supporting organizations that he confessed to assuming were communist-controlled, still signing petitions and protests, making speeches, still publicly supporting a China Welfare Appeal and participating in the Waldorf Conference.

The truth would seem to be that he felt as ambivalent as many others who appeared before the Committee. As he himself admitted, he had become aware of just how repressive the Soviet system was long before Khrushchev's speech that same year, 1956. His retreat from a Marxist stance had not been a Pauline conversion, but 'a slow process that occurred over years ... through my own work and through my own efforts to understand myself and what I was trying to do in the world'. His account of his changing views would have been unexceptional in another context. It was the fact that he offered this narrative of disillusionment before a Committee that had no interest in anything but supportive testimony and strategic confessions that was disturbing.

He was now given the names of two people who had allegedly attended meetings. The first was Arnaud d'Usseau, screenwriter and author of the anti-racist *Deep Are the Roots* (one of a group of writers, including Ring Lardner Jr and Budd Schulberg, who used to meet in the late 1930s), a work, incidentally, reviewed in *The Masses* by Matt Wayne. D'Usseau's wife had refused to answer questions about communist affiliation when asked by the Committee. The second was Sue Warren, who had allegedly proposed him for Party membership in 1943. He declined to answer. (In 2001, for the first time, he would admit to me: 'I have no recollection of d'Usseau or Warren being present', but, also for the first time, he would identify two of those who were.)

Oddly, as the proceedings now drew to a close he was asked why he did not direct 'some of that magnificent ability you have to fighting against well-known Communist subversive conspiracies in our country and the world'. He replied at length, making perhaps a necessary if, in the context, slightly demeaning declaration of loyalty and offering a denunciation of communism and his own past errors:

I think it would be a disaster and a calamity if the Communist Party ever took over this country. That is an opinion that has come to me not out of the blue sky but out of long thought ... We are living in a time of great uncertainty in this country. It is not a Communist idea: you just pick up a book-review section and you will see everybody selling books on peace of mind, because there isn't any ... I am trying to delve to the bottom of this, and come up with a positive answer, and I have had to go to hell to meet the devil ... I believe in democracy. I believe it is the only way for myself and for anybody that I care about; it is the only way to live; but my criticism, such as it has been, is not to be confused with a hatred. I love this country, I think, as much as any man, and it is because I see things that I think traduce certainly the values that have been in this country that I speak. I would like more than anything else in the world to make positive my plays, and I intend to do so before I finish. It has to be on the basis of reality.

As is evident from the fractured syntax, this was not a scripted speech. It was responsive to a context in which it was necessary for him to distinguish between his critical stance with regard to the drift of American society, and subversion. If the language was contaminated with boosterism, this is scarcely surprising. He had not come before the Committee to defend the Party, nor every gesture he had made towards his sense of justice and equity, in America and abroad. He had come with one thing in mind. He was prepared to stake out his own territory, confess to his own mistakes, defend his own beliefs, but not name others. Both sides in the hearing understood from the beginning that this was the principal issue.

Surprisingly, following Miller's declaration of loyalty and implicit admission of error, the chairman now himself confessed to making contributions to the Anti-Fascist Committee because, as he somewhat oddly remarked, 'they were moving Jews away from Germany', though this was merely the occasion for him to regret Miller's parallel failure to denounce Soviet anti-Semitism. Miller's response was to acknowledge a double regret, at the loss of an ideal and at a false allegiance:

> I think it is not only unfortunate, it was a great error. In the face of an overwhelming ideal it has been the common experience of mankind, both good people and bad people, that [the ideal] goes by the board and fades into the walls. I believe now in facts. I look at life to see what is happening, and I have no line. I have no preconception. I am devoted to what is going on. The hardest thing to do is to tell what is going on.

Representative Kearney now offered him the opportunity to represent himself as mere victim, albeit at the price of confessing a degree of naivety. 'Do you consider yourself,' he asked, 'more or less a dupe in joining these Communist organizations?' Miller's reply restored whatever dignity he might have risked in some of his previous statements. 'I wouldn't say so, because I was an adult. I was looking for [a] world that would be perfect. I think it was necessary that I do that, if I were to develop myself as a writer. I am not ashamed of this. I accept my life. This is what I have done. I have learned a great deal.'

The Chairman concluded with a statement that blended an implicit defence of the Committee with condescension. Addressing Miller across the piles of assembled documents he observed, 'You have learned a great deal and made a greater contribution to what we think you now stand for than you realize, because, by the errors that you committed, you are sounding a very loud note of warning to a lot of other people who might fall into what you did.'

When Miller had refused to name names, Representative Donald L. Jackson of California warned him that 'moral scruples, however laudable, do not constitute legal reasons for refusing to answer the question'.[41] Following the hearing, and under threat of contempt proceedings, Miller now sent a closely typed four-page letter to the Chairman Walter, in which not merely did he argue that others who had refused to name names had escaped censure but also outlined his own philosophy, reiterating in large part what he had already told the Committee. He was plainly naive to believe that Walter would be moved by such a confessional document but the process of writing it seems to have clarified his position in his own mind.

He was, he explained, a person devoted to democratic institutions and opposed to totalitarianism. He had attended meetings of the Communist Party but this had been at a time when the Party was legal and its candidates could freely run for public office. He could, he conceded, conceive that a man should inform if he had been tricked or misled by communists and was in possession of first-hand knowledge of plans to harm the country. In such circumstances, he 'could not condemn' the offering of names, itself an interesting formulation, of course, in that even in such circumstances he seemed to be reserving to himself the right to silence; but, he said, since he had no such knowledge the question did not arise. It was simply a matter that growing up when he did, with the Depression giving way to war, Marxism had seemed a logical and moral force that was bound to influence writers, among others. He had chosen of his free will to take part in communist meetings, but these had taken place at a time when authority of all kinds was being challenged and the social world was in a state of flux. He had come to the conclusion, however, that where he had looked for answers in the external world, the real change must come from within. By then, though, his name had become associated with a radicalism that was, in truth, simply an expression of the social forces of the day. The idea that he should name others who shared the same illusion would simply be to ignore this simple truth, to ignore history and the pressures to which all had been submitted.

He then proceeded, in the letter to Walter, to explain the nature of the meetings he had attended and his reasons for going to them. The meetings themselves had been essentially to do with literature and philosophy. They were not political meetings in the sense that they planned interventions in society. He went on to explore further his ill-formed sense of Marxism and to discuss the responsibility of the artist at such a time. He recalled stories and poems being read and plays and novels being discussed in the context of Marxist ideas. What he primarily learned from these meetings was that his work evidently had no place in the Marxist scheme.

He emerged, he explained, convinced that he was temperamentally opposed to Marxism. What he wished to protect, was not communists but his responsibility for his own actions. He was the sum of his actions, and therefore accepted bad choices as well as good as having shaped him. He was unequivocal that the Marxist analysis was wrong and its claims specious. He was even more certain of the damage it could do to the artist. But he was equally sure that only he could be called to account for his actions, while others must account for theirs. As he pointed out, if he had personally done damage, the naming of others could scarcely change that any more than a refusal to name them could exacerbate such damage. Quite why a refusal to name names should be regarded as a contempt of Congress was beyond him when the opposite might be said to be true. He could not point the finger at others to purge any fault of his own. To do so, he suggested, would demean not only himself but, ultimately, those who demanded his acquiescence.

This existential statement and plea for understanding is dated 6 July 1956. A day earlier, at his request, Sigurdur Magnusson, an Icelandic radio commentator, had sworn an affidavit in which he included a portion of an interview he had recorded with Miller nearly two years earlier. He was already building his case. In this interview he had remarked of the communist reaction to *The Crucible* that, while they knew it was an indictment of McCarthyism, they 'did not realize that it is an attack on any kind of fanaticism, so that the play is a ... protest against what has happened and what is happening in Russia and elsewhere where the communists have thrown their opponents on the "witch-fires".' Mentioning that the play had been inspired by a history course back in Michigan, he remarked, somewhat disingenuously and – given his conversation with Molly Kazan four years earlier – not entirely accurately:

> as you can see from that, the play is not first and foremost written against McCarthyism, as many people think, for that was non-existent then, but against all kinds of fanaticism, whatever their names, which try to get a foothold through inquisitions and a general reign of terror ... The shafts of flames from the 17th century witch fires are still seen against the sky and they cast somber reflections over our present atomic age.[42]

Despite such documents, four days later, on 10 July, in the Common Caucus Room where thirty-six years later he would receive the Kennedy Award, he was duly charged with contempt of Congress, the Committee voting unanimously in closed session. From there it would go to the full House. The precise grounds were that he had refused to answer two questions:

1. Can you tell us who was there when you walked into the room?
2. Was Arnaud D'Usseau chairman of this meeting of Communist Party writers which took place in 1947 at which you were in attendance?[43]

The next step was for the Justice Department to seek an indictment and prosecute, the maximum penalty being a year in prison and a $1,000 fine. His attorneys submitted a brief citing a dozen cases in which committees had failed to press contempt charges against witnesses who refused to testify against others; noting, too, that Miller had himself written to Committee

Chairman Walter explaining that 'I know myself to be a person devoted to democratic institutions and opposed to totalitarianism.'[44] An addendum to the brief noted court rulings that contempt actions could only be sustained when questions put to a witness were 'pertinent' to a valid legislative inquiry. Miller's was one of eight contempt citations dispatched by the House at the request of the Committee on 25 July, one of the others being that of the folk-singer Pete Seeger. Only the citation against Miller was debated. Three New York Democrats did speak up in his defence, but he was cited by 373 votes to 9. He was sentenced to thirty days in prison and a $500 fine.

As Richard Pells reminds us in *The Liberal Mind in a Conservative Age*, it is tempting to wish that Miller and others had responded to the Committee with the words of Woody Allen in his film *The Front*: 'Look, fellows, you don't have any right to ask me these questions. You can all go fuck yourselves.'[45] In fact, some did manage the equivalent. The stakes, though, were high and those called before HUAC were not untroubled by a certain private guilt about past actions and commitments. Despite his disdain for it, Miller was treated by the Committee with a degree of respect and responded, for the most part, in as open and rational a way as possible, while protecting those he was invited to betray. The problem was that despite its quasi-judicial air and seeming interest in rational process that was not what it was about.

In the context, he can perhaps be forgiven the touch of *schadenfreude* he felt at the fate of one of those who had put him through the ordeal of his appearance before HUAC, when the Chief Counsel of the Committee was dismissed following revelations that he had taken money from an anti-Semitic foundation in New York.

HUAC did not die. After an attack on Joe Papp (of New York's Public Theatre), who identified himself as Joseph Papirofsky in his appearance before the Committee in 1958, it moved on, in the 1960s, to attack anti-war protesters. By then, however, the balance of power had decisively swung and the Committee found itself confronting individuals who mocked and ridiculed it, deliberately turning hearings into low farce. Thus Jerry Rubin appeared dressed as a soldier of the Revolutionary War and Abbie Hoffman wearing a shirt made from the American flag, both accused of subversive involvement in disruption at the 1968 Democratic Party National Convention at which Miller had been an official delegate. Tom Hayden, like Miller a graduate of the University of Michigan, when asked what jobs he held, helpfully explained, 'I consider myself an organizer of a movement to put you and your Committee out of power, because I think you represent racist philosophy.'[46] Asked if his aim was to destroy 'the present American democratic system', he replied that he did not believe that such a thing existed, since it had been destroyed by the Committee. His wrong-footed interrogator then countered, 'Let us take the words "American" and "democratic" out of it.' And so it continued. The

House Committee on Un-American Activities was finally abolished in 1975.

When I asked him, in the mid-1990s, if he would name those who had attended the Communist Party meetings with him, Miller was still refusing: 'Most of the people I could have named . . . I barely knew at all, and the two I did know were utterly harmless people who, at the time I was testifying, were barely hanging on to jobs in television and it would have utterly destroyed them for absolutely no purpose whatsoever.'[47] Speaking to me in 2001, however, for the first time he offered two names, declaring that he had long since forgotten the rest. The man he was now prepared to name, forty-five years after the HUAC hearings, was the writer Millard Lampell, whom he had first met through his radio work. The other was Lampell's wife.

Lampell was Jewish. His father, an immigrant from Austria-Hungary, was a garment worker of a kind who might have worked in the Miller family company. Lampell himself had held a range of jobs, including silk-dyer and coalminer. He attended the University of West Virginia, where he wrote an article about fascist groups on campus. He then moved to New York where he was employed to spy on the American Destiny Party, a group of fascists led by Joe McWilliams who characterized himself as the anti-Jew candidate for Congress.

In New York Lampell met Pete Seeger. Together with Lee Hays, they formed a group called the Almanac Singers, which eventually included Sis Cunningham and Woody Guthrie. The group travelled America, playing at union meetings, and in 1942–3 Lampell wrote for several radio programmes, including *It's the Navy*. He met Norman Rosten and became a close friend. But his radio work came to a sudden halt. Pete Seeger explained:

> When Lee Hays and I and Mill Lampell formed the Almanac Singers, we got a lot of publicity in the Communist *Daily Worker* and were singing all around New York and then across the country. Woody Guthrie soon joined us. As Communists we were singing for trade unions and singing for peace in early 1941. But in the fall of '41 we were singing to support the war effort. In January of '42, the Almanacs were on a coast-to-coast network show directed by Norman Corwin called *This Is War*. The next day the headline in the *New York World-Telegram* said, 'Commie Singers Try to Infiltrate Radio', and that was the last job that Woody Guthrie and I got in 1942. In '43 he went in the Merchant Marine. In July '42 I went in the Army. People who participate in radical politics assume that you're going to lose jobs – it is nothing unusual. What happened in the 1950s, though, was a more extreme form of it: if you *knew* somebody who *knew* somebody, you got blacklisted.[48]

In 1944, Lampell wrote, produced and directed for CBS a series of radio programmes for the Army and Air Force called *First in the Air*. When he returned from the war, he abandoned music in favour of writing. In 1947 he published *The Hero* (later filmed as *Saturday's Hero*), about corruption in college athletics. Lampell was a communist, summoned by HUAC, who refused to cooperate. He was blacklisted in 1950. He explained:

> There was no way of getting proof that I was actually on a list, no easy way to learn the damning details. My income simply dropped from a comfortable five figures to $2000 a year. Finally I ran into an old friend, a producer who had downed a few too many martinis, and he leveled with me. 'Pal, you're dead. I submitted your name for a show and they told me I couldn't touch you with a barge pole.' He shrugged unhappily. 'It's a rotten thing. I hate it but what can I do?' And with a pat on my cheek: 'Don't quote me, pal, because I'll deny I said it.'[49]

Lampell did, however, go on to write novels, plays and films. He wote under four pseudonyms, producing two films and more than a dozen radio and television scripts. When he won an Emmy he used the occasion to denounce the blacklisting. In his acceptance speech he announced: 'I think I ought to mention I was blacklisted for ten years.'[50] He died in 1997, shortly before the four major Hollywood entertainment guilds offered an apology for the blacklisting they had practised.

Miller's naming of him at the time, had he done so, would hardly have made any difference. He was already squarely in the sights of HUAC and was unapologetic about his commitments. This merely underlines the extent to which the naming of names was, for the most part, a ritual. The point of the interrogation lay not in a search for information but in a display of power and a simultaneous assertion of the supposed extent of the communist conspiracy and of the Committee's power to address it. Miller could easily have named Lampell (and his wife), secure in the knowledge that he could do him no further harm. That he did not only serves to underline that his decision was, indeed, a principled one or, perhaps, as Twentieth Century Fox's Spyros Skouras thought, one based on pride. Miller had resisted joining the Party as much for aesthetic reasons as anything else. 'There were an awful lot of putative playwrights whose work I really detested, whose work was propaganda, and I didn't want to be in the same boat with them. I liked them as people, but they weren't really very good writers, and most of them were quick to sell out.'

Even in 1956, when the Committee had lost much of its power, few writers chose to stand up for Miller. One of those who did was John Steinbeck, who had earlier equivocated with respect to Kazan's naming of names. In a piece for *Esquire* he wrote:

> Law, to survive, must be moral. To force personal immorality on a man, to wound his private virtue, undermines his public virtue. If the Committee

frightens me enough, it is even possible that I may make up things to satisfy the questioners. This has been known to happen. A law which is immoral does not survive and a government which condones or fosters immorality is truly in clear and present danger. . . .

We have seen and been revolted by the Soviet Union's encouragement of spying and telling, children reporting their parents, wives informing on their husbands. In Hitler's Germany, it was considered patriotic to report your friends and relations to the authorities. And we in America have felt safe from and superior to these things. But are we so safe and superior?

The men in Congress must be conscious of their terrible choice. Their legal right is clearly established, but should they not think of their moral responsibility also? In their attempts to save the nation from attack, they could well undermine the deep personal morality which is the nation's final defense. The Congress is truly on trial along with Arthur Miller . . .

If I were in Arthur Miller's shoes, I do not know what I would do, but I could wish, for myself and for my children, that I would be brave enough to fortify and defend my private morality as he has. I feel profoundly that our country is better served by individual courage and morals than by the safe and public patriotism which Dr Johnson called 'the last refuge of scoundrels'.[51]

In thanking Steinbeck, Miller suggested that he was in fact the only writer publicly to defend him, sparking a letter by Steinbeck to his editor, Pat Covici:

When Artie told me that no one writer had come to his defense, it gave me a lonely sorrow and a shame that I waited so long and it seemed to me also that if we had fought back from the beginning instead of running away, perhaps these things would not be happening now . . . Please give him my respect and more than that, my love. You see we have had all along the sharpest weapons of all, words, and we did not use them, and I for one am ashamed. I don't think I was frightened but truly, I was careless.[52]

Marilyn spent the last few days of the hearing hiding from the press in Joseph Rauh's house. They were awkward times. She was anxious to be with Miller but it was hard for him to acknowledge her concern. She seems to have felt, in fact, that he was shutting her out. It had, he confessed, always been difficult for him to share his problems, just as his father had kept the news of his declining fortunes from his family as though the private shouldering of anxiety were a sign of strength. Miller explained in *Timebends*:

Something like fear was filling her up at my closing myself off. I was protecting a wound, defensively turning inward, but she glimpsed herself an unwanted wife cooped up for days in a strange house. I tried to see a good challenge in her need, if a somewhat scary one. It was the first time I had to apologize. Like a child, like me, she wanted to dissolve the boundaries of her mind and body in another person, in the world, and I had seemed to throw her back on herself.[53]

As soon as the HUAC hearings had been completed, Miller returned to New York where Marilyn was now waiting at Sutton Place as reporters milled around in the lobby. She stayed in her apartment, 8-E, where a repair man was working on her air-conditioning. It was he who confirmed to the press that the marriage was to go ahead. When Miller finally arrived they were interviewed outside the lobby and he revealed that they planned to marry before leaving for England, 'in July, before the 13th'. When she was asked if her plans would change in the event that her husband-to-be failed to secure a passport, she insisted that she would go ahead with her trip. Asked what he thought of the ruckus, he replied, 'It's good you only get married once', a remark that would thrill Freudians. As it happened, not only had he been married before but he was about to have two marriage ceremonies.

They then left for Roxbury, where they were joined by Miller's parents. There they planned the marriage that he had announced before the Committee. For her part, Marilyn decided that she wanted to marry according to the Jewish faith.

On 29 June, the day Miller had chosen for a press conference which the couple hoped would buy them some limited freedom, they drove, with Morton Miller (who had lived on Goldmine Road in Roxbury since 1950) at the wheel, from the Welton Road house in Roxbury that Miller had bought in the winter of 1947, to Westchester County, New York, to acquire a marriage licence. According to Morton, returning for the press conference, as they approached the house they heard the sound of a car crash. Through the rear-view mirror he could see the accident. A car had hurtled into a tree, throwing the passenger out. They hurried across to where Mara Scherbatof, a reporter from *Paris Match*, lay bleeding. There was nothing to be done but get to a telephone.

Miller's account differs in that he recalls encountering the crashed Chevrolet with Scherbatof already dead, her neck broken by the force of the collision. She had hitched a ride with an American photographer who then speeded after a car which they erroneously thought to be Miller's. Either way, what was to have been a celebratory moment was now clouded by this pointless death.

When, just before one o'clock, they arrived at Miller's home, Morton parked his green Oldsmobile and Miller and Marilyn ran for the house, she, according to Morton – though, speaking in 2003, Miller denied this – with blood on her sweater. Morton said: 'They were following us. This white car was following us and made the turn. You have to slow up. It's a sharp turn. We heard a crash. Behind us. We pulled over. We went back. There was a photographer and a girl. She was thrown out on the road. We tried to do what we could for them. She's bleeding. Arthur's calling the hospital right now.'[54] According to him, Scherbatof died in hospital. But dead on the road or at the hospital, it made no difference and, most disturbingly, seems to have had little impact on the gathered journalists, for whom a live movie star seemingly mattered more than a dead colleague. Miller was being ushered into a new moral universe.

The press conference went ahead, with the newsreel and still photographers granted twenty minutes, and reporters thirty. Miller and Marilyn were acutely conscious of the accident, and nervous. There were some four hundred journalists waiting.

Miller decided that it would be better to get the wedding over immediately and that same evening, 29 June, they drove to White Plains, New York, where they had found a judge, Seymour Rabinowitz, willing to conduct a civil ceremony at short notice. Two days later they married again, this time in a Jewish ceremony in Waccabuc, Westchester, in the home of his literary agent, Kay Brown. 'Marilyn had a yearning,' Miller said later, 'to belong. Her "conversion" was really little more than a conversation with a rabbi friend of mine with whom her connection was less religious than political and social.'[55]

After her supposed conversion, he recalled, she paid no attention to her new faith. Marilyn's conversion began and ended with the wedding ceremony, though she did once help Augusta Miller prepare chicken soup and matzo balls. The wedding ceremony was conducted by Rabbi Robert Goldberg of Congregation Mishkan Israel (in Hamden, Connecticut). There were some thirty friends and relatives present. At Hedda Rosten's suggestion, Marilyn wore not white but a 'bone-colored dress' with a veil 'dyed with tea leaves'.[56] As to Miller, according to Marilyn, 'he only has two suits – the one he got married in and the other one'.[57] Kermit and Hedda Rosten (who now joined Marilyn Monroe Productions at $2,000 a week) were attendants. Miller had to borrow his mother's ring (buying a new one the following week inscribed, 'A to M June 1956. Now is forever'). The guests shared lobster and champagne.

Milton Greene later alleged that Marilyn had changed her mind between the two ceremonies. 'Do you really want to go ahead?' he recalled asking her. 'No,' she had replied, then did so because it would disappoint the invited guests. It is an implausible suggestion, recalled by Greene's wife thirty-six years later and long after the acrimony that would come to characterize Marilyn and Miller's relationship with her husband.

On 3 July, the *New York Daily News* received an anonymous call from an individual described as well spoken and articulate and who, according to the FBI report swiftly generated (along with a note to conceal the *Daily News*'s role in passing the information on), 'sounded as if he knew what he was talking about'. It advised:

'MARILYN MONROE has drifted into the Communist orbit and her political education has been directed by NORMAN ROSTEN, who has been thrown out of TV and radio because of Communist activities.' The source advised that ROSTEN was one of the guests at both weddings of MONROE and ARTHUR MILLER. According to the source, Marilyn Monroe Productions was 'filled with Communists and money from MM Productions is finding its way into the CP'. The source stated that Irving Stein, a lawyer, is the legal advisor of MM Productions, and described STEIN as 'a Commie from way back'. Further, MILTON GREENE, the vice-President of MM Productions, has been mixed up with Communist activities. Further, ARTHUR MILLER has been and still is a member of the CP and still is their cultural front man. According to this source, the religious marriage ceremony and MILLER'S public statements are so much Communist cover up.

A note indicates that the FBI's New York office found nothing to corroborate the statements about any of the named individuals, except for Rosten, who had been identified as a communist during the 1940s. The same file reports a letter alleging that Monroe had been taken on a tour of Brooklyn by a *Life* magazine reporter who was a Party member.

This jumble of material is not untypical of the files kept on Miller and his wife but is indicative that in marrying Miller she, too, came under suspicion. In February 1962, when the marriage was over, confidential report MC 100-0 referred to a statement by Eunice Churchill, her interior decorator, describing Marilyn's visit to Mexico, a visit allegedly facilitated by Frank Sinatra. This reported that Marilyn had been disturbed by Miller's remarriage (to Inge Morath), feeling like a 'negated sex symbol', but that her social views were still those of her ex-husband. Talking to Robert Kennedy at Peter Lawford's home, she had reportedly challenged Kennedy 'on some points proposed to her by Miller'. Later, in conversation with President Kennedy, 'she had asked the President a lot of socially significant questions concerning the morality of atomic testing and the future of the youth of America'. The 'subject', the report concludes, 'still reflects the views of ARTHUR MILLER'.

Meanwhile, on 6 July 1956 a note was passed from the chief of the Passport Legal Division, Department of State, to the FBI, notifying it that Miller had been issued with passport number 129936.[58] It was to be valid for only six months and not to be extended without the express authorization of the Department of State. He now had his passport back and could go to England with his new wife. At the same time the State Department was letting him out on a short leash. With a contempt of Congress citation hanging over him, he could not be sure that on his return he might not lose more than his passport. In 1957, an FBI agent added yet another document to his growing file. This one was the transcript of a Walter Winchell broadcast which explained that 'Arthur Miller a prize-winning playwright and the husband of a well-known movie star was indicted this week . . . [His] pro-Red leanings are stale news to you listeners. I was the first to make them public.'[59]

Joyce Carol Oates begins her novel *Blonde*, a fictionalized account of the life of Marilyn Monroe, with a quotation from Jean-Paul Sartre: 'Genius is not a gift, but the way a person invents in desperate circumstances.' Marilyn may not have been a genius, but she was assuredly a product of her own desperation. Deeply insecure, she did, indeed, invent herself, only to become trapped in that invention, defined in the public eye by those very qualities that brought her success but which simultaneously seemed to deny her full access to her own needs. She existed in and through the films she made, aware that Marilyn was a persona, a mask, but increasingly finding that the membrane separating performance from being was far from impermeable.

She drew on her life to charge her roles with conviction while allowing her public image to bleed into a private life that was seldom private, not least because she feared the solitariness that was so often her fate. Perhaps as a result she formed a series of relationships, usually temporary, sometimes pragmatically designed to forward her career. She was driven by a neurotic energy and, when that failed her, by drugs to gift her sleep and to jump-start her dulled metabolism.

As noted earlier, deprived of a father, she looked to men who could play that role, guiding, protecting, educating, loving. Yves Montand was a mere five years older but Miller and Joe DiMaggio were both eleven years older; Kazan, seventeen. Johnny Hyde, whose death immediately preceded her first encounter with Miller, was 'older than my father – wherever he was',[60] as was Joe Schenk (aged seventy-one), one of the richest men in Hollywood (who, in the topsy-turvy world of Hollywood, was honoured for having gone to jail for bribing a union official to prevent a strike).

And that confusion of realms was revealing. Just as she often seems to have been looking for both roles in those to whom she was attracted, they, in turn, responded to a sexuality seemingly allied to a childlike naivety. But she wanted something else – protection, confirmation of her worth. Marriage itself appears to have been oddly beside the point. She seems repeatedly almost to have stumbled into it, surprised that the logic of relationships led to a permanence that she perhaps thought she valued, only to be disappointed when it failed to address her needs.

At first powerless, she traded in the only currency she possessed: herself.

As she began to accrete power, so she used it carelessly and occasionally ruthlessly. Yet even then there were few who could not see through the apparent disregard for others, the professional arrogance that left her fellow actors frustrated as she failed to arrive on the movie set, or kept friends waiting for hours. On and off screen she had the ability to command the eye. But she was also patently someone struggling to control her fear, her sense of her own inadequacies. Her sensitivities could sometimes seem extreme, almost parodistic. This was the Marilyn Monroe who pressed money into the hands of beggars but could be cruel to those closest to her, and who seems to have regarded sexual betrayal as an irrelevance.

Marilyn Monroe needed America and America needed Marilyn Monroe. Her first film came within two years of the end of the war. She offered glamour and comedy after a period of relative austerity. The apparently orphan girl turned movie star represented an embodiment of that American dream that was once more fuelling the American psyche. She was also, though, as Miller would later say, a foreshadowing of the 1960s. Her nude image on a calendar may have shocked some but for many more it was a sign of changing values, a change reflected in the emergence, in the early 50s, of *Playboy* magazine, whose first Playmate she was. She lived in the belief, Miller has suggested, 'that she was precisely what had to be denied and covered up by the conventional world'.[61] Hers was a sexuality openly displayed, indeed in some sense ironically and knowingly deployed. There was a conspiracy between the star and her public which had to do with a wide-eyed innocence coexisting with an open acknowledgement of sexual power.

Marilyn Monroe was projected to the world as pure sexuality; Arthur Miller as intellect detached from sensuality. The fact that neither image offered an accurate portrait of them was beside the point. As far as the public was concerned a dumb blonde was marrying an egghead, and since the dumb blonde had previously been married to one of the great sporting heroes of the age, amazement was mixed with some dismay. Even Miller recalled her performance in *Asphalt Jungle* as being that of the 'quintessential dumb blonde'.[62]

Marilyn suffered the fate of someone whose two-dimensional image was taken as an adequate account of her life. For all that her life has been investigated, dissected, explored for its pathologies, she still seems to emerge from such accounts as little more than a self-created orphan, desperate for respect and success, whose personal relationships took second place to her career and whose psyche collapsed under the strain of ambition wedded to insecurity. But, as Miller has said, if she had been that simple, it would have been easy to help her.

It is true that she was deeply insecure, afraid that the mental instability of her mother and grandfather would resurface in her. It is true, too, that she was intellectually uncertain and emotionally vulnerable, desperate for recognition. But there was a generosity that matched her occasional vindictiveness, an innocence at the heart of an apparent corruption, a resilience that did battle with an urge to surrender. She was deeply self-destructive, yet determined to succeed. For Laurence Olivier, she was schizophrenic, charming and aggressive by turns, wishing to be liked yet doing everything to alienate those with whom she worked. Sure that he was fated to have an affair with her when they first met, he was barely able to speak to her when they finished filming *The Prince and the Showgirl.*

Her problem was that it was precisely those who took advantage of her who despised and rejected her. There is evidence that she herself found little pleasure in sex, which is perhaps how she managed simultaneously to embody and parody it in her films. It was simply the currency in which she traded, the way in which she related to people. Afraid of being rejected, she ingratiated herself. Her innocence was both simulated and real. Abused, passed around foster homes as of no significance, she was desperate to be accepted and, in being so, invited further abuse. It was her very vulnerability, the damage she had sustained, that attracted Miller, who believed he could heal her, offer what she needed without the edge of contempt that others had brought to the relationship. She herself said, 'He was going to make my life different – better, a lot better. If I were nothing but a dumb blonde, he wouldn't have married me.'[63]

But Miller, too, had a public image. He was the intellectual, the liberal, a monument to integrity whom people likened to Lincoln. He was the social conscience of a country whose values he questioned through his art and his life. He was a signer of petitions, a supporter of liberal causes, a man who refused to betray his friends. It was as if he had no other life, as if there were no sensual dimension, no haunting anarchy to his experience. Much later he would admit to resentment at the role of moral 'pointman', which he had himself once willingly assumed.

Monroe and Miller went out of their way to deny the truth of their public images. 'I'm in love with the man,' insisted Monroe, 'not his mind. The Arthur Miller who attracted me was a man of warmth and friendliness. Arthur has helped me adjust myself. I've always been unsure of myself. Arthur has helped me overcome this feeling.'[64] For Miller, she 'sets up a challenge in every man. Most men become more of what they are natively when they are around her: a phoney becomes more phoney, a confused man becomes more confused, a retiring man more retiring. She's kind of a lodestone that draws out the male animal.' As to her rumoured reputation for promiscuity – 'I've known social workers who have had more of a checkered history than she has.'[65]

Yet in a sense both were equivocating. 'He attracted me because he is brilliant ... His mind is better than that of any other man I've ever known. And he understands and approves my wanting to improve myself,' Monroe said later.[66] Miller would acknowledge that she liberated and validated his sensual side. He may have seen talent in her as yet unrealized, but the role of bruised innocent, of sexual paradigm, was undoubtedly one to which he responded. Aware of his own repressions, he reacted to someone who seemed to him spontaneous and direct in her affections, who was, in effect, a natural force, asking little and giving much.

To a degree that neither wished to acknowledge, they were indeed drawn to one another in part because they accepted the images projected by the media, the roles in which they had separately been cast. This is not to say they were not in love. They were. Witness after witness attests to this. The ultimate failure of the marriage, however, surely owes much to the fact that neither of them could be adequately defined by those roles. Monroe was not just the simple, unaffected, girl-like woman, anxious only to offer love. Miller was not prepared just to be the moral and intellectual father to a woman bereft of family. Eventually, she came to think he condescended to her, failed to understand her professional needs or stand up for her in her disputes with the industry that exploited her. He came to feel the full force of her peremptory demands, the way she treated others, including himself, with contempt, had come to depend on drugs to get through a life in which her career became the centre around which everything was presumed to turn.

In time her affections would turn elsewhere. For a while, though, it seemed possible that both had, indeed, found in one another the answers they had been seeking. She discovered a temporary peace away from Hollywood, fulfilment in a pregnancy which she desperately hoped would gift her the child she believed she wanted. He found two aspects of his life come together for the first time in a relationship in which he rediscovered a sheer pleasure in living, free of guilt, no longer the object of blame.

For a time her sensitivity seemed to charge the everyday with a new significance, almost as though he were, indeed, father to a child discovering the world and not yet inured to a pain that age and experience would simultaneously engender and dull. But that hypersensitivity would later make her feel the victim of an uncaring world and an uncaring relationship.

It was hardly unusual for a playwright to marry an actress. O'Neill had done so, as had Clifford Odets. Sam Shepard would, along with David Mamet; indeed, the last two achieved the feat more than once. Nonetheless, despite by this time knowing something of the theatrical world, Miller remained largely ignorant of the pressures of Hollywood and in truth knew little of Monroe. He had never witnessed at first hand her behaviour on film sets, never fully understood how completely her sense of herself depended on the role she played in the public psyche. She might talk of her desire to be a housewife, of her wish that they should withdraw to the countryside to be alone, but she existed in and through the films she made even as the making of them was the source of her deepening anxiety. He knew little, either, of her dependency on prescription drugs and still less of her absolute need for unquestioning support.

It was not to be long before Miller began to realize just what he had taken on. Asked, some fifty years later, whether he was aware of any of the problems that would eventually destroy the relationship, he replied, 'If I had been sophisticated enough, I would have seen them. But I was not. I loved her.'[67] They may both have been carried away by the speed of events, but their affection was real enough and in the years to come there were idyllic periods. As Marilyn explained, 'I want some calmness, some steadiness, in my life, and for a time I had that in my life with Arthur. That was a nice time. And then we lost it.'[68] For Miller, the problems did not at first seem insurmountable. Speaking in the 1990s he said:

> I felt for a long time that they could be resolved, that she did not have to be destroyed by them, but gradually it became clear that, if she was going to remain an actress ... she was going to have these problems. They were basically unresolvable. You could not live a life and be at the mercy of that industry. You see, they did not regard her as an actress. They regarded her as a sex-pot ... She had very little confidence in herself. She had been exposing herself as an actress ... and this brought to a head all her sense of unworthiness. She felt she was being a faker and this led to a feeling that one was looking at somebody who, while she might be witty and funny ... had some profound sadness.[69]

The strains began to appear within weeks. Miller thought he was escaping the tensions of his first marriage, but quickly discovered that he had traded these for something infinitely more destructive. The price he would pay for the excitement, the glamour of a secret affair and then marriage to the most famous woman in America, was profound personal anguish and the momentary collapse of a career whose logic had seemed unstoppable. *All My Sons*, *Death of a Salesman*, *An Enemy of the People*, *The Crucible*, *A Memory of Two Mondays* and *A View from the Bridge* had followed one another in swift succession over an eight-year period. Only the young O'Neill and his contemporary Tennessee Williams could compare. Now that momentum was to be halted.

If Miller had thought that Marilyn might be a supportive figure in his life he was to discover that, on the contrary, it was he who would have to put his career on hold as he found himself used, publicly, as an intermediary between his wife and those with whom she was supposed to be collaborating. Privately, he was to become a paramedic, in-house psychotherapist and, increasingly, a focus for the anxiety, the anger and despair that seemed to wash over her and which would eventually reach out to include him. The man who had rejected the blandishments of Hollywood, who refused to compromise on the one script he had written for a studio, would now find himself working as script doctor on a film he despised and pulled into the psychodramas of the back lot. Eventually, he would write a screenplay for his wife in the desperate hope that it would simultaneously give her a chance to excel as an actress and mend a relationship already sliding towards collapse. The theatre, beyond a few false starts, fragments of plays that never quite cohered, was abandoned.

To be sure, audiences for his plays had begun to shrink and he found less and less common ground between himself and those he sought to address. He said later: 'I was just out of synch with the whole country ... I simply couldn't find a way into the country any more ... I had a sense that the time had gotten away from me.'[70] He found himself increasingly ostracized, but recognized in that sense of isolation not only a fate that he shared with others called before the Committee but one which the French writer Alexis de Tocqueville had identified well over a century earlier, when he noted the barriers to liberty of opinion in a country ready to punish the individual at odds with received opinion, an individual who was liable to find his friends silent and his enemies vocal in their hostility, until his own silence seemed the most logical if not the most moral recourse. No wonder he was fond of quoting de Tocqueville, whose *Democracy in America* had been reprinted at the end of the Second World War. Yet in the end it was not the loss of an audience that made him withdraw so much as the emotional demands of his new life which found him struggling to support a woman so much more profoundly damaged than he had ever imagined.

Removed from the pressures of their former life, they had discovered what they took to be, and was, for a time, a genuine happiness. But that came, in part at least, from the fact that they were escaping their problems, that they had abstracted themselves from a world they were about to rejoin. When they did take up their careers again, lay aside their fantasies of the future for the actualities of daily life and the pressures of the film industry, cracks quickly began to appear.

In July 1956, Miller put his Connecticut house up for sale. It went for $27,500. He was burning his bridges. At the same time there was unfinished business. Mary, whom he had first met as a radical young student in Michigan, who had borne him two children and shared his early failures and subsequent successes, now stayed behind in Brooklyn. She was financially secure – she had received their Brooklyn house on Willow Street plus a percentage of Miller's future earnings until she remarried, which she never did – but embittered. The newspapers were full of accounts of the glamorous life for which he had opted. The implication was that she had failed to offer what he needed. To her, he was choosing the very life he had once contemptuously dismissed as corrupt and corrupting. And there were the children to protect from the publicity.

Once they were old enough, she went back to university – City College – and obtained a masters degree in psychology, thereafter working as a psychological adviser with disturbed children in the public school system. She was based at the Northside Center in Harlem, founded and run by Dr Kenneth Clark. The pupils would come to her during school hours for help with their reading. She remained something of a radical, helping to form Union Local 1199 (a medical workers union), and had a distinguished career. When she retired, she continued to live in Brooklyn, having sold their old house and bought a large apartment. By then, though, she suffered from increasingly severe arthritis, which brought a halt to one of her favourite pastimes, walking in the city where she had come to live sixty years earlier.

Her life hardly closed down with the divorce. She travelled widely – Mexico, Japan, most of Europe – and remained active in a wide range of causes, including the Youth Center in Brooklyn. For many years she was on the board of her local library in Brooklyn Heights. But she remained bitter and angry; she felt, and played the role of the wronged wife, the victim. As a parent, though not strict, she was rigid in her views. As her son would later say, things were 'pretty much Black and White to her', in contrast to what he saw as his father's pragmatism. She might enjoy debate but she was not about to change her opinions, one of the reasons for the tension that had helped to undermine the marriage.

The effect of the divorce on the children, Miller conceded, must have been 'terrible', though he consoled himself with the thought that, as opposed to his own generation for which divorce carried a stigma, they lived at a time when 'people were divorcing all the time, especially in the level of society they were in. So I rather think that the impact was less than it might have been earlier.' That is not quite how his daughter Jane, a naturally reticent person, recalls it. 'At that time, of the kids that I knew, most of their parents were not divorced. In fact, off hand I can't think of any. So that alone was a little weird.'[71] And as David Mamet remarked of his parents, 'they got divorced in the 1950s and I didn't know anybody who'd been divorced . . . let alone have it happen to my family. So, there was a lot of trauma in my childhood.'[72]

At first, Jane went to a small school in Brooklyn, the largest class having six pupils, and then, not long after the divorce, to a school in Greenwich Village called the Little Red Schoolhouse. Though her father was now married to the most famous woman in America it was not something she wanted to talk about or even to be known. Under the divorce agreement, she and her brother saw their father once a week and every other weekend, if he was in New York. Robert recalls that his mother 'was always very scrupulous about making sure we were available and ready for these visits and seemed to genuinely encourage/support them within the boundaries of their agreement, at least ... However, if he'd cancel out at the last minute I would detect some annoyance or sarcasm.' But such occasions were rare. Robert could, though, feel the tension between them: 'Even the obligatory phone calls about one thing or another regarding us kids always seemed a bit strained to me, though they both seemed to listen attentively at those random times when I would mention something about one to the other.'[73] Miller conceded that 'Jane had a harder time, because there were probably some competitive feelings between her and Marilyn. It was inevitable.'[74]

At the age of fifteen she studied her father's plays in school and later went to his old university, at Michigan, for a year, majoring in music before dropping out. Having attended small schools she found the university intimidating. On returning to New York she did a series of part-time jobs and then went to the New School for Social Research, taking largely art classes. In 1965, she met a young sculptor, Tom Doyle, and in 1970 married him. They lived for many years in Three Springs, Pennsylvania, but then moved to Roxbury, building a house on land gifted to her by her father (land which had been part of his original Roxbury purchase but which he had retained when selling the house). Thirty acres were divided between Jane and her brother, Jane eventually buying his share since by this time he lived in California.

As for Robert, speaking in 2002:

I didn't try and keep quiet about Marilyn in the same way Jane did. I was a bit more naive as to what all the fuss was about – certainly in the beginning at least. I think as time went on and I began to get the hang of it, I developed a better sense of discretion – if that's the right word. To some degree I suppose I enjoyed some of the new-found attention it brought to me, but that rather quickly evolved into a somewhat healthier and realistic sense of scepticism as to how much of the fuss was really about ME. Finding the balance took some while and there were times when I'd go out of my way to avoid or protect that part of my life when dealing with outsiders, and at other times I suppose I'd play that card, if you will. It could be useful in a classroom situation, for example, to be able to speak from personal experience about an author.[75]

He attended casting sessions, rehearsals and openings of his father's plays whenever possible and remembers watching Kazan, Clurman and others, learning from them lessons he later put into practice when working in small theatres or directing TV commercials. He dropped out of college, where he had been involved in various student film projects, including briefly working on Brian De Palma's *Murder à la Mode*, and tried to make his way in film. He worked as a production assistant on *Midnight Cowboy* and *The Producers*. He did once rely on his father's help, to secure a job as gofer on *Up the Down Staircase*, but otherwise fought shy of using the connection until, with his father's agreement, he eventually set up the film version of *The Crucible*. Having originally moved to Eugene, Oregon, he then went to live in California where he also produced the film version of *Focus* in 2001.

The family now effectively reassembled itself, with one exception. The breach between Miller and Mary never healed. By 2001 she was suffering from what initially seemed like the early stages of Alzheimer's disease (though this may have been a series of small strokes), often getting lost as she ventured out on to the once familiar streets of Brooklyn where they had begun their married life just over sixty years earlier.

She subsequently moved to California. In later life, Miller met her only once, when they briefly encountered one another in a hospital when Kermit was ill. She had changed so much that he failed to recognize her until she spoke. Later, aware that part of his life was simply disappearing, he wondered what it would be like for them to meet again. He telephoned and suggested a meeting.

In the unpublished 'Constantine's Story', written in August 1985 and based in part on his own experiences, he had contemplated such a call and such a meeting. The story concerns a writer whose wife has been alienated by a brief affair, which he had once confessed. It was his only lapse. Her response has been coldness, a need for revenge. He has not seen her for over thirty years, and anyway believes their marriage was always a mistake. His own response to her accusations, he recalls, was to accuse her of a hardness of heart and an unforgiving nature.

Nonetheless, he calls her, seeking absolution, an absolution that would confirm her love for him in spite of everything, and thereby, paradoxically perhaps, his love for her, not now but in the past he is seeking to reinvent. He calls her and is shocked by her sixty-five-year-old voice. He asks whether she has time to see him. She replies, 'Why?' Because, he explains, they are both getting older and because . . . . He breaks off. In the story, the meeting takes place. In actuality, Mary refused.

11

MISFITS

For Miller and his new wife, the journey to England was about new beginnings. They hoped to find in one another an answer to their problems, a means of redefining themselves and their relationship to the world. 'I thought, and I think she did too, that we could build an open kind of existence, open in the sense that it was both spiritual, physical and even intellectual, because Marilyn was a very smart woman. She would have been capable, had her psychological problems been reduced – I don't think they could ever have been solved – of anything. She could learn anything instantly.' Though, in contradiction to others, he never saw her finish a book ('If they saw it, I never did'), he thought 'maybe she didn't have to. She was too distracted, though she did read two or three of my books. I think she read *Salesman* and she read *The Crucible*.'[1]

When they married they had had little time together. Theirs was a high-adrenaline relationship, charged with the excitement that initially came with secrecy. They had snatched hours, days together, but always under the pressure of events. The only relief had come when they retreated to the farm they bought at Roxbury, then much more isolated than today. Speaking in Roxbury in 2002, Miller recalled: 'Nobody bothered us here, but the echoes were always coming at you through the telephone. It's true. We were in a pressure cooker.' The hope was that in Europe things might be different. In the event, they were not. 'It happened that it was a terribly tense era in her life, and in my life, and it would have been a miracle for any marriage to survive that.'[2]

Two weeks after marrying, on 13 July 1956, they left for London. This was to be a working honeymoon and Miller's real introduction into what life with a filmstar wife would be like. They travelled with twenty-seven suitcases and excess baggage charges of $1,500, itself something of an initiation, for Miller, into a world of excess at odds with his own instincts.

They left the aircraft at Croydon, the old wartime airfield then London's main airport, both dressed in white, bringing with them, it seemed, a touch of California glamour to a still somewhat austere Britain. This was a glamour that was natural enough for Marilyn but scarcely for her husband, who had the air of an actor wearing his costume for the first time. They were welcomed by Olivier and his wife Vivien Leigh, she wearing a pert hat as if off to a garden party. Two sets of theatrical royalty met to the click of camera shutters and in the magnesium glare of flashbulbs so bright that, Miller later recalled, he could barely see the four hundred journalists gathered for the occasion. If he had expected the privacy denied them in the United States, he was quickly disabused, as they were greeted and pursued by press and public alike.

There was also a third person in their party, Paula Strasberg, to be employed for a minimum of $25,000 for ten weeks' work. Marilyn became ever more dependent on her as combination drama coach and psychotherapist, boosting the confidence of an actress on whom she increasingly relied for her own sense of self-importance. Olivier was not the first director to find her presence less than helpful. As he later remarked, 'Paula knew nothing, she was no actress, no director, no teacher, no adviser – except in Marilyn's eyes, for she had one talent: she could butter Marilyn up.' He recalled a car journey during which he had listened as she had told Marilyn:

> My dear, you really must recognize your own potential, you haven't even yet any idea of the importance of your position in the world, you are the greatest sex symbol in human memory, everybody knows and recognizes that and you should too, it's a duty which you owe to yourself and to the world, it's ungrateful not to accept it. You are the greatest woman of your time, the greatest human being of your time; of any time, you name it; you can't think of anybody, I mean – no, not even Jesus – except you're more popular.[3]

Colin Clark, third director (or gofer) on the picture, heard a similar encomium: 'All my life I've prayed for God to give me a truly great actress. You are that actress.'[4] Paula Strasberg's skills lay less in her abilities as a drama coach, he insisted, than in her fluency in sycophancy.

The flight had lasted an exhausting twelve hours and Miller and his wife felt drained as they were driven into the Surrey countryside, where they were to stay at Parkside House, owned by the publisher of the *Financial Times*, Lord North. They retired to bed only to be woken by a schoolboy choir serenading them.

Olivier visited them the following morning, 'on a fine English day that seemed full of hope'.[5] The same day Marilyn appeared at a press conference at the Savoy Hotel. Predictably, she was an hour late.

For the first few weeks, everything went well, with Miller working on *A View from the Bridge* in the music room and Marilyn filming at Shepperton Studios. Distance from the political turmoil of America seemed to offer the opportunity of a new start. As other American artists had discovered, Britain seemed immune to the kind of Cold War hysteria that had made life uncomfortable for so many.

By degrees, though, familiar problems began to emerge – familiar, that is, to those who worked with Marilyn, if not yet to her husband. If movie-making was her profession it was also a kind of agony for her as she tried to learn her lines and win what seemed to her necessary battles with those she believed belittled her. Having struggled for so long for respect, she seems to have convinced herself that this was a matter of power. If she was late on the set or demanded constant retakes, this placed her at the centre of attention. If it was necessary to propitiate her, it was obvious from this that she was the key ingredient in the film. She was also, though, nervous, unsure of herself even as she demanded praise. This was doubly true in a film in which the director and co-star had an unequalled reputation in the theatre and commanded respect for the serious roles he had played in the movies. One scene, in which she had to eat caviar, took two days of shooting, thirty-four takes and twenty jars of caviar. Olivier suggested that she should simply mime, rather than actually eat it, but she refused. She also refused to allow the substitution of apple juice for the champagne she was supposedly drinking. As a result she began to slur her lines. Another scene required thirty takes (which Olivier called 'an historic amount') as she repeatedly forgot her lines.

Colin Clark observed that she did not so much forget her lines as give the impression that she had never learned them in the first place. In the opening shot she had a hard time delivering the line 'Oui', in response to a question in French. Later she had trouble with the word 'No'. And as the tension mounted so she resorted to her habit of drinking gin with her morning tea and taking the 'uppers' she required to get through the day, supplies administered by the ever-attentive Paula Strasberg.

Nor had Miller and his new wife escaped public pressures, a fact which came as an unwelcome surprise: 'We were totally unprepared. In a desperate attempt to normalize life she wanted to go shopping in a department store. She had heard of Harrods but in order for her to go shopping they had to close the store, empty it out, at mid-day. I don't think the Queen of England could cause such a situation.'[6] Things were hardly helped when members of staff at Parkside House began leaking stories to the press.

As the film progressed, so the tensions increased Marilyn's sense of inse-curity. Simple fear led to sleepless nights, remedied by drugs, and difficult days in which she sustained herself with more drugs. She also deployed manipulative tactics designed to protect herself against what she increasingly felt to be the condescension of those around her, particularly that of Olivier, whose impatience was quickly hardening into anger. When she was late he demanded that she apologize to Sybil Thorndike, who had been waiting on set. As it happened, Sybil Thorndike was her greatest supporter, but the demand further soured the relationship between star and director. For Miller, this all came as a revelation and a shock as he found himself drawn into her battles with Olivier, who he was by no means convinced was at fault, a fact which she quickly detected and resented. Within weeks of their marriage they seemed, as a result, increasingly at odds. As he remarked in May 2002:

> I felt defeated, but I was also determined, and I believed it was possible that we could make a life together once this was over. But it kept getting more and more dense with difficulties and of course it played right into her main problem which was that she was abandoned and the least criticism, the most remote kind of criticism she immediately picked up on as a prelude to another abandonment, because that was the pattern she understood . . . the pathology set in fairly soon. Unfortunately, she was under tremendous pressure because she was performing with the fabulous Olivier, who at that time, to Americans anyway, represented the ultimate acting talent. Here she was trying to prove herself as a performer, so that she was scared. She needed all the reassurance she could get and there wasn't enough in the world to do that. Unfortunately, it was right after our marriage.[7]

After two weeks of filming he flew back to New York, via Paris, to see his children, using an assumed name in order to avoid press interest. (Nonetheless, the *New York Daily News* announced his arrival on 29 August and his departure on 12 September, a fact duly noted in his FBI file.)[8] Marilyn was not pleased and called a halt to filming, claiming to be suffering from colitis but in fact, it was assumed, resentful at being deserted at a time when she was feeling particularly vulnerable. There was, however, another reason. She had been told in late August that she was expecting a baby. She lost it almost immediately. With Miller absent, gofer Clark had assumed the unlikely and hardly credible role of comforter and adviser. In that role he had stayed in her room one night when she awoke in pain, immediately confessing that she was having a miscarriage: "'It was Arthur's,' Marilyn said, between sobs. 'It was for him. He didn't know. It was going to be a surprise. Then he would see that I could be a real wife, and a real mother.'" Asked how long she had been pregnant, she replied, "'Just a few weeks, I guess . . . I didn't dare mention it to anyone, in case it wasn't true.'"[9]

The FBI, meanwhile, did more than note Miller's movements. On 2 October a memo was sent from the Director of the Bureau to Assistant Attorney General William F. Tomkins in response to a request dated 21 September. It stated:

> The New Haven and Salt Lake City Offices should promptly review their files regarding subject and submit the results to the Bureau and New York, the office of origin . . . In view of the fact that the above action is being taken at the request of the Department of Justice and of the publicity which is

likely to be involved in any legal action concerning subject, any positive results obtained must be submitted in report form at the earliest possible date.

The memo was headed: 'ARTHUR ASHER MILLER SECURITY MATTER – FRAUD AGAINST THE GOVERNMENT – PER-JURY.'[10] The same day, a memo from the New York office noted: 'A review of defected Communists in the New York area suggested none who would logically be in a position to furnish information regarding ARTHUR MILLER.' The memo also noted that a woman (whose name is blanked out) 'refused to furnish any information and cannot be regarded as available to testify in this matter. A review of her case file and the case file on various Stuyvesant Clubs of the CP in the New York area reflected no former Stuyvesant Club members who could be considered as potential witnesses in captioned matter.'[11] The Los Angeles office was not to be requested to recontact an individual (whose name is also blanked out) 'inasmuch as information that informant could furnish on this matter would be only hearsay'.

Eight days later, a reply arrived from the Salt Lake City office stating that a 'review of the Salt Lake City Division files does not reflect any information tending to establish that MILLER falsified his affidavit [the one he had signed in applying for a passport].' A review of the New Haven files also turned up nothing of interest. On 11 October, somewhat belatedly, a memo was sent from the Director of the FBI to the Legal Attaché in London which stated that 'Subject MILLER is the new husband of MARILYN MONROE.' The nature of the request accompanying this statement is unknown, being blanked out, but it asked that the FBI be kept informed.

On his return to England, Miller found Marilyn angry not only with him, for his absence, and Olivier, for what she took to be his condescension, but also with Milton Greene, part-owner of her company. He was, she believed, buying antiques and shipping them back to America at her expense. She was accordingly disenchanted with the partnership and urged her husband to intervene while aware that to do so might disrupt their arrangement at a delicate time.

On 19 September, Marilyn declared that she was not satisfied with the car assigned to her. She wanted a Jaguar. Greene suspected that the request had actually come from Miller and that he would simply ship it back to America for his own use. The two men were increasingly at odds. Hearing that Greene was to be dropped from Monroe Productions, apparently at Miller's behest, Maurice Zolotow cabled him on 24 October asking him to confirm that this was, indeed, the case. Miller cabled a tart reply, saying that he had no connection with Marilyn Monroe Productions beyond the fact that its president was his wife. He had, he asserted, no more than a family interest in his wife's business affairs. He dismissed stories about a break with Greene as no more than space fillers for columnists with nothing else to hand.

What was not true then, though, would be later, as he was pulled ever deeper into Marilyn's affairs. Whatever he might be doing or not doing with antiques, Greene had negotiated a deal which left him with half the income from the production company. Against his better instincts Miller thus felt obliged to involve himself in his wife's business affairs as, equally reluctantly, he found himself party to her disputes with Olivier. In April 1957, Greene would sell his stock in Monroe Productions.

On 3 October, Lee Strasberg flew in from New York. Olivier was furious. Colin Clark noted him saying, 'I'm the fucking director of the film. I'm the producer, too. Fuck it. We aren't a bunch of psychoanalysts. We're making a film.' He told Greene that Strasberg should be banned from the set. By 30 October, however, he was lamenting that 'The bloody Strasbergs have won the day. It's a fucking nightmare.'

In the midst of all this, Miller found time to begin a short story, based on the two cowboys he had encountered in Nevada while establishing the residential requirement for his Reno divorce: *The Misfits*. He worked on the story even as he collaborated with Peter Brook on *A View from the Bridge*, turning the original one-act play into two acts while auditioning actors for the minor roles. 'Perhaps,' he later reflected, 'in the nearly two years since writing it, I had learned to suspend judgment somewhat and to cease holding myself apart from the ranks of driven men – and not as a matter of principle but for real.'[12]

Meanwhile, tension on the set of *The Prince and the Showgirl* mounted. Anthony Holden recounts an encounter between director and actress in which Olivier's patience finally cracked. 'Why can't you get here on time, for fuck's sake?' he asked, to which she replied, 'Oh ... do you have that word here in England, too?'[13] According to Miller, the disillusionment was shared. If Olivier had now long since forgotten that he had anticipated an affair, she was finding that he, who had once represented the purity of the theatre to her, was increasingly petulant and unappreciative of her qualities.

To her, this was an acting challenge in which she could draw on the lessons she had learned at the Actors Studio, reinforced by the presence of Paula Strasberg. For Olivier, it was a light comedy that required no more than her natural talent. To Marilyn, though, there was much more at stake. It was the beginning of a new phase in her work. Here, after all, was a film that was to be untainted by Hollywood values, made in a country whose theatrical tradition had always commanded American respect. Olivier carried no such baggage. As far as he was concerned, the film simply required the reproduction of a stage role he had already mastered, while as director all he demanded was professionalism of a kind he felt he had from his British cast but that he now despaired of finding in his American star.

From her point of view, if he seemed to lack sympathy as a director, as actor he was trying to vie for screen attention with her, and that was something she believed she understood. In his autobiography Miller noted that she came to think that he was 'trying to compete with her like another woman, a coquette drawing the audience's sexual attention away from herself'.[14] Indeed, looking back, he was inclined to think that Marilyn was probably correct in her belief that Olivier hated women. At the time, though, he still seemed the great actor Miller had admired in *Oedipus Rex*. The idea that he would wish to upstage his fellow star seemed absurd. Increasingly, he found himself defending a man with whom he felt a powerful affinity. Speaking in May 2002, he acknowledged that it was 'at that time that I thought, mistakenly, that I ought to enforce Olivier's standing with her, because after all he had to direct her and play scenes with her. She couldn't trash him too much or where would she be? She would be left with nobody on the set. And so I found myself defending him, and that was the worst possible thing I could have done. But I don't think any other course would have mattered, either.'

Nor, as far as he could see, was Olivier condescending to his American star. The problem went deeper and was, accordingly, the more serious. Two decades later he would offer an explanation for her behaviour and for the friction which, this early, began to enter their relationship:

> What gradually began to dawn on me . . . was her expectation of abandonment all over again; it was the blood of this terror that engorged what might have been a mere conflict of opinions. We were trying to hear each other through the echoes between two arguments – one about Olivier, and the deeper subterranean struggle against what she saw as her fate . . . She could not bear contradiction in any detail on this question of Olivier's knowing betrayal of her expectations, but far worse than that, she was laboring with how I fit into the pattern of disappointment. I could hardly help my alarmed protests for my own sake and the truth as I saw it. She was felled by my stubbornness, everything was over; if she was so opposed she could not be loved.[15]

He admitted that the dynamics of a movie set, the potentially competing systems of power, the vulnerabilities generated by performance under the exigencies of film-making, were as yet alien to him; that his own instinctive defence of Olivier might to some degree be a product of his own enthusiasms and commitments, and that Olivier was, perhaps, rather too arch in his comments and mechanistic in his direction. Nonetheless, under the pressures of filming Miller's relationship with his wife was already changing.

Alone together in a room in the Waldorf Towers, or her apartment at Sutton Place, they had seemed a mutual resource, a defence against their quite separate dilemmas. Each idealized the other, seeing in one another hope for a transformed future. Now, their pleasure in each other's company was tempered by new tensions. 'We had to learn how to live very close to our real feelings without burning up. Too much truth can kill ... Truth-telling, all that could rescue us both, could also be dangerous when she needed every shred of reassurance to get through a working day.'[16] She did not, he quickly came to realize, require an analytic mind or an objective overview. She needed unquestioning and absolute support and when it was not forthcoming was on the lookout for other evidence of betrayals.

It was during the shooting of the *The Prince and the Showgirl* that Marilyn allegedly discovered a note in which Miller had recorded his feelings about his new wife, expressing his sense of shock that he could have made the same mistake twice and confessing that he could think of no legitimate response to Olivier's growing anger and resentment at her. Certainly the Strasbergs, scarcely disinterested parties, claimed to have been told as much when they spent a weekend at Egham with the Millers. Lee Strasberg later remembered a tearful Marilyn telling him, 'It was something about how disappointed he was with me ... How he thought I was some kind of angel but now he guessed he was wrong. That his first wife had let him down, but I had done something worse. Olivier was beginning to think I was a troublesome bitch and that he (Arthur) no longer had a decent answer to that one.'[17] Colin Clark recounts a conversation, admittedly recalled forty years later, which seems to confirm this:

> Colin [she whispered], I have to tell you something. There is a part of me that is very ugly. Something which comes from being so ambitious, I guess. Something to do with all the things I've done – not bad things, but selfish things. I've slept with too many men, that's for sure. And I've been unfaithful so often I couldn't remember. Somehow sex didn't seem that important when I was a kid. But now I want people to respect me and to be faithful to me, and they never are. I want to find someone to love me – ugliness and beauty and all. But people only see the glamour and fall in love with that, and then when they see the ugly side they run away. That's what Arthur has done now. Before he left for Paris he wrote a note saying that he was disappointed in me. I saw it on his desk. I think he meant for me to see it ... Arthur says I don't think enough, but it seems I'm only happy when I don't think ... You don't think he's going to leave me, then? You think he'll come back?[18]

She allegedly told a similar story (minus the doubts about her husband returning) to Milton Greene, himself still at odds with Miller; and just such an incident occurs in *After the Fall* as the protagonist Quentin confesses that he has written 'a letter from hell' in an attempt to register and understand his feelings, a letter discovered by his wife Maggie, the character squarely based on Monroe. Miller long denied this, having, he insisted, invented the scene for the play. Later, however, he conceded that that July he had belatedly come to the conclusion that he had made a mistake and might have written something to that effect.

Back in Reno, he had listened over the phone to her complaints about a director and his failure to respect her. He knew nothing, then, of her reputation, though he was aware, at some level, of her fragility. In Washington, he had been confronted with her resentment when he appeared preoccupied with his appearance before HUAC and failed to share his worries with her. Then he had apologized. Now he was dismayed by what he witnessed and experienced. Her anger and resentment, initially directed at Olivier, had been turned on him.

The crisis seemed to pass, but already there was scar tissue. He found himself crossing the line between reassurance and uncritical praise, since this seemed what his wife needed, her insecurities proving immune to anything else. But this, in turn, meant the injection into their relationship of a new kind of deceit, a betrayal that was not sexual but in some ways more dangerous since it meant that they were edging towards a sense of unreality. For Miller, the 'worst of it was that any attempt to reduce the problem to reason implied that she was following a fantasy. And so the great wobbling wheel of emotions was setting itself into place, turning around the axial question of good faith.'[19] So bad did things become that, part of the way through the filming, Marilyn's psychoanalyst flew in from New York. Here was one more person in whom she could confide, one more defence against what she saw as Olivier's aggressive arrogance. Looking back, Miller said:

> I wasn't prepared for what I should have been prepared for, which was that she had literally no inner resources. If she sensed that Olivier had some underlying contempt – which I denied at the time, since I was trying to keep things happy, though she was right – once she had sensed that, or even any hostility, even though he would restrain it the best he could, because he wanted to get that picture finished, he wanted to act with her ... it was as though he had actually taken out a weapon and threatened her. You couldn't say to her: 'Everyone has hostile feelings of one kind or another, or envious feelings or anxious feelings. All that counts is what they act out, otherwise you would be in a constant state of suspicion about everyone and anyone.' That's not the way she could operate. As soon as there was any sign that she detected, sometimes real, sometimes not, it was as if somebody had actually attacked her, or was on the verge of attacking. This led to a life that was full of suspicion and it got to be very difficult very early on.[20]

Asked how long it was before he realized he had made a mistake in marrying, he replied:

Some months. But I expected that it would change. I figured she was under
terrible tension. As soon as that disappeared, the symptoms would disappear.
And they would at times. My tendency was to diminish any feelings of my
own that this was a dangerous situation, figuring ... that her real nature was
cheerful and optimistic. And it wasn't until we began to approach *The Misfits*
that I thought there was no hope for us, or for her. I remember thinking that
she couldn't go on indefinitely this way.

Miller and Olivier were drawn together not only by mutual respect but also
by the shared problems they were experiencing with their respective wives.
Vivien Leigh was mentally unstable and had a history of psychiatric problems.
She behaved increasingly oddly, her illness sometimes taking the form of
nymphomania. During the shooting of the film she also suffered a miscarriage.

To a degree the two men confided in one another, though, just married,
Miller was still inclined to defend his wife while feeling an increasing despair.
Then there was the question of his own work. It was already becoming clear
that Marilyn's problems were going to command time he would previously
have given to his work. To be sure, he continued preparations for the London
opening of *A View from the Bridge*, but he now found himself involved in the
daily business of supporting her in her struggles, real or imagined, and
emotionally drained by her demands that he defend her against those she
believed belittled and exploited her. For the moment, there was little she
could do about her suspicions of Olivier and Greene, with both of whom she
needed to cooperate, at least up to a point: but 'Toward me her disappointment
could flow, since she probably knew that I would take it and come back',
while she 'had no means of preventing the complete unraveling of her belief
in a person once a single thread was broken'.[21]

Things now took a further turn when, after a brief visit to the United
States, Paula was refused a work permit by the British immigration service.
Marilyn announced she would withdraw from the picture. After hectic nego-
tiations, the permit was forthcoming. The incident simultaneously revealed
her dependency and Paula's power. Miller, too, had his brush with the Home
Office, being summoned by an official anxious to know whether he planned
to stay beyond the shooting of the picture and the work he was doing with
Peter Brook. Such was the atmosphere in America that it seemed entirely
possible that he might choose to stay, thereby politically embarrassing the
British government.

He would hardly be the first. The director Joseph Losey, in flight from
HUAC, had already settled in England, as had the harmonica player and
composer Larry Adler, though in his case only to find that he was not entirely
immune even here. When the film of *Genevieve*, for which he wrote the
music, was due for release in America, the distributors demanded that his

name be removed from the credits. The Rank Organization complied. For Adler, though, this was an exception. When a Catholic organization called Val Parnell, impresario at the London Palladium, and demanded that Adler be dropped from the bill as a subversive, Parnell indignantly refused. The British government, though, was nervous enough to seek reassurance from Miller – the government which, that same year and under American pressure, decided against awarding a knighthood to Charlie Chaplin because of his supposed communist leanings.

Though their relationship had been damaged, for a time Miller and his wife retrieved something of their feelings of the previous year. He would cycle the ten miles to Shepperton Studios to see her, and in the breaks from filming they cycled together around the countryside and through Windsor Great Park as they had through Central Park and the streets of Brooklyn. The English summer was far removed from the heat of New York, and for a few hours they felt free of the political pressures at home and the problems on the film set. Once again she spoke of her wish to study literature and history and of the house they planned back in Roxbury. But it was only a momentary distraction.

He was also having problems with his work, having made his first acquaint-ance with one of the more arcane of British public offices, that of the Lord Chamberlain, who, until 1968, would have the power to censor plays. He had taken exception to *A View from the Bridge*, not because of the quasi-incestuous impulse at its heart but because Eddie Carbone chooses to humiliate Rodol-pho by kissing him on the mouth. Homosexuality was illegal in Britain, and since Eddie wishes to expose a man whose heterosexual rivalry he cannot acknowledge by implying that he is homosexual, the Lord Chamberlain took accusation for fact and saw the action as a provocation. He therefore refused to license the play for the public stage. There was a crisis.

Britain being what it was, however, where respect for art failed, legalistic hypocrisy prevailed. What was impermissible on the public stage became permissible in private, so that members of the audience were invited to pay a membership fee, supposedly to join a private club, before paying the normal ticket price. What was shocking thus became perfectly acceptable. It was an incident that opened Miller's eyes to the nature of the British theatre, as the British theatre, in turn, responded to the disturbing power of an American theatre for which sexuality was a natural subject and metaphor. Intrigued, Miller wondered where the extra money was going. The answer was, to the producer.

At Marilyn's suggestion, she, her husband and Olivier took an evening off to see a new play called *Look Back in Anger*, chosen by Marilyn purely on the basis of its title. It was a work that not only changed the direction of British theatre but was also to transform Olivier's career, as his initial hostility gave way to enthusiasm to the extent of his approaching its author, John Osborne, with a view to appearing in one of his subsequent plays. The result was *The Entertainer* which proved crucial to Olivier's desire to reinvent himself as an actor.

Ironically, the Royal Court Theatre, home to Osborne's play, chose this moment to host a meeting, to which Miller was invited, called 'Cause without a Rebel', in which British writers and critics including Colin Wilson, Wolf Mankowitz, John Whiting and Kenneth Tynan met to discuss what then seemed the weakness of the British theatre. For the previous ten years the American theatre had appeared to many in Britain to be the more compelling, unmired, as it was, in class presumptions and unhindered by censorship. But suddenly things were changing, and as a result of Marilyn's desire for a night out Miller had been present at what, retrospectively, was to seem a key moment in the history of postwar British theatre.

A View from the Bridge opened on 11 October 1956. Marilyn arrived in a scarlet satin gown so tight around the knees that the *Daily Mail* reporter was astonished she could walk. She was, she told reporters, 'just Mrs Miller tonight'. She sat between her husband and Olivier. For the most part, the play received excellent reviews, Kenneth Tynan greeting it as 'just short of being a masterpiece'. Harold Hobson, who had used the same word to describe the New York production, thought the expanded text less forceful but still 'very good'. Anthony Quayle, for all his suspect accent, was praised for his performance as Eddie.

The trip to England was briefly lightened by the arrival of Norman and Hedda Rosten, the latter, at Miller's urging, functioning as Marilyn's secretary. At the very least she would be another confidante, an alternative to Paula Strasberg who seemed to support Marilyn in her suspicions and her professional waywardness. With her training as a psychiatric social worker, Hedda could also see the strain they were both under. But even she fell foul of Marilyn's anger and frustration, not least because she was herself drinking heavily. She returned to Brooklyn before the film was complete.

There was also further trouble with Milton Greene. He had begun to discuss various projects with Jack Cardiff, cinematographer on the film. The idea was to establish a British offshoot of Marilyn Monroe Productions that would take advantage of subsidies on offer to British film-makers. Cardiff already held various options, including Henry James's *The Turn of the Screw*, which he would later direct under the title *The Innocents*, with Deborah Kerr in the role originally proposed for Marilyn. Greene, who had not discussed the idea with either Marilyn or her new husband, announced the plans to the press. The result was a widening of the gap between the two principal shareholders of the company.

Despite the delays, *The Prince and the Showgirl* was finished on time.

Olivier even had the luxury of two days of re-shooting, to which his star agreed, sensing weaknesses in the final product. Ironically, for a film in which no one quite believed, it turned out to be entirely serviceable and Monroe's performance, as Olivier was to admit, ultimately more satisfying than his own.

The film once in the can, in November the Millers left, following a public farewell with the Oliviers designed to squash rumours of discord. It was a carefully staged performance, wholly lacking in sincerity. Both Marilyn and Vivien Leigh were in a delicate mental state, while Miller and Olivier were acutely aware of the fragility of their marriages. For Miller, the trip, the Peter Brook production of *A View from the Bridge* aside, had been a disaster. As he was to remark, 'England ... had humbled both of us.'[22] Determined to start afresh, they first went on a two-week delayed honeymoon, to Ocho Rios in Jamaica – though, slightly oddly, with Morton Miller and his wife. It was a relaxing affair and their English experience began to seem an aberration. They walked on the beach together and watched as the fishermen landed fish, though the sight of those fish gasping for air on the sand distressed Marilyn. On returning to the city from Idlewild (now Kennedy) Airport they came across the body of a dog, run over by a car. According to Morton, 'Marilyn shut her eyes tight, covered her face with her hands, and shrieked.'[23] She was, Miller conceded, 'over the top about animals, children, old people. She could be fierce about protecting them. She would empathize, she would identify in a way that was total. She became a fish. She would get absolutely outraged that somebody had killed a fish. Although she ate fish, she didn't want to see them murdered.'[24]

It was this kind of sensitivity that Miller would see again later that year and which he would eventually capture in *The Misfits*, but it did not always extend to human beings. Not only was she peremptory with those she encountered on the movie set, but when a maid failed to follow orders to her satisfaction she was immediately fired. Also, as already noted, she had no compunction about keeping other people waiting. As Morton Miller recalled, 'In their apartment I can see her, an hour late already, fussing in the master bedroom, attended by her maid, dressmaker, hair stylist, and makeup man, while a group of us, party-dressed, waited. Surveying the assemblage Arthur tried to cover his embarrassment and quipped: "Looks like a bar mitzvah."'[25]

Miller and his wife now moved between their new apartment on 57th Street, with a room off the vestibule for May Reis, Marilyn's secretary inherited from Elia Kazan, and a summer home in Amagansett, on the southside of Long Island. Miller's old house in Roxbury had been bought by the critic John Aldridge (later it would be sold on to fellow playwright Tom Cole). Miller now looked for a new one, sometimes taking his son

Robert with him. In New York, Marilyn would spend mornings with her analyst Dr Kris, and afternoons with the Strasbergs who still gave her private lessons, both, coincidentally, living at 135 Central Park West. With *The Prince and the Showgirl* now behind her, it was as if the problems in England had been wished away, though the break-up of the partnership with Milton Greene as well as press stories about Marilyn's past affairs, meant that things were far from easy.

Miller now had to face the contempt proceedings that had been hanging over his head for a year. On 18 February 1957 he was indicted on two counts, one for each of the questions he had refused to answer, and released on a $1,000 bond. On 16 May, an affidavit by Miller was placed in the record of the Federal District Court by his lawyers. In this he denied ever having been under communist discipline. Richard Arens, Staff Director of the Committee, responded by asserting that a person who attended meetings to which only known communists were invited must have been under communist discipline. The hearings took place before Federal Judge Charles F. McLaughlin, who on 21 May rejected attempts by Miller's attorney, Joseph Rauh Jr, to introduce his client's relationship with Monroe into the hearing. Rauh had argued that Miller had been called as a witness merely in order to secure publicity. The judge found the motion to acquit on these grounds to be 'irrelevant and immaterial'.

That evening, William Hitz, Assistant US Attorney prosecuting the case, advised the Washington Field Office of the FBI that 'the defense was going to use an expert witness in an effort to refute Government testimony concerning the issue of how it can be determined if a person is under communist discipline. He [Hitz] requested identification of the defense witness if known to the Bureau, and any authoritative statements made by the Director relating to the issue of communist discipline.' He was duly advised that

> the identity of the defense witness was not known on the basis of available information and that the problem concerning Communist Party discipline was a problem which had been handled on previous occasions by Department attorneys in Smith Act trials [through] the use of former communists as witnesses and recorded statements of Marx and Lenin. It was suggested that he discuss this matter with Department experts in the Internal Security Division.

The attorney in the Internal Security Division also approached the Bureau requesting copies of the constitution of the Communist Party of the USA.

The Bureau contacted Hitz and explained that while they had no direct knowledge of the mystery witness, both the *Washington Post* and the *Times Herald* had suggested that it was Harry P. Cain, former member of the

Subversive Activities Control Board. Hitz rejected the idea, insisting that the story had been 'dreamed up' by a newspaperman and that there was no factual basis for it. However, he had learned from Miller's attorney that the witness was a former investigator who lived within a thousand miles of Washington, not, perhaps, an over-precise identification but one that he hoped would be sufficient. The witness, he added, would be arriving at two or three in the morning. A recess of a day was granted.

In order to prove that Miller had been under communist discipline, Hitz repeated his request for 'all the authoritative statements made by the Director on the existence of communist discipline and how to determine if a person is under communist discipline'. Alarm bells began to ring. The Bureau replied: 'It is not believed that such statements should be made available; it is doubtful if they could be introduced; if they were, they might well result in a request for the Director's appearance as an expert witness.' It was plainly more important to protect the Director than help the prosecution. The Bureau discretely reminded Hitz that it had no substantive jurisdiction in contempt-of-court cases. Hitz replied 'that he desperately needed this material'.[26]

In the *New Republic* of 27 May 1957, Harry Kalven Jr, professor of law at the University of Chicago, in an article that Miller's lawyers forwarded to their client, explored the possibilities. He noted, in particular, the irony by which the power to compel testimony before congressional committees had originally been supported by liberals – such as the then professor Felix Frankfurter – and opposed by conservatives on the grounds of individual liberty. The attitude tended to vary according to the subject of the investigation. He noted, too, the continuing debate over the scope and validity of such committees whose justification supposedly lay in gathering information for subsequent legislation.

Less than ten years before, in 1948, an attempt in the Court of Appeals to challenge investigative powers on the grounds of the First Amendment free-speech provision had foundered because public interest was ruled to take precedence. Nonetheless, the dissenting opinion of Judge Egerton was that 'Civil liberties may not be abridged in order to determine whether they should be abridged. The House Committee's investigation is both intended and likely to restrict expression of opinion that Congress may not prohibit. That it actually does so is clear and undisputed ... What Congress may not restrain, Congress may not restrain by exposure and obloquy.'[27] Despite the cogency of the argument, it seemed to Professor Kalven that it would fail again in Miller's case.

Miller's lawyers had already made it clear that they would contest the findings on another ground. The hearings had ostensibly been called to investigate a possible passport fraud by Miller. The question, therefore, was what relevance questions about other individuals attending Communist Party meetings would have to this, and, indeed, Judge McLaughlin had made it clear that this was the pertinent question. Kalven, however, believed that Miller had refused to answer the wrong questions. The questions he should have refused to answer were those relating to Communist China and Ezra Pound, which could hardly be said to be relevant either to the issue of his passport or to legislative requirements. Kalven's judgement was that Miller would lose, and he was right.

At the hearing Rauh duly flourished his witness, who had arrived from Florida. It was indeed former Senator Harry P. Cain. It was unusual for anyone other than the government to invoke expert testimony with respect to those believed to be under Communist Party discipline. The routine, as Miller explained, was usually 'an exact duplication of the use of clergy as experts on witchcraft in the Salem of 1692'. The Reverend Hale in *The Crucible* had ultimately defected from the prosecution's side and so had Harry Cain, who was, as Miller observed, 'one of a very few Red-hunters to have turned against the whole business'.[28] He had originally been supported by Senator McCarthy, had called for the deportation of Charlie Chaplin and had been head of the Subversive Activities Control Group (SACB) charged with keeping subversives out of government. When he had begun to doubt the validity of many of the accusations he processed, he was summarily fired. Now he appeared to assure the Court that Miller's plays showed no evidence of communist influence, in truth a rather curious strategy.

A memo to the Director of the FBI on 23 May reported that 'Hitz advised that the defense had former Senator Harry P. Cain, and former member of the SACB, qualified as an expert witness for the defense', but noted that

> Hitz does not feel that CAIN was a particularly good witness for the defense. When HITZ asked him how he (CAIN) would determine if a person was under CP discipline CAIN replied that he would study his life, his actions, his writings and his speeches. However, with respect to the defendant (MILLER) CAIN stated that as a professional writer it would only be necessary to study MILLER'S writings to determine if he were under CP discipline. HITZ pointed out that this was inconsistent with his previous statement.
>
> DONALD APPELL, HCUA, who was present during the questioning of CAIN, stated that it was his impression that CAIN was a better witness for the government than he was for MILLER.[29]

It seems they were both right. Certainly, on the 31st Judge McLaughlin of the District Court found Miller guilty on both counts on the authority of United States v. Watkins, a case still under appeal to the Supreme Court. He was sentenced to a $500 fine and a month in prison, with the prison sentence suspended, pending a probation report. Another man, Otto Nathan, was convicted alongside him. Twenty-four years later, as executor and trustee of the Albert Einstein estate he wrote to Miller recalling this moment and asking if he still had a letter of appreciation that Einstein had sent to him after reading his novel *Focus*.

With the trial over, Miller issued an extensive statement, making clear his position. Gone was the apologetic tone of the hearings, the anxiety to accommodate himself to the less contentious demands of the Committee. The press release he now issued was more like a manifesto:

> It should be easy for me to name those writers with whom I met some ten years ago. I am opposed to Communism and what ideology I profess is thoroughly democratic. Furthermore, I am and have been for some years now, on a blacklist which forbids the purchase of any of my works by motion picture or television companies in the United States. To get off this blacklist would mean a great increase in my income, and I can get off in the time it takes to say the half dozen or so names I remember of people I knew to be Communists. By uttering a certain number of syllables I would become what is called a 'good American', and I should then be permitted to earn my living as an American writer ordinarily does.
>
> I am not going to say those syllables. It would be well, I think, for the American people to understand why.
>
> 1. I did nothing illegal in associating at one time with Communists. The Government, in fact, does not even contend that it was illegal. It is merely using my refusal to lower myself in order to punish me and to destroy whatever influence my work exerts.
>
> 2. It is perfectly clear to me that the Government knows the names it is demanding of me, and this from its own informants.
>
> 3. The names of these people have no conceivable connection with national security, and I have had no connection with them for many years.
>
> 4. I do not believe that a person, under fierce pressure from Government, who professes patriotism is necessarily a patriot in his heart; and I refused to join those who have degraded patriotism by mouthing its praises on pain of being relegated to the twilight zone of their professions ...
>
> 5. I will not accede to the demands of the House Committee on UnAmerican Activities because in my case I believe those demands degrade the Government of the United States ...
>
> 6. The Committee's Chief Counsel, Mr Arens, recently held forth in New Haven, Connecticut. He took occasion severely to criticize a rabbi for

officiating at my wedding last summer, and at the same time called me a
dangerous Communist . . .

7. . . . The hope was expressed during my hearing in Washington that I
would write more 'positively' about America in the future. I am sorry to
say that I did not respond at the moment as I would have after reflection,
and as I do now. It is not the business of Government or any of its
officials what I write, how I write it, whether it is positive, negative, or
anything else . . .

8. A few days after my hearing in Washington, one of the members of the
Committee was quoted in the press as saying, in effect, that my indictment for contempt would be handed down just about the time I would
divorce the woman I had just announced I would shortly marry. I do not
detect in such a statement any sign of that moral authority to which I
might defer my own judgment of right and wrong, patriotism or treason,
or even ordinary decency . . .

9. I do not deny the right of Government to protect itself against a group
dominated by a slavish subservience to Soviet Russia or any other foreign
government. I affirm that right and that necessity. It happens that I am
not part of that or any other conspiracy, movement, or ideology devoted
to the advancement of Soviet ideas. But it does not follow that in the
name of anti-Communism a writer can be rightfully hounded, or that
Government has a right to defame him and attempt to bring him to his
knees. If I cannot stand up outside I will stand up in jail, if need be.

10. I take this position not to defy the Government but to correct its errors.
I do this because I love this country and will not be part of what I
conscientiously believe is a travesty upon its good name, and I ask of all
reporters and editors who print these words or résumés of them to print
with them this statement: The prosecution of me and the campaign to
destroy me does not represent the American spirit but only a deformation
of that spirit. I ask the people of the world not to conclude from my
troubles that freedom is dying here.[30]

Freedom may not have been dying, but the authorities continued their
efforts to prove that Miller had been a Party member, the FBI producing a
report on Sue Warren (the woman who, it was asserted, had enrolled him in
the Party in 1943). Warren, the report noted, had been Chairman of the
Communist Party at 132 East 26th Street. Nothing, however, came of the
inquiries.

The proceedings had cost Miller much time and money, though, in effect,
the Committee, while winning the day, had won only a Pyrrhic victory since
the conviction was later to be reversed on appeal. Indeed, on 28 June the

Supreme Court announced its opinion on the Watkins case and Miller was, as a consequence, acquitted of the second count on the grounds that he had raised the issue of pertinency (that is, relevance of the question to an investigation of misuse of passports). The other count, however, still stood, and his lawyers entered an appeal citing another case decided that same day, that of Singer v. United States, in which the Watkins case had been applied to a witness who had not raised the question of pertinency. This motion was rejected on 19 July and Miller's sentence was upheld. An immediate appeal was filed.

There seemed to be no end to the case. He found himself on probation for three months, which began with a two-and-a-half-hour interview with Maurice Sanders, Deputy Chief Probation Officer based in the US Court House in Foley Square, New York. In Sanders's office he was asked about his family background, his politics and his relationship with his wife, statements checked in a separate interview between Sanders and Marilyn. He was asked for a written account of his present attitudes, all of which he reported to his lawyer in a letter dated 10 June 1957, in which he also explained that he had just bought two hundred acres of land with a farm in Roxbury where they were to make a home. He hoped, he said, to raise bloodhounds that could scent a subpoena at a thousand yards and eat the person carrying it.

In a letter to Sanders he provided the information requested, outlining his personal history, from his birth to a well-to-do family, through the Crash and on to his university years. Interestingly, it was his experience of anti-Semitism that he chose to stress as a motivating force. He had, he explained, never been particularly sensitive as a Jew but in the 1930s and 40s was aware of a brief resurgence of domestic fascists. He himself had been attacked and vilified. Only the Left seemed interested. Communist propaganda emphasized the Party's opposition to anti-Semitic forces, while the Christian Front seemed to have free reign. The result was that he had been drawn to Marxism, for both the explanations and the empowerment it seemed to offer. As a result of this flirtation, he maintained, he felt stronger and clearer than those who had never questioned their values. He had embraced those on the Left because they had seemed to represent freedom, but it was freedom itself that concerned him and he had subsequently come to understand that democracy alone could guarantee it.

Quite what the Deputy Chief Probation Officer made of this is unclear but the probation order was signed on 19 July. It required Miller to report once monthly, pay $500 and 'Live a clean and temperate life'. It also required him to 'Keep good company and good hours. Keep away from all undesirable places' and not leave the city or town where he lived without notifying his probation officer, who also had the power to instruct and advise him regarding his 'recreational and social activities'.[31] The financial cost, in fact, went considerably beyond the $500 fine. When his lawyers' bill was finally presented, two years later, it itemised $2,000 for advice with respect to his passport in 1956, $2,000 for the Committee hearing, $9,000 for his trial and motions for acquittal, and $7,000 for the various appeals. It would be December 1960 before he would complete payment.

For all his exposed legal and political position, Miller did not back away from controversy. In delivering a lecture before the National Assembly of the Authors' League of America, he noted, that the State Department had interfered with the circulation of American books abroad, along with music and painting, while foreign scientists were banned from the country. People, it seemed to him, were being required to sacrifice their independence as writers and citizens: 'The mission of the written word is not to buttress high policy but to proclaim the truth.'

At a time that had seen the emergence of the 'organization man' and the 'lonely crowd' it became even more necessary for the writer to defend his freedom. 'What freedom we are using now,' he declared, 'we have not helped to make, and what is being eroded around us we are making no effort to protect.' These were truths he felt obliged to repeat 'because I have learned them at my cost, and because I wish none of you will have to learn them the same way'.[32] The irony was that it would now be many years before he exercised that freedom again in the sense of writing for the stage, though he would write *The Misfits*, itself a telling account of lost freedoms, if also of desperate hopes. It would be less the dictates of politicians that silenced him, however, than the demands of a relationship that would command much of his energy and mental resources.

In April 1957, Milton Greene was dismissed from Marilyn Monroe Productions. According to Marilyn's biographer Donald Spoto, Miller co-authored the press response supposedly from his wife: 'He knows perfectly well that we had been at odds for a year and a half and he knows why ... My company was not formed merely to parcel out 49.6% of all my earnings to Mr Greene, but to make better pictures, improve my work and secure my income.'[33] A new board of directors was named. Another source of contention, it seemed, had been removed, though Greene threatened a lawsuit which might amount to $2 million. He eventually settled for $100,000.

Miller and Marilyn found respite on Long Island, where they spent the summer of 1957 at their farmhouse at Amagansett. Willem de Kooning was a near neighbour, an artist whose portrait of Marilyn, in the Museum of Modern Art, Miller hated. Marilyn walked around the wooden-floored house in shorts and a polka-dot shirt. There was a badminton set and they fished and swam together, driving along the beaches and back roads in a jeep. Photographs show Miller, in baseball cap and swimming shorts, fishing, while

Marilyn, in white costume, runs in the surf. In one picture they lean on one another as they walk through the shallows.

Look magazine would report him as finishing a new play to be produced later in the year (there was none) but in fact it was there, working between nine and one, that he finished the short story version of *The Misfits* (at first turned down by a number of publications because of its length).

The couple strolled on the beach – Marilyn desperate that fishermen bringing their catch to land allowed some to die in the surf. This incident, along with her experience in Jamaica, Miller turned into a short story, 'Please Don't Kill Anything'. It is a story that seems to capture their relationship at that time, she, vulnerable, oversensitive, daughter-like; he, amused at her naivety but aware of her needs. Yet, published in 1960, before the final collapse of their relationship, it also hints at the tensions that would precipitate that collapse. 'Please Don't Kill Anything' has echoes of Hemingway's 'A Cat in the Rain' and 'Hills Like White Elephants'. It is the story of a relationship that seems to allude to the imminence of its own disintegration. Ostensibly a portrait of a loving partnership, it is a deal more disturbing, and perhaps more revealing, than it appears.

A man and a woman are watching as fishermen haul a net of fish on to the shore. He observes the process with a detached interest, she with an edge of nervousness, associating herself with the fish: 'Now they know they're caught! ... Each one is wondering what happened!'[34] When they spill out on to the sand, the fishermen sort through them, discarding those not suitable for market. They lie there, dying.

The woman is desperate to rescue them, yet at the same time her fastidiousness prevents her from effectively intervening, beyond throwing a single fish into the waves. 'If I had something to hold them with,' she cries, her helplessness being part of the appeal she directs at her companion. It is a plea for rescue, and not only for the fish. He overcomes his embarrassment and shame – shame at her sentimentality in the face of the men's professionalism, shame at his own, apparent, dependency – and sets about throwing the fish back into the sea where they do, indeed, quickly revive and swim off. At one stage a dog bounds into the waves and retrieves one of them; it finally escapes, though not before a smaller fish has slipped from its mouth, a reminder of the Darwinian principle she fears. The story ends with the two of them, hand in hand: 'He felt a great happiness opening in him that she had laid her hand on the fish which was now swimming in the sea because he had lifted them. Now she looked at him like a little girl, with that naked wonder in her face, even as she was smiling in the way of a grown woman ... he kissed her on her lips, blessing her ... "Oh, how I love you" she said with tears in her eyes.'[35]

The story is seemingly about a woman whose love for the natural world is of a piece with her love for the man, about the power of love to redeem. But there is plainly another logic which moves in a contrary direction, as the neurotic sensitivity of the woman, her empathic association with the plight of the fish, trapped and dying, suggests what may eventually destroy a relationship in which her emotional vulnerabilities already override everything else. Ostensibly about a touchingly sensitive woman persuading her companion to rescue dying fish, it is also about a sensibility and a relationship under stress. Compacted in this simple action is a personal history and a likely future. The fish are rescued; the relationship seems consolidated. But in fact the net seems to be tightening around the two lovers, so profoundly dissimilar, so unlikely to sustain a relationship in which one is fragile and demanding and the other substitutes tolerance for understanding. The fishermen's amused contempt, restrained and seemingly irrelevant, nonetheless carries the force of a normality against which this seeming epiphany is to be judged.

During the afternoons Marilyn would cycle to the Rostens, who lived nearby and who recognized, if not fully understanding, her mood swings. For a while she embraced domesticity, learning how to cook, hanging homemade pasta over the backs of chairs and drying it with a hairdryer. England now seemed no more than a bad dream. Their new relationship was apparently secured by another pregnancy. Norman Rosten later recalled that she was voluptuously overweight, lying in the sun. She was transformed by the possibility of a child. The woman who had seemed so at odds with her husband a year earlier, so wrapped up in her own emotional and psychological needs, now looked forward to the family she had always lacked. Miller felt more ambiguous about the impending birth but warmed to it, not least because it did seem to change their relationship. Here, it appeared, was what both had sought. He was no longer under the immediate threat of imprisonment. Hollywood was distant. They were together and now with the prospect of a child. They had a momentary if limited immunity.

The summer idyll on Long Island, which had done so much to heal the wounds opened up in England, suddenly came to an end on 1 August. While weeding the garden, Marilyn doubled over in pain and had to be rushed to hospital, a journey of some four hours. The pregnancy was soon revealed to be ectopic and, as a result, had to be terminated. It was not the first time she had lost a baby. It would not be the last. As Miller explained, she had gynaecological problems and 'had treatments with a very good doctor in New York but he finally couldn't manage it', adding 'in a way I'm not sure how good it would have been for her to have a child. It would have been an additional problem. In an ideal way she wished to have a family, but I'm not sure how it would have worked out in practice.'[36]

Miller felt helpless in the face of her despair until, on a visit to the hospital, where she was confined for ten days, he fell into conversation with the photographer Sam Shaw who had read 'The Misfits', by now published in *Esquire* magazine. It was he who suggested its possibility as a movie. A few days after he and Marilyn had been driven by ambulance back to Amagansett, Miller began work on it, the first extended project he had tackled since his marriage. It seemed to him that the script, now being radically rewritten from the short story, could be a gift to his wife, not merely a way of raising her spirits in the short term but a means both of offering the acting challenge she craved and of bringing the two of them together. Here was a film that would unite rather than divide them. Here was a chance to write a screenplay that would echo more profound aspects of her sensibility than were acknowledged by Hollywood.

Yet even now that other world intruded. Shortly after her return to Amagansett she was flown off to New York by helicopter to be photographed at an event celebrating *Life* magazine and then deposited back in Amagansett. It was a reminder that while they might be playing at happy families, just out of sight there were those who wanted to suck her back into that whirl of publicity, public adulation and exploitation that had caused them so much grief. It was also an indication that she remained resolute in her irresolution. Marilyn was then, as throughout her life, a series of contradictions. Yearning for love, she nonetheless watched constantly for signs of its limits. In search of anonymity, she would go shopping in dark glasses and a headscarf but travel from store to store in a stretch limo. Fully alive to her commercial potential, her power as movie star, she longed for artistic achievement, hoping one day to play roles in the classical repertory. Drawn, as she believed, to domesticity, she was frustrated by its limitations. Her post-operative depression was such, though, that Miller began to suspect that it might be better for her to get back to work sooner rather than later. *The Misfits* was not yet complete but Billy Wilder was already sounding her out for a project called *Some Like It Hot*.

Meanwhile, they took time out to go into New York for an interview and picture story with *Look* magazine. The story explained, none too accurately, that Marilyn, 'as a completely doting wife, has adopted her husband's city (New York), his faith, his future and his family as her own'.[37] In fact they were rarely in New York, she did not convert to Judaism, her commitment to his future was suspect; and though she did, indeed, get on well with Isidore Miller, the relationship between Augusta and Marilyn was frosty. Miller's own response to the magazine's questioning, in retrospect, seems somewhat ambiguous: 'This year has been the most learning of my life.' Marilyn said: 'His work will always be at the centre of our lives' but that she would 'keep working too', while he described their new Roxbury home as 'the place where we hope to live and die'.

It is tempting to read this interview ironically, but in fact this does genuinely appear to have been a time when their relationship blossomed. His testimony to her acting skills, though, again seemed to hint at something not expressed. It edges so far in the direction of hyperbole as to suggest that either he really was swept away or had learned the need to be unambiguous in his support for his wife. 'It's impossible to have a superficial relationship with her,' he affirmed. 'She's too honest and earthy for anything phoney. She has an enormous sense of play, inventiveness – and unexpectedness – not only as a wife but as an actress. She could never be dull. I took her as a serious actress even before I met her. I think she's an adroit comedienne, but I also think she might turn into the greatest tragic actress that can be imagined.'[38] As to her habit of taking four hours getting ready to go out, her husband, Marilyn explained, was the first man not to be exasperated with her, waiting patiently and puffing on his pipe.

The day after the interview, they attended the opening of *The Prince and the Showgirl*, braving memories of their British experience, but then quickly retreated to Amagansett. Here their idyllic few months were at an end. Whether it was the miscarriage itself or a continuing depression, she resorted more and more to drugs and day by day the tension between them grew. There was a profundity to her despair that he seemed unable to penetrate and she taunted him with his failure to rescue her. One evening, Miller came across her collapsed in a chair from an overdose of sleeping tablets and called the emergency services. On another occasion their friends the Rostens received a 3 a.m. call from Marilyn's maid. They rushed over to find her stomach being pumped after an overdose. She was attended by a private doctor. There was no publicity. All she could say was 'Alive. Bad luck.'[39]

The drugs, it seemed to Miller, were not merely a temporary response to the pressures of filming. They were now part of an emotional game she was playing with him as she simultaneously invited him to intervene and accused him of failing to do so. At times she seems genuinely to have wished to end her life; at others, she played out a melodrama in which she accused him of a failure of love. Meanwhile, as the drugs appeared to lose their potency, so she increased the dose until she was no longer clear how many tablets she was taking. Little by little the marriage, barely a year old, became more virtual than real. As Rosten said later, 'evenings with friends were often played out in a façade of marital harmony. Miller was more and more living with her in the third person, as it were, an observer.'[40] Susan Strasberg recalled an occasion on which Marilyn had treated her husband with contempt in front of a group of strangers. Yet she was also capable of throwing off her depression, forgetting the accusations and revelling in her new life. There were months at a time when both seemed to believe that theirs might yet prove a workable relationship.

They now retreated to their new Roxbury home, close to the property he had owned with Mary and where he had written *Death of a Salesman*. They had looked at a number of places, including some in New York State, before, with the help of Morton Miller, they settled on the Leavenworth homestead in Tophet Road, then a nondescript farmhouse set in 110 acres. They took joint title, with Morton as witness, and set about renovating it, even employing Frank Lloyd Wright whom Marilyn had met at the Plaza Hotel where he lived, to produce designs. Marilyn's own plans were grandiose, Miller's altogether more modest and practical. There was, Morton observed, a tension between 'Marilyn's lack of concern for money' and 'Arthur's frugality.'[41]

She wanted a swimming pool, perhaps somewhat redundant given the existence of a natural spring two hundred yards from the house which was later the basis for a pond where Miller was to swim every summer for nearly fifty years, but her ideas were based on the Hollywood she had, for a time, left behind. More than four decades later what were to have been the changing rooms for this pool are still visible, though now no more than sheds for garden tools.

In the 1990s, writing to an architect acquaintance, Miller recalled the designs produced by Wright. The watercolour sketches had shown a circular living room of sixty-foot diameter with stone columns. A swimming pool jutted out where the hillside fell away, necessitating large retaining walls. It was, it seemed to him, designed less for two people than for a corporation, and would have cost some $250,000. Consequently, they allowed the scheme to lapse and never took up Wright's designs. They simply went about the business of restoring the house to make it liveable as a weekend retreat. It would later become something more than a summer residence in the country for two; for the moment, though, what he had in mind was somewhere away from the pressures of the political world and Hollywood.

Marilyn arranged for stone setters to build a wall but in doing so they cut through the roots of a number of giant elms. Distraught, she and Miller hired specialists to inject proteins into the roots in an attempt to save them. Her sympathy for animals and for damaged individuals extended, it seemed, even to the plant kingdom. She did, though, urge her husband to buy the adjacent land, and though he was doubtful at the time he later described this as one of his wisest decisions. He had a split-shingle studio built fifty feet from the house where he would work on his plays for the next half-century. It looked out over a small wooded gully. When necessity dictated, he could stand on the back veranda and pee into the bushes below rather than trail back to the house.

At first, the very business of creating the house in which they were to live brought them together. It was in disrepair and still contained remnants of those who had been there before. Marilyn suggested installing sliding doors for the main room and hunted through nearby stores for cupboards and fittings. Now, each day was punctuated by the sounds of carpenters, plumbers and electricians. But the worm was already in the apple. In an undated poem whose refrain is 'When we began', Miller reflects, in the opening stanza, on the renovation of a house and the beginning of a marriage, speaking of a time when no window would open, the doors were stuck and the floors were bent. Then, as the house was reconstructed around them, they had lain together, as happy as mice. Three years later, with the house in perfect order, they lay apart, dreading the return of day, the marriage collapsing. In the final stanza the marriage is over.

Marilyn was now torn between trying for another baby and returning to movie-making. According to Rosten, she confided, 'I'd love my child to death. I want it, yet I'm scared. Arthur says he wants it, but he's losing his enthusiasm. He thinks I should do the picture ... After all, I'm a movie star, right?'[42] Whose idea it was mattered less than the fact that they had both begun to think of Hollywood as a solution rather than the root of the problem. Furthermore, the country was not quite as idyllic as she had presumed it would be. In his book on Marilyn, Fred Guiles describes an occasion in April 1958 when she saw a farmer loading a bull calf into a truck. A dairyman, he was shipping the animal to the abattoir. Desperate, she tried to offer him money to spare it, even as the teenage Mark Taylor, son of Miller's friend Frank Taylor (soon to work with him as producer of *The Misfits*), explained that a new bull calf would be produced every six months.

In nearby Bridgewater Norman Mailer tried to negotiate a chance to meet Marilyn, using Norman Rosten as an intermediary. Rosten recalled:

> Miller didn't want to set anything up with Mailer. He just didn't like the idea. Miller is a rabbi, and he didn't want this strange guy powering in ... I'm one of his oldest friends, but if I danced with Marilyn at a party and maybe held her a little too tight or whispered in her ear, he'd look at me and get a little nervous ... Norman used to say to me, 'Here I am in Bridgewater, here's this prick Arthur who won't even invite me over for a cocktail so I can meet Marilyn.'[43]

Hedda Rosten recalled Marilyn's own response: 'One writer is enough for me.'

Marilyn tried to act as a gracious hostess but found it far from easy. Miller recalled an occasion when they were to have dinner with friends Bob and Martha Whitehead. She delayed her appearance, staying in her room drinking, until at last she came down the stairs and fell, injuring her fingers. He passed it off as an accident but thought it a result not only of the drink but of her insecurity in trying to play the role of a hostess. Marilyn had her own rationalization: 'As long as I'm on time in the important areas, like making boats and planes or getting to the theater before the curtain goes up, it's all right with Arthur if I'm late to other places. He says it isn't necessary to be on time for most things because you just have to stay there longer if you do.'[44]

At Amagansett and later at Roxbury she read the emerging script of *The Misfits*, which took him six months to write (the first draft was completed on 28 October 1957), but already what had been designed as a gift was becoming a source of contention. Certainly, she did not immediately respond to the role of Roslyn, though he had specifically created it for her, a role which scarcely existed in the original story. At the same time, she began to see its commercial potential and to evidence that desire for control that was a feature of her attitude to movie-making. To Miller, he was giving her what she ostensibly longed for in the form of a serious acting role. That she did not immediately embrace it was hurtful. In the end she seemed inclined to allow the future of the project to turn on whether or not a major director would sign up for it, quite as if it were not a script by her husband, a man whose literary reputation had once attracted her. That Christmas she gave him a set of *Encyclopaedia Britannica*. Paula Strasberg received a pearl necklace with diamond clasp. John Strasberg was given her Thunderbird.

Meanwhile, the issue of Miller's contempt of Congress continued. When his case was considered by the Court of Appeals the Committee had released a copy of the Communist Party application form bearing Miller's name and address but not his signature. Miller called it either a forgery or a document prepared without his knowledge, and 'a transparent attempt to influence the course of my appeal'.[45] Whatever the truth of that, on 22 January 1958 the Court of Appeals ordered that the case be set for hearing en banc (before a panel of judges). On 21 February Miller filed his brief. The hearing itself was repeatedly deferred.

He also conducted a campaign through the press, on 11 February writing a letter to the *New York Times* in which he stressed that any investigating committee

> must take to heart the seriousness of any summons by one of its committee to a citizen to appear for investigation. It is simply an evasion of the truth to say, as many do, that merely to be summoned does not imply guilt. It does so imply in the public mind. It is easy to say that to be summoned does not mean one has committed a crime, but if one has not committed a crime why should one be summoned? ... If something less than a crime is at issue why must the atmosphere of crime be immediately foisted upon what might turn out to be non-criminal behaviour?

On 11 June Miller's lawyers presented their oral argument and a member of the firm, Daniel Pollitt, immediately dictated a memorandum praising Joe

Rauh for a magnificent oral presentation and suggesting that he had carried the Court. He guessed that Judge Burger would write the opinion for a unanimous Court, reversing the conviction on the grounds that Miller had never been directed to answer the question at issue. On 7 August, two years after the hearings, the Appeals Court duly found in his favour on the grounds that he had not been adequately informed that he risked contempt for refusing to answer that question. In the words of the final decision by the United States Court of Appeals:

> The question asked appellant to name the persons present with him at a meeting of 'Communist writers' in 1947. The record shows the witness urged the Chairman not to press the direction to answer the question and requested him to defer it until a later time. The Chairman agreed. The hearing terminated shortly thereafter without any unequivocally renewed direction or command to answer the 'suspended' question. Thus, the requirement of *Quinn v. United States*, that it be brought home to the witness that he risks the penalties of contempt if he refuses to answer the question, was not followed.[46]

The issue of the pertinence of the question was thus sidestepped and the original conviction was reversed with directions to enter a judgement of acquittal.

At last the process was over. In a statement released through his lawyer, Miller expressed the hope that his victory would make a contribution to eliminating the power of congressional committees. It did not, nor did it deflect the FBI's interest. The Bureau continued to add to his now extensive file, including a photocopy of a book by one Reverend Ginder in which the Reverend Edward A. Miller appears as 'Censor Librorum'. Evidently Miller had been confused with a catholic priest and a member of the Knights of Columbus.

The Millers now divided their time between Roxbury and their thirteenth-floor apartment on East 57th Street, living there during the week. Marilyn could work once again with the Strasbergs while he continued to develop *The Misfits* and had meetings with Norman Rosten, who was writing the screenplay of *A View from the Bridge*. At weekends they retreated to Connecticut, where Marilyn tried to ride a horse called Ebony bought from the Taylors.

A year later she was back in Hollywood to make *Some Like It Hot*, one of her best films. Miller remained in Connecticut but then flew in and stayed in a bungalow at the Beverly Hills Hotel. She quickly fell into what had become her normal routine, taking barbiturates and tranquillizers, and at odds with the director, Billy Wilder, and fellow actors Tony Curtis and Jack Lemmon. As ever, when she ran into difficulty with a scene she turned not to Wilder but to Paula Strasberg, leaving the director seemingly not in control of his own set. As Miller remarked, 'For any director to be kept waiting, even half an hour, was humiliating.'[47] One scene with Tony Curtis had to be retaken forty-two times when she had trouble with her lines.

When her husband wrote a tribute to her to accompany a series of Richard Avedon photographs in *Life* magazine, she objected to what seemed to her its confirmation of clichés about her naivety and sexuality. In his biography of Marilyn, Donald Spoto describes a letter which Miller sent to his wife in September 1959 in which he was apologetic about errors of omission and commission and remarked on discoveries about his own emotional life that had emerged from sessions with his psychoanalyst, Dr Loewenstein. For Spoto, the letter is crucial in that it 'contradicts the general tone and content of Arthur Miller's published memoirs in which he portrayed himself as the healthy-minded, long-suffering partner of a woman he saw as occasionally sweet and talented, but ever on the edge of madness'.

It is an odd remark in that it is clear that both were feeling vulnerable. She was briefly hospitalized. He flew out to see her. To Spoto, he brought with him an air of condescension. He quotes Billy Wilder as saying: 'There were days I could have strangled her . . . but there were wonderful days, too, when we all knew she was brilliant. But with Arthur it all seemed sour, and I remember saying at the time that in meeting Miller at last I met someone who resented her more than I did.'[48] Wilder was particularly angry when Miller argued that his wife should only work for half the day. There was, though, more going on than he knew at first. Marilyn was pregnant again. One day Miller approached him and reminded him of his wife's condition: 'Marilyn is pregnant. Can't you let her go home? It's nearly four o'clock' – to which Wilder replied, 'Arthur, it is now a quarter to four and I haven't got a shot.'

When the shooting was over, Wilder, who was himself ill during the filming, confessed: 'I am eating better. I have been able to sleep for the first time in months. I can look at my wife without wanting to hit her because she's a woman.'[49] The remark appeared in a column written by Joe Hyams in the *New York Herald Tribune* on 10 February 1959, in which Wilder explained: 'I am a glutton for friendliness and I had my hands full keeping up morale on the picture. No matter how high actors and crew are on a project, morale has a way of slipping when you wait on set for hours for a star who might never arrive . . . I hoped to finish the picture in seven weeks . . . the first two weeks were not too tough. It was the last two months that almost did me in.' Asked whether he would work with Marilyn again he replied that, having discussed the idea with his doctor and psychiatrist, he realized that he was too rich to need to do so. Despite the humour, the remarks struck home and Miller drafted a cable the next day demanding an apology. He could not, he insisted, let what he saw as a vicious attack on Marilyn go unchallenged. Wilder had, after all, been told that her pregnancy would prevent her working a full day, but had apparently chosen to ignore the fact. She had, Miller said, continued with the film out of a sense of responsibility, but twelve hours after the last shooting day had suffered a miscarriage. With its success now assured, it seemed, he now felt free to attack her. He accused Wilder of being unjust and cruel – but his comfort was, he added, that Marilyn's beauty and humanity continued to shine through.

A similar cable went to Joe Hyams. Miller was as angry and protective as he sounds. He knew all too well what her behaviour could be like but he also knew the pressure she had been under, especially now that she had lost another child.

By half past six the same night Wilder had replied at length:

DEAR ARTHUR: THIS IS A SMALL WORLD WITH VERY SHARP EARS. EVER SINCE THE EARLY DAYS OF SHOOTING, WHEN RUMORS OF MARILYNS UNPROFESSIONAL CONDUCT FIRST LEAKED OUT, I HAVE BEEN BESIEGED BY NEWSPAPERMEN FROM AS FAR AS LONDON, PARIS AND BERLIN FOR A STATEMENT. I HAVE STAVED THEM OFF. I HAVE AVOIDED THEM. I HAVE LIED TO THEM. AS FOR MR. HYAMS COLUMN, THE CONCLUSIONS HE HAD REACHED FROM HIS OWN RESEARCH WOULD HAVE BEEN TWICE AS VICIOUS HAD I NOT SUBMITTED TO THE INTERVIEW. OF COURSE I AM DEEPLY SORRY THAT SHE LOST HER BABY, BUT I MUST REJECT THE IMPLICATION THAT OVERWORK OR INCONSIDERATE TREATMENT BY ME OR ANYONE ELSE ASSOCIATED WITH THE PRODUCTION WAS IN ANY WAY RESPONSIBLE FOR IT. THE FACT IS THAT THE COMPANY PAMPERED HER, CODDLED HER AND ACCEDED TO ALL HER WHIMS. THE ONLY ONE WHO SHOWED ANY LACK OF CONSIDERATION WAS MARILYN, IN HER TREATMENT OF HER CO-STARS AND HER CO-WORKERS RIGHT FROM THE FIRST DAY, BEFORE THERE WAS ANY HINT OF PREGNANCY ... HER CHRONIC TARDINESS AND UNPREPAREDNESS COST US EIGHTEEN SHOOTING DAYS, HUNDRED OF THOUSANDS OF DOLLARS, AND COUNTLESS HEART-ACHES. I RECALL ONE TYPICAL MORNING WHEN SHE SHOWED UP TWO AND A HALF HOURS LATE, CARRYING A COPY OF THOMAS PAINES THE RIGHTS OF MAN, AND WHEN A SECOND ASSISTANT DIRECTOR KNOCKED ON HER DRESSING ROOM DOOR AND HUMBLY ASKED HER IF SHE WAS READY, HER HUMANITY SHONE THROUGH AND SHE REPLIED QUOTE DROP DEAD UNQUOTE. THIS HAVING BEEN MY SECOND PICTURE WITH MARILYN, I UNDERSTAND HER PROBLEMS. HER BIGGEST PROBLEM IS THAT SHE DOESN'T UNDERSTAND ANYONE ELSE'S PROB-LEMS. IF YOU TOOK A QUICK POLL AMONG THE CAST AND CREW ON

THE SUBJECT OF MARILYN [YOU] WOULD FIND A POSITIVELY OVER-
WHELMING LACK OF POPULARITY. HAD YOU, DEAR ARTHUR, BEEN
NOT HER HUSBAND BUT HER WRITER AND DIRECTOR, AND BEEN SUB-
JECTED TO ALL THE INDIGNITIES I WAS, YOU WOULD HAVE THROWN
HER OUT ON HER CAN, THERMOS BOTTLE AND ALL, TO AVOID A
NERVOUS BREAKDOWN. RESPECTFULLY – BILLY WILDER.

If anything, Wilder was still pulling his punches. The fact that he was telegraphing his reply meant that he had to be discreet. Marilyn's real response to the Second Assistant Director had actually been 'Go fuck yourself.' The 'thermos bottle' is a reference to the alcohol with which she complemented her drugs.

A couple of years later, Miller would be her writer and would experience precisely the problems encountered by Wilder. For the moment, though, the following morning he drafted yet another cable in reply. It was, if not more conciliatory, at least less angry. Once again he insisted that she had acted entirely professionally and that Wilder's responsibility had been to support her, even if her approach differed from his own. She had, he pointed out, excelled in the film. Her responsibility was not to bow to his authority but remain true to her talent. He was complaining at her treatment not simply because she was his wife but because hers was a unique talent, as was evident in the success of the film.

There was, of course, a fundamental truth to this, despite what might seem a temporizing argument. Why else, despite her behaviour, was she in demand? She herself had commented, 'A lot of people can be there on time and do nothing, which I have seen them do, and you know, all sit around and sort of chit-chatting and talking trivia about their social life. Gable said about me, "When she's there, she's there. All of her is there. She's there to work."'[50] But there is something in Miller's reply to Wilder which suggests his awareness that there was, indeed, a price to be paid for what she had to offer, and perhaps not only with respect to Hollywood. The exchange concluded with another cable from Wilder, sent that same afternoon:

DEAR ARTHUR IN ORDER TO HASTEN THE BURIAL OF THE HATCHET
I HEREBY ACKNOWLEDGE THAT GOOD WIFE MARILYN IS A UNIQUE
PERSONALITY AND I AM THE BEAST OF BELSEN BUT IN THE IMMORTAL
WORDS OF JOE E BROWN NOBODY IS PERFECT UNQUOTE SINCERELY
BILLY WILDER[51]

Marilyn had, in fact, been under stress throughout the shooting, and despite the presence on set of a doctor and psychiatrist she did have another miscarriage. Shooting had finished in November 1958, and she lost the baby on 17 December, in truth not quite the twelve hours after the end of shooting that Miller referred to in his cable. Once again she was plunged into depression, not least because she feared that the Amytal she had been taking might have been responsible. It was during the depths of this depression that Billy Wilder's remarks appeared in the *New York Herald Tribune*. Marilyn's response to Wilder had been rather more direct. She telephoned him and, finding him out, left a message with his wife: 'Would you please tell him to go fuck himself.'

Looking back on the Wilder incident from the distance of 2002, Miller was inclined to see the humour. By then, his experience with *The Misfits* had taught him how destructive her behaviour could be, both on and off set, but time had also made his own reaction seem disproportionate to the offence. Quite the most remarkable thing, though, was the fact that, whatever tension she suffered and created, her performance on *Some Like It Hot* contributed to making the film a classic of the American cinema.

In March 1959 the film's premiere was held at Loew's Capital Theatre on Broadway. Miller and his wife attended together, but in June she admitted: 'It's too late ... There's no communication between us anymore, and I feel so inferior around him. He seems so distant.'[52] Despite these tensions, however, neither felt inclined to walk away. The needs that had brought them together still existed and that same month she once again underwent gynaecological surgery, still with a view to having children as if this might yet hold them together. She continued to yearn for a family and was prepared to go through the humiliations of medical treatment and the repeated miscarriages to bring it about. Miller acknowledged her pain but in the end could do little about it.

From the vantage point of three decades later, it seemed clear to him that it was, indeed, at about this time that she had begun to despair of their relationship. Even his efforts to write had prompted suspicions, just as Mary had once seen his work as the source of a threat to their relationship. It was precisely his intellectual concerns that shut her out. She wanted to move things back on to her own territory, flirting with others and then accusing him of doing the same. After all, it was his reputation as a writer that had first attracted her. Why else would he be writing again unless he had some such on his mind?

In September 1959, the Millers met Yves Montand and his wife Simone Signoret. He was to star with her in Twentieth Century Fox's *Let's Make Love*. Montand and Signoret had appeared in the French version of *The Crucible*, a project brought to them by two French directors who had been victims of McCarthyism. They also featured in the film version, whose script, by Jean-Paul Sartre, Miller disliked with some intensity. Sartre, reportedly, had seen the play and said, 'This play was for me. Why didn't I do the adaptation?'[53]

Miller warmed to them, not least because their political beliefs were, at the time, similar to his own. They had only abandoned their pro-Soviet beliefs at the time of the Hungarian uprising in 1956. Both were radicals and had been denied visas to the United States during the McCarthy period. She was the granddaughter of a Polish Jew (Signoret was her mother's name); born Ivo Livi in a small Italian village, he came from the slums of Marseilles. They had both taken a stand against the French war in Indo-China, while she was a friend of Sartre's and, unlike Marilyn, a highly literate and cultivated woman. Later, in the eyes of some, Montand would move to the right – perhaps, Miller surmised, because America had begun to influence him. It was a relationship, though, that was to be strained by Marilyn's growing obsession with the French actor, though at first he seems to have had a mollifying effect on her.

She had fallen into her familiar routine, turning to sedatives and appearing late on set. It was clear to everyone that there was tension between her and her husband. Even her doctor was dismayed: 'I couldn't take it. All that bile, that recrimination.' Montand seemed to calm her down. As Miller remarked, 'Anyone who could make her smile came as a blessing to me.'[54]

At first Montand and Signoret, Miller and Monroe, formed a natural friendship, and all went well until Miller had to go to Ireland to see John Huston in connection with *The Misfits*. Then one day, as she continued to keep cast and crew waiting, Montand thrust a note under her door saying that he was not amused by 'capricious little girls'.[55] Unable to face him, Marilyn called Miller in Ireland, telling him to telephone Montand in bungalow 20 (Marilyn was in 21), a matter of feet away. Then Signoret went to Italy, to make *Adua et Ses Compagnes*, and Marilyn and Montand had a brief affair.

Later, Signoret would deny some of the reports that began to appear in gossip columns, but not the essential fact. She simply believed that it was nobody's business but those most immediately concerned. She had, she recalled, received a number of letters, many anonymous, not least because she had also been involved, during her husband's absence, in a manifesto in support of the Algerian people in their battle to throw off colonial power. To some of her anonymous correspondents the two issues became elided, so that she received letters suggesting that her husband had been right to prefer a blonde and that 'it served that Jew Miller right'. She was shocked and disturbed by the affair but nevertheless wished Marilyn well. 'Can *you* think of many men who wouldn't have responded to Marilyn's charm?' she asked.[56] She even regretted the fact that Miller went on to write about his wife in *After the Fall*.

Montand himself later wrote of what he chose to present as his seduction.

When Miller left, he complained to a friend, 'What am I going to do? ... He's leaving me with Marilyn. Do you think he doesn't know that she is beginning to throw herself at me? ... I'm a vulnerable man.'[57] His undoing, he explained, had been a goodnight kiss: 'I bent over to kiss her good night, but suddenly it was a wild kiss, a fire, a hurricane. I couldn't stop.'[58] He was, it seems, a victim of her passion and his will-less submission. Miller commented in *Timebends* on the difficulty Marilyn had in embracing the permanent relationships she believed she needed: 'The problem was that permanence with another person was a missing part of her.'[59] So it proved in relation to Montand, though in this case it was he who staged a rapid retreat, flying to France and refusing all her attempts to see him again.

By now, Marilyn was once more under psychiatric treatment, seeing her new doctor, Ralph Greenson, after one day's filming on *Let's Make Love*. She confessed to her regimen of drugs, supplied by a string of compliant doctors. She also complained about her husband's lack of response to her and his domination by his mother – accusations at odds with the psychoanalyst's own experience when he met Miller, and certainly at odds with the Miller who threw himself, against his better judgement, into all aspects of the production (including rewrites of the script during a writers' strike) despite his contempt for much of the material and the process in which he found himself increasingly involved. The columnist Sidney Skolsky complained: 'Arthur Miller, the big liberal, the man who always stood up for the underdog, ignored the Writers Guild strike ... his wife no longer looked up to him.'[60] There were certainly contradictory pressures on him.

Greenson sought to reduce her dependence on drugs, while acknowledging what seemed to him profound psychological problems. When he finally met Miller he found a man whose patience, unsurprisingly, was rapidly running out and who could no longer offer the unequivocal support she appeared to need – support which, as before, amounted to praise for her achievements and a shared animosity directed at any of those who she believed were denying her talents or were jealous of her accomplishments. And, as before, these tensions ebbed and flowed and the rift between the two narrowed, then widened. But, as Miller later remarked, most marriages are 'conspiracies to deny the dark and confirm the light',[61] and this playwright, for whom denial had always been a central theme, was a willing half of just such a conspiracy of two, alternately despairing and convincing himself that some kind of lasting relationship was possible.

But the fact was that they had both entered this relationship carrying with them their own histories and looking for some kind of absolution. If absolution was not, in fact, on offer this perhaps owed as much to their separate expectations as to their failure to find what they sought. Nonetheless, the result of those failures was a corrosive guilt. 'I had joyously accepted the role she had long been fashioning for someone who would save her,' he said, 'and so far I had not made it happen; just as she had seemed the all-forgiving and sensuous beloved that a self-denying life had been preparing me for long before she arrived.'[62] However, bad as things were, neither had, as yet, entirely given up on the marriage.

If Marilyn was keen to broaden her literary education and extend her abilities as an actress, she was also now alert to the political world. 1960 was election year and she had no doubts where her sympathies lay in a battle between Nixon and Kennedy. Nixon, she decided, had no soul. Otherwise she was divided between Nelson Rockefeller in one direction and Hubert Humphrey or Kennedy in the other. When the primaries began, the Democratic town committee that, eight years later, would send Miller as a delegate to the Chicago convention, named her as an alternate delegate. In spring, and following her husband's lifelong tendency to sign liberal documents, she joined Marlon Brando and other Hollywood stars in adding her name to those supporting the National Committee for a Sane Nuclear Policy (SANE). Her commitments were instinctive, but also owed something to her relationship with a man who was now working to complete *The Misfits* a film that would enable them to work togther. The irony was that it became the source of contention.

Norman Rosten recalled disputes between husband and wife over the script. In particular, he remembered a three-way telephone conversation in which she had attempted to enrol him in her attack on her husband. 'I want this speech rewritten,' she had said to Miller. 'Well, what are you going to do about it?' – 'I'm going to think about it,' replied Miller. – 'I object to the whole stupid speech,' she had said, 'and he's going to rewrite it!' Rosten later asked himself, 'Was she fighting him for script changes or putting the screws into him as a parting shot in a fading marriage?' In his view, it seemed clear that she was 'giving him the business, making him eat the Hollywood shit even as they made her eat it for so long. She was fighting the pain and humiliation of another rejection, of one more failure in love. She was aware that this was to be their last shared experience. She knew, too, that Miller wanted the film made even if it meant continuing the friction of their marriage.'[63]

The producer of *The Misfits* was to be Frank Taylor, who Miller had known when he worked at the same publishing house as his first wife, Mary. He had been the editor of his first book *Situation Normal* and his novel *Focus* before spending time with Twentieth Century Fox. He lived in Greenwich, Connecticut, and had one day come to call on Miller, who proceeded to tell him the story of *The Misfits*, playing each of the roles from memory and for some reason in a Southern accent, as the sound of Marilyn vacuuming reached them from the upstairs rooms. It was Taylor who suggested the director, a man who was respected by both Miller and his wife and who had done his best to protect her in Hollywood, to see her as an actress rather than another in a line of starlets: John Huston. Miller sent him an initial script which was forwarded to the George V hotel in Paris, where he was finishing work on *The Roots of Heaven*. He cabled Miller immediately: 'MAGNIFICENT.'[64] That film finished, he returned to his house at St Clerans in County Galway, Ireland, where, while nursing a broken leg, he was joined by Miller.

Huston had directed Marilyn in *The Asphalt Jungle*, before she earned her reputation for awkwardness, and had no qualms at the idea of working with her again. *Guardian* correspondent W.J. Weatherby interviewed Huston and Miller as they discussed the film. For Miller, America was suffering from a lack of transcendence and, though he denied an immediate application of his remarks to the forthcoming film, in fact they seem to bear directly on the plight of men baffled by a world of inverted values in which their skills are tainted by the interests they serve. Thus, he lamented the fact that 'certain things are not valued any longer unless they have some commercial use. Certain codes of behaviour can't be converted into money ... People degenerate when they only respond to things because there's a prospect of gain or usefulness.'[65]

Back in America, Miller awaited Huston's final decision. Marilyn, however, who had once, he recalled, clutched the script to her breast with delight, was becoming obdurate, announcing that she would not appear in the film without Huston. Miller, too, wanted Huston but her insistence went further than an expression of preference. It was an ultimatum. She was, he thought, announcing the limits of her commitment to him. Looking back in the year 2000, he recalled his sense of shock at her response even though she knew that he had put theatre on one side to write the script.

As it happened, Miller and Huston got on well together and the director signed on. They agreed that the film should studiously avoid Hollywood values, beyond assembling a first-rate cast. It was to be shot in black and white, thought by many in Hollywood to be uncommercial, appealing only to the art house audience. To Miller, colour would have made the scenery look too 'soft', too 'pretty'.[66] He was after a bleached-out quality, 'like drying bones'. It was to be set in Nevada, in a land from which all grace seemed to have been withdrawn, except a certain beauty menaced by modernity. This, after all, was the end of the line for many of those who went there to bring a quick end to relationships, acknowledge defeat, register the decay of old values and principles.

In March 1960 Miller had a correspondence with Aaron Copland, who he thought might compose the music. Copland wrote:

It was very good of you to sit down and write me about the script from the standpoint of its musical setting. What you said helped me a lot and makes me look forward to seeing a first rough cut of the film. At that time, we can make actual the various things you suggested in your letter.

Certain modes in music are easier to handle than others. For example, the notion of violence and the notion of serenity. The idea of reflecting 'misfittedness' is more difficult. But I feel sure one can suggest the essence of such a situation in some less precise way. One thing I should tell you: I have a prejudice, like most composers, for using music with a film only where it is absolutely essential, and I feel sure you would want that too.

As for the scenes where realistic jazz is required, I would think that the decision regarding Louis Armstrong would depend upon the kind of jazz you want to use. One should take into consideration what vintage jazz you want – whether it is a sound full of energy in a direct way; or tired and pooped in a grotesque way, or whatever. Armstrong does one certain kind of thing very well indeed, but if that's not what you want for the particular scenes in question, he does you no good no matter how big his rep.

On the other hand, I realize his value as a name in selling the picture.

Frank Taylor was to get back to him, but Copland wanted $55,000 for thirty minutes of music and the score was eventually composed by Alex North. Meanwhile, they began to assemble a cast that in itself might seem to guarantee success: Clark Gable, Marilyn's childhood hero, Montgomery Clift, Eli Wallach and Thelma Ritter. That line-up alone, however, served to expand the budget to three and a half million, over one and a half million going to the actors, including $750,000 for Gable and $300,000 to Monroe. Miller himself was to receive $225,000. Gable was almost sixty and at first leery of getting involved, not least because he found it hard to relate the script to anything he had appeared in before. He was, he complained, to be a cowboy in a film which seemed to have nothing to do with Westerns, but he was soon convinced.

Montgomery Clift was to prove an apt companion to Marilyn on the set. Like her, he was heavily dependent on prescription drugs: Nembutal, Doriden, Luminal, Seconal, the drugs which Tennessee Williams would insist 'we all took right through the 1960s'.[67] At a dinner with Miller and Monroe, Clift behaved so badly that she suggested: 'He's the only person I know who's in worse shape than I am.'[68] In the end it was she who was to prove in worse shape, as he behaved impeccably on the set while she had to be hospitalized as a result of her drug-taking.

The film was originally planned for the autumn of 1959 but delayed because Marilyn had agreed to make *Let's Make Love* and Gable would not be available before 1 October, the scheduled starting date for the Monroe film. As a result

The Misfits was moved to the spring of 1960 when it was further delayed as the result of an actors' strike, which pushed completion of *Let's Make Love* on by five weeks. Marilyn thus had to fly direct from Hollywood to New York for fittings and thence on to Nevada.

The ironies surrounding the shooting of *The Misfits* were soon to become apparent. It was set, though not filmed, in Reno, which boasted that it had processed five thousand divorces the previous year. For Miller, it brought back memories of another failed marriage. He explained in his autobiography: 'I knew by this time that I had initially expected what she satirized as "the happy girl that all men loved" and had discovered someone diametrically opposite, a troubled woman whose desperation was deepening no matter where she turned for a way out. By the start of *The Misfits* it was no longer possible to deny to myself that if there was a key to Marilyn's despair I did not possess it.'[69]

The short story had been written in the late 1950s when America seemed in disarray. Meeting the cowboys who had inspired it, in Nevada, he had felt a sudden sense of clarity. The very bleakness of the setting, far away from the political confusions of the East Coast, had brought him back to essentials, as it had for those who inhabited this place. The central characters in what became the film version were, like the cowboys, adrift, lacking in purpose and direction. They were all, as it seemed to him, trying to 'matter'. It was a film about trying to make sense of things. The mustang hunts, and the desperate reaching out of solitary individuals, were a part of that process. These characters were designed to exist as fact and as metaphor. In the story, two people are driven apart by their contrasting sensibilities, yet come together, finally, in a sense of their shared fate. Miller plainly hoped that the gap between his wife and the character she played would close, that she would find her way back from her deepening alienation. In the end it was another gap that closed: 'The simple fact, terrible and lethal, was that no space whatever existed between herself and this star. She was "Marilyn Monroe", and that was what was killing her.'[70]

The Misfits tells the story of Roslyn, in Reno to complete her divorce from a man whose principal crime lies in his emotional absence. Reno is a place of lost dreams, and not merely for her. She meets three men, each of whom has a life scarred by disappointment. Gay Langland himself has a broken marriage. His children make a fleeting appearance, but only to underscore the distance between them. Together with Guido, played by Eli Wallach, Gay likes to chase wild horses in the nearby desert, convincing himself that the world is as it once was, a place where a man can define himself by his battle with nature. Guido's wife has died and the house they were building is left unfinished. For him, too, the search for wild horses is the evidence that he is still free, that while he may work for wages for a while, this is merely temporary. The third member of the team is Perce, played by Montgomery Clift. He has been disinherited by his mother and now travels from rodeo to rodeo, picking up injuries, physical and psychological, struggling, like the others, to pretend that the West is as it once was.

The appearance of Roslyn changes all of them. Gay and Guido, in particular, compete for her attention. Gay has had a succession of relationships with the sad and lonely women who come to Reno to end their marriages, but Roslyn is different, as is his response to her. To his surprise, he feels himself drawn not only to her but to the idea of settling down. Together, they go in pursuit of the horses, hunting them down, though no longer on horseback but with the aid of a dilapidated plane and a truck. Despite their romanticizing of the hunt, it has long since been drained of meaning. There are few horses left, not enough, in fact, to make the project worthwhile, and when they are caught they are sold for dog food.

When Roslyn discovers the truth she is traumatized, not least because she feels an affinity with these animals, revelling in their freedom, and recognising in their desperation something of her own. She begs for them to be set free. To do so, though, is to strip Gay of the one thing left to him, to expose the lies he has told himself to justify his life. When a stallion is cut free he recaptures but then releases it. The gesture is simultaneously an acknowledgement that something has come to an end, and an acceptance of his love for Roslyn. The film ends as they drive across the desert under the night sky, seemingly brought together by their shared pain. Their joint future is not assured but does now seem a possibility.

Miller went to Nevada with some hope. The circumstances of this film were to be fundamentally different from any previous production. Marilyn had everything she wanted in terms of director and actors and, above all, a literate part which could at last display her talents as an actress. Beyond that, the role granted her dignity and, since it was based so closely on her own character, conceded that dignity to her off the screen as well. This was Marilyn stripped of vindictiveness, egotism, cruelty. Others may have taken advantage of her naivety and desperation, but she remained in some way untainted and pure. As he explained, 'Roslyn's dilemma was hers, but in the story it was resolved. I hoped that by living through this role she too might arrive at some threshold of faith and confidence, even as I had to wonder if I could hold on to it myself after we had both been let down from expectations such as few people allow themselves in a marriage.'[71]

The mood in which they settled into the Mapes Hotel in Reno was, at least on Miller's part, hopeful. Asked by me in May 2002 whether he had thought his marriage was in jeopardy at that moment, he replied:

Oh, no, I thought the opposite. It hadn't collapsed as far as I was concerned when the picture started. I thought, indeed, that now she could really start to function the way she had always wanted to function, with the director she wanted, with a cast she loved – Gable, after all, was her putative father and Monty was just lovely, and Eli – the conditions were absolutely perfect. I had brought in Frank Taylor, who had been an old friend of mine as the producer, so that she wouldn't have any problems with a producer. It was an independent picture, really. United Artists weren't going to interfere ... I thought that we were now going to function as I imagined we should. When I realized that she could not accept this good fortune, that's when it started to disintegrate.

She slowly alienated cast and crew, clinging only to the obsequious Paula Strasberg, who was now paid $3,000 a week and, unknown to anybody, was taking narcotics to treat the early stages of bone cancer. All Marilyn's old fears resurfaced while her husband, far from protecting her, seemed at first deputed to urge her to accept the discipline against which she was rebelling.

You know, there's a pattern in people's lives that gets repeated. If it doesn't get repeated, they're at a loss. She had to feel, when she was in the making of a film – it didn't matter if it was Billy Wilder or John Huston – that in some way they were persecuting her and I think in the very nature of being a director he has to correct her. In that relationship already rises the specter of expulsion. She did it with Olivier, with Wilder and with Huston. With Huston she had a hard time doing that because he simply backed off ... He knew he would have to wait her out, which he did. I think there was a pattern that she was simply helpless to change. George Cukor directed her in that stupid movie *Let's Make Love*. He had the same problem. He couldn't have been a milder director.

There was, he explained, no single moment when the marriage collapsed,

only a daily growing awareness that this was beyond her control. There was no way for me or anyone else, for that matter, to break through that pattern. She was simply bound to feel victimized. It wasn't just me, though. We had a cinematographer who never had more than one or two grips helping him. As he said, we need one light. He never delayed a shot for two seconds. She felt he was not treating her right. It became apparent that she was beyond reason. There was no way that anyone could penetrate this. At this point I thought I might be able to continue with the marriage, but I became increasingly aware that she was genuinely hostile to me.

For the first few days, shooting on *The Misfits* went well, though when Marilyn arrived, 20 July 1960, she was exhausted from *Let's Make Love*. She was, she pointed out, thirty-four years old, had been dancing for six months with no rest, and wanted to know where she was supposed to go from there. The answer, it soon seemed, was down a familiar path in which what turned out to be an excellent performance was won at the cost of her relationship with all those on the set and at the price of her own health. She even kept those who had gone to the airport to welcome her waiting for thirty minutes while she changed.

Kevin McCarthy (who plays Roslyn's estranged husband) has described his own experience of shooting the scene, early in the film, where he meets her on the steps of the courthouse immediately before the divorce hearing:

> We were rehearsing and she couldn't get all the lines done. This happened maybe six or seven times. My performance is going out the windows. I'm really trying to do my stuff but it gets interrupted. Whatever the secret I had for myself about how to play that stuff was gone. She finally was coming up the stairs toward me, and Huston is saying, 'I can't hear you, I can't hear you. Is she saying all the lines? I've got an idea. Let's run a line up Kevin's leg, get a microphone and put it under his tie. You won't be able to move, Kevin. Just stand there and do it.' And she still wasn't saying her little speeches. She came up maybe seventeen times. Huston says, 'She say them all?' And I say, 'Yeah, yeah, everything's all right.' And Huston said, 'Well, thanks, Kevin, nice working with you.'[72]

Marilyn's problem with the scene seems to have been that, with two divorces behind her, she was struck not by the similarity to her own experience as much as by the difference. 'I can't memorize this,' she complained. 'It's not the way it was.'[73] And the tension between the fictive and the real would trouble her as the film proceeded. Many of the lines she was required to deliver came directly out of her own life but were now aspects of a story that was in part her own but in part a product of her husband's desire to forge a new reality out of art.

Unusually, the film was shot in sequence, which made it easier for the actors to develop their roles. But Marilyn was arriving later and later for shooting. Susan Strasberg recalled her mother reassuring Marilyn that it was not her business to worry about production costs.[74] Paula Strasberg was nicknamed Black Bart, not least because she insisted on wearing an all-black outfit (black silk dress covered by black silk jacket, with black stockings, shoes, hat and veil), even when they were shooting in temperatures that could reach 120 degrees Fahrenheit. Inge Morath would describe her as looking like a mushroom. Strasberg's explanation was that she wore the outfit so as to be inconspicuous. The effect was quite the opposite. Whenever possible she would retreat into a parked limousine with its air conditioner powered by a 450 horsepower Cadillac engine. She wore multiple watches, set to different time zones (because, she said, she needed a reminder of when 'her' actors were performing around the world), and became increasingly unpopular with everyone on the set, particularly with John Huston who was not used to being confronted with intermediaries. As Miller recalled:

> John got really mad at one point and insisted that she didn't speak to him or to Marilyn anymore. Because by this time, he had to talk to the coach to communicate with Marilyn. She was completely distressed, so the coach was the interpreter. It was as if they spoke two different languages ... Marilyn was in such need of security ... That coach was a little crazy, she was an opportunist ... and not competent to help.[75]

In the middle of a scene Eli Wallach castigated Marilyn when she turned to Strasberg for help: 'What the hell is she telling you, you don't know?'[76] Upset by the evident hostility towards her, at the end of shooting Strasberg prepared, but did not release, this press statement:

> It's much more difficult to play yourself than someone you've never met. This is the most difficult part Marilyn has played, with the exception of one scene in *The Prince and the Showgirl* and *Some Like It Hot*. I believe it has been essential for me to be with her on this picture. It was essential because so much of it was close to her. Also, she is a creative actress, not just a personality. Almost every fine actor, including Walter Huston, always had someone to help them when they were working. Even Clark [Gable], in his first movies, had Josephine Dillon. I feel that I have contributed to every frame of *The Misfits* ... My work is evident on the screen.[77]

Rumours of the affair with Montand were rife at this point, and at one stage Marilyn defensively suggested that her husband might be having an affair with Angela Allen, the script supervisor. In early September, reports of the relationship with Montand began to appear in the Los Angeles newspapers and the actor himself went some way to confirm them, confessing that she had flown to Los Angeles from the set of *The Misfits* in order to see him, but that he had declined to meet her. As he explained, in an oddly elliptical comment to Hedda Hopper, 'She has been so kindly to me, but she is a simple girl without any guile. Perhaps I was too tender and thought that maybe she was as sophisticated as some of the other ladies I have known.' Even more oddly, he put developments down to the exigencies of his part in *Let's Make Love*: 'The only things that could stand out in my performance were my love scenes, so, naturally, I did everything I could to make them realistic.'[78] Shelagh Graham, in the *New York Mirror* on 4 September, even anticipated an announcement, presumably of their divorce, from Miller and his wife. Such reports, of course, found their way quickly to Reno.

Speaking to me Miller denied her flight to see Montand: 'That's a myth. She was in no position to do that. The only flight she took out was when

Huston arranged for her to be hospitalized for a week. She couldn't be photographed any more because the stuff she was taking was making her eyes look funny.' The truth is that when she was flown to the West Coast for medical treatment she had tried to see Montand at the Berverly Hills Hotel, but he was not there and did not respond to her note. The fact of the relationship, however, was common knowledge. Nan Taylor Abel, Frank Taylor's wife, speaking on a PBS programme in 2002, remarked: 'She had an affair with Yves Montand and they [Miller and Marilyn] were having a big fight about that. And at the same time he was supposed to be finishing a script and he was sitting there with his typewriter, but they were just arguing. So that's when I went down and got another room and said to Arthur, "Let's go over here where you can work".'[79]

Miller and Marilyn rarely spoke to one another on location. Huston took him aside and urged him to try to get his wife off drugs or he would feel guilty as long as he lived, only subsequently realizing the extent to which Miller had already exhausted himself in the effort to help her. On one occasion Marilyn abandoned him in the desert where they were filming rather than allow him in her car. He was rescued by Huston. Angela Allen later recalled, 'In the early scenes Arthur appeared besotted with her. I watched the disintegration of a marriage through the film ... Her behaviour was really despicable.' For Eve Arnold, on the set as a photographer from Magnum: 'She treated Miller very badly on the film ... She was very unhappy through that whole period. She took an overdose of pills. The dream was at an end.'

When W.J. Weatherby was invited to dinner with Miller, Marilyn openly expressed her boredom with her husband. Nor was it possible to conceal the rift from the actors who, apart from the daily evidence of estrangement, were aware of the extent to which the film itself bore directly on the relationship between author and star. Montgomery Clift observed: 'Arthur was doing some wish-fulfilment. He identified with the character played by Gable. Arthur wanted him to keep Marilyn because he wants to himself. But this marriage is over, and he might as well face it.' To him, the film's logic had more to do with Miller's desire to heal wounds, to propose a possible future, than it did with dramatic coherence. From his point of view, he and not Gable should have got the girl, though he recognized that, as written, this was scarcely possible:

My character represents something new, the future – Marilyn's future. Maybe Marilyn and I would have got together one day if we weren't so much alike. As it is, it's too much like brother and sister getting together. That's what's wrong with Gable going off with her in the end. When Marilyn first went to Hollywood, Gable was a father figure for her. It's like a girl going with her father. No, Arthur's got it wrong. Maybe that's what's wrong with his relationship with her. Maybe he was too paternal. I know she respected him too much, looked up to him. All idols fall eventually. Poor Marilyn, she can't keep anyone for long.[80]

It was an analysis that Miller himself might well have shared, at least in part. As he watched her perform the role of a woman disappointed in marriage, he could detect her own awareness of the irony. She was playing a woman who would eventually be reconciled with a man with whom she had argued but who offered her love. He remarked, 'it was far from accidental that by the end of the film Roslyn does find it possible to believe in a man and in her own survival'.[81] Marilyn herself believed in neither. As Eli Wallach observed, 'something happened in the relationship that was tearing it apart. She was conflicted between her real life and the acted life. Arthur had written her a valentine, a love piece. Each male in the movie spoke of how glamorous she was, how wonderful, how beautiful, how sensitive. And each one was going to resurrect and save that woman. That made her more unhappy.'[82]

The correspondence between actress and role was so close as to be disturbing. Marilyn said later: 'I didn't have enough ... distance from the character. Arthur wrote me into it and our marriage was breaking up during that period. Maybe I was playing *me* too much, some ideal me ... Maybe I was playing me, and Arthur was writing how he saw me instead of a character – or how he saw me before we broke up.' But, then, she had played that role before, off screen: 'When we were first married, he saw me as so beautiful and innocent among the Hollywood wolves that I tried to be like that. I almost became his student in life and literature, the way I'm Lee's student for acting. But when the monster showed, Arthur couldn't believe it. I disappointed him when that happened ... I put Arthur through a lot, I know. But he also put me through a lot.' For her, that was a natural product of relationships. He was private, she was social. He preferred a certain detachment: she liked company, noise, attention. 'It would have been easier for me with a more party-going kind of man, but that would be easy for one side of me.'

Miller had no answer when asked why his wife was failing to turn up for shooting. He half suspected that he might be the cause or the target of her tantrums. The fact that the two hardly communicated struck a young woman photographer, sent to cover the picture for the Magnum photographic agency which had been granted exclusive coverage, and for whom America was still a great adventure – she had driven to Reno from New York. Her name was Ingeborg Morath.

Inge had worked on several other films, including *Moulin Rouge* and *The Unforgiven*, but this, she said, 'was definitely the most fascinating film I've ever worked on, a very intense experience. You could easily see Marilyn was causing problems; she was always late, which was no fun for the others, and the film was falling behind schedule. But when she arrived, everyone was so pleased to see her.'[83]

She herself appears in a photograph taken by Henri Cartier-Bresson. In the foreground, Paula Strasberg, dressed in black, engages Marilyn Monroe in intense conversation. Sitting in a chair and studiously ignoring them is Miller. In the background is Inge, tousle-haired, in striped shirt, Leica strung round her neck, watching. Miller later recalled meeting Inge in the bar of the Mapes Hotel. He remembered 'a slender, noble-looking young woman with bobbed hair and a European accent, who seemed both shy and strong at the same time. I noticed the bob, her transparently blue eyes, and a conflicted sensitivity in her, but I was preoccupied by endings then, everything had gone out of control, and what words were spoken at the table I could never more than vaguely recall.'[84]

She remembered him as an impressive but remote figure, trying to persuade his wife to come to the set. Once or twice Inge was at the same dinner table, though Marilyn was absent. She recalled him saying, 'Ach! What a relief to get out of my hotel room!' Her own response was bafflement. 'I couldn't understand,' she explained, 'how anybody would be a slave to such a thing ... My mind is far too independent for this kind of stuff. If any of my lovers had wanted to sleep, I would just have left!'[85] On the other hand when she saw him in a swimming pool at a John Huston afternoon garden party, telling the story that became his play *Fame*, as he swam on his back, she thought him hilarious. 'I was very impressed with this, but then I forgot all about it because I had another boy friend at the time and Arthur was always preoccupied with Marilyn, getting her to the set.'[86]

For neither was this the start of an affair. Both were focused on the issues at hand. But if Inge was unaware of the extent of the breach between Miller and his wife, her pictures show otherwise. In one, against a sign on a white wall reading 'WAITING ROOM', Miller sits, pipe in mouth, staring ahead, while Huston slumps in the foreground as they wait for Marilyn to arrive. In another, Marilyn is lit for the courthouse scene while in the foreground Miller looks morosely ahead. In still another, Marilyn looks out of a hotel window as Miller stares emptily at her, cigarette in mouth, like figures in an Edward Hopper portrait.

Inge liked Marilyn, particularly what struck her as her dreamy quality, but it was difficult not to get a picture that looked posed, so aware of the camera was she.

Inge explained her approach to photography:

If you photograph you watch all the time. What interests me the most is not the vulnerability of people but their very person, not the way they pose for things. Marilyn posed a lot but I would wait for the moment when she wasn't posing, not to take a picture of her when she was tired, which I don't like, but when there was a moment when she was remarkably herself. It was wonderful to watch her. I would always watch when she was rehearsing or a little bit off the beaten track ... If you arrive at a certain stillness I think you see something about their being, in the photograph.

As far as she was concerned, Miller was no more than Monroe's husband, a man plainly preoccupied with the problems she was causing. She was a mystery, as was his relationship with her. 'I had no idea what was going on behind the scenes, but she didn't want to be photographed with Arthur.' Inge left *The Misfits* for Paris, where she was interviewed by *Marie Claire* magazine. Asked about Miller and Monroe she confirmed that they were perfectly happy. By the time the article appeared, they were divorced.

Huston began scheduling the daily start of shooting for noon, allowing for the lateness of his star, but even this was no guarantee. To him it was 'unthinkable for an actor not to start work at nine in the morning'.[87] Inevitably, as it seemed, there came a moment when it was no longer possible to shoot around Marilyn and filming had to stop. On Huston's orders, she was flown to hospital. In Los Angeles she was temporarily weaned from her sleeping tablets and given a tranquillizer, though this in turn induced a state of shock. Everyone awaited her return. To Miller's surprise, Gable was unworried, and not only because he was to be paid $25,000 for every extra day. He genuinely seemed to sympathize with Marilyn. To him, she was simply suffering from an illness, and needed treatment. On her return trip, she stopped off to see Joe DiMaggio in San Francisco.

In 1981, Miller began work on a brief memoir entitled 'Reno – '60' in which he recalled something of these events. He remembered, in particular, a telephone conversation with Paula Strasberg on the evening of one of the Nixon–Kennedy debates in the run-up to the presidential election. The phone rang in his room. She had called, she said, to tell him that Marilyn was asleep. He asked whether she was with her at all times because he had been told she had been seen wandering around the hotel, naked. (Marilyn had now permanently moved out of their room.) After a few moments Paula admitted that Marilyn had in fact been in the hotel elevator, travelling up and down, in the nude. His response was to settle down with a bottle of whisky. It was a new experience to be drinking alone.

Watching the Kennedy–Nixon debates had its own air of unreality, especially in the midst of several hundred people constructing a movie. They both appeared to him to be acting, the one sincerity, the other humility. After watching the debate and drinking the whisky, he sat in his room before vomiting in the bathroom for ten minutes. In the distance, the sky was orange from forest fires. He wandered down to the casino where Huston was gambling and where he himself had lost $600 in thirty seconds working on advice from a man who had just lost $40,000. He was looking for someone to have dinner with, preferably Montgomery Clift or Eli Wallach, who seemed to him to have retained their poise in the midst of the general chaos. He acknowledged the crew, though knew few by name since he had spent much of his time in his room, rewriting. Instead, he went to Huston at the gaming table and explained that Marilyn had moved out, thinking it best if he was the first one to admit to it. In return, Huston told him that Lee Strasberg would be flying out to see what he could do. They both had mixed feelings about it.

For her part, Paula continued to claim that she was no more than her husband's agent, a conduit to the man who really held the key to this wayward actress. But when Lee arrived he made no difference. Susan Strasberg later recalled a conversation between Miller and her father: "'What are you going to do about Marilyn?' Arthur demanded. We knew he thought Lee was a charlatan, so how could he expect him to save her? 'I'll talk to her later,' my father said, 'this comes first. I can't tolerate this behaviour toward Paula. She's an artist. She's worked with many stars and never been treated like this. If something doesn't change, I'm afraid I'll have to pull her off the picture. She has to be shown some respect.'"[88]

Beginning in 1978, Miller would attempt to capture this time in a work he would call *Finishing the Picture*, first for a reading and, in 2004 for a full production at the Goodman Theatre. If anything, the portraits of Paula and Lee Strasberg were now even more virulent (in a 2002 interview Eli Wallach indicated that he had offered to play Strasberg). Their only concern, in the final version, is with their own reputations and status. Kitty remains silent as far as the audience is concerned, though the other characters talk to her and hear her replies. It becomes a drama about a damaged woman but also about a wider dissolution. The sky is red from a distant fire. The cinematographer who sees this remarks that without fire the seeds buried in the earth will not sprout. Kitty's talent may, in like manner, have emerged from pain, a burned-over life; the problem is that the damage is by now beginning to seem terminal. Certainly relationships are strained to breaking point. Husband and wife are beyond talking to one another. As Paul (a self-portrait by Miller) suggests, they no longer like one another because they failed to save one another.

Back in the real Reno, one day Miller was led into Marilyn's bedroom by Paula in time to see a local doctor looking for a vein to inject Amytal. She screamed for him to leave. He retreated to continue work on the script. He made many small alterations, rewriting scenes overnight. In particular, he revised the ending. Since it had been designed in part as a fictional projection of a personal hope, that the gap between himself and Marilyn could be closed, he could not bring himself to allow it to end ironically, with the misfits left to go their separate ways. In the original version, Gay Langland, injured trying to catch a wild stallion, is found by Perce and Roslyn. As they head back to town she tells him she is confident he will find a way to live and insists that if he dies so will she. This version was revised in early September. Now Gay captures the freed stallion and ties it to the truck before releasing it, aware of the futility of the action. Roslyn and he are drawn together. A further revision followed in October.

For Marilyn, 'What they really should do is break up at the end.'[89] For her, the logic of the film should follow that of her own situation. But for Miller, even now, this was too implacable, a closure not only to the lives of his characters but also to his relationship with his wife – now, surely, damaged beyond repair but still not completely abandoned, at least by him.

More than thirty years later, Miller confirmed that the role she conventionally played, that of a woman whose sexuality conceals a vulnerability, almost an innocence, was close to the reality of her character: 'Oh, yes, she was just that way. She wasn't acting very much. Off-screen she was a lot like on-screen excepting that she got angry. She wouldn't show that, excepting I had her do it in the last scene of *The Misfits*, when she was furious at them for capturing the horses. Then she was quite a different person, and she became herself: quite paranoid.'[90]

As the film edged towards its conclusion, the strain – between husband and wife, actress and director, director and drama coach – became ever more obvious. Estranged from Miller, rebuffed by Montand, increasingly dependent on drugs, Marilyn, together with other members of the cast, spent an evening with Frank Sinatra at his nightclub. At the time she insisted that Sinatra was no more than a friend. Later, she was more equivocal. Miller recalled the time he had supposedly fallen between two beds when he was with Marilyn after their divorce. Either way, the trip to the club did little to restore her spirits.

Her attitude to Huston had also changed. Now she objected: 'He treats me like an idiot – "Honey, this" and "Honey, that".[91] The film, she insisted, was 'their movie. It's really about the cowboys and the horses. That's all they need. They don't need me at all. Not to act – just for the money. To put my name on the marquee.' *The Misfits* itself had become an insult: 'He could have written me anything and he comes up with this. If that's what he thinks of me, well, then, I'm not for him and he's not for me.' 'When I married him,' she explained, 'one of the fantasies in my mind was that I could get away from Marilyn Monroe through him, and here I find myself back doing the same thing, and I just couldn't take it … I just couldn't face having to do another scene with Marilyn Monroe.'[92]

Miller had his own doubts about the film, most especially about the way Huston chose to shoot it. He felt the director had stayed too close to the actors. He wanted more long shots that would 'remind us constantly how isolated these people are, physically and morally'.[93] Having spent time in Nevada while waiting for his divorce from Mary, he had been struck by the fact that the space was so vast, so oppressive that 'you're lost in it, you can spend a whole day without seeing anybody, not a car, nothing'. It was that feeling that he thought missing: 'That feeling should have gotten into the film. There's an irony between these people loving each other against that death, but we did not get that presence of death.' They were, after all, 'disconnected' and though 'it ends on a note of hopefulness, the story is basically tragic in its attitude toward the country and toward itself'. They were in this place because they 'were looking for something, they didn't know what. The whole state was full of misfits, people who did not fit anywhere.' It was to be a film 'about the total alienation of people from contemporary technology', people who reach out, as Biff Loman had done in *Death of a Salesman*, to a natural world as yet uncontaminated by modernity. But history is against them, as it was against him.

The Misfits, so much better than Miller feared while making it, is a powerful and moving work, no less so, perhaps, for our knowledge of the impending death of Clark Gable, so close in many ways to the character of Gay Langland, and of the end of Marilyn Monroe's marriage and career. For Miller, the experience was 'both sad and happy. What's very sad,' he explained, 'is that I had written it to make Marilyn feel good. And for her, it resulted in complete collapse. But at the same time,' he added, 'I was glad it was done, because her dream was to be a serious actress.'

Location shooting ended on 18 October. The previous day, a surprise birthday party had been thrown for Miller and Clift in the Christmas Tree Inn outside Reno. It ended with Marilyn shooting craps with John Huston. After the final shot of this film characterized by Miller as 'about people trying to connect and afraid to connect',[94] but in which Gay and Roslyn seem reconciled, Miller and his wife drove back to the hotel in separate cars, the gap between the fictional ending he had contrived and the reality he was living apparent to everyone. The production then moved back to Los Angeles where the film was completed in a Hollywood studio on 4 November, though not before Max Youngstein asked for script revisions. Gable, who had script approval, refused the changes. It was half a million dollars over budget and forty days over schedule.

Miller drove back to his Beverly Hills hotel once again on his own. Bewildered, he left Los Angeles for San Francisco, where he knew no one. He considered the idea of retreating to Connecticut and farming for a while, and, indeed, would go on to plant trees with the intention of selling them commercially, but instead found himself driving back to Los Angeles, spending a few aimless days there, emotionally drained and with no clear sense of what to do. A second marriage had sunk into the sand.

For her part, Marilyn remarked: 'I just had to get out . . . I just had to leave him. We had grown so distant, and he constantly ignored me. When I finally left him, I was such a nervous wreck and I wanted to get out so quickly that I even left behind my six jelly glasses' (thick, cheap glasses she had kept from her early days). 'I felt lonely and rejected,' she added, 'I drove myself into seclusion, and I worried myself sick. I felt that I was all alone in the world – just like I was during my childhood.'[95]

One week later, on Armistice Day, after meetings between the two of them in their apartment at 444 East 57th Street, Marilyn announced their separation. The announcement was carried in the *New York Times* the next day. *Life* magazine, for its part, noted that the 'most unlikely marriage since the Owl and the Pussycat has come apart', and that *The Misfits* had featured the very courthouse where Miller had divorced his first wife in order to marry Marilyn. So 'Pulitzer Prize-winning Playwright Arthur Miller, one of the country's foremost intellectuals, and Love Queen Marilyn Monroe, one of the country's foremost foremosts, were no longer as one.' It observed, too, that while Yves Montand had 'excited Marilyn's admiration' the separation had deeper causes: 'Marilyn's work requires her to live amid crowds while Miller needs solitude.' It quoted Marilyn: 'I'm always on the wrong end of the lollipop.'[96]

Their joint publicity release declared that they had 'amicably parted', the newspaper indicating that they had returned from the West coast on separate planes and were now living apart. In the *New York Times* a friend was quoted as saying: 'She's not just a star, she is an institution and must constantly be in the center of excitement and activity. The nature of Mr Miller's work requires him to be frequently alone and away from the stresses of show business.'[97] In an accompanying two-column article, the old stories were repeated. Unacknowledged 'friends and colleagues' were quoted as describing Marilyn as a woman of 'ferocious ambition' who was 'frightened', 'insecure', 'the beautiful woman who wants to be intelligent but is only shrewd', 'witty', 'ingenuous'. It concluded that it was 'her yearning for "serious" things and the intellectual life' that had been 'fulfilled by her marriage to Mr Miller'.[98]

He was aware of just how much the whole affair had undermined his confidence. Two weeks later, he was told by a friend that he should stop thinking of Marilyn and find someone else. In fact, that was precisely what he did, though a few weeks after his return he received a call from Marilyn asking him why he was not coming home. She was in their New York apartment. As he asked himself, 'had she forgotten her fury against me, or had it not meant to her what it did to me?' Her voice, he later recalled, 'had its old softness and vulnerability, as though nothing at all destructive had happened in the past four years'.[99] It was a curious incident, a call that seemed to come from nowhere and could lead nowhere.

'I still don't understand it,' he admitted. 'We got through it. I made a present of this [the film] to her, and I left it without her. I didn't even ride home with her on the last day.'[100] A few weeks later, the December issue of *Cosmopolitan* magazine published an article about their happy domestic life. It quoted Marilyn as saying, 'I'm delighted to have him close by',[101] and stressing that she was trying to be a good wife.

The Misfits was undeniably a personal work but the sense of alienation at its heart had a wider significance. Miller said later, 'I also feared dislocation for people of my generation' who had 'lost any orientation, politically, or socially, for that matter'. The old ideological matrix had been rendered irrelevant:

> I could not think of myself any longer as being allied with some working class or with the oppressed, because the oppressed were being middle-class. We were developing a classless society ... *The Misfits* was an attempt on my part to deal with the dislocation, with the sense that there was no root to anything, that we were a wandering tribe that was looking for some sense of values that was very difficult to locate. I do not think the picture succeeded in locating them. All it did succeed in conveying was the feeling that nothing was really connected to anything. And that is about the way I felt.

At the same time, it owed its existence to the wife he had already lost by the time the script was completed: 'I would not have written it except for Marilyn. I wrote it for her. It was the only time I did write anything for an actor and, had I not known her, I would not have begun such a thing. She had lost a child in early pregnancy, which really upset her a lot, so it was a kind of a gift. It was also the expression of some kind of belief in her as an actress.' But 'by the time we got to make the film ... we were no longer man and wife. The film was there but the marriage was not.'

Why? Nearly forty years on, he explained it in terms of divergent needs and ambitions:

> I really could not manage that kind of life, finally. I live a very quiet existence, despite appearances, and that whole show-business thing was more than I could take. And she was on her way. She wanted to do other things. She could not be happy settling down into a domestic kind of situation – nor should she have. But I think ... there was also a very destructive thing going on in her.

Could he not have saved her?

> She had two of the best psychoanalysts in the United States working with her at the same time, and if she could escape the ministrations of those two people, who had her best interests at heart and were very talented people, I do not see how anybody like myself could have reversed what was obviously taking place and which they knew was taking place. The self-destruction was terrifying, and certainly it was beyond me to master it. I could never do it, but I doubt that anybody could have.

What had she looked for in him? 'She wanted a father, a lover, a friend, an agent, everything, and, above all, somebody who would never criticize her for anything, or else she would lose confidence in herself. I don't know if that human being exists.'[102]

Barely a week after shooting on the film was finished, Clark Gable was dead of a heart attack. Clift would also die of a heart attack, in 1966. Marilyn would never make another film. Miller was back on the East Coast, ready to return to playwrighting. A period of his life was over. It would be thirty years before he again ventured into the world of film.

The Misfits was not, on the whole, well received. The League of Decency even did its best to have a scene in which Marilyn had embraced a tree eliminated on the grounds that it represented masturbation. Bosley Crowther in the *New York Times* found Marilyn 'completely blank', having nothing 'very exciting or interesting' about her, while the characters 'do not congeal' or 'add up to a Point'. He found the ending sentimental, and insisted that the picture as a whole 'doesn't come off'.[103] On the other hand, Gable thought it the best thing he had done, and Marilyn, too, ultimately recognized that in Roslyn she had at last found a part that offered her the challenges she had sought. There is nothing in Roslyn of the occasional cruelty and persistent egotism that had so undermined Miller's relationship with Marilyn. This is Marilyn as he had originally seen her, unaffected, the embodiment of a life force. But, as he later said of the film, 'it involves so much of her disappointment with people and her mistrust. She no longer believed that there could be a long-term relationship that didn't disintegrate.' Interestingly, in his comment on making the film he stressed not his own pain but hers: 'Artistically, it was a wonderful experience. It's just that personally it was terrible to see Marilyn go through such torture.'[104]

Marilyn returned to New York and every day for a week went through the hundreds of still photographs taken by Magnum photographers back in Nevada. She seems to have been in a strange frame of mind. Eve Arnold, who viewed the pictures with her, later recalled that during this week she had an interview with a European editor and she asked me to stay while she was interviewed. When she opened the door for the woman she was wearing a black diaphanous robe with nothing underneath and she had a hairbrush in her hand. While she was getting her tape recorder ready, Marilyn asked the woman whether she minded if she brushed her hair. No, of course not, said the woman. When she looked up, Marilyn was brushing her pubic hair.[105]

Provocation? Refreshing lack of inhibition? At the very least, having just finished a picture that had offered her a chance to escape her public image as sex goddess, here she was seemingly reinforcing that image, whether through calculation or inadvertence.

It is difficult to read this gesture as entirely rational, but then, Marilyn Monroe was never able to conceive of herself outside her role as movie star, literally an exhibitionist. At times Miller wondered whether this was anything more than a rationalization for a persistent narcissism or whether it was a product of fear and insecurity. She could not, it seemed, settle for a life out of the limelight, a domestic life, anonymous, with the small but real satisfactions of daily experience. As he asked himself, 'could we live an ordinary decompressed life down on the plain, far away from this rarefied peak where there was no air?'[106]

Meanwhile, though, the America of which he had despaired seemed to be changing. Opening a Sunday newspaper, he discovered that, along with a hundred and fifty other writers, scientists and artists, he had been invited to attend the inauguration of President-elect Kennedy, a fact which appeared to mark a change of style if not of direction. But he had good cause to be suspicious of Washington and the uses to which it might wish to put people such as himself. He was not even sure what the role of an intellectual might be in America.

He later commented that, given his experience with HUAC, he had doubts about going to Washington without a lawyer, but expressed the hope that he and the country had finally seen the end of a philistine decade. At least there was now a President capable of speaking and writing a complete English sentence and scientists could hold conferences to which their overseas colleagues could come without fear of being excluded for political reasons, though he suspected that the real cause of the invitation was the Soviet Sputnik, launched three years earlier and a shock to a complacent America. In other words, intellectuals were, perhaps, being enrolled once again as part of American foreign policy. Yet in truth he was more concerned with private rather than public matters.

By December, Marilyn was back in her old routine, seeing her psychoanalyst Marianne Kris in the mornings and taking classes at the Actors

Studio in the afternoons. Miller did visit her to retrieve one of his possessions. She seemed strange to him, and he to her. She tried simultaneously to be both pleasant and distant. He had not ceased to love her or at least to feel a sense of alarmed responsibility. He explained in May 2002:

> I had the illusion that if I didn't take care of her, she would come to a catastrophic end because she was living on the edge of her acceptance of life. Death was always on her shoulder, always. It was always there. After all, she had tried to commit suicide several times before we ever met and one time I brought in doctors to pump her out because she had swallowed enough stuff to kill her. As it turned out it took some years but it was beyond my powers or anybody else's to hold her back.

It had not, though, been all pathology. Looking back from the perspective of forty years, he insisted:

> she could be very funny. She had a terrific sense of humour, of irony, of generosity, to a fault. She would give anything away. We had a black cleaning woman, very tiny, and Marilyn gave her a black fur piece, black stockings, black shoes and a black cape. And one day we came in and there she was – Della her name was, I still correspond with her – and she was lying on a bed, her head propped up on one hand and dressed in all this clothing, and Marilyn said, 'Oh, you look wonderful, Della.' And Della said, 'Uh, uh. Too black.' She could be delightful to be with. She could be wonderfully kind.

But 'if she felt threatened, she could be very cruel and, of course, psychologically speaking she had a right to feel threatened because she had been threatened. So any sign of disagreement, even, raised the spectre of expulsion, of attack.'[107]

In the immediate aftermath of the filming Miller felt confused and exhausted, full of contradictory emotions, but – in retrospect, somewhat astonishingly – his despair lasted for only a short time. That was partly because, all else aside, he was suddenly freed of the arguments and accusations, and even, now she had chosen to leave him, of something of that sense of responsibility for her. More importantly, it was because he had met a woman who was not merely the opposite of Marilyn, being self-assured, unthreatened, supportive, but who would prove the single most important influence on his life, and therefore his art, for the next forty years.

By 14 December, just a month after separating from Marilyn, he was with Inge Morath, the Magnum photographer he had first encountered on the set of *The Misfits*. They had met again in New York. She was, clearly, an immediate and refreshing contrast to the person from whom he had just parted. It was a relationship that deepened quickly, and by early January he was beginning to ask himself about their impact on one another. For her part,

Inge was capable of being moved to tears by a relationship about which neither could yet be certain. Why, he asked himself, was she so disturbed by it? He surely could not think of marrying again after two calamities.

The crisis, if such it was, seems to have provoked a self-analysis that echoed his formal analysis of nearly a decade earlier. He began to write the play that would become *After the Fall*, feeling the need to capture and explore what had happened. It seemed to him that he had destroyed two marriages, if only because he had wanted to preserve part of himself, maintain a protected area which was his writing. Both women had seen this as a betrayal. Yet at the same time they, too, had destroyed him.

Looking back over his relationship with Marilyn (who, by now, was living with the Strasbergs), he felt that the accusations she and Mary had levelled at him had some justification. At the same time, his relentless self-examination was plainly wearing. By May he would be considering writing a play attacking analysis. On 28 January, meanwhile, he received a note from Laurence Olivier, then staying at the Algonquin, offering sympathy and understanding for the 'chaos' he had been through. It was only five years since they had exchanged confidences in England, recognizing something of their shared problems.

The relationship with Inge Morath continued, though both were tentative. He hovered between a temptation to end the affair before it got started and his sense of the peace she had brought him. He was not sure he could satisfy what seemed to him to be her high hopes. In fact, he was simply not sure about anything, being torn between resisting the new commitment, revelling in a new sense of freedom, and his fear of losing her. Moreover, it is by no means clear that he read the relationship correctly. Inge herself was far from convinced that she wished to commit herself to a man still seemingly in shock from the collapse of his marriage. It can hardly have been utterly intoxicating to enter into a relationship with someone who was privately considering ending it. For not all the cards, one suspects, were on the table as yet or, if so, not face up. She, also, had a failed marriage behind her. Meanwhile, he had begun to think more of the play he might write, about a twice-married man who meets another woman, and begins to understand his life.

On 11 January, he went to a screening of *The Misfits* which he thought beautiful, retrospectively acknowledging Huston's approach in allowing the actors virtual free rein. He made no comment on Marilyn or her performance. Nine days later, Marilyn flew to Ciudad Juárez in Mexico and secured a divorce. She declared that she and her husband had been living separately since November. It was the day of President Kennedy's inauguration. She assumed coverage of the event would relegate news of the divorce to inside pages. She was wrong. She returned the following day. Miller read the announcement in the newspaper and heard a report on the radio.

The divorce papers, dated 20 January 1961, indicate that Marilyn had appeared before the court with her counsel, Arturo Sosa Aquila, giving as grounds for the divorce 'the incompatibility of temperaments that exists between both spouses, which makes impossible the continuation of their married life' – a not unreasonable description of the failure of her third and longest marriage. Miller was represented by attorney Aureliano Gonzales Vargas to whom he had granted special power of attorney. There was, the document of divorce stated, 'no issue of this marriage', a phrase which, for Marilyn, must have recalled both her series of miscarriages and the ambulance ride from Amagansett that had ended in the loss of her child. The property rights having been settled, the marriage contracted on 13 June 1956 in White Plains was dissolved, leaving the parties 'legally free to enter into new matrimony'. The 'Plaintiffs former name: MARILYN MONROE' was declared 'restored to her'.[108] The relationship that had begun ten years earlier was now peremptorily ended, the divorce following just two months after their separation. Like his brother Kermit, Miller now had a Mexican divorce to his name.

The Misfits opened at a Broadway movie house on 1 February. Marilyn's companion for the event was Harry Belafonte. That same night, Miller attended a dinner at the home of the film's producer, Frank Taylor. His companion was Inge Morath.

Marilyn relinquished all rights to the Connecticut house. In volume 30 of the Roxbury Land Records is declared: 'KNOW ALL MEN BY THESE PRESENTS: THAT I, MARILYN MONROE MILLER . . . for divers good causes and considerations . . . have remised, released and forever quitclaimed . . . unto the said Arthur Miller . . . all such right and title . . . to the lands, premises and property situated in . . .'[109] This marked the final gesture of a marriage that had begun to founder within weeks of being contracted.

Miller commented in 1991:

> [Marilyn] would exhaust areas of her life. Simply exhaust them. Then she would go on. And this was one of them . . . the whole idea of a domestic existence . . . I can't live for too long in a tent and on the road. I have to have a steady domicile, and some peace and quiet, or I can't work. And she wanted that, too, with part of her psyche – wanted it desperately . . . And a child. But she also wanted something that made that very difficult to have. Which was this power. Star power. Because the opposite was to be destroyed.[110]

In February, under the name of Fay Miller and on the recommendation of Marianne Kris, Marilyn entered the Payne Whitney Psychiatric Hospital (to which Edmund Wilson, in 1938, had committed Mary McCarthy), unaware, apparently, that it was a mental hospital. She went there essentially because of her drug addiction but found herself stripped and placed in restraint.

Somewhere women were screaming. She sent a desperate letter to Lee Strasberg asking him to get her out, a letter years later put up for auction for $15,000, her iconic status making anything to do with her worth hard cash. (When the personal effects she left to Strasberg were auctioned in the 1990s they realized $13.4 million, $12.3 million of which went to Anna Strasberg, Lee's widow, a woman Marilyn had never met.) When Miller heard news of her hospitalization on 13 February 1961, he was distressed, knowing what impact it would have on her, the fear it would instil of repeating her mother's fate.

By then, however, she had been rescued by the ever-attentive Joe DiMaggio and taken to the Columbia Presbyterian Hospital, registering under the name, of Norma Jean Baker. She stayed there until 5 March complaining that it was impossible even to have a nervous breakdown in private. When she emerged she looked hunted, as the crowds gathered. This woman who had depended on her public to give assurance of her worth had also confessed that the public scared her. She had she explained, a fear of mobs. To Miller, it seemed that she had learned nothing of herself, that another collapse was inevitable, and that unless she was kept under constant treatment she would kill herself. He learned later that she had been angry at him for not visiting her in hospital. The truth is that he was afraid to, certain that it would lead to further disputes, but he was tempted and did send a note. Norman Rosten did see her. He told Miller that she was regressing.

Just one month later, at five in the morning of Tuesday, 7 March 1961, Miller's mother died. His father was due to be operated on the following Friday. In a scene that was later transferred almost precisely into *After the Fall*, Miller broke the news to him. At first, Isidore could do nothing but repeat, 'She was my right hand', saying that he had never known how to tell her he loved her and that he thought his own illness might have caused her death. An hour later, though, he had recovered, declaring that he would now be all the stronger. In fact, as Miller ruefully acknowledged, thereafter he would have to assume responsibility for the father with whom he had once been in contention.

Isidore called Marilyn, who attended Augusta's funeral service. He remarked, 'she had just been discharged from the hospital . . . and I was about to enter one myself. When I did, she called me every day after my operation, wiring flowers and phoning my doctors.'[111] At the funeral, Miller himself, knowing how she had hated his mother, found it hard to look either at her or at the roses she had sent.

Miller's relationship with his mother had not been easy. She had asked for help with her husband but he had resisted what seemed to him at the time a 'dull burden'. Now there was a rush of guilt and pity – guilt, for not feeling more deeply, pity for a man who now seemed rudderless. All depth of feeling, he confessed, had left him. Where there should have been unalloyed love there was self-accusation. His feelings about his mother were confused. This, after all, was the woman who had nurtured and encouraged him, had stood between him and his father's resentments when he had left Brooklyn, and a family in distress, to go to Michigan. This was the woman he had written to out of a need to explain himself, the woman who had loved him but whose love he had found it so difficult to return. Later, he acknowledged just how little of his life he had given her, and the thought led him, in 1993, to write a poem, a lament for her but also in a sense for himself at the recollection of the wall he had built between them to avoid drowning in her love. Now he wishes he could tell her everything that had happened since he lost her. She had sacrificed herself and tried to live through him. Perhaps, he suggests, she would have felt justified that he was what she had made.

He retreated to Roxbury. He had a new freedom, but it had hardly come on terms he could accept. Nor was he sure how to exercise it beyond surrendering it without knowing what the consequence might be. To commit himself again seemed likely to plunge him back into the same destructive turmoil; not to commit himself was to face a bleak future.

This was not quite the end of the story of Arthur Miller and Marilyn Monroe. One day she arrived at their Connecticut house to collect some of her things and show the house and land to her half-sister. He made them tea. As they said goodbye, standing in front of the garage where the driveway slopes down to the road, she showed him a bandage. This, she said, covered the wound from a pancreas operation, as though that might explain her behaviour back in Nevada, rather than, as he suggested in recalling this moment, indicating 'a consequence of immense dosages of barbiturates'.[112] In fact she had been operated on for impacted gallstones and an inflamed gall bladder at the Manhattan Polytechnic on 28 June.

So there they stood, outside the house where their separate dreams were to have been realized in some kind of golden alliance, feeling 'vaguely silly' as they met now on the other side of the marriage. She still seemed the child, anxious to justify herself, unaffected now, once removed from the tensions of Hollywood. And because this was that other Marilyn, what had happened in the intervening time seemed not forgotten but momentarily laid aside. Marilyn and her half-sister drove off, finally, and Miller turned back to his house.

Marilyn's memory directly conflicts with this account. 'I went to the country house,' she explained to Norman Rosten,

> with a small truck and a driver to pick up a few pieces of iron porch furniture. They were old sentimental pieces, not worth much, but they always followed me wherever I went, and I wanted them again. Maybe worth fifty dollars ...

So I called my ex about it, and he said sure come up any time and take them, if I'm not here you know where the key is. I told him when I'd be there, but when I got there he wasn't. It was sad. I thought he'd be there and maybe ask me in for coffee or something. We spent some happy years in that house. But he was away. And then I thought, maybe he's right, what's over is over, why torment yourself with hellos? Still, it would have been polite, sort of, don't you think, if he'd been there to greet me? Even a little smile would do.[113]

The one account has them concluding their relationship on a note if not of reconciliation then of mutual understanding and some regret; the other ends with a sense of abandonment, the absence that she had always insisted characterized men's relationships with her. She was the waif again, deprived of the father/lover. Asked in May 2002, about this discrepancy, Miller had no doubt that his own account was correct:

I helped load a few of the things she had left into her car. She was with her half-sister, Berneice Miracle. I had my Land Rover, which was new then, in the garage, and she had never seen one. In those days very few people had seen Land Rovers anyway. They were very distinctive, with the tyre mounted on the hood of the engine. It was very interesting to her. She wondered why I had gone to England to buy a jeep. We talked about that. I was here, most definitely.[114]

The answer was that there were two visits made by Marilyn. In July, she and Ralph Roberts, an actor and physiotherapist, drove there alone, collecting, among other things, a winter coat. But when she smelled another woman's perfume on it – Inge Morath's – she threw it in a rubbish bin. She later made another trip, the one recalled by Miller, in which she was accompanied by Berneice Baker Miracle. It is the former visit that Marilyn chose to recall. In August, she returned to Los Angeles.

Not even this, though, ended all connection with Marilyn, who had a genuine affection for Miller's father who had himself become seduced by the world into which his son had introduced him. They were drawn together, it seemed to Miller, by their common experience of abandonment. In February 1962 she had taken him for dinner at the Fountainebleau Hotel in Miami, primarily, it seems, in order to break the news of his son's impending marriage to Inge Morath. After she had left he found $200 she had slipped into his pocket. In May she invited him to accompany her to the Birthday Salute for President Kennedy, to be held in Madison Square Gardens, where she was, famously, to sing 'Happy Birthday to You'. She, who never had a father, found in Isidore one last tenuous connection with a world she had left behind since she, too, had found a new relationship – in her case with the President of the

United States, though Miller later noted that it was inevitable that both he and his brother would abandon her when it suited them.

Marilyn had interrupted work on her new film, *Something's Gotta Give*, for her trip east. The studio was not amused, not least because it was already in severe financial difficulty from the overspend on *Cleopatra*, starring Richard Burton and Elizabeth Taylor. The film, for Twentieth Century Fox, would never be completed, though nude pictures from a sequence shot in a swimming pool were released, with her approval, and appeared in *Playboy* magazine. Miller noted that she had lost none of her love of a publicly displayed sensuousness, even as her world fell apart. Marilyn herself remarked that 'we're all born sexual creatures. It's a pity many people despise and distrust this natural given.'[115] Now, though, she was making a statement, putting herself in the news, underlining her importance to the production. But the old problems had already resurfaced. She forgot her lines, turned up late, distrusted those who wished her well. And Miller could not forget her scorn at his failure to leave her, even as she had seen his desire to do so as further evidence of abandonment. She was, he now saw, trapped by her conflicting needs, playing out her desperation in the public eye.

On 1 June, her thirty-sixth birthday, she made her final appearance on the set of *Something's Gotta Give*. Six days later, she was fired by Twentieth Century Fox, no longer willing to put up with her behaviour, thereby sparking a legal battle, though later attempts were made to persuade her to return. She did not, though, withdraw from the world. She agreed to a number of photo shoots for magazines, seemingly determined to prove that she was still America's most glamorous actress. As ever, she was caught in the contradiction of taking pride in her physical attractions while being bitter that this was the primary cause of the condescension she felt she suffered. She had called for the firing of one actress because she was blonde and therefore a rival for attention, as she accused another of taping her breasts. Yet she demanded she be taken seriously as an actress. She had devoted her life to constructing this persona and could not abandon it.

Marilyn's own explanation for her lateness on set, on this film and others, was to relate it less to a desire for power than to her approach to life. 'I guess they think I'm late due to arrogance. I think it's the opposite. I also think I'm not in this great American rush. You've got to get there and what's there when you're there? I don't want to hold anybody up. I don't want to keep people waiting but I do want to be prepared when I get there.' Looking back, she said, 'I never used to be happy. It wasn't something I was counting on. I was brought up differently from the average American child. Happiness wasn't anything I ever took for granted. Fame and happiness seemed to me temporary, partial . . . it's not where I live.'[116] Quite where she did live, though, was no clearer than it had ever been.

Her last home was a small house at 12305 Fifth Helena Drive, Los Angeles, decorated, in an echo of her psychoanalyst's home, in Mexican style. She struck up a relationship with Frank Sinatra and seemed to be trying to put her life together again, but in the remaining weeks of her life her decline was evident to those around her. Various authors have attempted to trace her connection with John and Robert Kennedy and have suggested that the decision by both to distance themselves from her was a factor in this decline. In 1995, Miller would be visited by Seymour Hersh, who brought with him documents purporting to confirm the relationship and a deal to buy her silence. These turned out to be fraudulent. Whatever the immediate cause, though, she was once again heavily reliant on drugs, making repeated calls to her psychoanalyst Dr Greenson.

On the afternoon of 4 August, Norman and Hedda Rosten received a telephone call from Marilyn. She was

> bubbly, happy ... She spoke to both of us, an hour of talk, we passed the phone from one to the other. On the surface it was a happy exchange of news and hopes for the future: she was in great shape (not true); she was planning to begin a film in the fall (fantasy); her house was almost furnished (never to be); she planned to come to see us and then take a gala trip to Washington for the opening of Irving Berlin's new musical, *Mr President*; she was getting film offers from all over the world (doubtful) ... then she repeated How were we? How was I? And over and over ... Then a rush of new thoughts: it was time to put the past behind and begin to live, let's all start to live before we get too old; why don't I fly out for a visit and talk about the old days of Brooklyn.[117]

Just hours later, in the early morning of 5 August 1962, she was dead, face down on her bed, an empty bottle of Nembutal tablets beside her. There would also prove to be traces of chloral hydrate. It was almost certainly an accidental death. She had, reportedly, been planning to remarry Joe DiMaggio and left a letter to him expressing the hope that she would be able to make him happy. The letter broke off in mid-sentence.

In Miller's view, her days were probably numbered anyway: 'Marilyn was almost at the age when Hollywood would have dumped her. And she wouldn't have been able to take that. She would have turned to drink and drugs and killed herself. For her, movies were power. She would say that there were movies in which she had had a bit part that were still shown because she was in them. And she was right. She would have hated to lose that power. I can't see her having survived into old age.'[118]

Miller, by now deep into *After the Fall*, had watched her continuing career from a distance. In his play the central character, closely based on Monroe, might seem edging towards death, but, in actuality, as he wrote, all had seemed well with Marilyn, or at least no worse than usual when she was filming. When he saw the photographs of her in the swimming pool on the set of *Something's Gotta Give*, he wondered why she had chosen to return precisely to that version of herself that he had once hoped would be purged by *The Misfits*. Then he saw the story of her firing from the picture and began to feel anxious for her, though he had faith in her psychoanalyst who was her friend as well as her doctor. He was coming to the end of the first draft of *After the Fall* when news of her death reached him.

The producer Robert Whitehead has recalled Miller's excitement at being able to write again. 'When we first started meeting,' he recalled, 'Marilyn was still alive ... After Arthur finished the first act, in the summer of '62, we separated with a view to getting together after Labor Day.'[119] Marilyn's death changed the direction of the play and Whitehead felt that the second act was written too soon, before there had been a chance to assimilate the meaning of what had happened. When a reporter called to ask Miller for his reaction to his ex-wife's death, he replied, 'It had to happen. I don't know when or how, but it was inevitable.'[120] Asked if he would attend the funeral he said, 'She won't be there',[121] and hung up. The idea of being photographed next to a stone and in what he anticipated would be a media circus, seemed both pointless and repellent. Half a century on he said, 'I am sorry to say I don't particularly know how to deal with funerals. I have a tendency in general to separate matter from spirit in a way that makes it difficult to conceive of a relationship with a dead person. I feel that they are not there any more.'[122]

In the ensuing years interviewers would repeatedly ask him if he thought he might have saved her. His answer to Mel Gussow can stand for his several responses: 'She had the best analyst, Dr [Ralph] Greenson. He went beyond the normal professional relationship. She also had Dr Marianne Kris, who was supposedly one of the great analysts. The point had arrived where I didn't know how to do that. That's the tragedy. There's no way to intervene at a certain point ... A person's got to save himself. And sometimes you do and sometimes you don't.'[123]

Why did the marriage fail? Was it that she placed too great a strain on him and that he, in turn, could not stop the momentum of her self-destruction? Was it, as some publicly suggested, that they could simply not speak to one another, that they had been sexually incompatible? Miller's response, speaking a quarter of a century later:

> We had discovered something far deeper than they ever knew. We found plenty to talk about. She was a very politically interested person, interested in the society, interested in living. She wanted to survive into her middle and old age. She wanted children. I don't think there was any question of us being sexually incompatible. It was an attempt on my part and on hers to transcend

the barriers between two kinds of living – the one which was more sexual, the other more intellectual.[124]

In the end, their needs were too divergent. They were both deceived, as both deceived themselves. She was the patient who refused the ministrations of her psychiatrist-protector. He was the man whose will and imagination finally proved unequal to the task of rescuing her from the death with which she so assiduously flirted. She had attempted suicide in his presence, simultaneously underlining his failure to rescue her and his responsibility, as she saw it, for her condition. They failed each other. They changed nothing. Love, they both discovered, was not unconditional. But she would accept nothing less and he saw himself repeating the very failure that had led him to her in the first place, another disintegrated marriage sapping his morale.

There was a terror in her heart that he could never still until, in her eyes, he became its cause. When he saw her being injected with Amytal, just as the young O'Neill had come home from school to find his mother shooting up with heroin, it was hard thereafter to think that he could satisfy the dependency he had detected but whose depths he had not recognized in time. 'We had wonderful times,' Miller observed in 1987, 'I'd say out of five we had two good years, but her addiction to pills and drugs defeated me. If there was a key to her despair I never found it. I've never been any part of the drug culture. I didn't realize her addiction was the centre of her problem. The psychiatrists thought it was a symptom: they actually prescribed her pills.'[125]

Her analysts, it seemed to him, had failed to recognize her addiction to hard drugs for what it was and hence were confederate in her death. He was convinced that she had been on drugs in certain of her recordings and on the set of *Let's Make Love*. Her anger at him might even have been a consequence of his failure to join her, just as an alcoholic only feels comfortable, finally, in the company of other alcoholics. During the shooting of one of her films he had called in the head of the University of California Medical School in an effort to break her addiction. He had destroyed her drugs and for a few days it seemed to work, but there were always others who would supply what she needed and so she continued her spiralling decline.

In an untitled and undated story in which he tried to understand something of his relationship with his first two wives, he says of a character called Lorry (plainly Marilyn) that his conscience towards her is clear even as he acknowledges that they had conspired to destroy their life together. Their paths had not so much crossed as collided. They had come together out of need but that need had not been mutual. 'She'd ask for unconditional love,' Miller explained, 'but [could] not accept it. But I didn't feel I'd failed Marilyn. I felt I'd done all that anyone was capable of doing – more, in fact, and that it was just fate. You finally confront that old sky, and there it is.'[126]

There are certain photographs which suggest that for a while their love was, or at least seemed to them to be, unqualified. Friends and relatives might be amazed, even shocked, by the relationship, but they seem all to have agreed on the reality of the affection they felt for one another; as he said later, though, 'whether it finally cures anything is another thing'.[127]

Miller could never forget what the marriage had meant in terms of his work, the single most important part of his life. Asked later what he had written in those years, he replied, 'Hardly a word. It was impossible.'[128] Speaking in 2001, he said, 'I spent four years doing nothing, except *The Misfits*. There was no gratitude. It just increased her contempt. All of her relationships ended that way. There were times when it was agony, for her especially, but of course for everybody around her.'[129] The marriage over, he had begun to write almost immediately. Besides beginning *After the Fall* he also set to work on a play about a man called Rojas, later refashioned as a novel. In a three-week period in April 1961 he wrote a story called 'The Prophecy.'

Asked by the director Harry Rasky, for his 1980 film *Arthur Miller: On Home Ground*, to speak about the relationship between Roslyn and Gay in *The Misfits*, Miller offered what was, in effect, an account of his own relationship with Marilyn:

> She wants stability. She wants things not to change. She wants to rely on people while at the same time she is terribly suspicious of them and will probe until she discovers that point at which they will turn against her, that point of unreliability. His viewpoint is that, yes, that is true but that is life. Life is unreliable but in order to love you have to accept and even embrace the tension between expectations which must never be lost and their disappointment, which is inevitable. He is saying that everybody disappoints you but that there is always someone who won't. Gable and she, off-screen and on, exemplified these positions. He lived a life of enormous vigour and expectation at the same time as he was sceptical about practically everything. She couldn't believe in anything and she believed in everything.

As to Marilyn's death:

> It just seemed to me such a monstrous waste. She was in a terrific struggle for herself. She was always playing with suicide. She was trying to get as close as she could get [but] I always thought it was an accident. I can't believe she went over voluntarily. She needed a little luck, not even a lot, to keep her that day. She just didn't have it. I guess she was the original of all those who declared themselves a free soul and at the same time was suffering a kind of repression within, even as they were declaring that freedom and acting it out … Things possessed her that she couldn't disengage from. She was quite the opposite of a free soul. A little blessing would have deflected it.

Quite the most complete, honest and direct analysis of the relationship between Miller and Marilyn is the one he himself gives in the outline for a film version of his 1964 play *After the Fall* referred to earlier, a film that was never made. This comes closer even than the play to expressing the nature of their lives together, from their first encounter through the pain of the later years. It is also a document that in many ways sums up Miller's own journey from a childhood disillusionment with family, through the days of an earnest commitment to socialist values, the collapse of his first marriage and on to the moral quagmire and calculated persecutions of HUAC. It deals with his struggle to rebuild his personal life with Marilyn and the ultimate failure of that dream.

By the time he sketched this outline, he was no longer denying the relevance to himself. In the play the central female character, Maggie, is a singer. Here she is an actress. The distance between Maggie and Marilyn shrinks to nothing. In the first 'movement or phase' of the film, Quentin, the figure based on Miller, still exhibits a desire for the old leftist solidarity that had shaped him and which gifted a curious sense of moral superiority. This had been analogous to that feeling of solidarity which, as a child, he had believed to exist within the family and whose shattering was a major factor of his youth. That faith in unity had also, he explains, underlain his first marriage, the belief that relationships are unconditional. That had ended, however, when his wife and he in effect disposed of one another, just as those on the Left had broken apart as a consequence of betrayals and the revelation that what they had taken for principle was a form of naivety.

As for Maggie/Marilyn, Quentin/Miller sees a kind of freedom in her. She seems to him to be a form of truth, demanding nothing. She responds to him because he believes in her rather than trying to seduce her. And this gives her a confidence in herself that others cannot offer. She also responds to a man with social commitment, who seems to care about others. He represents an escape from her own past which is one of abandonment and humiliation.

At this point, the Committee subpoena him, and this he knows is a consequence of his relationship with Maggie, who alone can guarantee them the publicity they seek. An executive arrives from her studio, as Spiros Skouras had in Miller's case, to insist that he will destroy her career if he refuses testimony. There are suggestions that her contract can be broken on moral grounds. Before the Committee he refuses to name names and when he speaks we are told that it is as if he were addressing himself, precisely as Miller had seemed to speak to himself as much as to those who sought to interrogate him.

For Quentin/Miller, Maggie/Marilyn is someone who identifies herself with the downtrodden and represents and embodies sexual fulfilment. What follows, though, is the collapse of good intentions, as a worm enters the apple.

As his wife, she begins with the aim of supporting him in his career but is acutely alert to signs of rejection and becomes increasingly angry when he fails to set his work aside to support her in her battle with directors and the media.

As for him, his freedom is not forthcoming. He cannot stand by as the studio exploits her, but he comes to realize that she wants something more than this. She demands total commitment and when, in her eyes, he fails to exhibit this, a kind of contempt is born.

Meanwhile, he remains under threat from the Right and his wife detects his fear, which in turn deepens her contempt and self-doubt since he was the one who had affirmed her talent. He thereby becomes a threat to her. What she fears above all is being abandoned, and he now becomes the embodiment of that abandonment. She can no longer sleep – in fact her fear of death inhibits sleep. Meanwhile, Quentin is forced to acknowledge his failure to understand her, to rescue her. He becomes aware of the fraudulence associated with his messianic impulse.

There would be those who said of the play that it was Miller's attempt to absolve himself of responsibility. Quite the opposite is true. Though these notes for a film version are more direct and explicit, they and the play constitute in part an analysis and in part a confessional. What chills him especially is his own failure with Marilyn, not least because it replicates those earlier failures – with his family, with Mary, indeed even with the political ideals that had become implicated in his personal relationships. It is clear in the play; it is even clearer here.

Maggie/Marilyn's career begins to slide. She sleepwalks through a film, surrounded by people she pays. Quentin/Miller is faced with the bald fact that without her income they cannot live in the style they do, but that anything less will probably hasten her destruction because what she 'is' now is made in great part of these accoutrements of success. Quentin now makes the same mistake that Miller had made with Mary and with Marilyn. He blurts out the truth. It is as destructive as Miller's own earlier attempt. It is seen as a further betrayal. He confesses that he had originally thought of her as a pretentious tart, and that despite his subsequent realization of her value, he had been seduced by the thought that he could save rather than love her.

She continues to decline. More and more she resorts to drugs, taking them to bed like a lover. He feels the need to leave her, as she has indicated he should. His very impulse to leave is, Miller writes, like his impulse to give way to the Committee, an impulse he hates but is forced to recognize. And there it is worth pausing a second. Did Miller in fact feel such an impulse with respect to HUAC, and did Marilyn detect it if he did? The notes continue, in effect retrieving some of the more painful moments of Miller's life with Marilyn, as they describe his attempt to wrest the pills away from her. Acknowledging her suicidal drive, he nonetheless sees in himself a desire to let it take its course even as he intervenes.

The screenplay ends as his relationship with Marilyn did not, but nonetheless with a symbolic truth. Their parting is brought forward. There is no reference to miscarriage and nothing here of *The Misfits*. The notes end as Quentin watches Maggie emerge from a hotel and the press and fans surge forward. A maid walks behind her with whisky in a paper cup. The camera catches her frightened eyes. She stumbles and then gets into a limousine. He watches as she sits in the back seat, her head thrown back. He walks away.

Here, in a dozen pages, is the story of Miller's relationship with Marilyn Monroe, conveying his sense of how the failure of that relationship seemed to him connected with other failures, the collapse of other dreams. In the play version there is redemption, as a character based on Inge Morath restores him to himself and offers a way of understanding the private and public worlds. The screenplay, by contrast, ends on a note of irony and regret. It seems designed both to present and to seal off a phase in his life. It is a farewell to a woman whom he seems genuinely to have loved but whom he misread, as she did him. But if it was so designed, it seems not to have achieved its objective for, in notes scattered in his papers, he continued to return to those years as if, for all the contentment that his life brought him, this remained in some way unfinished business, a story whose ending may, in retrospect, have been inevitable but whose meaning still in some way eluded him.

A decade and a half after his relationship with her had ended, he contemplated the idea of writing a short piece about her called 'The Other Marilyn', thinking that perhaps he still owed her a debt. It was never written. Two years later, though, he was still puzzled by a woman whose life he had shared. Holidaying in Nantucket in 1978, he recalled how close Marilyn's story had been to that of Jean Harlow. Indeed, in a photo shoot for Richard Avedon in 1958 she had actually dressed as Harlow. It was convincing, Miller suggested, not because she was particularly like her but because she felt a natural sympathy for her tragic life. Ironically, he recalled how pleased Marilyn had been when she was told how like Harlow she was. A month later she was still on his mind, still a mystery, as he thought of her passing from him to Sinatra, to the Kennedys, chasing some dream that could never be grasped.

In 1984 he was still recalling this phase of his life, a time of so many unsolved riddles, baffled that he could ever have considered she might be a wife, angry that he should have allowed himself to abandon his career in the belief that he could save her from her demons. In truth, though, it was something more than the emotional pressure of those years, and time spent working on *The Misfits*, that had kept him from the theatre. Here he echoes an earlier comment:

I was quite out of synch with the whole country. I would have had a long period of that type whether I had married Marilyn or not. I simply couldn't find a way into the country. This was the great American Century ... what someone has called the twenty-year century. I never believed it would last. I didn't believe the values they were espousing. I didn't think it had a future. I thought we would pay for it one way or another, which we did in Vietnam. I couldn't begin to speak of it. It was as though I were living in a different world. I couldn't speak of it as an artist. I didn't know how to do it.[130]

Besides which, he suspected that if Marilyn had not been the agent of his alienation, he would have found another way to destroy himself.

In the years that followed he continued to dream of her. Somehow, he had never been able to mourn her when she died. There were too many conflicting emotions at play. It was twenty years after her death before he could cry at the thought of her death.

Despite the bitterness between them, Marilyn kept all the letters he ever sent her. They were found bundled together on her death. Asked by me, in 2002, what mementoes he retained from their relationship, Miller could list only four or five letters. Otherwise there was nothing to show for twelve years that had turned his life around. Then he stopped and pointed through the house they had planned together to the garage, which opens off the back of the kitchen, and added, 'Those and her bicycle. It's been hanging up in there for forty years.'

And there it was, and is, the bicycle she had ridden when the two of them had gone on their secret rides together, chasing love through Central Park, over which he had looked out as a boy, fireflies floating down from the roof of the family's expensive apartment building to the limousines below. This was the bicycle on which she had ridden beside him through the Brooklyn where he had grown up, when the family money had gone and his parents turned against one another in their despair at lost dreams; the Brooklyn where he had once delivered bread at four-thirty in the morning, discovered communism in a street corner conversation, and at the age of seventeen sketched out his first short story, born of his father's despair, a story about an ageing salesman, his head full of tainted dreams, facing the last day of his life.

12

INGE

Towards the end of the Second World War, British aircraft flew over Berlin dropping not bombs, but leaflets. A young woman watched as they floated down as if part of some bizarre ticker-tape celebration. She snatched one from the air as the planes droned on and the anti-aircraft guns thudded around her, and found herself staring at a photograph that was almost as surreal as the scene itself. Here were enemy planes that had flown halfway across Europe to fill the air with floating pictures, pictures, she realized, of shoes, mountains of shoes: men's shoes, women's shoes, children's shoes. Amidst the broken buildings of Berlin had come this snowstorm of images, each with a caption that turned the surreal into the real. All the owners of these shoes, it said, had been killed in the concentration camp at Maidanek.

She had heard rumours of concentration camps, but this was the first evidence of what they might mean. She never doubted the truth of the photographs, never forgot the shock she felt. It was not what was in the pictures, but what was not. She felt the pressure of that absence. Even to hold the leaflet in her hand, however, was to risk arrest, and the knowledge of that fact in itself seemed to offer confirmation of its truth. It never occurred to her to dismiss it as simple propaganda. The image and the caption had the power to change her sense of the world, to remove what lingering doubt she had about the forces that had shaped her life.

Ingeborg Morath was born on 27 May 1923 in Graz, southern Austria, near the borders of Czechoslovakia, Hungary and Yugoslavia. Somewhere beyond, lay Russia. She was educated in two further countries, while marriage would take her to two more. Her mother's family came from Lower Styria, today's Slovenia, where they had lived in Windischgrät, now Slovenj Gradec. The crossing of borders, the shifting of national identities, was part of the family's experience, as it would be part of the experience of many in 20th century Europe. In 1919 the border between Austria and Slovenia was redrawn. The family were forced to leave, abandoning almost everything. Inge was a traveller by nature, aware simultaneously of similarity and difference. As a child she read Russian fairy-tales while Prince Gagarin, who had fallen on hard times, taught her father Russian and told her about his old country. Russia was to become a central interest. She went there with Arthur Miller in 1965 and then again, on her own or with him, in 1967, 1986, 1988, 1989 and 1990.

She was the daughter of two scientists, her mother working as assistant to her father. Bizarrely, the couple, raised as Catholics, had converted to Protestantism before their marriage as a guarantee that they could divorce if they wished, though, as Inge recalled, 'they were the couple most in love all the years they were married'.[1] The quick conversion was a scandal in 1920s Graz.

Inge's early years were spent moving from place to place, from one language to the next, as her parents' careers advanced. She went from Graz to Munich to Freiburg and attended ten different schools, the first, in France, run by nuns. They spent time, too, in Darmstadt, in an apartment a few hundred yards from the Mathildenhöhe, where there was an artists' colony originally established by the Grand Duke of Hesse. Partly composed of art nouveau buildings alongside a contrasting Russian chapel, this, she said later, represented her first important visual experience and stayed with her, as did visits to the theatre. She recalled in particular seeing her first opera there, *Mignon* by Ambroise Thomas, as she did hearing the jazz records of a family friend and meeting her father's Indian students.

Far from being disturbed by this succession of schools and countries, both Inge and her brother revelled in it. The positive side was that she managed to avoid mathematics while learning languages (she would eventually speak seven). On the other hand, it did have its drawbacks. She learned how to write in France. When they moved to Germany she was put into a school next to their house and also to the local prison – and hence with a fair number of prisoners' children – where she spelled her German in the French way. As a result, for six months she received poor marks for her spelling. In retrospect, she believed that her love of language came from her desperate attempts to prove that she was not the backward child her German teachers presumed.

For all this movement between countries, however, she was always clear about her nationality. She was Austrian. Vacations were spent with her grandparents, who had vineyards and a large house. Her world was privileged but it was also various. During her youth there were few clouds. Her parents may have been scientists but they also enjoyed the arts, and Inge found herself being taken to museums and exposed to literature from her parents' library. The family house, and the houses of her grandparents and aunts, were full of art. She recalled, in particular, her mother's love of Dürer. For someone who would later become a photographer there were also cameras to hand – from her grandfather's, before which she would pose, to the Contax on top of her father's microscope, a camera owned by her mother who took the photographs used by her husband in his lectures. Towards the end of the 1930s the family moved to Berlin, where she attended the Luisenschule in Ziegelstrasse, near the Friedrichstrasse Station, while living outside the city. This necessitated a two-hour commute by cycle and train. They later moved to the suburb of Wilmersdorf.

Her mother, known to the family as Titi, hated the Nazis, it seems partly for aesthetic reasons. As Inge later recalled, 'She couldn't stand this brown' that they wore, though her brother, Werner, thought that her disaffection had only come when it was clear that the war was lost. Her father, Edgar, was more ambivalent. He had been a fighter pilot in the First World War. For him, that war had not been without its gallantry. He and his fellow fliers respected their British opponents. In his mind he was now 'back there in his beautiful uniform, gallant. There was a great mystique born out of that.'[2] He had respect for the past, for the Habsburgs, but at first failed to understand what was happening in the new Germany of the 1920s and 30s. He had simply proceeded with his university career. Inge had always believed that he had never been a Nazi Party member, and it was not until 2000 that her brother corrected her. Their father had joined the Party early out of a sentimental nationalism. There was, indeed, a photograph of him in Nazi uniform. Serving in the Austrian air arm, he was receptive to Nazi promises of a returned greatness. Later, he volunteered and flew supply planes into Stalingrad. He urged his daughter to join the Party, even late in the war when defeat was beginning to seem inevitable. Miller later characterized him as politically naive and guessed at what he was sure must have been his bitterness when his daughter married a Jew.

Edgar Morath seems, though, never to have been anti-Semitic, simply finding this a baffling aspect of Nazi ideology. Indeed, in the late 1930s he advised a number of their Jewish friends to leave. There were, at that time, still Jewish professors in the universities and American visiting professors, who continued to come after the outbreak of war. A Jewish couple lived in the basement of the family home for part of 1939, by which time Inge herself was becoming more politically conscious. He once transported a Jewish colleague out of the country into Switzerland in the boot of his car, a gesture that could at the very least have landed him in prison and which, more likely, could have earned him a place in a concentration camp.

Speaking later, Miller saw him as a man who responded to authority, irrespective of its ideological complexion. He had been invited to go to Russia as a forestry specialist, expert in the manufacture of plywood and paper. 'They offered a good salary and he pressed his wife to go with him. It was only her resistance that stopped him going. He was as much of a leftist as the Kaiser, but it had nothing to do with that.' As Inge explained, the full horror of the political situation just 'didn't gell. The only time I quarrelled with him was over political aspects. We had violent quarrels. But he disappeared very early in the war. People were drafted, even in the reserves. He began flying transports into Russia and I saw very little of him.' At the end of the war, according to Miller, 'he was practically psychologically inert as he found out what had gone on in the camps'.[3]

Inge's brother was drafted into the Luftwaffe at the age of sixteen and a half and was shot down by the British on his first mission in the Mediterranean. He ended up in an Egyptian prisoner-of-war camp, though was posted as missing for some time, the family unsure whether he was alive or dead. He made several escape attempts, some not entirely untouched with farce: 'One of his best attempts came from the fact that the British left their aircraft standing around at night, so they decided that they were simply going to take one of these and fly to Tunisia. They dug a tunnel for months, got in the airplane and then realized that none of them could read English, so they couldn't read the instructions.'[4]

In a public lecture in Berlin in 1994, Inge spoke of the increasingly oppressive atmosphere of late 1930s Berlin in which certain books had to be concealed and jazz records removed.[5] Her mother's distaste for the Nazis and their uniforms, she explained, could only be mentioned among friends, and then at some risk. As for art, this was now censored, though ironically she was introduced to the avant garde as a result of the first 'Degenerate Art' exhibition, held in 1937, in which the paintings were interspersed with slogans denouncing them: 'Reproductions of the "infamous" paintings showed up in school corridors to instil in us the obligatory feelings of hatred.' The effect was quite otherwise: 'I found a number of these paintings exciting and fell in love with Franz Marc's *Blue Horse*.' Only 'negative commentary' was permitted and, as she explained:

> thus began the long period of keeping silent and concealing thoughts out of which a more intense way of visually observing came to pass ... I learned everything about modern art [from this exhibition] because we were forced to go there. We were supposed to say that it was terrible but I just said nothing, and I learned by heart those paintings that I wanted to remember. I went home and I drew the compositions and then threw them out. So I memorized paintings.[6]

Olivia Lahs-Gonzales recalls that Inge was drawn to 'Ernst Ludwig Kirchner's street scenes, Paul Klee's fantastic landscape and fish paintings, and Oskar Schlemmer's *Frauentreppe* (Women on a Staircase, 1925).'[7] All this was a relief from a visual world of propaganda, with its authorized images to which the observer was invited to do no more than submit.

Inge was then, and remained, a dedicated reader: Mann, Dostoevsky, Gogol, Musil. She was an admirer of André Breton's surrealist novel, *Nadja* (1928) and that surrealist influence surfaced from time to time in her photographs. Books were also to prove her way into the countries she visited. In later years her preparation for a foreign shoot consisted of learning the country's language and reading its literature, and many of her photographs were to be of writers, their houses, the scenes in which they set their novels. It was as if photography could bridge a gap, was itself an act of translation. Whatever else Inge Morath derived from these years, at the very least she was taught the significance of books, burned in 1933, and the centrality of paintings, put to the torch in 1939. She herself explained that in a world in which you had to learn to keep your mouth closed, it became necessary to look with greater attention. She always took seriously Goethe's observation that we are born seeing but are required to look.

It now became necessary to speak in code, if at all. Publicly, what was required was subservience, and not only to political but also to cultural edicts. Theatre and concerts were still available but listening to foreign radio stations was forbidden, if practised. Repression and denial became civic virtues; the private conscience, the hermit's cell.

Inge passed her final school examination but before proceeding to university had to work first in a daycare centre for workers' children and then do six months of *Arbeitsdienst* (labour service) at Grossborken in eastern Prussia. This was a prerequisite for university admission and was designed as part of the process of indoctrination in National Socialism. Reading was punishable with extra work, which she was accordingly obliged to do. Mail was censored, clothes required to conform to regulation length and type, while critical remarks were to be reported to the authorities. Sympathy with those singled out for punishment was itself seen as subversive.

The procedures and practices of totalitarianism were designed to secure something more than mere obedience. What Miller would call human charity was eroded in the name of a necessary uniformity of national purpose. The individual conscience, and hence the individual, was to be superfluous. What mattered was that the mass should grant legitimacy to power. This was the principle behind the choreographed rallies, the operatic stages on to which the leader would step to the ecstatic, yet controlled, cries of those who rendered up the tribute of their souls.

Despite the difficulties, Inge returned to Berlin and entered the university, where, as the city became a target for enemy bombers, she studied romance languages. Three cousins she had played with as a child were killed. 'I studied where I could, in the University and the Underground stations that served as air raid shelters. I did not join the *Studentenschaft* (students' organization) and one day, in the subway, one of [my] professors, his name was Pfeffer, bent down and whispered into my ear, "We'll get you yet."' Membership was not legally required but was an expectation. There was intense pressure to conform. Nonetheless, she refused to join. The risk was that, like others who refused, she would be sent to the anti-aircraft batteries in eastern Prussia, 'which was a place where you absolutely did not want to be'.[8] Among the books she read at this time, crouched in the shelters, and in a city where literature was censored and freedom constrained, were Tolstoy and Dostoevsky. On another continent, Arthur Miller, too, read Dostoevsky as he travelled on the subway.

Inge's mother continued to work in the laboratory, while taking her daughter into the countryside from time to time to buy food, a venture that led to them being denounced by an anonymous informer and hence losing their ration cards for a number of weeks. They too had to confront the corrosive impact of those who named names. Speaking in Berlin in 1994, Inge recalled three vivid images from those days. One was of returning from a bomb shelter to find the front of their building blown away (they slept there that night, nonetheless). Another was attending a performance of the second part of Goethe's *Faust*, with Gustaf Gründgens as Mephistopheles. The third was of the falling leaflets that had brought her news of Maidanek.

In 1944 she passed her exams but was immediately drafted to work in a factory at Tempelhof. (Years later, travelling by ferry across the Rhine with her new husband Arthur Miller, she met the man responsible for sending her there. He offered no apology, simply asking whether she could help him publish a book he was writing.) She worked on an assembly line, 'like Charlie Chaplin in *Modern Times*', sometimes given food by the regular workers. Her grey identity card at Tempelhof, she later recalled, was stamped with the slogan 'Until the victorious end of the war'. Injured in an accident after a bombing, she was forced to treat herself by pressing coal dust into the wound. The impregnated dust left a dark scar that would remain with her for the rest of her life – not, to be sure, like the tattooed numbers on the forearms of concentration camp victims, but a reminder, nonetheless, of a time of privation and some despair. But she never confused her own suffering with that of those in the camps. Indeed, for many years she felt a burden of guilt that plainly did not afflict many of those directly responsible for such atrocities though that guilt may also have derived from the fact that, according to Regina Strassegger, who co-wrote the text of the 2003 *Inge Morath: Last Journey*, she also undertook translation work for the Nazi Foreign Ministry.

In the spring of 1945, when the game was manifestly up, she had a meeting with her father who tried to convince her to join the Nazi Party, saying that it would be safer for her. The two had a violent argument. She knew he lacked political judgement but this suggested that he lacked moral judgement as well, and certainly that he failed to understand his own daughter who had known clearly enough the conseqences of her own earlier stance, indeed was still suffering from them. The two parted with the gap between them not closed.

With the Russians now pressing towards Berlin, she decided that the time had come to leave. A gate had been smashed by the bombs, and she simply walked out. For want of any other destination she set herself to go to Salzburg, where her family now lived. There was little transport available. At first she walked along city streets and country roads littered with dead people and animals, a surreal *mise-en-scène*. The roads were crowded with refugees, deserters, soldiers from the east. The military were ordered to destroy the bridges. At one they waved her over before detonating the explosives. She had to scavenge for food. When a sausage was stolen from her it seemed a disaster. From time to time she would fight her way on to the crowded platform of a railway station and cling on to a train for a few miles until Spitfires plunged down and raked them with cannonfire, scattering everyone into the ditches and fields.

The chaos was more than physical. To her, it seemed like the end of the world. Though these people shared a common plight, they were still afraid to talk openly to one another, even of their despair. In her 1994 lecture in Berlin, scene once of her broken youth, she explained, with an affecting simplicity, the plight to which she had been reduced. There was no water to drink, no water to wash with, no place to relieve herself. She decided to drown herself in a river, but was pulled down from the parapet of the bridge by a soldier back from the Russian front, a man who had lost a leg in the fighting and who told her that she had no right to kill herself. The war was anyway almost over. The description is flat, matter of fact. It had simply seemed logical to die.

She walked on. It was 'a slow procedure', not least because her companion was now a man with a wooden leg. They finally reached Salzburg, but the effect of what she had undergone had been to destroy her memory. She was exhausted and bewildered:

> We arrived in Salzburg, at the railway station, which was a kind of camping ground for refugees. The soldier kept on saying to me, 'Where is that house you've been talking about? Are you sure it's in Salzburg?' Yes. I looked so dirty that he took me to all the poor neighbourhoods. We were walking around the city. But our house was outside, on a very beautiful and elegant alley, with rather elaborate houses. Then I remembered that it was somewhere in that direction. We finally got to the house, which is set maybe thirty metres back from the road, and he said, 'All right, go ahead and try it', because he thought I was crazy trying to go there. My mother opened the door, and we had a long embrace and when I turned round he had disappeared. I ran after him. I ran in the alley, but I never saw him again. It's a mystery.[9]

In later years Miller wondered whether the soldier had even existed. Perhaps, he thought, he was summoned up by her mind as she tried to find the strength to make her way back across a ruined Germany. Perhaps he was one side of a debate she was having with herself as she struggled to find some reason for living. In the speech he delivered in April 2002 at her memorial service, he told the story of her return home from Berlin but left out the figure of the soldier, in part because it seemed inappropriate to the occasion and in part because he did indeed suspect he had been a fantasy, albeit one that enabled her to survive.

Asked what the long-term effects of these experiences had been, Inge replied:

> I think it was two things: one, that you really felt terrible having survived; two, since you had survived, you might as well survive well. There was a curious state of mind, then. Everyone was very hungry and dirty, but there was a certain euphoria, as there is when you face danger. So, suddenly things were possible that hadn't been possible practically since I was a child. You could read things that had been forbidden. You could see movies that you were never allowed to see. You could see art. To me, painting was the thing I loved. It was a great liberation.

For the moment, the thrill of new possibilities chased out other concerns. Later, though, the guilt of the survivor, the guilt, even, of speaking the language of Nazi Germany, would lead her to the gates of a concentration camp. Even as she had been suffering from the accumulating consequences of her own resistance, she had been acquiring an irrational feeling of responsibility for the crimes of those she hated.

Shortly after her return to Salzburg the American 3rd Division swept into the city and the war was effectively over. Food was scarce and work scarcer but soup kitchens were set up and American soldiers, billeted in the family home, let them have supplies. She was struck by the friendliness of the occupiers, so at odds with the propaganda to which she had been exposed for so long. By now her father had returned but the family had no money. It was he who saw an advertisement in a local paper, now publishing again, calling for interpreters to work for the Information Services branch of the occupying American forces. She had taken some courses in journalism and she had added Romanian to her English, French and Italian. Nonetheless, she was hesitant to apply, not least because she had greater ambitions for herself than being a translator. But, at her father's urging, she did so.

She found herself in a room of fifty people, all older than her and, as it seemed, 'learned'. Her English was not good. She had had poor teachers, none of whom could themselves pronounce 'th'. What she was, though, was a great deal prettier than the others – even after the privations of the war and her journey back to Salzburg. Dark-haired, slight, she had a vivacity that compelled attention, and it was doubtless for this reason that, as she turned to leave, the American officer in charge urged her to apply. She got the job, which was, as it turned out, not as a translator but as a journalist writing brief feature stories. When the unit moved to Vienna in 1946 she moved with it.

Life remained difficult in postwar Austria. To travel from Salzburg to Vienna meant crossing from the American to the Russian zone. On one side people were sprayed with DDT while on the other, on occasion, their documents were challenged and they were pulled off the train. In her apartment block she had to share a bathroom with the widow of a Nazi official. But the world was opening up again. Vienna 'was fantastic. Modern art was flourishing' as was music, with Webern and Schönberg. 'It was a dream.'

As Miller had done in America just a year or two earlier, she wrote radio plays, in her case for the Rot-Weiss-Rot network, and articles for various illustrated magazines, including *Wiener Illustrierte*. She was asked to supply photographs with her stories but at the time had no interest in photography and knew no photographers. Her visual world was defined by paintings and drawings. For a decade, photography had been in the service of propaganda. It still seemed tainted.

She rapidly grew dissatisfied with her work for the Americans and was employed briefly as editor on a literary magazine, the *Optimiste*; in the process she met a number of young writers who for visuals stole drawings from the *New Yorker*, which had now become available again. Always 'a theatre fan', she began to write theatre reviews, just as Miller briefly had in New York. When the magazine folded after three months, she was again approached by the Americans who were looking for a picture editor for *Heute*, the first American picture magazine to be published in Bavaria. She admitted to knowing nothing about photography but they continued to press her, the editor asking her to divide up a pile of photographs purely according to her own taste. He gave her five minutes. When she had finished, he looked through the two piles and hired her. Until this moment she had never even taken an amateur photograph, but here she was, the picture editor of a magazine. Her first step, a shock to those in the office, was to take on a male secretary.

Part of her job was to identify photographs that could accompany the stories she wrote. Accordingly, she began to buy *Life* magazine along with photographic books, in a crash course on photography. Desperate to find photographers, she hired the boyfriend of an actress friend of hers. He was Hans Hass. Later she hired Lothar Rübelt and Franz Hubmann. After a time she teamed up with Hass, she as writer, he as photographer: 'We did terrible stories. We didn't know anything at all about journalism.' Then, in the summer of 1949, they published a story about Austrian prisoners of war

returning from Russia. They had shown their other stories to *Heute* editor
Warren Trabant and he had dismissed them, but this one appealed to him so
much that he sent it to Robert Capa, who two years earlier, in a small Paris
apartment, had founded the Magnum picture agency. He cabled for them to
go to Paris. With Hass she set off by train from Vienna on Bastille Day 1949,
loaded down with food but with little in the way of financial resources. 'I
bought a hat,' she said, 'which I thought essential for going to Paris, and went
on a third-class train.'

In four years she had journeyed from private despair in a devastated
Germany, now to arrive in Paris, though still as a writer rather than a
photographer. She had taken with her the Contax camera her mother had
used to take the photographs for her father's lectures though she did not use
it for a further two years. She settled for writing brief stories or captions to
accompany the photographs now arriving in Paris from the agency's photographers around the world. Then she began working on the contact sheets,
slowly learning the craft she was subsequently to practise: 'I really learned
more from editing the contact sheets than from being taught.' In particular,
she was struck by the work of Henri Cartier-Bresson.

Magnum was a male-dominated group, happy to see the office brightened
with attractive young women but not at first entirely certain that they should
be equals. Nonetheless, her foot was more than in the door. These were early
days for the agency and she was in a position to grow with it. Among her
friends in Paris were Russian émigrés still fired, like many of her French
friends, with memories of the Revolution. Yet she was aware, too, of those
for whom its failure and perversion were the source of a disappointment
deepening into despair. She set herself to reading Blok, Mayakovsky and
Tsvetayeva. Meanwhile, in Vienna and Paris, she would visit Russian churches
at Easter and Christmas, watching their Byzantine rituals. It is hardly surprising that she later seized every opportunity to go to Russia.

In 1951, in France, she met Lionel Birch, an English journalist who worked
for *Picture Post*, and together they did a story on Konrad Adenauer, who was
so impressed with her that he asked her to become his secretary. She then
moved to England where she shared an apartment with Derek Monsey, whose
girlfriend was the actress Yvonne Mitchell. After a time, she and Birch
married. He was, she explained, 'a good looking man who had been married
three times by the time I met him. I was number four and then there were
two more.' He was 'brilliant and knew the theatre very well'. Indeed, he went
to the theatre virtually every day. He seemed to possess what she had come
to feel were the virtues of the British, only to discover that he also possessed
the vices. For a time she was entranced, seeing Shakespeare in English for
the first time and meeting actors and actresses (including Dorothy Tutin),
but it was not a successful marriage. 'I really knew it was stupid.' She felt

excluded from the world in which she now found herself moving, the world of an ex-public school boy whose friends reflected his upbringing:

> The British are so snobbish. I didn't know anything about all these schools. You had to wear your college tie as a belt. You had to stutter. You had to drink sherry when you went to a party. It didn't amuse me one bit. I had a wonderful Dior sweater from Paris. It was black and blue stripes. It turned out to be the Eton colours. So he said, 'How can you wear Eton colours?' I said, 'This is really going too far.' Then I had an accent and they told me I wasn't very bright if I have an accent.[10]

Birch seemed to have few expectations of her beyond domestic functions at which she scarcely excelled. Years later, when she married Miller, she could, she confessed, barely boil an egg. Nor did England, curiously pinched and inward-looking, have much to offer. Also, she was aware that her native language was that of the enemy, and acknowledged that the stories she wrote in French and English seemed not to 'touch the root'.[11] The image, as opposed to the word, thus had its own attractions, operating as it did in its own language.

No longer accompanied by photographers on her assignments, 'the world around me seemed to be filled with things that wanted to be photographed'. Her contacts with the photographic world, though, seemed to atrophy until, on a brief holiday in Venice in 1951, where two homosexual friends of her husband ran a *pensione*, she called Capa and asked him to send a photographer to capture what seemed to her the remarkable light of Venice in the rain. He was unreceptive, pointing out that the rain would have stopped by the time any photographer arrived and suggesting that she should take the pictures herself.

She retrieved her Contax camera from her room, but knew so little about the practicalities that she had to have a camera shop install the film for her. For speed and setting, she followed the instructions on the film pack. 'I looked through my viewfinder and, when people, columns, pigeons, presented themselves in a rhythm I would have liked to see on a photograph, I pressed the shutter. It was instantly clear to me that from now on I would be a photographer. I had finally found my language. [I had] discovered my own possibility to express what interested or obsessed me in a way with which I could live.'[12] 'I knew that the instantaneous thing was what I wanted to do. I also knew that I would probably have to leave Mr Birch. So I just said, "I'm sorry. This is not what I want to do." He didn't like it at all, but I was just determined. I didn't feel very bad about it because I figured it didn't really matter all that much.'[13] In 2003, her brother contradicted this story, insisting that Birch had initiated the divorce and that Inge had simply accepted it. Whatever the truth, the divorce took three years.

Birch was not the only man to have proposed marriage. A Spanish duke from a pro-Franco family wanted to marry her and gave her the Spanish apartment which she and Miller would later use. She insisted on paying for it, using money borrowed from her brother.

On returning to London she found a new flat and sought out Simon Guttman, the somewhat eccentric originator of the photo-essay, who, as a Jew, had emigrated from Germany and arrived in England in the early 1940s. Now in his sixties, he had ill-fitting teeth and lived on top of layers of newspapers in a small London flat. He had once been the head of a photographic agency and involved in the early days of the *Berliner Illustrierte*, with Robert Capa as one of his apprentices. Now he worked for *Picture Post* and again ran his own picture agency. Inge showed him the contact sheets from her work in Venice and he took her on, at first as little more than a secretary, though he pointed out to her that all the letters he gave her to type were relevant to the craft and art of photography. Nonetheless, she spent much of her day sweeping the floor and even heating his shaving water, putting a shilling in the electricity meter from time to time. He also had a tendency to misplace his teeth, which she was expected to find. Slowly, however, she learned to develop and print as well as to make enlargements. She went on small assignments – the opening of a film, a fire in Smithfield Market. Eventually, he told her that he had no more to teach her and suggested that she should return to Paris, which she did, earning her living by writing and eventually by selling her own photographs.

This marked the beginning of a new career. She bought a second-hand Leica and started to sell her work, at first under the name of Egni Tarom, Inge Morath in reverse: 'Egni Tarom, the talented Swede'. She recalled receiving letters saying, 'Dear Mr Tarom, you have a good eye but your technique . . .'.

Back in Paris she felt more at home. It was here that she received a commission from a Catholic magazine to produce a photographic essay about worker priests, then operating in factories to bring Christianity to the masses. She worked on the story for three months. When she had finished, she took the results to Robert Capa at Magnum, at first not telling him that the pictures were her own. He asked to see her other work and employed her, first as an associate and then as a full member. There was, she recalled, some initial consternation: 'I had been the nice girl who was not in competition.'[14] Now she was part of the team, at first taking on assignments that nobody else wanted, such as covering a Paris flower show for $100.

After several small projects, Capa sent her to London to do a photo story on the shooting of *Moulin Rouge*, directed by John Huston, whom she was to meet again in the United States on the set of *The Misfits*. He befriended her and secured for her several rolls of film, then difficult to find. She had gone on the assignment with a single roll. The result was a double spread in *Life* and a picture in *Paris Match*. When she returned she was set to working for magazines, beginning with a story on Mayfair for *Holiday* magazine. She was still, though, to some degree an apprentice. She worked alongside Henri Cartier-Bresson with whom she shared an interest in art and, it seems, later something more. It was plainly a relationship that had been important to her and which she could never quite surrender.

By degrees she found herself accepted as part of Magnum, a photographic collective in which each photographer was free to select his or her own stories, while coming together for certain assignments such as *The Misfits* shoot, which involved a whole team. Capa's role, beyond his own projects, was to locate work for others. Inge found herself working in England and Spain, for which she learned Spanish. Her time in Paris she described as 'fantastic'. In the evenings Capa and Cartier-Bresson would go with her to a café where they met Sartre and Simone de Beauvoir. It was while in Paris that she saw a performance of *The Crucible* with Simone Signoret and Yves Montand.

When she first entered the United States, she was required to fill in a form that asked her colour. Baffled, she wrote, 'pink'. Straight away, she was offered an insight into a paranoid culture. German scientists and doctors, some deeply implicated in war crimes, might have been spirited out of immediately postwar Germany and into America, but immigration officials were alert to those on the left who might be arriving with subversion in mind. Inge Morath found herself being interrogated by an immigration official suspicious that a book in her suitcase, *Stardust in Hollywood*, about movie stars, published by the Left Book Club, indicated communist leanings. She was detained for several hours and questioned about her politics. Among the questions posed was whether she had committed adultery – doubtless presumed to be a particularly European vice. On finally passing through immigration she was confronted by a woman handing out leaflets calling on people to report anyone suspected of un-American activities. It stirred memories of Nazi Germany.

One commission was to meet the artist Saul Steinberg, whose work regularly appeared in the *New Yorker*. In 1959, he greeted her at his Manhattan house wearing a brown paper bag over his head on which he had drawn a caricature of himself. The sequence of photographs she took that day was still to be seen on the walls of her Roxbury home at the time of her death, and often featured in exhibitions of her work.

It was another commission, however, that proved most significant. In 1960 she went to Reno, Nevada, and met Arthur Miller. When she returned to New York, en route to Argentina, she encountered Miller again, at the Magnum office where he had gone in search of photographs of *The Misfits*. By now he was living at the Adams Hotel in Upper Manhattan. Afterwards he telephoned her, already entranced by this woman who seemed to be everything that Marilyn had not been – self-reliant, an intellectual, alive with energy – but she was constantly on the move, rarely more than a few days in one place. He invited her for lunch. 'I thought, this man, having just been left by Marilyn, or having left . . . I hate to be the Red Cross. I had enough of husbands complaining about wives. So I took Henri with me.' She was afraid that he would spend his time talking about his failed marriage. When Miller ordered a Bialystok roll she assumed it must be some elegant and exotic food. It turned out to be a bagel. At the end of the meal, Miller invited Inge and Cartier-Bresson to Roxbury where she provided evidence that American domestic technology was as yet beyond her.

'I pretended that I understood an ironing machine and promptly burned my fingers. Then he started to ask me out to dinners and lunches, though I was travelling constantly, and I was really not interested. I had a terrific guy and all the money I wanted. I just liked the man a lot but I also liked my independence. I had a wonderful place in Paris. But we slowly started to rely on each other and understand each other. But I didn't think I wanted to live in America. I was very Austro-French. I loved New York, but as a visitor.'[15]

Inge continued to disappear on assignments, to France and elsewhere, leaving him to a privacy that was the condition of his work, something he had been denied for several years now but which, ironically, he no longer desired, at least so far as she was concerned. One solution was to pursue her, which he did in travelling to Paris where *A View from the Bridge* was to be filmed by Sidney Lumet and where Inge was working on the set as a photographer. He had earned sufficient royalties in England to buy a Land Rover (the one he had taken back to Roxbury and shown to Marilyn) and drive it to Paris. He admitted in *Timebends*: 'That all this was a ruse to meet Inge I was perfectly aware, but sometimes even weak self-delusion is better than none. The truth was that I simply wished to praise the day and hope another one would follow, and Inge was a fine partner for that . . . Perhaps I also longed to see Inge again because she so respected muddle, but being an artist herself, she could easily combine muddle with resolve.'[16] His marriage to Marilyn had forced him to live his private life publicly. After the pain and the artifice he was now looking for peace, privacy and a restored sense of the real. He told himself that he was afraid of committing himself again. Yet this did battle with another conviction, that he could not survive on his own, and that perhaps 'Ibsen had been wrong: he is not strongest who is most alone, he is just lonelier.'[17]

After the Fall was about surviving but it was also about his discovery of, and redemption by, Inge, who was herself a survivor. She had the enthusiasm for life that is a consequence of surviving the knowledge of the immediate possibility of death. She was not, like Marilyn, a recidivist when it came to suicide attempts. Her own moment, balanced on the parapet of a bridge, had, after all, been a logical enough conclusion to literal chaos. Having stepped down from the edge, she had chosen to revel in life, her photography embodying a desire to capture its multifaceted qualities, to record, sustain, memorialize, celebrate. There was a democracy to her commitments, though she assured Miller that in other respects she was a snob. What she meant by this, however, was not an arrogant preference for her own taste but a respect for the best.

In New York, Inge had made a practice of staying at the Chelsea Hotel since 1956, when Mary McCarthy secured her a room. In 1961 Miller moved in, too, breakfasting at the nearby automat at 23rd and 7th Avenue. Slowly, their relationship deepened, though Miller recognized that after the failure of her first marriage she was prepared to live her life alone. They were both aware of the potential fragility of relationships. 'We never thought of anything terribly permanent,' Inge observed, 'I know we got married, but it was like a gift . . . that you could live with someone with whom it was fun and interesting to live without putting any weight on either side.' It was, she conceded, a little like her parents' situation in so far as they had mentally considered that things might not work out: 'I was not banking on this marriage being for ever. Arthur was astonishing because my husband was a cheater. He was charming but he lied. Arthur, on the other hand, is very honest, a very straightforward person. I was impressed by his sense of humour. I thought he would be very drear. All I had seen was *The Crucible!*'

Miller, too, was cautious:

> only because the whole idea of marrying seemed a little doubtful, but the idea of getting out of her life, or her getting out of my life, was worse. She brought life. I could easily have slipped into a complete negativism. I probably would have gone on writing because I have always been a writer, but I think it would have been a different kind of writing, more defeated. Inge was a great relief, because she didn't need anybody nursing her along. I went into it with great doubts. As I told her, 'I'm probably not the person to be married to anybody.' But she had her own independence. She wasn't waiting for me to come out of the room. She was busy doing something herself. She was working in Latin America. She was working in Europe.[18]

They had difficulty conducting their affair because Miller was still pursued by the press. As Inge explained; 'We had to hide all the time from the reporters so we had to find a moment when we could escape somewhere to get married in the bushes. We had to postpone things all the time.'[19]

The ceremony was finally conducted in February 1962, in Milford, Connecticut, by Justice of the Peace Robert Spatola. It was a marriage that was to prove crucial, rescuing him, as it did, from the confusion and despair that he felt after his second marriage came to an end and the various plays on which he had worked since *A View from the Bridge* appeared to founder. As Miller remarked thirty-five years later:

> I did not believe I could ever relate to anybody for very long, any more. I was already a middle-aged man by that time. But she is terrific, that she could bear being with me for that long ... Without her I do not know what the hell would have become of me. She helped me reconstruct a whole existence that had never existed before in my life ... She is just a tremendous force for good in my life. She has kept me sane (as sane as I am). She has a wonderful combination of aesthetic sensibility and a practical view of life.[20]

For her part: 'By that time I really thought that it might be nice to stay in one place ... Eventually. Having a baby was really what clinched the deal. But then I thought I could leave it with my mother. I had so no idea about babies that I bought a doll's carriage.'[21] That child was Rebecca, born on 15 September 1962, the year of their marriage, one year after the divorce from Marilyn Monroe and a month after Marilyn's death. Curiously, on a visit to Spain, and before she showed any signs of pregnancy, a gypsy had told Inge both that she was pregnant and that the child would be a girl. It was while she was pregnant with Rebecca that the two of them struggled up the hillsides around their Roxbury home carrying buckets full of tree seedlings, the same trees that have now grown tall and dense. Back in New York, Inge continued to work right to the moment of her delivery. Miller recalled her taking photographs from a crane overlooking the Brooklyn Navy Yard where he had once worked, hours before she went into labour, convinced that she still had ten days to go.

The marriage between Arthur Miller and Inge Morath was to flourish in part because each respected the other's career, and each learned from the other. Inge continued to travel, and her exhibitions increasingly took her abroad. Travel was central to her:

> It takes you out of everything that you're used to. I am very curious about the world and if you go on a trip alone, you are so open to meeting people, to taking your own time. It's a different experience. There are certain places in the world about which I am very curious so I've tried to get to those. But to travel with Arthur is wonderful because then you can share the experience and very often he sees something I don't see, or he insists I should see something I don't see right away. I show him things which he passes by. The vision of a writer is very often of a great help because you have some additional thinking that you can translate into visual terms sometimes. Both sides have their excitement but I have probably caused Arthur to travel more than he would have on his own. But he got something out of that as well.[22]

She also discovered 'that photographic discoveries can be made in one's backyard':

My new life was simply included in what my eyes registered and what my camera documented. I changed some routines and worked closer to home and discovered the enrichment of living with a writer. His rhythm of work is different from mine: he has to take his time to formulate thoughts and words. For me a missed moment is irretrievably lost. But in the course of the years, his way of pondering about an event helped me to different ways of seeing.

His stories about the 'old timers' amongst whom he lived during his first years in Connecticut made it possible for me to photograph my new surroundings with a lot more insight. One only sees what is in one to see, and good writing contributes endlessly to the enrichment of the inner eye.[23]

Miller said: 'I got more acutely aware of art, of painting, and of images in movies, and so on. I've met some of her friends who are terrific talkers about this, like Henri Cartier-Bresson with whom she worked for many years and who is, of course, a master of this. We have had marvellous talks together. I was educated by Henri about how to look at things. He does not know that, but it is true.'

If Marilyn had been, in some senses, a prototypical American, severed from the past, concerned above all for the moment, Inge represented a historical continuity. She came from a continent with a history that bore on the present. Her sense of independence shared nothing with Marilyn's, being forged out of a suffering that was more than personal. If both women had been brought to the point of contemplating suicide, Inge's despair had been rooted in an experience so harrowing that it had seemed to contain its own logic, a logic reaching out beyond a private despair. A year after their meeting she and Miller travelled to Austria and Germany, two people as yet unsure of the commitment they were tempted to make, aware of a history of failure and now journeying through a country where that failure seemed of a piece with other, more profound disasters.

It was on this trip that the two of them went to Mauthausen, a visit that was to prove deeply influential and which changed the direction of Miller's work as he now made a direct connection, through Inge, with events he had observed from afar. It brought him face to face with a subject that had been virtually suppressed, not only in America but in Israel, not only by non-Jews but by Jews. It was not until the 1960s that the subject of the Holocaust was fully engaged and, largely unremarked as it is, Miller was one of the first American writers to tackle it.

The camp was not, then, a place of pilgrimage. A visitors' centre was not opened until 2003. It was virtually deserted. They had to rouse a keeper to open the gate. What struck Miller first of all was that it was plainly designed to be permanent:

> It had a stone wall that was several feet thick and twenty feet high. This was not barbed wire. There were big iron gates. They intended to go on killing people for a long time, and they would probably have done that once they had eliminated all the Jews. That wouldn't have taken very long. I think they were going to put all the Poles in there. They were going to kill the Poles as a nation, and maybe some of the other East Europeans.

Asked why Inge had taken him there, he replied, 'I think she wanted to confront herself . . . She had to get sorted out about all this.'[24] Over twenty-five years later he recalled their visit: 'Inge moved very straight, saying little, but pale and fighting her fear. Tears were constantly threatening the rims of her eyes. The builders of this place and the indifference we saw about us now – to say the least – had destroyed her youth and laid on her for the rest of her life a debt that she did not owe and could never pay.'[25] And here, of course, she was alongside a Jew who knew that this fate could very well have been his own. She may have suffered at the hands of those who contrived this fate, but her first language was German and she came from a country that had enthusiastically embraced the Nazis.

She considered her decision to go to Mauthausen a necessity: 'If the past wants you, you have to face it. Mauthausen was the only concentration camp I was vaguely aware of and it was in Austria. It was an Austrian camp. I wanted to face this myself.' It was a painful experience, 'but it was supposed to be'. She took her husband 'because it was important that he should know everything'. It was a critical moment. The fact that she had suffered under the regime 'didn't matter, because you still had a German accent. I couldn't write in German for a while. Photography was a saving grace because you didn't have to speak.'[26]

She was aware that while he had engaged with American traumas, she suffered from a European one. It seemed to her, though, that he understood the European sensibility and, perhaps because of his Jewishness, was responsive to what she was going through. She was laying before him her own past and the past of her country. She was accepting responsibility for events over which she had had no control, but in that she was expressing the dilemma of a generation.

For Miller, his time in the camp made everything 'very concrete. The tragedy of it became very poignant because she suffered in the war and certainly I hadn't suffered, and here I was, the Jew, and I had come through without a scratch but she had damn near starved to death.' Beyond that, this was a time when the Holocaust had not become the coinage it later became. It was the period when the whole Nazi thing was slipping into history. If you had asked almost anybody at that time whether people were going to remember any of this in ten years they would have told you no. The German educational system had obliterated the whole thing. It never happened. So a whole generation had gone through school knowing nothing. And here's this monstrous building, standing there, but deserted. I could easily put myself in a position of walking through the gate into that place. There were rooms in there that were obviously torture rooms. Stone slabs with a drain in them, clearly for the blood to be drained out. They were knocking the gold out of the teeth and probably operating on people alive. They were ghouls in charge of a country. It made me certain that I had to write about this. What was interesting to me was that ... the whole thing described the death of love, people incapable any more of the human connection.[27]

The American journalist Fred Friendly had been present at the liberation of Mauthausen. He wrote a letter home and asked that it should be read out loud to his family every Yom Kippur. Speaking of the horrors he had seen, he added, 'If there had been no America, we, all of us, might well have carried granite at Mauthausen.'[28] Essentially that same truth came home to Miller on his visit. He returned to continue work on *After the Fall*, now with the tower of a concentration camp dominating the action.

It was this visit that enabled him to finish the play. It was this visit, too, that introduced an element into his work that had simply not been there before – not merely a European dimension, which would lead to *Incident at Vichy*, *The Archbishop's Ceiling* and *Broken Glass*, but an urge to press beyond the social and the psychological to the metaphysical. It may also have played a role in persuading him to step into the international arena when, three years later, he accepted the presidency of International PEN. Inge had changed the direction of his work and of his life.

She died on the morning of January 30, 2002, of lymphoma. In a letter sent to her brother, Miller wrote: 'I am still astonished by the happiness that was ours for forty years. And what happiness! I try to keep reminding myself of it, also how much she gave me. I can only hope she experienced something similar regarding me. I think she did. She was a courageous, fine woman.'[29]

There was always an element of the French *oppositionnel* about Arthur Miller. Partly, that came from the political logic he pursued, but perhaps it also had deeper roots. It was Freud, after all, who remarked that 'being a Jew, I would always be in the opposition.'[30] For Jean-Paul Sartre, 'one of the functions of the artist and the intellectual in a given society, is a critical function ... A culture is designed to manifest the freedom of man who concurrently expresses, questions, contests and stimulates the society in which he lives.'[31] This is a good description of Miller's attitude to his art and his society. Albert Camus preferred a different formulation. We should want, he explained, to think and live in our history: 'It seems to me that the writer must be fully aware of the conflicts of his time and that he must take sides every time or know how to do so.' He believed that a work should 'give a form to the passions of his time'.[32] This, surely, was also Miller's conviction.

However, often cast in the role of an intellectual in a society that has little use for or understanding of such a term, he was in fact less concerned to engage with abstract ideas than with observed lives. Most of his plays are rooted in lived experience, as if that were a guarantee of authenticity. Though this seldom pushed him in the direction of realism, it did lead him to create drama in which the integrity of the self was method as well as subject. What he derived from Sartre and Camus was the need to discover the basis for moral action.

Miller, in Irving Howe's striking phrase, was an historian of moral consciousness. His plays proved immediately responsive to ethical questions equally implicit in the shifting social and political environment and in the processes of daily living. Once he had thought that values might be embodied in the geometry of ideology, as his grandparents had believed they might be contained within God's eye and his parents in the promises America offered to immigrants who had cut themselves adrift, desperate to believe in the inevitability of their rescue. His aim had once been to change the world. He had, he admitted, been an 'impatient moralist'.[33] Later, he was more modest. People, it seemed to him, did not change, or hardly. He acknowledged that his characters had had a tendency to move towards disaster, particularly those of the 1940s and 50s. But then, so, he noted, did the protagonists of tragedy; and the tragic impulse, always part of his sensibility, precisely underlines that sense of a victory born out of apparent defeat that was the essence of his commitment, in and out of the theatre.

Perhaps the best description of what Miller's work aspires to is that offered by Seamus Heaney in seeking to describe a crucial function of poetry, not least because the poet was strong in Miller. The poet, Heaney explained in his Nobel Prize address in 1995, seeks

> [to] touch the base of our sympathetic nature while taking in at the same time the unsympathetic reality of the world to which that nature is constantly exposed. The form of the poem, in other words, is crucial to poetry's power to do the thing which always is and always will be to poetry's credit: the power to persuade that vulnerable part of our consciousness of its rightness in spite of the evidence of wrongness all around it, the power to remind us that we are hunters and gatherers of values, that our very solitudes and

distresses are creditable, in so far as they, too, are an earnest of our veritable human being.[34]

Ignazio Silone once remarked that most writers keep telling the same story over and over again; 'it is the story that releases their controlling sense of existence, their springs of anxiety and dilemma'.[35] There is a sense in which Miller did tell the same story throughout his career. It is an account of the struggle to find in the business of living the reason for living. It is an account of the effort to justify life to itself and of the responsibilities born out of a social existence. It is the story of men and women alone, with no believable promise of redemption, condemned to be their own creators, obliged not to discover a hidden meaning but to create it from a lived life, from their own wills and imaginations and from those with whom they stare into the past that formed them and the future that may yet transform them.

Henry Luce's American century turned out to be one in which Miller would find himself a victim of domestic repressions and at odds with America's myths and political imperatives. However, decades later, and listening to Solzhenitsyn's denunciation of American values, delivered at Harvard University, this most critical of American playwrights felt prompted to celebrate the culture with which he had so often been in contention. The Americans, he insisted, despite evidence of decay, had nonetheless determined the very spirit of the century. It seemed to him that no other country had so excelled in the arts, in medicine, science, engineering. He also celebrated America's social and moral responsibility, stressing the work done by Americans around the world. If it was guilt that provided the spur, it also seemed to stem from a genuine sense of obligation to the human race. The Un-American, it appears, was American after all, if also a citizen of something more than a once revolutionary state now seemingly content with its discontents. Perhaps the tears supposedly shed by Marilyn Monroe on evidence of his patriotism were real tears, as was the loyalty he expressed to the society with which he spent a lifetime arguing.

In 1995, Miller responded to an invitation to write about a day in his life for a British newspaper. The brief piece did, indeed, offer a glimpse of a day in his Connecticut home with Inge Morath. It also gave an insight into his sense of himself as a writer, then eighty years old:

> In the warm weather, Inge and I swim in the little lake behind the house, then we have breakfast together in the kitchen. Living together is the most difficult thing there is, because it is about constant tolerance and forgiveness. Fortunately, Inge is an artist, so she understands that I need to shut myself away to work. I cross the garden to my hut and Inge goes to her studio. I bought this house with Marilyn in 1956. Many things still remind me of her, but I have no desire to escape my past. I use it all the time.

Maybe because I have less time left, my writing has changed. It's denser, more concise. I don't want to listen to myself going on and on. I'm not really a moralist, I just make the assumption that certain things we do lead to catastrophe. I am trying to find out why people destroy themselves the way they do. Each of my plays is begun in the belief that it will unveil an unrecognized truth.

I have no formal religion but there's a space in my head for it. Maybe I would believe in God if he believed in me. But we live in a reality that is so difficult to understand. In the last seventy-five years the human race has been humiliated in a way we've never known before. We can't predict anything. Uncertainty seems to be the only true principle.[36]

Like his father before him, he had travelled not just in hope but in the conviction that meaning is created and not imminent. A play is a construction but so, too, is a life, to be formed out of an imagination distilled into pure being. In the end Miller's satisfaction lay not in a fluctuating reputation – in truth, always secure as his plays continued to be performed around the world, rediscovered and reinvented by every generation – but in the making of things, the shaping of plays, the crafting of stories, the forming of daily objects from trees felled on his own Connecticut hills.

His daughter Rebecca, herself an artist, writer, actress and director, has said that he was happier talking with craftsmen than with famous actors or directors. The fact is that Miller saw playwrighting as continuous with the craftsmanship that shapes wood into useful objects. It was a way of creating form.

In speaking of *King Lear*, he observed that form *is* art, its truth-to-itself, and its falsity-to-life. Lear's pain is reshaped into meaning. Yet the second half of that sentence is also important in so far as he acknowledges a tension between his commitment to language and his commitment to the lived lives of those he places on stage, his desire to earth art in experience. His characters, shaped to serve dramatic function, still bear the marks of their humanity just as the furniture he built carried the grain of the wood. It is obedient to its own contingent necessities. Beyond that, his carpentry, like his drama, was functional, unelaborated, with clear and defining limits. The dining table in his Roxbury home was shaped to the elegance of a mathematical formula that enabled fourteen people to engage in a single conversation, much as he saw the theatre as facilitating the same shared experience and once saw it as engaging in a conversation with America.

He explained the satisfaction he derived from his craftsmanship in an unpublished poem, itself sculpting order out of language. It is called 'Making', and can stand as his own epitaph for what he spent a lifetime creating, bringing the past into the present, finding not only coherence and purpose but meaning in the seeming randomness of creation. He was content, finally, to leave all traces of himself in what he had made. As the poem's last line suggests, through his work he endures even as he disappears. That poem was read by his daughter Rebecca from the stage of the Majestic Theatre in Manhattan in 2005, in a memorial service that also brought the past into the present in giving thanks for the life of a man born in Harlem, raised in Brooklyn, educated in Michigan, who went on to write plays that continue to live on the pulse in the twenty-first century.

There is never a moment when an Arthur Miller play is not being staged somewhere in the world. There is never a moment when a man does not declare that he is John Proctor still, or stand, exhausted, in the doorway of his home carrying two suitcases and wondering what became of the dream that was not his alone but that of a country in which everything had once seemed possible.

When he was dying, Arthur Miller asked to be driven back from New York to New England, where he had written most of his plays. He died in the bed he had made with his own hands, surrounded by his family. It was 10 February 2005. The right-wing magazine *New Criterion* marked the occasion with an article headed 'Arthur Miller, Communist Stooge'. The *Wall Street Journal's* obituary was headed 'The Great Pretender: Arthur Miller Wasn't Well Liked – and With Good Reason'. Even in a new century, and at such a moment, it seemed, old battles were not forgotten. Such views, however, now seemed aberrant. On Broadway, lights were dimmed. Across the Atlantic, in England, the editor of the *Independent* newspaper cleared the whole front page judging that there was no news more pressing than the death of a writer on another continent who may have been made by America but who belonged to everyone.

NOTES

1 FROM HARLEM TO BROOKLYN

1. Robert A. Martin and Steven R. Centola, *The Theater Essays of Arthur Miller* (New York, 1996), p. 193.
2. Mark Schechner, *The Conversion of the Jews and Other Essays* (London, 1990), p. 1.
3. *Ibid.*, p. 9.
4. Irving Howe, *World of Our Fathers* (New York, 1976), p. 25.
5. Nancy Foner, *From Ellis Island to JFK: New York's Two Great Waves of Immigration* (New Haven, 2000), p. 10.
6. Jennifer L. Hochschild, *Facing Up to the American Dream: Race, Class, and the Soul of the Nation* (Princeton, 1995), p. 229.
7. Jacob Riis, *How the Other Half Lives* (Cambridge, 1970), p. 70.
8. *Ibid.*, p. 72.
9. Email from Ross Miller to the author, 8 January 2007.
10. Interview with the author.
11. Christopher Bigsby, *Writers in Conversation*, vol. 1 (Norwich, 1999), p. 169.
12. Foner, *From Ellis Island to JFK*, p. 29.
13. *Ibid.*, pp. 75, 80.
14. *Ibid.*, p. 31.
15. Samuel Huntington, *Who Are We? The Challenges to America's National Destiny* (New York, 2004), p. 189.
16. Arthur Miller, *Timebends: A Life* (1987), p. 9.
17. Abraham Cahan, *The Rise of David Levinsky* (New York, 1960), pp. 88–9.
18. Howe, *World of Our Fathers*, p. 45.
19. *Ibid.*, p. 73.
20. *Ibid.*, p. 59.
21. *Ibid.*, p. 82.
22. *Ibid.*, pp. 87, 69.
23. Huntington, *Who Are We?*, p. 74.
24. Foner, *From Ellis Island to JFK*, p. 44.
25. *Ibid.*, pp. 43, 44.
26. Samuel Joseph, *Jewish Immigration to the United States from 1881 to 1910* (New York, 1967), p. 192.
27. Foner, *From Ellis Island to JFK*, pp. 75–80.
28. *Ibid.*, p. 85.
29. Email from Ross Miller, 8 January 2007.
30. Riis, *How The Other Half Lives*, p. 86.
31. Interview with the author, 2001.
32. Interview with the author, 1984.
33. Vivian Gornick, *The Romance of American Communism* (New York, 1977), p. 119.
34. Howe, *World of Our Fathers*, p. 161.
35. Foner, *From Ellis Island to JKF*, p. 42.
36. Miller, *Timebends*, (1990), p. 126.
37. Arthur Miller, 'After the Fall', *Saturday Evening Post*, 237 (1 February 1964), p. 37.

38. Arthur Miller, *After the Fall* (New York, 1964), p. 17.

39. Miller, *Timebends*, (1990), p. 594.

40. Howe, *World of Our Fathers*, p. 131.

41. Foner, *From Ellis Island to JFK*, p. 42.

42. Jeffrey S. Gurock, *When Harlem Was Jewish: 1870–1930* (New York, 1979), p. 45.

43. Howe, *World of Our Fathers*, p. 155.

44. Interview with the author, 2001.

45. Miller, *Timebends*, (1990), p. 20.

46. Interview with the author, 1984.

47. Michael N. Dobkowski, *The Tarnished Dream: The Basis of American Anti-Semitism* (Westport, 1979), p. 129.

48. *Ibid.*, pp. 124–5.

49. Letter to the author, 7 November 2002.

50. Interview with the author, 2001.

51. Arthur Miller, *The American Clock* (London, 1982), pp. 5, 16.

52. Last two quotations, interview with the author, 1995.

53. *Ibid.*

54. Hochschild, *Facing Up to the American Dream*, p. 35.

55. Interview with the author, 1995.

56. Interview with the author, 2001.

57. Arthur Miller, *I Don't Need You Any More* (London, 1967), p. 11.

58. Last two quotations from ibid., pp. 51, 47–8.

59. Interview with the author, 1995.

60. Arthur Miller, 'The Story of Adam and Eve', in *Genesis: As It Is Written, Contemporary Writers on Our First Stories*, ed. David Rosenberg (San Francisco, 1996), p. 35.

61. *Ibid.*, p. 36.

62. Quotations from Miller, *Timebends* (1990), pp. 24, 25, 26.

63. Gurock, *When Harlem Was Jewish*, p. 119.

64. Miller, *Timebends* (1990), pp. 42–3, 338.

65. Studs Terkel, *Hard Times* (New York, 1970), p. 6.

66. Carol Brightman, *Writing Dangerously: Mary McCarthy and Her World* (New York, 1994), pp. 113–14.

67. *Arthur Miller: on Home Ground*, directed by Harry Rasky, CBC, 1980.

68. Interview with the author, 1995.

69. Miller, *After the Fall* (1964), pp. 20, 41.

70. Email from Ross Miller, 3 January 2007.

71. Gurock, *When Harlem Was Jewish*, pp. 145–6.

72. Alfred Kazin, *A Walker in the City* (London, 1952), pp. 126–7.

73. Interview with the author, 1995.

74. Beth S. Wenger, *New York Jews and the Great Depression: Uncertain Promise* (New Haven, 1996), p. 14.

75. Interview with the author, 1995.

76. *Ibid.*

77. Arthur Miller, 'Grandfather and Emperor Franz Joseph', *New Currents*, June 1943, p. 9.

78. Miller, *The American Clock* (1983), p. 69.

79. Miller, *After the Fall* (1964), p. 17.

80. Miller, *The American Clock* (1983), p. 81.

81. Miller, *Timebends* (1990), p. 113.

82. Arthur Miller, *Echoes Down the Corridor: Collected Essays 1944–2000* ed. Steven R. Centola (New York, 2000) p. 128.

83. Interview with the author, 2001.

84. Miller, *Timebends* (1990), pp. 62, 63.

85. Interview with the author, 1995.

86. *Ibid.*

87. Miller, *Timebends* (1990), pp. 111.

88. Eric Homberger, *American Writers and Radical Politics, 1900–39: Equivocal Commitments* (London, 1986), p. 149.

89. Interview with the author, 1995.

90. Miller, *Timebends* (1990), p. 115.

91. Miller, *The American Clock* (1983), p. 46.
92. Vivian Gornick, *The Romance of American Communism* (New York, 1977), p. 29.
93. *Ibid.*, p. 8.
94. Miller, *Timebends* (1990), p. 112.
95. Interview with the author, 1999.
96. Interview with the author, 1995.
97. Arthur Miller, 'A Boy Grew in Brooklyn', *Holiday*, March 1955, 54–5, 117, 119–20, 122–4.
98. Miller, *Timebends* (1990), pp. 4.
99. Interview with the author.
100. Wenger, *New York Jews and the Great Depression*, p. 73.
101. Interview with the author, 1995.
102. Interview with the author, 2001.
103. Interview with the author.
104. *Ibid.*
105. Miller, *The American Clock* (1983), pp. 34, 36.
106. Interview with the author, 1984.
107. Wenger, *New York Jews and the Great Depression*, p. 22.
108. 'Bulletin Board: Miller's City College Secret', *New York Times*, 31 October 2001, p. 9.
109. Miller, *Timebends* (1990), p. 217.
110. *Ibid.*, p. 314.
111. Wenger, *New York Jews and the Great Depression*, p. 1.
112. Alfred Kazin, *Starting Out in the Thirties* (London, 1966), pp. 3, 12.
113. *Ibid.*, p. 13.
114. *Ibid.*, p. 5–6.
115. Irving Howe, *A Margin of Hope* (London, 1983), p. 53.
116. *Ibid.*, p. 5.
117. Miller, *After the Fall* (1964), pp. 67–8.
118. Arthur Miller, 'No Villain', typescript at the University of Michigan, p. 36.
119. Interview with the author, 2001.
120. Email from Ross Miller, 2 January 2007.
121. Interview with the author, 2001.

2 MICHIGAN

1. Carol Brightman, *Writing Dangerously: Mary McCarthy and Her World* (New York, 1994), p. 274.
2. Arthur Miller, 'The American Writer: The American Theater', in *The Writer's Craft: Hopwood Lectures, 1965–81* (Ann Arbor, 1982), pp. 254–5.
3. Miller, *Timebends* (1990), p. 213.
4. Arthur Miller, 'Steinbeck', in Stephen K. George (ed.), *John Steinbeck: A Centennial Tribute* (Westport, 2002), p. 65.
5. Miller, *Timebends* (1990), p. 92.
6. Ellen W. Schrecker, *No Ivory Tower: McCarthyism and the Universities* (New York, 1986), pp. 88–9, 110.
7. *Ibid.*, p. 312.
8. Enoch Brater, *Arthur Miller: A Playwright's Life and Works* (London, 2005), pp. 13–14.
9. Arthur Miller, *The American Clock* (London, 1983), p. 43.
10. Arthur Miller, 'Concerning Jews Who Write', *Jewish Life*, 2, 5 (March 1948), p. 9.
11. Email from Ross Miller to the author, 2 January 2007.
12. Interview with the author, 2001.
13. Arthur Miller, *Echoes Down the Corridor: Collected Essays 1944–2000*, ed. Steven R. Centola (New York, 2000), p. 16.
14. Schrecker, *No Ivory Tower*, p. 28.
15. Interview with the author, 2000.
16. Alan M. Wald, *The Rise and Decline of the Anti-Stalinist Left from the 1930s to the 1980s* (Chapel Hill, 1987), p. 246.
17. Interview with the author.
18. Irving Howe, *Steady Work* (New York, 1966), p. 358.
19. Miller, *Timebends* (1990), p. 95.
20. Brater, *Arthur Miller: A Playwright's Life and Works*, p. 19.

21. Miller, *Timebends* (1990), p. 211.
22. Interview with the author, May 2001.
23. Miller, *Timebends* (1990), pp. 212, 213.
24. Interview with the author, May 2001.
25. Miller, *Timebends* (1990), p. 212.
26. Letter to the author, 13 January 2004.
27. Rasky, *Arthur Miller: On Home Ground*.
28. Mel Gussow, *Conversations with Arthur Miller* (London, 2002), p. 78.
29. Leonard Dinnerstein, *Anti-Semitism in America* (Oxford, 1994) p. 103.
30. Miller, *Timebends* (1990), p. 253.
31. Miller, 'The American Writer: The American Theater' (1982), p. 257.
32. These papers are held at the University of Michigan.
33. Rasky, *Arthur Miller: On Home Ground*.
34. Miller, *Timebends* (1990), p. 224.
35. Miller, 'The American Writer: The American Theater' (1978), p. 259.
36. *Ibid*.
37. This and the next seven quotations: Kenneth Rowe, *Write That Play* (New York, 1939), pp. 41–2, 44, 45, 48, 50, 156, 53, 170.
38. James McFarlane, ed., *The Cambridge Companion to Henrick Ibsen* (Cambridge, 1994), p. 229.
39. *Ibid*.
40. Arthur Miller, 'An American Reaction', *World Theater* (New York, 1951), pp. 21–2.
41. Interview with the author, 2001.
42. Alfred Kazin, *Starting Out in the Thirties* (London, 1966), p. 81.
43. Miller, *Timebends* (1990), p. 228.
44. Miller, 'The American Writer: The American Theater' (1982), p. 256.
45. Miller, *Timebends* (1990), p. 228.
46. *Ibid*., p. 230.
47. Interview with the author, 2001.
48. Ellen N. Schrecker, *Many Are the Crimes: McCarthyism in America* (New York, 1998), p. 14.
49. Interview with the author, 1995.
50. Miller, 'The American Writer: The American Theater' (1982), p. 256.
51. Papers at the University of Michigan, Arthur Miller Collection.
52. Reports from Federal Theatre Archive at George Mason University.
53. Interview with the author, 2001.
54. Arthur Schlesinger Jr, *The Vital Center* (London, 1950), p. 54.
55. Richard Crossman, ed., *The God That Failed: Six Studies in Communism* (New York, 1965), p. 233.
56. This quotation and the next: Vivian Gornick, *The Romance of American Communism* (New York, 1977), pp. 240, 241–2.
57. Alfred Kazin, *A Walker in the City* (London, 1952), pp. 60–61.
58. Vivian Gornick, *The Romance of American Communism* p. 104.
59. Crossman, *The God That Failed*, p. 30.
60. Schlesinger, *The Vital Center*, p. 54.
61. Miller, *Timebends* (1990), pp. 264–5.
62. Interview with the author, 1995.
63. Leonard Dinnerstein, *Anti-Semitism in America* (Oxford, 1994), p. 89.
64. Interview with the author, 2001.
65. Sidney Fine, *Sit-Down: The General Motors Strike 1936–1937* (Ann Arbor, 1969), p. 115.
66. Schrecker, *Many Are the Crimes*, p. 71.
67. Fine, *Sit-Down*, p. 117.
68. *Ibid*., p. 158.
69. *Ibid*., p. 205.
70. *Punch Press*, no. 6, University of Michigan archive.

71. Miller, *Timebends* (1990), p. 267.
72. Miller, *The American Clock* (1983), pp. 64–5.
73. Fine, *Sit-Down*, p. 338.
74. Interview with the author, 2001.
75. Arthur Miller, speech for the Prince of Asturias Award, 2002.
76. Miller, *Timebends* (1990), p. 101.
77. Crossman, *The God That Failed*, pp. 244–5.
78. Natalie Robins, *Alien Ink: The FBI's War on Freedom of Expression* (New York, 1992), p. 76.
79. Kazin, *Starting Out in the Thirties*, pp. 82–3, 86.
80. Interview with the author, 2001.
81. Stanley Weintraub, *The Last Great Crusade: The Intellectuals and the Spanish Civil War* (London, 1968), p. 228.
82. Letter to the author.
83. This quotation and the next few, Miller, *Timebends* (1990), pp. 294, 295, 296.
84. Interview with the author, 2001.
85. Arthur H. Landis, *The Abraham Lincoln Brigade* (New York, 1968), p. 308.
86. *Ibid.*, pp. 315–16.
87. *Ibid.*, pp. 219, 321.
88. *Ibid.*, p. 368.
89. Peter N. Carroll, *The Odyssey of the Abraham Lincoln Brigade* (Stanford, 1994), p. 173.
90. *Ibid.*, p. 426.
91. *Ibid.*, p. 323.
92. Albert Camus, trans. Justin O'Brien, *Rebellion, Resistance and Death* (London, 1961), p. 58.
93. Arthur Miller, 'Rip Van Winkle Spanish Style', *New York Times*, 9 July 1972.
94. *Ibid.*
95. Germaine Brée, *Camus and Sartre: Crisis and Commitment* (London, 1974), p. 57.
96. Schrecker, *No Ivory Tower*, p. 31.
97. Arthur Miller, 'Forward', *Toward the Radical Center: A Karel Čapek Reader*, ed. Peter Kussi (New Haven, Conn., 1990), pp. 1–2.
98. Judges' reports held at the University of Michigan Library.
99. Arthur A. Miller, 'You Simply Must Go to College', *The Gargoyle*, October 1937, pp. 12, 24.
100. Art Miller, 'The Rosten', *The Gargoyle*, January 1938, p. 24. Bentley Historical Library, University of Michigan.
101. Interview with the author, 2001.
102. James Carroll, *Constantine's Sword: The Church and the Jews* (Boston, 2001), p. 520.
103. Interview with the author, 2001.
104. *Ibid.*
105. Miller, *Echoes Down the Corridor* (2000), p. 30.
106. Miller, 'The American Writer: The American Theater' (1982), p. 263.

3 BEGINNINGS

1. Miller, *The American Clock* (1983), p. 63.
2. Miller, *Timebends* (1990), p. 396.
3. Interview with the author, 2001.
4. Email to the author from Ross Miller, 2 January 2007.
5. Interview with the author, May 2002.
6. George Kazacoff, *Dangerous Theatre: The Federal Theatre Project as a Forum for New Plays* (New York, 1989), p. 39.
7. *Ibid.*, p. 41.
8. *Arthur Miller: On Home Ground*, a film by Harry Rasky, CBC, 1980.
9. Thomas Gordon and Max Morgan Witts, *Guernica: The Crucible of World War II* (Chelsea, 1975), p. 288.
10. Typescript held at the Harry Ransom Humanities Research Center, University of Texas at Austin.

11. Gornick, *The Romance of American Communism*, pp. 122–3, 250.

12. Elia Kazan, *A Life* (New York, 1988), p. 244.

13. Kazin, *Starting Out in the Thirties*, pp. 139, 140–1.

14. Interview with the author, 1995.

15. Ellen W. Schrecker, *No Ivory Tower: McCarthyism and the Universities* (New York, 1986), p. 56.

16. Solomon Schwartz, 'The New Anti-Semitism of the Soviet Union: Its Background and Its Meaning', *Commentary*, vol. 7, p. 541.

17. Malech Epstein, *The Jew and Communism: The Story of Early Communist Victories and Ultimate Defeats in the Jewish Community, USA, 1919–1941* (New York, 1959), p. 321.

18. Wenger, *New York Jews and the Great Depression*, p. 199.

19. Arthur Miller, *The Golden Years* and *The Man Who Had All the Luck* (London, 1989), p. 107.

20. *Ibid.*, 'Afterword', p. 223.

21. Howard Blue, *Words at War* (Lanham, 2002), p. 82.

22. Miller, 'Afterword', *The Golden Years* (1989), p. 222.

23. Interview with the author, May 2002.

24. Quoted in Cooney, *The Rise of the New York Intellectuals*, p. 238.

25. Interview with the author, 2001.

26. Alfred Kazin, *New York Jew* (New York, 1978), p. 4.

27. Lionel Abel, *The Intellectual Follies* (New York, 1984), p. 40.

28. Dinnerstein, *Anti-Semitism in America*, p. 136.

29. Miller, *Timebends* (1990), p. 72.

30. Interview with the author, 1999.

31. *Ibid.*

32. Miller, *Timebends* (1990), p. 77.

33. *Ibid.*, p. 82.

34. Interview with the author, 1998.

35. Miller, *Timebends* (1990), p. 70.

36. *Ibid.*, p. 70.

37. Interview with the author, 2001.

38. Matthew Barton, 'Arthur Miller – A View from the Field', *Folklore Center News*, winter/spring, vol. xxvii, nos 1–2.

39. *Ibid.*

40. Interview with the author, October 2003.

41. Recording in Library of Congress.

42. Interview with the author, October 2003.

43. Interview with the author, 2001.

44. These quotations are from recordings held in the Library of Congress.

45. Barton, 'Arthur Miller – A View from the Field'.

46. Library of Congress recording.

47. Barton, 'Arthur Miller – A View from the Field'.

48. Arthur Miller, *The Pussycat and the Expert Plumber Who Was a Man*, in *One Hundred Non-Royalty Radio Plays*, ed. William Kozlenko (New York, 1941), pp. 29, 26.

49. Peter Manso, *Mailer: His Life and Times* (New York, 1986), p. 98.

50. Interview with the author, 1995.

51. Blue, 'Words at War', p. 377.

52. *Ibid.*, pp. 165–6.

53. Unless otherwise noted, this and subsequent quotations from Miller's radio plays derive from typescripts held at the Harry Ransom Center or from contemporaneous recordings.

54. Miller, *Timebends* (1990), p. 203.

55. Erik Barnouw, *Radio Drama in Action: Twenty-Five Plays of a Changing World* (New York, 1945), p. 268.

56. Arthur Miller, 'Sacajawea', typescript in the Harry Ransom Center, University of Texas at Austin.

57. Interview with the author, 1995.

58. *Ibid.*

59. Miller, *Timebends* (1990), p. 206.

60. Arthur Miller, *Thunder in the Hills.* Broadcast on *Cavalcade of America*, 28 September 1942. Copies held at the Harry Ransom Center, University of Texas at Austin, and at the Billy Rose Theater Collection of New York Public Library.

61. Arthur Miller, *Glider Doctor*, transmitted 20 June 1944. Typescript at the Harry Ransom Center, University of Texas at Austin.

62. Arthur Miller, *The Magic Drug.* Transmitted 3 July 1945. Typescript held at the Harry Ransom Center, University of Texas at Austin.

63. Untitled, undated memo (though clearly dating from 1945) at Harry Ransom Center, University of Texas at Austin.

64. Arthur Miller, *Mare Island and Back*, 19 June 1945, at Harry Ransom Center, University of Texas at Austin.

65. Arthur Miller, 'The Plaster Masks', *Encore*, vol. 9 (April 1946), p. 429.

66. Arthur Miller, *Lips for a Trumpet*, typescript at the Harry Ransom Center, University of Texas at Austin.

67. Arthur Miller, *Men of Our Merchant Marine*; script #1 'The Crew'. This typescript seems to be a draft and is to be found at Harry Ransom Center, University of Texas at Austin.

68. Blue, *Words at War*, p. 351.

69. In Joseph Liss, ed., *Radio's Best Plays* (New York, 1947), p. 303.

70. Interview with the author, May 2002.

71. Interview with the author, 4 October, 2003.

72. Elia Kazan, *A Life* (London, 1988), p. 245.

73. Louis Harrap, *Creative Awakening: The Jewish Presence in Twentiwth-Century American Literature 1900–1940s* (New York, 1987), p. 135.

74. Robins, *Alien Ink*, p. 310.

75. FBI file 100–57673.

76. Robins, *Alien Ink*, p. 114.

77. Margaret Mayorga, ed., *The Best One-Act Plays of 1944* (New York, 1945), p. 47.

78. *Ibid.*, p. 58.

79. Miller, *Timebends* (1990), p. 223.

80. *Ibid.*, p. 223.

81. Letter from J. B. Walker, Commandant of the Brooklyn Navy Yard, in Arthur Miller's private papers.

82. Interview with the author, 1995.

83. Miller, *Timebends* (1990), p. 278.

84. Miller, 'The Plaster Masks' (April 1946), p. 424.

85. Quoted in Howe, *A World More Attrative*, p. 264.

86. Miller, *Timebends* (1990), p. 280.

87. Arthur Miller, *Situation Normal* (New York, 1944), pp. 166, 167.

88. Miller, *Timebends* (1990), p. 286.

89. Jackson J. Benson, *The True Adventures of John Steinbeck, Writer* (London, 1984), p. 701.

90. Arthur Miller, 'Ernie Pyle: G.I.', *New Masses*, 15 May 1945, pp. 23–4.

91. Miller, *Situation Normal* (1944).

92. This and the following quotations from *ibid.*, pp. 28, 40, 91, 116, 117, 118, 119, 120.

93. Quoted in Harrap, *Creative Awakening*, p. 137.

94. This and the following quotations, unless otherwise indicated, are from *Situation Normal* (1944): pp. 145, 149, 155, 157, 157, 157, 158, 157, 161, 162, 162, 162, 162, 160, 161.

4 ALL MY SONS

1. Letter from Paul Streger of Leland Hayward, 14 April 1944, in Arthur Miller's private papers.
2. Miller, *Timebends* (1990), p. 90.
3. Interview with the author, 1995.
4. Letter from William A. Hart, E.I. DuPont de Nemours & Company, 8 March 1945. Presumably this is a mistype for 1944 in Arthur Miller's private papers.
5. Interview with the author, 2000.
6. John Chapman, *New York Daily News*, 24 November 1944.
7. *Berkshire Eagle*, 21 July 2001.
8. Michael Kuchwara, 'Arthur Miller's "Luck": A Fortunate Revival', *Morning Call*, 29 July 2001.
9. Bruce Webber, 'Deflation of an Optimist by a Young Writer', *New York Times*, 24 July 2001.
10. Arthur Miller, 'Introduction', *The Collected Plays* (New York, 1957), p. 14.
11. Burns Mantle, ed., *The Best Plays of 1944 5* (New York, 1946), p. 8.
12. Email to the author from Ross Miller, 2 January 2007.
13. Letter from Bud Bohman, 31 December 1944, in Arthur Miller's private papers.
14. Miller, *Timebends* (1990), p. 105.
15. Arthur Miller, 'Shattering the Silence, Illuminating the Hatred', in *Writers on Writing*, vol. II, ed. Jane Smiley (New York, 2003), p. 163.
16. Robins, *Alien Ink*, p. 314.
17. FBI file LA 100–19333.
18. Interview with the author, 1995.
19. Dinnerstein, *Anti-Semitism in America*, p. 122.
20. Michael N. Dobkowski, *The Tarnished Dream: The Basis of American Anti-Semitism* (Westport, 1979), p. 242.
21. Dinnerstein, *Anti-Semitism in America*, p. 114.
22. Miller, *Echoes Down the Corridor* (2000), p. 206.
23. Miller, 'Shattering the Silence', in Smiley, *Writers on Writing*, pp. 164–5.
24. Alfred Kazin, *New York Jew* (New York, 1978), pp. 27, 28.
25. Eric Bentley, ed., *Thirty Years of Treason* (London, 1971), p. 804.
26. *Ibid.*, p. 805.
27. Kazin, *New York Jew*, pp. 31–2.
28. Irving Howe, *The Critical Point: On Literature and Culture* (New York, 1973), p. 110.
29. *Ibid.*, p. 111.
30. 'Should Ezra Pound Be Shot?', *New Masses*, 25 December 1945, pp. 6, 5, 6, 6.
31. Bentley, *Thirty Years of Treason*, p. 805.
32. Miller, *Echoes Down the Corridor* (2000), p. 207.
33. Quoted in Dinnerstein, *Anti-Semitism in America*, p. 138.
34. Arthur Miller, 'The Face in the Mirror: Anti-Semitism Then and Now', *New York Times Book Review*, 14 October 1984, p. 3.
35. Jean-Paul Sartre, *Anti-Semite and Jew*, trans. George J. Becker (New York, 1965), p. 21. The next four quotations: *ibid.*, pp. 22, 27, 54, 72.
36. Arthur Miller, 'His Jewish Question', *Vanity Fair*, October 2001, p. 365.
37. *Guardian*, 11 March 2002, p. 7.
38. Mihail Sebastian, *Journal 1935–1944* 'Introduction' by Radu Ioanid (Chicago, 2000), pp. xii–xv, 78.
39. Miller, *Timebends* (1990), p. 223.
40. Bellow, *Dangling Man*, p. 22.
41. Arthur Miller, 'On Censorship and Laughter, Chicago's First Annual Humanities Festival', 11 November 1990.

42. Miller, 'Shattering the Silence', in Smiley, *Writer on Writing*, pp. 166–7.
43. Miller, 'The Face in the Mirror' (14 October 1984), p. 3.
44. Interview with the author, 1995.
45. Dinnerstein, *Anti-Semitism in America*, p. 151.
46. Richard Pells, *The Liberal Mind in a Conservative Age: American Intellectuals in the 1940s and 1950s* (New York, 1985), p. 45.
47. I am indebted to Nathan David Abrahams for this information, who in turn credits Andrew Hemmingway and notes confirmation as coming from Lloyd Brown, former managing editor of *New Masses*.
48. FBI file 100–57673.
49. Interview with the author in *Miller Shorts*, BBC TV, 2000.
50. *Ibid.*
51. *Ibid.*
52. *Ibid.*
53. James McFarlane, ed., *The Cambridge Companion to Henrik Ibsen* (Cambridge, 1994), p. 227.
54. Arthur Miller, *A View from the Bridge, All My Sons* (Harmondsworth, 1961), p. 107.
55. Interview with the author.
56. Kazan, *A Life*, p. 340.
57. *Ibid.*, pp. 339–40.
58. *Ibid.*, p. 339.
59. Jay Williams, *Stage Left* (New York, 1974), p. 166.
60. Miller, *Timebends* (1990), p. 275.
61. Kazan, *A Life*, p. 341.
62. Miller, *Timebends* (1990), p. 133.
63. Arthur Miller, 'It Takes a Thief', *Collier's*, 8 February 1947, pp. 23, 75–6.
64. In Gerald Weales, *The Crucible: Text and Criticism* (New York, 1971), p. 397.
65. *Ibid.*, p. 398.
66. Miller, *Timebends* (1990), p. 406.
67. Richard D. G. Crockatt, *British Documents on Foreign Affairs: Reports and Papers from the Foreign Office Confidential Print*, part IV, vol. 2 (Washington, 2001), pp. 27, 28, 29.
68. Schrecker, *Many Are the Crimes*, p. 38.
69. Letter to the author, 11 July 2002.
70. Howard Barnes, 'Two More Duds', *New York Herald Tribune*, 30 January 1947.
71. Robert Coleman, '"All My Sons" Not Very Convincing', *Daily Mirror*, 30 January 1947.
72. John Chapman, 'A Lot Goes On But Little Happens in Backyard Drama "All My Sons"', *Daily News*, 30 January 1947.
73. Louis Valta, 'All My Sons Wins Critics' Laurels', *New York Times*, 22 April 1947.
74. Quoted in Thomas H. Pauly, *An American Odyssey: Elia Kazan and American Culture* (Philadelphia, 1983), p. 76.
75. FBI file NY 100–57673.
76. FBI file dated 14 August 1947.
77. *Ibid.*
78. Brooks Atkinson, 'No Compromise', *New York Times*, 21 September 1947.
79. Bentley, *Thirty Years of Treason*, pp. 443–5.
80. *Ibid.*, pp. 518–9.
81. *Ibid.*, p. 524.
82. Letter to the author.
83. HUAC Files, 'Testimony of Jack L. Warner, Lino Regal – CC 58.'
84. FBI file NY 100–57673.
85. Kazan, *A Life*, p. 348.

5 DEATH OF A SALESMAN

1. Interview with the author, 1995.
2. Interview with the author, 2002.
3. Miller, *Timebends* (1990), pp. 143–4.

4. *Investigation of So-Called 'Blacklisting'*, pp. 5260, 5263, in FBI file 100–22169, dated 14 November 1956.

5. FBI file NY 100–50870.

6. Bentley, *Thirty Years of Treason*, p. 820.

7. *Ibid.*, p. 799.

8. Walter Goodman, *The Committee* (London, 1969), p. 70.

9. Letter from William Green, 19 May 1947, in Arthur Miller's private papers.

10. Arthur Miller, *Story from the Stars*, 8 May 1947. Typescript in Harry Ransom Center, University of Texas at Austin.

11. Bentley, *Thirty Years of Treason*, p. 798.

12. *Ibid.*, p. 800.

13. Goodman, *The Committee*, p. 191.

14. Bentley, *Thirty Years of Treason*, p. 800.

15. Goodman, *The Committee*, p. 181.

16. Miller, *Timebends* (1990), p. 145.

17. Miller, *After the Fall* (1964), p. 28.

18. Miller, *Timebends* (1990), p. 155.

19. *Ibid.*, p. 156.

20. *Ibid.*, p. 158.

21. *Ibid.*, p. 167.

22. This quotation and the following ones from Arthur Miller, *I Don't Need You Any More* (London, 1967), pp. 54, 56, 56, 57, 60, 65, 66, 79, 70, 70.

23. Miller, *Timebends* (1990), p. 176.

24. This and preceding quotations from Arthur Miller, 'Concerning Jews Who Write', *Jewish Life*, 2, 5 (March 1948), pp. 7–10.

25. FBI File NY 100–57673.

26. Letter to the author, 7 November 2002.

27. Interview with the author, September 2001.

28. *Ibid.*

29. Arthur Miller, 'Waiting for the Teacher', *Harper's*, July 1998, pp. 56–7.

30. This and the preceding quotation: Miller, *Timebends* (1990), pp. 179, 182.

31. *Ibid.*, p. 185.

32. Cheryl Crawford, *My Fifty Years in the Theatre* (Indianapolis, 1977), p. 213.

33. Peter Novick, *The Holocaust and Collective Memory* (London, 1999), pp. 112–3.

34. Gussow, *Conversations with Arthur Miller*, p. 143.

35. Arthur Miller, 'Mildred Dunnock', *Theater Week*, 29 June 1991, pp. 12–13.

36. *New York Times*, 6 February 1949.

37. Arthur Miller, 'Classics in Words and Music', *The Times*, 1 February 1999.

38. Arthur Miller, *Salesman in Beijing* (New York, 1984), p. 197.

39. Telegram from Irene Selznick to Arthur Miller at the Morosco Theatre, 10 February 1949, in Arthur Miller's private papers.

40. *New York Times*, 6 February 1949.

41. Brooks Atkinson, '*Death of a Salesman*, a New Drama by Arthur Miller, Has Premiere at the Morosco,' *New York Times*, 11 February 1949.

42. Robins, *Alien Ink*, p. 312.

43. Earl Shorris, *The Nation of Salesmen: The Tyranny of the Market and the Subversion of Culture* (New York, 1994), p. 325.

44. If the play were set at the time of its composition the scenes from the past would date back to 1931, but we have Miller's assurance that 'For Willy it meant the American 1920s, the time when it all seemed to be coasting, expanding opportunity everywhere, the dream in full bloom' (Miller, *Salesman in Beijing* (1984), p. 108).

45. Typescript, Harry Ransom Research Center, University of Texas at Austin.

46. This and the following quotations: Miller, *Timebends* (1990), pp. 122, 123, 124, 126, 131.

47. *Death of a Salesman* Notebook, Harry Ransom Center, University of Texas. Subsequent references are to this notebook.

48. Arthur Miller, *Death of a Salesman* (New York, 1998), p. 2.

49. Miller, *Salesman in Beijing* (1984), p. 7.

50. Jo Mielziner, *Designing for the Theatre: A Memoir and a Portfolio* (New York, 1965), p. 25.

51. *Ibid.*, p. 33.

52. Miller, *Salesman in Beijing* (1984), p. 210.

53. Robert A. Martin and Steven R. Centola, eds, *The Theater Essays of Arthur Miller* (New York, 1996), p. 423.

54. Kenneth Thorpe Rowe, *A Theater in Your Head* (New York, 1960), pp. 48–9.

55. Miller, *Salesman in Beijing* (1984), p. 27.

56. Miller, *Timebends* (1990), p. 184.

57. This and the next two quotations from Miller, *Salesman in Beijing* (1984), pp. 49, 27, 27.

58. Eric Bentley, *In Search of Theatre* (London, 1954), p. 85. Interestingly, in another book, *What Is Theatre?*, he argues that there is a confusion between the political and the sexual realm: the key scene is the one with the tape recorder if it is a policital play, or the one set in the Boston hotel room if it is a sexual play, as though the two acts of betrayal and denial were wholly separate.

59. Matthew C. Roudané, *Conversations with Arthur Miller* (Jackson, 1987), p. 15.

60. Rasky, *Arthur Miller: On Home Ground.*

61. Gussow, *Conversations with Arthur Miller*, p. 26.

62. Rhoda Koenig, 'Seduced by Salesman's Patter', *Sunday Times*, 20 October 1996.

63. Gussow, *Conversations with Arthur Miller*, p. 102.

64. This and the next quotation from Miller, *Salesman in Beijing* (1984), p. 20, 69.

65. *Ibid.*, p. 69.

66. *Ibid.*, p. 78.

67. *New York Times*, 9 May 1999, Arts section, p. 7.

68. *Ibid.*

69. Peter Applebome, 'Arthur Miller: Present at the Birth of a Salesman', *New York Times*, 29 January 1999.

70. Gussow, *Conversations with Arthur Miller*, p. 39.

71. Mary McCarthy, *Sights and Spectacles: 1937–1958* (London, 1959), pp. xxiii, xv.

72. Miller, *Timebends* (1990), p. 182.

73. Miller, *Salesman in Beijing* (1984), p. 40.

74. Gussow, *Conversations with Arthur Miller*, p. 50.

75. Interview with the author, 2002.

6 THE WALDORF

1. This and the next quotation from Donald Windham, ed. *Tennessee Williams' Letters to Donald Windham 1940–1965* (New York, 1977), pp. 232, 258.

2. Stanley Kauffman, *Persons of the Drama: Theater Criticism and Comment* (New York, 1976), pp. 143–4.

3. Robert Brustein, *Who Needs Theatre?* (London, 1989), pp. 48–9.

4. Robert Brustein, *The Theatre of Revolt* (London, 1965), pp. 24–5.

5. Miller, *Timebends* (1990), p. 194.

6. Kazan, *A Life*, pp. 389–90.

7. Interview with the author, September 2001.

8. 'Dangerous Thoughts' an unpublished, undated manuscript at the Harry Ransom Center, University of Texas.

9. FBI file NY 100–57673.

10. Arthur Schlesinger Jr, *A Life in the Twentieth Century: Innocent Beginnings, 1917–1950* (New York, 2000), p. 506.

11. Irving Howe, *Celebrations and Attacks: Thirty Years of Literary and Cultural Commentary* (New York, 1979), p. 113.

12. Interview with the author, 2001.

13. Miller, *Timebends* (1990), p. 234.

14. Abrams, 'Struggling for Freedom', quoting from Columbia Oral History Research Project, p. 945.

15. Miller, *Timebends* (1990), p. 234.

16. William Barrett, 'Culture Conference at the Waldorf', *Commentary*, vol. 7, p. 487.

17. *Ibid.*, p. 489.

18. *Ibid.*, p. 490.

19. Arthur Schlesinger Jr, *The Vital Center: The Politics of Freedom* (London, 1950), p. 81.

20. *Ibid.*, pp. 83–4.

21. *Ibid.*, p. 102.

22. Abrams, 'Struggling for Freedom', p. 123.

23. Schlesinger, *The Vital Center*, p. 507.

24. William Phillips, *A Partisan View: Five Decades of the Literary Life* (New York, 1983), p. 153.

25. Frances Stonor Saunders, *Who Paid the Piper?* (London, 1999), p. 201.

26. Carol Brightman, *Writing Dangerously: Mary McCarthy and Her World* (New York, 1994), p. 324.

27. Alexander Bloom, *Prodigal Sons: The New York Intellectuals and Their World* (New York, 1986), p. 261.

28. Peter Manso, *Mailer: His Life and Times* (New York, 1986), p. 136.

29. Interview with the author, 2001.

30. Irving Howe, *A Margin of Hope: An Intellectual Biography* (London, 1983), p. 157.

31. Robins, *Alien Ink*, p. 279.

32. Saunders, *Who Paid the Piper?*, p. 51.

33. This quote and the next from Miller, *Timebends* (1990), pp. 235.

34. Howard Fast, *The Naked God: The Writer and the Communist Party* (London, 1958), p. 78.

35. This and the next quotation, Miller, *Timebends* (1990), pp. 237, 239–40.

36. Arthur Miller, 'The Year It Came Apart', *New York* (1974), p. 36.

37. W. Scott Lucas, 'Revealing the Parameters of Opinion: An Interview with Frances Stonor Saunders', in *The Cultural Cold War in Western Europe 1945–1960* (London, 2003), p. 29.

38. This and the next quotation, Miller, *Timebends* (1990), pp. 237, 239.

39. Interview with the author, September 2001.

40. Saunders, *Who Paid the Piper?*, p. 48.

41. Irving Howe, 'The Culture Conference', *Partisan Review*, vol. xvi, no. 5, p. 505.

42. Robert Crossly, *Olaf Stapledon: Speaking for the Future* (Liverpool, 1994), p. 37.

43. FBI file NY 100–57673.

44. Barrett, 'Culture Conference at the Waldorf', p. 493.

45. Abrams, 'Struggling for Freedom', p. 183, quoting from Columbia Oral History Project, p. 945.

46. Robert Warshow, letter to the editors, *Partisan Review*, 21 (1954), p. 235.

47. Eleanor Clark, 'Theater Chronical', *Partisan Review* XVI, vi, p. 633.

48. Brightman, *Writing Dangerously*, p. 323.

49. Saunders, *Who Paid the Piper?*, p. 42.
50. *Ibid.*, p. 12.
51. W. Scott Lucas, 'Beyond Freedom, Beyond Control: Approaches to Culture and the State–Private Network in the Cold War', in Lucas, *The Cultural Cold War* p. 59.
52. Quoted in Christopher Lasch, *The Agony of the American Left* (London, 1970), pp. 100–1. The article originally appeared in the *Saturday Evening Post* of 20 May 1967.
53. *Ibid.*, p. 100.
54. *Ibid.*, p. 60.
55. Miller, *Timebends* (1990), pp. 235–6.
56. Lasch, *The Agony of the American Left*.
57. Joel Kotel, 'Youth Organizations as a Battlefield in the Cold War', in Lucas, *The Cultural Cold War*, p. 185.
58. Frances Stoner Saunders, *Who Paid the Piper?* p. 136.
59. Crossman, *The God That Failed*, p. 82.
60. Arthur Miller, letter to the editor, *New York Herald Tribune*, 27 May 1949.
61. Philip S. Foner, *Paul Robeson Speaks* (New York, 1978), p. 211.
62. FBI file NY 100–57673.
63. *Ibid.*
64. Camus, *Resistance, Rebellion and Death*, p. 172.
65. This quotation and the next from interview with the author, September 2001.
66. Solomon M. Schwartz, 'The New Anti-Semitism of the Soviet Union: Its Background and Its Meaning', *Commentary*, vol. 7, p. 535.
67. *Ibid.*, p. 544.
68. Doris Lessing, *Walking in the Shade* (London, 1997), pp. 45–6.
69. Miller, 'The Year It Came Apart,' p. 31.
70. *Ibid.*, p. 294.
71. This and the next quotation, Kazan,

A Life, pp. 428, 429.
72. James Kaplan, 'Miller's Crossing', *Vanity Fair*, November 1991, p. 149.
73. This and the next quotation, Miller, *Timebends* (1990), p. 312.
74. Miller, *Echoes Down the Corridor* (2000), p. 131.
75. *Ibid.*, p. 138.
76. This and the next few quotations, Miller, *After the Fall* (1964), pp. 40, 40–1, 42, 57, 60.
77. Kazan, *A Life*, p. 392.
78. Miller, *After the Fall* (1964), p. 61.
79. *Ibid.*
80. Memorandum dated 16 August 1950 to the Director of the FBI from SAC New York.
81. SAC [Special Agent in Charge] Los Angeles 100–40559.

7 MARILYN

1. This and the next two quotations from Miller, *Timebends* (1990), p. 372.
2. Marilyn Monroe, *My Story* (New York, 1974), pp. 16, 16, 19.
3. *Marilyn on Marilyn*, BBC Television, 2000.
4. Maurice Zolotow, *Marilyn Monroe* (London, 1961), p. 39.
5. Interview with the author, 1995.
6. Zolotow, *Marilyn Monroe*, p. 62.
7. *Ibid.*, p. 45.
8. *Ibid.*, p. 60.
9. Monroe, *My Story*, p. 60.
10. *Ibid.*, p. 47.
11. Donald Spoto, *Marilyn Monroe: The Biography* (London, 1993), p. 136.
12. Zolotow, *Marilyn Monroe*, p. 77.
13. *Marilyn on Marilyn*, BBC TV, 2000.
14. Kazan, *A Life*, p. 801.
15. Spoto, *Marilyn Monroe: The Biography*, p. 161.

16. Roger G. Taylor, ed., *Marilyn on Marilyn* (London, 1983), p. 57.
17. This and the next few quotations, Miller, *Timebends* (1990), pp. 293, 294, 299, 302.
18. Morton Miller, 'My Moments with Marilyn: P.S. Arthur Was There, Too', *Esquire*, June 1998, p. 167.
19. Typescript at Harry Ransom Humanities Research Center, University of Texas at Austin.
20. This and the next quotation from Miller, *Timebends* (1990), pp. 303.
21. This and the next several quotations, Kazan, *A Life*, p. 432, 434, 431–2, 436, 435.
22. W.J. Weatherby, *Conversations with Marilyn* (New York, 1992), p. 144.
23. This and the next quotation, Miller, *Timebends* (1990), pp. 303, 304.
24. Kazan, *A Life*, p. 437.
25. Miller, *Timebends* (1990), p. 302.
26. Anthony Summers, *Goddess: The Secret Lives of Marilyn Monroe* (London, 1985), p. 77.
27. Kazan, *A Life*, pp. 436–7.
28. Taylor, *Marilyn on Marilyn*.
29. Griffin Fariello, *Red Scare: Memories of the American Inquisition, An Oral History* (New York, 1995), pp. 120–2.
30. Kazan, *A Life*, p. 440.
31. Fariello, *Red Scare*, p. 122.
32. Interview with the author, May 2002.
33. Fariello, *Red Scare*, p. 342.
34. This and the next quotation, Miller, *Timebends* (1990), pp. 305, 308.
35. Interview with the author.
36. Miller, 'On Censorship and Laughter, Chicago's First Annual Humanities Festival', 11 November 1990.
37. This and the next two quotations, Kazan, *A Life*, pp. 441, 442, 443.
38. Miller, *Timebends* (1990), p. 307.
39. Kazan, *A Life*, pp. 442–3.
40. Arthur Miller, 'After Kefauver –

what?' *New York Daily Compass*, March 25, 1951. Compass Magazine and Special Articles Section, 11, 2, 4.
41. This quotation and the next, Miller, *Timebends* (1990), pp. 307, 327.
42. *Ibid.*, p. 328.
43. Arthur Miller, 'The Year It Came Apart', in *New York* (1974), p. 32.
44. Miller, *Timebends* (1990), p. 320.
45. *Ibid.*, p. 321.
46. This and the next quotation, Kazin, *New York Jew*, pp. 19, 20.
47. Miller, *Timebends* (1990), p. 315.
48. *Career of a Salesman*, Columbia Pictures, 1951.
49. Miller, *Timebends* (1990), p. 316.
50. FBI File 100–333798.
51. Miller, *Timebends* (1990), pp. 322–3.
52. Brenda Murphy, *Congressional Theatre: Dramatizing McCarthyism on Stage, Film, and Television* (Cambridge, 1999), p. 137.
53. This and the next quotation, Miller, *Timebends* (1990), p. 326.
54. Alan Judd, *The Quest for C: Mansfield Cumming and the Founding of the Secret Service* (London, 1999), p. 11.
55. Miller, *Echoes Down the Corridor* (2000), p. 193.
56. This and the next few quotations, Miller, *Timebends* (1990), pp. 326–7, 327, 327, 328, 328.
57. Robert Lewis, *Slings and Arrows* (New York, 1984), p. 221.
58. Interview with the author, 1995.
59. *Ibid.*
60. Miller, *Echoes Down the Corridor* (2000), p. 193.
61. Lewis, *Slings and Arrows*, p. 222.
62. Miller, *Timebends* (1990), p. 332.
63. Kazan, *A Life*, p. 391.

8 THE CRUCIBLE

1. Interview with the author, 2003.

2. Arthur Miller, *The Crucible in History and Other Essays* (London, 2000), p. 30.

3. At the Harry Ransom Center, University of Texas.

4. Gussow, *Conversations with Arthur Miller*, pp. 87, 89.

5. Interview with the author.

6. Tennessee Williams, *Five O'Clock Angel: Letters of Tennessee Williams to Maria St Just 1948–1982* (London, 1991), p. 54.

7. Victor Navasky, *Naming Names* (London, 1982), p. 36.

8. *Ibid.*, pp. 201–2.

9. Kazan, *A Life*, p. 495.

10. Navasky, *Naming Names*, p. 202.

11. *A Life*, p. 494.

12. Jeff Young, *Kazan on Kazan* (London, 1999), p. 119.

13. *Ibid.*

14. Interview with the author, January 2002.

15. *Ibid.*

16. Robins, *Alien Ink*, p. 122.

17. Kazan, *A Life*, p. 222.

18. This and the next quotation, Navasky, *Naming Names*, pp. 272, 393.

19. Kazan, *A Life*, p. 504.

20. *Ibid.*, pp. 734–5.

21. Saunders, *Who Paid the Piper?*, pp. 282–3.

22. Kazan, *A Life*, p. 497.

23. Bentley, *Thirty Years of Treason*, p. 485.

24. Young, *Kazan on Kazan*, p. 118.

25. *Ibid.*, p. 492.

26. Interview with the author, May 2002.

27. WNET, *Arthur Miller, Elia Kazan and the Blacklist: None without Sin*, New York, 3 September 2003.

28. Navasky, *Naming Names*, pp. 204–6.

29. Jackson J. Benson, *The True Adventures of John Steinbeck, Writer* (London, 1984), p. 722.

30. *Ibid.*, p. 746.

31. WNET, *Arthur Miller, Elia Kazan and the Blacklist: None without Sin.*

32. David Garfield, *The Actors Studio: A Player's Place* (New York, 1984), p. 87.

33. Letter from Elia Kazan to Cheryl Crawford, Cheryl Crawford files, NYPL-LC, quoted in Garfield, *The Actors Studio*, pp. 88–9.

34. Saunders, *Who Paid the Piper?*, p. 283.

35. Navasky, *Naming Names*, pp. 154–5.

36. *Ibid.*, p. 208, 221.

37. Robins, *Alien Ink*, p. 92.

38. Bentley, *Thirty Years of Treason*, p. 529.

39. *Ibid.*, p. 531.

40. FBI file 100–333798.

41. This and the next two quotations, Alvah Bessie, *Inquisition in Eden* (New York, 1967), pp. 245, 246, 272.

42. Fariello, *Red Scare*, p. 120.

43. Bentley, *Thirty Years of Treason*, p. 665–6.

44. Navasky, *Naming Names*, pp. 271–3.

45. This and the following quotations, Kazan, *A Life*, pp. 508, 521, 538, 538–9, 569, 525, 570.

46. Navasky, *Naming Names*, pp. 327.

47. Peter Charles Hoffer, *The Salem Witchcraft Trials: A Legal History* (Lawrence, 1997), p. 38.

48. Henry Hewes, 'Arthur Miller and How He Went to the Devil', *Saturday Review*, XXXVI, (31 January 1953), p. 24.

49. Marion Starkey, *The Devil in Massachusetts: A Modern Enquiry into the Salem Witch Trials* (London, nd), p. 12.

50. *Ibid.*, p. 10.

51. *Ibid.*, p. 11.

52. Miller, *Timebends* (1990), p. 331.

53. Bigsby, *Arthur Miller and Company*, pp. 80–1.

54. Arthur Miller, *The Crucible* (Harmondsworth, 1968), p. 38.

55. *Ibid.*, pp. 122–3, 125.
56. Bentley, *Thirty Years of Treason*, p. 820.
57. Letter from Laurence Olivier in Miller's private papers.
58. Arthur Miller, 'Salem Revisited', *New York Times*, 15 October 1998.
59. Arthur Miller, 'Steinbeck', in *John Steinbeck: A Centennial Tribute*, ed. Stephen K. George (Westport, 2002), p. 64.
60. Walter Kerr, *New York Herald Tribune*, 23 January 1953.
61. Joseph T. Shipley, 'Arthur Miller's New Melodrama Is Not What It Seems to Be', *New Leader*, XXXVI (9 February 1953), pp. 25–6.
62. Eric Bentley, *New Republic*, CXXVIII (16 February 1953), p. 22, reprinted in Bentley, *What Is Theatre?* (New York, 1968), pp. 62–5.
63. *Ibid.*, p. 64.
64. Robert Warshow, 'The Liberal Conscience in "The Crucible": Arthur Miller and His Audience, *Commentary*, XV, (March 1953), p. 266.
65. *Daily Worker*, 28 January 1953, in FBI file NY 100–57673.
66. Miller, *Timebends* (1990), pp. 347–8.
67. WNET, *Arthur Miller, Elia Kazan and the Blacklist: None without Sin*.
68. Arthur Miller, 'The Night Ed Murrow Struck Back', *Esquire*, December 1983, p. 465.
69. Arthur Miller, 'It Could Happen Here – And Did', *New York Times*, 30 April 1967.
70. Arthur Miller, 'Again They Drink from the Cup of Suspicion', *New York Times*, 26 November 1989, p. 36.

9 A VIEW FROM THE BRIDGE

1. Kazin, *New York Jew*, p. 188.
2. Irving, Kristol, 'Civil Liberties 1952 – A Study in Confusion: Do We Defend Our Rights by Protecting Communists?' *Commentary* 13 (March 1952), p. 236.
3. Richard Pells, *The Liberal Mind in a Conservative Age: American Intellectuals in the 1940s and 1950s* (New York, 1985), p. 288.
4. Fariello, *Red Scare*, p. 421.
5. *Ibid.*, p. 422.
6. Mary McCarthy, *On the Contrary* (London, 1962), p. 49.
7. *Ibid.*, p. 233–4.
8. Saunders, *Who Paid the Piper?*, p. 161.
9. Mary Sperling McAuliffe, *Crisis on the Left: Cold War Politics and American Liberals 1944–1954* (Amherst, 1978), p. 116.
10. Nathan David Abrams, 'Struggling for Freedom: Arthur Miller, The Commentary Community and the Cultural Cold War', PhD thesis, University of Birmingham, July 1998.
11. Robert Warshow, *The Immediate Experience: Movies, Comics, Theater and Other Aspects of Popular Culture* (New York, 1962), pp. 141, 145.
12. Irving Howe, *A Margin of Hope: An Intellectual Biography* (London, 1983), p. 217.
13. Norman Podhoretz, *Breaking Ranks* (New York, 1979), p. 4.
14. Irving Howe, *Steady Work* (New York, 1966), p. 328.
15. Howe, *A Margin of Hope*, p. 215.
16. Abrams, 'Struggling for Freedom', p. 53.
17. Norman Podhoretz, 'The Issue', *Commentary*, 29 (1960), pp. 182–3.
18. Saunders, *Who Paid the Piper?*, p. 250.
19. Arthur Schlesinger Jr, *A Life in the Twentieth Century* (New York, 2000), pp. 519–20.

20. Howard Brick, *Daniel Bell and the Decline of Intellectual Modernism* (Madison, 1986), p. 21.

21. Miller, *The Crucible in History* (2000), p. 15.

22. Fariello, *Red Scare*, p. 140.

23. *Ibid.*, p. 141.

24. Ronald Radosh, 'Arthur Miller's McCarthy Fantasy: The Crucible and the 1950s', *Front Page* magazine, 26 July 2000.

25. Saunders, *Who Paid the Piper?* p. 162.

26. Victor Navasky, *Naming Names* (London, 1982), p. 56.

27. Saunders, *Who Paid the Piper?* pp. 157, 207.

28. Kristol, 'Civil Liberties 1952 – A Study in Confusion', p. 236.

29. Alfred Kazin, *Starting Out in the Thirties* (London, 1966), p. 156.

30. McCarthy, *On the Contrary*, p. 311.

31. Mary McCarthy, *Sights and Spectacles: 1937–1958* (London, 1959), p. xxv.

32. *Ibid.*, p. 292.

33. Kazin, *Starting Out in the Thirties*, p. 156.

34. Eric Bentley, *In Search of Theatre* (London, 1954), p. 86.

35. Eric Bentley, *The Dramatic Event* (London, 1954), pp. 257, 258.

36. Abrams, 'Struggling for Freedom', p. 187.

37. Sidney Hook, *Out of Step: An Unquiet Life in the Twentieth Century* (New York, 1987), pp. 495–6.

38. Gerald Bordman, *The Oxford Companion to American Theatre* (Oxford, 1984), p. 477.

39. Bigsby, *Miller and Company*, p. 228.

40. *Ibid.*

41. Miller, *Timebends* (1990), p. 353.

42. John Mortimer, 'Thoroughly Modern Miller', *Daily Telegraph*, 10 October 1987.

43. Arthur Miller, *A Memory of Two Mondays* (New York, 1955), pp. 5–6.

44. Miller, *Timebends* (1990), p. 220.

45. Arthur Miller, 'Picking a Cast', *New York Times*, 21 August 1955, section 2, p. 12.

46. Miller, *Timebends* (1990), p. 354.

47. Interview with the author, 1995.

48. Miller, *Timebends* (1990), pp. 150, 152, 152.

49. Martin and Centola, *The Theater Essays of Arthur Miller*, p. 220.

50. Miller, *Timebends* (1990), p. 356.

51. Bigsby, *Miller and Company*, p. 112.

52. Martin and Centola, *The Theater Essays of Arthur Miller*, p. 219.

53. *Ibid.*

54. Bigsby, *Miller and Company*, pp. 110–13.

55. Letter to the *New York Post*.

56. Letter from Murray Kempton, undated but probably 4 January 1956, in Arthur Miller's private papers.

57. Eric Bentley, 'Theater', *New Republic*, 19 December 1955, p. 21.

58. Brooks Atkinson, 'A View from the Bridge', *New York Times*, 9 October 1955.

59. Martin and Centola, *The Theater Essays of Arthur Miller*, p. 57.

60. Bigsby, *Miller and Company*, p. 111.

61. *Ibid.*, pp. 110–11.

62. FBI file NY 100–50870.

63. Norman Mailer, *The Time of Our Time* (London, 1998), p. 300.

64. Arthur Miller, 'Concerning the Boom', *in International Theatre Annual*, no. 1, ed. Harold Hobson (London, 1956), pp. 85–8.

65. Martin and Centola, *The Theater Essays of Arthur Miller*, pp. 57–8.

66. This and the next quotation, *Ibid.*, pp. 57–8, 59.

67. Interview with the author, September 2001.

68. Interview with the author, 2001.

69. Summers, *Goddess*, p. 70.

70. Kazan, *A Life*, p. 435.

71. Summers, *Goddess*, p. 71.
72. Spoto, *Marilyn Monroe: The Biography*, pp. 204–5. Guiles, *Norma Jean: the Life and Death of Marilyn Monroe*, p. 122.
73. Zolotow, *Marilyn Monroe*, p. 168.
74. Spoto, *Marilyn Monroe: The Biography*, p. 299.
75. Sam Shaw and Norman Rosten, *Marilyn among Friends* (London, 1987), p. 38.
76. This and the next three quotations, Zolotow, *Marilyn Monroe*, pp. 209, 210, 211, 147.
77. *Ibid.*, p. 208.
78. Spoto, *Marilyn Monroe: The Biography*, p. 330.
79. *Ibid.*, p. 353.
80. *Ibid.*, p. 361.
81. Bigsby, *Miller and Company*, p. 224.
82. *Ibid.*, p. 118.
83. Miller, *Timebends* (1990), p. 359.
84. This and the next three quotations, F. Scott Fitzgerald, *The Great Gatsby* (Harmondsworth, 1950), pp. 105, 106, 156, 187.
85. Summers, *Goddess*, p. 190.
86. Morton Miller, *Vanity Fair*, November 1991, pp. 149–50.
87. *Ibid.*, p. 150.
88. Anthony Holden, *Olivier* (London, 1988), p. 304.
89. Summers, *Goddess*, p. 219.
90. This and the next two quotations, Laurence Olivier, *Confessions of an Actor* (London, 1982), pp. 169, 306, 169.
91. Miller, *Timebends* (1990), p. 354.
92. Robert Lewis, *Slings and Arrows* (New York, 1984), p. 244.
93. Miller, *Timebends* (1990), p. 356.
94. Morton Miller, 'My Moments with Marilyn: P.S. Arthur was There, Too', *Esquire*, June 1998, p. 161.
95. WNET, *Arthur Miller, Elia Kazan and the Blacklist: None without Sin.*
96. Bentley, *Thirty Years of Treason*, p. 794.
97. Walter Goodman, 'How Not to Produce a Film', *New Republic*, 26 December, 1955, p. 13.
98. *Ibid.*
99. *Ibid.*
100. *Ibid.*
101. This and the next two quotations, Arthur Miller, 'Bridge to a Savage World', *Esquire*, vol. 50 (October 1958), pp. 185, 189, 190.
102. Jeff Kisseloff, *On the Box: An Oral History of Television 1920–1961* (New York, 1995), pp. 428–9.
103. Arthur Miller, 'The Bored and the Violent', *Harper's*, vol. 225 (November 1962), pp. 50–6.
104. Abrams, 'Struggling for Freedom', pp. 188–9.
105. FBI file 100–27055–31.
106. This and the next quotations, Miller, *Timebends* (1990), pp. 359, 359, 360, 366, 369.
107. Shaw and Rosten, *Marilyn among Friends*, p. 95.
108. David Garfield, *The Actors Studio: A Player's Place* (New York, 1984), p. 121.
109. FBI file 100–333798.
110. Miller, *Timebends* (1990), p. 378.
111. FBI file 100–333798.
112. Arthur Miller, interviewed by John H. Richardson, 'What I've Learned', *Esquire*, July 2003, p. 110.
113. Zolotow, *Marilyn Monroe*, p. 269.
114. This and the next few quotations, Miller, *Timebends* (1990), pp. 380, 380, 381.
115. FBI file 100–333798.
116. Miller, *Timebends* (1990), p. 391.
117. FBI file 100–333798.
118. Morton, Miller, 'My Moments with Marilyn', p. 161.
119. Interview with the author.
120. Taylor, *Marilyn on Marilyn*, p. 48.
121. Morton, Miller, 'My Moments with Marilyn', p. 163.
122. Summers, *Goddess*, p. 212.
123. Miller, *Timebends* (1990), p. 400.

124. *Ibid.*, p. 405.
125. Bigsby, *Miller and Company*, pp. 108–9.
126. Spoto, *Marilyn Monroe: The Biography*, p. 433.
127. Susan Strasberg, *Marilyn and Me* (New York, 1992) p. 80.
128. Summers, *Goddess*, p. 213.
129. Norman Rosten, *Marilyn: A Very Personal Story* (London, 1973), p. 31.
130. *Newsweek*, vol. 48 (July 1956), p. 22.
131. FBI file 100–333798.

10 HUAC

1. Interview with the author, 1995.
2. Miller, *Echoes Down the Corridor* (2000), p. 197.
3. FBI file 100–57673.
4. Walter Goodman, *The Committee: The Extraordinary Career of the House Committee on Un-American Activities* (London, 1969), p. 1.
5. Schrecker, *Many Are the Crimes*, p. 40.
6. Goodman, *The Committee*, p. 14.
7. Bentley, *Thirty Years of Treason*, p. xv.
8. Schrecker, *Many Are the Crimes*, p. 91.
9. *Ibid.*, p. xv.
10. Interview with the author.
11. Victor Navasky, *Naming Names* (London, 1982), p. 355.
12. Goodman, *The Committee*, pp. 173–4.
13. Kazan, *A Life*, p. 451.
14. Goodman, *The Committee*, p. 217.
15. Duncan Campbell, 'Hollywood Owns Up', *Guardian Weekly*, 16 February 2002, p. 45.
16. Navasky, *Naming Names*, p. 153.
17. Schrecker, *Many Are the Crimes*, p. 330.
18. Arthur Schlesinger Jr, *The Vital Center* (London, 1950), p. 25.
19. Irving Kristol, 'Civil Liberties 1952 –
A Study in Confusion', *Commentary*, 13 (March 1952), pp. 234–5.
20. Larry Ceplair and Stephen Englund, *The Inquisition in Hollywood: Politics in the Film Community 1930–1960* (Berkeley, 1979), p. 423.
21. Bentley, *Thirty Years of Treason*, p. 144.
22. Goodman, *The Committee*, p. 301.
23. This and the next two quotations, Miller, *Timebends* (1990), pp. 309, 309–10, 310.
24. Bentley, *Thirty Years of Treason*, p. 537.
25. Kazan, *A Life*, p. 496.
26. This and the next quotations, Bentley, *Thirty Years of Treason*, pp. 532, 773, 778–9, 779, 784, 785–6, 774, 782, 775, 776, 782, 784, 787, 788, 789.
27. Miller, *Echoes Down the Corridor* (2000), p. 133.
28. Robins, *Alien Ink*, p. 315.
29. Murphy, *Congressional Theatre*, p. 42.
30. Goodman, *The Committee*, p. 389.
31. Bentley, *Thirty Years of Treason*, p. 794.
32. Interview with the author, 2001.
33. This and the next few quotations, Bentley, *Thirty Years of Treason*, pp. 798, 799, 799.
34. *Ibid.*, p. 802.
35. This and the next three quotations, Miller, *Timebends* (1990), pp. 407, 407, 410.
36. Bentley, *Thirty Years of Treason*, pp. 805–6.
37. *Ibid.*, p. 806.
38. *Ibid.*, p. 807.
39. Schlesinger, *The Vital Center*, p. 199.
40. This and the next six pages' quotations, Bentley, *Thirty Years of Treason*, pp. 808, 810, 813, 813, 814, 816, 817, 817, 818–9, 820, 821, 821, 803, 823–4, 824, 824, 824–5.

41. Harry Kalven Jr, 'A View from the Law', *New Republic*, 27 May 1957, p. 8.
42. Sworn deposition by Sigurdur Magnusson dated 5 July 1956, in Arthur Miller's private papers.
43. *Report 2922 84th Congress 2nd Session, House of Representatives: Proceedings Against Arthur Miller.*
44. 'House Unit Asks Miller Citation', *New York Times*, 6 July 1956.
45. Richard H. Pells, *The Liberal Mind in a Conservative Age: American Intellectuals in the 1940s and 1950s* (New York, 1985), p. 264.
46. Bentley, *Thirty Years of Treason*, p. 882.
47. Interview with the author, 1995.
48. Griffin Fariello, *Red Scare: Memories of the American Inquisition, an Oral History* (New York, 1995), p. 363.
49. Navasky, *Naming Names*, p. 348.
50. *Ibid.*, p. 328.
51. Benson, *The True Adventures of John Steinbeck, Writer*, pp. 812–13.
52. *Ibid.*, p. 813.
53. Miller, *Timebends* (1990), p. 412.
54. Zolotow, *Marilyn Monroe*, p. 278.
55. Letter to the author, 22 June 2001.
56. Morton, Miller, 'My Moments with Marilyn', p. 164.
57. Taylor, *Marilyn on Marilyn*, p. 51.
58. FBI file NY 100–57673.
59. Robins, *Alien Ink*, p. 118.
60. Kazan, *A Life*, p. 432.
61. Miller, *Timebends* (1990), p. 366.
62. *Ibid.*, p. 302.
63. Taylor, *Marilyn on Marilyn*, p. 51.
64. Summers, *Goddess*, p. 190.
65. *Ibid.*
66. *Ibid.*, p. 78.
67. Interview with the author, 1995.
68. Weatherby, *Conversation with Marilyn*, p. 188.
69. Interview with the author, 1995.
70. Bigsby, ed. *Miller and Company*, p. 123.
71. Interview with the author, 2001.
72. Leslie Kane, ed., *David Mamet in Conversation* (Ann Arbor, 2001), p. 168.
73. Interview with the author, 2002.
74. Interview with the author, 2001.
75. Interview with the author, 2002.

11 MISFITS

1. Interview with the author, May 2002.
2. *Ibid.*
3. Olivier, *Confessions of an Actor*, p. 172.
4. *The Prince, the Showgirl and Me*, BBC Television, January 2004.
5. Miller, *Timebends* (1990), pp. 415.
6. Interview with the author.
7. *Ibid.*
8. FBI file NY 100–57673.
9. Colin Clark, *My Week with Marilyn* (London, 2000), pp. 130–1.
10. FBI file dated 2 October 1956.
11. FBI file 100–333798.
12. Miller, *Timebends* (1990), p. 412.
13. Holden, *Olivier*, p. 308.
14. Miller, *Timebends* (1990), p. 418.
15. *Ibid.*, pp. 418–19.
16. *Ibid.*, pp. 419, 421.
17. Fred Lawrence Guiles, *Norma Jean: The Life and Death of Marilyn Monroe* (London, 1969), p. 227.
18. Clark, *My Week with Marilyn*, p. 112.
19. Miller, *Timebends* (1990), p. 421.
20. This and the next quotation, interview with the author, 2001.
21. Miller, *Timebends* (1990), pp. 422, 424.
22. *Ibid.*, p. 436.
23. Morton, Miller, 'My Moments with Marilyn', p. 164.
24. Interview with the author, 2001.
25. Morton Miller, 'My Moments with Marilyn', p. 167.
26. FBI file 100–333798.
27. Kalven, 'A View from the Law'.
28. Miller, *Timebends* (1990), p. 453.

29. FBI file 100–23181, dated 23 May 1957.

30. Statement by Arthur Miller on being indicted for contempt of Congress for refusing to answer certain questions. Arthur Miller's personal papers.

31. Conditions of Probation, Arthur Miller, docket no. 164–57, 19 July 1957.

32. Arthur Miller, 'The Writer's Position in America', *Coastlines*, August 1957, p. 40.

33. Spoto, *Marilyn Monroe: The Biography*, p. 431.

34. Miller, *I Don't Need You Any More* (1967), p. 72.

35. *Ibid.*, p. 77.

36. Interview with the author, 2001.

37. 'Marilyn's New Life', *Look*, vol. 21 (1 October 1957), p. 110.

38. *Ibid.*, p. 114.

39. Rosten, *Marilyn: A Very Personal Story*, p. 69.

40. *Ibid.*, p. 72.

41. Morton, Miller, 'My Moments with Marilyn', p. 164.

42. Rosten, *Marilyn: A Very Personal Story*, p. 66.

43. This and the next quotation, Peter Manso, *Mailer: His Life and Times* (New York, 1986), pp. 538, 539.

44. Taylor, *Marilyn on Marilyn*, p. 115.

45. Goodman, *The Committee*, p. 394.

46. United States Court of Appeals for the District of Columbia, no. 14057, decided 7 August 1958.

47. Guiles, *Norma Jean: the Life and Death of Marilyn Monroe*, p. 247.

48. This quotation and the next, Spoto, *Marilyn Monroe: The Biography*, pp. 446, 448, 252.

49. Joe Hyams, 'Marilyn Monroe – Upsetting', *New York Herald Tribune*, 10 February 1959, p. 25.

50. Taylor, *Marilyn on Marilyn*, p. 114.

51. Zolotow, *Marilyn Monroe*, p. 307.

52. Robert F. Slatzer, *The Life and Curious Death of Marilyn Monroe* (New York, 1982), p. 157.

53. Catherine David, *Simone Signoret* (London, 1992), p. 89.

54. Interview with the author.

55. Guiles, *Norma Jean: The Life and Death of Marilyn Monroe*, p. 249.

56. Simone Signoret, *Nostalgia Isn't What It Used to Be* (New York, 1978), pp. 302, 120.

57. Guiles, *Norma Jean: The Life and Death of Marilyn Monroe* p. 274.

58. Spoto, *Marilyn Monroe: The Biography*, p. 464.

59. Miller, *Timebends* (1990), p. 460.

60. Spoto, *Marilyn Monroe: The Biography*, p. 459.

61. Miller, *Timebends* (1990), p. 460.

62. *Ibid.*

63. Rosten, *Marilyn: A Very Personal Story*, pp. 76–7.

64. James Goode, *The Story of the Misfits* (New York, 1963), p. 21.

65. Weatherby, *Conversations with Marilyn*, p. 19.

66. Arthur Miller and Serge Toubiana, *The Misfits: Story of a Shoot* (London, 2000), p. 33.

67. Patricia Bosworth, *Montgomery Clift: A Biography* (New York, 1978), p. 330.

68. *Ibid.*

69. Miller, *Timebends* (1990), p. 466.

70. *Ibid.*, p. 483.

71. *Ibid.*, p. 466.

72. *Making The Misfits*, produced and directed by Gail Levin for Thirteen WNET and Channel 4; copyright 2001; first transmitted, 2002.

73. Shelly Frome, *The Actors Studio: A History* (Jefferson, 2001), p. 130.

74. Susan Strasberg, *Marilyn and Me: Sisters, Rivals, Friends* (New York, 1992), p. 210.

75. Miller and Toubiana, *The Misfits: Story of a Shoot*, p. 16.

76. Strasberg, *Marilyn and Me*, p. 167.

77. *Ibid.*, p. 168–9.

78. Goode, *The Story of The Misfits*, p. 128.
79. This and the next two quotations, Levin, *Making The Misfits*.
80. Weatherby, *Conversations with Marilyn*, pp. 75–6.
81. Miller, *Timebends* (1990), p. 464.
82. This and the next few quotations, Levin, *Making The Misfits*, pp. 174, 187.
83. Miller and Toubiana, *The Misfits: Story of a Shoot*, p. 70.
84. Miller, *Timebends* (1990), p. 493.
85. James Kaplan, 'Miller's Crossing,' *Vanity Fair*, November 1991, p. 151.
86. This and the next two quotations interview with the author, 2001.
87. Goode, *The Story of The Misfits*, p. 123.
88. Strasberg, *Marilyn and Me*, p. 219.
89. Miller, *Timebends* (1990), p. 474.
90. Interview with the author, 1995.
91. This and the next two quotations, Taylor, *Marilyn on Marilyn*, pp. 57, 88, 52.
92. Spoto, *Marilyn Monroe: The Biography*, p. 494.
93. This and next few quotations, Miller and Toubiana, *The Misfits: Story of a Shoot*, pp. 13, 30, 32, 15–16, 27, 40, 44.
94. Levin, *Making The Misfits*.
95. Slatzer, *The Life and Curious Death of Marilyn Monroe*, pp. 201–2.
96. 'End of a Famous Marriage', *Life*, vol. 49 (21 November 1960), p. 88A.
97. *New York Times*, 12 November 1960, p. 14.
98. *Ibid.*
99. Miller, *Timebends* (1990), p. 521.
100. Goode, *The Story of The Misfits*, p. 300.
101. *Ibid.*, p. 302.
102. Interview with the author, 1995.
103. Bosley Crowther, 'Screen: John Huston's The Misfits', *New York Times*, 2 February 1961.
104. *The Making of the Misfits*.
105. Eve Arnold, 'Indecent Exposure', *Telegraph Magazine*, 8 June 2002, p. 46.
106. Miller, *Timebends* (1990), p. 482.
107. Interview with the author, 2002.
108. Juzgado Civil Del Distrito Bravos, 1 Distrito Judicial, Estado de Chihuahua, Sentencia de Divorcio, Copia Certificada. Actor: Marilyn Monroe Miller. Demando: Arthur Miller. File no. 406/961 23 January 1961.
109. Morton, Miller, 'My Moments with Marilyn', p. 167.
110. James Kaplan, 'Miller's Crossing,' *Vanity Fair*, November 1991, p. 151.
111. Spoto, *Marilyn Monroe: The Biography*, p. 515.
112. Miller, *Timebends* (1990), p. 507.
113. Rosten, *Marilyn: A Very Personal Story*, p. 83.
114. Interview with the author, May 2002.
115. Taylor, *Marilyn on Marilyn*, p. 37.
116. *Ibid.*, p. 114.
117. Shaw and Rosten, *Marilyn among Friends*, p. 190.
118. Interview with the author, 2001.
119. Kaplan, 'Miller's Crossing,' p. 151.
120. Summers, *Goddess*, p. 421.
121. Miller, *Timebends* (1990), p. 531.
122. Interview with the author.
123. Gussow, *Conversations with Arthur Miller*, p. 95.
124. John Ezard, 'Life, Love and Marilyn', *Guardian*, 5 November 1987.
125. Mortimer, 'Thoroughly Modern Miller'.
126. Mick Brown, 'Still Not Laid to Rest', *Sunday Times*, 8 November 1987.
127. *Ibid.*
128. Mortimer, 'Thoroughly Modern Miller'.
129. Interview with the author, 2001.

130. Interview with the author, 1984.

12 INGE

1. Interview with the author, 1995.
2. *Ibid.*
3. Interview with the author, 2001.
4. Author's interview with Inge Morath, 2001.
5. Lecture at the Residenztheater, Berlin, October 1994.
6. *Ibid.*
7. Olivia Lahs-Gonzales, 'To Unseal the Deeper Nature', in *Inge Morath: Life as a Photographer*, ed. Sabine Folie and Gerald Matt (Munich, 1999), p. 61.
8. Interview with the author, 2001.
9. This and the next few quotations, interview with the author, 1995.
10. Interview with the author, 2001.
11. Inge Morath, 'About Myself', in Folie and Matt, *Inge Morath: Life as a Photographer*, p. 14.
12. *Ibid.*
13. Interview with the author, 2001.
14. *Ibid.*
15. *Ibid.*
16. Miller, *Timebends* (1990), p. 504.
17. *Ibid.*, p. 502.
18. Interview with the author, 2001.
19. *Ibid.*
20. Interview with the author, 1995.
21. Kaplan, *Vanity Fair*, November 1991, p. 151.
22. Inge Morath, 'About My Photographs', *Michigan Quarterly Review*, Fall 1998, p. 695.
23. *Ibid.*, pp. 695–6.
24. Interview with the author, 2001.
25. Miller, *Timebends* (1990), p. 524.
26. Interview with the author, 2001.
27. *Ibid.*
28. Peter Novick, *The Holocaust and Collective Memory* (London, 1999), p. 66.
29. Regina Strassegger, *Inge Morath: Last Journey* (New York, 2003), p. 176.
30. Alfred Kazin, *New York Jew* (New York, 1978), p. 45.
31. Germaine Brée, *Camus and Sartre: Crisis and Commitment* (London, 1974), p. xvii.
32. Albert Camus, *Rebellion, Resistance, and Death*, trans. Justin O'Brien (London, 1961), p. 169.
33. Miller, *Timebends* (1990), p. 145.
34. Seamus Heaney, *Opened Ground: Poems 1966–1996* (London, 1998), p. 467.
35. Irving Howe, *Celebrations and Attacks: Thirty Years of Literary and Cultural Commentary* (New York, 1979), p. 213.
36. Arthur Miller, 'A Day in the Life of Arthur Miller', *Sunday Times*, 3 December 1995.

BIBLIOGRAPHY

Arthur Miller's works are in chronological order.

Abel, Lionel, *The Intellectual Follies* (New York, 1984)

Abrams, Nathan David, 'Struggling for Freedom: Arthur Miller, The Commentary Community and the Cultural Cold War', PhD thesis, University of Birmingham, July 1998

Applebome, Peter, 'Arthur Miller: Present at the Birth of a Salesman', *New York Times*, 29 January 1999

Arnold, Eve, 'Indecent Exposure', *Telegraph Magazine*, 8 June 2002, p. 46

Atkinson, Brooks, 'No Compromise', *New York Times*, 21 September 1947

——, '*Death of a Salesman*, a New Drama by Arthur Miller, Has Premiere at the Morosco', *New York Times*, 11 February 1949

——, 'A View from the Bridge', *New York Times*, 9 October 1955

Barnes, Howard, 'Two More Duds', *New York Herald Tribune*, 30 January 1947

Barnouw, Erik, *Radio Drama in Action: Twenty-Five Plays of a Changing World* (New York, 1945)

Barrett, William, 'Culture Conference at the Waldorf', *Commentary*, vol. 7, p. 487

Barton, Matthew, 'Arthur Miller – A View from the Field', *Folklore Center News*, winter/spring, vol. xxvii, nos 1–2

Bellow, Saul, *Dangling Man* (Harmondsworth, 1963)

Benson, Jackson J., *The True Adventures of John Steinbeck, Writer* (London, 1984)

Bentley, Eric, *In Search of Theatre*, (London, 1954)

——, *The Dramatic Event* (London, 1954)

——, 'Theatre', *New Republic*, 19 December 1955

——, *What Is Theatre?* (New York, 1968)

——, ed., *Thirty Years of Treason* (London, 1971)

Bessie, Alvah, *Inquisition in Eden* (New York, 1967)

Bigsby, Christopher, ed., *Arthur Miller and Company* (London, 1989)

——, *Writers in Conversation*, vol. 1 (Norwich, 1999)

Bloom, Alexander, *Prodigal Sons: The New York Intellectuals and Their World* (New York, 1986)

Blue, Howard, *Words at War* (Lanham, 2002)

Bordman, Gerald, *The Oxford Companion to American Theatre* (Oxford, 1984)

Bosworth, Patricia, *Montgomery Clift: A Biography* (New York, 1978)

Brater, Enoch, *Arthur Miller: A Playwright's Life and Works* (London, 2005)

Brée, Germaine, *Camus and Sartre: Crisis and Commitment* (London, 1974)

Brick, Howard, *Daniel Bell and the Decline of Intellectual Modernism* (Madison, 1986)

Brightman, Carol, *Writing Dangerously: Mary McCarthy and Her World* (New York, 1994)

Brown, Mick, 'Still Not Laid to Rest,' *Sunday Times*, 8 November 1987

Brustein, Robert, *The Theatre of Revolt* (London, 1965)

——, *Who Needs Theatre?* (London, 1989)

Cahan, Abraham, *The Rise of David Levinsky* (New York, 1960)

Campbell, Duncan, 'Hollywood Owns Up', *Guardian Weekly*, 16 February 2002, p. 45

Camus, Albert, trans. Justin O'Brien, *Rebellion, Resistance and Death* (London, 1961)

Carroll, James, *Constantine's Sword: The Church and the Jews* (Boston, 2001)

Carroll, Peter N., *The Odyssey of the Abraham Lincoln Brigade* (Stanford, 1994)

Ceplair, Larry, and Englund, Stephen, *The Inquisition in Hollywood: Politics in the Film Community 1930–1960* (Berkeley, 1979)

Chapman, John, 'A Lot Goes On But Little Happens in Backyard Drama "All My Sons",' *Daily News*, 30 January 1947

Clark, Colin, *My Week with Marilyn* (London, 2000)

Clark, Eleanor, 'Theater Chronicle', *Partisan Review*, XVI, vi, p. 633

Coleman, Robert, ' "All My Sons" Not Very Convincing', *Daily Mirror*, 30 January 1947

Cooney, Terry A., *The Rise of the New York Intellectuals: Partisan Review and Its Circle* (Madison, 1986)

Crawford, Cheryl, *My Fifty Years in the Theatre* (Indianapolis, 1977)

Crockatt, Richard D.G., *British Documents on Foreign Affairs: Reports and Papers from the Foreign Office Confidential Print*, part IV, vol. 2 (Washington, 2001)

Crossly, Robert, *Olaf Stapledon: Speaking for the Future* (Liverpool, 1994)

Crossman, Richard, ed., *The God That Failed: Six Studies in Communism* (New York, 1965)

Crowther, Bosley, 'Screen: John Huston's The Misfits', *New York Times*, 2 February 1961

David, Catherine, *Simone Signoret* (London, 1992)

Dinnerstein, Leonard, *Anti-Semitism in America* (Oxford, 1994)

Dobkowski, Michael N., *The Tarnished Dream: The Basis of American Anti-Semitism* (Westport, 1979)

Epstein, Malech, *The Jew and Communism: The Story of Early Communist Victories and Ultimate Defeats in the Jewish Community, USA, 1919–1941* (New York, 1959)

Ezard, John, 'Life, Love and Marilyn', *Guardian*, 5 November 1987

Fariello, Griffin, *Red Scare: Memories of the American Inquisition, an Oral History* (New York, 1995)

Fast, Howard, *The Naked God: The Writer and the Communist Party* (London, 1958)

Fine, Sidney, *Sit-Down: The General Motors Strike 1936–1937* (Ann Arbor, 1969)

Fitzgerald, F. Scott, *The Great Gatsby* (Harmondsworth, 1950)

Folie, Sabine, and Matt, Gerald, eds, *Inge Morath: Life as a Photographer* (Munich, 1999)

Foner, Nancy, *From Ellis Island to JFK: New York's Two Great Waves of Immigration* (New Haven, 2000)

Foner, Philip S., *Paul Robeson Speaks* (New York, 1978)

Frome, Shelly, *The Actors Studio: A History* (Jefferson, 2001)

Garfield, David, *The Actors Studio: A Player's Place* (New York, 1984)

George, Stephen K., ed., *John Steinbeck: A Centennial Tribute* (Westport, 2002)

Goode, James, *The Story of The Misfits* (New York, 1963)

Goodman, Walter, 'How Not to Produce a Film', *New Republic*, 26 December 1955, p. 13

——, *The Committee: The Extraordinary Career of the House Committee on Un-American Activities* (London, 1969)

Gordon, Thomas, and Max Morgan, Witts, *Guernica: The Crucible of World War II* (Chelsea, 1975)

Gornick, Vivian, *The Romance of American Communism* (New York, 1977)

Guiles, Fred Lawrence, *Norma Jean: The Life and Death of Marilyn Monroe* (London, 1969)

Gurock, Jeffrey, S., *When Harlem Was Jewish: 1870–1930* (New York, 1979)

Gussow, Mel, *Conversations with Arthur Miller* (London, 2002)

Harrap, Louis, *Creative Awakening: The Jewish Presence in Twentieth-Century American Literature 1900–1940s* (New York, 1987)

Heaney, Seamus, *Opened Ground: Poems 1966–1996* (London, 1998)

Hewes, Henry, 'Arthur Miller and How He Went to the Devil', *Saturday Review* XXXVI (31 January 1953), p. 24

Hobson, Harold, ed., *International Theatre Annual*, no. 1 (London, 1956)

Hochschild, Jennifer L., *Facing Up to the American Dream: Race, Class, and the Soul of the Nation* (Princeton, 1995)

Hoffer, Peter Charles, *The Salem Witchcraft Trials: A Legal History* (Lawrence, 1997)

Holden, Anthony, *Olivier* (London, 1988)

Homberger, Eric, *American Writers and Radical Politics, 1900–39: Equivocal Commitments* (London, 1986)

Hook, Sidney, *Out of Step: An Unquiet Life in the Twentieth Century* (New York, 1987)

Howe, Irving, 'The Culture Conference', *Partisan Review*, vol. xvi, no. 5, p. 505

——, *Steady Work* (New York, 1966)

——, *A World More Attractive: A View of Modern Literature and Politics* (New York, 1970)

——, *The Critical Point: On Literature and Culture* (New York, 1973)

——, *World of Our Fathers* (New York, 1976)

——, *Celebrations and Attacks: Thirty Years of Literary and Cultural Commentary* (New York, 1979)

——, *A Margin of Hope: An Intellectual Biography* (London, 1983)

Huntington, Samuel, *Who Are We? The Challenges to America's National Destiny* (New York, 2004)

Hyams, Joe, 'Marilyn Monroe – Upsetting', *New York Herald Tribune*, 10 February 1959, p. 25

Joseph, Samuel, *Jewish Immigration to the United States from 1881 to 1910* (New York, 1967)

Judd, Alan, *The Quest for C: Mansfield Cumming and the Founding of the Secret Service* (London, 1999)

Kalven Jr, Harry, 'A View from the Law', *New Republic*, 27 May 1957, p. 8

Kane, Leslie, ed., *David Mamet in Conversation* (Ann Arbor, 2001)

Kaplan, James, 'Miller's Crossing', *Vanity Fair*, November 1991, pp. 149–51

Kauffman, Stanley, *Persons of the Drama: Theater Criticism and Comment* (New York, 1976)

Kazacoff, George, *Dangerous Theatre: The Federal Theatre Project as a Forum for New Plays* (New York, 1989)

Kazan, Elia, *A Life* (New York, 1988)

Kazin, Alfred, *A Walker in the City* (London, 1952)

——, *Starting Out in the Thirties* (London, 1966)

——, *New York Jew* (New York, 1978)

Kisseloff, Jeff, *On the Box: An Oral History of Television 1920–1961* (New York, 1995)

Koenig, Rhoda, 'Seduced by Salesman's Patter', *Sunday Times*, 20 October 1996

Kozlenko, William, ed., *One Hundred Non-Royalty Radio Plays* (New York, 1941)

Kristol, Irving, 'Civil Liberties 1952 – A Study in Confusion: Do We Defend Our Rights by Protecting Communists?' *Commentary* 13 (March 1952), pp. 234–6

Kuchwara, Michael, 'Arthur Miller's "Luck": A Fortunate Revival', *Morning Call*, 29 July 2001

Kussi, Peter, ed., *Toward the Radical Center: A Karel Čapek Reader* (New Haven, 1990)

Landis, Arthur H., *The Abraham Lincoln Brigade* (New York, 1968)

Lasch, Christopher, *The Agony of the American Left* (London, 1970)

Lessing, Doris, *Walking in the Shade* (London, 1997)

Levin, Gail, dir., *Making the Misfits*, Thirteen WNET and Channel 4, copyright 2001, first transmitted 2002

Lewis, Robert, *Slings and Arrows* (New York, 1984)

Liss, Joseph, ed., *Radio's Best Plays* (New York, 1947)

Lucas, W. Scott, *The Cultural Cold War in Western Europe 1945–1960* (London, 2003)

Mailer, Norman, *The Time of Our Time* (London, 1998)

Manso, Peter, *Mailer: His Life and Times* (New York, 1986)

Mantle, Burns, ed., *The Best Plays of 1944–5* (New York, 1946)

Martin, Robert A., *The Writer's Craft: Hopwood Lectures 1965–81* (Ann Arbor, 1982)

——, and Centola, Steven R., eds, *The Theater Essays of Arthur Miller* (New York, 1996)

Mayorga, Margaret, ed., *The Best One-Act Plays of 1944* (New York, 1945)

McAuliffe, Mary Sperling, *Crisis on the Left: Cold War Politics and American Liberals 1944–1954* (Amherst, 1978)

McCarthy, Mary, *Sights and Spectacles: 1937–1958* (London, 1959)

——, *On the Contrary* (London, 1962)

McFarlane, James, ed., *The Cambridge Companion to Henrik Ibsen* (Cambridge, 1994)

Mielziner, Jo, *Designing for the Theatre: A Memoir and a Portfolio* (New York, 1965)

Miller, Arthur A., 'You Simply Must Go to College', *The Gargoyle*, October 1937, pp. 12, 24

Miller, Art, 'The Rosten', *The Gargoyle*, January 1938, p. 24; Bentley Historical Library, University of Michigan

Miller, Arthur, 'Grandfather and Emperor Franz Joseph', *New Currents*, June 1943, p. 9

——, *Situation Normal* (New York, 1944)

——, 'Ernie Pyle: G.I.', *New Masses*, 15 May 1945, pp. 23–4

——, *Focus* (New York, 1945)

——, 'The Plaster Masks', *Encore*, vol . 9, April 1946

——, 'It Takes a Thief', *Collier's* 8 February 1947

——, 'Concerning Jews Who Write', *Jewish Life*, 2, 5 (March 1948), pp. 7–10

——, letter to the Editor, *New York Herald Tribune*, 27 May 1949

——, 'An American Reaction', *World Theater* (New York, 1951), pp. 21–2

——, 'A Boy Grew in Brooklyn', *Holiday*, March 1955, pp. 54–5, 117, 119–20, 122–4

——, 'Picking a Cast', *New York Times*, 21 August 1955, section 2, p. 12

——, *A Memory of Two Mondays* (New York, 1955)

——, *The Collected Plays* (New York, 1957)

——, 'The Writer's Position in America', *Coastlines*, August 1957, p. 40

——, 'Bridge to a Savage World', *Esquire*, vol. 50 (October 1958), p. 185

——, *A View from the Bridge, All My Sons* (Harmondsworth, 1961)

——, 'The Bored and the Violent', *Harper's*, vol. 225 (November 1962), pp. 50–6

——, *After the Fall* (New York, 1964)

——, 'After the Fall', *Saturday Evening Post*, 237 (1 February 1964)

——, *I Don't Need You Any More* (London, 1967)

——, 'It Could Happen Here – And Did', *New York Times*, 30 April 1967

——, *The Crucible* (Harmondsworth, 1968)

——, 'Rip Van Winkle Spanish Style', *New York Times*, 9 July 1972

——, 'The Year It Came Apart,' *New York* (1974), p. 36

——, 'The American Writer: The American Theater', in *The Writer's Craft: Hopwood Lectures, 1965–81* (Ann Arbor, 1978), pp. 254–5

——, *The American Clock* (London, 1982)

——, 'The Night Ed Murrow Struck Back', *Esquire*, December 1983

——, *Salesman in Beijing* (London, 1984)

——, 'The Face in the Mirror: Anti-Semitism Then and Now', *New York Times Book Review*, 14 October 1984, p. 3

——, *The Golden Years* and *The Man Who Had All the Luck* (London, 1989)

——, 'Again they drink from the Cup of Suspicion', *New York Times*, 26 November 1989, p. 36

——, *Timebends: A Life* (London, 1987)

——, 'Mildred Dunnock', *Theater Week*, 29 June 1991, pp. 12–13

——, 'A Day in the Life of Arthur Miller', *Sunday Times*, 3 December, 1995

——, *Death of a Salesman* (New York, 1998)

——, 'Waiting for the Teacher', *Harper's*, July 1998, pp. 56–7

——, 'Salem Revisited', *New York Times*, 15 October 1998

——, 'Classics in Words and Music,' *The Times*, 1 February 1999

——, *Echoes Down the Corridor: Collected Essays 1944–2000* (New York, 2000), ed. Steven R. Centola

——, and Toubiana, Serge, *The Misfits: Story of a Shoot* (London, 2000)

——, *The Crucible in History and other Essays* (London, 2000)

——, 'His Jewish Question', *Vanity Fair*, October 2001, p. 365

——, interviewed by John H. Richardson, 'What I've Learned', *Esquire*, July 2003, p. 110

——, 'Shattering the Silence, Illuminating the Hatred', in *Writers on Writing*, vol. ii, ed. Jane Smiley (New York, 2003)

Miller, Morton, 'My Moments with Marilyn: P.S. Arthur Was There, Too', *Esquire*, June 1998, p. 167

Monroe, Marilyn, *My Story* (New York, 1974)

Morath, Inge, 'About My Photographs', *Michigan Quarterly Review*, Fall 1998, p. 695

Mortimer, John, 'Thoroughly Modern Miller', *Daily Telegraph*, 10 October 1987

Murphy, Brenda, *Congressional Theatre: Dramatizing McCarthyism on Stage, Film, and Television* (Cambridge, 1999)

Navasky, Victor, *Naming Names* (London, 1982)

Novick, Peter, *The Holocaust and Collective Memory* (London, 1999)

Olivier, Laurence, *Confessions of an Actor: An Autobiography* (London, 1982)

Pauly, Thomas H., *An American Odyssey: Elia Kazan and American Culture* (Philadelphia, 1983)

Pells, Richard H., *The Liberal Mind in a Conservative Age: American Intellectuals in the 1940s and 1950s* (New York, 1985)

Phillips, William, *A Partisan View: Five Decades of the Literary Life* (New York, 1983)

Podhoretz, Norman, 'The Issue', *Commentary*, 29 (1960), pp. 182–3

——, *Breaking Ranks* (New York, 1979)

Radosh, Ronald, 'Arthur Miller's McCarthy Fantasy: The Crucible and the 1950s', *Front Page* magazine 26 July 2000

Rasky, Harry, dir., *Arthur Miller: On Home Ground*, CBC, 1980

Riis, Jacob, *How the Other Half Lives* (Cambridge, 1970)

Robins, Natalie, *Alien Ink: The FBI's War on Freedom of Expression* (New York, 1992)

Rosenberg, David, ed., *Genesis: As It Is Written, Contemporary Writers on Our First Stories* (San Francisco, 1996)

Rosten, Norman, *Marilyn: A Very Personal Story* (London, 1973)

Roudané, Matthew C., *Conversations with Arthur Miller* (Jackson, 1987)

Rowe, Kenneth, *Write That Play* (New York, 1939)

Rowe, Kenneth Thorpe, *A Theater in Your Head* (New York, 1960)

Sartre, Jean-Paul, *Anti-Semite and Jew*, trans. George J. Becker (New York, 1965)

Saunders, Frances Stonor, *Who Paid the Piper? The CIA and the Cultural Cold War* (London, 1999)

Schechner, Mark, *The Conversion of the Jews and Other Essays* (London, 1990)

Schlesinger Jr, Arthur, *The Vital Center: The Politics of Freedom* (London, 1950)

——, *A Life in the Twentieth Century: Innocent Beginnings, 1917–1950* (New York, 2000)

Schrecker, Ellen W., *No Ivory Tower: McCarthyism and the Universities* (New York, 1986)

——, *Many Are the Crimes: McCarthyism in America* (New York, 1998)

Schwartz, Solomon M., 'The New Anti-Semitism of the Soviet Union: Its Background and Its Meaning', *Commentary*, vol. 7

Sebastian, Mihail, *Journal 1935–1944* (Chicago, 2000)

Shaw, Sam, and Rosten, Norman, *Marilyn among Friends* (London, 1987)

Shipley, Joseph T., 'Arthur Miller's New Melodrama Is Not What It Seems to Be', *New Leader*, XXXVI (9 February 1953), pp. 25–6

Shorris, Earl, *The Nation of Salesmen: The Tyranny of the Market and the Subversion of Culture* (New York, 1994)

Signoret, Simone, *Nostalgia Isn't What It Used to Be* (New York, 1978)

Slatzer, Robert, F., *The Life and Curious Death of Marilyn Monroe* (New York, 1982)

Smiley, Jane, ed., *Writers on Writing*, vol. II (New York, 2003)

Spoto, Donald, *Marilyn Monroe: The Biography* (London, 1993)

Starkey, Marion, *The Devil in Massachusetts: A Modern Enquiry into the Salem Witch Trials* (London, nd)

Steiner, George, *Errata* (London, 1997)

Strasberg, Susan, *Marilyn and Me: Sisters, Rivals, Friends* (New York, 1992)

Strassegger, Regina, *Inge Morath: Last Journey* (New York, 2003)

Summers, Anthony, *Goddess: The Secret Lives of Marilyn Monroe* (London, 1985)

Taylor, Roger G., ed., *Marilyn on Marilyn* (London, 1983)

Terkel, Studs, *Hard Times* (New York, 1970)

Valta, Louis, 'All My Sons Wins Critics' Laurels', *New York Times*, 22 April 1947

Wald, Alan M., *The Rise and Decline of the Anti-Stalinist Left from the 1930s to the 1980s* (Chapel Hill, 1987)

Warshow, Robert, 'The Liberal Conscience in "The Crucible": Arthur Miller and His Audience', *Commentary* XV (March 1953), p. 266

——, letter to the Editors, *Partisan Review*, 21 (1954), p. 235

——, *The Immediate Experience: Movies, Comics, Theater and Other Aspects of Popular Culture* (New York, 1962)

Weales, Gerald, *The Crucible: Text and Criticism* (New York, 1971)

Weatherby, W.J., *Conversations with Marilyn* (New York, 1992)

Webber, Bruce, 'Deflation of an Optimist by a Young Writer', *New York Times*, 24 July 2001

Weintraub, Stanley, *The Last Great Crusade: The Intellectuals and the Spanish Civil War* (London, 1968)

Wenger, Beth S., *New York Jews and the Great Depression: Uncertain Promise* (New Haven, 1996)

Williams, Jay, *Stage Left* (New York, 1974)

Williams, Tennessee, *Five O'Clock Angel: Letters of Tennessee Williams to Maria St Just 1948–1982* (London, 1991)

Windham, Donald, ed, *Tennessee Williams' Letters to Donald Windham 1940–1965* (New York, 1977)

WNET, *Arthur Miller, Elia Kazan and the Blacklist: None without Sin*, New York, 3 September 2003

Young, Jeff, *Kazan on Kazan* (London, 1999)

Zolotow, Maurice, *Marilyn Monroe* (London, 1961)

ACKNOWLEDGEMENTS

My greatest debt is to Arthur Miller himself. For more than twenty-five years he and Inge offered me gracious hospitality whenever I visited Roxbury, and Arthur submitted to many hours of interviews. For two years he gave me free and exclusive access to all his published and unpublished materials, work which would after the completion of this text, subsequently make its way to the Harry Ransom Center of the University of Texas. I have benefited greatly from his generosity and the openness with which he spoke to me.

I am also grateful to the members of his family who submitted to interviews: his sister Joan Copeland, his brother Kermit and sister-in-law Frances, his son Robert and two daughters, Jane and Rebecca. Arthur's nephew, Ross Miller, was also generous with his time and gave me permission to reproduce his father's letters, as Dr Rodney M. Cook also gave me permission to reproduce Professor Rowe's letters.

I benefited greatly from the various librarians who have assisted me at the Special Collections room of the University of Michigan and at the Harry Ransom Center. I am also grateful for the help offered by the Billy Rose Collection of New York Public Library, and to the Arts and Humanities Research Board for their research leave grant.

I acknowledge with thanks the permission granted to reproduce material by Elia Kazan; two unpublished letters from John Steinbeck to Arthur Miller, and two letters which originally appeared in *The True Adventures of John Steinbeck, Writer*, ed. Jackson J. Benson (Heinemann: London, 1984); and the letter from Laurence Olivier (CMG Worldwide). Where I have been unable to locate copyright owners I am very happy to make acknowledgement in any subsequent edition.

PICTURE CREDITS *t=top, b=bottom, c=centre*
Associated Press/PA Photos: 22t, 24t; Bentley Historical Library, University of Michigan: 1b, 2–3; © Ian Berry/Magnum Photos: 24b; Bettmann/CORBIS: 1t, 4t, 4c, 5c, 9t, 10, 14t, 19t, 20, 21t, 22t; © John Bryson/Sygma/CORBIS: 17t; © Clifford Coffin/Condé Nast Archives/CORBIS: 5t; © Ernst Haas/Getty Images: 21b; Hagley Museum & Library (DuPont *Cavalcade of America* Photograph Collection no. 1985259_0550): 7b; Hulton Archive/Getty Images: 5b, 16b; Photofest: 4b, 8t, 8b, 9b, 11t, 13t, 13b, 16t, 17b, 19b, 23; Rex Features/Everett Collection: 14b; Time & Life Pictures/Getty Images: 6t, 6b, 7t, 11b, 12b, 15; Topfoto/PA Photos: 22b; Underwood & Underwood/CORBIS: 18

INDEX